INSIGHT GUIDES

SCANDINAVIA

*Hope you enjoy your trip —
Don't worry about me in the
Kennel — — I'm sure I'll survive!
Luv
DASH*

DISCOVERY
CHANNEL

APA PUBLICATIONS
Part of the Langenscheidt Publishing Group

INSIGHT GUIDE
Scandinavia

Editorial
Project Editor
Jane Hutchings
Managing Editor **Tom Le Bas**
Editorial Director
Brian Bell

Distribution

UK & Ireland
GeoCenter International Ltd
The Viables Centre, Harrow Way
Basingstoke, Hants RG22 4BJ
Fax: (44) 1256 817988

United States
Langenscheidt Publishers, Inc.
46–35 54th Road, Maspeth, NY 11378
Fax: (1) 718 784 0640

Canada
Thomas Allen & Son Ltd
390 Steelcase Road East
Markham, Ontario L3R 1G2
Fax: (1) 905 475 6747

Australia
Universal Publishers
1 Waterloo Road
Macquarie Park, NSW 2113
Fax: (61) 2 9888 9074

New Zealand
Hema Maps New Zealand Ltd (HNZ)
Unit D, 24 Ra ORA Drive
East Tamaki, Auckland
Fax: (64) 9 273 6479

Worldwide
**Apa Publications GmbH & Co.
Verlag KG (Singapore branch)**
38 Joo Koon Road, Singapore 628990
Tel: (65) 6865 1600. Fax: (65) 6861 6438

Printing

Insight Print Services (Pte) Ltd
38 Joo Koon Road, Singapore 628990
Tel: (65) 6865 1600. Fax: (65) 6861 6438

©2003 Apa Publications GmbH & Co.
Verlag KG (Singapore branch)
All Rights Reserved
First Edition 2001
Updated 2003

CONTACTING THE EDITORS
We would appreciate it if readers
would alert us to errors or out-
dated information by writing to:
**Insight Guides, P.O. Box 7910,
London SE1 1WE, England.
Fax: (44) 20 7403-0290.
insight@apaguide.co.uk**

www.insightguides.com

ABOUT THIS BOOK

This guidebook combines the interests and enthusiasms of two of the world's best known infor- mation providers: Insight Guides, whose titles have set the standard for visual travel guides since 1970, and Discovery Channel, the world's premier source of non-fiction televi- sion programming.

The editors of Insight Guides pro- vide practical advice and general understanding about a destination's history, culture and people. Discovery Channel and its popular web site, www. discovery.com, help millions of viewers to explore their world from the comfort of their home and encourage them to explore it first hand.

How to use this book

This first edition of *Insight Guide: Scandinavia* is carefully structured to convey an understanding of the countries of Denmark, Norway, Sweden and Finland and their cul- tures as well as to guide readers through their sights and activities:

◆ The **Features** section, indicated by a yellow bar at the top of each page, covers the history and culture of the countries in a series of infor- mative essays.

◆ The main **Places** section, indicated by a blue bar, is a complete guide to all the sights and areas worth visiting. Places of spe- cial interest are coor- dinated by number with the maps.

◆ The **Travel Tips** sec- tion, with an orange bar,

EXPLORE YOUR WORLD®
Discovery
CHANNEL

Map Legend

▬ ▪ ▬	International Boundary
▬ ▬ ▬	Province/County Boundary
⊖	Border Crossing
▬ ▪ ▬	National Park/Reserve
▬ ▬ ▬	Ferry Route
Ⓜ Ⓣ	Metro
Ⓢ	S-Tog (S-Train)
Ⓣ	Tunnelbanan
✈ ✈	Airport: International/Regional
🚌	Bus Station
🅿	Parking
❶	Tourist Information
✉	Post Office
† ⛪	Church/Ruins
†	Monastery
☾	Mosque
✡	Synagogue
🏰	Castle/Ruins
∴	Archaeological Site
∩	Cave
⚐	Statue/Monument
★	Place of Interest

The main places of interest in the Places section are coordinated by number with a full-colour map (e.g. ❶), and a symbol at the top of every right-hand page tells you where to find the map.

provides a handy point of reference for information on travel, hotels, shops, restaurants and more.

The contributors

Insight Guide: Scandinavia was edited by **Jane Hutchings**, under the guidance of managing editor **Tom Le Bas**. The book builds on the solid foundations laid by the late **Doreen Taylor-Wilkie**, editor of the original Insight Guides to each of the four countries. This version has been fact-checked and updated by **James Proctor**.

The history of Scandinavia was the work of **Rowlinson Carter**. Art historian **Kathryn Boyer** wrote about Scandinavia's culture and from her base in Trollhättan covered Sweden's West Coast and Great Lakes. Stockholm-based journalist **Amy Brown** contributed the feature on the Great Outdoors, and the chapters on Stockholm, Southern Sweden and Dalarna. The writer **Debra Williamson** provided her comments on The Swedes and the Insight on the Vikings. From Arjeplog in Lapland **Illona Fjellström** covered Northern Sweden. **Joanie Rafidi Oxhammar** compiled the Insight on the Stockholm Archipelago.

From Århus, Denmark, journalist **Jack Jackson** wrote about the Scandinavian passion for food and drink and contributed chapters on The Danes, Copenhagen and Jutland, and the Insight on Danish Design.

The chapters on Norway were compiled by the journalist and author **Michael Brady** with the assistance of **Samtext** in Oslo. Brady, a longtime resident of Norway, has written extensively about the country. Other contributors included **Lance Price** and Olso columnist **Yngve Kvistad**.

Joan Gannij, an Amsterdam-based American journalist and "Finnatic", contributed the chapters on Finland and The Finns. She also compiled the Insight on the Hurtigruten in Norway. Writers whose text has been adapted from individual *Insight Guides* to the countries include: Denmark, **Fradley Garner**, **Bryan Wilder**; Norway, **Anita Peltonen**, **Robert Spark**, **John Harley**; Sweden, **Philip Ray**; Finland, **Anne Roston**, **Sylvie Nickels**, **Robert Spark**.

The Travel Tips section was compiled by **Anna Lia Bright** in Copenhagen, **Liv Bente T. Dybfest** in Oslo, **Elisabet Lim** in Stockholm and for Finland, **Joan Gannij**. The section was edited by **Sue Platt**.

Thanks also go to **Susannah Wight** and **Sylvia Suddes** for proofreading the book and to **Penny Phenix** for indexing it.

Insight Guide
Scandinavia

CONTENTS

Maps

Scandinavia	**78**
DENMARK	**92**
Copenhagen	**94**
Zealand	**114**
Bornholm	**118**
Funen	**124**
Jutland	**130**
Greenland	**138**
Faroe Islands	**142**
NORWAY	**156**
Oslo	**158**
Oslo Fjord	**168**
South & Cent. Norway	**174**
Bergen	**186**
Northwest Norway	**206**
Norway's Far North	**212**
SWEDEN	**228**
Stockholm	**230**
Around Stockholm	**242**
Southern Sweden	**250**
Sweden's West Coast	**256**
Göteborg	**258**
Sweden's Great Lakes	**262**
Dalarna	**268**
Central Sweden	**272**
Northern Sweden	**278**
FINLAND	**296**
Helsinki	**298**
Lakes & South Finland	**316**
Turku	**324**
Tampere	**332**
Finland's West Coast	**338**
Karelia & Kuusamo	**342**
Lapland	**346**

Introduction

Introduction **15**

History

Decisive Dates **18**
Beginnings **21**
War and Peace **31**
The Modern Age **39**

Features

Art and Culture **51**
Food and Drink **61**
Great Outdoors **65**

People

The Danes **89**
The Norwegians **153**
The Swedes **225**
The Finns **293**

Insight on ...

The Vikings 28
Danish Design 110
Hurtigruten Voyage 202
Stockholm Archipelago 246
Finnish Saunas 312

Information panels

Royal Families 42
Scandinavian Style ....:.... 54
Sami and the Outdoor Life 70
Christiania 106
Andersen and Nielsen.......... 127
Heroes of Telemark 180
Stiklestad 209
Drottningholms Slott............ 245
Gotland 253
Göta Kanal......................... 265
Helsinki's Art Nouveau 306
Åland Islands 321
Canoeing 335

Travel Tips

Denmark 354
Norway 368
Sweden 385
Finland 404

◆ **Full Travel Tips index
is on page 353**

MAIN PICTURE: Vibrant
colours in springtime,
southern Sweden.

Places

DENMARK
Introduction 87
Copenhagen 97
Zealand 113
Bornholm 118
Funen 123
Jutland 129
Greenland 137
The Faroe Islands 141

NORWAY
Introduction 151
Oslo and its Fjord 161
Southern Norway 173
Bergen 185
The Heart of Norway 191
Norway's Northwest Coast ..205
Norway's Far North
    and Svalbard................... 211

SWEDEN
Introduction 223
Stockholm and Around 233
Southern Sweden 249
Sweden's West Coast 255
Sweden's Great Lakes 261
Dalarna 267
Central Sweden 271
Northern Sweden 277

FINLAND
Introduction 291
Helsinki 301
Southern Finland 315
Turku 323
Finland's Lakeland 327
Finland's West Coast 337
Karelia 340
Lapland 345

NORTHERLY NEIGHBOURS

At the top of the map, but no longer aloof, the
Scandinavian countries are Europe's best-kept secret

To fly over Scandinavia is to discover a vast, sparsely inhabited, natural landscape of sparkling fjords and rocky mountains, glassy lakes and rushing rivers, dense forests and frozen tundra, extending from temperate Denmark far north to the land of the Sami and including Greenland and the Faroe Islands.

Norway, Denmark, Sweden and Finland are among Europe's most ancient civilisations. Theirs is an eventful shared history of prowess and intrigue. Early Norse traders ventured deep into Asia leaving graphic runic inscriptions on stones which provide clues as to their exploits. Later, the infamous Vikings who pillaged their way round the coasts of Ireland, Britain and France laid the foundations for kingdoms and Christianity across Scandinavia. They were followed by kings, queens and tsars who schemed and battled. Borders shifted, unions came and went, and by the start of the 20th century four distinct nations emerged which have grown into the modern, highly individualistic countries we know today.

The Danes are probably the most garrulous of the Scandinavians, though all will ensure the visitor receives a warm welcome. The Nordic reputation for cool reservedness has had its day, but not for cool design. Everything from beer bottle openers to the latest building has the stamp of chic understatement.

The Scandinavian capitals of Copenhagen, Oslo, Stockholm and Helsinki are vibrant cities housing some of the most inspirational museums and finest art collections in Europe, with concerts and festivals bringing music and life to the streets. In fact, at the slightest excuse Scandinavians will take to the outdoors, whether on a bicycle along the winding lanes of Denmark, skiing on floodlit trails around Oslo, escaping to little red-painted waterside cottages in Sweden, or plunging from sauna to ice pool in Finland. An inherent love of nature is deeply rooted within the national psyches. Perhaps this has to do with the long dark days of winter and the need to soak up the summer light. Arrive in any of the Scandinavian countries in mid to late June and you'll find the locals dancing and feasting around Midsummer maypoles and bonfires.

Transport and communications are excellent: roads join southerly Denmark with the North Cape, railways penetrate Lapland, ferries ply the fjords and link remote islands and lakeside villages, and planes cut the journey times. And with the opening of the Øresund bridge in 2000 from Denmark to Sweden, Scandinavia is just a short step from its European neighbours. ❑

PRECEDING PAGES: Danish football supporters in high spirits; a moment's contemplation, Hustad, Norway; winter festivities, northern Sweden; a Sami and his reindeer, Rovaniemi, Finnish Lapland.
LEFT: on the water – boating is a way of life in Scandinavia.

Decisive Dates

EARLY HISTORY: 10,000 BC–AD 800

From 10,000 BC Hunter-gatherer tribes follow the melting ice northwards, establishing settlements and farming communities in southern Scandinavia. Tribes from Eastern Europe settle the Arctic coast.

1500 BC Trade routes are forged through the rivers of Eastern Europe to the Danube.

c.500 BC–AD 800 Iron Age "Grauballe Man" and "Tollund Man" are buried in peat bogs in Denmark to be unearthed in the 1950s in remarkable condition.

c.AD 100 The historian Tacitus mentions the Fenni

(the Sami of Finland) in his *Germania* and describes the Sveas who inhabit what is now central Sweden.

c.AD 400 Suomalaiset (Baltic Finns) cross the Baltic and settle in Finland. Sweden's influence over its "eastern province" begins. In Norway farmers push inland; forts have been found on Lake Mjøsa.

THE VIKING AGE

800–1060 The Scandinavian Vikings earn a reputation as sea warriors. In 862, at the invitation of the Slavs, Prince Rurik leads the Swedish Vikings (Varangians) east to bring order to the principality of Novgorod. They soon control the trade routes to Byzantium.

830 A Benedictine monk, Ansgar (801–865), lands on Björkö in Sweden and founds a church.

861 Vikings sack Paris.

866 After repeated raids along the English and French coasts and the plundering of monasteries, the Vikings control most of England and Normandy.

940–95 Harald Bluetooth brings Christianity to Denmark; Olav Tryggvason uses force in his attempts to convert the Norwegian Vikings.

1001 The sagas relate that it was Leifur Eiríksson who discovered Vinland (America).

1030 Battle of Stiklestad in Norway and the death of King Olav Haraldson who later becomes St Olav.

1050 Harald Hardrade of Norway founds Oslo.

1066 Defeat in England at the Battle of Stamford Bridge brings the Viking Age to an end.

MIDDLE AGES C.1100–1500

1100 The first bishoprics appear, among them the see of Nidaros (Trondheim) in Norway.

1155 King Erik of Sweden launches a crusade into Finland; further Swedish invasions take place in 1239 and 1293 subjugating large areas of the country.

1319–43 Inter-Scandinavian royal marriages produce a joint Norwegian–Swedish monarchy.

1362 Finland becomes a province of Sweden.

1397 A union is forged by Queen Margarethe and signed at Kalmar which unites the kingdoms of Norway, Denmark and Sweden.

1417 Eric VII of Denmark makes Copenhagen his capital and builds a palace at Helsingør.

1460 Kristian I secures the duchies of Schleswig and Holstein for Denmark.

WARS AND REFORMATION

1520 Kristian II of Denmark invades Sweden and massacres the nobility in the "Stockholm Bloodbath". Gustav Vasa drives him out and the Kalmar Union is disbanded. Norway remains under Danish rule.

1523 In Sweden, Gustav Vasa (1523–60) ascends the throne, marking the start of the Vasa dynasty (1523–1720), which also holds power in Finland. Under Gustav II Adolf (1611–32) Sweden becomes a great European power, only to decline during the reign of Karl XII (1697– 1718), the "warrior king". Fine arts flourish under Gustav III (1771–92).

1530 The Reformation passes through the Scandinavian countries and the Lutheran faith is introduced. In Finland Mikael Agricola's translation of the Bible forms the basis of Finnish literary language.

1536 Norway ceases to be an independent kingdom as the Danes take control.

1588–1648 Denmark flourishes under the long rule of Kristian IV (1577–1648). Attempts to regain territory lost to Sweden end in failure.

1625–57 The Thirty Years War launched by the Danish king, Kristian IV, to check Swedish expansion ends in defeat for Denmark.

1714–41 "Great Wrath" and "Lesser Wrath": Russia and Sweden battle over Finland. Under the Treaty of Turku (1743) Russia moves its border westwards.

NINETEENTH-CENTURY MANOEUVRES

1801–14 During the Napoleonic Wars English fleets twice bombard Copenhagen. Denmark sides with Napoleon and suffers further defeat. In 1814 the victorious powers dissolve the Denmark–Norway union and Norway is ceded to Sweden (1815–1905). A new Norwegian constitution is adopted at Eidsvoll.

1807–1905 Tsar Alexander I occupies Finland in 1807. The Treaty of Hamina cedes Finland to Russia. A programme of "Russification" is introduced in Finland; in 1899 the composer, Jean Sibelius, is forced to publish his *Finlandia* as *Opus 26, No 7*. Finnish resistance grows. In 1905 events in Russia lead to a degree of autonomy for Finland.

1812 Tsar Alexander makes Helsinki Finland's capital.

1815–1907 In Sweden, Jean Baptiste Bernadotte, French marshal of Napoleon, succeeds to the throne as Karl XIV Johan (1818–44). The great exodus to the United States takes place.

1864 Denmark and Prussia at war. Denmark loses Schleswig-Holstein.

MODERN TIMES

1905 Referendum in Norway leads to the end of the union with Sweden. The Danish prince Håkon VII is invited to be King of Norway.

1906 Finnish women become the first in Europe to be given the vote.

1917–19 Finland declares its independence from the new Soviet Union, but is plunged into civil war in 1918 over attempts by radicals to introduce a Russian-style revolution. The White Guard (government troops) under General Mannerheim, defeats the Red Guard.

1919 The Republic of Finland comes into being under its first president, K.J. Ståhlberg.

1919 Denmark recovers Schleswig, not Holstein.

1930s Sweden and Denmark establish welfare states.

1939–48 Soviet territorial demands spark off the Winter War between Finland and the Soviet Union. The Continuation War follows. Finland is forced to cede land to the USSR. War reparations are severe. In 1948 Finland and the Soviet Union sign the Treaty of

Friendship, Co-operation and Mutual Assistance. Sweden remains neutral in World Wars I and II. Norway proclaims neutrality in World War II, but is attacked by the Germans, who also occupy Denmark.

1949 Denmark becomes a founding member of NATO.

1951–86 In Sweden, Social Democrats hold office for several years at a time; the monarch's constitutional powers are removed. In 1986 Olof Palme, Swedish prime minister and international peacemaker, is assassinated.

1955 Finland is admitted to the United Nations. Helsinki becomes a centre for international peace and arms limitation talks in the late 20th century.

1960s Norway begins oil exploration in the North Sea

and by the end of the 20th century is a major oil exporting nation. Later Denmark begins to exploit its North Sea oil reserves.

1972 Denmark joins the EEC (now European Union).

1995 Finland and Sweden join the European Union. Norway votes against membership (1972 and 1994).

1999 Sweden closes one of two nuclear reactors at Barsebäck following intense pressure from Denmark.

2000 Øresund bridge opens between Denmark and Sweden, establishing new links across Scandinavia.

2002 Finnish parliament gives permission for a new nuclear power station to be built, against the trend of winding down nuclear power in Scandinavia.

2003 Intense debate in Sweden over whether or not to join the Euro. ❑

PRECEDING PAGES: Sweden loses Finland at the battle of Poltava, 1709. **LEFT:** King Gustav Vasa of Sweden.
RIGHT: Marti Ahtissari, Finland's president until 2000.

BEGINNINGS

As the ice floes retreated, so the hunter-gatherers moved north,
colonising the Nordic lands and giving rise to the Viking Age

For 1.6 million years, Scandinavia languished under an ice-sheet that oozed out of the Jostedalsbreen in Norway, stretched as far as the British Isles and Moscow, and was 3,000 metres (9,800 ft) thick. When eventually it melted, nomadic hunters and gatherers went after the plants and animals that surfaced in its wake. Some 12,000 years ago, the peninsula celebrated its final liberation from the crushing weight of the ice by rising like bread in an oven. Unleavened Denmark, however, remained barely above sea level, the land bridge with Norway and Sweden broken.

The first inhabitants

Some of the earliest arrivals in this re-sculptured land brought with them tame dogs, knew how to make leather boats, and kept a well-stocked armoury of bows, arrows, harpoons and spears. Not much else is known about them, so a case has been made for recognising the nomadic Lapps, also known as Sami, as Scandinavia's quasi-aboriginals. Other schools of thought put them down as comparatively recent arrivals from Siberia. In any case, Lapp women and children these days generally live in houses while their men in shrinking numbers drive reindeer herds over a territory which encompasses parts of Norway, Sweden, Finland and the Russian Kola Peninsula.

As for the Finns, the second group of somewhat exceptional Scandinavians, a 19th-century scholar, M.A. Castren, suggested that they and anyone else speaking a Finno-Ugric language, which includes Hungarians, Estonians and indeed Lapps, hailed from Outer Mongolia and could therefore claim kinship with the likes of Genghis Khan. After searching self-examination, an increasing number of Finns see themselves as indigenous Baltic folk who drifted into their present location between the

Bronze Age and the start of the great European migration in the 5th century AD.

The real majority of Scandinavians are legendary types, like the 11th-century Norman crusader Bohemund who stopped in Constantinople on his way to the Holy Land. "Like no other man ever seen in the Byzantine Empire

whether barbarian or Greek," gushed the emperor's daughter, Anna Comnenus, "so tall in body that he exceeded even the tallest man by almost 50 centimetres... so narrow in the belly and flanks... so broad in the chest and shoulders... so strong in the arms. His whole stature could be described as neither constricted nor over-endowed with flesh, but blended as perfectly as possible."

Nevertheless, there were always significant numbers of shorter, darker people with more rounded skulls in the region, although more so in Denmark than in the northern forests and fjords. Lapps and Finns aside, they all spoke the same Primitive Nordic language, one of the

LEFT: Viking raiding party sets out across the North Sea, 9th century.
RIGHT: latter-day Viking in traditional garb at one of Denmark's popular re-enactments.

Germanic group, and had common notions of religion, law and culture. Bronze Age rock-carvings reveal a well-appointed world of horse-drawn carts, ships with curious beaks at either end, weapons and a religion devoted to the worship of the sun and fertility.

Travellers' tales

In 500 BC, however, a drastic turn in the weather killed off livestock which had previously spent the whole year outdoors, wrecked agriculture and forced men into trousers instead of belted cloaks. In the meantime, sun-drenched Athenians were building the Parthenon and,

healthy respect for wealth, recognised a king "with an unchallengeable right to obedience", and built powerful ships "unusual in that there is a prow at each end". Augustus and Nero sent expeditions to find out more, and it was through contact with Rome that the Scandinavians were inspired to produce their own alphabet.

Jordanes, the 6th-century historian of the Goths, was the first to identify "Dani" among the local tribes, all of whom were said to be taller than Germans and ferocious fighters. The Old English epic *Beowolf* planted the popular but erroneous idea that Scandinavians wore horned helmets, and Procopius, the Byzantine

like most Europeans, had no idea whatsoever of Scandinavia until the voyager Pytheas of Marseilles returned a little before 300 BC with tales of a land north of Britain where it was either dark for six months at a time or light enough, even at midnight, to pick lice out of a shirt. The local population were barbarians who lived on millet, herbs, roots and fruit because, he noticed, they had hardly any domestic animals, and threshing generally had to be done indoors. Nevertheless, grain fermented with honey produced a giddy drink they enjoyed.

Four centuries later, the Roman historian Tacitus reported significant improvements. The Suiones (Uppland Swedes) had developed a

historian, singled out the Lapps as people who had neither crops nor wine and wore animal skins held together with sinews. Lapp babies, he said, did not touch milk. Put into skin cradles and left dangling from trees while their mothers worked, they tucked into bone marrow. He also described hunters on skis and an excessive enthusiasm for human sacrifice.

Raiding parties

In 789, however, the Scandinavians spoke up for themselves. Three ships of an unfamiliar design appeared off the coast of Dorset in southwest England and the local magistrate ambled down to welcome them. Heavily armed warriors leapt ashore and subjected the hapless man to a fate known as "kissing the thin lips of the axe". As his head rolled, they stormed off to fill their ships with whatever caught their fancy, including a number of attractive natives, and were gone. The bemused *Anglo-Saxon Chronicle* could only say that they were apparently "Northmen from Hordaland" (Norwegians from the Bergen area). They returned four years later. As committed pagans, the raiders were unaffected by the sanctity of Chris-

> ### RUNIC WRITING
>
> To facilitate carving in wood or stone, the runic alphabet consisted of permutations of straight lines. It was used initially only for names and invocations against evil spirits.

navigable grid between the Gulf of Finland and the Caspian and Black seas. At the far end lay Constantinople, the richest city on earth and an inexhaustible market for northern products like amber, furs, weapons and above all fresh-faced European slaves. The Arab traveller and diplomat Ibn Fadlan was impressed by the usual attributes of the Swedes – "perfect physical specimens, tall as date palms, blond and ruddy" – but had reservations about their insistence on exercising seigneurial rites over the

tian monasteries stuffed with valuables. Beginning with Lindisfarne in Northumbria, they murdered monks and ransacked coastal monasteries all around the British Isles, and repeated the performance every summer. Prayers went up everywhere for delivery from so-called Northmen. They, however, called themselves Vikings, whose meaning is disputed.

At more or less the same time, Swedish counterparts were capitalising on the fact that lakes and rivers formed an almost uninterrupted

---

LEFT: Bronze Age Sun Chariot, National Museum of Denmark, Copenhagen.
RIGHT: rock carvings at Hjemmeluft, Sweden.

merchandise in public and en masse. "A man will have sexual intercourse with slave girls while his companions look on," he said.

On a third contemporary front, Charlemagne's crusade against the heathen Saxons of northwest Germany brought him into contact with their Danish neighbours on the other side of the Eider, whose look he liked even less. As the Danes felt exactly the same way about him and his Franks, they built the Danevirke wall across the Jutland peninsula to keep them at bay and to secure the border town of Hedeby, the trade bridge between the North Sea and the Baltic. Thus were sown the seeds of the Schleswig-Holstein imbroglio, a territorial dispute of such complexity that any-one dragged into it even 1,000 years later, according to a 19th-century British prime min-ister himself involved, was in danger of going mad or dying.

Al-Tartushi, another Arab traveller, went to see Hedeby, "a large town at the farthest end of the world ocean." The car-casses of sacrificed animals swung from poles, but the main food was fish "as there is so much of it".

Both men and women used eye make-up, he said (not that anyone else ever noticed),

NO LOVE LOST

In Arthurian romances the Vikings were described as being "wild and savage and had not in them the love of God nor their neighbours".

and women could unilaterally divorce their husbands whenever they felt like it.

Taken together, these developments across three fronts signalled the start of the "Viking Age" in which they went abroad to conquer most of the British Isles, carve a Norman province out of France, invade Germany, Spain and Italy, settle Iceland and Green-land, discover America, terrorise the Mediter-ranean, dominate the Baltic region, Poland, Russia and Ukraine, fight for and against Byzantium, attack the Muslim Caliphate in

VIKING SHIP DESIGN

A Viking's ticket to foreign parts was the latest evolution of the ship design first shown in Bronze Age rock carvings. The prows at either end were the extremities of a keel made out of a single oak. It could twist like a tree in the wind, hence its immense strength. A fighting ship of the type found at Gokstad in Norway was 25 metres (82 ft) long, 6 metres (19 ft) wide, and carried a crew of 70. Clinker-built, caulked with tarred animal hair or wool, it had a hinged steering oar that swung out of the way so the ships could be aimed at a beach at full speed. An important innovation was the use of sail. Viking ships could cross the North Sea to England in 72 hours.

Baghdad, and contribute to the liberation of Jerusalem. Meanwhile, the pack of warring chieftainships and petty kingdoms at home was being shuffled and cut down to form the sepa-rate states as exist today.

Trade with Byzantium

Various factors combined to produce this explo-sive energy. The disruption of traditional trade by the 9th-century Muslim conquests in Europe, for one, encouraged the Swedes to open up the alternative routes through Russia. They put it about that the Slavs begged them to take over the running of the territory. "Our land is large and fruitful but it lacks order," the message allegedly read. "Come over and rule us." By 900, Swedish influence radiated throughout Eastern Europe from their strongholds at Novgorod and Kiev. The Swedes were soon assimilated under the weight of Slavic numbers, but they left an indelible mark in the name by which they were locally known, Rus.

Polygamy and primogeniture were also forces behind the Viking Age. Big as Scandinavia was, only a tiny proportion of the land was actually habitable, and the useful land in remote valleys or fjords could only be subdivided so many times. As the whole of a patrimony generally went to the eldest son, or

foray in 844 opened with a rebuff at La Coruña on Spain's Atlantic coast, improved with the sacking of Lisbon, Cádiz and Seville, and ended with the loss of two ships crammed with gold, silver and prisoners to the Moors.

Terrorising the Mediterranean

Back again in 859 with a fleet of 62 red-sailed ships, Hasting negotiated the Straits of Gibraltar, sacked Algeciras, spent a week in Morocco rounding up "blue men" for subsequent sale in Ireland and then wintered on La Camargue in the Rhone Delta, "causing great annoyance and detriment to the inhabitants." Come spring, he

rather the eldest surviving son, Swedish kings with 40 women in their harem, or Norwegian earls with a dozen sons by various wives and concubines, were sure recipes for orgiastic fratricide. Harald Fairhair's ascendancy, c.890, went a long way towards defining Norway, but it necessarily involved stripping and disbanding numerous lessers dynasties, whose scions had no real choice but to try their luck abroad.

To begin with, Viking enterprise abroad was a matter of independent initiative, as epitomised by a certain Hasting. Born in Denmark, his first

LEFT: Viking burial ground, Jutland, Denmark.
ABOVE: runic script, National Museum, Copenhagen.

was ready for Italy. After looting Pisa, he turned south and came across a city of such marbled magnificence that it could only be Rome.

Hasting dispatched messengers with the story that their leader, a Christian of unparalled piety, was dying, and his last wish was to be given a Christian burial in such hallowed ground as now lay before them. Permission granted, the gates admitted a coffin followed by a long procession of mournful Vikings. As the local bishop was praying over the coffin it flew open and out leapt Hasting himself. The startled bishop was on his back, run through with Hasting's sword, as the mourners went off to reduce the city to ashes. Only then did Hasting learn that he had destroyed Luna, not Rome, and felt so cheated that he ordered the massacre of all male prisoners. His next port of call was Alexandria in Egypt. The campaign closed in 862 with an overland march to sack Pamplona.

England under attack

Three years later, in 865, Hasting appeared at the mouth of the Thames with a new fleet of 80 ships just as "a big heathen horde", according to the *Anglo-Saxon Chronicle*, arrived elsewhere in England under Ivar the Boneless. Their immediate mission was to avenge a private grievance, the cruel death of their father

Ragnar in a pit full of snakes, but with Hasting's fleet and other Danish private armies dotted around the country, the show took on the appearance of a concerted Danish conquest. The outcome was a Danish kingdom in England and the imposition of a stiff tax, Danegeld.

Ironically, Harald Bluetooth of Denmark (c.910–985) was in turn obliged to prostrate himself. His *bête noire* was the crusading Holy Roman Emperor Otto I, a German, who could be appeased only by Harald's submission to Christian baptism. Most of Europe had been Christian for five centuries or more, but Scandinavia was not inclined to abandon paganism. Harald's son and successor, Swein Forkbeard,

brushed aside his father's baptism as an aberration. The Norwegian king Olav Tryggvason (c.965–1000), a hell-raising pirate from the age of 12, was supposedly convinced by a wise hermit in the Scillies in England, but the methods he then employed to convert his subjects were pure Viking. Sweden remained true to paganism by turning Christian missionaries into martyrs. Sacrifices in the golden temple at Uppsala continued into the late 11th century.

Norman conquest

In France, Vikings who sailed up the Seine and attacked Paris were given 3,000 kg (3 tons) of silver by Charles the Bald of France to go away, while his successor Charles the Simple was ready to cede an entire province as protection money to Rolf (or "Rollo") the Ganger, a Viking too big to ride any horse. The province became the Duchy of Normandy, and within two centuries it was the springboard for the 1066 Norman conquest of Anglo-Danish England. But if the conquest was a great triumph for Norman arms, it also accelerated the end of the Viking Age.

Harald Hardrade of Norway (1015–66), the "Thunderbolt of the North", had tried to preempt William's seizure of England with an invasion of his own, and it was not long before Danish and Norwegian forces attempted to unseat William. But England under the Normans was a tough nut to crack; Normandy itself was no longer open to disgruntled Scandinavians, and Iceland was full. Greenland was the next possibility, and it was from here that Leifur Eiríksson set sail to see if he could find something better in the unknown world to the west.

As it was Leifur's own father who had coined the deceptive tease "Greenland", sceptics might have wondered about the son's tales of Vinland, a land of warm sunshine, trees, grass and, as the name implied, grapes. But his brother Thorvaldur believed him, followed his directions, and on landing in Vinland walked straight into an Indian arrow. The next assessment of the land's potential was by a fearsome woman, Freydis, who murdered most of her party en route. She was not over-impressed. The future America, she thought, was not more than "all right". ❏

LEFT: Lejre Iron Age village, Roskilde, Denmark.
RIGHT: Odin, the mythological Norse god of wisdom, war, culture and the dead.

MEDIEVAL THUGS OR MERCHANT TRADERS?

The Vikings plundered their way into the annals of Scandinavian history. But archaeology reveals there's more to these raiders than meets the eye

At first glance the Viking legacy appears to be little more than an impressive catalogue of violence and piracy. Archaeological finds have, however, shed light not only on the way the Vikings lived (everything from the food they ate to the clothing they wore) but also on their burial traditions. Today, the Vikings are recognised for their skills as craftsmen, traders and of course as sailors.

The Viking longship, essential for both raiding and trading, was also used to bury kings and chieftains. Superb examples can be seen at the Viking ship museums in Roskilde, Denmark, and in Oslo, Norway, where textiles, household utensils and other artefacts excavated from the burial mounds around the Oslo Fjord are also on display. In Denmark, Funen's Ladby Ship Museum houses a magnificent burial ship with a dragon's head and tail.

Sites and open-air museums such as those at Birka outside Stockholm *(see right)*, and Denmark's Fyrkat and Trelleborg, offer a unique look into the daily lives of the Vikings. Other places of interest include the burial ground at Lindholm Høje, Jutland and Jelling in Zealand, with its runes and burial mounds, often referred to as Denmark's "birth certificate". With a host of activities and re-enactments, these sites offer visitors a chance to relive the Viking experience first-hand.

▷ **BURIAL SHIP**
The Oseberg ship in Oslo's Vikingskipshuset is thought to be the tomb of a queen buried in 834 with her maidservant and most valued possessions.

△ **ANCIENT LIFESTYLE**
Reliving life the Viking way in Fyrkat, Denmark. Viking re-enactments are popular attractions in Jutland.

▽ **GRAVE OBJECTS**
Tools found in the graves at Birka, Sweden, are testimony to the society of skilled craftsmen who lived in the town.

▷ **CARVED IN STONE**
The Vikings would commemorate an event or a death on runestones like this one on Öland.

△ **DWELLING PLACE**
The reconstructed longhouse at Fyrkat, in Denmark, where four earth fortifications enclosed 16 large houses.

▽ **SAILING ONWARD**
Unlike other burial sites, graves at Lindholm Høje, Denmark, were marked by stones. This one is in the shape of a ship.

△ **MONEY MATTERS**
Danish, Frankish and Arabic coins were found at Birka. This one depicts a trading vessel.

◁ **HAIR CARE**
Combs were popular items. Many fine examples were found in the graves excavated at Birka.

△ **SHIPSHAPE**
Manoeuvrability and speed were the key features of Viking ship design. A number of replicas have been built in Norway, like this one in Oslo harbour.

THE VIKING SILK ROUTE

This bishop's crosier from Ireland, pictured above, was found at the site of Sweden's first Viking town, Birka. Situated 30 km (19 miles) west of Stockholm, Birka was founded towards the end of the 8th century.

Archaeological excavations have revealed trade networks stretching east to Byzantium and as far as China. The finds, which include silks from the Far East, Arabic coins and glass beads from the Arabic Caliphate, have challenged the belief that the Viking age was all murder and mayhem. They point instead to a burgeoning, prosperous society made up of merchants, traders and farmers.

Birka was the first town in Sweden to come into contact with Christianity. But the town was never evangelised and in some graves Thor's hammer was found alongside a crucifix.

The museum at Birka is open between May and mid-September. Boats leave from outside Stockholm City Hall, at Stadshusbron.

WAR AND PEACE

From the end of the Viking Age to the dawn of the 20th century, kings battled for supremacy, land changed hands and unions were made and broken

As the Viking Age drew to a close in the 11th century, the kings of Norway, Sweden and Denmark – "all handsome and big men, of noble looks and well-spoken" – met at Konghelle on the Göta River in 1098 to acknowledge one another's legitimacy and to adopt a common policy on robbery and theft, ever the crimes of greatest concern. To seal the pact, King Magnus of Norway – known as "Barelegs" since returning from Scotland sporting a kilt – married Inge of Sweden's daughter Margaret, hence "The Peace Maiden".

Five years later, however, Magnus fulfilled one of his own favourite sayings – "a king stands for his country's honour and glory, not for a long life" – by being killed in action in Ireland. Norway was then carved up among his three young sons, thereby undoing not only the single Norwegian kingdom hammered together by Harald Fairhair but also any real prospect of smooth Scandinavian co-existence.

Converting the heathens

Denmark's particular difficulty was not fragmentation but a succession of kings so ineffectual (e.g. "Harald the Hen") that several were simply taken out to sea and drowned. In Sweden, the throne bobbed between two dynasties who routinely murdered the opposing encumbent. Next to these goings-on, the princes of the new power in the land, the Church, looked purposeful. As comfortable in the saddle as the pulpit, Bishop Absalon of Roskilde (1128–1201) personally sorted out "the heathen Wend", a tribe of defiant Baltic pagans whose headquarters were on Rügen island. Smashing the four-headed god Svantevit, he offered everyone the choice of embracing Christ or dying immediately. The island then became part of his booming diocese. With bishops like Absalon around, ambitious kings were obliged to demonstrate their religious credentials by "taking the

Cross" and joining a crusade. Sigurd of Norway, one of Barelegs' sons ("not good-looking but well-grown and manly; his few words were most often not friendly") went to the Holy Land. Valdemar I (1131–82), a more dashing king than Denmark had seen for some time, fought 28 battles against heathens of one sort or

another. His successor Valdemar II concentrated on Estonians, and in spite of a fleet of 1,000 ships was only rescued from one certain defeat by the miraculous apparition of a red-and-white banner in the heavens. It became Denmark's national flag.

Sweden annexes Finland

Erik I of Sweden did his crusader service among the Finns during the 12th century, marking the start of Sweden's 700-year annexation of Finland and Erik's climb to the status of his country's patron saint. But aggrandisement was all too easily reversed, as occurred in Denmark on Valdemar II's exit. "The crown fell off the

LEFT: Gustav Vasa (1523–60), first king of the Vasa dynasty, laid the foundations of the Swedish state.
RIGHT: Kristian II of Denmark (1513–23).

head of the Danes," a chronicle wailed, "and they became the laughing stock for all their neighbours through civil wars and mutual destruction."

In Sweden, the saintly Erik I was murdered by the son of the king he had removed, Sverker, leaving Erik's son in no doubt about what was expected of him. He did not disappoint.

Like the Church, German and Dutch Hansa traders recognised the chaotic absence of government as an excellent opportunity for themselves. The obvious fact

THE DANISH FLAG

The oldest national flag in the world is a source of pride among Danes. It must never touch the ground and only a pennant version may be flown at night.

Fishing vessels raced from all over Europe until some 40,000 were crammed into the Sound, temporarily loosening the Hansa's grip on the market. The 14th-century king, Valdemar IV of Denmark, launched a snap invasion of the Hansa's base at Visby in Gotland and, flushed with success, assumed the title of "King of the Goths". The Hansa were neither impressed nor amused. Throwing the resources of their 77 towns and cities into a military alliance with Sweden, they bounced Valdemar off his Danish throne and

of Scandinavian economic life was an abundance of fish versus a shortage of grain. By tying up the markets in both commodities, and the shipping in between, the Hansa had a goose of pure gold, and it gave them a network of strategic ports and market towns across the continent. But if Scandinavia was sapped by an extortionate exchange rate between fish and grain, it was then poleaxed by the Black Death in 1349. With the population of Norway, for example, cut by more than half, economics reverted to the Stone Age.

One interlude in the slow reconstruction process was the arrival of shoals of herring so dense that fish could be caught with bare hands.

invited applications. Margarethe, the young wife of King Håkon VI of Norway, proposed their son Oluf. He was five years old.

A scheming queen

Margarethe, who had married in 1363 at the age of 10 and given birth to Oluf at 17, knew what she was doing. With Denmark under Oluf's little belt and the Norwegian crown bound to follow in due course, she encouraged him to think of himself as "the true heir to Sweden" as well, a presumption that infuriated Albrecht, the reigning king of Sweden.

Nevertheless, Margarethe (described as "of dark complexion and somewhat masculine in appearance") had to think again when Oluf died at 17. While personally keeping the Danish throne warm, she persuaded the Norwegian nobility to recognise her grandnephew Erik of Pomerania as Oluf's successor. Erik, too, was five at this turning point in his career. Margarethe went behind Albrecht's back to offer the Swedish nobles perpetual rights to their property and privileges in exchange for their support against him. Albrecht could take no more. Raising an army of German mercenaries, he demanded satisfaction at Falkoping. A chronicler was surprised by the outcome: "God gave an unexpected victory into the hands of a woman."

of a war with Holstein when she collapsed. The Danish nobility were inclined to ask aloud whether their interests might be better served by Erik's nephew, Christopher of Bavaria, and the talk in Sweden was of a separate constitution and a fresh crowned head. Meanwhile, Erik retired to Visborg Castle in Gotland and applied himself, privately and very profitably, to the business of piracy.

Stockholm Bloodbath

After more than one trial separation Denmark and Sweden were together again under the Danish king, Kristian II (1481–1559). Anti-

Margarethe's grand scheme was at last realised at Kalmar in 1397 when Eric, now 14, donned the three crowns of Norway, Denmark and Sweden. "Rash, violent and obstinate," he faced the tall order of running an empire from the Arctic Circle (including Swedish Finland) to the Eider, and west to Greenland, with no money or support from the wary nobility. Margarethe had her hands full nursing the damage caused by Erik's railings against these constraints, and she was addressing the aftermath

---

LEFT: the Swedish army is defeated by Peter the Great of Russia at the battle of Poltava, 1709.
ABOVE: a depiction of medieval life at Turku Castle.

Danish feeling was growing apace in Sweden when the Swedish assembly voted to burn the fortress of the Archbishop of Sweden, a pro-Dane, Gustav Trolle. In the event Trolle was merely imprisoned, but in 1520 the Papal Court excommunicated the Swedish regent, Sten Sture the Younger, for this act. Kristian II had the justification he sought for invading Sweden. He invited Sweden's leading nobles to a feast in Stockholm at which he chopped off the heads of 82 of Sweden's finest. This "Stockholm Bloodbath" provoked a rebellion.

Kristian was driven out of Sweden and Gustav Vasa, a nobleman whose family had been victims in the massacre seized power.

Thus began a Swedish dynasty of exceptional distinction and durability.

Hounded out of Denmark, Kristian II sought refuge in the Netherlands. Norway's clergy, staunchly loyal to Rome, made him an offer of the Norwegian throne, which provoked violent intervention by Danish and Hanseatic forces with far-reaching consequences. Kristian spent the rest of his life in Sonderborg Castle, while the Norwegian church was purged of Roman Catholics to make it Lutheran, and the Norwegian monarchy was abolished. Norway was thereafter a mere province of Denmark. The tripartite Kalmar Union was dead.

squadrons crossed the ice and a resounding victory cost Denmark all its territory on the Swedish side of the Sound.

The warrior king

In Karl XII (1682–1718), Sweden seemed to acquire a reincarnation of the Vikings who fought and caroused their way across Russia. Taking over the mantle of the traditional Germanic *Drang nach Osten* (drive to the east), he collided with Peter the Great of Russia.

The Russians eventually got the better of a titanic struggle, putting Karl in the impossible position of trying to rule Sweden from his bolt-

Battle on ice

Kristian IV (1577–1648) was on the Danish throne for 52 years, building palaces and towns, trebling the size of the navy, and sending explorers to investigate the possibility of a northwest passage to Asia. He took an avuncular interest in Norway, renaming Oslo after himself ("Kristiania"), but never managed to achieve friendly relations with Sweden or his counterpart, Gustavus II Adolphus.

Inevitably they entered the Thirty Years War on opposite sides, but the Swedish king was quicker off the mark when the Sound (Øresund) between the two countries froze over during the winter of 1657. Two cavalry

hole in Turkey. Finally, he rode home with two companions, a journey of 1,300 miles, only to find that in his absence Sweden had been stripped of all his recent gains. His plan to put matters right began and ended with a siege of Frederiksten in southern Norway. The bullet through his head may have been fired by a genuine enemy sniper or a contracted assassin, but in any case Sweden decided to give absolutism a rest and explore constitutional government.

Denmark's first taste of quasi-constitutional government was deferred until the 1770s and even so only materialised in strange circumstances. Kristian VII's increasingly erratic behaviour clearly needed medical attention, a task entrusted to a German doctor, Johann Friederich Struensee. The patient was off his head, Struensee decided, so the best he could do was to run the country himself. And so he did.

In little more than a year, Struensee drew up 1,069 bills introducing freedom of speech and the press, a national budget, the decriminalisation of fornication and adultery, and the abolition of capital punishment for all but the most unspeakable crimes.

He could not have envisaged, as he extended his stately role to touch on the void in Queen Caroline Matilde's conjugal life, that he would be dragged out of bed at dawn and charged with

Britain bombarded Copenhagen, Tsar Alexander I occupied Finland, bringing the ages-old Swedish rule initiated by St Erik to a close.

Russia wins Finland

Russia later changed sides and was sitting with the victors when reparations were decided after the Battle of Waterloo (1815). Russia was allowed to keep Finland; Norway was detached from Denmark and handed to Sweden, albeit not as a colony but as a supposed equal in a union under a common crown.

The king in question was a curious choice: Jean-Baptiste Bernadotte was French and not

just such a crime, one that still carried the supreme penalty. Locked up in Kronborg Castle at Helsingør, his partner in crime was rescued from her fate by an English warship sent by George III, himself showing signs of instability but her brother nonetheless.

The same navy was again under the guns of Kronborg Castle at the outbreak of the Napoleonic War in the early 19th century, in this instance because Denmark had sided with Russia, at that stage Napoleon's ally. While

LEFT: the Swedish royal palace of Drottningholm, designed in the 17th century by Tessin the Elder.
ABOVE: *Conversation at Drottningholm*, 1779.

THE GREAT EXODUS

The 19th century witnessed a mass exodus of Scandinavians in search of a better life in the New World. "Potatoes, peace and vaccination" were blamed for a population explosion at home which contributed to an outflow of 750,000 Norwegian and 1 million Swedish emigrants – a quarter of the Swedish population.

The new settlers sent back glowing accounts of their lives in America, and money to support those left behind. These signs of prosperity and other factors such as The United States Homestead Act of 1862, which promised land almost free to settlers who dared to travel west, encouraged others to follow.

only a former general of the French Revolution but a key member of Napoleon's staff. If taking the name Karl Johan was meant to help him to blend into his new surroundings, this was offset by his refusal to speak anything but French.

Thus reorganised, the Scandinavian states stepped into the frenzy of romantic nationalism that swept across Europe and inspired phenomenal scientific progress and a flowering of the arts. In these respects Scandinavia did its bit and more. Sweden was especially strong in the sciences;

> ### TROUBLED UNION
>
> Sweden typically bribed North African pirates not to attack their ships, but to plunder those of the Norwegians who insisted on sailing under their own colours.

consider, for one, Linnaeus, the naturalist *(see box, below)*. Denmark's most notable contributions were the writer Hans Christian Andersen *(see page 127)* and the philosopher, Søren Kierkegaard. Norway offered Edvard Grieg (composer), Henrik Ibsen (dramatist) and Edvard Munch (painter), and Finland (pre-Sibelius) contributed the *Kalevala*, an epic which Elias Lönnrot compiled from old ballads and songs to reinvent his country's hitherto elusive past.

Language became a vexing issue in Finland and Norway. Mikael Agricola, the Bishop of Turku, had produced a Finnish translation of the Bible as early as 1642, and although Finnish had always been spoken by the majority of the population, it had no official status. The Russians even banned books written in Finnish.

In Norway, Old Norse had gone to Iceland with the Viking settlers, while the language in Norway itself had been affected by Danish connections. Pure Danish was used for official business, in literature and by the educated classes. In the 19th century Norwegian nationalists wanted to revert to untainted Norwegian. They concocted a cocktail from Norway's surviving rural dialects called "New Norwegian".

Friends and foes

One 19th-century development was that Swedish, Danish and Norwegian (but not yet Finnish) historians could at last get together for a chat without coming to blows, and in this spirit Swedish and Danish university students took advantage of the atrocious winter of 1838, when the Sound again froze over, to walk across the ice, meet in the middle, and improvise odes to Scandinavian solidarity.

If this was reminiscent of Magnus Barelegs and company at Konghelle, the dream was again upset by events in Norway, where the union with Sweden was in trouble. Norway strengthened its fortifications along the Swedish frontier, and Sweden had its army on alert before a compromise was worked out. The union dissolved and, as Norway went shopping for a new king, Scandinavia braced itself for the 20th century. ❑

LINNAEUS, THE PLANTSMAN

Carl Linnaeus (also known as von Linné), the Swedish naturalist who devised the modern classification system for plants and animals, was one of the great scientists of 18th-century Scandinavia. Born in 1707, he studied medicine at the University of Lund and botany at Uppsala. He travelled widely and was a leading figure in the founding of the Swedish Academy of Science. As chair of botany, dietetics and *materia medica* at Uppsala, he pursued his research into nomenclature. His publications included *Systema Naturae* (1735), *Philosophia Botanica* (1750), and *Species Plantarum* (1753). Linnaeus died in 1778. His house and botanical garden can be visited at Uppsala.

LEFT: Alfred Nobel (1833–96), Swedish chemist, inventor of dynamite and founder of the Nobel Prizes.
RIGHT: Sami girls in traditional costume, 1898.

THE MODERN AGE

*Two world wars took their toll on the Nordic countries, but by the end of the
20th century they had emerged as sophisticated economic powers*

The 20th century dawned with not only the union of Sweden and Norway on the rocks but also the special relationship between Finland and Russia. A new tsar, the ill-fated Nicholas II, did not share his predecessors' fond view of Finland as a separate grand duchy and liked even less the privileges that went with it. So while breakaway Norway recruited Håkon VII, né Prince Carl of Denmark, as its first independent king for 600 years, Finland was delivered into the hands of Nikolai Ivanovich Bobrikov, a hard-boiled martinet whose previous assignment had been to knock some sense into Russia's wayward Baltic provinces.

King Håkon accepted the job only after a plebiscite indicated that three-quarters of the Norwegian population wanted him. Bobrikov did not bother with such trifles. Having abolished the Finns' exemption from service in the Russian imperial forces, he was systematically shredding the freedom of speech and other rights when he was met on the staircase to the Senate by Eugen Schauman, a civil servant. Schauman put three bullets into the brute before turning the revolver on himself.

The onset of World War I

Fortunately for Finland, the tsar was too involved in war with Japan and later in the St Petersburg uprising to avenge Bobrikov's murder. Every one of 40 previous wars with Russia had gone badly for the Finns, but they were always ready to try again. The first whiff of World War I saw volunteers flocking to Germany to join a special "Jagar battalion" which duly entered the field against Russia alongside Kaiser Wilhem's forces.

For their part, the three kings of Scandinavia met at Malmö in Sweden in December 1914 and declared their neutrality. However, putting the proclamation into practice was not so easy. After centuries of anguish over Schleswig-

Holstein, Denmark was not Germany's greatest admirer, but it was in no position to defy the kaiser's orders to mine Danish sea-lanes against the British navy. Conversely, Norway received a warning from Britain that selling fish, iron pyrites or copper to Germany would not be tolerated, and Sweden was in fact blockaded,

eventually to suffer acute food shortages, for trading too eagerly with Wilhem. The worst blow, though, was Germany's declaration of unrestricted submarine warfare in 1916. Hundreds of Scandinavian ships and crews "on charter" to Britain had in fact been commandeered, but they went to the bottom all the same and with heavy losses.

On Russia's withdrawal from the war after the Bolshevik revolution in 1917, Lenin made a direct appeal to sympathisers in Scandinavia and Finland in particular. "Rise, rise instantly," he cried, "take over the government in the hands of organised labour." The Finnish Red Guard, about 30,000 strong, accordingly seized

LEFT: flag-waving during the annual National Day celebrations in Norway on 17 May.
RIGHT: evacuated Finnish family, 1939.

government offices in Helsinki and proclaimed a Socialist Workers' Republic. The government's response was to raise a White Guard, including the Jagar battalion, Swedish volunteers and 12,000 German troops, under the command of General Baron Gustaf Mannerheim, a former White Russian cavalry officer. The revolution lasted less than four months, but there were 24,000 casualties and a comparable number of Red sympathisers were subsequently executed or left to die in internment camps.

Consideration was then given to turning Finland into a kingdom with one of Kaiser Wilhem's sons on the throne, but Germany's

MED WAFFEN-*SS* OG
DEN NORSKE LEGION
MOT DEN FELLES FIENDE.....

UNDERCOVER OPERATIONS

The Resistance movement in Denmark and Norway was crucial in undermining the German campaign during World War II. Anders Lassen epitomised the 20,000-strong Danish Resistance. By the time he died aged 24, he had fought in France, Greece, the Balkans and Italy. His commanding officer said, "Anders caused more discomfort to the enemy over five years of war than any other man of his rank and age." Other heroes included the Norwegians who knocked out the heavy water plant at Rjukan (*Heroes of Telemark, see page 180*). Two museums, Frihedsmuseet, Copenhagen, and Norges Hjemmefront-museum, Oslo, document the movement's history.

---

defeat in the war turned opinion in favour of a republic under the presidency of Kaarlo Juho Stahlberg, a local professor of law. The Soviet Union raised no objection to Finland's independence and signed the Treaty of Tartu to that effect, but Finland's fanatical Christian fundamentalists, the Lapua pietists, were determined to clear the nest of vipers. Suspected communists were kidnapped, beaten and dumped at the Soviet border. The pietists forced the government to ban communism completely and were arming themselves for a full-scale *coup d'état* when the army decided they had been around too long for any good they were doing.

Sweden sailed through the post-war years on a wave of international demand for Swedish steel and ball bearings, Ericsson telephones and Electrolux vacuum cleaners. While also doing well, Norway and Denmark clashed over Greenland and the Arctic islands of Svalbard (Spitzbergen) and Jan Mayen, which raised issues rooted in Viking times. Asked to arbitrate, the international court at the Hague gave Greenland to Denmark, the islands to Norway.

Scandinavia emerged from the second crisis of the inter-war years, the Great Depression, with improved political systems. The severity of the situation forced small parties with narrow interests – farmers' parties being a prime example – to remove their blinkers and join broader coalitions, the front runners generally calling themselves "Social Democrats".

World War II

With the Depression out of the way it was not long until the storm clouds of World War II gathered. Hitler's rise was especially worrying to Denmark because Germany had never formally agreed to the Schleswig-Holstein border as defined by plebiscite after World War I. Accepting his surprising offer of a non-aggression pact, Denmark nevertheless joined Sweden and Norway in another declaration of neutrality.

Finland was again a special case. When Hitler invaded Poland, Stalin assumed Russia would be next and seized a strip of Finnish territory to strengthen the defences around Leningrad. The 1939 Nazi-Soviet pact removed this threat, but at the same time it allowed Stalin

---

LEFT: World War II poster published during the German occupation of Norway, 1941.
RIGHT: German aircraft on Finland's tundra, 1941.

a free hand in Finland, and he ordered an invasion. Marshal Mannerheim, now in his seventies, came out of retirement to lead Finland in what came to be known as the Winter War.

Almost invisible in the white uniforms against driving snow, Finnish troops went into action on skis against Russian tanks. As Swedish volunteers arrived to help, Hitler had to restrain Mussolini ("that great man across the Alps") from sending in the Italian air force to give Stalin one in the eye. What really mattered, though, was the collapse of the Nazi-Soviet pact and Germany's invasion of Russia. The Finns went in at the same time to recover their recent losses (the "War of Continuation") and were therefore stigmatised as Hitler's allies.

German aggression

The German invasion of Denmark and Norway began on 9 April 1940. Some troops crossed the Jutland border into Denmark, others emerged from hiding in German merchant ships in Copenhagen harbour, and paratroops landed at key points around the country. The Danish army was in barracks, the navy was too surprised to fire a single shot, and the air force was destroyed on the ground. If nothing else, the Royal Life Guards at Amalienborg Palace in

THE DEMON DRINK

Stringent laws on the purchase of alcohol in Norway and Sweden have been somewhat at odds with the figure these countries have wanted to cut in the modern world. The time-honoured yearning for drink can be blamed on long winter nights, but ancient Scandinavians also drank like fish because their food was preserved with lashings of salt. King Sverre of Norway experimented with prohibition as early as the 12th century. In 1775, however, King Gustav III of Sweden turned the distillation and sale of spirits into a royal monopoly and encouraged his subjects to drink because he needed the money. Against this backdrop, 20th-century prohibitionists had problems. The conundrum in Norway was that France, Spain and Portugal, major consumers of Norwegian fish, had always bartered with wine or brandy. The issue of prohibition led to the downfall of three successive governments in the early 20th century.

Sweden, however, put its faith in the "Bratt Liquor Control System", a certain Dr Ivan Bratt having worked out exactly how much alcohol an individual could consume according to age, physique and other considerations, with the result that it was almost impossible for a married woman to qualify for a single drink in any circumstances. Today, as in Gustav III's time, the sale of wines and spirits in both countries, as well as in Finland, is a state monopoly.

The Royal Line

I t used to be said, not so long ago, that there would soon be just five kings left in the world: of England, clubs, hearts, spades and diamonds. Come the turn of the millennium, however, there were still six monarchies alive in Europe, three of them in Scandinavia. Moreover, the royal families of Denmark, Sweden and Norway were probably as secure and popular as ever they had been.

Monarchy could hardly be more entrenched than in Denmark. Queen Margrethe II is the 52nd in an unbroken line of sovereigns spanning more than

1,000 years. Sweden, too, has had more than 50 kings since 980. The present King Carl Gustaf may be "XVI" but his direct line begins with Jean Baptiste Bernadotte, the French marshal who was installed on the throne in 1810. Norway's royal line ceased when Norway became a Danish province and the monarchy was only restored, after a referendum, following the dissolution in 1905 of the subsequent union with Sweden. The present king, Harald V, is the third of the modern line, the "V" notwithstanding. Finland also considered a monarchy on breaking away from Russia, but chose to become a republic instead.

Nevertheless, not a little craft has gone into keeping the Scandinavian monarchies in robust health. When Carl XVI Gustaf ascended the Swedish throne in 1973, the Constitution began with: "The King alone shall govern the realm..." Lest he got the wrong impression, this was hastily changed to: "All public power in Sweden emanates from the people..." The king decided his own official motto ought to be: "For Sweden – in Keeping with the Times". This was the cue for changing the rules of succession so that they no longer discriminated against daughters. Consequently, next in line is Crown Princess Victoria rather than her younger brother. Their mother, Queen Silvia, is the daughter of a German businessman.

Carl Gustaf is not averse to tearing around in a Ferrari and was reported to the police in Denmark for doing an alleged 250 kph (155 mph) on the Copenhagen expressway. Nonsense, the king retorted. He admitted having a lot to do on his way to Queen Margrethe's 60th birthday but had not exceeded 150. In contrast, King Harald loves boats – and has represented his country at the Olympic Games – but would not be seen dead in a Ferrari. He uses public transport. Harald works hard at being uninteresting, a quality Norwegians apparently like in their kings. Queen Sonja is the daughter of an Oslo shopkeeper and their children went to state schools. Fittingly, the Crown Prince found himself a bachelor flat in an unfashionable part of Oslo but let the side down, as it were, by sharing it with a waitress, and her three-year-old son by a man who was in prison for drug offences; they are now married.

If conscientious exercises in non-charisma go down well in Norway, Queen Margrethe could not hope to do the same in Denmark. She has been showered with genuine academic honours from the likes of Cambridge, Oxford and the London School of Economics. While trying unsuccessfully to hide her distinguished output as a painter, writer and designer behind a string of aliases, she has at least persuaded her friends to call her Daisy. Crown Prince Frederik, her heir, is not much better at disguise. Dressing down for a night on the town, he turned out so scruffy that the bar refused to let him in. The situation was saved by an extremely attractive stranger, one Bettina Odum, stepping forward to say that he was with her. As a trained soldier, no mean dancer and the leader of a husky-drawn expedition across Greenland, Frederik looks set to retain his position with the voters as Denmark's "Man of the Year" for some time to come. ❑

LEFT: the ever-popular Queen Margarethe of Denmark celebrating her 60th birthday in 2000.

Copenhagen prevented the Germans from capturing King Kristian X just long enough for him to order a surrender. Denmark remained in theory a sovereign state under German protection, but when the king ignored Hitler's effusive greetings on his birthday in 1942, the pretence was dropped. A new government was expected to jump at Hitler's whim, but it refused to sanction death sentences on members of the increasingly active Resistance movement and made arrangements to smuggle Denmark's endangered Jews to safety in Sweden.

Norway is overrun

In Norway's case, gunners in an old fortress on Oslo fjord had the satisfaction of sinking the German cruiser *Blucher* on the first day of the invasion, killing or at least drenching the bureaucrats earmarked to run the country with Hitler's local stooge, Vidkun Quisling, the leader of the National Socialist Party. King Håkon and most members of the government escaped to Tromsø in northern Norway and remained there while a combined force of British, French, Polish and Norwegian units recaptured the iron-ore port of Narvik. The sudden collapse of France, however, created a greater demand for the expeditionary force elsewhere, so as the Allies withdrew the king and his entourage were evacuated to England.

Neutral throughout the war, Sweden took in 300,000 refugees. The Swedish Red Cross, led by Count Folke Bernadotte, a nephew of the king, secured the release of 30,000 prisoners of various nationalities from German concentration camps, and the diplomat Raoul Wallenberg played "Schindler" to Jews in Hungary. But it was also the case that German troops and materials were given permission to cross Sweden on their way to Norway in 1940 and thereafter when they went on leave. Moreover, Sweden supplied iron ore critical to the German war machine. These are matters which Norwegians to this day cannot easily forget.

Peacetime recovery

The last stage of the war, with German forces scorching the earth in their retreat from the advancing Soviets, hurt northern Norway but was utterly devastating in Finland. The latter,

RIGHT: the great long-distance runner Paavo Nurmi lights the Olympic flame at the 1952 Helsinki Games.

then, could hardly have been in a worse position to meet Soviet demands for US$600 million in reparations. These were to be paid within 10 years in goods other than what remained of the Finnish economy, namely trees. Barred by Moscow from accepting Marshall aid, Finland nevertheless beat the deadline by creating a diversified industrial economy from scratch.

Reparations out of the way, the bottomless Soviet market kept these new industries – shipbuilding, oil refineries, textiles – working flat out, with the extra bonus that the USSR paid for goods in dirt-cheap oil. So the eventual collapse of the Soviet Union was politically a pleasure but

at the same time a threat to the Finnish economy – until, among numerous aspects of the country's second economic miracle, Nokia recognised the potential of the mobile phone and Porsche decided to build its new Boxster model in Finland. By the turn of the millennium, Finland was a member of the European Union.

A new way of life

Recovery from the war in Denmark and Norway was set in motion by the Marshall Plan, and within a decade or so they were able to join Sweden in presenting a seemingly united Scandinavian front to the outside world. In certain quarters, the image was a paradox, a combination of beautiful and talented people, an enviable standard of living, robust health, exceptional generosity to the Third World – and at the same time rather too much promiscuity, self-righteousness and suicide.

At the heart of all this lay the desire to find a compromise between capitalism and socialism, in Sweden's case "the Middle Way". While Denmark and Norway joined NATO after the war, Sweden remained nonaligned and spent a huge proportion of the national budget on its arms industry in the belief, or at least hope, that its products would therefore never be required.

To begin with, Scandinavians were willing to live with the punitive taxation needed to cover the cost of their vaunted "cradle-to-grave" social security if only because memories of bitterly hard times without it were still fresh. But if new generations were less susceptible to these fears and consequently concerned about the enormous cost of maintaining the safety, in Norway and Denmark it suddenly didn't matter. They struck oil.

The new oil-rich nations

Denmark's agriculture was always on its toes. Characteristically quick to breed a pig that produced the streaky bacon popular on British breakfast tables, and companies like Lego,

Bang & Olufsen and Carlsberg, which proved adept at exploiting particular market niches, it was the first time the country had enjoyed the luxury of natural resources since the herring shoals in the 14th century. Ironically, Denmark's North Sea windfall arrived in the middle of concerted efforts to start "wind farms", fields full of power-generating turbines.

Measured against population, the prize in Norway was much bigger and triggered lavish expenditure on items such as road tunnels through solid rock which served no indispensable purpose that anyone could think of. At one point it looked as if Norway might have blown more oil revenue than existed under the North Sea, but new discoveries, especially of gas, put such fears to rest.

Deprived of any share of the North Sea bonanza, Sweden's Middle Way showed signs of turning into a cul-de-sac. Industry had long been pampered with low taxes on profits while individual taxpayers were bled white. Companies like Volvo had a proud international profile but even they complained loudly of burdens like the costs attached to each employee in the form of national insurance, shorter working weeks, longer holidays and so on. Nevertheless, most Swedes were astonished and dismayed when Saab was swallowed by General Motors, Volvo by Ford, and a regiment of other prestigious companies decamped abroad.

Bridge to the future

While more than one proposed business merger along pan-Scandinavian lines tripped up on mutual misgivings as ancient as the Kalmar Union, the new millennium found a cure for the oldest schism of all. The Øresund road and rail bridge rejoined Denmark and Sweden in 2000, a connection broken by the cataclysmic convulsion at the end of the Ice Age. Although the bridge has strengthened pan-Scandinavian links, it has conversely fuelled the traditional suspicion of the European Union, symbolised by the Euro. In September 2003 a public referendum will be held in Sweden to decide the most far-reaching issue the country has faced in decades – whether to join the single currency and consequently loosen ties with neighbouring Denmark, which has opted to stay outside the new currency. ❑

LEFT: Olof Palme, prime minister of Sweden and international peace campaigner, assassinated in 1986.
RIGHT: Øresund bridge linking Denmark and Sweden.

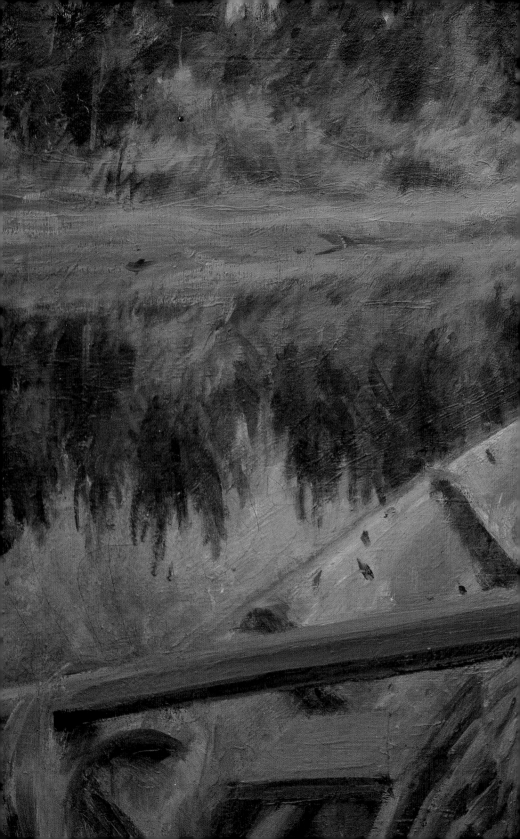

ART AND CULTURE

Rich in art, music and literature, and pioneers of modern design,
Scandinavians are justifiably proud of their cultural heritage

The history of Denmark, Norway, Sweden, and Finland has been so intertwined through the centuries that, while each country possesses a unique culture, there are strong similarities, perhaps best seen in design and an overall "feel" for visual expression. A bias towards simplicity pervades with clean lines, natural materials and a lack of pretence.

Although much of what is considered Scandinavian style is a product of the 20th century *(see page 54)* there is an underlying cultural heritage that complements the modern look. Exceptions exist, such as work commissioned by royalty with French design in mind, but the tastes of the people over the past 200 years make the strongest impression on the visitor.

DENMARK

The rich cultural history of Denmark finds expression in centuries-worth of art and artefacts, including Viking treasures, numerous castles and manor houses, churches (many from the Middle Ages), fortresses, stimulating museums, and some of the finest contemporary design in the world.

Denmark's strongest art tradition is literary, reaching back to sagas and medieval folk songs, to the most popular Danish playwright, Ludvig Holberg (1684–1754) in the Age of Enlightenment, the Romantic poet Adam Oehlenschläger (1779–1850) and, in the 19th century, to Hans Christian Andersen (1805–75) and Søren Kierkegaard (1813–55).

Thanks to stories such as *The Little Mermaid*, Andersen is probably the most widely read Danish writer today. His children's tales – including *The Ugly Duckling*, *The Emperor's New Clothes* and *The Princess and the Pea* – gained him world-wide fame, and their popularity has not waned as a source for plays, ballets, films, visual arts and bedtime reading. In

the 20th century, Karen Blixen (1885–1962), working under the pseudonym Isak Dinesen, gained international recognition for her 1937 memoir of her years in Kenya, *Out of Africa*, which became a Hollywood movie in 1985.

The Danish philosopher Søren Kierkegaard, known as the father of existentialism, wrote in

the first half of the 19th century, but his work had the most impact in the mid-20th century, when in translation it became an important source for existentialists.

Masters of dance

More than a third of the state funds allocated for the theatre in Denmark finance the Det Kongelige Teater (Royal Theatre) in Copenhagen, founded in 1748. This building also houses the Royal Danish Opera, the Royal Danish Orchestra and the Royal Danish Ballet. The ballet company, formed 150 years ago, is one of the most influential worldwide. It has attracted great masters such as August Bournonville

---

PRECEDING PAGES: Norwegian composer Edvard Grieg; *Midnight* by Sweden's Anders Zorn, 1891.
LEFT: *The Girl in the Kitchen*, Anna Ancher, 1883–6.
RIGHT: Karen Blixen, Denmark, author of *Out of Africa*.

(1805–79), creator of today's "classical ballet" and choreographer of more than 50 productions, including the popular *La Sylphide*.

The big screen

Denmark's Nordisk Film Kompagni, founded in 1906, is the oldest film company still in operation. Carl Theodor Dreyer (1889–1968), a master of psychological realism who started his career here, produced classics such as *The Passion of Joan of Arc* (1928) and *The Word* (1955). Today the government-supported Danish Film Institute is the heart of a vibrant Danish film industry. *Babette's Feast* (1986), based on a story by Karen Blixen, directed by Gabriel Axel, and *Pelle the Conqueror* (1987), directed by Bille August, both won Academy Awards for Best Foreign Film. In the 1990s Lars von Trier's *Breaking the Waves*, Thomas Vinterberg's *The Celebration* and Søren Kragh-Jacobsen's *Mifune's Last Song* have attracted international acclaim. These directors are signatories (along with Kristian Levring) of the Dogma 95 Manifesto. This set of "chastity" rules, which holds that films should be made on location without artificial lighting or sound, using hand-held cameras, was intended as a personal challenge to help to reinvigorate film.

LOUISIANA MUSEUM OF MODERN ART

Small museum treasures may be found throughout Denmark, but the most complete and satisfying of them all is the Louisiana Museum of Modern Art, situated in a sublime spot in Humlebæk, 35 km (22 miles) north of Copenhagen. Louisiana houses a splendid collection of 20th-century art, including pieces by Pablo Picasso, Andy Warhol, Alberto Giacometti and Asger Jorn. It lies on the water's edge, and the extensive sculpture garden, featuring work by Henry Moore and Alexander Calder, that surrounds the unassuming building (much of its space is underground) is backdropped by exquisite coastal scenery and landscaping (www.louisiana.dk).

The Skagen painters

In the visual arts, Denmark's most notable contributions were produced in the 19th and 20th centuries. C.W. Eckersberg (1783–1853), the father of Danish painting, and those who studied under him absorbed the artistic lessons offered from France, particularly a sense of classical nature. At the end of the 19th century, a group of artists – including P.S. Krøyer (1851–1909) and Michael and Anna Ancher (1859–1935) – based themselves in Skagen at the northernmost tip of Jutland. Known as the "Skagen painters", they turned away from Impressionism, the favoured French style of the day, while still being highly indebted to it. Their works captured the special northern light within images of the maritime landscape.

In the middle of the 20th century, Asger Jorn (1914–73), a member of the CoBrA art movement (including artists from Copenhagen, Brussels and Amsterdam), created large, bold, brightly coloured paintings. His expressionistic and experimental works on canvas and ceramics played a key role in the development and promotion of modern Danish art.

SWEDEN

Along with being the conqueror rather than the conquered throughout history, Sweden

King", took many of his cues from the royal court of France and was a great patron of drama and the arts. In 1773, he built the Kungliga Teatern (Royal Theatre, known today as the Royal Opera), and Kunliga Dramatiska Teatern (Royal Dramatic Theatre or *Dramaten*) in 1788. In addition, he hired Swedish actors and singers, forming the basis for a tradition of opera and drama performed in Swedish instead of in the original French or Italian.

The most notable of Swedish dramatic venues is Drottningholms Slottsteater (Drottningholm Court Theatre), in the grounds of Drottningholm Palace outside Stockholm. Built

developed strong cultural traditions, particularly in theatre, music and dance.

Diplomatic as well as commercial ties with European cultural centres provided conduits for importing styles that left their mark on architecture and the performing arts. The prosperity of the Swedish monarchy resulted in the patronage of cultural venues, theatre troupes and court painters. Their private collections became the basis for national art museums.

King Gustav III (1771–92), the "Theatre

LEFT: Drottningholms Slottsteater, near Stockholm, built by "Theatre King" Gustav III in the 18th century.
ABOVE: interior at Sundborn, Sweden, by Carl Larsson.

in 1766 and rediscovered and restored in the mid-20th century, every summer this intimate stage draws spectators from all over the world eager to see baroque and rococo productions in an intact 18th-century theatre, complete with original backdrops and stage machinery.

Award-winning writers

One of the best-known (at least among Swedes) and still popular writers of the past is Carl Bellman, a troubadour, whose lyrics and poems immortalised daily life in the 18th century.

Works such as *The Red Room* by August Strindberg (1849–1912) and *Gösta Berlings Saga* by Selma Lagerlöf (1858–1940), two of

Cool looks

Say "Scandinavian design"and most people visualise furniture, glass and domestic ware with pure forms and simple, clean lines. The aesthetic is immediately recognisable, especially since the Swedish home-furnishing giant IKEA invaded the world.

Elegant, light, sparse – these are all descriptive of the Scandinavian look – along with a respect for natural materials and superb craftsmanship. The key is not only good looks, but also utility. This picture of Scandinavian design, while having roots in

traditional crafts, is very much a product of the 20th century and the age of Functionalism.

Taking off in the 1920s, led by architects and artists such as Le Corbusier in France and Walter Gropius in Germany, Functionalism applies to various movements such as the International Style and Bauhaus. In Scandinavia it has been a source of inspiration since the 1930s.

The move away from ornamentation in favour of clean shapes and lines, allowing for the pure expression of the essence of structures, was more than a mere change in taste. Adherents to this style, which manifested itself in new materials (tubular metal, steel and glass), also embraced a vision for a new world, one where architecture and design could contribute to the levelling out of injustices in modern society. In Scandinavia, not only were the aesthetics of the modern, international style eagerly adopted, the social agenda behind the style was also very popular.

Earlier in the 1900s, Carl and Karin Larsson, taking their cue from the English Arts and Crafts movement, revived an interest in traditional Swedish crafts and craftsmanship. Their home at Sundborn, now a museum of Swedish country style *(see page 269)*, features textiles with simple checked and striped patterns, against a background of sparse wall designs, wooden floors, striped rag runners and furniture brightened with uncomplicated embellishments.

The influences of Art Nouveau were an important inspiration, but in the hands of Danish designers in the mid-20th century, the fluid lines that had served as mere decoration in southern countries became the impulse behind the quest for a satisfying form that fitted a function, as seen in the chairs of Hans Wegner and Arne Jacobsen from the 1940s and 1950s *(see page 110)*. Designers also began to heed ergonomic research that long at the service of industrial companies like the car-makers Saab and Volvo. Today, the adage "form follows function" is taken to a high science in Scandinavia. Aesthetics are fused with efficiency for everything from utensils to welding equipment, as seen in the products of Ergonomi Design Gruppen (Sweden). Numerous pieces from the early 20th century remain as popular as ever, for example, stools by the Finnish architect and designer, Alvar Aalto.

The success of Nordic design has made it a standard far beyond the boundaries of Northern Europe – from time-tested pieces, such as the Stokke Tripp Trapp chairs by the Norwegian, Peter Opsvik, to the works of the multitalented Stefan Lindfors, whose output includes designs for Finnish companies Arabia (porcelain) and Marimekko (textiles); from glass and crystal designed for Kosta and Orrefors (Sweden) by Ulrika Hydman-Vallien to Nokia telephones (Finland) by Frank Nuovo.

In a part of the world forsaken by the sun for half the year, Scandinavians exploit interiors to maximise light. Even national characteristics may be seen as a source of style. Just as their design is characterised as rather stark, cool, unadorned, the Scandinavian character is often reserved, sombre – hardly excessively embellished. ❑

LEFT: contemporary furniture design at the Kunstmuseet Trapholt, Kolding, Denmark.

the country's finest writers, set the foundation for modern Swedish literature. Strindberg, whose personal life was marked by a series of failed marriages, alcoholism and instability, produced books, stories and screenplays that often featured social criticism, satire and emotional angst.

The creative output of Lagerlöf, the first woman to win a Nobel prize for Literature (1909), is sharply distinct from Strindberg, depending more on legend, history and tradition, and childhood memories (*Jerusalem*, 1901–02, *The Wonderful Adventures of Nils*, 1906).

Other Swedes have been honoured with Nobel Literature prizes (Verner von Heidenstan, 1909; Erik Axel Karlfeldt, 1931; Pär Lagerkvist, 1951; Eyvind Johnson and Harry Martinson, 1974), and many other novelists have had their work translated for publication abroad, such as Vilhelm Moberg, whose four-volume novel, beginning with *The Emigrants*, is the inspiration for the hit musical *Kristina from Duvemåla*.

Undoubtedly the most widely read Swedish writer, both at home and abroad, is Astrid Lindgren, the indefatigable creative mind behind *Pippi Longstocking*, *Emil in Lönneberga*, and many other free-spirited child heroines and antiheroines.

Swedish design

The "Swedish look", as it is understood today, is greatly indebted to the graphic work and paintings of Carl Larsson (1853–1919) as well as to the design of his home at Sundborn (*see box, page 269*). Larsson's images are marked by strong outline, subdued colours, and a gentle curvilinear quality.

Today, however, Swedish visual arts are extraordinarily multifaceted and bear little resemblance to preconceived notions of the Swedish look. Artists such as Ann-Sofi Sidén, Elin Wikström and Carl Michael von Hausswolff work in a variety of media, addressing complex contemporary issues. These trends can be seen at the Moderna Museet in Stockholm, which reopened in 1998 in a new building by Rafael Moneo. The museum has a fine collection of modern Swedish and international art.

RIGHT: Ingmar Bergman, internationally acclaimed Swedish playwright and film producer.

> ### THE SOUND OF JOIK
>
> *Joik* is a form of singing traditional among the Sami. Composed in response to an event or emotion, it sounds like a yodelling chant.

NORWAY

After being a world power during the Viking Age, Norway went through various unions with and occupations by Denmark and Sweden until independence in 1905. Over the centuries the country's culture was suppressed rather than enhanced by those of Denmark and Sweden. Culture with a capital "C" was something the overlords brought with them from foreign capitals. And it was something they took away with them when they left. Under Danish rule Norwegian

> ### INGMAR BERGMAN
>
> Although Sweden was a cinematic powerhouse in the age of silent films, since the advent of sound it has been a relatively small player, with the exception of exports such as Greta Garbo and Ingrid Bergman, and one of the giants of film and theatre, Ingmar Bergman.
>
> Born in 1918, Bergman made his breakthrough with *Smiles of a Summer Night* in 1955. Among his most acclaimed films are *The Seventh Seal* (1956), *Wild Strawberries* (1957) and *Cries and Whispers* (1973). *Fanny and Alexander* (1982) was his final film, but he has remained active in the theatre. His work offers a very personal perspective on what is Swedish, yet universal.

"dialects" were forbidden for official documents and communications. As a result, the heritage of Norwegian culture is identified in the arts and crafts of rural populations.

The recreation of a national identity began in earnest in the 19th century. Not surprisingly, inspiration came from the sublime nature, ancient verbal traditions, and heroic sagas of a mighty Norway and Viking lords of long ago.

Henrik Ibsen (1828–1906), wrote many plays inspired by folklore. His best-known works include *Peer Gynt* (1867), *A Doll's House* (1879) and *Hedda Gabler* (1890). Ibsen delved into the individual struggle for freedom and self-knowing. He commented on Norway's relationship with Denmark and Sweden as well on the individual's relationship with a society which would have him conform.

Rustic arts

The country's ancient stave churches represent some of the most distinctive examples of Norwegian artistic production. The rich ornamental carvings on door frames, around windows and on capitals in the interior owe more, stylistically, to the design motifs of the Viking period – dragons, tendrils, leaf patterns – than to Christian iconography found in carvings elsewhere in Europe. The most famous stave churches still standing can be seen in Borgund, Heddal and Urnes.

Another very "Norwegian" visual expression is found in the *rosemaling* or "rose painting" (more aptly called "rustic painting") of which there are as many styles as villages, since each isolated community developed its own interpretation. This decorative painting, used to adorn household utensils as well as interiors, features organic patterns and flowers, figurative representations and even geometric design. Most "genuine" *rosemaling* dates from the early 18th century to the late 19th century, but today many artisans continue the traditions of this very native art.

Golden age of music

Norwegian music flowered in the early 19th century, mainly as a result of the union with Sweden and the influence of the Royal Swedish Court. The violin virtuoso Ole Bull (1810–80), "The Nordic Paganini", proved a model for musicians and writers alike.

The 1870s and 1880s became known as the Golden Age of Norwegian music with such prominent composers as Halfdan Kierulf (1815–68), Edvard Grieg and Johan Svendsen (1849–1911). Generally, they incorporated elements of folk music in their work, including Grieg (1843–1907), who fused folk music with Romanticism.

Today, Oslo, Trondheim and Bergen all have philharmonic orchestras, and the latter hosts the Bergen International Music Festival each May.

EDVARD MUNCH

Edvard Munch (1863–1944), perhaps Norway's most reproduced artist, is honoured with a museum in Oslo dedicated to his work, as well as an entire floor of the National Gallery.

A forerunner of Expressionism, his introspective, symbolist and angst-ridden paintings and prints, such as *The Scream* (1893), *The Kiss* and *The Vampire* (both 1895), verge on the dark side and are a product of Scandinavian themes, artistic developments in France and Germany where he studied, as well as personal idiosyncrasies and obsessions (Munchmuseet, Oslo; tel: 23 24 14 00; Nasjonalgalleriet, Oslo; tel: 22 20 04 04).

LEFT: *The Scream* by Edvard Munch, 1893.
RIGHT: the Alvar Aalto Museum, Jyväskylä, celebrates the work of Finland's renowned architect-designer.

FINLAND

What may properly be called "Finnish culture" has existed for only a little over a century. Until the late 19th century, the arts in Finland fell under the influence of the invading powers of Sweden and Russia. Prior to Finnish independence (from Russia) in 1917, talented artists and composers normally studied and worked in Stockholm or St Petersburg.

Today, Finnish architecture and design are the nation's most influential cultural exports

> **TURNING POINT**
>
> The 19th-century artist Akseli Gallén-Kallela was a seminal figure in Finnish culture whose contribution laid the foundations for contemporary Finnish design.

(*see box, below*). Purely modern and very Scandinavian, they combine a love of natural materials and purity of form and functionalism with an exquisite aesthetic.

As is true for all the Nordic countries, the innovations that emanated from France and Germany preoccupied Finland's artists, with Finnish nature and themes lending the art a special character. Albert Edelfelt (1854–1905) was one of the nation's greatest artists of the 19th century. Later the national style created by Akseli Gallén-Kallela

FINNISH ARCHITECTURE AND DESIGN

One of the more prominent architects of Helsinki is Carl Ludwig Engel (1778–1840) from Germany, who designed much of the capital, including Senate Square and the cathedral. But despite the neoclassical imprint of this import, his creations are not representative of what is considered Finnish architecture, which, by many definitions, is no more than a century old.

The National Romanticism of Armas Lindgren (1874–1929), Herman Gesellius (1874–1916) and Eliel Saarinen (1873–1950) defined Finnish architecture of the late 19th and early 20th century, gradually turning from a Gothic look to embrace Art Nouveau.

Alvar Aalto (1898–1976), Finland's most celebrated architect, designed the Finnish Pavilion at the New York World's Fair in 1939, gaining international recognition for himself and the unadorned Functionalist style. He designed many buildings around the world. In Finland he left his mark on housing, schools, governmental and industrial buildings, theatres and churches. His finest building, Helsinki's Finlandia Hall, was built in 1971 during his "white" period.

Possibly Aalto's most indelible imprint on the world is not from architecture but furniture design. His simple solutions for chairs and stools are classics (Alvar Aalto Museo, Alvar Aallonkatu 7, Jyväskylä; tel: 014 624 809).

(1865–1931) became so popular that Finnish painters in the early 20th century tended to ignore foreign influences. The peasant and the landscape were considered to be representative of true Finnish qualities.

Musical notes

Although Jean Sibelius (1865–1957) still ranks as the most notable Finnish name in music, the contemporary scene is teeming with internationally acclaimed composers, conductors, opera singers and classical

LEFT: the composer Jean Sibelius (1865–1957) set the scene for modern music in Finland.

OPERA FESTIVAL

Even the most recalcitrant sopranos come home for the annual Savonlinna Opera Festival. Held in a 500-year-old castle, it is one of the most delightful summer opera festivals in the world.

musicians. Sibelius exemplified 19th-century Romanticism in his compositions, which drew inspiration from Finnish nature, folk music and poetry. His career began while Finland was still under Russian rule, and works such as *Finlandia* (1899; revised 1900) provoked such patriotic and nationalistic feelings that they were banned by the Russian authorities. His early symphonies, such as *Kullervo*, used material and motifs from Elias Lönnrot's classic poem *Kalevala*.

A generous policy of funding for musicians, musical institutes (of which there are nearly 130), conservatories and the celebrated Sibelius Academy has spawned a remarkable pool of

modern talent. Supporting this talent are numerous professional and semi-professional or chamber orchestras and ensembles. Finnish artists such as the principal conductor Esa-Pekka Salonen, the opera singers Peter Lindroos and Karita Mattila, and cellists Arto Noras and Erkki Rautio appear the world over. At home, musical festivals abound, of which the Savonlinna Opera Festival and the Pori Jazz Festival, both in late July, have become international attractions.

Literary heritage

Precious little writing in the Finnish language exists from prior to the early 19th century. Until Sweden ceded Finland to Russia in 1809, the Swedish language dominated Finnish culture.

In 1835, after many years of studying and collecting folk poetry and ballads, Elias Lönnrot (1802–84) published his remarkable poem, *Kalevala*. The work is a heroic epic on the scale of *The Odyssey* or *The Iliad* as well as a ragbag of narratives and light interludes, existing to preserve old customs and songs. The context – sea, farm, forest – is entirely Finnish.

The *Kalevala* has had an enormous impact on Finnish literature, art and music, not only in the 19th century where it inspired a nationalistic surge in writing in Finnish, but even today it continues to be a source of inspiration.

At the same time that Lönnrot was working, Aleksis Kivi (1834–72) wrote the first proper Finnish novel set in Finland, *Seven Brothers*, which celebrated rural life and contributed to a burgeoning national consciousness. The stage performance of Kivi's *Leah* in the late 19th century marked the beginning of Finnish drama. The Finns love theatre and even amateur groups perform to capacity audiences.

F.E. Sillanpää (1888–1964) took home the country's sole literary Nobel prize, in 1939.

Today, international audiences are probably most familiar with the books about the Moomintrolls by Tove Jansson. However, contemporary literature is vibrant and more introspective and critical than the roots of Finnish literature. ❑

RIGHT: Ingrid Bergman (1915–82), Swedish actress.

FOOD AND DRINK

Brace yourself for a gastronomic treat: fresh seafood, wild berries and succulent mountain meat washed down by fiery aquavit is the order of the day

Scandinavian food gets down to the basics of nature, finding deep flavour in simple and healthy ways. Meats and fish might be smoked, then served with little else than steaming new potatoes, fresh dill, rich butter and tart redcurrants. The general rule says "less is more", and Scandinavian cooks – from the fanciest restaurant to the basic home kitchen – make good use of native fruits and vegetables, grains, fish, meat and game.

Fruits of the sea

Denmark, Sweden, Norway and Finland each have their own food cultures, but they share some gastronomic ground. Seafood is king, and this king spreads its rule into society. In Denmark, for example, model ships hang in every church, as if to remind parishioners to give thanks for the fruits of the sea. The North and Baltic seas have provided a solid economic base for strong fishing industries – and the societies that have revolved around them.

Herring might be the fish most associated with the region, and each country prepares it in variations on the same themes: marinated in sugar and vinegar with onions and herbs, or spiced with sandalwood (like *matjes*, which the Swedes frequently eat with boiled potatoes and sour cream); fried and then marinated; seasoned with mustard, curry, or sherry; smoked; salted; or baked. Usually, the dishes are eaten cold, and washed down with aquavit.

A Swedish summertime favourite is the smelly *surströmming*, fermented Baltic herring, eaten with raw onion, cheese and potatoes. Norwegians have a similar dish, *rakfisk*, a pungent cured trout. The uninitiated to these dishes run for cover in the opposite direction.

Other fish have their place on the dinner table or in the finest local restaurants, including plaice, cod, haddock, mackerel and eel. *Klippfisk*, a salty splitcod, is hung and dried in the open air in Norway's coastal villages. Salmon is king in Finland, where it is commonly made into a simple, tasty soup. *Fraavi lohi*, salmon marinated for a day in salt and herbs, is sometimes called the Finnish version of *sushi*. Danes, Swedes and Norwegians eat sweet, cured gravlax as a lunch-time delicacy.

Feasting on open sandwiches

Fish is the focus of a Danish or Swedish lunch-time feast. In Denmark the *smørrebrød* (open sandwiches) start with rye bread. Extremely dense and packed with all kinds of seeds and grains, this bread could be used to build walls if one ran out of bricks. Sliced and spread with goose lard or butter, the Danish rye is topped with arty combinations of foods and eaten with knife and fork.

Some restaurants, most notably Slotskælderen in Copenhagen, feature *smørrebrød* menus on scrolls several feet long. But certain unwritten rules apply to the feast, even at home: "You must have two or three kinds of herring,"

LEFT: an appetising spread of seafood and smoked meat toppings for Danish open sandwiches.
RIGHT: a Scandinavian buffet-style *smörgåsbord*.

explains Hanne Christensen from Funen. Her husband, Carl, adds that fiery shots of cold aquavit must "go down like hail stones".

"Then you need a little warm dish, like fried fish with lemon and remoulade," Hanne says.

"Sliced meats," adds Carl. "Small tenderloin steaks. Danish meatballs with red cabbage."

"And then cheese and fruit salad at the end," says Hanne.

The Swedish *smörgåsbord* and Finnish *voileipäpöytä* are equally artistic and elegant, with cold and hot dishes – similar to those eaten at a Danish lunch – laid out buffet-style on a table, to which guests visit five times. Special to these countries are dishes such as roasted reindeer, Swedish meatballs and a baked anchovy-potato-cream casserole called "Jansson's Temptation". The Finnish dishes tend to be less sweet than those in Sweden, and Finns serve a greater variety of bread.

In Norway, a large selection of breads and toppings comes at breakfast, *frokost*, with copious amounts of cold meats, crispbreads, cheeses, caviar from a tube and black coffee. *Myseost* is a food of national pride, a type of brown, sweet, goats' and cows' milk cheese flavoured lightly with caramel. At home and at celebrations Norwegians also enjoy *rømme*, a

SKÅL! TO THE SPIRIT OF LIFE

No herring dish in Scandinavia is complete without aquavit, literally "water of life". Distilled from potatoes or grain and flavoured with a variety of herbs and seasonings – such as caraway seed, cumin, fennel, dill or St John's wort – ice cold aquavit warms the body (and mood). One of the best versions is Norway's Løiten Linie, which is matured partly by a sea voyage in oak casks across the equator and back (each bottle carries details of its "voyage" on the label). The Finns tend to pour bigger glasses of the drink, but they are also masters at distilling and drinking vodka.

To gain instant friends in Scandinavia, lift your drink and say the word for cheers: *"skål"* (pronounced *"skoal"*). The correct way to *skål* is to look at the person, say the word, lift the glass slightly, drink and look at the person again. There are some rules about when to *skål* at formal occasions. Never drink until the host has given a welcome toast. A gentleman must ensure that the woman on his right has something on her plate and in her glass. She must be the first he *skåls*, followed by the woman on his left. The host will *skål* each guest. The hostess may also *skål* her guests. It is not good form to *skål* a person who is older or of higher rank. Let them take the initiative and return the gesture within three minutes. A gentleman should *skål* the man sitting on the left of his partner, as well as her.

thick and extremely rich porridge made from cream, butter and milk. At Easter, the Finns eat *mämmi*, a whipped rye and malt porridge that takes up to a day to make.

Sausage fare

Sausage is common in all four countries, and its flavour and consistency depends upon the region where it is made. In Tampere in southwest Finland, *mustamakkara* (black sausage) is flavoured with spices, barley and blood. The Danes also make a blood sausage, *blødpølse*, which is seen commonly

CRAYFISH SEASON

Crayfish is eaten widely in Finland and Sweden in July and August, where it is boiled and peeled and served at outdoor parties.

liver and kidney and cooked for hours at a time, is another Finnish speciality.

Fruits of the forest

Along the same lines, nearly all Scandinavians do a hunting of a different sort in the summer and autumn – that is for mushrooms, which appear in several dishes, or berries (from raspberries to cloudberries and blueberries). Some restaurants have even gained fame for their use of foraged foods sold to them by local enthusiasts, fresh back from the woods or heath.

around Christmas; the south Jutland *ølpølse* (beer sausage) is a tasty snack found at the local butcher. Swedes eat little pork links (*prinskorv*) at a *smörgåsbord*.

Besides elk and venison, the Norwegians, Swedes and Finns eat reindeer, which can be found on the menus of fine restaurants – as well as stocked up in freezers across the area.

After a bracing trek in the Finnish wilderness, try the hearty *poronkäristys* (reindeer casserole). Karelian stew, made of meats,

FAR LEFT: Norway's celebrated Løiten Linie aquavit.
LEFT: Danish open sandwiches (*smørrebrød*).
ABOVE: baked salmon is popular in Finland.

Sweet treats

It almost goes without saying that the traditional Danish pastry (*weinerbrød*) became famous for a reason. When in Denmark, visit a bakery and try a rich, chewy "chocolate snail" pastry in the morning, or a layered cream cake in the afternoon. Danish waffle cones filled with ice cream, marshmallow topping and marmalade are also not to be missed.

The Finns eat *pulla* (wheat buns) with their coffee and indulge in cream cakes topped with strawberries. In Skåne in southern Sweden, *spettkaka* is a local speciality, a tower-shaped confectionery of sugar, eggs and potato flour baked over an open fire. ❏

THE GREAT OUTDOORS

Scandinavians are passionate about nature and the outdoor life.
Unfazed by the weather they hike, ski, skate, sail, fish and climb

The people of the Nordic countries are so at home in their natural surroundings that they seldom pause to consider how intertwined their daily lives are with the climate, the seasons, and the amazing and diverse beauty of the northern landscape. In winter, they take to their skis to traverse fields and forests, and pull on skates to blaze paths across icy lakes. They'll fish through the ice and even climb a frozen waterfall. Winter poses no obstacle to the hardy Scandinavian. In spring and summer, the mountains will beckon backpackers to scale their heights while the Swedish archipelago will be dotted with thousands of sailing boats, and the forests of the Nordic countries will be full of berry-pickers, picnickers, and hikers.

Danes will head for their magnificent beaches while Swedes, Norwegians, and Finns will celebrate the cool refreshing plunge of the thousands of lakes that dot the landscape. Come autumn, the people of the Nordic lands are combing the forests for mushrooms and admiring the gold- and red-hued foliage of the forest.

For Scandianvians, the great outdoors is a reflection of their national identity, an expression of their individuality and sporting spirit, and a valuable national asset that they will go to great lengths to protect. Some of the world's strongest green movements are to be found in Denmark, Sweden, Norway and Finland.

Country retreats

In a region where winter days are short and nasty weather can crop up any time of the year, comfort translates to secure shelter, often your own. A quarter of Norway's households own a holiday home, or *hytte*, a cottage or cabin.

In Sweden, many families save for years in order to buy a *stuga* (cottage) in the country or on the coast. Others are lucky enough to have inherited their little spot in a meadow. Most

LEFT: Norway, Sweden and Finland offer exciting opportunities for winter sports enthusiasts.
RIGHT: jet-boarding off Bornholm, Denmark.

Swedes are only a generation or two away from rural life and many have relatives who still live in their original home districts.

At the water's edge

Denmark and Sweden offer varied coastlines and a beach-life that is unique to each coun-

try's topography. There are 8,000 km (5,000 miles) of coastline in Sweden, offering clean, if often chilly, water to swim in, and rocks to sun on (but few sandy beaches). The most spectacular seascape is the Stockholm archipelago, with its 24,000 islands, but nearly as thrilling are the waves crashing on the rocks of Bohuslän's archipelago.

The Danes, on the other hand, are blessed with sandy beaches. With more than 7,400 km (4,600 miles) of coastline, the waters surrounding Denmark are a playground for outdoor activities. No point in the country is more than a 45-minute drive from the sea and many inland waterways or fjords are even closer.

Kayaks, canoes, rowing boats, smaller sailing or motor craft may be hired at resorts along the coasts or on the larger lakes. The air is hardly still in Denmark, and the windsurfing is excellent. Seasoned surfers may prefer the exhilaration of the North Sea, while beginners can try their hand in the lee of a fjord, bay or on a lake.

Norway has its fjords, which can be explored by steamers in summertime. In winter, when the fjords freeze over, families take Sunday "walks" on skates among the rocks and islets. Increased tourism along Finland's lake system is bringing the steamers back into business. There are now regular passenger routes on several of the lake systems, but the oldest and probably the most romantic are those across Saimaa's vast expanse.

Hitting the trails

The Nordic region is known for its great open landscapes and is a mecca for hikers and backpackers. The greatest proportion of Sweden is virgin country. You can stroll for miles along tracks without seeing another human being, or drive a car on serpentine gravel roads and never have to pass another vehicle, or cycle through untouched land on special bicycle trails.

Norwegians are quite at home in their wild,

FREEDOM TO ROAM

The freedom to explore nature is considered a birthright of most Scandinavians, and the politicians have seen fit to put that inheritance into law. Since 1957 Norway has had a *Lov om friluftslivet* (Outdoor Recreations Act), which states succinctly that: "At any time of the year, outlying property may be crossed on foot, with consideration and due caution."

In Sweden, it's called *Allemansrätten* (Everyman's Right), an old custom that permits you to camp anywhere for a night, or to walk, ski or paddle a canoe anywhere, as long as the area is not fenced in or in close proximity to a private home.

unspoilt country, and have a great feeling for its mountains. Finland also offers pristine wilderness, quaint historical attractions, peace and quiet and free access to practically anywhere – all forests are potentially yours for trekking, berry- and mushroom-picking or short-term camping.

The Danish countryside is a appealing patchwork of dense forests, coastal dunes, marshes, moors and meticulously manicured farmland. In every type of landscape walkers will find paths or trails that stretch for miles, and a labyrinth of winding country roads.

Throughout Sweden, there's an excellent network of waymarked footpaths. Close to

Stockholm is the 850-km (530-mile) Sörmlandsleden (Sörmland trail), starting at Björkhagen underground station. Carefully laid out, the trail offers hikers constantly changing vistas of deep forest, historic sites, lookout points and lakes. It passes several camps where you can eat, rest and buy supplies, with shelters at regular intervals. Sörmlandsleden is an easy hike, but it offers plenty of excitement. You rarely meet another soul, particularly in spring, autumn and winter, but you will spot deer, elk, capercaillie, hawks and grouse. The area is full of mushrooms and berries to pick. For the most exotic views, however, head for the Kungsleden trail which runs for more than 500 km (300 miles) between Abisko and Hemavan.

Waymarked footpaths are found in the more scenically outstanding areas like the national parks. These areas are often well away from towns and villages, and as a result many of them have a chain of mountain stations set a day's walk from one another along the footpaths, providing shelter for walkers. Most of the mountain stations are equipped with cooking facilities, a shop and comfortable beds. Some even have a self-service restaurant and a sauna. They are not hotels, but simple accommodation designed to provide a haven at the end of the day for tired walkers.

In Norway, the bulk of the trails and lodges are conveniently in the middle of the triangle bounded by the cities of Oslo, Bergen and Trondheim. A central entry point is Finse, situated above the timber line at 1,200 metres (4,000 ft). Finse's main street is the station platform; there are no cars because there are no roads. When a train has gone and the last passengers have left, Finse returns to normal, a speck in a seemingly infinite expanse of rock, ice and snow.

Accessible mountaineering

To the north of Finse lie the Jotunheimen mountains, the range that took its name from Norse mythology, literally "Home of the Giants". The name is appropriate: peaks jut a

FOLLOW THE SIGNS
In Sweden and Norway, the extensive networks of walking and hiking trails are marked by a red "T". Lodges and cabins offer accommodation along the way.

kilometre and more skywards from lake-studded, moraine-strewn flats, all above the timber line. Nonetheless, even the loftiest of the Jotunheimen peaks, Galdhøpiggen and Glittertind, which are the highest in Northern Europe with summits rising more than 2,400 metres (7,900 ft), rank low on the international scale of noteworthy mountains where sheer altitude, not challenge, is the main criterion. Though this fact has led to relative anonymity – few Norwegian peaks appear in the classic mountaineering literature

– it does mean that you can ascend the equivalent of the Matterhorn or Mont Blanc without having to cope with the problems of altitude. Most Jotunheimen trails meander from around 900–1,200 metres (3,000–4,000 ft) above sea level and there are no acclimatisation problems at that height.

Some of the glaciers that hewed the Norwegian landscape left offspring. One, Jostedalsbreen (Jostedal Glacier), is the largest on the mainland of Europe. Jostedalsbreen and its siblings throughout the country are the places to see crampon-shod parties wielding ice axes from spring until autumn.

Contact with the ice that shaped their land is

LEFT: the "Sjaelland Rundt" yacht race circumnavigates the Danish island of Zealand.
RIGHT: climbing in the mountains of Norway.

currently the Norwegians' fastest-growing wilderness recreation and many centres now organise specialist courses.

Wilderness experience

In Finland, you can enjoy some of the region's best hiking along the Karelian Circle Trek, Finland's longest trekking route with approximately 1,000 km (620 miles) of marked trails. The Karelian Circle Trek offers genuine wilderness routes, variety in four different national parks, and the possibility to combine walking with mountain biking or canoeing. Fishing gear is common, and some even carry a hunting gun.

This is a friendly wilderness, with no fear of dangerous wild animals. Bed-and-breakfast accommodation is available, as are free wilderness huts (or ones that have to be reserved in advance). Pitching a tent is legal (and free) almost everywhere along this route.

On two wheels

Visitors to Denmark will notice within minutes of their arrival two signs of the country's greenness: windmills and bicycles. Windmills dot the landscape – including the area around Copenhagen's airport – churning out clean energy. The bicycle, meanwhile, is an important mode

NATIONAL PARKS

The Nordic region has many national parks, each with its own claim to unique native flora and fauna. Hiking trails are marked and it's often possible to engage a guide. Large areas of Norway have been designated as national parks to protect special habitats and support biodiversity.

In Sweden, strict laws protect the rarer mammals such as the bear, wolf, wolverine, lynx, musk-ox, Arctic fox and otter. Among the more common animals, roe deer live in the forest and only in Scandinavia will you see the traffic sign "Danger, Elk". National parks cover highland and lowland regions. To see herbaceous flora and listen to birdsong in Sweden, Dalby Söderskog near Lund in Skåne

is at its best in the spring, while Store Mosse in Småland is worth a detour for birdwatchers interested in whooper swans, marsh harriers and cranes.

Denmark's national parks include the heather-covered Svanninge Bakker on Funen and the beech and conifer woods of Rebild Bakker in North Jutland.

Finland's park network is mostly administered by the Forest and Park Service, which controls 30 or so national parks, including the rugged rift valley of Hiidenporrttin Kansallis-puisto in Karelia and the Ramsholmen Nature Reserve on the Åland Islands. The organisation rents interesting accommodation in isolated wilderness cottages.

of transport for Danes and visitors alike. Bikes outnumber cars in some city areas, where the streets have bicycle lanes and traffic lights.

Denmark has thousands of miles of foot and cycle paths and bikes may be taken on most trains and ferries. Tourist offices can provide detailed maps of routes. Hærvejen is a bicycle and walking trail that stretches from the German border to Viborg in north-central Jutland. Traders and travellers beat this path a few thousand years ago, and much of it still looks as it did during Viking times. All along the route there are inns, hotels or hostels, as well as shops for provisions.

there is the Sverigeleden (Sweden Bicycle Route), from Stockholm to Göteborg – a distance of 2,576 km (1,600 miles).

Cast your line

Anglers are beginning to appreciate the wealth of excellent fishing that Scandinavia provides.

One of the most remarkable and most accessible places to fish is right in the centre of Stockholm, in the fast-moving Strömmen channel which links the freshwater of Lake Mälaren with the Baltic Sea. A clean-up programme has brought salmon and sea trout back to the very heart of the capital. What is more, the fishing

Cycling and, in recent years, mountain biking, are also popular outdoor sports for Swedes, and there are many well-designed and well-lit cycle routes all over the country. You could spend a week touring the island of Gotland on a bike. Keen cyclists also head for Östergötland, particularly along the banks of the Göta Kanal where the towpaths make ideal cycling tracks. Bikes can be hired at several places, and the most popular route for cyclists is between Berg and Borensberg. For the truly ambitious,

here is completely free of charge. Big salmon and sea trout can also be caught almost anywhere in Sweden – in world-famous waters like the Mörrum River in southern Sweden and, above all, in the large and wild rivers of northern Sweden, as well as along the coast when the fish are on their migration.

The salmon season varies between rivers, but it usually starts during the summer and continues well into the autumn. The sea trout tend to arrive a little later. Both spinning and fly-fishing can produce good salmon catches, but sturdy tackle is advised.

To Norwegians, fish is the standby staple. Even in modest markets, the variety of fish and

LEFT: the wide open spaces of northern Sweden and Finland offer superb wilderness trekking.
ABOVE: the Danes and Swedes are keen cyclists.

Life in Lapland

They call themselves "the people of the eight seasons". They are the Sami who live in Sweden, Norway, and Finland's most northerly provinces: vast wildernesses where nature and reindeer set the course of the year. Traces of their presence stretch back more than 8,000 years. They have their own language, religious traditions, and customs. While the life of the Sami has changed in modern times, the annual cycle of the reindeer – rutting, herding, separating, slaughtering, calving, marking – continues to shape the Lap-

land calendar. The winter round-ups are among Europe's most colourful events, resembling scenes from a Wild West film transposed to an Arctic setting. Visitors can enjoy this ancient culture at festivals and ceremonial occasions held throughout the year, where one can sample reindeer delicacies and marvel at Sami handicrafts.

A vivid way to experience the Sami lifestyle and landscape is to get outdoors. In spring and summer the mountains blossom with Sami heather, globe flowers, cloudberries and countless other species, inviting the visitor to take to the trails and woods of the many national parks in the Sami regions of Scandinavia. One not to miss is Padjelanta, the biggest national park in Europe. The name comes from a Sami word that means "the higher mountain", and it is one of Sweden's most beautiful areas, with rolling plains, gently rounded mountain massifs, and huge lakes, such as Vastenjaure and Virihaure. Almost the entire park is above the tree line. There are many small streams, which the Lapps call *jokk*, and it has always been an important pasture for their reindeer herds.

For golf enthusiasts, nothing can quite top the thrill of golfing under the Midnight Sun in the glorious days of summer, where (depending on latitude and cloud cover) the sun is visible for up to 70 summer days. Anglers will find a true paradise in the primeval wilderness of the north, laced by swift rivers and streams and punctuated by lakes and pools. Big salmon and sea trout can be caught almost anywhere in northern Scandinavia.

To enjoy the wintry wilderness in an entirely different way, try dog-sledging, which is offered by many firms in northern Scandinavia. Drive the dog-sledge yourself or sit back in the vast silence of the mountains and be driven by a team of huskies. Your guide will tell you how to take care of a sledge dog and share bits of trivia, like the fact that in the Inuit language there are 18 different words for snow. Dog-sledging, common in Greenland, is now well established in Sweden and is growing in popularity in Finland's northern wilderness around Muonio.

The Sami winter vistas can also be enjoyed on reindeer sleigh rides and snowshoe treks. Ice climbing is popular, too. Fishing through the ice is common on most lakes and rivers.

To really soak up the hard life of the Sami, the visitor can stay in the world's largest igloo, the Jukkasjärvi Ice Hotel in Sweden. Each autumn, as the Arctic temperature plummets, Laplanders rebuild this celebrated igloo from thousands of tons of snow and ice. Inside it houses a church, hotel, gallery, golf room, cinema and bar named appropriately Absolut Ice. Guests sleep in warm sleeping bags on mattresses of spruce bough and reindeer skins. Temperatures average –4°C (25°F). The hearty fare served from the kitchen and the activities waiting outdoors don't leave guests much time to feel cold. Next morning, the hotel will issue a certificate of survival. It's not quite the same as herding reindeer, but it brings you one step closer to understanding how climate, custom, and sheer human persistence have made the Sami what they are today. ❑

LEFT: a young Sami boy from northern Sweden dressed for winter in a traditional pom-pom hat.

fish products is amazing, and Norwegians look on a proper fresh fish shop as an asset to a community. It is not surprising, then, that Norway is a country of fishermen of all kinds, both commercial fishermen and anglers.

The long coastline is a mecca for saltwater angling, yet freshwater angling is the more popular pastime, and there are a quarter of a million fishable inland lakes and ponds. The most common of around 40 freshwater species are trout and char; in the northernmost parts, and in lakes and ponds at higher elevations, they are the only fish. Grayling and pike are more common in larger lakes and rivers in eastern and central areas.

Ice fishing is a prime winter-time hobby. It's a straightforward form of angling, which requires only a baited hand line or short pole and line, warm clothing, and lots of patience.

Sporting nations

Norway, Denmark and Finland consider sport both a pleasure and an athletic pursuit. Sweden is one of the world's most sporting nations, with nearly half the population engaged in some form of sport or outdoor recreation. One in four Norwegians competes in a sport.

From the broad base of people for whom sport is a major leisure activity come the élite, competitors who enter the many national championships and represent their countries in international sports meetings. In Sweden, great athletes like Björn Björg have made Swedish tennis prowess legendary.

The runner, Paavo Nurmi (1897–1973), put Finland on the map, breaking multiple world records and winning four gold medals, Nurmi first competed in the 1920 Olympics. Variously known as the Flying Finn, the Phantom Finn and the Phenomenal Finn, he is still remembered for his extraordinary running style, speed, and tough character.

These days the Finns are better known for being world-class rally drivers. Mika Hakkinen, Tommi Mäkinen, Ari Vatanen and Hannu Mikkola may be known only to lovers of motor

> ### TEEING OFF
>
> Golf is the fastest-growing sport in Scandinavia, and its popularity has exploded in Denmark in recent years. In Scandinavia's far north enthusiasts like to play golf under the Midnight Sun.

sports, but probably more non-Finns could name one of these sportsmen than could identify Finland's current prime minister.

Traditionally, Norwegian prowess has been in winter sports and in sailing, but they have also won international medals in a wide range of events, including , weight lifting, women's football, cycling, boxing, marathon running, wrestling, handball, karate, canoeing, rowing, and shooting.

All the Nordic countries share the European

passion for football. Clubs are supported through funds from the football pools and from the sale of players to major European leagues, in particular the Englishand Scottish Premier League.

Winter sports

Not surprisingly, given the long winters and the beckoning snow-topped mountains, Swedes, Norwegians and Finns all excel at winter sports.

Downhill skiing in Sweden attracts a growing number of visitors thanks to the more reliable snowfall, the reduced risk of avalanches compared to Alpine resorts, and the variety of slopes. While slalom champion Ingemar Stenmark put Sweden on the international skiing

RIGHT: the Scandinavian countries are an angler's dream with numerous lakes, rivers and a varied coastline all offering a good catch.

map, it is Pernilla Wiberg, the World and Olympic champion skier, who is keeping the country in the spotlight. As a result, Swedish downhill resorts such as Åre *attract skiers from all over Europe. Sälen is the largest ski resort in Sweden with various Alpine and cross-country skiing facilities. World Cup Ski Championships are held in Åre, so there are hundreds of top-class, superbly groomed pistes served by high-speed lifts and cabins. Half-pipes and snow parks are available for snowboarding fanatics.

Norway has witnessed a reawakening of interest in the style of skiing called Telemark,

which evolved in Morgedal, in the southern county of Telemark. In the mid-1800s, Sondre Norheim, a young farmer, devised bindings (devices that hold ski boots to skis) that were firm and were the first to give the feet control over the skis. He also gave the skis what is known as "sidecut", the slight hourglass profile of a ski seen from above. Sidecut is what enables skis to run true and turn easily, even to this day.

Norheim and his fellow Morgedal skiers used the new designs to perfect new skiing manoeuvres, including landing from airborne flights off snow-covered rooftops and natural outcrops. Soon, they were ready to show off their new

skills and this led to the first ski-jumping contest in 1879. The bent-knee stance with one ski trailing soon became known as the "Telemark".

In modern Telemark skiing, the heel is free to lift up from the ski and turns are steered, with one ski trailing and at an angle to the other. Competitive Telemark ski races are now held on packed slopes, as are Alpine ski races, but true Telemark skiing has spawned the revival of skiathlons, in which competitors must ski jump, ski through a slalom course, and run a cross-country ski race, all on the same pair of skis.

The Vasaloppet

Another world-famous ski competition takes place in Mora, in the Dalarna region of Sweden. The Vasaloppet, an 85-km 85-km (85-km) cross-country skiing race, is the most popular sporting event in the country. It is held every March to commemorate King Gustav Vasa's flight from his enemies in the 16th century. Each year the race includes more than 15,000 competitors, who in the past have included the present king, Carl XVI Gustaf. The first Vasaloppet was run on 19 March 1922. A victory in Vasaloppet is regarded by most of the world's best skiers as highly as a podium place in the Olympic games or the World Championships.

Skiing is also one of the top sports in Finland, and the sport most readily associated with this snow-covered nation. Along with its Scandinavian neighbours, Finland has produced champion cross-country and downhill skiers, who benefit from an extended winter season in which to perfect their sport.

Skiing is not the only winter sport in which the nation excels. Ice hockey is one of the most important team sports in Finland. Almost all males participate at school, and the élite are filtered through and chosen for the best teams. Ice hockey is highly commercialised: one of the leading teams, Jokerit (the Jokers, referring to a deck of cards rather than humour) is run like a large company. Teams in Helsinki, Tampere and Turku are usually the best and spectators can number up to 10,000 for a game. Many Finns play in the North American NHL and many foreigners play in Finnish teams. ❑

LEFT: skiing, both downhill and cross-country, is a national sport in Norway, Sweden and Finland.
RIGHT: hikers enjoy the solitude of the far north.

PLACES

A detailed guide to the Scandinavian countries, with principal sites cross-referenced by number to the maps

Whether you're in a car or coach, on a bicycle, boat or train, on foot or on skis, the Scandinavian countries of Denmark, Norway, Sweden and Finland have an enormous variety of sights and scenery to beguile the visitor.

Denmark is neatly beautiful rather than grand, with its white sand beaches, well-groomed farmland and gentle hills. Nurtured by the mild climate, the countryside in spring glows with fruit blossom and sharp yellow rape seed, and in late summer with the golden tinge of harvest fields. Brightly painted half-timbered buildings echo nature's colours and Renaissance castles dot the landscape. Copenhagen is one of Europe's most enjoyable cities, a relaxed place with pedestrianised streets, pavement cafés, superb shops and enterainment. This is the cultural as well as the political capital, but every Danish town has its museum and art gallery, every castle its collection.

Far out to sea, remote from the rest of Scandinavia but part of the Danish realm, lie the Faroe Islands – a paradise for bird-watchers – and Greenland, a fascinating destination for the adventurous.

As if to compensate for the flatter terrain of its neighbours, Norway is made up of mountains, not craggy like the Alps, but curved and etched with beautiful fjords and dramatic valleys. From the beaches and pastures of the south, the coastline stretches far north to the Arctic Circle and beyond, dotted with islands, fishing villages and historic towns such as Bergen. Inland, the rugged landscape beckons walkers and skiers. The capital, Oslo, offers all the attractions of a European city, but with a very Norwegian imprint.

A short journey from Copenhagen across the *Øresund bridge brings you to southern Sweden, the rolling landscape of Skåne and the sunny islands of Öland and Gotland. At the heart of Sweden lie two vast lakes, Vänern and Vättern linked by the Göta Kanal, a pleasure-boaters' mecca. Further north the folklore province of Dalarna gives way to lakes and forests, winter-sports centres and the rugged landscape of Lapland. Stockholm lies majestically on an archipelago of Baltic islands, the most sophisticated of the Scandinavian capitals.

For many centuries Finland came under Sweden's wing; later the Russians took control. Remnants of both cultures can be found, but with independence Finland's own identity has emerged. The south coast is a summer playground of islands and beaches, fortresses and painted towns. The capital, Helsinki, with its wealth of architecture, new and old, is known as the "Daughter of the Baltic". Lakes and forests cover central Finland, while easterly Karelia is a hiker's delight. Lapland, land of the Midnight Sun, attracts anglers, white-water enthusiasts and those in search of true peace and solitude. ❑

PRECEDING PAGES: modern reproductions of typical Norwegian boats at the Sunmore Boat Museum, Ålesund.
LEFT: the spectacular Dalsnibba panorama at Geirangerfjord, Norway.

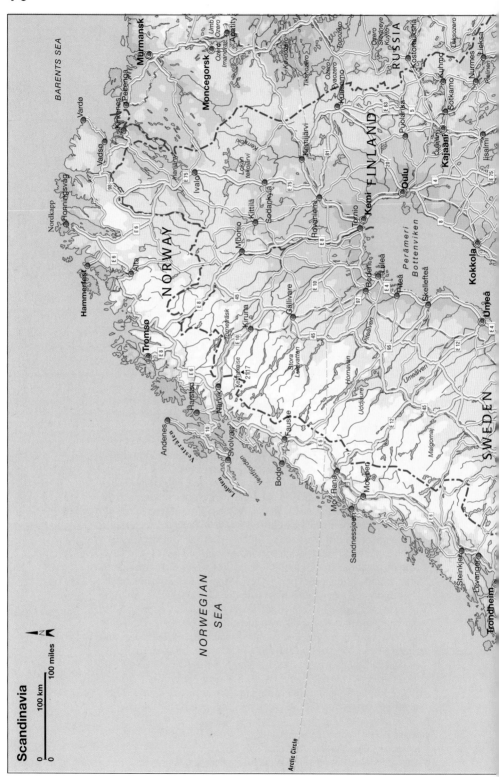

Scandinavia

N

0   100 km
0   100 miles

BARENTS SEA

NORWEGIAN SEA

Arctic Circle

NORWAY

SWEDEN

FINLAND

RUSSIA

Bottenviken

Perämeri

Murmansk
Pecenga
Kirkenes
Vardø
Vadsø
Nordkapp
Honningsvåg
Hammerfest
Alta
Tromsø
Andenes
Harstad
Narvik
Svolvær
Bodø
Fauske
Mo i Rana
Mosjøen
Sandnessjøen
Steinkjer
Levanger
Trondheim
Ivalo
Mbono
Kittilä
Sodankylä
Gällivare
Kiruna
Kebnekaise 2117
Stora Lulevatten

Moncegorsk
Apatity
Umb
Ozero Imandra
Kandalaksa
Ozero Pyaozero
Kuusamo
Kemijärvi
Rovaniemi
Tornio
Kemi
Oulu
Luleå
Piteå
Skellefteå
Umeå
Kokkola
Pudasjärvi
Kajaani
Iisalmi
Suolijärvi
Kuhmo
Sotkamo
Nurmes
Lieksa
Kostomuksha
Eksozero

Inarijärvi
Kemijoki
Lokan tekojärvi
Ofoten
Hornavan
Uddjure
Pitealven
Umealven
Malgomaj
Stora Lelevatten
Torneträsk

N O R W E G I A N   S E A

Vesterålen
Lofoten
Vestfjorden

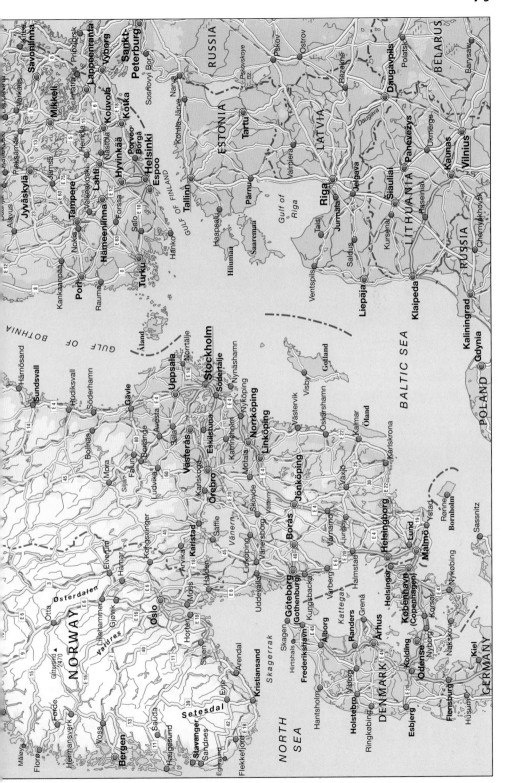

DENMARK

Small, but perfectly formed, Denmark is a country of
fun-loving, environmentally conscious people

Hamlet was wrong – there is nothing rotten in the State of Denmark. Yes, the winters can be dreary, but they're not biting cold and there is little snow – the Danes go to Sweden and Norway to ski – and summers can be sunny, with long hours of daylight. Yes, the tax rate is among the world's highest. But taxes are reinvested to help make this a country "where few have too much and fewer too little".

The world's oldest kingdom may be no empire as of yore, but the sons of those Vikings continue to pack plenty of clout. These days they're spreading their seed far and wide in canisters of frozen nitrogen: Denmark is the biggest supplier of meticulously screened and frozen human sperm on the planet – and a major purveyor of computer elements and electronic devices, windmills, agricultural products, arts and crafts and skilled professionals.

Denmark is also a nation of cyclists (two-wheelers outnumber bipeds) and recyclers – more than half the country's rubbish is turned into district steam heat for homes and other new things, nuclear plants excepted. Natural gas and windmills are the preferred energy sources of this windy country.

Nowhere is very far away, especially now that a network of motorways, railway lines and spectacular bridges link west to east from Germany, through Denmark to Copenhagen and across the Øresund to Sweden. Ferries still play their part, linking islands and crossing "fjords" as the Danes call their larger lakes, for this is a nation with a strong seafaring past.

Zealand, in the east, holds the capital, Copenhagen, Scandinavia's liveliest city, and Hamlet's castle, Kronborg at Helsingør (Elsinore). Jutland, in the west, is Denmark's link with mainland Europe. The North Jutland seascapes have captivated artists over the centuries; west-coast sands stretching as far as the eye can see draw summer holiday-makers. East Jutland has an intricate lake system, well-used for canoeing and water sports, and also Århus, Denmark's second city, with an international arts festival in the autumn. Funen, sandwiched between Jutland and Zealand, is the "garden of Denmark", with Odense, the birthplace of Denmark's most famous writer, Hans Christian Andersen. Out in the Baltic is the island of Bornholm, home to craftspeople and a popular holiday destination.

Far to the west and north lie the outposts of the Danish kingdom; the windswept Faroe Islands ("Sheep Islands"), a favourite haunt for birdwatchers; and Greenland, a true adventure travel destination offering stunning scenery and a pristine natural environment. ❑

PRECEDING PAGES: mustard field, Djursland; Den Gamle By, the historic old town of Århus, Jutland; Valdemars Slot (castle) on the island of Tåsinge, Funen Archipelago.
LEFT: Amagertorv and the Stork Fountain in Copenhagen's main shopping area.

THE DANES

They're generally warm, witty and welcoming. But they can also be cool and reserved. It depends where you meet them

Danes have two reputations in the world; one at home and another abroad. Outside their homeland, Danes are known as warm, curious, friendly, funny, charming. In their modest way, Danish travellers bring on laughs and a sense of pure enjoyment for life. They try not to act too offended when, outside Europe, one too many people ask: "Is Denmark the capital of Sweden?" or "What language do you speak – Dutch?" A short, firm geography lesson is given on the spot, but modesty usually prevents the Dane to say that Denmark is the oldest monarchy in the world, dating from AD 935.

At home, Danes are seen by foreign visitors as distant, sombre, even cold. They keep to themselves. Danes blame this image on the wet, cool climate. "Not much of our social life happens on the pavements or out in front of the home," says Frans Kjær Nielsen, a teacher. "We spend much of our time indoors with our families and friends."

Cosiness prevails

Inside this thin barrier of social contact, Denmark is one of the warmest countries in the world. People are genuine. They speak their minds. They thrive on making life cosy, relaxing and enjoyable – from festive occasions to mundane coffee breaks. This is what Danish *hygge* is all about. *Hygge* (pronounced **whoo-guh**) stands for any and every sense of cosiness, and it is found everywhere in Denmark. A good meal has *hygge*, a house can have *hygge*, a story, a walk in the woods, a meeting at a café, even a person can have *hygge*.

Parties for weddings, birthdays, anniversaries and the like have *hygge* at their core. Tables are decorated with flowers and candles and creatively folded napkins. A three-course meal is usually interspersed with songs and speeches, which end in a collective "Hurrah!" Wine flows freely. As the Danish poet and troubadour

Benny Andersen wrote in a song well known among Danes: "One must keep the mood wet. I'm drunk and I'm feeling great."

Six hours into such a celebration and filled with spirits, a party-goer has a chance to get up from the table, dance a bit, then fetch some coffee and cookies and sit down again. Later, the

DENMARK: THE ESSENTIALS

Population 5.3 million.
Capital Copenhagen (pop. 1.1 million).
Notable towns Århus, Odense.
Climate Average maximum temperature in July: 22°C (71°F). In February: 5.5°C (42°F).
Top museums Nationalmuseet, Louisiana Museum of Modern Art, Vikingeskibshallen.
Famous home Hans Christian Andersen Hus, Odense.
Historic sights Christiansborg, Copenhagen; Kronborg, Helsingør; Roskilde Cathedral; Vikingeborgen, Trælleborg.
Natural wonders Råbjerg Mile sand dune; cliffs of Møn.
Tourist information www.visitdenmark.com

LEFT: a farmer practises the traditional art of canal-jumping in low-lying southwestern Denmark.
RIGHT: the modern face of Danish industry.

hosts serve the final course, called "get out food", and guests gradually take the hint.

Hygge was born, no doubt, indoors during the grey winter months. From November to February, Danes go to work in darkness and return home in darkness. Warm candlelight fills flats, homes and offices in natural defence. During *Jul* (Christmas), live candles decorate Christmas trees indoors, around which families join hands and sing carols. Local ferries light up the black water with strings of white lights. On New Year's Eve, the Queen gives her annual talk to the nation on television, and fireworks spark and pop, lighting up the midnight sky.

A whiff of spring

By February, winter seems to drag on forever. In his essay, *Oh! To be Danish*, the author Klaus Rifbjerg writes of this time: "Sure, it can be grim, and now and then we might want to turn our collar up and jump in the river. But then the light suddenly changes and there's a melody in the air, a whiff of spring to come, the smell of the sea and a blackbird singing on a rooftop."

Fields of fluorescent yellow winter rape blossom in May, and the days turn longer. In spring and summer, urban Danes cycle out to their garden houses on the edge of town, and rural Danes collect dead branches and greenery

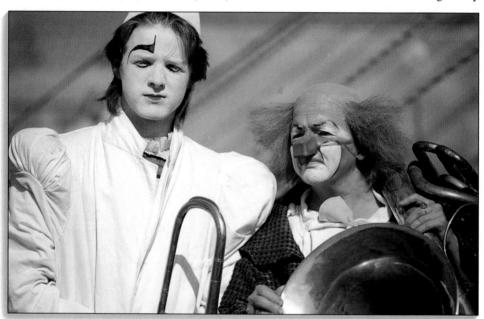

EQUALITY FOR ALL

Denmark is a society of non-extremes where, as Danes themselves say, "few have too much and fewer have too little". The welfare system gives everyone the same opportunities: free health service, education, support for the elderly and handicapped, unemployment benefits, pensions, and more.

The system carries a price: goods and services are taxed at 25 percent, and 50–70 percent of income is taxed. This equality carries through to social mores. Everyone is on first-name terms. The formal address, *De*, being reserved mainly for the Queen. Dress is casual and a tie in the workplace is rare.

into huge piles on the beaches and in the countryside. On the evening of 23 June, Midsummer's Eve, those piles of wood are topped with an effigy of a witch and set on fire to drive bad spirits from the land as Danes gather around the bonfires and sing. In July, nearly the whole country goes on holiday for three weeks. Barbecues are lit andbathing-suits donned.

By late summer, farmers' tractors haul grain and hay, holding up traffic. Towns hold harvest festivals, children start school and families hunt for mushrooms and berries in the beech and oak forests. People complain about the diminishing light and increasing rain, and soon the frost hits and temperatures can drop so low the sea freezes solid. So, the Danes light a candle, make some *hygge* with hot cocoa and buns, and look forward to *Jul* again.

A sense of togetherness and looking out for each other can be felt not only in family *hygge*, but in society as well, starting with the generous welfare system. Workers unions are strong, and the co-operative spirit prevails. Only four out of 100 Danes do not belong to an association.

"We have a joke that if two Danes sit

MANY VOICES

More than 100 dialects are spoken in Denmark. Some vary greatly. People in South Jutland are hardly understood by the residents of Copenhagen.

democracy, traditions, norms and welfare system were suddenly thrown into question by new-comers and Danes alike. Denmark found itself unprepared in how to deal with cultural misunderstandings, how to teach Danish effectively to thousands of immigrants, and how to help integrate them into the job market and society.

When Frans Kjær Nielsen began to teach Danish in Århus in 1985, the only option for foreigners was a local night school, which also offered hobby classes like painting and gardening. Only a couple of

together for five minutes, they will start an association," says Frans Kjær Nielsen.

The new Danes

In the 1960s and 1970s, Denmark experienced the first recent wave of immigrants – Turkish "guest workers". It was not until the early 1980s, however, that the effects of immigration on the Danish culture were felt, when refugees from the Far East, Middle East, the Balkans, Somalia, and elsewhere came to the country. The Danish social

---

LEFT: arts and music festivals are regular fixtures on the Danish cultural calendar.
ABOVE: looking to the future.

Danish text books were available. Fortunately, things got better. The country passed immigrant education laws and improved teacher-training. Yet unemployment remains high among immi-grants, who have tended to congregate into their own neighbourhoods.

While politicians and public officials have tried to work things out on paper, the greater part of Danish society seems to be tolerant – it takes personal effort from both sides, many have pointed out. However, immigration remains an emotive issue. It was at the top of the political agenda in the 2001 elections, at which the right-wing, anti-immigration Danish People's Party increased its share of the vote. ❏

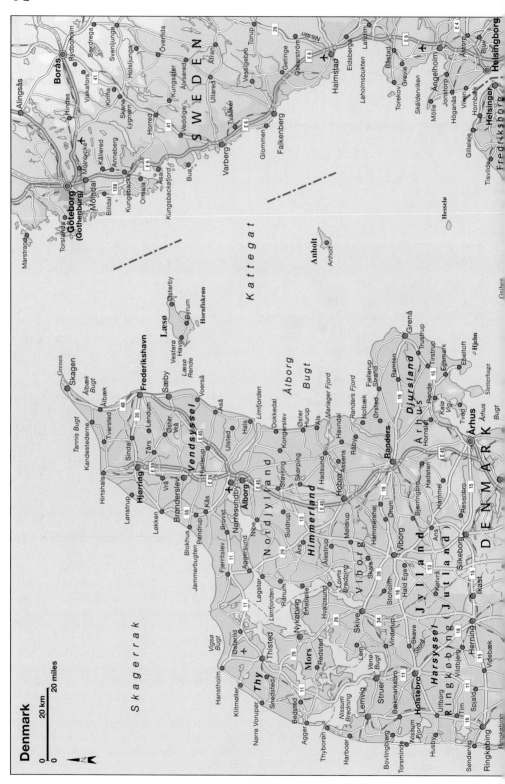

Denmark

N

0   20 km
0   20 miles

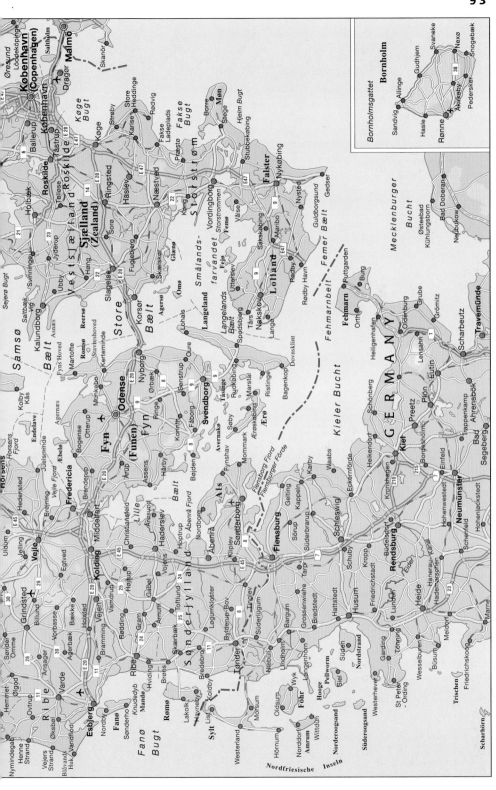

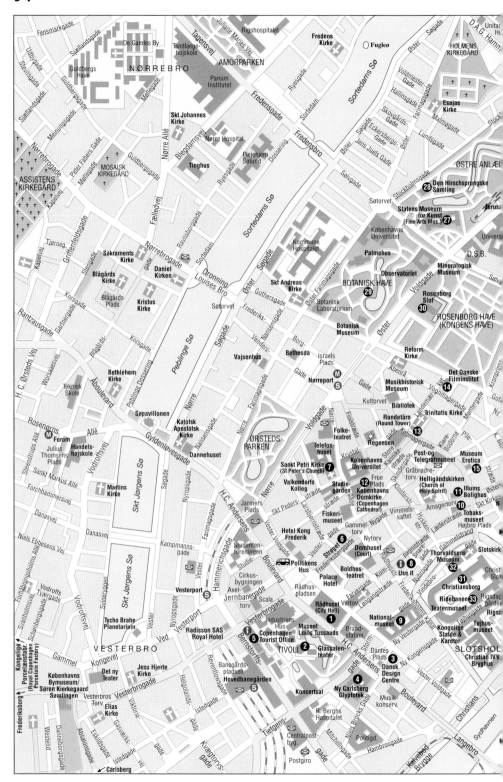

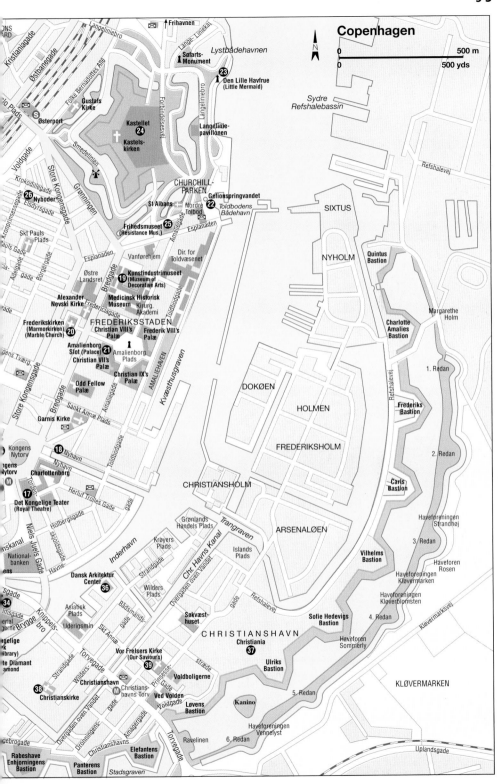

Copenhagen

0   500 m
0   500 yds

Frihavnen

Lystbådehavnen

Søfarts-Monument

Den Lille Havfrue
(Little Mermaid)

Sydre
Refshalebassin

Gustafs
Kirke

Østerport

Kastellet

Kastels-
kirken

Langelinie-
pavillónen

Refshalevej

CHURCHILL-
PARKEN

Gefionspringvandet

SIXTUS

St Albans
Nyboder

Nordre
Toldbod

Toldbodens
Bådehavn

Frihedsmuseet
(Resistance Mus.)

Esplanaden

NYHOLM

Quintus
Bastion

Skt Pauls
Plads

Vanførehjem

Dir. for
Toldvæsenet

Esplanaden

Margarethe
Holm

Østre
Landsret

Kunstindustrimuseet
(Museum of
Decorative Arts)

Charlotte
Amalies
Bastion

Alexander
Nevski Kirke

Medicinsk Historisk
Museum

Kirurg.
Akademi

1. Redan

Frederikskirken
(Marmorkirken)
(Marble Church)

FREDERIKSSTADEN

Christian VIII's
Palæ

Frederik VIII's
Palæ

Frederiks
Bastion

Amalienborg
Slot (Palace)

Amalienborg
Plads

Christian VII's
Palæ

DOKØEN

HOLMEN

2. Redan

Christian IX's
Palæ

Odd Fellow
Palæ

Garnis Kirke

FREDERIKSHOLM

Kongens
Nytorv

Nyhavn

Nyhavn

Charlottenborg

CHRISTIANSHOLM

Carls
Bastion

Det Kongelige Teater
(Royal Theatre)

Herluf Trolles Gade

Holbergsgade

Haveforeningen
(Strandhøj

National-
banken

Grønlands
Handels Plads

Trangraven

ARSENALØEN

3/ Redan

Krøyers
Plads

Islands
Plads

Vilhelms
Bastion

Haveforen
Rosen

Dansk Arkitektur
Center

Strandgade

Haveforeningen
Kløvermarken

Asiatisk
Plads

Wilders
Plads

Haveforeningen
Kløverblomsten

Uderigsmin

Ski Anna

Søkvæst-
huset

Sofie Hedevigs
Bastion

4. Redan

te Diamant
amond

Vor Frelsers Kirke
(Our Saviour's)

CHRISTIANSHAVN

Christiania

Haveforen
Sommerly

Ulriks
Bastion

Christianshavn

Voldboligerne

KLØVERMARKEN

Christianskirke

Christians-
havns Torv

Ved Volden

Løvens
Bastion

Kanino

5. Redan

Rabeshave
Enhjorningens
Bastion

Panterens
Bastion

Elefantens
Bastion

Ravelinen

6. Redan

Haveforeningen
Vennelyst

Uplandsgade

Stadsgraven

COPENHAGEN

*Denmark's capital city is the most exuberant in Scandinavia.
Pedestrians and cyclists rule, shopping is a pleasure,
cultural sights abound, and by night the city buzzes*

Map
on pages
94–95

Copenhagen (København) is the "city of green spires". Copper plates, etched green by salt air, clad the spires of castles and churches in the old city, and tower over the medieval street network and newer houses. The Old Town you visit today would have looked different but for two devastating fires and a terrible bombardment. Blazes in 1728 and 1795 licked and leaped along the straw-roofed houses and turned most of the half-timbered medieval town to ashes. Only a few solidly built structures survived – among them, the Rundetårn (Round Tower). When Admiral Lord Nelson and the British fleet bombarded Copenhagen in 1807 the toll was also heavy. The old Copenhagen Cathedral was a victim.

Copenhagen is the liveliest – and many claim the most fetching – of the Scandinavian capitals, with things to see and do all the time. With Europe's longest pedestrian mall, this was the first capital to offer the pleasures of ambling through a network of streets free of motor vehicles and exhaust fumes.

A good way to get a first feel of Copenhagen is from the water. Take one of the 50-minute canal boat trips from Gammel Strand (open Apr–mid-Dec: every 30 minutes from 10am; tel: 70 15 65 65). If you're the adventuresome type you could explore the waterways in a kayak for two hours, starting at the same place.

LEFT: the bright lights of Tivoli.
BELOW: dressed for the carnival.

FACT FILE

Situation Copenhagen is located on the east coast of Zealand facing the sound between Denmark and Sweden.
Population 1.8 million in the Copenhagen area.
Climate Afternoon temperatures in February average 5.5°C (42°F); in July they are around 21 or 22°C (70–72°F).
Transport Metro, bus and S-train network; bike hire.
Discount card Buy a Copenhagen Card for free entrance to museums, galleries, and free transport.
Best sightseeing tour Guided Walking Tour *(see panel, page 103)*; canal boat trip from Gammel Strand.
Best shopping Strøget, Europe's longest pedestrian mall.
Top attraction Tivoli Gardens (open summer, Christmas).
Finest building Rosenborg Slot (Castle).
Best museums Nationalmuseet, Ny Carlsberg Glyptotek, Statens Museum for Kunst (National Museum for Fine Arts), the ruins of Absalon's castle beneath Christiansborg.
Best views of the city Rådhuset tower; Rundetårn (Round Tower); Vor Frelsers Kirke, Christianshavn.
Best *smørrebrød* Slotskælderen, Fortunstræde 4, tel: 33 11 15 37.
Tourist information office Bernstorffsgade 1 (opposite the Central Railway Station); tel: 45 70 22 24 42; www.visitcopenhagen.dk; touristinfo@woco.dk

A guide paddles ahead of you (Copenhagen Adventure Tours; tel: 40 50 40 06).

Rådhuspladsen (City Hall Square) is the nexus of Copenhagen, grandly lit up at night with its coloured signs, digital news headlines and blinking neon, with the enormous **Rådhuset ❶** (City Hall; open Mon–Sat 8am–5pm, free; tours in English, 3pm, for a fee; tel: 33 66 25 82) at its heart. Constructed in the National Romantic style, its inspiration was drawn from medieval Danish and Norwegian architecture with a touch of the Palazzo style of northern Italy. The facade and interior are trimmed with historic details from Nordic mythology. Looking for a bird's-eye view of the city's spires and towers? The 106-metre (347-ft) tower (open daily; entrance fee) is for you.

Inside the foyer, look for the entrance to **Jens Olsen's World Clock** (open Mon–Fri 10am–4pm, Sat 10am–1pm; entrance fee). Its star dial mechanism shows the path of the pole star in re-settable periods, making it the "most accurate and complicated clock in the world", according to the *Guinness Book of World Records*.

Bordering the square to the east on Vester Voldgade are two of Copenhagen's fine traditional hotels. Closest to City Hall is the **Palace Hotel**, one of the few buildings in the Jugendstil (Art Nouveau style), and further north, past the square, **Hotel Kong Frederik** with the smart and pricey Queen's Pub restaurant.

To the west, on H.C. Andersens Boulevard, it's hard to miss a castle-like red-brick building nicknamed "Little Rosenborg". There's an entrance to **Tivoli Gardens ❷** (open late Apr–late Sept Sun–Thur 11am–midnight, Fri and Sat 11am–1am; also at Christmas; entrance fee; tel: 33 15 10 01; www.tivoli.dk) and **Museet Louis Tussaud's** (open May–Sept 10am–10pm; Oct–Apr 10am–5pm; entrance fee; tel: 33 11 89 00). Although smaller than Madame Tussaud's in London, the waxworks museum offers a line-up including all the kings and

BELOW: the palace of Christiansborg, Denmark's seat of government.

HISTORIC TRADING POST

Before 1167, Copenhagen was just a trading post called Havn (Harbour), which gave easy access to Skåne (Scania) across the Sound. Skåne is now part of Sweden, but in those days southern Sweden was part of Denmark, and the village of Havn enjoyed a position in the middle of the kingdom. As wars and unrest changed the geography of Denmark, København (Merchant's Harbour) gradually moved to its point on the eastern shore of Zealand.

In 1167, King Valdemar I commanded the local bishop, Absalon of Roskilde, to fortify Havn in order to protect it against Wendic pirates. Absalon built a fortress on the spot where the Parliament building now looms across the canal from Højbro Plads (Square). Copenhagen was on the way to becoming Denmark's biggest and most important town. The fortress became Christiansborg, *borg* meaning castle. Centuries later, it remains the seat of Danish politics, housing the Folketing (Parliament).

During the long reign of Kristian IV (1588–1648), Copenhagen solidified its role as the country's seat of power. This visionary town planner built Børsen, said to be the oldest stock exchange in Europe, a Renaissance structure with a spire of four entwined dragons, steep copper roofs, tiny windows and gables galore.

queens of Denmark and many other notables, historic and contemporary.

Tivoli is a Scandinavian rainbow of gardens, open-air amusements, restaurants, cafés, theatres, an open-air stage and a major concert hall, home of Sjællands Symphony Orchestra. Tivoli is also the place to enjoy a good meal, coffee and cake, or a drink. The park has more than 20 restaurants. For children, the greatest thrills come from the rides, roller coasters and merry-go-rounds. In recent years the lake has been machine-frozen for winter ice-skating, and the pleasure mecca's portals are thrown open for an old-fashioned market at Christmas time.

Danish design

A two-minute walk south of the City Hall on H.C. Andersens Boulevard is the **Danish Design Centre** ❸ (open Mon–Thur 9.30am–6pm, Fri 9.30am–7pm, Sat 10am–4pm; entrance fee; tel: 33 69 33 69), with ongoing Danish and international exhibitions *(see Insight on Danish Design, page 110)*.

Across the road and a block to the southeast is **Ny Carlsberg Glyptotek** ❹ (open Tues–Sun 10am–4pm, closed Mon; entrance fee, Sun and Wed free; tel: 33 41 81 41). This exquisite museum offers a grand art collection begun by the brewer Carl Jacobsen and maintained by the New Carlsberg Foundation. There are collections of ancient Egyptian, Greek, Roman and Etruscan sculptures, as well as some French masterpieces from Cézanne, Gauguin and Rodin. The lush, palm-lined indoor Winter Garden has a wonderful café.

On Bernstorffsgade, across from Tivoli's west entrance, is **Hovedbanegården** (Central Railway Station). Beyond it to the west lies **Vesterbro**, one of Copenhagen's old residential districts, today a multicultural community, vibrant

Map on pages 94–95

The tall tubes in front of the Moorish-style palace restaurant in Tivoli contain bubbling water. This unusual sculpture was designed by the Danish nuclear physicist Niels Bohr.

BELOW: City Hall dominates the bustling central square of Rådhuspladsen.

TIP

You'll find local news and listings in the weekly English-language tabloid newspaper, *The Copenhagen Post*, distributed free at some hotels and sold at Danish State Railway kiosks and 7-Eleven stores.

with bizarre shops, exotic restaurants and its red-light boulevard, **Istedgade**.

The **Copenhagen Tourist Office ❺** lies across the street from Central Station on Bernstorffsgade, near the corner of Vesterbrogade. This travellers' ganglion has it all: information on sights, cultural activities, transport, eating places, events. A prime source is the free magazine *Copenhagen This Week* (www.ctw.dk).

The medieval city

If Rådhuspladsen is the heart of Copenhagen, then **Strøget ❻**, the 1.8-km (1-mile) pedestrian shopping street, is the spine. It has endless shops, street vendors and buskers and cellar galleries. Strøget *("stroy-yet")* is where Copenhageners and visitors alike go to shop or just to promenade. The mainstream shops and eateries are on Strøget proper, while the more quirky boutiques, cafés and restaurants are situated on any of the quieter side streets.

Starting at Rådhuspladsen, Strøget meanders through five streets and four squares before it runs into Kongens Nytorv, the largest square in the old town. Good landmarks and meeting places are the squares at **Gammeltorv** (Old Square) and at Strøget's major crossroads, the crane fountain at **Amagertorv**. Here, another main pedestrian artery, **Købmagergade**, branches off to the north.

Near Gammeltorv, the area behind **Vestergade** is one of the few remaining residential areas in the inner city. Living in the picturesque neoclassical houses is a mixture of old-time Copenhageners, artists and students, and here you find some of the more exotic clothes shops and galleries – try Skt Pedersstræde for starters. **Sankt Petri Kirke ❼** (St Peter's Church), on the corner of Nørregade and Skt Pedersstræde, is the oldest church in Copenhagen, its chancellery built in 1450. Hans Christian Andersen lived in No. 19 Vestergade when, as a young man, he first arrived in Copenhagen from Odense. Another famous Dane, the 19th-century philosopher Søren Kierkegaard, lived in the house on the corner of Nytorv and Frederiksberggade at Gammeltorv.

One block south and running parallel to Strøget, is **Kompagnistræde**, with shops specialising in antiques, china and pewter. At Rådhusstræde 13 you'll find - **Use It ❽** (tel: 33 73 06 20; www.useit.dk), an extremely helpful information centre for tourists on a low budget. Pick up its excellent guide, *Playtime*.

Two blocks south, across from the canal on Ny Vestergade, is Denmark's **Nationalmuseet ❾** (National Museum; open 10am–5pm, closed Mon; entrance fee, Wed free; tel: 33 13 44 11), highly recommended for its collections of ancient "bog" finds from the Stone, Bronze and Iron Ages. A fascinating and well-structured museum that takes days to cover, it has an interesting section on Danish cultural history.

From Nytorv, continue along Strøget towards Amagertorv. For a close encounter of the rich and sweet, stop at one of Copenhagen's premier confectioner's, **Konditori La Glace**, a few stops from Strøget at Skoubogade. Here, cream-layer cakes reign supreme. For tobacco aficionados, Amagertorv 9 is one of those rare places you find where you least

BELOW: a touch of the tropics in the indoor Winter Garden of Ny Carlsberg Glyptotek.

expect it. W.Ø. Larsen is a smokers' emporium and houses the **Tobaksmuseet** ❿ (Tobacco Museum; open Mon–Thur 10am–6pm, Fri 10am–7pm, Sat 10am–5pm; free; tel: 33 12 20 50), with its display of ancient pipes, tobaccos and smoking history. The opposite side of Amagertorv is occupied by the shops most often visited by tourists: **Illums Bolighus** ⓫, showcase for superb Danish and international design; and the flagship stores of **Royal Copenhagen Porcelain** and **Georg Jensen** silver.

Map on pages 94–95

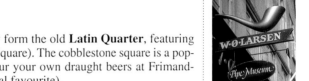

Latin Quarter

The streets to the north of Amagertorv form the old **Latin Quarter**, featuring the cosy **Gråbrødretorv** (Greyfriar's Square). The cobblestone square is a popular place to enjoy lunch (you can pour your own draught beers at Frimandskvarter) or dinner (Peder Oxe is a local favourite).

The streets just to the north hold **Københavns Domkirke** ⓬ (Copenhagen's Cathedral) and the main building of the **University of Copenhagen**. The seat of the University Board, beside Nørregade, dates from 1420 and is the oldest building in Copenhagen. A fun stop for children is the sweet factory on Nørregade 36, **Sømod's Bolcher**, where confectioners make old-fashioned boiled sweets by hand (demonstrations Mon–Fri 9.15am–3pm; tel: 33 12 60 46). **Fiolstræde** is known for its antiquarian bookshops, and **Krystalgade** is the site of Copenhagen's synagogue. Try a sandwich from the busy, bowler-hatted organic butchers, **Slagteren ved Kultorvet** (Coal Square), on the open plaza near the Nørreport subway station, at the top of traffic-free Købmagergade.

On Købmagergade itself is one of Copenhagen's most fascinating buildings. The **Rundetårn** ⓭ (Round Tower; open Sept–May 10am–5pm;

A whiff of tobacco: W.Ø. Larsen's museum in Strøget.

BELOW: enjoying a break in Skt Anne's Passage.

For a taste of brewing, visit the famous Carlsberg Brewery and stables, Gammel Valby Langgade 1, Valby, and sample a glass of the best (open 10am–4pm, closed Mon; free; tel: 33 27 27 27).

BELOW: time for a beer on the quayside at Nyhavn.

June–Aug 10am–8pm; tel: 33 73 03 73) was built in 1642 as an observatory for Denmark's world-renowned astronomer, Tycho Brahe. It still has a viewing platform on the top which offers a breathtaking panorama on clear days and nights. The tower stands 36 metres (118 ft) high, and to reach the roof one walks up a 209-metre (685-ft) spiral ramp. In 1716 Tsar Peter the Great drove a horse and carriage to the top.

Around the corner off Landemærket is the **Det Danske Filminstitut ⑭**, home of Cinemateket, which celebrates Denmark's trailblazing successes in cinematography, and shows a programme of international and Danish films (performances Tues–Sun 9.30am–10pm; tel: 33 74 34 12).

A few blocks south on Købmagergade is **Museum Erotica ⑮** (open May–Sept 10am–11pm; Oct–Apr 11am–8pm; entrance fee; tel: 33 12 03 11), one of the best examples in town of the liberal-minded Danes. Here sex and sensuality are not an issue – they *are* the issue.

Haunts of the rich and famous

The last section of Strøget, from the Crane Fountain to Kongens Nytorv, is the home of the exclusive and expensive: fashion shops, furriers and jewellers.

At the end of Strøget, facing **Kongens Nytorv** (King's New Square), stands the grand old hotel of the city, **Hotel D'Angleterre ⑯**. The majestic buildings dominating Kongens Nytorv are **Det Kongelige Teater ⑰** (Royal Theatre) – the national stage for ballet, opera, and drama. The present building was designed in the 1870s, taking the Parisian Opera as its ideal. Next door is **Charlotten-borg**, since 1754 the home of the **Royal Academy of Fine Arts**, where painters, sculptors and architects receive their formal training.

Nyhavn quayside

At the narrow waterway of **Nyhavn** ⑱, a famous landmark from 1673, colourful old wooden schooners line the quay, and the north side is a charming combination of sailors' bars and new restaurants. The south side was always "the nice side" but the north side used to be "the naughty side" where sailors on shore leave would spend their liberty drinking, whoring, and getting tattooed. Times have changed, and Nyhavn is now one of the most popular spots in town for a different type of visitor.

From Nyhavn, Bredgade and its parallel twin, Store Kongensgade, are the main shopping streets of the residential **Frederiksstaden** to the north. The area was planned and built in the 18th century for the well-to-do who wanted stately homes close to the centre.

At Bredgade 68 is **Kunstindustrimuseet** ⑲ (The Danish Museum of Decorative Art; open Tues–Fri 10am–4pm, Sat–Sun noon–4pm; entrance fee; tel: 33 18 56 56) which features not only European and Oriental works, but classic Danish design as well. The building dates from 1757 and was originally a hospital. Opposite the museum, three domes tower over **Alexander Nevski Russian Orthodox Church**, which was built in 1881 by the Russian government and contains a number of fine icons.

Close by, there is almost no way one can miss the grand copper dome of **Frederikskirken** ⑳, popularly known as the **Marble Church**. The church was meant to be a majestic rococo monument, but the king, Frederik V, ran out of money and the project was cancelled in 1770. The church was not completed until the 1870s. When the project was resumed it was built not in marble but in limestone. From the dome, which is accessible to visitors (open mid-June–Aug

Nyhavn still retains some of the character of bygone days, when it was a haunt for sailors on leave.

BELOW: the Round Tower, built in 1642, offers good views of the city.

THE WALK OF THE TOWN

On your feet is the best way to discover this old town of narrow streets and cobbled courtyards. The "Guided Walking Tour of Copenhagen" starts outside the Tourist Information Office on Bernstorffsgade, across from Central Station (all year Sat–Sun 11am, also June–Aug: Thur and Fri 11am; tel: 70 22 24 42).

The first stop is Rådhuspladsen, where the western wall came down in the 1850s to let the city expand, "it was dirty and terribly crowded inside." The guide sets off along streets following the curve of the canal which once extended to Strøget – now Europe's longest pedestrian mall – pausing at the City Court House, profiled like a Greek temple. By the canal a buxom woman serves fishcakes. Over Amagertorv looms a Dutch Renaissance building from 1616, the mayor's residence taken over in 1911 by Royal Copenhagen Porcelain. Today, side by side, are Royal Copenhagen, Georg Jensen silver, Holmegaard glass, and Illums Bolighus with Danish gifts and furnishings. Then there's the Royal Theatre and the elegant Hotel D'Angleterre, where Victor Borge stays. And Nyhavn, where you can take a canal tour. What's this – Amalienborg Palace? Just in time for the noon-time changing of the guard. Have two hours really passed?

daily 1pm and 3pm; Sept–early June Sat–Sun 1pm and 3pm; entrance fee), there is a splendid view across the Sound to Sweden. The statues outside the church represent important Danish churchmen and theologians.

Royal residence

Amalienborg Slot ㉑ (Palace), directly across Bredgade towards the harbour, is the residence of the Royal Family, one of Europe's less assuming royal domiciles, built in the 18th century. The Royal Guard are always on duty, and the changing of the guard at noon every day attracts both children and adults. If the flag is flying, then the Queen is in residence and the full ceremony will take place. The exquisite equestrian statue in the middle of the square represents Frederik V and was made by the French sculptor Jacques Saly. Det Østasiatiske Kompagni (East Asiatic Company), one of Denmark's most prosperous trading companies of the day, promised to finance the statue, but there was disagreement between the artist and his backers and it took 20 years to complete the work.

Along the promenade

The other end of the east–west axis through the plaza ends in **Amaliehaven**, a modern park donated to the city by the A.P. Møller shipping company in 1983. Following the promenade to the north, you will find the dazzling fountain, **Gefionspringvandet ㉒**, dedicated to the Nordic goddess Gefion.

At the start of Langelinie is *the* symbol of Copenhagen, **Den Lille Havfrue ㉓** (The Little Mermaid). This bronze statue of the character from the Hans Christian Andersen fairy tale was created by Edvard Eriksen in 1917.

The quay of Langelinie follows, and Europe's busiest cruise ship pier is to the

BELOW: royal guards on duty at Amalienborg Palace.
RIGHT: rococo splendour at the Marble Church.

north of this at **Frihavnen** (Free Harbour). Renovations have been taking place to rejuvenate the area. The most architecturally interesting of the new buildings is **Paustians Hus**, designed by Jørn Utzon, who also designed the Sydney Opera House. Paustian is one of Copenhagen's finest furniture stores and the building also houses a good restaurant.

Map on pages 94–95

War resistance

Return to the city centre via **Kastellet ②** (The Citadel), a fortification that has kept its old ramparts intact. Part of the area is still military property.

Churchillparken, a tiny park just south of Kastellet, provides a home for **Frihedsmuseet ②** (Danish Resistance Museum; open May–mid-Sept Tues–Sat 10am–4pm, Sun 10am–5pm; mid-Sept–Apr Tues–Sat 11am–3pm, Sun 11am–4pm; entrance fee, Wed free; tel: 33 13 77 14), which commemorates the Danish underground fighters of World War II.

Continue past Store Kongensgade to visit Denmark's oldest housing development, **Nyboder ②**. The long rows of ochre-coloured houses were built in 1638 by Kristian IV as quarters for the Danish Royal Navy, and the 616 apartments are still used for staff and retired officers.

Nearby, where Øster Voldgade and Sølvgade meet, is the superb **Statens Museum for Kunst ②** (National Museum for Fine Arts; open Thurs–Sun and Tues 10am–5pm, Wed 10am–8pm; entrance fee; tel: 33 74 84 94). An extension was completed in 1999, housing four storey of modern art within stunning glass and whitewashed walls. Other Danish and European works are displayed permanently, along with changing international exhibitions. Behind the museum and across the park is **Den Hirschsprungske Samling ②** (Hirschsprung Col-

Lille Havfrue (the Little Mermaid), by Edvard Eriksen, was modelled on his wife.

BELOW: the Royal Library's shining "Black Diamond" extension.

CHRISTIANIA – THE ALTERNATIVE CITY

In a beautiful position on Copenhagen's waterfront, Christiania offers a way of life far removed from the bustle of a city

In 1971, a group of alternative thinkers founded Christiania, a 41-hectare (84-acre) "Free City" with woods, dirt roads, workshops, restaurants and funky houses. The hippie playground in the heart of the city – only 1 km from the Parliament buildings – retains the spirit of the Woodstock era.

You will find the area in Christianshavn in what was previously an abandoned 19th-century military barracks. The Christianites have converted barrack blocks, workshops and powder magazines into a place where they can live and work.

About 1,000 people of all ages, cultures and income levels live in this working collective, but its existence is still a subject of controversy in the Danish Parliament. It was given official status as a social experiment in 1981.

There are only three rules here: no hard drugs, no cars, no weapons or violence. As part of their belief in their way of life, the Christianites refuse to condemn the open sale of hashish and marijuana, and they have successfully campaigned against hard drugs. The area's suggestively named "Pusher Street" does, however, get visits from the city police.

From the entrance on, Christiania is a sensory overload. Buildings are painted with rainbows, spiritual figures and politically defiant graffiti. There are barefoot cyclists, their baskets full of vegetables; earthy-smelling organic markets; recycling warehouses; workshops; and stables. Resident children play in an "organic kindergarten", where modern equipment is replaced with nature. Houses along the leafy path have names such as "The Blue Banana" or "The Pyramid".

"The more secure people have felt to be here, the more money they have spent to restore the houses," says tour guide Nina Pontoppidan. "We take care of our own buildings, so the politicians look between their fingers. If they put the people in social housing, they would have to spend a lot of money."

Christiania has some of the best restaurants in the city, including SpiseLoppen (The Eating Flea), in the warehouse by the front entrance. In the same building is Loppen, a music club. Månefiskeren (The Moon Fisher), a café in the heart of the collective, serves excellent coffee in a "far-out" atmosphere.

For an inexpensive walking tour, meet at the front entrance hourly between noon and 3pm – this is the best way to see the Free City and get a broader perspective. In addition, *Nitten*, Christiania's free tourist guide, provides a detailed history and self-guided walks. ❑

TOP LEFT: murals decorate many of Christiania's buildings. **LEFT:** relaxed lifestyle. **TOP:** child of the New Age. **ABOVE:** the streets are car-free.

lection; open Wed–Mon 11am–4pm; entrance fee; tel: 35 42 03 36), a commendable private collection of 19th-century Danish art – including many of the originals from the Skagen painters.

Map on pages 94–95

Gardens and jewels

The **Botanisk Have ㉙** (Botanical Gardens) are just across the street, along Sølvgade and Øster Voldgade (open summer 8.30am–6pm; winter: 8.30am–4pm; free; tel: 35 32 22 40). Visit the rosarium, the perennials and a huge conservatory with tropical and subtropical plants.

One of Copenhagen's most attractive sights is **Rosenborg Slot ㉚** (opening times vary; entrance fee; 33 15 32 86), the fairy-tale castle across from the Botanical Gardens. King Kristian IV's exquisite palace in Dutch Renaissance style is now a museum, and contains three centuries-worth of royal treasures, as well as the crown jewels. The garden surrounding it, **Kongens Have**, has been a favourite with Copenhageners for centuries.

For treasure and trash visit the city's antique and flea markets. Try Israels Plads on Saturday, 8am–2pm, and Gammel Strand, Friday and Saturday 9am–4pm.

Centre of government

To the southeast of Strøget and the main shopping area lies **Slotsholmen** (Castle Island). Surrounded by canals, the island is the seat of the Danish Parliament and government ministries. The imposing **Christiansborg ㉛**, built on the same spot as the original old castle of Copenhagen, contains Parliament, the Prime Minister's office, the Supreme Court and the Royal Reception Chambers. The public may join free conducted tours of the **Folketinget** (House of Parliament), and the **Royal Reception Chambers** (tel: 33 92 64 93).

Bishop Absalon built a fortress on this little islet in 1167, and from 1416 it was the home of the Danish king. Absalon's fortress was replaced by a new castle in 1367 and in the 1730s King Kristian VI ordered a new palace. This one, a magnificent baroque building, burned in 1794 and was replaced yet again with a new palace which, ill-fated as it was, burned down in 1884. The present version of Christiansborg is less than 100 years old, built between 1907 and 1928. The granite facade was made from stones gathered in every parish in the country. The equestrian statue, erected on the Palace Square, depicts King Frederik VII (1843–63).

The **Ruins of Absalon's Old Fortress** (open May–Sept daily 9.30am–3.30pm; Oct–Apr Tues, Thur, Sun 9.30am–3.30pm; entrance fee) and the medieval castle are now accessible to visitors and make an interesting "underground" visit.

The **Palace Chapel**, erected in 1826, is located to the north of Christiansborg. Behind the chapel is **Thorvaldsens Museum ㉜**, which contains the works of Denmark's great sculptor, Bertel Thorvaldsen (1770–1844), who lived and worked in Rome for 40 years (open Tues–Sun 10am–5pm; entrance fee; - tel: 33 32 15 32).

In front of Christiansborg is the **Ridebanen ㉝**, the royal riding grounds from the 1740s bordered by the only surviving buildings from the first Christiansborg. The royal horses are still exercised here and their stables can be visited on the southeast side of the

BELOW: exploring Copenhagen's waterways by boat.

Map on pages 94–95

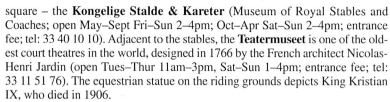

The 17th-century Vor Frelsers Kirke on Christianshavn.

BELOW: the city's Botanical Gardens.
RIGHT: Carlsberg Brewery drayman.

square – the **Kongelige Stalde & Kareter** (Museum of Royal Stables and Coaches; open May–Sept Fri–Sun 2–4pm; Oct–Apr Sat–Sun 2–4pm; entrance fee; tel: 33 40 10 10). Adjacent to the stables, the **Teatermuseet** is one of the oldest court theatres in the world, designed in 1766 by the French architect Nicolas-Henri Jardin (open Tues–Thur 11am–3pm, Sat–Sun 1–4pm; entrance fee; tel: 33 11 51 76). The equestrian statue on the riding grounds depicts King Kristian IX, who died in 1906.

East of Christiansborg is another of Copenhagen's best-known buildings, **Børsen** ❸ (Stock Exchange), built in 1619 in Dutch Renaissance style by Kristian IV. Its prominent spire is formed by the entwined tails of dragons representing Denmark, Sweden and Norway. On the southeast side of the island is **Det Kongelige Bibliotek** ❸ (Royal Library) and its "Black Diamond" – an architectural wonder of old and new. Det Kongelige Bibliotek dates back to 1482 and is the largest library in Scandinavia, with more than 2½ million volumes. The Black Diamond, completed in 1999, is a modern extension in black polished granite perched on the water's edge.

Colourful Christianshavn

Cross the harbour via the Knippelsbro bridge to reach **Christianshavn**, one of Copenhagen's oldest and most colourful residential areas. Christianshavn was built on an island in 1617 by Kristian IV and is surrounded by the original star-shaped ramparts. Along the harbour wall, one of the meticulously restored warehouses is well worth a visit, the **Dansk Arkitektur Center** ❸ (Danish Architecture Centre; open daily 10am–5pm; free; tel: 32 57 19 30), which features various exhibitions, a bookshop and café.

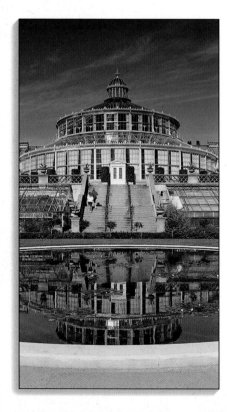

Until recently a run-down, working-class area and the site of Denmark's largest shipyard, Christianshavn has changed its appearance greatly and now features a quaint mixture of smartly renovated 18th-century city houses, big apartment blocks, old and new industry and a good deal of the state's administration.

Take a stroll down the streets of Christianshavn and glance into the courtyards of some of the old houses on **Strandgade**. Amagergade 11, at the other end of Christianshavn, is said to have the finest courtyard in town, and is surrounded by old galleries.

Christianshavn is also the home of **Christiania** ❸, the hippie-style "free city" *(see Christiania, page 106)*. The main entrance is on Prinsessegade.

Two of Copenhagen's more notable churches are on Christianshavn. **Christianskirke** ❸ in Strandgade is a rococo building from 1754. It was built as a theatre with boxes, including one for the royal family. **Vor Frelsers Kirke** ❸ (Church of Our Saviour; open Mon–Sat 11am–4.30pm, Sun noon–4.30pm, closes 3.30pm Sept–Mar; tower closed in winter) in Prinsessegade attracts the most attention. Built in red brick in 1694, its tall copper-clad tower with a spiralling, external stairway can be seen from all over the city. For a magnificent view over Copenhagen, the tower is open to visitors who dare to climb through a maze of roof timbers and up the 150 gilded steps. It's the perfect place to get an overview of the city of spires. ❑

A FLAIR FOR DESIGN: FUNCTION WITH FORM

*When a nation of craftsmen mixed with a late
move towards industrialisation in the 1900s,
an influential new school of design was born*

A chair may be
something to sit in, and
a lamp may help to
light up a room, but
Danish designers have
made these objects
more than ordinary
over the past 50 years.
Behind glass in
museums and in use in
a wide range of places
from conference rooms to homes, Danish design
has brought a sense of elegance to everyday life.

"It always starts with a task," says designer
Hans J. Wegner. "I never say to myself I'm going
to make a piece of art. I tell myself I want to
make a good chair" (Wegner's Round Chair,
above). Danish designers "subtract and subtract"
unnecessary elements from products and tools to
find true function and form, says Jens Bernsen of
the Danish Design Centre. "Sometimes these
designs even turn out to be beautiful."

In Copenhagen, you should visit the Danish
Museum of Decorative Art, Bredgade 68 (open
Tues–Fri 10am–4pm, Sat–Sun 12–4pm, closed
Mon; entrance fee; tel: 33 18 56 56), and the Danish
Design Centre, H.C. Andersens Boulevard (open
Mon–Thur 9.30am–6pm, Fri 9.30am–7pm, Sat
10am–4pm, closed Sun; entrance fee; tel: 33 69 33
69). A good place for furniture is Illum's Bolighus.

△ URSULA
Ursula Munch-Petersen
designed this well-loved
table service for Royal
Copenhagen.

▽ PH LAMP
Poul Henningsen saw a light
fixture as more than just
light, but something to
create a sense of space.

▽ CYLINDA LINE
The architect Arne Jacobsen designed this stainless steel line
of household objects for the company Stelton, and it is now
one of the most recognised in Denmark.

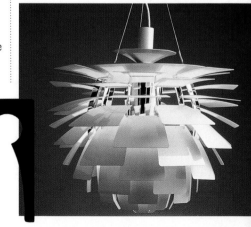

DESIGN IN THE HOME

For all its elegance, Danish design is not something limited to galleries and museums. In Denmark, it is found everywhere – hotels, restaurants, cafés, offices, and most importantly, homes. Nearly every Dane, it seems, has some sort of sleek designer lamp hanging over the dinner or coffee table.

For special occasions, such as weddings, birthdays and office receptions, Danes give presents such as arty salad sets, candle holders, salt and pepper grinders, pot holders – even mixing bowls *(pictured above)*.

"The kitchen drawer is good design's enemy number one," says Erik Bagger, whose wine serving tools are well known in Denmark. Danish-designed products are meant to be used, however, meaning that Denmark probably has the most stylish contents of kitchen drawers anywhere in the world.

The visually striking sound systems designed by Bang & Olufsen are praised worldwide, and are found in many a Danish home. Even such prosaic items as cupboard handles and other household fittings are given due attention by Danish designers.

◁ **EGG CHAIR**
Many of Arne Jacobsen's designs were intended for specific buildings or, in this case, hotel lobbies.

▽ **IC3 TRAIN**
Gone are the days of lumpish locomotives. Even Danish trains have a high quality of design.

ZEALAND

*Venture north from Copenhagen to Hamlet's castle at Helsingør,
or south to the white cliffs of Møn, and discover Zealand,
a colourful land rich in culture and tradition*

Map
on page
114

The island of Zealand is Denmark's largest, yet it is still compact and most of its many attractions make ideal day-trips from the capital. The area north of Copenhagen makes a classic tour for visitors, with its undulating countryside, beech forests, lakes and good beaches, as well as castles, manor houses, royal hunting lodges, art galleries and museums. The southern and western areas of Zealand have traditionally been the port of entry for new people and ideas coming from the Continent. This side of the island is an enchanting expanse of rolling hills, woodland and some wonderful seaside scenery.

Historically, Zealand played an important political role in the development of Denmark. The Viking influence was strong and the town of Roskilde, a trading post in Viking times, became the seat of kings and an important religious centre.

The Danish Riviera

The coast road from **Copenhagen ❶** to Helsingør is officially called Strandvejen, but is also known as the "Danish Riviera" for its stylish houses and fine views across the Øresund to Sweden. Small protected harbours shelter working fishing boats and millionaires' yachts alike, and converted marine buildings now house fresh fish restaurants.

While it's true that the essence of North Zealand can be glimpsed in a day, it really warrants more time, either by an overnight stop at a charming Danish *kro* (inn) or by taking several day tours from Copenhagen.

Starting from Copenhagen, drive north through fashionable Charlottenlund to **Klampenborg ❷** where just 15 minutes from the city centre you come to an ancient deer park, **Klampenborg Dyrhaven** (open daily), first mentioned in official documents in 1231. You can leave your car here and take a horse and carriage through the woods and parkland. Forest walks are indicated by yellow spots painted on trees.

In another part of the deer park lies what is claimed to be the world's oldest fun fair, **Bakken. Peter Lieps'** rustic restaurant in the forest is the place where the locals go to drink hot chocolate or beer after winter walks. Art lovers will enjoy the quiet elegance of the nearby **Ordrupgaard** (Vilvordevej 110; open Tues–Sun 1–4pm; entrance fee; tel: 39 64 11 83). It has a permanent collection of Danish and French paintings, which include major works by Matisse, Corot, Manet, Renoir, Sisley and Gauguin.

Out of Africa

A further 12 km (7 miles) brings you to **Rungsted ❸**, site of **Rungstedlund** (open May–Sept daily 10am–5pm; Oct–Apr Wed–Fri 1–4pm, Sat–Sun 11am–4pm; entrance fee; tel: 45 57 10 57), the family home of

LEFT: the chalk face of Møns Klint.
BELOW: the chapel at Frederiksborg.

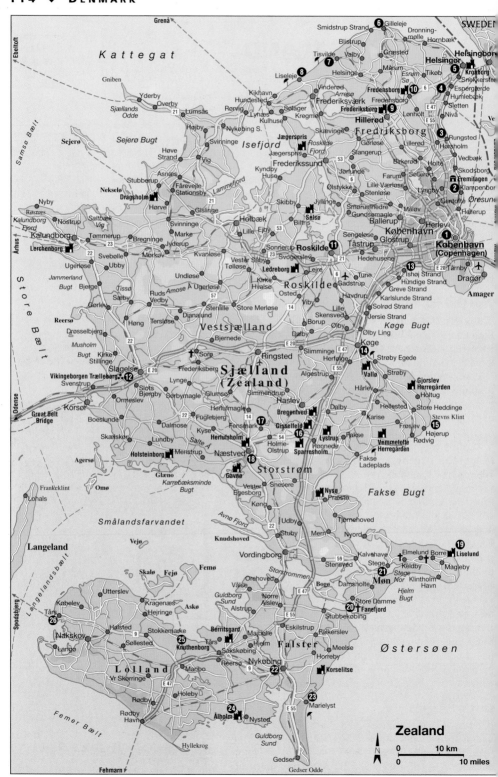

Zealand

0 — 10 km
0 — 10 miles

Karen Blixen, the Danish writer known as Isak Dinesen whose best-selling book, *Out of Africa*, became a film starring Meryl Streep and Robert Redford.

At **Humlebæk ④**, art lovers could easily spend an entire day at the **Louisiana Museum for Moderne Kunst** (Louisiana Museum of Modern Art, Gl. Strandvej 13; open Thurs–Sun 10am–5pm, Wed until 10pm; entrance fee; tel: 49 19 07 91). A rich permanent collection is supplemented by frequent international exhibitions held in a breathtaking setting overlooking the Øresund to Sweden. Sculptures adorn the gardens and there is a children's wing *(see box, page 52).*

Map on page 114

Hamlet's Helsingør

Helsingør ⑤ is best known for its massive Renaissance-style **Kronborg**, Hamlet's "Castle of Elsinore" (open May–Sept daily 10.30am–5pm; Oct–Apr Tues–Sun 11am–4pm; entrance fee; tel: 49 21 30 78). Originally built by King Eric of Pomerania when he introduced the "Sound Dues" (fees paid to the Danish crown by all ships passing through to the Baltic), Kronborg has been rebuilt several times. It has provided a backdrop for many productions of Shakespeare's *Hamlet*. Inside, the richly decorated King's and Queen's chambers and the 62-metre (203-ft) long Great Hall are worth seeing.

Taking on the elements: a Zealand skipper.

Helsingør is one of Denmark's most historic towns, with entire streets of colour-washed buildings. The 15th-century **Skt Mariæ Kirke** and the **Carmelite Kloster** (Convent) are among the best-preserved Gothic buildings in the world. Hans Christian Andersen described it as "one of the most beautiful spots in Denmark, close to the Sound, which is a mile wide and looks like a blue stream swelling between Denmark and Sweden".

BELOW: author Karen Blixen lived at Rungsted.

The coast road leads on to **Gilleleje ⑥**, the most northerly town of Zealand, a small working fishing port. **Hos Karen og Marie**, in an unpretentious green-painted wooden building, is one of the best fish restaurants.

If the weather is good, you could stop at the sunworshippers' beaches of **Tisvilde ⑦** or **Liseleje ⑧**.

As one turns towards Copenhagen, Denmark's National History Museum is at **Frederiksborg ⑨** (open Apr–Oct daily 10am–5pm; Nov–Mar daily 11am–3pm; entrance fee; tel: 48 26 04 39), built between 1605 and 1621 on the outskirts of **Hillerød**. The most notable rooms are the Council Hall, Knights' Hall and the chapel with its original Compenius organ, built in 1610. North of the lake is one of the best baroque gardens in Northern Europe.

Just 9 km (5 miles) from Hillerød is the royal palace of **Fredensborg ⑩**. The palace was built in Italian style in 1722, and is now used as a residence for the Danish Royal Family in spring and autumn (guided tours, July daily 1–4.30pm; tel: 33 40 31 87).

Viking town

A major highlight of Zealand is the town of **Roskilde ⑪**, the island's second-largest town, 20 minutes by train west of Copenhagen. The **Domkirke** (Cathedral), built in 1170, is the burial place of generations of Danish monarchs. The **Vikingeskibshallen** (Viking Ship Museum; open daily 10am–5pm; entrance fee; tel: 46 30 02 00) is one of the great

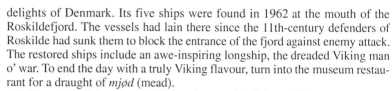

Kronborg, Hamlet's "Castle of Elsinore" at Helsingør.

delights of Denmark. Its five ships were found in 1962 at the mouth of the Roskildefjord. The vessels had lain there since the 11th-century defenders of Roskilde had sunk them to block the entrance of the fjord against enemy attack. The restored ships include an awe-inspiring longship, the dreaded Viking man o' war. To end the day with a truly Viking flavour, turn into the museum restaurant for a draught of *mjød* (mead).

Still on the Viking theme, **Vikingeborgen Trelleborg ⑫** (open May–Oct daily 10am–5pm; entrance fee; tel: 58 54 95 06), near Slagelse in western Zealand, is an abandoned Viking fortress some 1,000 years old. It was once a huge fortified camp that housed 1,000 Vikings. One of the houses has been reconstructed and on a cold spring day it is easy to understand how tough the life here must have been, despite the Vikings' reputations as hardy souls.

Southern Zealand

The first stop for modern art enthusiasts south of Copenhagen is the sleek white **Arken Museet for Moderne Kunst** (open Thurs–Sun and Tues 10am–5pm, Wed until 9pm; entrance fee; tel: 43 54 02 22) at **Ishøj ⑬**. For a summer holiday atmosphere, **Køge ⑭** is popular for its bathing beaches, crowded with sun-loving Danes. Inhabitants claim that Køge has more half-timbered houses than any other town in Denmark. The oldest, dated 1527, stands at 20 Kirkestræde. **Skt Nikolai Kirke** has one of Denmark's most beautiful town church interiors. Not far from the market place is **Hugo's Vinkælder**, an historic inn serving good old-fashioned draught porter.

BELOW: Arken, the modern art museum at Ishøj.

The cliffs of **Stevns Klint ⑮** on the south headland of Køge Bay may not be quite as dramatic as those on the island of Møn, but they are impressive when the sun illuminates them in brilliant hues of white.

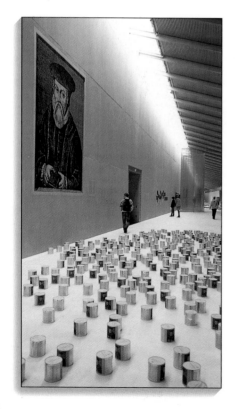

Inland, 5 km (3 miles) south of the ancient town of **Haslev**, Hans Christian Andersen is said to have found inspiration for what is perhaps his most famous story, *The Ugly Duckling*, in **Gisselfeld Slot ⑯** (grounds and stables open daily), a castle built in 1554. To the west of Gisselfeld at **Fensmark ⑰** is the **Holmegård Danish Glassvæk** (Glassworks; tours Mon–Fri; entrance fee; tel: 55 54 50 00), a popular target for tours from Copenhagen. Here, visitors can watch fine pieces being formed. The **Glass Museum** has a notable collection, and at the museum shop, seconds often make superb bargains.

Næstved ⑱, 5 km (3 miles) southwest of Fensmark, has been an important trading town for most of its history and has an attractive city centre. About 6 km (4 miles) to the southwest is **Gavnø Slot** (open May–Aug daily 10am–5pm; entrance fee; tel: 55 70 02 00), situated among magnificent gardens on a tiny island linked by road. In the 13th century it was used as a pirates' castle; today it houses Scandinavia's largest privately owned picture collection.

Cliffs of Møn

The island of **Møn** ("The Maid") to the east is linked to Zealand by road bridges. According to legend, its spectacular stretches of luminous white chalk cliffs, topped with beech woods and studded with fossils, became a refuge for the most powerful of Nordic gods, Odin, when Christianity left him homeless. Over the past 200 years, most of the invaders of Møn have been writers and painters, lured there by the inspiration of its beauty and drama.

Liselund Slot ⑲ (open May–Oct; guided tours; entrance fee; tel: 55 81 21 78) is a thatched mini-château, built in 1796. Hans Christian Andersen wrote his tales *The Tinder Box* and *The Little Match Girl* in a summer house on the estate.

Møn's churches are noted for their frescoes, particularly those at **Keldby**, **Elmelund** and **Fanefjord** ⑳, the last standing on an isolated hill overlooking the narrows of Grønsund. Beside the church is the longest barrow grave in Denmark, **Grønjægers Høj**. The main town of **Stege** ㉑ has medieval ramparts.

Falster and Lolland

The Farø bridges connect Zealand to the island of **Falster**, and the ferry routes to Germany. The main town on the island is **Nykøbing** ㉒, noted for the **Czarens Hus** (Tsar's House; open Mon–Sat 11am–10pm; entrance fee; tel: 54 85 28 29), where Peter the Great stayed in 1716. The area around **Marielyst** ㉓, to the southeast, has miles of white sand dunes where families take beach holidays.

There is a choice of road bridges from Falster to **Lolland**, to reach one of the island's main attractions, **Aalholm Slot** ㉔ (open July–Aug daily 10am–5pm; Sept–June Sat and Sun 11am–5pm; entrance fee; tel: 54 87 10 17), near the old seaport of **Nysted**. The castle dates from the 12th century and was once known as the robber's castle. It has a fine collection of rare cars. From Aalholm, the road north and west runs past beautiful lakes to **Knuthenborg** ㉕ (open May–Sept: 9am–5pm; entrance fee; tel: 54 78 80 88), a safari park. In the far west, the **Tårs** ㉖ to **Spodsbjerg** crossing connects the island with Langeland and Funen. ❑

Map on page 114

TIP

On Midsummer's Eve along the coast north of Copenhagen, beach bonfires and fireworks light the skies and a procession of ships passes through the Øresund, blasting their horns to celebrate the peak of the short Danish summer.

BELOW: farmland landscape, North Zealand.

Map
below

BORNHOLM

*Denmark's Baltic island of Bornholm is a haven for both
artists and holiday-makers, attracted by its climate,
peaceful lifestyle and natural beauty*

Bornholmers, and for that matter most Danes, will be happy to relate the tale
of creation of Bornholm: when God had finished making Scandinavia, he
had a few leftovers from the very best features of the regions, so he
gathered them all up and tossed them into the Baltic Sea. The tale perfectly
illustrates the island's nickname, "Scandinavian in a nutshell", since Bornholm
features a variety of landscapes typical to different areas of Scandinavia.

The enchanting island stands in the middle of the Baltic Sea between
Sweden and Poland, seven hours away from Copenhagen by ferry, and 30
minutes by plane. It is a peaceful place, home to about 48,000 Bornholmers.
There are no large towns and almost no industry; visitors have a perfect
opportunity to relax, although from early July until the end of August the population swells fourfold with holiday-makers.

Living history

BELOW: Olsker,
one of Bornholm's
medieval round
churches.

Bornholm was a maritime centre in the Baltic Sea during the Iron Age.
Jewellery, coins, and relics from as far away as Rome and the Near East have
been discovered and two forts, both known as **Gamleborg**, found in
Paradisbakkerne (The Hills of Paradise) and at **Almindingen Skov**, date from

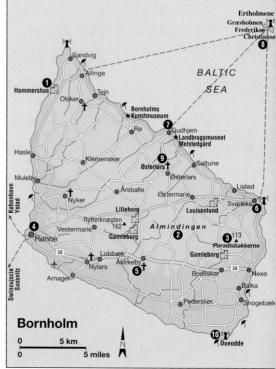

the Viking period. It is generally believed that Bornholm became a part of the Kingdom of Denmark at around that time.

Hammershus ❶ (open May–Sept daily 10am–5pm; Apr & early–mid-Oct daily 10am–4pm; free; tel: 56 48 24 31) was built around 1250 to defend the island against attack, and is today Scandinavia's largest fortified castle. Impressive ruins remain on a huge, rocky knoll on the northwest corner of the island. At the time the castle was built, Bornholm was owned by the Archbishop of Lund (in what is now southern Sweden, but then part of Denmark); he was openly at war with the kings of Denmark. Strong separatist feelings still exist among some Bornholmers. Their banner is a Danish flag with a green cross instead of the familiar white one.

The variety of plant life on Bornholm is almost overwhelming. The northern part of the island is extremely rocky and, by radiating heat picked up from the sun, the rocks keep the surface warm enough for figs, grapes, mulberry trees and other plants from southern Europe to grow well. Sweet cherry trees blossom in June and give a colourful show. Red orchids are common on the banks in the river valleys and thousands of woodland flowers, especially blue, yellow, and white anemones, cover large areas. About 20 percent of Bornholm is woodland: **Almindingen ❷**, in the centre of the island, is Denmark's third-largest forest. **Paradisbakkerne ❸** is wilder in vegetation than Almindingen and is best enjoyed on foot. Small farms are scattered all over the island.

Around Bornholm

Rønne ❹, with 15,000 inhabitants, is the largest town on Bornholm, and its harbour is one of the largest provincial ports in Denmark. Some parts of the town

Bornholm is a centre for Danish applied arts and handicrafts. Every village has its silversmiths, wood turners, jewellers, textile artists and more. Potteries and glass-blowing workshops are often open to the public.

BELOW: Bornholm is a favourite with holidaymakers.

have been well preserved, especially in the area just east of **Skt Nikolai Kirke**. The beautiful **Kastellet** (citadel) is on the east side of town; today it is a military museum, **Forsvarsmuseet** (open June–Sept Tues–Sat 11am–5pm; entrance fee; tel: 56 95 65 83).

Bornholm has inspired many Danish painters, as well as having produced a few of its own: Oluf Høst is the best known. **Bornholms Museum** (Skt Mortensgade 29; open Apr–Oct Mon–Sat 10am–5pm; Sept–Mar Tues–Sat 1–4pm; entrance fee; tel: 56 95 07 35) and its collection of paintings and exhibits from pre-history onwards relating to the island's past, is worth visiting.

Åkirkeby ❺ (pop. 1,400) is the main town in the southern part of Bornholm, and the only one of the larger towns situated inland. It was an ecclesiastical centre and its church, **Åkirke**, was built around 1150 as a chapter house in the Archbishopric of Lund. The large tower was extended around 1200, and at the same time it was fortified with walls even heavier than those of Hammershus. It is notable for its sandstone baptismal font depicting the life of Christ in 11 relief carvings; the figures are explained in runic script, and end with the signature of the stonecutter, "Sighraf, master".

The easternmost town in Denmark, **Svaneke ❻**, prospered with the success of its shipping captains. The largest buildings were originally merchants' houses. North of the town is an old Dutch mill, and nearby an untraditional water tower, built by the architect Jørn Utzon in 1951.

Cycling downhill is forbidden in **Gudhjem ❼** ("good home"), a very pretty place, built on steep slopes down to the water. Windmills around the town once provided electricity. The former railway station has been converted into a model train museum, **Bornholms Model Jernbane Museum** (open May–Sept Sun–Fri 1–5pm; free; tel: 56 47 04 85), and provides an excellent way of exploring local history. There is an agricultural museum, **Landbrugsmuseet Melstedgård** (open May–Oct Tues–Sun 10am–5pm; entrance fee; tel: 56 48 55 98), just southeast of Gudhjem at **Melsted**, a settlement which first gained prominence as an important trading centre during the Middle Ages.

Fortress in the sea

From Gudhjem Harbour one can sail to the group of islands collectively known as **Ertholmene**. The largest of these are **Christiansø ❽** and **Frederiksø**. A naval base was constructed here in about 1864, but today only fishermen and their families live on this "fortress in the sea". It makes an interesting place to visit. The islands are rocky, with castle towers, batteries, and cannon serving as reminders of the past.

Round churches

Østerlars Kirke ❾ (consecrated to St Laurentius), just over 4 km (2½ miles) southwest from Gudhjem, is the largest of the four medieval "round churches" of Bornholm, which include **Nylars**, **Nyker** and **Olsker**. When the Slavic Wends ravaged the island they were occasionally used as places of refuge and in the 14th–16th century Hanseatic merchants from northern Germany would move in during the herring season. At

Bornholm celebrates classical music with a festival from mid-July to September, which attracts music lovers from around the world.

BELOW:
a great breakfast.

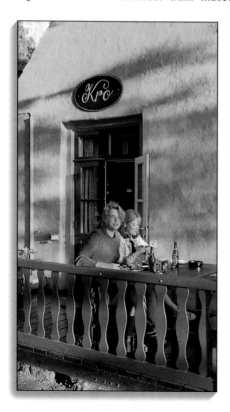

Map on page 118

Osterlars the enormous support pillars create the impression of a fortress, which was the second purpose of the structure. Inside the church (built around 1150), the vault is painted with fine frescoes of biblical scenes. On the north wall of the oval-shaped choir, stone steps lead to the second storey, where the hollow central pillar has two entrances. The outer wall has a watchman's gallery. The double altarpiece was painted by the local artist Poul Høm.

Edible delicacies

During the summer months, freshly landed herrings are delivered to the island's smokehouses. Here they are turned from their original silver colour into the "golden Bornholmers" dearly loved by Danes, which can often be seen drying on stands outside. Elderwood gives them their special taste. You can eat them warm from the oven or put them on black bread, sprinkle them with salt, and add chopped chives, radishes and an egg yolk on top.

Pickled herrings are a lunchtime speciality. The best spiced herrings are produced on Christiansø. Baltic salmon, said to be the finest edible fish in the world, is normally available, too.

Bornholm by bike

The best way to travel around Bornholm is by bicycle. An extensive network of cycle paths has been established and its easy to find houses, hotels, and campsites en route. Residents often rent rooms or houses to visitors. but remember to book accommodation in advance in summer, especially in the southeast part of the island where the wonderful beaches of **Dueodde** ❿ and **Balka** in particular attract crowds of holiday-makers in high season. ❏

A cheerful sign attracts diners. Try a delicious "golden Bornholmer", the island's smoked herring speciality.

BELOW: Gudhjem village, on the north coast.

FUNEN

Bridging the water between Zealand and Jutland is the island of Funen, the "Garden of Denmark", with the buzzing cultural centre of Odense at its heart

Map on page 124

Denmark's central island of **Funen** (*Fyn* in Danish) is known for its natural beauty, flowered gardens, castles and manor houses. Danes call it "the Garden of Denmark". Cycling tours take you along hundreds of kilometres of marked routes. Here, too, lies historic Odense, the birthplace of author Hans Christian Andersen *(see page 127)*. South Funen and the island archipelago are a paradise for anglers and yachtsmen.

The Funen circle

When coming from Copenhagen, the usual way to reach Funen is by train or car across the mighty Store Bælt bridge to Nyborg on Funen's east coast. The Lille Bælt bridge links it to east central Jutland on the opposite side. Your choice then is circling the islands from Nyborg or Middelfart, and basing yourself either in Odense or Svendborg to make excursions. Driving is easy, but the most satisfying way to see Funen is on a bicycle. You can lean your bike beside one of the little whitewashed churches to take a look inside, and inhale the scent of the wild flowers that lie beneath roadside rose hedges.

Before heading north out of **Nyborg ❶** for Kerteminde and the Hindsholm Peninsula, take a look at **Nyborg Slot** (open Mar–May & Sept–Oct daily 10am–3pm; June & Aug daily 10am–4pm; July daily 10am–5pm; entrance fee; tel: 65 31 02 07), which dates from 1170. It was built to defend the country from the Wends of North Germany and, during the Middle Ages, was the meeting place for the three ruling powers of monarchy, nobility and clergy. However, in 1722, much of Nyborg Slot was demolished to provide building materials for Odense Castle. Part of the original ramparts and moat remain, and the castle has a fine interior of great echoing, empty rooms.

About 15 km (9 miles) north from Nyborg, near Kerteminde, are the underground remains of a Viking chieftain's burial ship at **Ladby ❷** (open June–Aug daily 10am–5pm; Mar–May & Sept–Oct daily 10am–4pm; Nov–Feb Wed–Sun 11am–3pm; entrance fee). With him in his 22-metre (72-ft) Viking ship, the chief took what he prized most: his weapons, hunting dogs and 11 horses.

Kerteminde ❸ is Funen's foremost fishing village, with old half-timbered houses. Most towns in Funen have craftspeople of many different skills, and Kerteminde offers stoneware and pottery at local shops.

Odense

In the centre of Funen lies the quaint but lively capital of Funen, **Odense ❹**, Denmark's third-largest city (pop. 200,000). Its name stems from Old Norse and means "the sanctuary of Odin", the wise and mighty

LEFT: young visitor at Hans Christian Andersen's house in Odense.
BELOW: decorative doorway in Ærøskøbing

The Kerteminde landscape has attracted some of Denmark's most renowned artists. Their work can be seen at the village's Johannes Larsen Museum in Møllebakken (tel: 65 32 11 77).

chief god. So the place was important enough to be worthy of Odin's protection before the Christian conversion of Denmark. The Gothic cathedral, **Skt Knuds Domkirke**, is one of the most beautiful landmarks of Odense. It was named after King Knud (Canute) II, who was murdered in the town in 1086 by his rebellious subjects and later canonised by the Pope. It's adorned with a gilded altarpiece made by Claus Berg in Germany in 1521. In the crypt lie the remains of Skt Knud.

Munkemøllestræde, west of the cathedral, is the cobblestone street with the house where the storyteller Hans Christian Andersen grew up in the early 1800s (open Apr–Sept daily 10am–5pm; Oct–Mar daily noon–3pm; entrance fee). Northeast of the cathedral is the outstanding **Hans Christian Andersen Museum** (Hans Jensens Stræde 37–45; open Sept–mid-June Tues–Sun 10am–4pm; mid-June–Aug daily 9am–7pm; entrance fee; tel: 66 14 88 14). The museum's collection is devoted to the writer's life, with manuscripts, and other personal belongings.

Denmark's foremost composer, Carl Nielsen (*see page 127*), spent his early years in the city and the **Carl Nielsen Museet** (Claus Bergs Gade 11; open

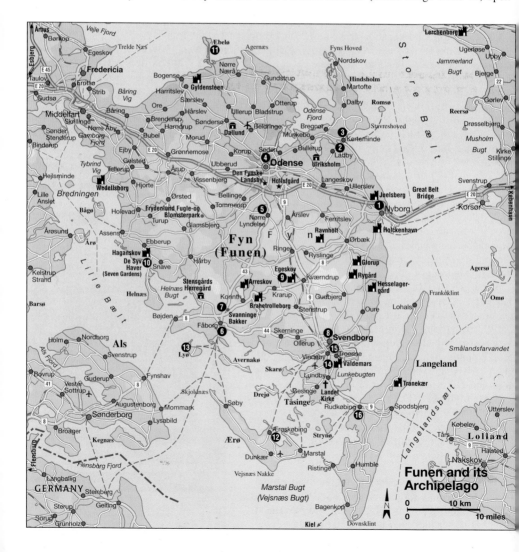

Funen and its Archipelago

June–Aug Tues–Sun noon–4pm; Sept–May Thur–Sun noon–4pm; entrance fee; tel: 66 14 88 14) is devoted both to his life and work and to that of his wife, Anne Marie Nielsen, a sculptor. His childhood home can be visited at **Nørre Lyndelse 5** (open May–early Sept Tues–Sun 11am–3pm; entrance fee; tel: 66 14 88 14), south of Odense.

Few other cities have a river that is clean enough to offer amateur fishermen both sea trout and eel. This is an accomplishment for what was once a polluted industrial centre. Today, the quarter around the old factory buildings at Kongensgade and Vestergade has been revitalised and is a popular magnet for young people. The former textile mill, **Brandt's Klædefabrik**, off Vestergade, is now a multipurpose building for concerts, complete with the **Museet for Fotokunst** (Museum of Photographic Art); the **Kunsthallen** art gallery, featuring a varied programme of exhibitions; **Dannmarks Grafiske Museum** (Danish Museum for Printing); and **Tidens Samling** (Time Collection) which follows daily life and fashion since 1900 (all open 10am–5pm, closed Mon except July–Aug; entrance fee).

Just south of Odense is a delightful spot, **Den Fynske Landsby** (Funen Village, Sejerskovvej 20; open Apr–Oct daily 10am–5pm; mid-June–mid-Aug daily 9.30am–7pm; entrance fee; tel: 66 14 88 14). It contains old farm buildings from different areas, with a vicarage, workshops, a windmill and water mill.

Map on page 124

Gardeners admire De Syv Haver, the Seven Gardens southeast of Assens inspired by different countries.

Tuneful Fåborg

Fåborg 6 on south Funen is a lovely little town where **Klokketårnet**, a carillon, chimes out a hymn four times a day. It's the largest carillon in Europe and the town's main landmark. If you could choose only one place to visit in Fåborg, it must be **Fåborg Museum for Fynsk Kunst** (Grønnegade 75; open Apr–Sept daily 10am–4pm; Nov–Mar Tues–Sun 11am–3pm; entrance fee; tel: 62 61 06 65), an art gallery featuring the "Funen artists" (1880– 1920), including Peter Hansen, Fritz Syberg and Johannes Larsen, with sculptures by Kai Nielsen.

The heather-covered **Svanninge Bakker 7**, about 10 km (6 miles) north of Fåborg, is a national park. Heading eastwards, **Svendborg 8** is a beautiful market town and a good centre for touring. Along with Fåborg, it is the gateway to the southern islands.

Egeskov Slot 9 (open May–Sept daily 10am–5pm, closes later in summer; entrance fee; tel: 62 27 10 16), 14 km (9 miles) north of Svendborg, is one of Denmark's most famous historic sights, set in magnificent baroque and Renaissance gardens. Egeskov means oak forest, and the oaks were felled around 1540 to form the piles the castle stands on. The grounds also feature a re-creation of its 200-year-old **maze**. This "labyrinth", as it is called, has 1.6 km (1 mile) of paths screened by 2,200 bamboo shoots. There is a **Veteranmuseum** (Veteran Motor Museum; open as for Egeskov Slot above) with a fine collection of old cars, aircraft, motor cycles, and horse-drawn carriages.

Along the west coast

From Fåborg, turn northwest to explore Funen's west coast. At Ebberup, south of Assens, are **De Syv Haver 10** (The Seven Gardens; open Easter–Oct daily

BELOW: book sale on Funen.

Map
on page
124

TIP

Whether driving, cycling or walking, follow the "Daisy Routes" marked by a flower sign. These guide you past some of the most beautiful scenery in Funen.

BELOW: Egeskov Slot, built in the 16th century.

10am–5pm; entrance fee; tel: 64 74 12 85), outstanding gardens created by Tove and Gunner Sylvest. Around 15 km (9 miles) north from Assens on the road to **Middelfart**, a broad west-facing bay at **Tybrind Vig** is a site for underwater archaeology. North of Middelfart dramatic steep cliffs line the shore.

About 3 km (2 miles) east of **Bogense** is the castle of **Gyldensteen**, a late-Renaissance building with an impressive gatehouse (closed to the public). Here, Karen Blixen (pen name Isak Dinesen), author of *Out of Africa*, wrote some of her books during the German Occupation of Denmark in World War II. From Bogense, you can complete the Funen circle by touring along the sparsely populated north coast to the Hindsholm Peninsula and Kerteminde. At low tide you can walk to the island of Æbelø **⓫**, an unspoilt landscape rich in wildlife.

To the islands

You could spend a lifetime trying to visit all the islands of the Funen Archipelago and still miss a few. Only 19 are inhabited permanently. Even the largest islands hold no more than a few thousand people, and others just a couple of families. All summer the harbours are full of boats. You can take day trips aboard wooden sailing ships or longer cruises through the archipelago. This is also an angler's paradise.

From Fåborg, it is just a short trip to the most beautiful island of all, Ærø. Hire a bike for the short cycle run from Søby to **Ærøskøbing ⓬**, the main town, and on to the old naval port of **Marstal**. Cycling is easy and the roads wind past fertile fields and thatched farmhouses, medieval churches and windmills. The American author, Temple Fielding, said that Ærøskøbing was one of the five places in the world one should see. Certainly, the cobbled streets with their brightly coloured houses almost seem like a film set.

From Fåborg, ferries also run to the smaller islands of **Avernakø** and **Lyø ⓭**, both of which have good, inexpensive inns.

Svendborg is the ferry port for the southern islands. The first island, reached by a narrow bridge, is **Tåsinge**, with some 5,000 inhabitants. **Valdemars Slot ⓮** is one of Denmark's oldest privately owned castles, with a wonderful view over Svendborgsund (open May–Sept daily 10am–5pm; entrance fee; tel: 62 22 61 06). It was built in 1640 by King Kristian IV for one of his sons, Prince Valdemar Kristian. Most interesting is the castle church, with an excellent restaurant beneath. The Tea Pavilion, mirrored in its own lake overlooking **Lunkebugten Bay**, is now a café. The loveliest village on Tåsinge is **Troense ⓯**. Sitting on the veranda of the **Troense Inn** as the slim masts of the sailing boats gather in the harbour against a darkening sea, is one of the pleasures of a Funen summer.

Langeland, literally "long land", is connected to Tåsinge by a causeway-bridge. One of its famous sons was H.C. Ørsted, the discoverer of electromagnetism, who was born in the main town of **Rudkøbing ⓰**. Another famous resident was N.F.S. Grundtvig, a clergyman and founder of modern Danish education. To the south, **Ristinge** and **Bagenkop** both have excellent bathing beaches. In fact, nowhere along the coast of Funen and its islands are you far from good places to swim and sail, ❑

ANDERSEN AND NIELSEN: FUNEN'S FAMOUS SONS

In the 19th century, two Funen boys, the storyteller Hans Christian Andersen and the the composer Carl Nielsen, set off to make their fortunes in the world

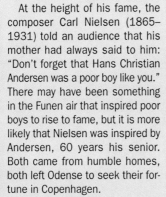

Two of Denmark's most noted literary and musical figures, Hans Christian Andersen and Carl Nielsen respectively, were born on the island of Funen.

At the height of his fame, the composer Carl Nielsen (1865–1931) told an audience that his mother had always said to him: "Don't forget that Hans Christian Andersen was a poor boy like you." There may have been something in the Funen air that inspired poor boys to rise to fame, but it is more likely that Nielsen was inspired by Andersen, 60 years his senior. Both came from humble homes, both left Odense to seek their fortune in Copenhagen.

Andersen (1805–75) was born in Odense and spent his childhood in a small half-timbered house in Munkemøllestræde, now a museum. Quite apart from his skill as a writer, Andersen had a good singing voice and gifts as an artist. At the age of 14 he set off to Copenhagen to attend the Royal Theatre School. The Theatre Board recognised his skills and he was found a place at a grammar school in Helsingør.

After school, Andersen travelled widely; *Shadow Picture of a Journey to the Harz Mountains and Saxony* (1831) was the result of his early adventures. Through his life he continued to write poems, novels and plays. His autobiographical novel, *The Improvisatore*, described the rise to fortune of a poor Italian boy. His early fairy tales, including *The Tinder Box* and *The Princess and the Pea* (1835), brought him immortality. In 1840 he met and fell in love with the singer Jenny Lind, "The Swedish Nightingale", though she

always called him "brother". His fairy tale, *The Nightingale*, was inspired by her.

When he was made an honorary citizen of Odense in 1867, Andersen said it was "an honour greater than I had ever dreamt of".

Carl Nielsen was born at Nørre Lyndelse, now a museum devoted to his life. His father was a folk musician and Carl played the violin. His earliest compositions, at the age of eight, were two dance tunes. Like Andersen, Nielsen wrote an autobiography, *My Childhood*.

At the Royal Theatre Orchestra in Copenhagen, where Nielsen became second violinist, the Norwegian conductor, Johan Svendsen, encouraged him to compose. At 25, Nielsen won a fellowship which allowed him to travel, and went to Dresden to steep himself in Wagner's ideas.

Nielsen composed two operas: the dark drama, *Saul og David*, and a comic opera, *Maskarade*, along with symphonies and choral works, such as *Hymnus Amoris*. ❑

TOP LEFT AND RIGHT: composer Carl Nielsen.
ABOVE LEFT: Hans Christian Andersen.
RIGHT: actor Ejnar Han Jensen plays Andersen.

JUTLAND

The dune-fringed shores of Jutland have captured the imagination of both painters and holiday-makers, while music lovers head for Århus, "the world's smallest big city"

Map
on page
130

Jutland *(Jylland)* is the Danish peninsula that juts up above Germany, the "mainland" in this nation of islands. When Copenhageners talk about the provinces, they usually mean Jutland. With its rolling hills crisscrossed with rivers and creeks, patched with forests, crusted by sand dunes and scattered with palaces, Viking monuments and remains, Jutland is a land of contrasts.

Jutland's capital city is **Århus ❶**, a lively college town known for its music, theatre, ballet, art and cafés, as well as its fun Festival Week every autumn. Denmark's second-largest city – with a population of 280,000, only a fraction of Copenhagen's size – this harbour town is noted for its nearby forests, beaches and castles. The pointed spire of **Domkirken**, the Cathedral of St Clement (open May–Sept daily 9.30am–4pm; rest of year daily 10am–3pm; free), is 93 metres (316 ft) high and offers one of the best views in the city from its belfry. Nearby are the winding, cobblestone streets of the Latin Quarter, with quirky boutiques and trendy cafés and restaurants. The **Århus Kunstmuseum** (Museum of Art; open Tues, Thurs–Sun 10am–5pm, Wed until 8pm; entrance fee; tel: 86 13 52 55) gives an overview of Danish art from the 18th, 19th and 20th centuries. The **Rådhus** (City Hall) was built in 1941 and designed by Arne Jacobsen, one of Denmark's most notable architects and designers.

Den Gamle By (The Old Town; open all year; times vary; entrance fee; tel: 86 12 31 88), is an open-air, national museum of urban culture and history, featuring reconstructions of 75 Danish urban buildings. From the front entrance onwards, the museum is a sensory overload in an environment that feels genuinely historic – with merchant and artisan houses and workshops, gardens, shops and stalls, streets and alleys.

One of the best museum exhibits in Denmark is the 2,000-year-old Grauballe Man at the **Forhistorisk Museum** (Museum of Prehistory; open Apr–Sept Tues–Sun 10am–5pm; Oct–Mar Tues–Sun 10am–4pm; entrance fee; tel: 89 42 11 00) at **Moesgård ❷**, 8 km (5 miles) south of Århus. To stand face to face with the grimacing man, who was found perfectly preserved in a peat bog in 1952, is a chilling experience.

The ruins of the **Kalø Slot ❸**, built in 1313, are situated on a small island on the edge of a cove on the north side of Århus bay. The nearby hills of **Mols Bjerge ❹**, where Viking relics abound in beautiful nature, are well worth a visit. Several artists have set up shop on the pretty Djursland peninsula.

Island haven

Just south of Mols Bjerge is the immaculate town of **Ebeltoft ❺**, with its small, unaltered town hall from 1789. The island of **Samsø** can be seen from here,

LEFT: dappled forest of East Jutland.
BELOW: beach life, West Jutland.

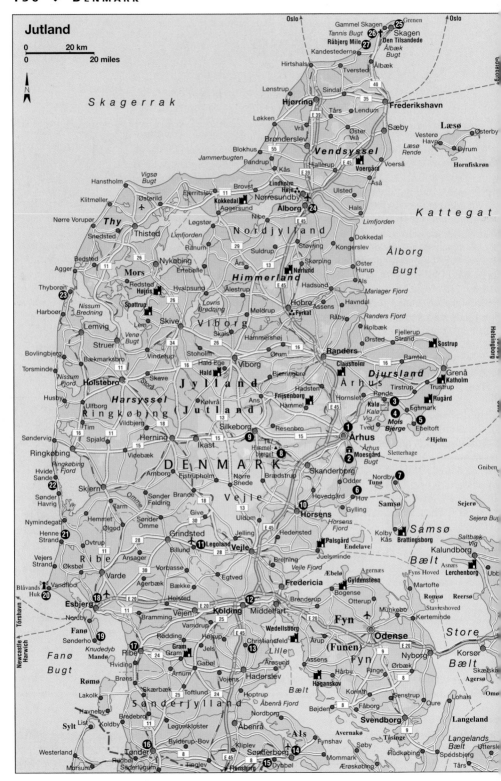

Jutland

0   20 km

0   20 miles

N

Skagerrak

Oslo
Gammel Skagen · 25 Grenen · Oslo
Tannis Bugt · 26 Skagen
Råbjerg Mile · 27 Den Tilsandede
Kandestederne · Ålbæk Bugt
Hirtshals · Tversted · Ålbæk
Lønstrup · Sindal · 40
Hjørring · 35 · Frederikshavn
Løkken · Tårs · Lendum
Vrå · Øster Vrå · Sæby · Læsø
Brønderslev · Vesterø Havn · Østerby
Blokhus · 55 · Læsø Rende · Byrum
Jammerbugten · Pandrup · Vendsyssel · Hornfiskrøn
Hansholm · Vigsø Bugt · Fjerritslev · Brovst · Kås · Hjallerup · Voergård · Voerså · Aså
Klitmøller · Østerild · Kokkedal · Lindholm Høje · Ulsted
Nørre Vorupør · Thy · Aggersund · Nibe · Ålborg · 24 · Hals · Kattegat
Snedsted · Thisted · Limfjorden · Løgstør · Nordjylland · Limfjorden · Dokkedal
Bedsted · Ranum · 29 · Suldrup · Støvring · Kongerslev · Ålborg Bugt
Agger · 11 · Nykøbing · Års · 13 · Skørping · Øster Hurup
Thyborøn · 23 · Mors · Redsted · Ertebølle · Nørlund · Als · Mariager Fjord
Harboør · Nissum Bredning · Højris · Hvalpsund · Ålestrup · Hadsund · Havndal
Lemvig · Spøttrup · 26 · Lovns Bredning · Møldrup · Hobro · Assens · Randers Fjord
Struer · Venø Bugt · Skive · Skals · Hammershøj · Fyrkat · Råby · Holbæk · Fjellerup Strand · Sostrup
Bovlingbjerg · Bækmarksbro · Vinderup · Stoholm · Viborg · Ørum · Randers · Ørsted · Ramten
Torsminde · Nissum Fjord · 11 · Skave · Hald Ege · Bjerringbro · Clausholm · 16 · Djursland · Grenå
Husby · Holstebro · Hald · Hadsten · Århus · Tirstrup · Trustrup · Katholm
Ulfborg · Harsyssel · Kølvrå · Ans · Frijsenborg · Rønde · Rugård
Tim · Ringkøbing (Jutland) · Vildbjerg · 18 · Hammel · Kalø Vig · Egsmark
Søndervig · 16 · Spjald · 11 · Silkeborg · Resenbro · Tved · Mols Bjerge · Ebeltoft
Ringkøbing · Videbæk · Ikast · 15 · Århus · Hjelm
Hvide Sande · Ringkøbing Fjord · Arnborg · Fjstrupholm · Nørre Snede · Brædstrup · Skanderborg · Nordby · Gniben
22 · Skjern · Omme · Sønder Brande · Odder · Tunø · 7
Sønder Havrig · Tarm · Sønder Felding · Vejle · Hovedgård · Hov · Samsø · Sejerø
Nymindegab · Hemmet · Ølgod · Sønder Omme · Uldum · Horsens · Gylling · Samsø · Sejerø Bugt
Henne Strand · 21 · Ovtrup · Grindsted · Jelling · Hedensted · Horsens Fjord · Kolby Kås · Brattingsborg · Saltbæk Vig
Vejers Strand · Øksbøl · 11 · Ansager · Billund · Legoland · Vejle · Brejning · Juelsminde · Endelave · Kalundborg
Blåvands Huk · 20 · Vandflod · Varde · Vorbasse · Egtved · Vejle Fjord · Æbelø · Agernæs · Bælt · Lerchenborg
Esbjerg · 18 · Agerbæk · Bække · Holsted · Fredericia · Brenderup · Bogense · Gyldensteen · Romsø · Reersø
Nordby · Bramming · Vejen · 25 · Vamdrup · Middelfart · Otterup · Munkebo · Staveshoved · Kerteminde
Fanø · 19 · Rødding · Højrup · Kolding · E20 · Fyn · Odense · Store
Sønderho · Christiansfeld · Årup · Nyborg · Korsør
Fanø Bugt · Knudedyb · Ribe · Gram · Jels · Lille Bælt · (Funen) · Ørbæk · Bælt · Skælskø
Mandø · Hviding · Gabøl · Å+sund · Assens · Fyn · Ringe · Agersø
Rømø · Brøns · Arnum · Vojens · Haderslev · Bælt · Håganskov · Korinth · Senstrup · Lohals · Omø
Lakolk · Skærbæk · Toftlund · 24 · Hoptrup · Bøjden · Fåborg
Havneby · Bredebro · Løgumkloster · Åbenrå Fjord · Nordborg · Svendborg · Langeland
Sylt · List · Koldby · 11 · Bylderup-Bov · Åbenrå · Als · Avernakø · Tåsinge · Langelands Bælt
Westerland · Tønder · 16 · Kliplev · Søby · Rudkøbing · Spodsbjerg · Uttersl
Rudbø · 8 · Tinglev · E45 · Sønderborg · 14 · Dybbøl · Tårs
Mørsum · Søderlugum · Flensburg · 15 · Mommark · Ærøskøbing

Skagerrak

Kattegat

Store Bælt

Samsø

DENMARK

Himmelbjerget · 8

147

Moesgård Bugt · 2

Århus · 1

Sletterhage

Helsingborg

Göteborg

Tørshavn · Newcastle Harwich

but it must be reached by ferry from **Hov ⑥**, 25 km (15 miles) south of Århus. A haven for artists, farmers and nature lovers alike, Samsø is renowned for its new potatoes and cheese. **Nordby ⑦**, on the northern tip, contains a wealth of colourful, crossbeam houses, as well as small art galleries. Also worth a visit in Nordby is **Samsø Labyrinten**, the world's largest maze (open June–Aug daily 11am–5pm; weekends only May, Sept and Oct; entrance fee; tel: 86 59 66 59 for times). Its 5 km (3 miles) of passages wind through a dense fir forest covering 6 hectares (15 acres). In the south of the island, **Brundby Rock Hotel**, owned by a group of Danish rock musicians, is a festive place to have dinner and hear live music.

Map on page 130

Lake District

A series of lakes snake through forested hills west of Århus, and a fun way to see them is from the paddle steamer *MS Hjejlen*, which has carried passengers from Ry to Silkeborg since 1861. For a bird's-eye view, climb **Himmelbjerget ⑧** (Sky Mountain), at 147 metres (482 ft) one of Denmark's highest "mountains". The nearby town of **Silkeborg ⑨** features the **Silkeborg Kunstmuseum** (Museum of Art; open Apr–Oct Tues–Sun 10am–5pm; Nov–Mar Tues–Fri noon–4pm, Sat–Sun 10am–5pm; entrance fee; tel: 86 82 53 88), which is built around the glorious, playful work of the painter Asger Jorn and others from the 20th-century CoBrA (Copenhagen, Brussels, Amsterdam) group.

Miniature world: Lego was developed by Ole Kirk Christiansen and his family in Billund in 1949.

Further south, historical **Horsens ⑩** hosts an annual Middle Ages Festival in the autumn, which is highly recommended. At **Billund**, 50 km (31 miles) southwest of Horsens, more than a million people a year visit **Legoland ⑪** (open June–Aug daily 10am–6pm; Apr, May, Sept & Oct daily 10am–5pm; entrance fee; tel: 75 33 13 33), coming to marvel at the miniature world created from more than 35 million of the studded plastic bricks.

BELOW: timber-framed cottages, Ebeltoft.

A good salami

South Jutland has some of the most patriotic Danes in the country, particularly the generations who remember the area when it was officially part of Germany's Schleswig duchy from 1864 to 1920. **Kolding ⑫** was a border town on the Danish side at the time, and historical sights abound. Particularly of interest are the remains of **Koldinghus Slot** (open daily 10am–5pm; entrance fee; tel: 76 33 81 00), a castle built in 1208, and the **Kunstmuseet Trapholt** (Trapholt Museum of Art; open daily 10am–5pm; entrance fee; tel: 76 30 05 30) with a fine collection of modern art.

Driving south 15 km (9 miles), the Danish Moravian town of **Christiansfeld ⑬** is famous for its scrumptious honey cakes. Further south, close to the German border, **Sønderborg ⑭** is a striking town on **Als Island**, with a colourful harbour and the mighty **Sønderborg Slot** (open May–Sept daily 10am–5pm; Apr & Oct daily 10am–4pm; Nov–Mar: 1–4pm; tel: 74 42 25 39), a fortress built around 1100. Provincial Sønderborg happens to have one of the best cafés in Denmark, **Café Druen**, not far from the castle. South Jutland is known for its meats – particularly salamis. Stop at a local butcher to try a beer sausage.

Just to the west, **Dybbøl** ⑮ played a major role in the 1864 war with Germany. At a national historic park, the **Dybbøl Mill**, restored and painted white, and its museum are open to the public (Apr–Oct daily 10am–5pm; free; tel: 74 48 69 91).

On the western side of South Jutland is **Tønder** ⑯, a lace-making centre in the 17th century, documented in **Tønder Museum** (open June–Aug daily 10am–5pm, Sept–May closed Mon; entrance fee; tel: 74 72 26 57). Tønder has an attractive 17th- and 18th-century townscape, and many houses have distinctive painted doorways. At **Møgeltønder**, 3 km (2 miles) to the west, the village street is lined with lime trees – a beautiful sight. This is home to Prince Joachim (second in succession) and Princess Alexandra at **Schackenborg Slot**.

Night watchmen

Ribe ⑰, built around its 12th-century cathedral, ranks high on the list of historic centres in Scandinavia. Its brick and half-timbered houses, courtyards and *kroer* (inns) are much as they were hundreds of years ago.

Ribe Domkirke (Cathedral; open June–Aug Mon–Sat 10am–6pm, Sun noon–5pm; May & Sept Mon–Sat 10am–5pm, Sun noon–5pm; Oct–Apr Mon–Sat 11am–4pm, Sun noon–4pm; entrance fee) stands on the site of one of Denmark's earliest wooden churches, built around AD 860. The "Cat Head Door" was said to be the entrance for the Devil. The choir has been stunningly decorated by CoBrA artist Carl-Henning Petersen. There are splendid views from the tower.

Ribe continues the Middle Ages tradition of night watchmen. On summer evenings at 10pm, the watchman walks around singing the traditional songs that once told the people that they could sleep soundly, all was well.

HARALD BLUETOOTH WAS HERE

Viking sights abound in Jutland. **Lindholm Høje** (open Apr–Oct daily 10am–5pm; Nov–Mar Tues–Sun 11am–4pm; entrance fee; tel: 98 17 55 22), just north of Ålborg, is a necropolis with 700 graves, a reconstructed village from the early Iron Age and Viking times, and a museum. Many of the graves are in the shape of Viking ships.

Elsewhere, near Hobro, is the Viking fort of **Fyrkat**. Four earth fortifications once enclosed 16 large houses on the site, and one of these longhouses has been reconstructed. Finds from Fyrkat are on display in **Hobro Museum** (open Apr–Oct daily 11am–4pm; entrance fee; tel: 98 51 05 55). On the Mols peninsula near Århus is the **Poskjær Stenhus** barrow, which lies along the road from Agri to Grønfeld.

A memorial referred to as Denmark's "birth certificate" can be found in Jelling. The **Jellingstenene** (Jelling Stones) are covered with runic script carved by King Harald Bluetooth 1,000 years ago to proclaim his conversion to Christianity, and in honour of his parents, King Gorm the Old and Queen Thyra Danebrod, who were buried in the mounds beside Jelling town church. For a flavour of life in Viking times, re-enactments, including battles and blood oaths, can be experienced at Moesgård, and in Jels in July.

Western shores

West Jutland has a sense of space and time different from the rest of the region. In winter, the weather can be rugged, with storms blowing in off a turbulent North Sea. In summer this part of Denmark, with its sandy beaches, is popular with holiday-makers.

Esbjerg ⑱ is the biggest port town on the coast, the main gateway for ferries from Britain. A 20-minute ferry ride away is the island of **Fanø**, a major ship-building centre in the 18th and 19th centuries. **Sønderho** ⑲ village in the south of the island has colourful thatch-roofed cottages, an inn and Seamen's Church (1782). The island is characteristic for West Jutland: a superb stretch of white sandy beach, dunes, heath and forest.

Back on the Jutland coast, 30 km (19 miles) northwest, is **Blåvands Huk** ⑳ lighthouse, a popular holiday spot with a nature reserve nearby. At the beach during low tide if you see people standing in water up to their ankles staring down, don't be alarmed. They are hunting for nuggets of amber, a golden-coloured petrified tree resin that frequently washes ashore here.

Some 25 km (16 miles) to the north, at **Henne** ㉑, Denmark's television chef Hans Beck Thomsen runs the **Henne Kirkeby Kro** (tel: 75 25 54 00) in summer.

A narrow strip of land runs north from Nymindegab to Søndervig, separating the sea from **Ringkøbing Fjord**, a broad, shallow, saltwater "lake". Driving north towards the fishing village of **Hvide Sande** ㉒, the crashing waves from the North Sea can be heard but are hidden from view by tall sand dunes. No matter how many times one walks to the top of these dunes, the experience is breathtaking: an incredibly long, narrow beach stretches out of sight in each direction, a stiff, salty breeze slaps you in the face, and the churning ocean melts into the horizon.

Map
on page
130

The night watchman of Ribe who recounts the town's history in song on his rounds.

BELOW: re-enacting the Middle Ages.

Map on page 130

Shell-covered house at Thyborøn.

BELOW: church in the sands. **RIGHT:** Hennes Strand.

From here to the northern tip at Skagen, the scenery is similar, broken by several attractive fishing villages and bathing resorts. At **Thyborøn ㉓**, a native has decorated a house with shells, covering all surfaces, inside and out. Take the 10-minute ferry from here across the Limfjorden to Vendsyssel, north Jutland.

At its advantageous location for trade on the Limfjorden, **Ålborg ㉔** – Denmark's fourth-largest city with a population of 155,000 – is full of historical buildings, castles and Viking monuments. The most well-known building in town is the opulent six-storey **Stenhus** (Stone House) on Østerågade, built in 1624 by a merchant, Jens Bang, to show off his wealth. Bang was annoyed that he had never become a town councillor; on the south facade of Stenhus is a carving of him sticking his tongue out at the town hall across the street. Also across the street lies the tourist information centre (tel: 98 12 60 22). The town's main entertainment artery is **Jomfru Ane Gade**, lined with restaurants and bars in courtyards and half-timbered buildings. This is the place to try Ålborg's most famous product: *aquavit*, the strong aperitif flavoured with caraway seeds that accompanies the traditional Danish *smørrebrød* (open-faced sandwiches).

Nordic light

Situated on a narrow piece of land with the North Sea on one side and the Baltic on the other, **Skagen ㉕** has a magical quality to it. The air shimmers with a certain light that must be experienced in person to believe it. This was an irresistible lure to the Skagen painters, who made it their home in the second half of the 19th century, with Brøndums Hotel as their rallying ground. Works by artists from this period, such as Anna and Michael Ancher, P.S. Krøyer, and Viggo Johansen can be seen in **Skagens Museum** (open Apr, May & Sept Tues–Sun 11am–4pm; June–Aug daily 10am–6pm; Nov–Mar Wed–Fri 1–4pm, Sat 11am–4pm, Sun 11am–3pm; entrance fee; tel: 98 44 64 44), and **Anchers Hus** (Ancher's House; open Apr daily 11am–3pm; May–Sept daily 10am–5pm; Nov–Mar Sat & Sun 11am–3pm; entrance fee; tel: 98 44 30 09), bought by the Anchers in 1884. The artists' colony still lives on in Skagen. A few kilometres southwest is **Gammel Skagen** (Old Skagen), a cosmopolitan resort known for its sun-yellow homes with red-tiled roofs and its gourmet fish restaurants.

Just west of Gammel Skagen, **Den Tilsandede Kirke ㉖** (Sand-Covered Church; open June–Aug daily 11am–5pm; entrance fee) peeps out of the dunes with only its steeple visible. (another church is on the way to a more dramatic end at **Lønstrup** on the west coast. Here, the powerful waves are eating away at the cliffs under Mårup Kirke, starting with its cemetery.) To see migrating dunes up close, you need go no further than **Råbjerg Mile ㉗**, 10 km (6 miles) south of Skagen. Pushed by the wind and sea, the dunes travel as much as 20 metres (65 ft) every year.

For a thrilling experience of nature moving at its own rhythms, go to **Grenen**, 5 km (3 miles) north of Skagen, continental Europe's northernmost point. At the tip, you can actually see the North and Baltic seas crash into each other. The experience of standing here with one foot in each sea is exhilarating. ❑

GREENLAND

In spring and summer when the ice retreats and the temperature rises, Greenland's spectacular landscape becomes accessible for some of the most awesome adventure travel

Map
on page
138

The world's largest island is a place of stunning natural beauty, dramatic weather and fascinating culture. Greenland, like the Faroe Islands, is a former Danish colony that has become a member of the kingdom, but with its own home-rule government.

Greenland is like no other place. Its vast Arctic solitude is profound and its silence almost consumes you. Here, where the North Atlantic meets the Arctic Ocean, is the cleanest environment in the world, and measurably the oldest. Where else can you sip a drink cooled by a 1,000-year-old ice cube?

Greenland is called Kalaallit Nunaat (the land of the people) by its own people. They number only about 45,000 (plus an additional 10,000 Danes) in an area of 2,175,600 sq km (840,000 sq miles). The distance north to south is 2,670 km (1,655 miles), and the widest part east to west is 1,000 km (620 miles). Its closest neighbour is Canada. The capital is **Nuuk ❶** (Godthåb) on the west coast.

Greenlanders are Inuit and live in small towns around the coasts, mainly on the milder western side. Most of these people still earn their livelihoods by fishing and hunting. But thanks to its long association with Denmark, Greenland has a modern infrastructure and burgeoning tourist industry.

More than four-fifths of the country lies under 3 km (2 miles) of pack ice, but the southern coastal regions, especially to the west, are green and mild during late spring and summer. Daytime temperatures here can climb to a balmy 21°C (70°F) or more, but northerly winds in winter can make the mercury plunge to a bone-cracking -32°C (-25°F). Conditions in spring and summer make for excellent hiking and camping, not to mention some of the best fishing anywhere.

Adventure tours

The classic way of touring Greenland is by dog sled. You can hire a team and driver for a short sightseeing tour or for a longer journey. The season is usually from late February to May. In western Greenland it is possible to arrange trips from **Sisimiut ❷**, **Qeqertarsuaq ❸** (Disko Island) and points further north. On the barely populated east coast, you can dog sled from **Tasiilaq ❹** and **Ittoqqortoormiit ❺**.

A classic, though physically demanding, dog sled tour is the eight-day trip between Sisimiut and **Kangerlussuaq ❻** at Søndre Strømfjord on the west coast, which is best done in March, April or early May. The route takes you through the vast and beautiful landscapes of mid-Greenland, across frozen lakes and over hilly terrain. You sleep in hunting huts or tents.

Boat tours also offer breathtaking scenery and wildlife. Summer cruises to towns along the east and west coasts take you through sparkling seas alive with

LEFT: Greenland coastal settlement.
BELOW: fisherman's hideaway.

Arctic foxes are common in Greenland's coastal areas; other species found in the harsh environment include polar bear, musk ox and caribou.

seals and other marine life, even whales. You can disembark at harbours and settlements for hiking trips, or dog sled tours in season. Between ports, you sail past icebergs and glaciers. On land you might see reindeer and musk oxen, and polar bears have been spotted. Bird life is not abundant in Greenland, but you can encounter Arctic terns, ravens, peregrine falcons and eagles.

Helicopters are an important, often essential, means of transport here. Chopper tours are a breathtakingly beautiful way to travel around Greenland.

A novel way of exploring Greenland's nature is aboard a sturdy Icelandic pony. From Kangerlussuaq, you can join riding tours over gentle or demanding terrain, past lush flora and fauna, and inspiring scenery.

This vast, half-frozen island draws an increasing number of anglers each year. They come to fish for trout and Arctic char in the lowland lakes, rivers and streams. Off the coast and sometimes through ice, they reel in Greenland halibut, Norway haddock, catfish and cod. Fishing licences are required.

Among the spectacular natural phenomena in Greenland are the Northern Lights and the Midnight Sun. The *aurora borealis* occurs all year long but is only visible in a clear night sky in autumn and winter. These ethereal lights can appear as colourful curtains, veins of silk ribbon, or as ghostly souls flying to heaven. In summer, the midnight sun keeps the night sky blue.

Ruled by the weather

The only way to travel to Greenland is by air, either via Copenhagen; Keflavik, Iceland; or Ottawa, Canada. Once in Greenland, sailing is an option year-round, but schedules are highly dependent on the changing weather. The same applies to air services. In a climate which changes from hot sun and clear bright air to

BELOW: dressed in traditional costume.

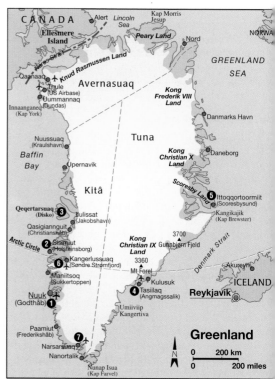

a deluge of rain in a moment, the weather decides whether it's possible to keep to a plan made the day before. Many a visitor has been forced to "overnight" at **Narsarsuaq** in the south because aircraft couldn't land.

Most towns in Greenland have modern hotels in various categories of comfort. These and the local tourist offices are the best places to book excursions. The more footloose visitor may prefer a hostel, seaman's home, or a cabin. Camping sites are appearing and tent-roughing is permitted virtually everywhere, so long as campers observe the rules of nature and common politeness.

Fruits of the sea

Heart disease is a rarity for Greenlanders, thanks to a diet based heavily on the sea. Greenlandic specialities also include fowl, game and berries. The national dish is *svaassat*, seal meat cooked with rice and onions. A particular delicacy is *mattak*, pieces of whale skin with a thin layer of blubber. Slow chewing brings out its nutty flavour. If your taste buds are more "Western", try musk ox steak or Greenlandic lamb cutlets, considered to be some of the best in the world. The reindeer venison and honey-roasted eider duck breast aren't bad, either.

Then, of course, there is any kind of fresh Greenlandic seafood. This includes trout, salmon, Atlantic halibut, redfish, whale, bay scallops and the world-renowned large Greenlandic prawns. Smoked fish is a traditional lunch.

In the summer, families take to the highlands to cook in traditional Greenlandic style. This involves building a raised, flat stone base, gathering heather and branches for a fire and placing a pot or a piece of meat directly on the stone. Soon comes the delicious aroma of heather smoke and cooking fish or seal meat. ❑

Map on page 138

TIP

If you travel to Greenland in summer, it's wise to take shorts, gloves, and everything in between, plus waterproof clothing. Light waterproof hiking boots are the most appropriate footwear.

BELOW: Greenland's icy waters.

THE FAROE ISLANDS

The fruits of the sea have brought prosperity to the far-flung Faroe Islands. Visitors are attracted by the natural beauty and remarkable bird life

Map on page 142

The remote Faroe Islands lie far to the north of mainland Europe, halfway between Iceland and the Shetland Islands. The sailing distance between this self-governing Danish outpost and Copenhagen is around 1,500 km (900 miles). The sea is serious business here, and nothing shows that more clearly than **Tórshavn's ❶** harbour. It is stuffed with boats of all kinds – visiting ships, inter-island ferries, sailing boats and other pleasure craft and, most numerous of all, the fishing boats which disgorge their cargoes at one of the big fish processors scattered around the islands' coasts.

The fishing fleet is one of the most modern in Europe. Fish products make up more than 95 percent of the country's export earnings and the not-to-be missed tang of fish permeating the harbour is also the smell of money.

Although the Faroe islanders are prosperous with a high standard of living – they claim to have more cars and more video recorders per head than anyone else in Europe – everything is relative. Only 48,340 live on the 18 inhabited islands – a dozen more are home only to the huge colonies of birds. Much of the surface area is virtually bare rock, and only a few areas are habitable. As though to contrast with the muted blues, greens and greys of rocks, sea and hills, modern Faroese favour brightly painted houses. Traditional, living, green turf roofs are becoming popular once more.

Warm and wet

Far north as the islands are and feel, the Gulf Stream keeps the climate mild and moist. In the coldest month the average temperature is around 3°C (37°F), although wind chill makes it feel much colder. In the warmest, it reaches only 11°C (52°F). The weather is very changeable; one minute the sun is warm against the back, the next there is driving rain and mist.

No self-respecting tree could grow to a reasonable height against the islands' constant wind – though, as a joke, the Faroese call the small copse in the shelter of the park in the capital, Tórshavn, the islands' "forest".

The islands' name in Faroese, Føroyar, means "sheep islands" – even today, there are thousands more sheep than people, and lamb is a basic staple. The amount of arable land is extremely limited. Small kitchen gardens have robust plants, leeks, cabbages, carrots. Outside, people hang fish and lamb to dry in the wind.

On the trail

The inland trails cover a wonderland of stunning terrain. Footpaths crisscross all the islands and were originally the main routes between settlements. Most of the paths are marked by cairns, but some of them are not regularly maintained, and it's imperative to carry a map and compass. Campers may pitch tents

LEFT: the turf-roofed church at Saksun set against the green Faroese landscape.
BELOW: fishing boats at anchor in Tórshavn harbour.

The puffin is a Faroese delicacy, caught during the open season in July. The meat has a distinctively tangy flavour.

virtually anywhere, but many a tent has been swept into the North Atlantic by powerful gusts, so remember to find a sheltered spot and weight the tent down.

Bird cliffs

Although the Faroe Islands have few mammals, the bird life is outstanding. The towering faces of the stacks and cliffs are home to thousands of sea birds and in the sheltered pools live phalaropes and red-throated divers. The stiff-winged flight of the fulmars follows the boats without ever tiring and clown-faced puffins gaze solemnly from cliff burrows. The Faroese national bird, the black and white oystercatcher, calls worriedly from every hillock.

For the seafaring adventurer, boat operators sail from **Vestmanna** on an excursion of the islands to view the **Vestmannabjørgini** ❷, or **Enniberg** bird cliffs. The restored sloop, *Urðardrangur*, takes visitors on a tour of the islands, sailing into fjords and grottoes; and the island of **Mykines** ❸ attracts birdwatchers from many lands.

Anglers may find great challenges in the brooks and lochs which hold trout and salmon. The season extends from 1 May to 31 August. Contact the tourist office in Tórshavn for permits and details (tel: 31 57 88).

Early settlers

BELOW: fish hanging up to dry – a common sight on the Faroe Islands.

The islands' first substantial settlers came from Norway in the 9th century. Even before that time, an early township, **Kirkjubøur** ❹, had been the centre of life for a group of Irish friars who colonised the islands around the 8th century. In 1380, as Norway came under Danish Rule, the islands, too, became part of Denmark and, when the union dissolved in 1814, the Faroes continued

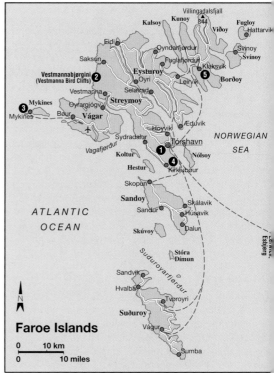

Faroe Islands

0   10 km
0   10 miles

Map on page 142

as a Danish county. The present system of Home Rule dates from 1948 and the Faroe Islands also send two representatives to the Danish Parliament.

The islands' long seafaring history is traced in the **Fornminnissavn** (National Museum; open mid-May–mid-Sept Mon–Fri 10am–5pm, Sat–Sun 2–5pm; mid-Sept–Apr Sun only 3–5pm; entrance fee) at Hoyvik, 2 km (1 mile) north of Tórshavn, and also in the **Norðoya Fornminnissavn** (North Islands Museum; open mid-May–mid-Sept daily 1–4pm) at **Klaksvík ❺**, on **Borðoy** island.

Dancing with the Faroese

The Faroese are proud of the rich culture and traditions of their islands, where the language, costumes and customs are kept very much alive. On festive occasions everyone joins in the Faroese chain dance, a slow, hypnotic dance accompanied by chanting. An older tradition that is still practised is the "door schnapps". Visitors are greeted at the door with a horn full of schnapps *(akvavit)* and everybody takes a sip before entering.

When visiting the **Roykstovan** (Smoke Room; open June–Aug Mon–Sat 10am–5.30pm, Sun 2–5pm) in Kirkjubøur, the first order of the day is a nip from the horn. The building is allegedly the oldest wooden structure in the world, built from logs that were towed from Norway.

In the summer months a series of events encompassing literature, music, theatre and, of course, chain dancing – known as the **Faroese Cultural Evening** – is held on the island of **Eysturoy** and at Tórshavn. In late June and July the **Summartónar Music Festival** is staged at venues around the islands. The **Tórshavnar Jazz, Folk and Blues Festival** is a four-day event held from the end of July to early August, and the **Folk Music Festival** takes place in mid-July in Tórshavn. ❑

TIP

For the thirsty, Faroe is not the easiest place to find a drink. Alcoholic beverages are sold only at state-run monopoly stores *(Rúsdrekkasøla Landsins)*. Hotels generally have fully stocked bars, as do restaurants.

BELOW: stacking hay Faroese-style.

NORWAY

Breathtaking scenery, historic sights and modern cities
are the big attractions for the traveller to Norway

The Norwegian landscape is both beautiful and brutal, hospitable and hostile; barren rock submits to soft fertile plains, majestic mountains tower above mysterious fjords; harsh winters are relieved by glorious summers; and long polar nights give way to the radiant Midnight Sun. One of the oldest civilisations in Europe has become one of its youngest nations. The Norwegians themselves have adapted rather quickly. The lusty Vikings have turned into global peacemakers. Norway has urban excitement and rural tranquillity; shopping malls and Mercedes rub shoulders with compass and rucksack; hi-technology parallels steadfast tradition.

A thriving offshore oil industry has brought prosperity, and as a consequence, social habits are changing rapidly, though, in a society where the divorce rate is high and cohabitation the norm, the home and family still remain important. Murray's *Handbook for Travellers in Norway* described the Norwegians in 1874 thus: "Great patriotism and hospitality are two of the leading characteristics of the Norwegians; they are often cold and reserved, and combine great simplicity of manner with firmness and kindness. 'Deeds, not words' is their motto." Today, little has changed.

Norway is a long narrow strip of a country, stretching north from mainland Europe far into the Arctic. The ancient capital of Trondheim is 500 km (350 miles) from the modern capital of Oslo, yet only a quarter of the way up the country's jagged coast. The southern coast is as far from Monaco as it is from the Nordkapp (North Cape), and Norway's northernmost outpost, the islands of Svalbard (Spitsbergen), are hundreds of kilometres further still. With a population of less than 4½ million, Norway has, above all else, space.

Yet travel is not difficult. From early times, the Norwegians were magnificent sailors, and this old way of travel continues today through the Hurtigruten coastal steamers and other ferries that link coastal communities. The Gulf Stream warms the western coastline so that the seas are ice-free all the year round. On land, the Norwegians have achieved the seemingly impossible, connecting even the most isolated settlements by building railways, roads and bridges across their fjords and by tunnelling deep into mountains and under the sea. Oslo, Stavanger, Bergen, Trondheim and Tromsø are small manageable cities that make good use of the surrounding countryside.

Norwegians are an outdoor people, and Norway a country where inhabitants and visitors alike can make the most of limitless space for walking, skiing, touring and just breathing in the clear air.   ❏

PRECEDING PAGES: rocky outline of the Lofoten Islands; the reindeer reigns supreme in the far north; Art Nouveau architecture in the fishing town of Ålesund. **LEFT:** intrepid settlers built their homes in the most secluded spots.

THE NORWEGIANS

Forget the stereotypical image of a cool Scandinavian, visitors to
Norway can be assured of a warm and friendly welcome

Even to their nearest neighbours in Scandinavia, the Norwegians are a bit of a conundrum. To visitors from further afield they offer so many, often conflicting, faces that many leave Norway feeling they haven't even come close to understanding the people.

They can be cool almost to the point of rudeness when you first meet them, but once they've got to know you a little their warmth and hospitality are unmistakable. They are slow to offer opinions but when they do their views are forthright. They pride themselves on their internationalism and yet can be incredibly inward looking. They have strong cultural and economic links with the rest of Europe but stubbornly insist on staying outside the European Union. Where many people have national pride, for the Norwegians it's a passion. Their way is the best in just about everything and if the rest of the world hasn't noticed, well too bad.

One Hans Christian Andersen character proclaims: "I'm a Norwegian. And when I say I'm Norwegian, I think I've said enough. I'm as firm in my foundations as the ancient mountains of old Norway... It thrills me to the marrow to think what I am, and let my thoughts ring out in words of granite."

Andersen was a Dane, and he was teasing the Norwegians, as their Scandinavian neighbours are still apt to do.

Many people put this self-reliance down to history and to resentment over centuries of foreign rule and neighbourly condescension. Others use one word to explain it: oil. These days the Norwegians can afford to go it alone and say a polite "*nei takk*" ("no thanks") to the advice of outsiders.

Proud self-reliance

Historically, Norway is one the oldest nations in Europe, if not the oldest. Its people can trace an unbroken line of descent from those who inhabited the area in prehistoric times.

During the era of the Vikings (*circa* 800–1050), Norway controlled an enormous territory from Russia to the British Isles, and the common European tongue was Old Norse. Yet today's Norway was reconstituted as late as 1905 when the union with Sweden was

NORWAY: THE ESSENTIALS		

Population 4.5 million, including 30,000 Sami.
Capital Oslo (pop. just over 512,000).
Notable towns Bergen, Stavanger, Trondheim, Tromsø.
Climate Afternoon temperatures in January are around –2°C (28°F), but lower in the north; July, 20°C (68°F).
Top museums Vikingskipshuset, Nasjonalgalleriet, Oslo.
Historic sights Gamle Bergen; Trondheim Cathedral; Røros; stave churches including Borgund and Heddal.
Natural wonders Fjord coastline; Preikestolen (Pulpit Rock); Lofoten Islands; North Cape.
Outdoor activities Water sports, hiking, skiing, fishing.
Tourist information www.visitnorway.com

LEFT: patriotism runs strong in Norway where national sport – whether football or skiing – is concerned.
RIGHT: young face of Norway.

finally dissolved. The dominance of Old Norse may have gone but today's Norwegians have regained their pride.

World War II, and the Nazi occupation, was a massive shock to the Norwegian psyche. Still today there's a deep felt anger against the supposedly neutral Swedes for permitting the transit of German troops into Norway. After the war, the Norwegians realised with some reluctance that strategically they had no choice but to seek the protection of others. So they signed up to NATO, not least as protection against Russia, another unreliable neighbour in the north. But they turned their backs on the European

Union. The importance of fishing and the security of the oil revenues meant that economically they preferred to go it alone.

At times it seems that the enthusiasm of so many Norwegians to resume commercial whaling has less to do with its value as an industry and more to do with a hatred of being told what to do by the international community.

It's too easy, however, to equate this self-reliance with xenophobia. Norwegians don't fear or dislike foreigners. Their foreign aid budget puts many other developed nations to shame and they play a role on the world stage, particularly in the field of conflict resolution, that is impressive for a country of only five million people.

Home comforts

Hospitality is second nature to a Norwegian, whether he or she lives in Oslo or in the remotest corner of Finnmark. If you're planning to visit people at home be prepared – there's a lot of coffee to be drunk and usually cakes to be eaten.

Traditionally the host would light a candle as the guest arrived. It still happens, though not so religiously these days, and probably harks back to the days when, compounded by the long hours of winter darkness, houses shuttered against the cold were rather gloomy. The food will be plentiful and wholesome; your host will expect nothing in return except some appreciative comments about the welcome and maybe the décor.

Thanks to all that oil, and a very generous social security system, there is next to no poverty in Norway. But nor are they at all ostentatious about their wealth and, especially in rural areas, life can still be very simple.

The more enigmatic aspects of the Norwegian character – including the Nordic gloom which can descend after a drink too many – have been famously scrutinised by native, Norwegian, Henrik Ibsen. He was brought up in small communities and, during a long exile, turned his critical eye on the experience. One of the themes running through Ibsen's work is the double-edged nature of life in such a community: mutual support in adversity weighed against a suffocating lack of privacy at other times.

The lesser-known Aksel Sandemose wrote Ten Commandments for village life, the essence being humility bordering on self-abasement. They included: "You must not think that you are worth anything; you must not think that you are better than anyone else; you must not think yourself capable of anything worthwhile; and you must not think that you are in any way exceptional."

Land of many dialects

The essentially rural nature of so much of Norway has compounded one of their thorniest problems, language. The issue has split the country for over a century. Throwing off the Danish dominated *bokmål* (book language) was crucial to the independence activists of the 19th century. Unfortunately there was no Norwegian alternative on offer, just a variety of often very divergent dialects. Various attempts were made to bring these together into a truly national language known as *nynorsk* (new Norwegian) but these were never more than a partial success and even now there are huge regional variations in the spoken tongue.

Most Norwegians speak English extremely well and are more than happy to do so. Long before the French, for example, they realised it was taking national pride too far to deny the pre-eminence of English. Indeed many an urbanite will claim to find it much eas-

HONOURED GUESTS

An American student visiting Norway for the first time summed up his stay – and his increased body mass – with the three words "coffee and cakes".

mountains, which were easier to cross in winter on skis than in summer, they effectively lived in worlds apart. Families managed on their own, a resourcefulness which still runs in the blood. It is not unknown for young couples living in Oslo today to solicit the help of friends to build their first home with their own hands.

Whether it's the outdoor life or all the fish in the diet, Norwegians enjoy amazing longevity. They manage to look remarkably healthy all their lives, and the octo-

ier to understand a foreigner speaking English than one of their own compatriots speaking in their regional dialect.

Worlds apart

Norway's geography and its sparse population has entrenched cultural and economic fragmentation too. Rural lives depended on agriculture, and the land was too poor to support more than a family or two in a single valley. Separated from their neighbours by

LEFT: conscripts undergoing winter training in the far north of Norway.
ABOVE: enjoying the spring sunshine.

genarian grandmother whizzing by on skis is not entirely a myth. Yet one more reason why they feel rather pleased with themselves.

The Swedish king who reluctantly oversaw Norway's independence predicted that bureaucratic incompetence would soon have Norwegians begging to be returned to the fold. That, of course, never happened and modern Norway is a strong, successful and highly efficient state. But they've never forgiven the patronising attitude of their eastern neighbours.

So, if even now they're reluctant to admit that they're capable of making a mistake, it may just be that they're still trying to prove that Swedish king wrong. ❏

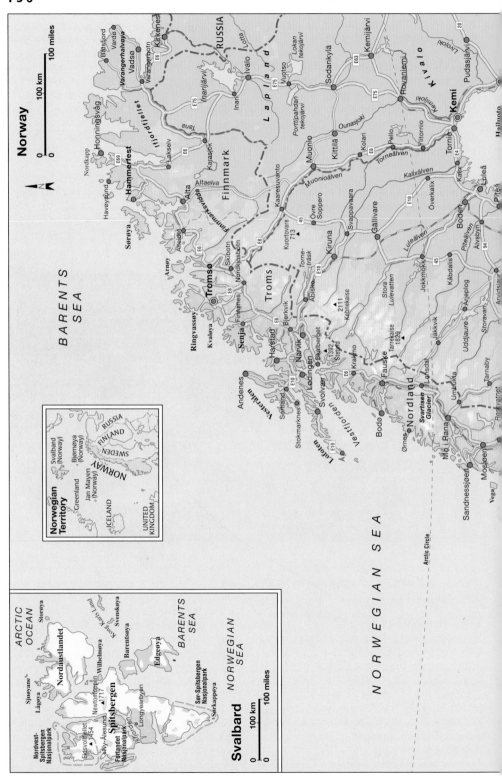

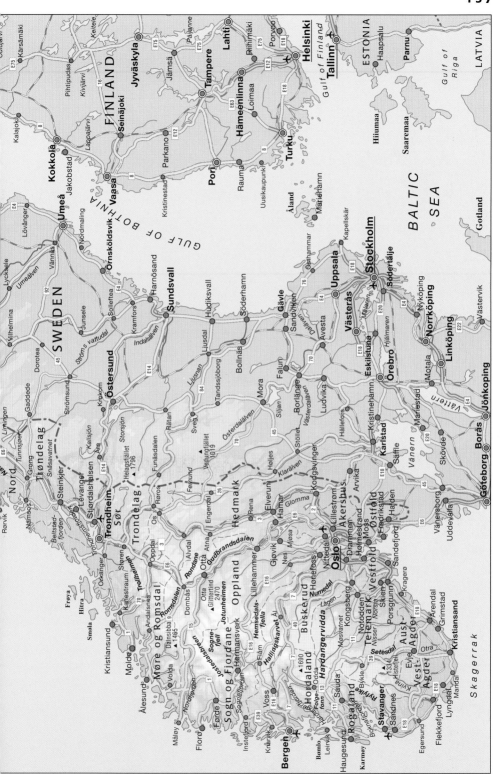

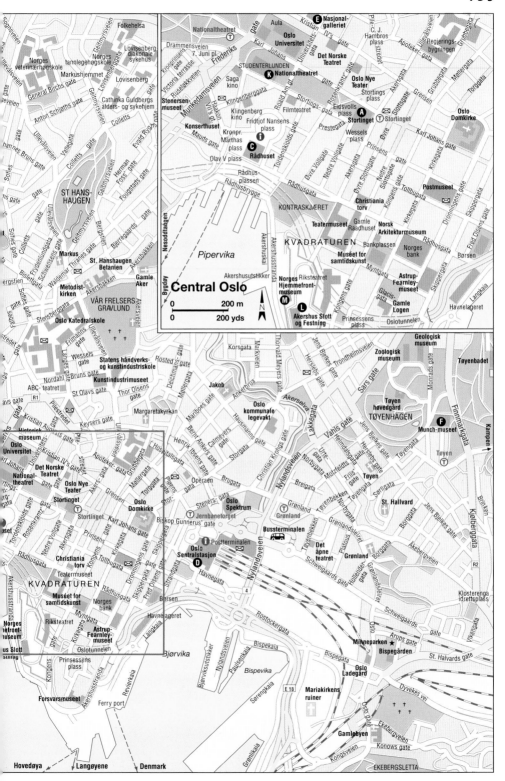

OSLO AND ITS FJORD

Norway's capital offers a lively mix of galleries, museums, shops, restaurants and nightlife, with magnificent forests, ski trails and the beautiful Oslo Fjord close at hand

Maps:
City 158
Area 168

O slo: the name has an English connection. According to the *Snorre Saga*, the city was founded by Harald III (1015–66), the half brother of Olaf II (later St Olaf). Crowned in 1045, Harald ruled so harshly as to earn the nickname Hardrade (Harsh Ruler). In 1066, he invaded England to claim its throne following the death of Edward the Confessor. The attempt failed; he was killed at Stamford Bridge on 25 September, barely three weeks before the Battle of Hastings that so changed English history.

Back home, Harald's subjects kept the name Oslo for six centuries, until 1624, when King Christian IV of Denmark and Norway immodestly renamed it Christiania. In 1877, at the height of the national romantic period following the dissolution of the union with Denmark in 1814, the government officially Norwegianised the spelling to Kristiania, and the city followed suit in 1897. State and municipal bureaucrats were obliged to use the new spelling, but the citizenry were divided and arguments raged. In 1924, the Storting (Parliament) settled the argument by reinstating the name Oslo. But the pronunciation has yet to settle down. The British say "Ozlo". The natives say "Osslo" or Oschlo, depending on whether they are East Siders or West Siders. Linguistic purists do it straight: "Os-lo", with two distinct syllables. Ask two Osloites to pronounce

LEFT: sculpture by Gustav Vigeland in Vigelandsparken.
BELOW: cafés spill out onto the street in summer.

FACT FILE

Situation Oslo lies in southeast Norway at 59°55'N.
Size 454 sq km (175 sq miles).
Population just over 512,000
Climate Average afternoon temperature in winter: –2°C (28°F); in summer: 21°C (70°F). Annual precipitation: 763 mm (30 inches).
Transport T-bane (underground), tram, bus, boat and commuter rail services. Trafikanten information, tel: 177.
Airports Gardermoen, 51 km (32 miles) north, and Torp at Sandefjord, 117 km (73 miles) south.
Biggest attraction Frogner Park, featuring works by the sculptor Gustav Vigeland in stone and bronze.
Newest attraction Aker Brygge (Aker Quay) gentrified former shipyard with trendy boutiques and eateries.
Finest building Akershus Slott og Festning (Castle), 1300.
Best view of the city Tryvannstårnet (Tryvann Tower).
Best museums Vikingskiphuset, Norsk Folkemuseum, Skimuseet, Barnekunstmuseet (Children's Art Museum).
Annual events Ski Festival (Mar); Jazz Festival (Aug).
Best ski resort Oslomarka, 2,500 km (1,553 miles) of cross-country ski trails. Snow report, tel: 82 05 20 20.
Tourist Information Fridtjof Nansens plass 5 and Oslo S Railway Station, tel: 23 11 78 80; www.visitoslo.com

The classical facade of Oslo's Det Kongelige Slott (Royal Palace).

the city name and you trigger debate. Today the dialects of the city are declining, under the influence of television and an ever more mobile population.

The industrial complex that lined the banks of Akerselva (Aker River) from the 1840s is no more. The city's remnant heavy industry, the Aker Shipyards, where 550 ships were built, closed in 1982. In its place is Aker Brygge (Aker Docks), a gentrified complex of trendy boutiques, international eateries and luxury apartments overlooking the fjord.

Likewise, civil servants and service-sector professionals have displaced industrial workers as the stalwarts of the city. The myth of the blond, blue-eyed Viking weakens, as an influx of foreigners enriches the city. Oslo has the country's greatest percentage of immigrants. The East Side, in the city districts of Torshov, Grünerløkka, Dælen, Tøyen, Grønland and Gamlebyen, has become the international palette of the country, where daily life and business are conducted as much in Turkish, Vietnamese and Urdu as they are in Norwegian. Here are most of the city's ethnic eateries and shops, as well as mosques and Islamic organisations to serve the burgeoning Muslim population. Should you visit Oslo during traditional Norwegian holidays and find establishments closed, go east of the Aker River for shopping and sustenance.

The 19th century today

BELOW: more than 200 sculptures by Gustav Vigeland are on display in Vigelandsparken.

In many ways **Oslo ❶** retains the features of the ideal city of the 19th century. Within easy walking distance, nestled around the northern tip of the fjord, are all the accoutrements of a capital: **Stortinget Ⓐ** (Parliament; tours in English July & Aug 10am & 1pm; free; tel: 23 31 35 96), **Det Kongelige Slott Ⓑ** (Royal Palace; park open all year; free; changing of the guard daily 1.30pm),

Rådhuset **C** (City Hall; open May–Aug Mon–Sun 9am–5pm; Sept–Apr 9am–4pm; entrance fee; tel: 23 46 16 00), **Oslo Sentralstasjon** **D** (Oslo Central Station), **Nasjonalgalleriet** **E** (National Gallery; open Mon, Wed & Fri 10am–6pm, Thur 10am–8pm, Sat 10am–4pm, Sun 11am–4pm; free; tel: 22 20 04 04), government ministries, courts, embassies, larger hotels and shops. The attractions not in this compact grid of streets are just a few stops away on the T-Bane (underground).

   Munch-museet **F** (Munch Museum; open June–mid-Sept daily 10am–6pm; mid-Sept–May Tues–Fri 10am–4pm, Sat–Sun 11am–5pm; entrance fee; tel: 23 24 14 00), near the Tøyen underground station to the east of the city centre, is dedicated to the works of Edvard Munch (1863–1944), the painter and graphic artist who fathered German expressionism. His most known work, *Skrik* (The Scream), in the National Gallery, is probably Scandinavia's most famed work of art. The ever increasing popularity of Munch's works may be attributed to his violent, emotionally charged style and themes of fear and anxiety, that communicate as well today as they did a century ago *(see box, page 56)*.

   One of Munch's contemporaries, sculptor Gustav Vigeland (1869–1943), also communicates through time. His works dominate **Vigelandsparken** **G** (Vigeland Park; open year-round; entrance free) at Frogner Park to the west of the city centre. Nowhere else is there so extensive a display of the scope of human life and emotion cast in stone and bronze. No matter that English novelist Evelyn Waugh called it a "subhuman zoo"; it remains one of Scandinavia's most visited attractions, drawing more than a million visitors each year.

   At Frøen, a short stroll north from Frogner Park, is another one of its kind: **Det Internasjonale Barnekunstmuseet** **H** (International Museum of Children's

Maps:
City 158
Area 168

👁 **TIP**

Buy an Osloskortet (Oslo Pass), for free admission to the city's museums, free public transport and parking, discounts at shops, restaurants and on car hire. Obtainable from tourist offices and hotels.

BELOW: youngsters are well catered for in Oslo with their own museum of art.

A CHILD'S-EYE VIEW OF ART

All too often, children's art – a subtle but essential trigger of the creative impulse – is overlooked or discarded. Yet were it not a tangible force, art could claim neither Chagall nor Picasso, nor other greats, who heeded its impetus. Indeed, Pablo Picasso once remarked that "when I was 18, I had Raphael's expertise. The rest of the time I spent learning to draw like a child."

   In the world, there is one permanent walk-through monument to Picasso's mandate for artistic expression, **Barnekunstmuseet** (Museum of Children's Art) in Oslo. Founded in 1986 by Rafael Goldin (1920–94), an émigré Russian film director, it is dedicated to seeing the world from the eye of a child. The museum exhibits paintings, sculpture, ceramics, collages, tapestries and other items from its collection of the works of children from more than 150 countries. Moreover, it's a place of action where visiting children and adults can take part in artistic activities, from drawing to playing African drums.

   Det Internasjonale Barnekunstmuseet, Lille Frøens vei 4, near the Frøen T-Bane station, is open July–mid-Aug Tues–Thur, Sun 11am–4pm; late-Sept–June Tues–Thur 9.30am–2pm, Sun 11am–4pm; closed Mon, Fri–Sat and mid-Aug–mid-Sept; entrance fee; tel: 22 46 85 73.

Art; *see box, page 163)*. A few blocks uphill from Barnekunstmuseet near Slemdal T-Bane station is the **Emanuel Vigeland Museum**  (Grimelundsveien 8; open Sun noon–4pm; entrance fee; tel: 22 14 57 88). Emanuel Vigeland (1875–1948), Gustav Vigeland's brother, made his living painting the great personages of his time. But like Edvard Munch, he was fascinated by themes of life and death, and used them in the alfresco decoration of a crypt, entitled *Vita* ("life"), the museum's major attraction.

Children will enjoy the old-fashioned candy store and horse and carriage rides at the Norsk Folkemuseum (Museumsveien 10; open daily; tel: 22 12 37 00), where more than 150 historic timber houses and a stave church are on display.

Back to the city centre, on the south side of Drammensveien from Dronningsparken, **Ibsen-museet** ❶ (Ibsen Museum; open Tues–Sun noon–3pm; tours noon, 1pm & 2pm; entrance fee; tel: 22 55 20 09) is located partly in the flat once occupied by Henrik Ibsen (1828–1906), Norway's most noted playwright and one of the world's outstanding pioneers of social drama. A statue of Ibsen stands in front of the **Nationaltheatret** ❷ (National Theatre, Johanne Dybwads plass 1), a rococo theatre built in 1899, with four stages, and the venue of the annual international Ibsen Festival in August.

History and the outdoors

The river that divides the city shares the root of its name with **Akershus Slott og Festning** ❸ (Akershus Castle and Fortress; bastions and ramparts open 6am–9pm; free entrance to grounds), a major complex begun in 1300, finished in 1308 and extended through the 15th century. It was built principally to defend the city against attack from Sweden. The fort remains an imposing symbol of past military importance. **Norges Hjemmefrontmuseum** ❹ (Norway's Resistance Museum; open Sept–May Mon–Sat 10am–4pm; June–Aug Mon–Sat 10am–5pm, Sun 11am–7pm; entrance fee; tel: 23 09 31 38) is located here,

BELOW: off duty at the Royal Palace.

near the place where members of the Resistance were executed during World War II. It illustrates the intense story of occupied Norway.

Map on pages 158–159

Capital sports

For an Osloite, saying you ski is as exciting as saying you drive a car – unless, of course, you are a world-class competitor in the sport. And that many Norwegians are: Norway leads the world in the number of medals won in the Olympic Winter Games.

High on the hills overlooking the city is **Holmenkollbakken**  (Holmenkollen Ski Jump; open all year; free except during ski meets), venue of the annual Holmenkollen Ski Festival, among the world's oldest sporting events. Adjoining the ski jump is **Skimuseet O** (Ski Museum; open May & Sept daily 10am–5pm; June–Aug daily 9am–8pm; Oct–Apr daily 10am–4pm; entrance fee; tel: 22 92 32 00), featuring 4,000 years of skiing history. Alongside the arena there is a statue of King Olav V (1903–91) in a cross-country skiing pose, because here skiing is the sport of commoner and king alike. Indeed, Oslo is so much a "ski town" that an Olympic Winter Games (1952) and two World Nordic Ski Championships (1966 and 1982) have been held within the city limits.

Oslo's sporty profile is due in part to the closeness of outdoor recreation. On one side there's the fjord, a broad, sheltered expanse of water ideal for windsurfing and boating. On the other side is a huge woodland recreation area known as **Oslomarka** (Oslo's fields), covering some 1,700 sq km (656 sq miles). Here there are 2,500 km (1,550 miles) of ski trails marked with red-painted slashes on trees and rings round sign-poles at trail intersections. The total length of the summer-time walking trails is even longer; they are marked in

Akershus Slott, built to defend against attacks from Sweden.

BELOW LEFT: high-tech facade. **BELOW RIGHT:** the city's ski jump.

blue, the difference being that red-marked trails can cross lakes and marshes frozen in the winter, while blue-marked trails cannot.

Some 110 km (68 miles) of ski trails are illuminated with their trailheads at car parks or underground stations, for ease of after-dark access. All the illuminated trails, as well as some 500 km (300 miles) of other trails, are regularly maintained with tracks set by machine. Trail use is free, as cross-country skiing is regarded as part of public recreation. Along the trails, there are some 20 staffed lodges with lounges, cafeterias and toilets; most are open at weekends and during school holidays, and in the winter, some are open in the evening. There are also 16 Alpine ski lift hills and 48 ski jumps.

For details, contact Skiforeningen (tel: 22 92 32 00), or Skogvesen (Oslo Municipal Forestry Service; tel: 22 08 22 00), which maintains trails, and operates the illuminated trails and 11 of the trailside lodges. In winter *føremelding* (snow conditions) for the Oslo area are recorded daily, tel: 82 05 20 20.

Although Norway gave the word "ski" (meaning "piece of split wood") to the world, the language has no verb equivalent to the act of skiing.

Great explorers

The pines and waters of Oslo were the training ground for Fridtjof Nansen (1861–1930) and Roald Amundsen (1872–1928), two of the greats of the heroic age of polar exploration. Their ships, *Fram* and *Gjøa*, are preserved in two museums on the **Bygdøy** peninsula, **Frammuseet ℗** (Fram Museum; open May, Sept & Oct daily 10am–4.45pm; June–Aug daily 9am–6.45pm; Nov–Apr daily 11am–2.45pm; entrance fee; tel: 23 28 29 50) and **Norsk Sjøfartsmuseum ℚ** (Norwegian Maritime Museum; open May–Sept daily 10am–6pm; Oct–Apr daily 10.30am–4pm; entrance fee; tel: 23 28 41 70). Nearby, the **Kon-Tiki Museum ℝ** (open Apr, May & Sept daily 10.30am–5pm; June–Aug daily 9.30am–5.45pm; Oct–Apr daily 10.30am–4pm; entrance fee; tel: 23 08 67 67) has a fine collection of Easter Island artefacts as well as detailed displays of the preserved *Kon-Tiki* and *Ra II* craft used by ethnographic explorer Thor Heyerdahl (1914–2002), and **Vikingskipshuset ⑤** (Viking Ship Museum; open May–Sept daily 9am–6pm; Oct–Apr daily 11am–6pm; entrance fee; tel: 22 13 52 80) features the world's best-preserved collection of the elegant long ships of the Viking Age.

BELOW: old-style country store at the Norsk Folke-museum on the Bygdøy peninsula.

Historic coat of arms

An event during the era of the city's founding is depicted in its coat of arms. One day, Hallvard Husaby (*d.*1053), came upon a young, pregnant girl being pursued by three men. He took her in his boat in an attempt to escape on the fjord. But the villains caught and slew them both, tied a millstone around his neck, and tossed the bodies into the fjord. A few days later, Hallvard's body was found floating on the fjord, millstone still securely tied to his neck. A saint was born. City coats of arms and seals depicting St Hallvard have been in use since the 14th century. The current version, designed in 1924, shows Hallvard on a lion throne, the three lethal arrows in his left hand, the millstone in his right, and the girl at his feet. Around the periphery is the Latin motto: *Unanimiter et Constanter* (Unanimous and Eternal).

Can an increasingly multicultural city be unanimous about anything? Perhaps. In the late 1980s, the public transport authorities decreed that trams were to be repainted red to promote visibility in traffic. The citizens were not pleased. Adamant that trams in Oslo are blue, preferably the cobalt blue of the city flag, they obliged the authorities to surrender. Cobalt blue now is the standard tram colour.

And the eternal? It also survives, subliminal in the soul of the city. Novelist Knut Hamsun (1859–1952), awarded the Nobel Prize for Literature in 1920, observed in his novel *Sult* (*Hunger*, 1888) that Oslo is "a strange city that nobody leaves without being marked by it". Translated to today's idiom, Oslo might be said to be memorable because it is a different sort of city.

Maps:
City 158
Area 168

Southward and outward

If you stand at a vantage point in Oslo and look south down the fjord, almost everything in view is in Akershus county. Further south, the fjord is flanked on the east by Østfold county and on the west by Vestfold county. Aside from being home to one in three residents of the country, the city and these counties play a key role in contemporary events and history.

In Akershus county, some 67 km (42 miles) north of Oslo lies **Eidsvoll ❷**, a town that grew around the iron works built in 1624. The works closed in 1825; Eidsvoll might be just another post-industrial town, save for the happenings of the spring of 1814. Following the dissolution of the union with Denmark, 112 representatives convened at the headquarters of the iron works, then the only convenient large building, to draw up the Norwegian Constitution. **Eidsvoll-byningen** (Memorial Building; open May–Sept daily; Apr–Oct weekends only; Nov–Mar: by appointment; entrance fee; tel: 63 92 22 10) is now a museum to

The excellent Kon-Tiki Museum displays Thor Heyerdahl's Kon-Tiki and Ra II craft as well as artefacts from Easter Island.

BELOW: outdoor café, Aker Brygge.

Traditional architecture in Drøbak, south of the capital.

the constitution and includes the room where the document was signed on 17 May 1814. The country's first railway, built in 1845, connected Oslo and Eidsvoll, and it's now on the E6 highway, the major north-south artery.

Historic provincial cities and towns are scattered throughout Østfold and Vestfold counties. The best way to explore the counties, whether you travel by bus, car or boat, is via **Drøbak** ❸. If you choose road, you will pass Vinterbro, at the junction of the E6 and E18 highways, the location of **TusenFryd** ❹, the country's major amusement park (open June–Aug daily 10.30am–7pm; May & Sept weekends only; entrance fee; tel: 64 97 66 99).

The village of Drøbak was once a fishermen's settlement. Fishing vessels still dock here to sell fresh prawns and fish on the quayside. Places of interest include the **Follo Museum** (Heritage Museum; open Tues–Fri 11am–4pm, Sat–Sun noon–5pm; entrance fee; tel: 64 93 99 90) and the **Oscarsborg Festning** (fort) out in the fjord, whose cannons sunk the German heavy cruiser *Blücher* on the day the country was invaded in 1940 (guided boat trips from the harbour). Another point of pride is the cross-timbered **Drøbak Kirke** (church; built 1776; open all year; entrance free), with an elaborately carved model of a ship inside, a common church decoration in seafaring towns.

Further south, **Fredrikstad** ❺ is a gem among Østfold towns, and Scandinavia's only completely preserved fortress town, dating from 1567. History and prehistory figure largely hereabouts. The **Oldtidsveien** (Highway of the Ancients), the 18-km (11-mile) stretch of National Highway 110 between Fredrikstad and Skjeberg, has three **Helleristningsfelt** (literally "rock wall carving areas"; open all year; free access to grounds) with Bronze Age pictographs.

Halden ❻, south of Skjeberg and close by the Swedish border, is dominated

Map on page 168

by **Fredriksten Festning** (fort), a largely intact ruin with many of its buildings serving as small theme museums. The streets below were laid out along the cannons' blast lines to give the fortress's defenders freedom to fire. In summer, passenger launches travel the **Haldenkanal** (canal) that runs east and then north, through several sets of massive locks. The **Kanalmuseum** (Canal Museum; open mid-June–mid-Aug daily noon–6pm; Sept–Apr times vary; entrance fee; tel: 69 81 10 21) at the locks at **Ørje** ❼, displays the implements of canal operations. It also arranges charter tours on the *Engebret Soot*, named after the designer of the canal and now the world's oldest propeller-driven steamship in service.

Throughout Østfold, *Olsok* (St Olav's day, 29 July) is celebrated with a great show of folk costume, music and dance. One of the best displays is at the **Borgarsyssel Museum** (open mid-May–Aug Tues–Fri 10am–7pm, Sat–Sun noon–5pm; entrance fee; tel: 69 15 50 11) in **Sarpsborg** ❽, north of Skjeberg.

Viking Vestfold

The Moss-Horten car ferry connects Østfold and Vestfold in just under an hour. The **Marinemuseet** (Naval Museum; open May–Sept daily noon–4pm; free; tel: 33 03 33 97) at **Horten** ❾, home port of Sjøforsvaret (the Royal Norwegian Navy), bulges with maritime history. There are also museums of photography and veteran cars in Horten (both open all year; entrance fee).

To the south lies the heart of eastern Viking country, and **Borre Nasjonalpark** ❿ (open all year; free access to grounds), en route to Tønsberg, contains large turf-covered mounds concealing the graves of Viking kings. Keeping to the coastline along Road 311, **Munch's Lille Hus** (Munch's Little House, open June–Aug, times vary; entrance fee; tel: 33 08 21 31) at **Åsgårdstrand** ⓫ is

TIP

A pleasant way to travel to fjord towns is by boat. Contact any travel agent or Trafikanten at Oslo S station for information on ferry and launch services (tel: 177).

BELOW:
Drøbak, a fishing port on Oslo Fjord.

Map
on page
168

TIP

Oslo has a wide variety of restaurants, both Norwegian and international. Cafés and *konditoris* offer coffee and pastries. For low-budget meals, look for a *kafeteria*.

BELOW: stave church at the Norsk Folkemuseum.
RIGHT: Kragerø, the summer home of Edvard Munch.

where the artist lived when he returned to Norway from abroad. It was a setting for many of his paintings.

Between Åsgårdstrand and Tønsberg is a burial mound, **Oseberghaugen** ⑫, the most important Viking site yet discovered (open all year; grounds free). Oslo's Vikingskipshuset *(see page 166)* contains the finds, including the 20-metre (65-ft) arch-ended wooden ship. Only the mound itself, near Slagen church, remains, but as a symbol Oseberghaugen has a subtle, magnetic power.

Just south is historic **Tønsberg** ⑬, established in the 9th century. On the 65-metre (200-ft) high **Slottsfjellet** are the fortress remains and tower. The main street, **Storgata**, is flanked by Viking graves. These were excavated and incorporated, under glass, into the ground floor of the new library.

The most renowned king to hold court in Tønsberg was Håkon Håkonson IV (1240–63). The ruins of his court can be seen on **Nordbyen**, a street with old houses hunched along it. A more recent native son is Roald Amundsen, the polar explorer. Less known outside Norway is Svend Foyn, the Tønsberg whaling captain who invented the explosive-powered harpoon.

The steamship *Kysten I* (built 1909), moored on Byfjorden near the old customs house, operates a three-hour islands tour.

Summer playground

To the south of Tønsberg, along the eastern side of the fjord, the islands of **Nøtterøy** and **Tjøme**, and the skerries, are fantastic summer hangouts. **Verdens Ende** ⑭ (World's End) is at the end – but for a few boulders – of the chain. The old lighthouse here is a beautifully simple structure made of stone.

On the other side of Tønsbergfjorden lies **Sandefjord** ⑮, a whaling town. The sea still dominates life here. One of the main industries is marine paint production. The town centre is compact, and near **Badeparken** are the former spa and the old town. **Preståsen** is the hilly park above it.

Just outside Sandefjord is another burial site, **Gokstadhaugen** ⑯ (open all year; May–Sept guided tours; entrance free to grounds), in which the *Gokstad* ship, now in Oslo's Vikingskipshuset, was discovered in 1880. The **Vesterøy** peninsula is a supremely peaceful place, ideal for walking, cycling and boating.

Larvik ⑰ was home to two legendary boat lovers, ethnographic explorer Thor Heyerdahl and master boatbuilder Colin Archer (1832–1921), designer of the polar ship *Fram*. Archer's first house was at Tollerodden, on the fjord. At Larvik's back is Farris lake and **Farriskilde** (Farris Spring), the country's only natural mineral water spring.

People who live around Oslofjorden have a strange modesty-pride complex. They are the first to point out that the fjords of the west are more beautiful, the central mountain ranges far higher. But once these are out of the way, the superlatives begin to flow. The birthplaces of the most intrepid explorers are here, as are the best sailing races, the warmest summers, the finest archaeological discoveries, the best drinking water and summer resorts; for when it comes to this part of Norway neither modesty nor pride is false. ❑

SOUTHERN NORWAY

Map on pages 174–175

Norway's southern beaches and picturesque seaside towns are a magnet for summer visitors. The west coast is blessed with glorious fjords and the oil-rich city of Stavanger

Draw an upward arc on the map from Oslo in the east to Bergen in the west, and south of it you see the part of Norway where the bulk of the natives take their home country holidays. Here is where much of the history of the country happened and where the myriad roots of the contemporary Norwegian character remain intact. In clockwise order starting at Oslo, Southern Norway can be divided into the principal regions of **Sørlandet** (Southern country) comprising Telemark, Aust-Agder and Vest-Agder counties and their coasts around to about 7 o'clock; **Rogaland** county centred at the city of Stavanger on the west coast; and **Hordaland** county around Bergen.

Sørlandet

Kristiansand ❶ is the unofficial capital of the southern coast, and rightfully so. In 1639, King Christian IV of Denmark and Norway selected the site of the city for a fort to control the approaches to the North Sea and the Baltic. Much survives of the first of many forts built there, such as **Christiansholm Festning** (fortress; open May–Sept daily 9am–9pm; free; tel: 38 07 51 50). Present-day Kristiansand, a pleasant city laid out in a rectangular pattern by Christian IV's directive, invites strolling. The nearby **Kristiansand Dyrepark** (zoo and amusement park; open late June–mid-Aug daily 10am–7pm; entrance fee; tel: 47 38 04 97 00), which includes the miniature town of Kardemomme By (Cardamom Town), is the most-visited theme park in Norway.

West of Kristiansand, the **Lindesnes Fyr ❷** (lighthouse; open all year; entrance fee to museum) marks the southernmost point of Norway. The last town before Vest Agder rises to meet Rogaland is the port of **Flekkefjord** and the idyllic island of **Hidra**. The terrain is mountainous, with many splendid waterfalls, especially around **Kvinesdal ❸**.

Coastal journey

The principal centres along the coast east from Kristiansand are, in order, Lillesand, Grimstad and Arendal. **Lillesand ❹** is a popular holiday town with a fine selection of cafés and restaurants around the harbour. **Grimstad ❺** is indelibly associated with Ibsen. It was here that he served his apprenticeship to a chemist. Ibsen and his works are commemorated in the **Grimstad Bymuseum** (Town Museum: open May–Sept daily 9am–5pm; Oct–Apr Mon–Fri 9am–2pm; entrance fee; tel: 37 04 46 53). **Arendal ❻** was struck by fire in 1863, and lost the houses on stilts that had earned it the nickname "Little Venice". Now overflowing onto a number of small islands, it retains its lovely setting. The **Arendal Bymuseum** (Town Museum; open Tues–Fri 9am–3pm, Sat 10am–2pm;

LEFT: Preikestolen (the Pulpit Rock), one of Rogaland's best-known landmarks. **BELOW:** cascading waters of the southwest.

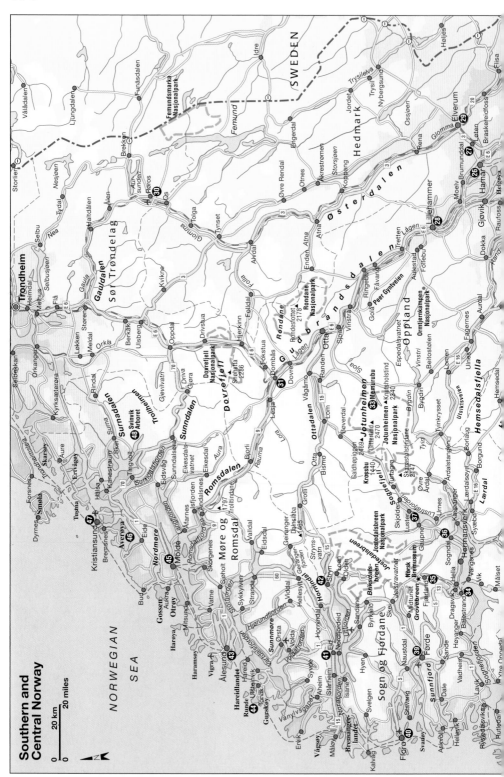

Southern and Central Norway

SWEDEN

NORWEGIAN SEA

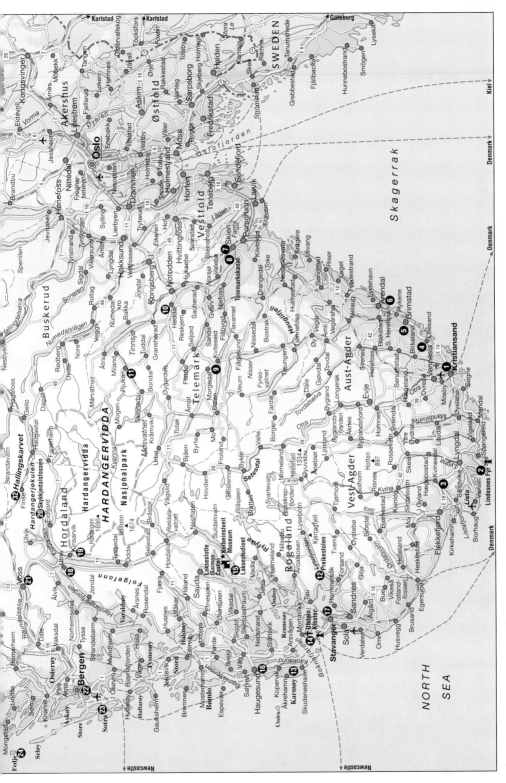

TIP

Signatur express
trains speed between
Oslo and Kristiansand
in 4 hours and 4
minutes, and between
Kristiansand and
Stavanger in 2 hours
and 25 minutes.

entrance fee; tel: 37 02 59 25) has extensive displays delineating local history, and the **Rådhus** (Town Hall), previously the home of a merchant, is said to be one of the largest wooden buildings ever constructed in Norway.

Telemark

Travelling northeast, the capital of Telemark is **Skien ❼**, which originally came into existence on the back of an industry producing stone projectiles for military slingshots. Norway's great playwright, Henrik Ibsen (1828–1906) spent his childhood here and his home, Venstøp, forms part of the **Telemark Museum** (Brekke Park; open May–Aug daily 10am–6pm; entrance fee; tel: 35 52 35 94), where tulips bloom en masse in the gardens in summer.

Northwest of Skien lies **Ulefoss**, a village that until the end of the 19th century was a major exporter of ice, which was transported along waterways that became the **Telemarkskanal ❽**, which is still trafficked by passenger launches, such as the *MV Victoria* and *MV Henrik Ibsen* (May–Sept; tel: 35 90 00 30).

Although a finger of Telemark reaches the sea at **Kragerø**, not far from the mouth of Oslofjorden, the county is most associated with its inland terrain. Indeed, whenever a modern skier performs a Telemark turn, homage is done to the village of **Morgedal ❾**. It was there that Sondre Norheim (1825–97), the son of a sharecropper, first improved utilitarian skis and ski bindings for greater control in turns and consequently became regarded as the father of modern downhill skiing.

One of the major attractions west of **Notodden**, along Road 11, is at **Heddal ❿**, where the **Heddal Stavkirke** (stave church) is the country's largest (open May, June & Sept Mon–Sat 10am–5pm; July–Aug Mon–Sat

BELOW: southerly
Mandal's popular
bathing beach.

9am–7pm, Sun 1–5pm; entrance fee; tel: 35 02 08 40). Its ornate carvings are rivalled only by the beautiful period rose paintings in the Ramberg room of the nearby **Heddal Bygdetun** (rural museum; open May–Sept; entrance fee).

About 10 km (6 miles) further on, Road 37 branches north past Tinnsjø lake towards **Rjukan ⓫**. The principal attraction of Rjukan is the hydroelectric plant where heavy water once was produced; see "Heroes of Telemark" *(page 180)* for an account of the daring sabotage that took place there in 1943. Today, the plant is the **Norsk Industriarbeidermuseum** (Norwegian Industrial Workers Museum; open May–Sept daily 10am–4pm; entrance fee; tel: 35 09 90 00). Rjukan lies in the shade of the surrounding mountains and from **Gvepseborg**, (860 metres/2,800 ft), it is said that one can see about one-sixth of Norway.

Rogaland

Though Bergen is known as the capital of fjord country, Rogaland county, centred on the west-coast port of Stavanger, has some of the country's more spectacular fjord and mountain sights. It also has the country's highest average temperature, and in winter there is little snow and the fertile fields are green for most of the year. The Ryfylke area northeast of Stavanger is true fjord country. It starts with Lysefjorden and stretches north past long narrow lakes that once were open fjords, until it reaches Vindafjorden, Saudafjorden and Suldalsvatn. Every visitor should try to walk out through the heather moor to stand on the top of **Preikestolen ⓬** (The Pulpit), a rock outcropping 597 metres (1,958 ft) above Lysefjorden, the country's most famous vantage point.

The sheltered bay north of Stavanger, and outer islands such as **Karmøy ⓭**, protect Ryfylke's inshore islands from the North Sea. Christianity flourished

Map on pages 174–175

The ornate altar at the Heddal Stavkirke, Norway's largest stave church.

BELOW: sheltered marinas dot the south coast.

COUNTRY AFLOAT

To the world, Norway and seafaring are synonymous. From the age of sail until after World War II, the Norwegian merchant fleet was one of the world's largest, and Norwegian could be heard in ports worldwide.

Norwegians seem happiest when they are in, on or around the sea. Each year, more than a third of the population spend their summer holidays partly or completely in craft that range from small dinghies to motor launches and ocean-going yachts. In all, there are more than 400,000 boats over 4.5 metres (15 ft) in length, and an untold number of smaller boats in the country. Most are motor boats, though sailing is popular on the fjords and as a competitive sport.

Geography and topography are the deciding factors. There are thousands of islands, and the fjords and coastal archipelagos are a paradise for competitive and recreational sailors, king and commoner alike. King Olav V (1903–91), the father of present King Harald V, won a Gold Medal in sailing in the 1928 Olympic Games, which made him the world's only Olympic medallist monarch.

Norway's first sailing club was founded in 1868 in Tønsberg, since when the nation has been a major force in championship sailing and regattas worldwide.

early here under the protection of the bishops of Stavanger and the islands have many churches. The 12th-century **Utstein Kloster**  on **Mosterøy** makes a beautiful setting for concerts (open May–Oct, closed Mon; entrance fee).

The many lighthouses are not only landmarks for islanders and seafarers but make excellent bird-watching sites. The waters around these peaceful islands are a sea kingdom for sailors with enough coastline to give every boat a bay to itself and many yacht harbours. Most of the island grocers also provide boat services, and it is easy to hire rowing boats and small craft with outboard engines.

Following chemical analysis, it has been confirmed that the copper used to cover New York's Statue of Liberty came from one of the old Visnes mines on the island of Karmøy.

In the northeast highlands of Rogaland the fjords, lakes and rivers are rich in fish and fine for sailing and canoeing. All these inland, eastern areas of Rogaland have good cross-country skiing tracks in winter and excellent Alpine slopes.

Among the best holiday areas is the Suldal district, stretching from Sand on the Sandsfjorden, along the Suldalslågen River – where the rushing waters have produced large salmon. At the Sand end of Suldalslågen is **Laksestudioet**  (open mid-June–mid-Aug daily 10am–6pm; mid-Aug–mid-Sept daily noon–4pm; entrance fee; tel: 52 79 72 84), an observation studio built under a waterfall where visitors look through a large window at the salmon resting before their next leap up the fish ladder. Where river meets lake is **Kolbeinstveit Museum** (Rural Museum; open June–Aug Tues–Sun 11am–4pm; entrance fee; tel: 52 79 72 84) with a 13th-century farm, Guggedalsloftet Bygdetun.

Back to the coast

BELOW: Utstein Kloster (cloister) on Mosterøy.

The sea route to **Bergen** is a popular way to see the coast. By taking an express boat (a cross between a catamaran and a hydrofoil) you can drop off at any of the harbour stops and stay a night or a week according to your whim. Karmøy,

the island at the south of the outer islands chain, is big enough to merit its own boat service, which goes to Skudeneshavn in the south, an idyllic old port with white, wooden houses along narrow streets. The north of the island is linked to the mainland just south of **Haugesund** , the first sizeable coastal town north of Stavanger. Haugesund has long been a centre for fishing, shipping and farming. Today its harbour is filled with pleasure boats; the town has also become a festival and congress centre and host to the International Trad Jazz Festival and the Norwegian Film Festival (both in Aug; Tourist Office tel: 52 73 43 00).

Map on pages 174–175

Stavanger

The sea has blessed **Stavanger** ⑰, Norway's oil capital and fourth-largest city; as one source of prosperity waned, another arose. It has taken the city's ships and citizens round the world and has in turn brought foreigners to Stavanger. Today, nearly one in ten of its 108,000 inhabitants was born abroad. This is a truly cosmopolitan city, international restaurants abound and in the fish market and the fruit and flower market nearby you will hear many many languages.

In the 19th and early 20th centuries, Stavanger was the principal port of embarkation for the great waves of Norwegian emigration to the United States, the history of which is documented at **Det Norske Utvandrersenteret** (Emigration Centre; open daily; free). In midsummer the centre stages the Emigration Festival with exhibitions, concerts, folk dancing and a crafts market. The highlight of the festival is the re-enactment of the 1825 sailing of the *Restauration*, the 38-ton sloop that carried the first 52 emigrants across the Atlantic.

The Stavanger *siddis* (colloquialism for a person from Stavanger, a contraction of "citizen" in English) claim to be the oldest true Norwegians, tracing

The Anglo-Norman cathedral at Stavanger dates from the 12th century.

BELOW: the harbour at Stavanger.

The Heroes of Telemark

The most celebrated act of resistance in Norway during World War II was the sabotage of the Vemork heavy water plant at Rjukan, in Telemark, in February 1943. No visitor to Rjukan, dwarfed and darkened by mountains all round, could fail to be awed by the audacity of the saboteurs. More importantly, the production of heavy water in the plant, if it had not been stopped, could conceivably have aided German development of an atomic bomb.

The operation was originally planned for a joint force of Norwegian volunteers and British commandos in two towed gliders. It ended disastrously when both gliders and one of the aircraft towing them crashed 160 km (100 miles) from Rjukan.

The next attempt was an all-Norwegian affair. "Gunnerside" was the code name for six men who had been trained in England.

They parachuted onto a frozen lake where they joined up with "Swallow", an advance party on the ground.

They skied to the ridge above Rjukan for the perilous descent on foot and slithered down, up to their waists in snow. Just after midnight, the covering party took up positions while the six-man demolition team cut a chain on the gates and crept forward to the basement of the concrete building where the most vital equipment and the heavy water storage tanks were located. All agreed that no lights would be carried; weapons would be unloaded and anyone captured would take his own life.

The best way in appeared to be a funnel carrying cables and piping. Two went through it. The solitary Norwegian guard was astonished but agreed to lead them to vital components. "I had placed half the charges in position when there was a crash of broken glass behind me," one of the pair wrote later. The other members of the team, not realising that their leaders had managed to get in, had decided to smash in through a window. With the rest of the charges laid, the six began a rapid withdrawal. The party had only gone a few yards when there was what members later variously described as "a cataclysmic explosion" and "a tiny, insignificant pop".

Five members of the parachute team reached Sweden after a 400-km (250-mile) journey on skis in indescribably difficult conditions; the sixth stayed on for another year. Of the Swallow party, Claus Helberg had the liveliest time. He was chased through the mountains by German soldiers, but escaped. Then he fell over a cliff and broke an arm. The next day he walked into a German patrol but had a good enough story to be taken to a hotel to await treatment. Most of the hotel guests (but not the injured Norwegian) were turned out of their rooms to make way for Reichskommissar Joseph Terboven (the Nazi who ruled Norway). Later, and through no fault of his own, he was bundled along with the remaining guests "into a bus and sent off to the Grini concentration camp". Helberg jumped from the bus. Later, he turned up in Britain, reporting for further duties. ❑

LEFT: Kirk Douglas played a saboteur in the 1965 film *The Heroes of Telemark*.

their lines to the Battle of Hafrsfjord. This decisive battle that first united the country under King Harald I Hårfagre, *c*.880, took place at a bay just southwest of the city. On the shore there is a monument to the event, **Sverd i fjell**, three larger-than-life Viking swords seemingly thrust into bedrock.

Map on pages 174–175

The heart of modern Stavanger is the area around **Breiavatnet**, the small lake in the middle of the city, near the **Domkirken** (cathedral). Work began on the cathedral in 1125 in the Anglo-Norman style. Massive interior pillars give it a feeling of austere strength and contrast with the elegant arches of the chancel. One of the finest pieces is the ornate 16th-century pulpit by Andrew Smith.

Northwest of the cathedral are the winding cobbled streets and old timber houses of **Gamle Stavanger** (Old Stavanger), one of the most coveted places to live in the town.

Around 1870, as fishing and shipping were in decline, the fishermen turned their attention to *brisling* (small herring), which were cured and canned in the town and sent as Norwegian "sardines" all over the world. Stavanger thrived on sardines through the 1950s. Today, **Hermetikkmuseet** (Canning Museum; open June–Aug daily 11am–4pm; Sept–May Sun only 11am–4pm; entrance fee; tel: 51 84 27 00) is a reminder of the former smell of money.

Violas growing wild by the roadside in southern Norway.

In 1966, the city became the base for oil exploration in the North Sea. The black gold has brought prosperity to Stavanger – the city is second only to Saudi Arabia in oil exports. Visit the interactive **Norsk Oljemuseum** (Norwegian Petroleum Museum; open May–Aug daily 10am–7pm; Sept–Apr daily 10am–5pm; entrance fee; tel: 51 93 93 00) for an insight into this source of energy. Sadly, not all advances come without their disasters: in the suburb of **Kvernevik** the **Alexander Kielland Minnesmerke** (monument) commemorates the loss of 123 lives when the Alexander Kielland offshore oil platform capsized in 1980.

BELOW: sardines, once the lifeblood of Stavanger.

Hordaland

Hordaland county includes two of the country's prime natural attractions: **Hardangervidda**, the central mountain plateau at 1,300 metres (4,500 ft) above sea level and **Hardangerfjorden**, which gave its name to Norway's national musical instrument, the eight-stringed Hardanger fiddle, and provided inspiration for the composer Edvard Grieg (1843–1907), and the violinist Ole Bull (1810–80). Among these mountains and fjords, Grieg and Bull travelled on foot and horse, absorbing the old melodies of the land. Like the visitors of today, they came to Hardanger for its waterfalls, for the secret beauty of smaller fjords that lead almost to the plateau above, and for glaciers and mountains that rarely lose their snowcaps, contrasted with orchards lining the fjordside.

In days gone by, the fjords provided West Norway's main transport arteries, and **Utne** ⑱ was an important junction between east and west. Two establishments there that sum up Hardanger life over the past centuries are the **Hardanger Folkemuseum** (open daily; entrance fee), and the **Utne Hotel**, founded in 1722, the oldest hotel in Norway still in operation.

A ferry service connects Utne with **Kinsarvik** ⑲ on the east side of Sørfjorden, an arm of the

Map
on pages
174–175

*Edvard Grieg used to
visit a small "hytte"
poised on the edge of
Hardangerfjorden,
near the village of
Ullensvang, where
with piano and
writing desk at hand,
he would compose
surrounded by the
beauty of the
Norwegian fjords.*

BELOW: Heddal
Stave Church.
RIGHT: dramatic
Hordaland fjord.

Hardangerfjord. Heading northeast on National Highway 13, you'll find a beautiful stretch of water, Eidfjorden. It cuts far into the dramatic landscape that includes **Skykkjedalsfossen ⑳**, Norway's highest waterfall.

Hang-gliding to skiing

If you loop back northwest, crossing Eidfjord by ferry and continuing on Highway 13, you come to **Voss ㉑**, which lies next to a lake, Vangsvatnet, in the middle of rich farmland. The Voss *kommune* (district) makes full use of its surroundings to attract visitors. In summer they come for touring, fjord excursions, mountain walking, parachuting, hang-gliding and paragliding from Hangurfjell, and fishing and watersports on Vangsvatnet. In winter, everything changes and Voss becomes one of the best centres for Alpine and cross-country skiing.

The top station of the cable car up Hangurfjell at 610 metres (2,000 ft) gives one of the best prospects of Voss in its bowl-shaped valley. The town has long been a centre for artists and musicians, and their monuments are scattered around. It is one of the best places to hear the Hardanger fiddle and see the old dances performed in beautiful costumes. On the main street is a shop where you can buy the ornate silver belts and jewellery that go with the traditional Norwegian costume.

Around Bergen and north

From Voss the E16 highway or the train take you to **Bergen ㉒** *(see page 185)*. Bergen's islands are linked so closely together that sometimes it is hard to realise that you have crossed water, but those such as **Askøy** and **Osterøy** to the north of the city have their own character, and the area round the Bjørnafjorden (Bear Fjord) to the south is particularly mild and green.

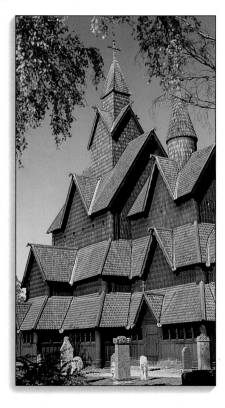

The long narrow island of **Sotra ㉓** shelters Bergen from the North Sea. It is a good base for sea canoeing in and out of the small offshore islands and rocks and, in good weather, as far as the open sea to combine canoeing with ocean fishing. In any case, shelter is never far away.

North of Bergen is **Nordhordland**, a district of islands that stretches as far north as Sognefjorden. Today, fish farming is the prime livelihood and the region exports salmon and trout all round the world. Fish farmers are now attempting to rear cod, halibut and other species. Some fish farms are open to the public. There is good sea fishing for cod and coalfish, and rosy-coloured trout inhabit many of the lakes. Diving and sub-aqua fishing, as well as treasure hunting, are easy in these transparent waters. Oil is a modern, though not conflicting, industry in this area with the Mongstad refinery illuminated at night.

To the north and most remote of all is the island of **Fedje ㉔**, an important navigation point for many centuries with two 19th-century lighthouses still in use today. Norwegian maritime rules insist that all ships must carry a Norwegian pilot, which here is vital, as tankers serving the Mongstad refinery navigate through the ever-changing waters. ❑

BERGEN

Gateway to the fjords, mountains and islands, Norway's western seaport has a relaxed atmosphere, stunning setting and vibrant cultural life

Map on page 186

Should you tell a Bergenser that your spouse or a good friend hails from the city, the spontaneous response may be "how fortunate". Mirth is the currency of life in Bergen, humour among its better-known exports. A Bergenser wants you to laugh at a local joke, but seldom forewarns you that in laughing you might find yourself caught in a mental mousetrap.

During the city's official 900th anniversary celebrations in 1970, King Olav V visited an archaeological excavation and asked Councilman Knut Tjonneland "How old is the city, really?" "That depends, your majesty," replied Tjonneland, "on the amounts appropriated for further excavation."

Although Bergen is said to have been founded in AD 1070 by the Viking king, Olav Kyrre, the city is probably older. Recent archaeological finds have dated the earliest settlements to 50 BC or earlier. The name Bergen derives from the old Norse *Bjørgvin*, still the name of the diocese.

International connections

Surrounded by seven mountains, Bergen is now a major port with 10 km (6 miles) of dockside. Until the railway eastwards over the high mountain plateau to Oslo was opened in November 1909, Bergen was isolated from the rest of Norway. Scotland by ship was closer than Oslo, England less distant than Copenhagen. As the western-most city in Scandinavia, Bergen soon became a crossroads of the north and, in the 13th century, the capital of a united Norway. Its favourable location with respect to the other ports of Europe drew Hanseatic tradesmen, who established a commercial community at the harbour.

Fullriggers plied the port, with peak traffic in 1644, when more than 400 ships docked from Scotland alone. Many current everyday objects first came to Norway on ships docking here – not least wallpaper, which first appeared in the late 17th century in the homes of ships' captains who plied the Oriental trade routes. With nine centuries of maritime tradition, it is hardly surprising that most "real" Bergensers have their roots elsewhere. Composer Edvard Grieg's family of diplomats, writers and musicians, for example, is an offspring of the Scottish McGregor clan.

Street and place names ring the register of central European origins. Even the crisp Bergen dialect bears the indelible stamp of international influence. To most Norwegians, an Englishman is an *engelskmann*, but to the Bergenser, an *englender*, from the German *Engländer*. A parade in Bergen is a *prosesjon*, from the English "procession"; the rest of Norway says *tog*.

Individuality prevails. Edvard Grieg was a Bergenser, a self-professed misfit at the 130-year-old Tanks

LEFT: shopfronts in Bryggen.
BELOW: selling fish in Bergen's famous fish market.

School, where he was known as Pupil No 139. Yet, today, annual summer concerts attract music lovers from all over the world to his home, **Troldhaugen**, 8 km (5 miles) south of the city (open May–Sept daily 9am–6pm; Oct–Apr times vary; entrance fee; tel: 55 92 29 92), and the **Grieghallen** ❶ music hall is renowned in Europe as the home of one of the world's oldest orchestras, Harmonien, founded in 1765, as well as of the annual Bergen Music Festival.

Most of the time, the city's backdrop is the glacial quiet of the mountains, but music, one is frequently reminded, is very much a part of its heritage. "Rat-a-tat-tat, rat-a-tat-tat." The sound pierces the mind. It's the **Buekorps**, an organisation for 10–20-year-old boys. They're easily recognised by their natty tunics and tasselled tam-o'-shanter caps dating from the 1850s, when the organisation was founded in emulation of the home guards, then the backbone of the country's defence. From mid-April until 17 May, when the boys march in formation in the annual Constitution Day parade, they practise before going to school, which makes early morning sleep a rarity.

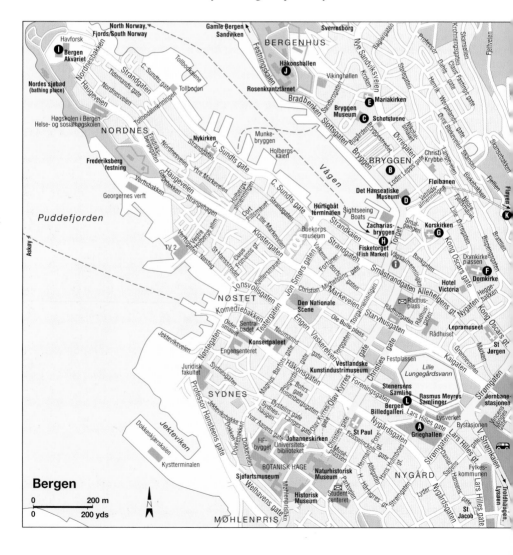

Water, water...

The Gulf Stream blesses Bergen with a benign climate and a harbour that is ice-free year round. But it also brings rain, some 2,250 mm (89 inches), making Bergen the country's wettest city. A local saying holds that "*I Bergen by, går alle med paraply*" ("In Bergen town, everyone carries an umbrella"). In other parts of the world, in other parts of Norway, teenagers refuse to carry umbrellas no matter how wet the weather. In Bergen, they are customary confirmation gifts.

Map on page 186

Reminders of the city's seafaring tradition abound. The magnificently preserved full-rigged *Statsraad Lehmkuhl*, named after Christopher Lehmkuhl, a Bergenser and a man of the sea who ultimately became a cabinet minister, has her home port in the city. Today, Bergen is a port of call for cruise ships heading to and from the fjords. As the American movie producer Woody Allen said, "There is enough scenery for a dozen films." Quite rightly, the city calls itself the capital of fjord country.

Moreover, many of the Hanseatic **Bryggen** ❸ buildings remain – a film set in themselves, meticulously preserved and listed as a UNESCO World Heritage Site. A walk through Bryggen is a step back in time, to before the Reformation. Here are galleries, craft shops, fashion boutiques and eating places, interspersed with sailmakers, a freight company and a scrap metal dealer.

King Harald Harfegre sculpture at Bryggens Museum.

The earliest archaeological remains are in **Bryggens Museum** ❻ (open May–Aug daily 10am–5pm; Sept–Apr Mon–Fri 11am–3pm, Sat noon–3pm, Sun noon–4pm; entrance fee; tel: 55 58 80 10). Guides from the museum conduct tours through the row of Hansa houses and warehouses that line Bryggen. These were built after the great fire of 1702, which destroyed many buildings. One key to understanding the Hansa merchants' way of life is to visit the **Hanseatiske Museum** ❼ (open June–Aug daily 9am–5pm; Sept–May daily 11am–2pm; entrance fee).

Nearby is the oldest building still in use in the city, **Mariakirken** ❺ (St Mary's Church), built in the early 12th century and justly proud of its rich baroque pulpit. The other medieval churches to survive the periodic fires are the present **Domkirke** ❺ (cathedral) and **Korskirken** ❻, both of which merit a visit.

BELOW: statue of the violinist Ole Bull.

Fish for sale

To buy fish year-round in the open-air **Fisketorget** ❽ (Fish Market) on the nearby harbour is to walk in and out of a continuous conversation. Fishmongers from as far afield as Asia ward their solid masonry tanks teeming with live cod or crawling with crustaceans. To the Bergenser, a fresh fish is one with the tail still flipping.

Bergen's shopping centre is situated south of the Fish Market around **Torgalmenningen**, a broad, traffic-free street where many of the best shops are to be found. Crowded in summer, these thoroughfares, known as *almenning*, were deliberately built wide to prevent flames from spreading to the opposite side of the street.

The view from the Nordnes peninsula over the town to the mountain of Fløyen is characterised by the contrast between the green woodland, blue sea and the mainly white-painted wooden houses. At the point of the peninsula is **Bergen Akvariet** ❾ (Aquarium;

The summer home of Edvard Grieg (1843–1907) at Troldhaugen.

BELOW:
Bergen, seen from Fløyen mountain.

open May–Sept daily 9am–8pm; Oct–Apr daily 10am–6pm; entrance fee; tel: 55 55 71 71), one of the most extensive collections of sea life in Europe.

Historic highs

Håkonshallen ❶ (open mid-May–Aug daily 10am–4pm; Sept–mid-May noon–3pm; entrance fee; tel: 55 31 60 67), northwest of Bryggen, is an imposing Gothic festival hall built in 1261. It is arguably the best example of middle-age profane architecture remaining in Scandinavia. In it resides the fierce pride of the Bergenser. During World War II, Håkonshallen was nearly levelled to the ground when the *Voorbode*, a Dutch ship carrying German munitions, blew up in the harbour. The explosion flung parts of the ship 25 km (16 miles) from town and killed or injured its crew, dozens of Russian prisoner dock workers and more than 5,000 townspeople. One of the *Voorbode's* anchors still lies where it hit the ground, on **Fløyen mountain** ❹, some 300 metres (1,000 ft) higher than where the ship had been docked. A small park has been built around the anchor. Stand there, and you can tell the true Bergenser among the many elderly who pass by on their Sunday strolls: they're the ones who doff their hats.

A funicular, **Fløibanen** (open daily 7.30am–11pm, Sat from 8am, Sun from 9am; May–Aug closes at midnight) connects the city centre to Fløyen mountain and panoramic views of Bergen. At the top there is a restaurant and the start of eight marked walking routes. Concerts are held here on summer evenings.

Lakeside galleries

Bergen has several strong art collections, mostly centred on Lille Lungegårdsvann, an octagonal-shaped lake near Grieghallen. Here are the **Bergen Billedgalleri**

L (Municipal Art Gallery) with a large collection of Norwegian painting; the **Rasmus Meyers Samlinger** (Rasmus Meyer Collection), which also specialises in Norwegian art, including Edvard Munch; and the **Stenersens Samling**, with work by Munch, Picasso and Klee among others (all open June–Aug daily 11am–5pm; Sept–May closed Mon; entrance fee; tel: 55 56 80 00).

The outgoing nature, taste for trade and concern for others typical of Bergensers are best reflected in Thoralf Rafto (1922–86). Before the fall of communism, Rafto dedicated his energies to awakening the West to the human rights abuses in the East, particularly of Soviet Jews. An annual Rafto Prize for Human Rights commemorates his work; fittingly it is administered at **Raftohuset – Menneskerettighetenes Hus** (Rafto Human Rights House, Menneskerettighetenes Plass 1; open Mon–Fri 9am–5pm; tel: 55 21 09 30).

Excursions from Bergen

Not to be missed is the **Fantoft Stave Church**, 8 km (5 miles) south of the city in Paradis (open mid-May–Sept daily 10.30am–2pm, 2.30–6pm; entrance fee; tel: 55 28 07 10). It was built around 1150 and is one of the oldest wooden buildings in Europe. In 1992, it burned down, but has since been completely restored.

A short ferry ride across Lysefjorden brings you to the beautiful island of **Lysøen** (Island of Light) and the onion-domed summer residence of the violin virtuoso Ole Bull (1810–80). Bull called the villa, built in 1873, his "Little Alhambra" and often invited fellow musicians and artists. In summer, the old music room resounds to the music Bull played here with violin recitals and small ensembles (open mid-May–Aug Mon–Sat noon–4pm, Sun 11am–5pm; ferry from Buena quay; entrance fee; tel: 56 30 90 77). ❑

Map on page 186

TIP

The Hotel Terminus, across Kaaes Gate from Bergen's railway station, is known for putting on one of the country's most sumptuous breakfast tables.

BELOW: National Day celebrations.

THE HEART OF NORWAY

Central Norway encompasses a remarkable landscape from the shimmering fjords of the west across the peaks, plateaux and valleys that have inspired great writers and composers

Map on pages 174–175

The heartland of Norway is the upper part of the southern bulge of the country, extending from above Oslo and Bergen to below Trondheim. The area encompasses the highest mountains in Scandinavia, and freshwater lakes and watercourses abound. To the east there are two long valleys, Østerdalen (literally "Easterly Valley") and **Gudbrandsdalen**, orientated roughly parallel to the border with Sweden and knifing through the high interior cordillera to provide the major north–south land transport arteries. In the middle there are the lofty peaks and high plateau of the Rondane and Jotunheimen ranges, and to the west lies the coast with its fjords and archipelago in waters plied by boats since the land was first settled. Indeed, this part of the country embodies the *fjord og fjell* (fjord and mountain) landscape so deeply etched in the Norwegian ethos.

Lake Mjøsa, a slender jewel

The glaciers that gouged the fjords also worked the inland and left **Mjøsa ㉕**, a jewel of a lake. Its southern end is at Minnesund just north of Eidsvoll, and its northern tip is at Lillehammer, 101 km (63 miles) to the northwest. It's slender – only 15 km (9 miles) at its broadest – and like a fjord, deep – up to 449 metres (1,472 ft). Around Mjøsa lies some of the most arable land in the country, and its shores greet undulating countryside with large farms backed by densely forested hills. One of the best ways to enjoy the lake and its surroundings is a trip on the *Skibladner*, the world's oldest paddlewheel steamship still in service, named after a sailing ship of Nordic mythology. In summer, the *Skibladner* carries up to 230 passengers on excursions six days a week; contact any tourist information office in the region or her home port at **Hamar ㉖** for schedules (tel: 61 14 40 80).

Hamar was a medieval centre of Roman Catholicism in Norway and the seat of a bishop. It is still a bishopric, but only ruins remain of its imposing cathedral, now protected under a glass canopy at **Hedemarksmuseet og Domkirkeodden** (Hedemark Museum and Cathedral Point; open mid-May–mid-Sept daily 10am–4pm; entrance fee). In the 19th century Hamar became a railway junction with a locomotive works. The works are gone, but there's a reminder: **Jernbanemuseet** (National Museum of Railway Transport; open May–Sept; entrance fee), with stations, railway buildings and vintage rolling stock. There are regular excursions on a narrow-gauge steam train.

Fertile local lands long ago led to cities and towns producing comestibles. Most stimulating, perhaps, is that seven of the country's eight distilleries are located hereabouts. One of them, **Løten Brænderi** (guided

LEFT: Ålesund abounds with Art Nouveau buildings. **BELOW:** legendary Norwegian troll.

Lillehammer's coat of arms reflects a national pastime.

tours; entrance fee; tel: 62 59 49 10), at **Løten ㉗**, 18 km (11 miles) east of Hamar, is open to the public. A fascinating one-man show (Fri, Sat & Sun 6pm, entrance fee) recounts the history of the distillery and the production of *akevitt*, the Norwegian liquor made from potato and caraway seeds. Also worth visiting on the same site is **Løiten Lys** (open Mon–Fri 10am–8pm; Sat–Sun noon–6pm), a candle factory with a display of candles in every conceivable shape and size.

Two weeks of fame

Lillehammer ㉘ is best known in the world of winter sport as the venue of the 1994 Olympic Winter Games. Many of the Olympic facilities still stand, such as the ice event rinks at Hamar and Gjøvik. Other Olympic facilities include a new Alpine ski area at nearby **Hafjell**, and some 500 km (300 miles) of cross-country skiing tracks. The cross-country arena now is the finish for the annual trans-mountain Birkebeiner race, one of the world's oldest citizens' races.

For summer visitors, the biggest attraction is the open-air museum, **Maihaugen** (open June–Aug daily 9am–6pm; May & Sept daily 10am–5pm; entrance fee), with some 120 vintage buildings brought into the 40-hectare (100-acre) site from all over Gudbrandsdalen, including a stave church and two farms. The museum was the life work of Anders Sandvig. He came to Lillehammer in 1885 suffering from tuberculosis and with a life expectancy of just two years. Whether or not it was his interest in the museum he founded in 1887 which kept him alive, he lived another 65 years. The **Norsk Vegmuseum** (Road Transport Museum) at **Fåberg**, to the north of Lillehammer on the E6 highway, has everything from horse-drawn sleighs to modern cars (open mid May–Aug daily 10am–6pm; Sept–mid May Tues–Sun 10am–3pm; free).

BELOW: the historic copper-mining town of Røros.

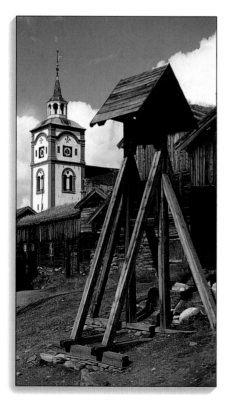

RØROS

Røros, a UNESCO World Heritage site on the E30 north of Alvdal, was until recently the archetypal company town, with life and society revolving around the mining business. Isolated, exposed, nearly 600 metres (2,000 ft) above sea level and surrounded by mountains, it owed its existence to copper, which was mined here from 1644 to 1972. Now the inhabitants make their living from sawmills, furniture making, wool processing and reindeer meat, as well as tourism. It is a harsh spot; the lowest temperatures in the whole of Norway are often recorded here.

By some miracle Røros escaped the fires that so often laid waste to the wooden buildings in Norwegian towns, and it has retained much of its mining town atmosphere. The wealthy folk lived to the east of the river in Bergmannsgate, while the miners had to make do with the area beneath the slagheaps and the smelter. Picturesque log houses remain, while the crooked houses in Slaggveien are particularly interesting. The most noticeable feature is the stone church, "the pride of the mining town", which was dedicated in 1784. Paintings of clergymen and mining officials decorate the interior. The smelter was the focal point of the town and has been restored as a museum.

Østerdalen

To the east of Mjøsa lake lies **Østerdalen**, carved through the mountains by the Glomma – the country's longest river – stretching 617 km (383 miles). The valley carries one of the north–south railway lines as well as National Highway 3. It starts at **Elverum** ㉙ in the south and continues northward for 250 km (150 miles) becoming broader and more open further north. Just south of **Aursunden**, one of the source lakes for the Glomma River, lies the old copper-mining town of **Røros** ㉚ *(see box, page 192)*, a UNESCO World Heritage site.

Gudbrandsdalen

To the west of Østerdalen lies **Gudbrandsdalen**, the country's second-longest valley, cut by the River Lågen flowing south to Lillehammer. Perhaps because mountains surround it, the valley has a long tradition of folk dancing and folk music and is known for its wood carving and rose painting, sold by handicraft shops in the villages.

For Norwegians everywhere, as well as for curious visitors, Gudbrandsdalen is best remembered as the place where the indigenous Norwegian *geitost* (whey cheese made from goat's milk) was first made in the mid-19th century. The real variety, *ekte geitost*, made entirely of goat's milk, is still produced in the valley and elsewhere in the country. Tribute to the original cheese is paid in the name of *Gudbrandsdalost* (Gudbrandsdalen cheese), made from 10 percent goat's milk and 90 percent cow's milk, the cheese most likely to adorn all breakfast tables, from humble bed and breakfasts to the best of hotels.

About midway along the valley lies **Dombås** ㉛, a principal rail and road junction just southwest of the **Dovrefjell** (Dovre Mountains). The Dovre

The unsung hero of the Gudbrandsdalen valley is Anne Haav, the "budeia" (farm maiden) who first made the uniquely Norwegian "geitost" (goat's cheese) in the 19th century.

BELOW: canoeing is a popular pastime in summer.

A local hazard for drivers: elk on the road.

summits are lofty, but even the highest, **Snøhetta**, at 2,286 metres (7,498 ft), is lower than the peaks of the Jotunheimen. Yet the Dovre Mountains have a place in the national psyche like no other, embodied in the saying about the strength of the country, *"Enig og tro til Dovre Faller"* ("United we stand till Dovre falls"). Fittingly, the name Dombås derives from *Domba*, the name of a river, and *ås*, meaning "mountain ridge".

Home of the Giants

South of Dombås is an extensive area of peak and plateau. The Norwegian mountains are made for walking. As explorer Paul Belloni Du Chaillu observed in *Land of the Midnight Sun* (1881): "The difference between the mountains of Switzerland and Norway is this: those of the former are much higher, more bold and pointed, and sharp in the outlines of their thousand forms. On the other hand, the Norwegian mountains have a grave and sombre character, appearing like a gigantic stony wave, with a peak here and there, impressing more by their vastness than their height and ruggedness."

This "gigantic stony wave" has many hiking trails marked by red letter Ts painted on rocks and cairns. They meander between *hytta* (lodges), mostly above the timberline, between 950 and 1,600 metres (3,100–5,250 ft) above sea level, and the highest summits are around 2,400 metres (7,900 ft). Hence the lack of mention in mountaineering anthologies, where sheer elevation is the criterion. Therein lies part of the secret: you can enjoy the high-altitude experience without needing high-altitude lungs.

Moreover, in summer you can travel to the heart of the range in only a few steps, by boarding one of the passenger launches that ply the waters of lakes

BELOW: carved ravens offer protection over this household in Stordalselva.

Gjende and Bygdin. That joy has long been acknowledged by urban natives. In the late 19th century, the composer Edvard Grieg remarked that "when I contemplate the possibility of a future visit to the [Jotunheimen] mountains, I shudder with joy and expectation, as if it were a matter of hearing Beethoven's Tenth Symphony." That attraction was in part why Grieg wrote the incidental music for Henrik Ibsen's play *Peer Gynt*, based on a traditional legend of Gudbrandsdalen, in which braggart Peer leaps astride a reindeer, from a knife ridge into the lake below. The knife ridge and the lake are real: **Besseggen** and **Gjende** in the Jotunheimen, literally "Home of the Giants". The reindeer are equally real, as herds of them still graze here. One reminder of them is the reindeer pattern on the Gjende brand biscuits, sold throughout the country.

Out of this world

Accessibility is another allure of these wilderness areas. To the south of the Jotunheimen lies the hamlet of **Finse** ❷ the highpoint at 1,225 metres (4,000 ft) on the Oslo–Bergen railway line. Its high street is the station platform; trains are the local traffic, as there are neither cars nor roads. It's a small speck in a seemingly boundless expanse of ice and snow. So remote yet accessible is this place that it was chosen for the filming of the initial sequences of *The Empire Strikes Back*, the *Star Wars* film depicting battles fought on the Ice Planet Holth.

Finse has the country's largest *hytta* for hikers and skiers, as well as a full-service hotel, as suits its location as the junction between two giant trail networks, north to the **Jotunheimen** and south to **Hardangervidda** (Hardanger Plateau). As the crow flies, the trail networks stretch 225 km (140 miles) to the north and 100 km (60 miles) to the south, and in all have more than 5,000 km

Map on pages 174–175

One of the best views in the region is from Besseggen in the Jotunheimen Mountains, the ridge immortalised by Henrik Ibsen in his play "Peer Gynt".

BELOW: finding warmth in a cosy snow hole.

(3,000 miles) of T-marked hiking trails and at Easter-time, some 2,000 km (1,240 miles) of ski trails, marked by poles in the snow.

To the north and east of the Jotunheimen, on the other side of the Gudbrandsdalen valley, lies the **Rondane** range, which offers some of the country's finest hiking and cross-country skiing. Here the trails are not steep, the peaks not as high, the walks not as long and the *hytta* not as numerous as in the Jotunheimen. But the connection to the Gudbrandsdalen legend remains, as there is a Peer Gynt *hytta* here. Moreover, to the south and on the west flank of the valley there is a **Peer Gyntveien** (Peer Gynt Way) which leads from Gausdal north of Lillehammer to Golå south of Vinstra. A hike or drive along it affords views of much of the central cordillera.

Easy hiking

The trails and the *hytta* reflect the Norwegian view of wilderness: it is for everyone. Pristine perhaps is the best word; only the red Ts and an occasional electric power line belie modern times. Little has changed since three English adventurers, with the pseudonyms Skipper, Essau and John, came to the Jotunheimen in the 1880s. Their subsequent book, *Three in Norway by Two of Them*, became one of the classic travelogues of the Victorian age. The remnants of their camp are carefully preserved near **Memurubu** ❸ on Lake Gjende in the Jotunheimen, one of the *hytta* that dot these wilderness areas.

The *hytta* are one of the secrets of Norwegian mountain hiking and skiing. The word has the same root as "hut" in English, but there the similarity ends. One need carry only a light sleeping bag for overnighting, because there are comfortable bunk beds in the *hytta* and meals are provided in most of them. Indeed, "full-service lodge" would be the best translation.

You need not stay at the *hytta*; many people carry packs with a full array of gear to be self-sufficient. But after a few days on the trail, or even on their first night, they camp near one of the *hytta* for a good meal and the conviviality of evenings there.

Most of the *hytta* are owned and operated by Den Norske Turistforening (DNT) and its affiliated local organisations; hence the red Ts on rocks and cairns. You need not be a DNT member to stay in a DNT *hytta*, but membership is a good investment, as the price is soon offset by the accumulated discounts on accommodation. You can join DNT at any of the *hytta* or at the head office in Oslo (tel: 22 82 28 00).

From Sogn to Nordfjord

The county of **Sogn og Fjordane** lies between the coast and the Jotunheimen mountains. Narrow fingers of water push inland from the main fjords to reach far into the mountains, and waterfalls tumble hundreds of metres into the fjords below. In the past, the terrain was impassable in winter. Today travel is easier thanks to the network of ferries, tunnels and bridges. The county is easily accessible from Bergen. Indeed, until 1918, it was named Nordre Bergenhus (Northern Bergen Province).

The **Sognefjorden** is unmatched. On both sides of it small villages cling to the land, each with its

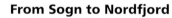

own atmosphere. **Balestrand** 🟤 has been a favourite since the 19th century and has an English church, St Olav's. A narrow side-fjord leads to **Fjærland** 🟤 near the two southernmost tongues of the **Jostedalsbreen Glacier**. Nestling at its base is the **Norsk Bremuseum** (Norwegian Glacier Museum; open Apr–Oct daily 10am–4pm; June–Aug daily 9am–7pm; entrance fee; tel: 57 69 32 88), where interactive models, displays and films provide an insight into Europe's largest glacier.

Going east from Balestrand, a short crossing takes you to **Hella** and past the glistening arc of **Kvinnfoss** (Lady's Waterfall) close to the main road. At the head of the fjord, **Sogndal** 🟤 is the centre for trade and administration. It swells considerably during term-time because it is also a centre for education, with universities and Norway's oldest folk high school.

Map on pages 174–175

Cool, green waters

In **Luster** 🟤, 25 km (15 miles) to the northeast of Sogndal, is another of Sogn's many stave churches, **Urnes Stavkirke**. Built around 1130 and believed to be the oldest stave church in Norway, it is now a UNESCO World Heritage site (open June–Aug daily 10.30am–4pm; entrance fee).

Aurlandsvangen, Flåm and Gudvangen lie along the innermost recesses of the fjord, which stretches south from the main fjord like an upside-down "Y". Not to be missed is the mountain railway from **Flåm** 🟤 which spirals up the steep mountain gorge to meet the Bergen Line at **Myrdal**.

Heading northwest from Balestrand towards **Førde** 🟤 and the coast, you cross a region of many lakes – Jølstravatnet – that penetrate the foothills of the high tops in the east and feed into the fjords in the west. One of the rivers, the

The railway from Flåm to Myrdal winds through spectacular mountain scenery.

BELOW: fjords punctuate the landscape in Sogn og Fjordane.

Jølstra, said to be one of the best salmon rivers in the area, drops precipitously before reaching Førde on **Førdefjord**. Here is **Sunnfjord Museum** (open June–Aug: Mon–Fri 10am–6pm, Sat & Sun noon–5pm; Sept–May: Mon–Fri 10am–3pm; entrance fee; tel: 57 72 19 35), a collection of 24 historic buildings.

Oddly, **Florø** ⓰, the only community in this large county big enough to be called a town, lies on the remote edge of the sea, but not so odd considering that Norway has always depended on the sea for food, trade and transport. The **Sogn og Fjordane Kystmuseet** (Coastal Museum; open all year; entrance fee; tel: 57 74 22 33) in Florø has a fine collection of old boats.

Inland along Nordfjorden

Nordfjorden is 100 km (60 miles) shorter than the Sognefjorden. With so many side-fjords, lakes and valleys it is easy to get into the mountains or make the journey up **Briksdalsbreen**, one of the most beautiful glaciers in the fjord country. Even better is that you can climb up to the base of the glacier in the two-wheeled farm carriages, *stolkjaerrer*, pulled by small sturdy, cream-coloured *fjording* (fjord horses) native to Nordfjord.

The traditional home of the *fjording* is the Eid district, centred around Nordfjordeid, where Nordfjorden proper has already divided itself into Eidsfjorden and Isefjorden. **Eid** ⓫, which is also connected to the coast by Road 15, is known for Firdariket, the seat of the last Viking chief. The town has white-painted buildings, and the church, which dates from 1849, is decorated with beautiful rose painting.

Further along you reach the Inner Nordfjorden, where the fjord system ends at Stryn, Loen and Olden, the start of three spectacular valleys stretching up to the northwest edges of the Jostedalsbreen. Nowadays, three tunnels out of the

BELOW: remote farmstead in the mountainous hinterland.

FJORD FORMATION

Fjords are found in Alaska, Canada, Chile, Greenland, New Zealand, Norway and Scotland. But nowhere are they more prominent than in Norway. A direct line along the coast measures 2,650 km (1,568 miles), but the stretch of the entire coastline, including the archipelago, is 57,260 km (33,880 miles), a third more than the distance around the earth at the equator. The coast of Norway is more jagged than any other, and Norway gave the word fjord to other languages of the world.

The fjords were formed about 100,000 years ago, during the last ice age. Glaciers gouged valleys from the land, to depths that lessened at the coast, where the ice was thinner. When the ice retreated, the sea inundated. So a typical fjord is deepest at its midpoint and far less deep at its mouth: the Sognefjord, for instance, reaches a depth of 1,244 metres (4,080 ft), but is only 158 metres (518 ft) deep at its mouth.

The fame of these fjords has made them part of the myth of science fiction. In *The Hitch-Hikers Guide to the Galaxy*, the venerable planet-builder Slartibartfast recalls "…doing the coastlines was always my favourite, used to have endless fun doing all the little fiddly bits in fjords…did you ever go to a place…I think it's called Norway?"

Stryn valley cut right through the mountain to the renowned **Geirangerfjorden** to the north. **Stryn ㊷** is known for summer skiing on the northeast of Strynsvatn, where the ground rises to Tystigbreen. Until you watch, it is hard to imagine skiers in swimsuits or shorts and T-shirts with deep tans, but there they are enjoying every moment.

Møre og Romsdal

Coastal vessels have long called at Ålesund, Molde and Kristiansund on their way to Trondheim and the north. Looking at the coastline, islands and fjord mouths on a map, it is difficult to distinguish where sea and islands end and fjords and mainland begin. Yet move inland and half the area lies above 600 metres (1,800 ft).

Ålesund ㊸ is Norway's largest fishing town. Yet it is best known for its Art Nouveau architecture, built in 1904 after fire destroyed its centre. First to the rescue came Kaiser Wilhelm II of Germany, who sent four ships laden with supplies and building materials. With help and donations from all over Europe, the people of Ålesund completed the rebuilding of their town.

Until the 1950s, fishing supported Ålesund, and *klippfisk* (traditional Norwegian split dried cod) was its principal export. But as fishing changed so did Ålesund, which added fish processing and aquaculture. Many former warehouses are now offices and restaurants, where you can try one of the more unlikely local specialities such as *bacalao*, made from boned *klippfisk*.

Bird island

To the southwest of Ålesund is **Runde ㊹**, the island that draws naturalists from around the world, as more than 200 bird species have been recorded there. One

TIP

Explore the colourful Art Nouveau town of Ålesund: guided walks depart daily from the Tourist Information Office (Rådhuset; June–Aug; tel: 70 15 76 00).

BELOW: the magnificent setting of Geirangerfjorden.

Map on pages 174–175

Detail from the marble church on the island of Giske, near Ålesund.

BELOW: Molde is the "Town of Roses".
RIGHT: at the foot of the Jostedalsbreen Glacier.

of the best ways of seeing the island is by taking a four-hour tour on boats departing from **Ulsteinvik** daily from June to August. As a bonus, the waters round the island close over myriad wrecks; in 1972, divers found a hoard of gold and silver coins on board the *Akerendam*, a Dutch vessel that sank in 1725; it was one of the largest finds of sunken treasure ever.

Roses, jazz and ocean driving

Molde ㊺, halfway along the coast from Ålesund north to Kristiansund, is part of an archipelago sheltered from the Norwegian Sea; its mild climate, lush vegetation and rose gardens earn it the title "Town of Roses". It is known at home for the might of its football team and for the annual Molde International Jazz Festival (mid-July; many free concerts; tel: 71 20 31 50).

From **Bud** on the coast west of Molde, a road leads to the **Atlanterhavsveien** (Atlantic Road) to Kristiansund, over **Averøya** ㊻, the biggest island in the area. It heads north across the rim of the ocean, so driving seems like a voyage. Averøya deserves more than the view from a car window. Archaeologists believe that this was one of the first places to be settled after the last Ice Age, and their finds include remnants of the early Fosna Culture that existed around 7000 BC.

The *klippfisk* capital

Unlike Ålesund and Molde, **Kristiansund** ㊼ has little protection from the worst the North Atlantic can do. It is right on the coast, with weather-beaten rocks pounded by the sea, yet not far inland are grassy areas and small woods. This is the *klippfisk* town, for long the biggest exporter of Norwegian dried cod. A recent census counted only 17,000 inhabitants but, because of the centuries-old links with other countries through its sailors and fishermen, and the foreign merchants who settled here, the atmosphere is cosmopolitan. Like most Norwegian towns with "Kristian" in their title, Kristiansund was named after King Christian VI. A good introduction is by *sundbåtene*, the harbour boats that for more than 100 years have linked the town's three islands.

Mellemverftet, once one of four shipyards in Vågen, is working again as a centre for preserving the craft of shipbuilding, carefully restoring the beautiful lines of traditional Norwegian boats.

Land of the trolls

Inland, the northern part of Møre og Romsdal ends in a crisscross of fjords eating into the islands and peninsulas which lead to **Trollheimen**, the "Home of the Trolls", where the mountains reach nearly 1,600 metres (5,000 ft).

This haunt of climbers and skiers is bounded by two important valleys, Surnadalen and Sunndalen, with between them the tiny Todalfjorden. Beside the latter is the surprise of the **Svinvik Arboret** ㊽ (arboretum), beautiful gardens with thousands of rhododendrons, conifers and other plants (open May–Sept; entrance fee). Despite the northern latitude, plants from all over the world grow at Svinvik, owned and run today by the University at Trondheim. ❑

NORWAY'S MOST BEAUTIFUL VOYAGE

The splendid coastal voyage from Bergen to the North Cape and beyond has long been regarded as one of the great sea journeys of the world

To travel on board the Hurtigruten (literally "swift route") steamships is to partake in what has been described as one of the world's most beautiful voyages. What began in 1891 as an idea to provide an express shipping service along the rugged Norwegian coast between Trondheim and Hammerfest has evolved into a lucrative form of tourism. Yet part of the charm is watching a working ship going about its business. Out of season, it reverts to its traditional role of carrying west-coast Norwegians, who treat it as a bus, for business and pleasure.

PORTS OF CALL

In spring and autumn, the 12-day round trip from Bergen across the Arctic Circle to the Nordkapp (North Cape) and Kirkenes lets you feast on the dramatic seasonal changes. In May, the fjord valleys are brilliantly in bloom, and the hills and the mountains of the north are still covered with snow. Returning south one meets the swift Norwegian summer marching north.

The Hurtigruten makes 34 ports of call along this ever-changing coast, some at places no bigger than a handful of houses round a harbour, others at cities such as Trondheim and Tromsø with time ashore to explore.

▷ **FULL STEAM AHEAD**
Captain Ernstsen, *M/S Nordlys*, and his crew, along with those of the other ships in the fleet, ensure generally smooth sailings in and out of the islands along the coast.

▷ **OUTWARD BOUND**
In the summer months the Hurtigruten take on the trimmings of cruise ships with dancing, film shows and day trips. Guides are on hand for hikes and vigorous climbs.

▽ **TEMPTING TREATS**
No matter what season, the meals on board offer a feast of Norwegian specialities, with abundant buffets, assorted cheeses and a mouthwatering selection of desserts.

◁ **STUNNING SCENERY**
Tranquil Trollfjorden: from fjords to open sea, fertile land to barren rock, fishing hamlets to cities, the voyage is a mix of the workaday and the spectacular.

△ **ARCHITECTURAL SIGHT**
Ishavskatedralen, the Arctic Ocean Cathedral at Tromsø, is a symbol of the north. Built in 1964, the cathedral features one of Europe's largest works of stained glass.

△ **VIEW FROM THE DECK**
With thousands of islands and skerries, mountains and glaciers, the landscape is constantly changing and no two days are alike.

◁ **NIGHT SKY**
The Northern Lights (Aurora Borealis) is a fascinating spectacle, whether a sparkling multicoloured vision or dancing white streaks.

COMMUNICATIONS REVOLUTION

Over the past century more than 70 ships have served in the Hurtigruten fleet.

These diverse vessels led a communications revolution, enabling the population and industries along the rugged Norwegian coast to keep in touch in a new way. Previously, it took three weeks in summer or five months in winter to send a letter from Trondheim to Hammerfest; the Coastal Express reduced this time to a few days.

Places such as the Lofoten Islands, Trollfjorden and the North Cape *(symbol pictured above)* became accessible to travellers who wanted to see the Midnight Sun, and so the tourist business began to grow. Nature lovers and bird-watchers are attracted by the scenery and the many bird colonies, which include puffins, kittiwakes and guillemots

As time went by, ships were built specifically with cold storage and freezer rooms, vehicle roll on/roll off capacity and conference facilities, as well as comfortable cabins.

Two companies now run 11 ships, ranging from the grand old *M/S Harald Jarl* to the *M/S Nordnorge*, built in 1997.

THE NORTHWEST COAST

North of Trondheim, Norway's religious and cultural capital, lies a beautiful but often harsh landscape that crosses the Arctic Circle into the land of the Midnight Sun

Map on page 206

The northwest coast is where Norway gets thinner, from Trondheim – a large city for its latitude and the gateway to the north, up to Bodø, which lies beyond the Arctic Circle. The land along this narrow conduit is mostly forested, with the benign influence of the Gulf Stream ensuring temperate conditions persist far to the north.

Trondheim ❶ is a name rooted in Nordic mythology: *Trond* comes from the Old Norse "*throendr*", the name of the people of the region and meaning "strong and virile", and *heim* comes from the word for habitation. It is a pleasant city, with clean air, wide streets, low buildings and a compact centre. Its relatively modest population of 151,000 swells by nearly a sixth in term-time, as this is a university town, as well as the country's leading hi-tech research centre. It is, as American sociologists have proclaimed, a most ideal city to live in.

As with all Norwegian cities, the outdoors is close at hand. Trondheim's back garden is Bymarka to the west, where **Gråkallen** (Old Man) at 520 metres (1,700 ft) high is a favourite walking and cross-country skiing area. Indeed, outdoor sports are a leading local pastime, and the city has acted as host to the World Nordic Ski Championships. The River Nidelva is known for the size of its salmon, and the fjord itself is ideal for sea fishing from boat or shore.

LEFT: overview of the city of Trondheim. **BELOW:** Nidaros Cathedral, venue for Norwegian coronations.

NIDAROS CATHEDRAL

In 997 the settlers of Nidaros could not have known, but the sheltered site they picked at the mouth of the Nid River was to become a pivotal city in Europe.

In the late 11th century, work started on a major church at Nidaros, erected over the grave of St Olav, the king who brought Christianity to the Vikings *(see page 209)*. Apparently the Pope found that fact auspicious, as he appointed an archbishop there and made the bishops of Greenland, Iceland, the Isle of Man, Orkney and the Faroe Islands, and the bishops in Norway responsible to him.

The church became a cathedral, one of the holy sites of Europe and the goal for many pilgrimages. It has become the national shrine and the venue for the coronation of Norwegian kings.

The name Nidaros endured; the cathedral is Nidarosdomen (Nidaros Cathedral). The city that grew up around it became Trondhjem, a name rooted in Nordic mythology. In January 1930, when the city celebrated its 900th anniversary, the origin of the cathedral was honoured by changing the city name to Nidaros. The re-naming triggered a debate that ended in March 1931 when the name reverted to Trondheim, with the spelling "*hjem*" amended to "*heim*" to please linguistic purists.

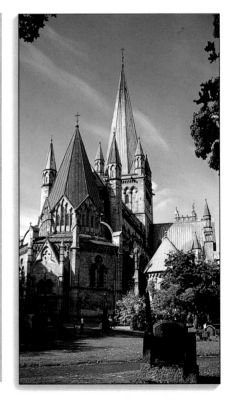

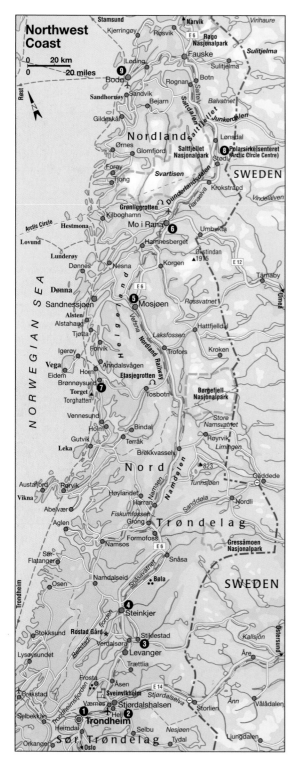

Northwest Coast

Viking city

The well-preserved buildings of the old harbour, the imposing **Nidarosdomen** (cathedral; *see box, page 205*; open daily: hours vary; entrance fee includes admission to adjacent Archbishop's Manor) and the statute of a Viking king, Olav Tryggvason, on a high pedestal in the centre of the city, belie the heritage of more than a millennium. Tryggvason founded the city in 997, and his successor, Olav Haraldsson, brought Christianity to the country (*see page 209*). It was Haraldson's martyrdom that triggered the building of the cathedral, where Norwegian kings are crowned, most recently King Harald V in 1991. The **Norwegian Crown Jewels** (open June–Aug Mon–Fri 9am–6pm, Sat 9am–2pm, Sun 1–4pm; Sept–May times vary; entrance fee) are kept in the cathedral, and the regalia for king, queen and crown prince are on display in a chapel.

Through history, the cathedral also had influence on secular life. In pre-Reformation Europe, kings would often extend the powers of the clerics to civil and mercantile matters, including the issuing of coins. At Nidaros, that happened in 1222, when young King Håkon Håkonsson issued an edict empowering Archbishop Guttorm of Nidaros to mint and circulate coins. The archbishop and his successors exercised that right until 1537, when the Reformation ousted the last archbishop. Examples of the coins struck at the archbishop's mint were found in the following centuries, then in the early 1990s archaeologists discovered the mint beneath the ruins of a building that had burned down in 1640. The mint, the oldest found in Europe, forms part of the exhibits at **Erkebispegården** (the Archbishop's Manor) next to the cathedral.

Giving cyclists a lift

Trondheim has done much to relieve traffic congestion, including implementing a toll ring round the city. Cycling is encouraged on a network of dedicated cycle paths. Yet topography challenges cycling: the flat centre is surrounded by steep hills. So in 1995, the resourceful

Map
on page
206

city built **Trampe**, the world's first bicycle lift, 130 metres (426 ft) up Brubakken hill. The lift operates like a ski tow, and cyclists pay using keycards at the bottom of the hill. Not surprisingly, the annual **Styrkeprøven** (Trial of Strength) trans-mountain bicycle race held in June starts in Trondheim. It finishes 540 km (336 miles) south, in Oslo.

And you can go to...

Some Norwegian words tempt double entendre in English, most notably the name of the village closest to Trondheim's Værnes airport. It's **Hell ❷**. Notwithstanding the derivation of the name from the Old Norse word for cavern, postcards of the railway station at Hell sell astonishingly well. So when in Trondheim, you can indeed go to Hell; it's only 33 minutes east by commuter train. The station here must be one of the most photographed in the country. In September Hell hosts an annual blues festival which attracts international stars and fans to this otherwise quiet settlement.

St Olav's battleground

Many European countries claim histories highlighted by a decisive medieval battle. For Norway, it's the **Battle of Stiklestad** on 29 July 1030, some 36 years before England's momentous Battle of Hastings. Unlike Hastings, which enabled the winning Normans to conquer the country, at **Stiklestad ❸** it was the loser who ultimately won. The forces of King Canute of Denmark and England were victorious and King Olav Haraldson of Norway was slain. Olav was later to become a saint *(see page 209)*. Stiklestad, located east of the E6 highway about 100 km (60 miles) north of Trondheim, is the venue for the annual

Northern road signs appear in Norwegian and Finnish.

BELOW: Bodø, port of call for the coastal steamers.

Map on page 206

Olsokspelet (St Olav's Play) performed every July in an open-air amphitheatre during the St Olav Festival. A 12th-century church marks the spot where King Olav died, and a museum (St Olav's Kulturhus) chronicles the events.

Trade essential

Despite their reputation as marauders, the Vikings were principally farmers and traders who settled and worked the land wherever they went. **Steinkjer ❹**, the first sizeable town north of Trondheim, reflects this. Its name comes from the Old Norse word for a river dam built to trap fish, and indeed in Viking times it was a trading centre. In 1857 it became an export port for timber and agricultural produce, a status that underscores the comparatively mild climate of the region, as here at 64°N the land is fertile and forests abound.

North of Steinkjer, the railway and the E6 highway follow the sheltered Namdalen valley to **Mosjøen ❺** at the head of the Vefsnfjorden and then to **Mo i Rana ❻** at the head of Ranafjorden. The word *Mo*, which means sand or gravel flats, is a common place name in Norway. Consequently, Mo at the head of Ranafjorden is called Mo i Rana to distinguish it from other towns named Mo. As for Steinkjer, trade triggered the first settlement of Mosjøen and Mo i Rana. Today the towns support heavy industries, starting in the mid-1950s with the **Norsk Jernverk** iron works at Mo i Rana and **Mosjøen Aluminumverk** aluminium plant at Mosjøen. From a business viewpoint, the locations of these industries in small, northern towns may be questioned. They are there as part of the government's efforts to provide jobs that keep people in the region. A similar effort is the more recent centralisation of the nine principal government registers at **Brønnøysund ❼**, on the coast south of Mosjøen. If, say, you take out a loan to buy a car anywhere in Norway, the relevant details will be registered at Brønnøysund.

The Arctic Circle at 66°N is defined not by temperature, but by light. It is the latitude at which the sun is above the horizon at noon on 21 June. At Bødo, the "Mørketid" (Arctic Night) lasts from 15 to 29 December.

BELOW: the bus runs whatever the weather.

Crossing the Arctic Circle

Most people experience an inexplicable thrill as they cross the **Polarsirkel** (Arctic Circle). You cannot see it, but it's there. Perhaps the reason is celestial: unlike the Equator, set by geometry, or the International Date Line, drawn by timekeepers, the Arctic Circle delineates the southern boundary of a different sort of world, the land of The Midnight Sun.

The only building in this landscape is **Polarsirkelsenteret ❽** (Arctic Circle Centre; open May, June & Aug daily 9am–8pm; July daily 8am–10pm; Sept daily 10am–6pm; free). Situated on the Circle, alongside the railway and the E6 highway, it has a cafeteria, gift shop and exhibitions, including Europe's largest stuffed polar bear. Outside stands a memorial to the thousands of World War II prisoners of war who built the railway and perished in the bitter winter conditions.

Further north, **Bodø ❾** was founded as a trading centre, to compete with Bergen. It competed unsuccessfully, but today the Hurtigruten coastal steamers *(see Insight on Hurtigruten, page 202)* call on their way from Bergen. Bodø is the northern end of the rail network and a staging post for summer visitors. As the crow flies, it is as far from Kristiansand, the southernmost station, as Kristiansand is from Paris. ❏

STIKLESTAD: THE MAKING OF A SAINT

The site of the Battle of Stiklestad near Trondheim in 1030 marks a pivotal point in the history of the Norwegian nation and the adoption of Christianity

Stiklestad, north of Trondheim, is a name which is revered by Norwegians. This ancient battlefield is the place that saw the foundation of Norwegian unity and the adoption of the Christian faith.

In the 11th century Norway was a country constantly disrupted by disputes between rival chieftains. The ambition of the reigning king, Olav Haraldsson, was a united Norway. He also wanted to create a Christian country with Christian laws and churches and clergy.

He was not the first to attempt this. In the previous century Olav Tryggvason had been converted to Christianity in England. He returned to Norway in 995 with the express purpose of crushing the chieftains and imposing his new-found faith. But Olav Tryggvason's conversion had not swept away all his Viking instincts and in his zeal he used great cruelty to convert the populace. His chieftains became disenchanted and Olav was killed in the Battle of Svolder in the year 1000.

Olav Haraldsson ascended the throne in 1015, but like Olav Tryggvason he foolishly made too great a use of the sword to establish Christianity. King Canute of Denmark and England, with his eye on the Norwegian throne, gave support to discontented factions within the country and in 1028 invaded Norway, forcing King Olav to flee to Russia.

Undaunted, Olav returned with a few followers, but his support had dwindled. He met his end on 29 July 1030 at the Battle of Stiklestad. Olav's corpse was taken to the then capital, Nidaros, and buried on the banks of the Nidelva river. When the body was disinterred a year later, it showed no signs of corruption: his face was unchanged and his nails and hair had grown. This was taken as a sign of sanctity.

Following this revelation, Olav was proclaimed a saint and his body placed in a silver shrine in Nidaros Cathedral. Faith in the holiness of King Olav – St Olav – spread and his shrine became a centre of pilgrimage.

Canute's victory at the Battle of Stiklestad was brief. He ceded power to his son, Svejn, but as rumours of Olav's sanctity grew, popular support for Canute evaporated and Svejn was exiled to Denmark in 1035. Meanwhile, St Olav's son, Magnus, had been in exile in Russia. Norway now invited him to return and accept the crown.

From that time Stiklestad has been a place of pilgrimage. It now has a beautiful open-air theatre, and on the anniversary of the battle a cast of 300 actors, choristers, dancers and musicians re-enact the events of July 1030. ❑

TOP LEFT: statue of St Olav. **ABOVE LEFT:** a rune stone marks the place where King Olav died. **TOP RIGHT AND RIGHT:** the annual St Olav's Play.

NORWAY'S FAR NORTH

Far removed from the rest of Europe, Norway's spectacular north extends through Arctic latitudes from the rugged Lofoten Islands to the Russian border. Beyond is the remote archipelago of Spitsbergen

Map on pages 212–213

T he far north of Norway, comprising Troms and Finnmark counties and the Lofoten Islands, is unique in the Arctic, thanks to the warming currents of the Gulf Stream. Here lies more than a third of the land of Norway, which one resident in 20 calls home.

Imposing wall, tricky waters

Viewed from the mainland across Vestfjorden north of Bodø, the **Lofoten Islands** present an imposing wall of rugged peaks rising from the sea. On the west, these mountains form a mighty shield against the onslaught of Norwegian Sea weather, so most of their habitation is along their east coasts, facing the mainland. **Svolvær ❶**, the main town, has been a trading and fishing centre since the 17th century. Fishing has long been the traditional calling of the islanders, and today *Lofot torsk* (Lofoten cod) remains choice throughout the country. Between February and April, **Kabelvåg**, to the south, is the undisputed fishing capital of northern Norway. Up to 10,000 vessels make for Vestfjord during these months for the colourful *Lofotfiske*, the annual cod-fishing event.

The southernmost of the larger Lofoten Islands, **Moskenesøya** is the most photographed, perhaps because of the picturesque fishing village of **Reine ❷**. Between Lofotodden, its southern cape, and the islet of Mosken lies **Moskenstraumen ❸**, a 4-km (2½-mile) wide, shallow channel. Here tidal currents reach speeds of up to 6 knots in their alternating flow between the Norwegian Sea and Vestfjorden, and water always swirls around a submerged rock in the middle of the channel. Sailing here is risky, as Dutch navigators first noted on maps published in 1595 in *Mercator's Atlas*, where the current was called "*Maelstrom*". Internationally, it has since been known by that name, and writers, including Jules Verne and Edgar Allan Poe, have amplified it to a huge whirlpool that engulfs ships and men. Maelstrom now is a synonym for a whirlpool treacherous to navigation and by extension turbulent confusion.

Paris of the North

Tromsø ❹ has long been a leading city in northern Norway and now is regarded as the region's unofficial capital. International trade and influence came early, and by the 1860s the women of the town were so stylishly dressed as to cause a visiting tourist to remark that the city seemed to be "The Paris of the North". That nickname persists, and now may apply as well to Tromsø's abundant and varied nightlife, with an average of one seat in an eatery or place of entertainment for every three residents. The city is built mostly on an island between the mainland and the larger coastal

LEFT: sunset by a frozen waterfall on the Lofoten Islands.
BELOW: a tribute to the explorer Roald Amundsen.

ROALD AMUNDSEN
1872 - 1928

island of **Kvaløya**. The sheltered location made it an ideal port for commercial operations in Arctic waters as well as the last port of call for polar expeditions. Intrepid polar explorers are the centre of attention at the **Polarmuseet** (Polar Museum; open June–Aug daily 10am–7pm; Sept–May daily 11am–3pm) in the historic harbour area.

The city is the cultural centre of the North. The **Nordnorsk Kunstmuseum** (Art Museum of Northern Norway; open Tues, Wed & Fri 10am–5pm, Thur 10am–7pm, Sat & Sun noon–5pm; entrance fee) has been going from strength to strength since moving in 2001 to its first permanent home facing Roald Amundsens Square. Sami and Northern Norwegian art is well represented in the permanent collection. The museum has some excellent visiting exhibitions throughout the year as well. The **Tromsø Museum** (open June–Aug daily 9am–8pm; Sept–May Mon–Fri 9am–3.30pm, Sat & Sun 11am–5pm; entrance fee; tel: 77 64 50 00) has a splendid collection of Sami art and contains a reconstructed Viking longhouse.

For panoramic views of Tromsø, take the Fjellheisen cable car 420 metres (1,378 ft) above sea level. It even operates through the night when the Midnight Sun is shining.

Just over the bridge on the mainland, is the striking **Ishavskatedral** (Arctic Ocean Cathedral; open June–Aug daily 10am–8pm; Sept–May times vary; entrance fee), a daring and impressive modern work by the architect Jan Inge Hovig. Its entire east wall, 23 metres (75 ft) high, consists of a *dalle* (French for "flagstone") technique stained glass window by the artist Victor Sparre.

Tromsø is also home to Europe's northernmost brewery, **Mack** (tel: 77 62 45 00), established in 1845. Here you can sample its famous Arctic Ale, *Mackøl*.

Though it is in the Arctic, the city enjoys a benign climate. The average midday temperature in January is the same as in Oslo and summer temperatures are about the same as in Trondheim.

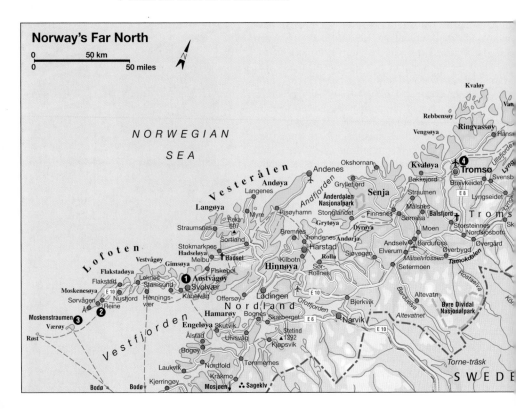

Norway's Far North

Heritage of the centuries

Alta ❺, the largest town in Finnmark, is known among fishermen for having one of the world's best salmon rivers. It is also home to the **Alta Museum** at **Hjemmeluft** (open June–Aug daily 8am–9pm; Sept–May times vary; entrance fee) on the southern outskirts, a collection of rock carvings dating from 4200 to 500 BC. These remarkable "stories in pictures" depicting people, animals (particularly reindeer), boats and weapons, are now a UNESCO World Heritage site.

South of Alta on the E93 lies **Kautokeino** ❻, a centre for the Sami, the indigenous people of northern Scandinavia and the Kola Peninsula of Russia. They are sometimes called Lapps, but prefer their own name Sami, which designates the land where they have lived for thousands of years. The size of the Sami population is not known, but is conservatively estimated at 70,000, of which about half live in Norway. Their native languages are related to Finnish, Hungarian and Estonian and have little in common with Norwegian. Traditionally, the Sami have been hunters, fishermen and reindeer herders. Some still follow the traditional callings, while others practise more modern trades. One of the more famous among them is film director Nils Gaup, whose *Pathfinder* (1987), the first feature-length Sami film, was nominated for an Academy Award. Like indigenous minorities elsewhere, the Sami were long suppressed, but now have their own flag and own parliament, *Sameting*, at **Karasjok** ❼.

After two months of winter darkness, Vardø, Norway's easternmost town, celebrates the return of the sun around 20 January with a gun salute on the first day that the entire disk is visible above the horizon.

Northernmost point

Nordkapp ❽ (The North Cape) at 71°10'21"N is considered by many to be the most northerly point of mainland Europe. But in fact the tip of **Knivskjelodden**, a low, slim peninsula to the west of Nordkapp, lies 47 seconds of latitude farther

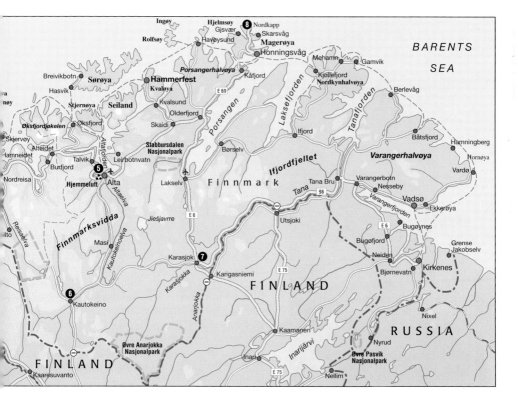

Map on pages 212–213

Part of the Children of the World Monument at the North Cape.

BELOW: polar bear on Svalbard.
RIGHT: Sami woman rounds up reindeer.

north. No matter; the North Cape, a name first used in 1553 by English sailor Richard Chancellor, is the imposing headland that draws visitors from around the world. Residents further south know the annual signs: in early summer, a stream of cars with southern European number plates heads north, many of them with "To the North Cape" written on their boots. Later, the stream reverses, and the cars come south, reindeer horns strapped to their roof racks. They have attained their goal. Tablets attest that even royalty have been here, King Oscar II of Sweden in 1873, King Chulalangkorn of Thailand in 1907.

Nordkapphallen (North Cape Hall; open Apr–early Oct times vary; mid-June–early Aug daily 9am–2pm; entrance fee) has a café, restaurant and other facilities for visitors. The **Nordkappmuséet** (North Cape Museum; open June–Aug Sun–Fri 11am–8pm; Sept–May Mon–Fri 12.30–4pm; entrance fee; tel: 78 47 72 00), near the Hurtigruten quay in **Honningsvag**, has a variety of displays about the cape and its history.

North to Svalbard

The **Svalbard** (Spitsbergen) archipelago lies 640 km (400 miles) north of the mainland. It was first mentioned in 1194 by Icelandic sailors. In 1596, the Dutch navigator Willem Barents, searching for the Northeast Passage, sighted the largest of its four main islands, which he called Spitsbergen (Pointed Peaks). Indeed, the terrain resembles that of the Alps, and Spitsbergen covers an area almost as large as Switzerland. In 1920, an international treaty gave Norway sovereignty over Svalbard and granted 35 signatory countries the right to exploit its resources. Only three countries have exercised their right on a commercial scale. In 1906, John Longyear, an American industrialist, founded the Arctic Coal Company on Spitsbergen. Today, the principal village, **Longyearbyen** (pop. 1,300) is named after him, but only Norway and Russia remain as mine operators.

The climate is relatively mild for the Arctic: midday temperatures at Longyearbyen average −7°C (19°F) in February and 7°C (45°F) in July. But permafrost prevails year-round. In 1998 it made the international news, when Canadian pathologists exhumed the well-preserved corpses of six Svalbard coal miners who had died in the 1918 influenza pandemic, to search for clues that might reveal its origin.

Today, hi-tech is supplanting mining as a leading livelihood. The **Svalbard Satellite Station** near Longyearbyen is positioned to download images from all earth observation satellites in polar orbits, and the **Svalbard Rocket Range** at **Ny Ålesund** is now instrumental in weather research.

With daily flights between Tromsø and Longyearbyen, tourism is growing. In summer, the stark mountains around the village are offset by a valley which has meadows spangled with flowers. Here you will find cassiope and purple saxifrage, and, perhaps, a patch of boreal Jacob's ladder, *Polemonium boreale*, an Arctic rarity. The polar winter is another matter. The sun does not rise above the horizon and everything is locked in darkness, lit only by the moon and the multicoloured rays of the **Aurora Borealis**, the Northern Lights. ❑

SWEDEN

From sophisticated Stockholm to mountain wilderness,
Sweden offers the traveller immense variety

A subtle change in Swedish attitudes has been emerging in recent years. Not so long ago the country was an introverted Fortress Sweden perched uneasily on the edge of Western Europe. Indeed, many Swedes still talked about travelling "to Europe" as if it was on a different continent. All that changed with the country's admission to the European Union in the 1990s and the opening in 2000 of the Öresund bridge across the straits separating Sweden from Denmark. The Swedes have finally become "good Europeans".

As such, Sweden is attracting many more visitors, not just to the bustling big cities and cultural centres of Stockholm, Göteborg and Malmö, but also to the rural regions and the vast wilderness areas of Lapland and the Bothnian coast. Where else can you stay in an hotel made entirely from ice, play golf under the Midnight Sun or dance with abandon around a maypole at Midsummer?

It is an ideal country for those who like the great outdoors and activities such as angling, golf, riding, fell-walking, skiing, sailing or canoeing. Even Greater Stockholm, which covers a much wider area than you might expect for its 1.6 million population, is a region of sea, lake and open spaces, and never far from the thousands of islands that form its archipelago, reaching out into the waters of the Baltic.

The southern provinces, including Skåne, were for centuries part of Denmark and a faintly Danish accent persists. Much of south central Sweden is dominated by the great lakes of Vänern and Vättern, the heart of a network of waterways that make it possible to cross this widest part of Sweden by boat along the Göta Kanal, which links Stockholm to Göteborg.

Further north, the geographical centre of Sweden holds Dalarna, the folklore province where old customs linger. At the end of the long road or rail route north are the mountains. This is home to Scandinavia's second race, the Sami, whose wanderings with their reindeer herds take little account of national boundaries.

Culturally, well-preserved sites like the remains of the Viking capital of Birka, state-of-the-art museums, and the homes of artists such as Carl Larsson, who inspired the clean lines of contemporary Swedish design, are all open to the visitor. On the musical front, Göteborg's Symphony Orchestra is in the top rank of world orchestras. Sweden has even become a centre of gastronomic excellence.

This northern land is also a popular year-round destination. The winter climate is less harsh than many people imagine and the period around Christmas, with its traditional markets, brightly decorated streets and St Lucia processions, is a magical time of year. ❑

PRECEDING PAGES: the smooth rocks of the Bohuslän coast; Swedish paratroopers cool off after a sauna in Jukkasjärvi; Stockholm, city of islands. **LEFT:** decorative ironwork at Stockholm's Royal Palace.

THE SWEDES

Beneath the cool, sophisticated exterior, the surprisingly mirthful Swede harbours a deep commitment to nature, tradition and schnapps

Contrary to popular opinion, Swedes do have a sense of humour. Armies of dissenters will no doubt beg to differ and sceptics will balk at the very idea. But the Swedish sense of humour is a peculiar thing: as elusive as Garbo and as fleeting as a Swedish summer. Blink and you'll miss it. Their reputation for being dry, sombre and painfully serious is itself the cause of much mirth for these Scandinavian jokers. And when the uninitiated confuse Sweden with Switzerland, it always raises an eyebrow and just the smallest trace of a knowing smile.

But don't let the cool exterior of this Scandinavian fool you. They may certainly seem calm and collected on the outside, but they're every bit as prone to hysterical fits as the next person. Even if they do recover much faster and the smile that flashed across those solemn features vanishes as quickly as it came.

Blond and beautiful

When it comes to Sweden, popular misconceptions are rife. It is commonly held that most people in Sweden are blond, at least 6ft 3in tall and drive Volvos. In fact, only half the population are natural blonds, the average male is 5ft 10in and the BMW is the preferred mode of transport for upwardly mobile Swedes today. Though the more stereotypical images of Sweden – leggy blonde beauties, pickled herring, meatballs and seemingly unflappable tennis players – certainly run true to form, Sweden today is a country of growing cultural and social diversity. A country in which the traditional mingles with the ultramodern and in which society and the political arena have been shaped by a strong democratic tradition.

First encounters with Swedes can be somewhat confusing. They are a baffling blend of the cosmopolitan and the provincial. For this sophisticated urbanite is every bit at home in

the concrete jungle, sipping cappuccinos at a pavement café, as going barefoot at their place in the country. It's no exaggeration to say that Swedes are potty about nature. It's somehow a part of the Swedish soul. They are quick to wax lyrical about the grassy plains of Skåne, expound the virtues of lakeside Dalarna and

SWEDEN: THE ESSENTIALS

Population 8.9 million.
Capital Stockholm (pop. 750,000).
Notable towns Göteborg, Malmö.
Climate Average afternoon temperatures in Stockholm in July are 22°C (71°F); in January, −1°C (30°F).
Top museums Vasamuséet, Nordiska Muséet, Skansen, Stockholm; Rooseum, Malmö; Silvermuséet, Arjeplog.
Historic sights Drottningholm Palace, Gripsholms Slott, Uppsala Cathedral, Gammelstad, Luleå.
Best midsummer festivity Dalarna.
Outdoor activities watersports, hiking, fishing, skiing.
Tourist information www.visitsweden.com.

LEFT: time off to unwind in the sauna, an essential part of Swedish life.
RIGHT: growing up in modern Sweden.

remind you that theirs is the only true wilderness left in all Europe. Ask any Swede to recount tales of their childhood and they'll dreamily recall summers spent in the country with a noticeable softening of facial expression, a voice tinged with more than just a hint of nostalgia and a faraway look in their eye.

National pride

Next to nature, there's nothing Swedes like to talk about more than Sweden itself. Get them started on this subject at your peril. This is not to say that Swedes are braggarts, far from it. A more humble, self-deprecating tribe you'd be hard pushed to find. But their modesty is a thin veil in the face of such obvious national pride. For all young Swedes are well versed in the achievements of their countrymen, be it Alfred Nobel or August Strindberg; even the exploits of their marauding ancestors are today taught in schools with pride.

At first glance a Swede may appear a very cool customer. But underneath that composed exterior and self-satisfaction with all things Swedish, you'll find a warm, friendly individual, who having decided to let their guard down and befriend you, will be a friend for life.

The image of the bloodthirsty Viking,

WINING AND DINING

Oddly enough, this "vodka-belt" nation has a rather uneasy relationship with alcohol. The liberalism that once made Sweden the envy of more conservative societies makes the prevailing attitude towards drinking, with its moral pontificating, all the more perplexing.

Despite EU membership and its initial effects, alcohol remains a contentious issue. Exorbitant prices and an unyielding state monopoly have conspired to create a sense of deprivation and prohibition. A Friday evening ritual is played out at state off-licences up and down the country, in which Swedes queue with stoical aplomb to buy a bottle of wine and a six-pack. It's not so strange then that when the chance to indulge presents itself, Swedes have few qualms about throwing themselves into the fray.

Whatever your take on the Swedes' drinking habits, when it comes to dining their manners are impeccable. Be it state banquets or family get-togethers, Swedes are sticklers for etiquette. From arriving punctually to observing the niceties of fine dining, the formalities are upheld to the last drop of schnapps. At birthdays and anniversaries, coffee and cake are served with the precision of a military exercise. Yet Swedes will happily tuck into a crayfish feast, ripping off claws with their hands and clashing beer glasses in a fashion reminiscent of their Viking forebears.

plundering all in his path, is one the Swedes have taken centuries to live down. Nowadays the little red cottage is Sweden's most enduring image and there's nothing Swedes like better than to take off to the country for a spell. An affinity for the land runs deep within the Swedish soul and they are never happier than when they can kick off their shoes, swim naked and bond with nature.

Life in Sweden is intrinsically linked to the natural rhythms of the changing seasons.

SKÅL!

Friendships are often sealed over schnapps. Delicately flavoured with fruits or spices, schnapps is a perennial favourite and every Swede can name his or her tipple.

soaking up the first warming rays of spring. Summers are woefully short, often hot and always much longed for.

Swedes today come in a variety of creeds and colours. Immigration continues to influence the country's social, cultural and political landscape. During the turbulent 1990s Sweden was forced to re-evaluate its global position in the face of new economic challenges and growing questions of social inequality. The high standard of living once enjoyed by Swedes and

Swedish winters are famous for their longevity, Arctic temperatures and the sun's prolonged absence. But Swedes have learnt how to make the most of it and winter sports are popular with Swedes of all ages. They eagerly await the spring and the return of sunlight with all the excited anticipation of children at Christmas. Like hibernating animals re-emerging after winter, sun-starved Swedes are wont to stand on street corners, at crossings, in traffic lights, and any other spot with a south-facing aspect,

LEFT: Swedish fathers are more involved than their European counterparts in caring for their children.
ABOVE: male voice choir prepares for a performance.

their enviable cradle-to-the-grave welfare system has come under increasing pressure.

Looking to Europe

For years Swedes championed the causes of others, but their own increasingly precarious position has forced them to abandon, albeit unofficially, their policy of neutrality and take closer steps to the Continent. Sweden's entry into the European Union in 1995 was part of an effort to bring Sweden in line with a changing Europe. New social and economic policies are helping the country adapt to a global economy, while the Swedes themselves are learning to adapt to their new role – as Europeans. ❑

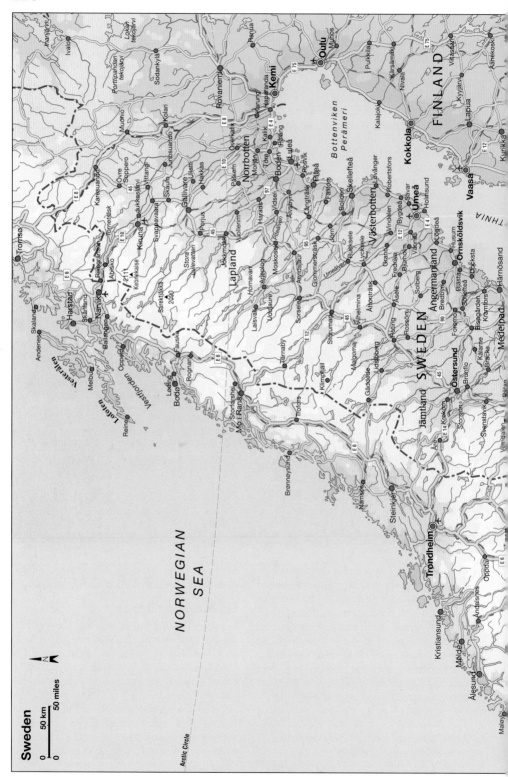

Sweden

0   50 km

0   50 miles

N

Arctic Circle

NORWEGIAN SEA

FINLAND

SWEDEN

Lapland

Norrbotten

Västerbotten

Ångermanland

Jämtland

Medelpad

Bottenviken Perämeri

Vesterålen

Lofoten

Oulu

Muhos

Kemi

Rovaniemi

Haparanda

Torneå

Kalix

Överkalix

Boden

Luleå

Piteå

Skellefteå

Umeå

Kokkola

Vaasa

Ivalo

Sodankylä

Portipahdan tekojärvi

Lokan tekojärvi

Raqua

Muonio

Kolari

Kaaresuvanto

Övre Soppero

Junosuando

Hakkas

Pajala

Morjärv

Töre

Råneå

Posvik

Luvånger

Robertsfors

Lövånger

Sävar

Holmsund

Örnsköldsvik

Härnösand

Östersund

Trondheim

Steinkjer

Namsos

Brønnøysund

Mo i Rana

Storforshei

Fauske

Rognan

Bodø

Loding

Oppeid

Ballangen

Narvik

Rikkegransen

Abisko

Kebnekaise 2111

Riksgränsen

Kiruna

Svappavaara

Vittangi

Jukkasjärvi

Torneträsk

Gällivare

Jällett

Skaulo

Porjus

Stora Lulevatten

Sarektjåkkå 2089

Jokkmokk

Vuollerim

Harads

Vidsel

Älvsbyn

Langträsk

Pålljobo

Boliden

Jörn

Arvidsjaur

Moskosel

Pinvejaur

Arjeplog

Sorsele

Ammarnäs

Gunnarsbyn

Rusfors

Lycksele

Vindeln

Granö

Bjurholm

Fredrika

Åsele

Solberg

Bredbyn

Fjällsta

Bredbyn

Bispgården

Kramfors

Nordmaling

Husum

Logdeå

Björna

Docksta

Ullånger

Laisvall

Vuodjaure

Tärnaby

Vojmsjön

Stensele

Storuman

Vilhelmina

Dikanäs

Klimpfjäll

Dorotea

Gäddede

Lidsjöberg

Hoting

Ankarede

Rossön

Flåsjön

Föllinge

Krokom

Brunflo

Brätche

Kälarne

Storsjön

Svenstavik

Vemdalen

Ljusnan

Foss

Trofors

Andalsnes

Oppdal

Kristiansund

Molde

Ålesund

Maloy

Reine

Melbu

Andenes

Skalans

Harstad

Skånland

harrjärvi

Pulkkila

Kalajoki

Nivala

Lapua

Kärsämäki

Kähekoski

Kurikka

Vasa

Rättvik

Kauhava

E 75

E 4

E 8

E 10

E 6

E 12

E 14

45

97

95

90

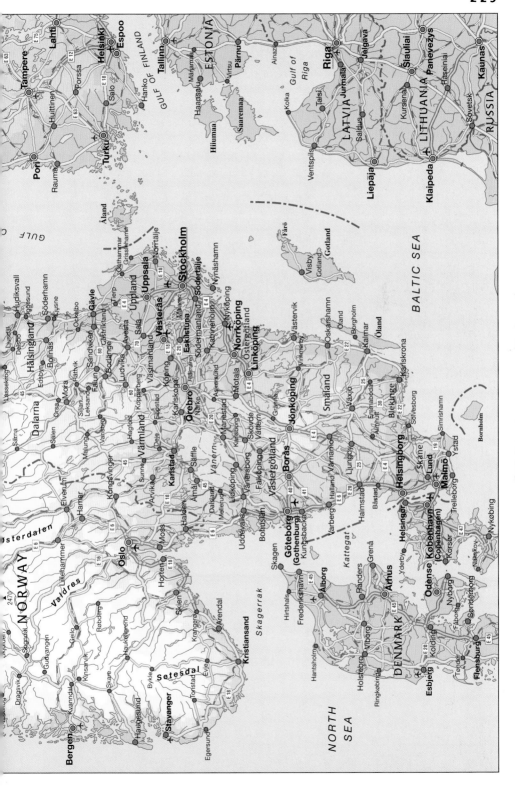

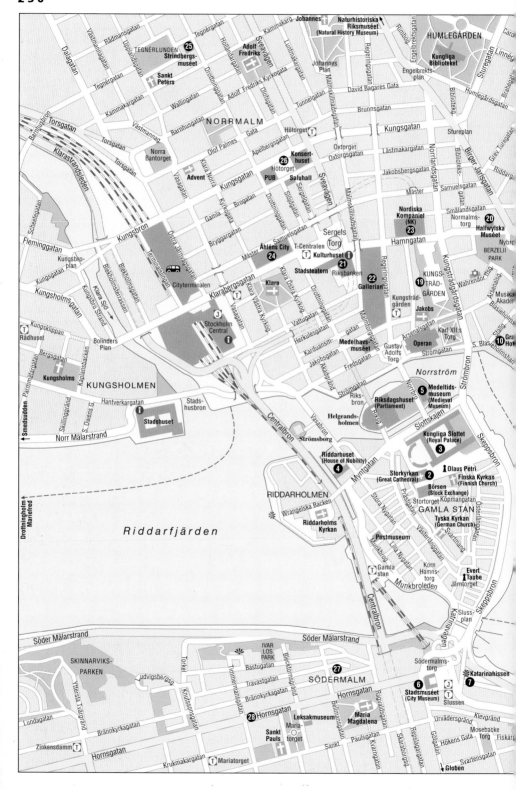

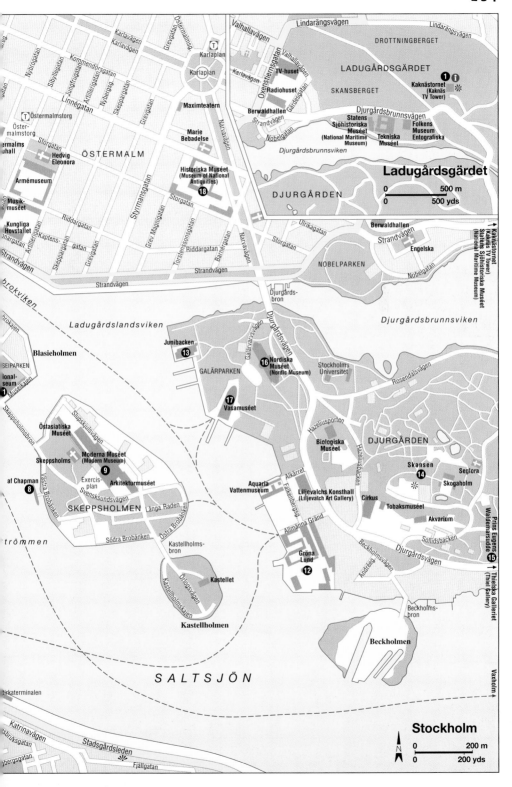

Stockholm

STOCKHOLM

*Sweden's capital is a city of islands where palaces and peaceful
hideaways line the shores, and where cobbled streets lead
to chic shops, cafés and lively cultural attractions*

Map
on pages
230–231

The novelist Selma Lagerlöf called Stockholm "the city that floats on water".
Nowhere do you see this more clearly than from the dizzy observation
platform on top of the **Kaknästornet ❶** (Kaknäs Television Tower; open
May–Aug daily 9am–10pm; Sept–Apr daily 10am–9pm; entrance fee; tel: 08
667 21 05), Ladugårdsgärdet, which rises 155 metres (508 ft). Below, Stockholm
spreads out in a panorama of blue water, the red of the old buildings contrasting with the stark white and glass of the new, and swathes of trees and grass.

Fresh and salt water are separated by the island of Gamla Stan (Old Town) and
the great lock gates of Slussen at the southern end. This island barrier is where
Stockholm originated some time before the 13th century. Today, with a population of 1.6 million, Stockholm is a modern and sophisticated metropolis,
famous for Scandinavian design in furniture, textiles and interiors and a hotbed
for innovation in information technology – Europe's Silicon Valley. The city features some of the most exciting cuisine in Europe. Stockholm's nightlife has
exploded into an array of young, hip clubs and older, more sedate nightspots.
Infusing the old with the new is a speciality of today's vibrant Stockholm.

Stockholm's history starts in **Gamla Stan** (Old Town), which still has the
character of a medieval city. Its narrow lanes follow the same curves along

LEFT: Gamla Stan,
the old town of
Stockholm.
BELOW: outdoor
café, Stortorget.

FACT FILE

Situation On a cluster of Baltic coast islands between the
sea and Lake Mälaren.
Population 1.6 million people live in the Stockholm area.
Climate In summer the daytime temperature can reach
20–25°C (68–77°F); in winter –7°C to +2°C (19–36°F).
Transport Comprehensive bus and Tunnelbanan (under-
ground) network; ferry services; sightseeing boats.
Best ferry ride Djurgårdsfärjan (Slussen to Djurgården).
Essential purchase Stockholmskortet (Stockholm Card),
for free admission to museums and free public transport.
Top attractions Drottningholms Slott; Historiska Muséet;
Kungliga Slottet (Royal Palace); Moderna Muséet; Stads-
huset; Vasamuséet; Ekoparken.
For children Skansen; Junibacken; Aquaria; Gröna Lund.
Views Fjällgatan, Södermalm; Katarina Hissen, Slussen.
Annual festivities Walpurgis Night (end Apr); Midsummer
celebrations, Skansen (late June); St Lucia celebrations
(mid-Dec).
Best coffee Vete-Katten, Kungsgatan.
Best smörgåsbord Ulriksdals Slottspark; tel: 08 85 08 15.
Tourist information Stockholm Information Service,
Sweden House, Hamngatan 27; tel: 08 789 24 90/24 95;
www.stockholmtown.com

TIP

See more and pay less with a Stockholm Card, available from Sverigehuset (Sweden House), Hamnagatan 27. It offers free admission to museums and sights, free travel, discounts and a guide book.

BELOW: Stadshuset, the City Hall, on Lake Mälaren.

which the seamen of former times carried their goods. The best place to start a tour is **Stortorget**, the centre of the original city, from which narrow streets fan out in all directions.

The Vasa capital

In medieval times, Stortorget was a crowded, noisy place of trade, where German merchants, stallholders, craftsmen, and young servant girls and boys jostled and shouted. In the cobbled square, people laze on benches or sit at one of the outdoor cafés, and it is hard to visualise that in 1520 the cobbles ran with blood during the Stockholm Bloodbath. Despite a guarantee of safety, the Danish King Kristian II, known as The Tyrant, murdered 82 people, not only nobles but innocent civilians unlucky enough to have a shop or a business nearby. This gory incident triggered the demise of the Kalmar Union, which had united Sweden with Denmark and Norway. Three years later, Sweden's first heroic king, Gustav Vasa, put an end to the union and made Stockholm his capital.

From the square, it's a short walk to **Storkyrkan ②** (cathedral; open mid-Sept–mid-May daily 9am–4pm; mid-May–mid-Sept 9am–6pm; entrance fee; tel: 08 723 30 16). This awesome Gothic cathedral is the oldest building in Gamla Stan, in part dating to the 12th century. It has high vaulted arches and sturdy pillars stripped back to their original red brick. Its most famous statue is St George and the Dragon, the largest medieval monument in Scandinavia, a wooden sculpture carved by Bernt Notke in 1489, which has retained its original colouring.

Gamla Stan's **Västerlånggatan** is a favourite shopping street for locals and tourists alike. Here and on nearly every other cobbled lane in the Old Town

A CITY AND ITS SYMBOL

From any part of Stockholm that lies south of Lake Mälaren, Stadshuset (City Hall) dominates the skyline. Situated on the lake shore overlooking Riddarfjärden, Stadshuset is the work of architect Ragnar Östberg. A massive square tower rises 105 metres (450 ft) from one corner of the elegant building. Constructed of decorated brickwork with an open-fronted portico facing the lake, the building is topped with spires, domes and minarets. The roofs are clad in copper. Above them gleam the Tre Kronor, the three golden crowns that symbolise the city.

Östberg began work in 1911 and devoted the next 12 years of his life to the City Hall. It was formally opened in 1923 and used 8 million bricks and 19 million gilded mosaic tiles, the latter mostly in the famous Golden Hall. The effect is stunning. The walls are entirely clad in gilded mosaics. The gardens of the southern terrace feature a statue of the 15th-century Swedish patriot, Engelbrekt, who championed the peasants in his native Dalarna.

A procession of St George and the Dragon emerges twice a day as the bells play a medieval tune. Guided tours are available Sept–mid-May 10am & noon; mid-May–Sept 10am, noon & 2pm; entrance fee; tel: 08 508 290 00.

you will find shops, restaurants and cafés to suit every taste. Particularly enjoyable are the cellar restaurants with their musty smell and stone walls. It's easy to imagine the Swedish troubador Evert Taube (1890–1976) raising a beer stein to his compatriots as he composed yet another lyric to the Swedish way of life.

The present **Kungliga Slottet** ❸ (Royal Palace; open mid-May–Aug daily 10am–4pm; Sept–Apr Tues–Sun noon–3pm; entrance fee; tel: 08 402 61 30) was built on the site of the Tre Kronor Palace, which burnt down in 1697, some say not without the help of Nicodemus Tessin the Younger, who had already built a new northern wing and who obviously relished the glory of rebuilding the palace to his Renaissance designs. His father, Nicodemus the Elder, had been architect to the old Tre Kronor palace, and the grandson, Carl Gustaf, was responsible for supervising the completion of the new palace many years later. The palace comprises 608 rooms. Various suites are open to the public and the oldest interiors from the 1660s are in the north wing.

For more of Sweden's aristocratic heritage, head for **Riddarhuset** ❹ (House of Nobility; open Mon–Fri 11.30am–12.30pm; entrance fee; tel: 08 723 39 90) on the nearby island of **Riddarholmen**, built in 1641 as a meeting place for the nobles. It is arguably the most beautiful building in Gamla Stan, with two pavilions looking out across the water. Inside, the erstwhile power of the nobles is matched by the grandeur of the Main Chamber, where the nobles deliberated, watched from above by a painting of Mother Svea, who symbolises Sweden.

The refurbishment of the Swedish **Riksdaghuset** (Parliament building) on Helgeandsholmen to the north of Gamla Stan some years ago led to a remarkable archaeological find and a new museum. When the builders started to excavate the Riksdaghuset terrace to form an underground car park, they discovered

Map on pages 230–231

Royal guardsman on duty outside the Royal Palace.

BELOW: ceremonial display at the Royal Palace, Gamla Stan.

Doorman at Stockholm's famous Grand Hotel.

layer upon layer of the past, including part of the medieval wall and the cellars of an apothecary shop. Stockholm's **Medeltidsmuseum** ❺ (Medieval Museum, Strömparterren; open July–Aug Tues–Thur 11am–6pm, Fri–Mon 11am–4pm; Sept–June: Tues–Sun 11am–4pm, Wed until 6pm; entrance fee; tel: 08 508 317 90), incorporates the old wall and other treasures uncovered during the excavations.

From the southern end of Gamla Stan it is worth making a detour to visit Stockholm's **Stadsmuseet** ❻ (City Museum, Ryssgården; open June–Aug daily 11am–7pm; Sept–May Tues–Sun 11am–5pm, Thur until 9pm; entrance fee; tel: 08 508 316 00). While Stockholm received virtually no mention until the 13th century, the museum makes it clear that this strategic spot had been inhabited for many centuries. After the museum, it would be a pity not to make a quick trip up **Katarinahissen** ❼ (open Mon–Sat 7.30am–10pm, Sun 10am–10pm; entrance fee), a 19th-century lift rebuilt in 1935 that carries you to the heights of Södermalm.

Stockholm's playground

From Gamla Stan, it is just 10 minutes by boat across the harbour to the island of **Djurgården**. Once a royal deer park, much of Djurgården is still in its natural state, with paths and woods where you may spot small creatures, both everyday and rare, such as hares and the occasional deer. The island is part of **Ekoparken**, the world's first city national park *(see page 239)*. A good way to get around is to hire a bike at the bridge which forms the road entrance.

BELOW: gilded tiles decorate the walls of the Golden Hall, Stadshuset.

Between Djurgården and Gamla Stan lies **Skeppsholmen**. The sleek schooner moored off the island is the 100-year-old *af Chapman* ❽, now a youth hostel and a café. Also on the island is the spectacular new building of the **Moderna**

Muséet ❾ (Modern Museum; open Tues–Thur 11am–8pm, Fri–Sun 11am–6pm; entrance fee; tel: 08 519 552 00), designed by the Spanish architect Rafael Moneo, with a collection of 20th-century art that is considered one of the finest in the world, including works by Dali, Picasso and Magritte among others. Its large restaurant-café offers a beautiful panorama of the city skyline.

Northwest of Skeppsholmen is the **Blasieholmen**, waterfront area where the sumptuous big building is one of Scandinavia's most famous hotels, the **Grand** ❿. Nearby is the **Nationalmuseum** ⓫ (National Museum of Fine Arts, Södra Blasieholmshamnen; open Tues & Thur 11am–8pm, Wed, Fri–Sun 11am–5pm; entrance fee; tel: 08 519 543 00) featuring Sweden's national collection of art, with most of the great masters from 1500–1900. Rembrandt is particularly well represented. In summer, the National Museum holds concerts in the evening, a lovely setting for music.

As the ferry slides into the Djurgården quay, there is no mistaking that this is an island devoted to enjoyment. On the right is **Gröna Lund** ⓬, an amusement park with its roots in the 18th century (open May–mid-Sept: hours vary; tel: 08 587 501 00; www.gronalund.com).

Fans of Astrid Lindgren's children books should not miss **Junibacken** ⓭ (open June–Aug daily 10am–5pm; Sept–May Tues–Sun 10am–5pm; entrance fee; tel: 08 587 230 00), a museum dedicated to her life's work. An electrically operated indoor tram, with narration in English, allows the rider to experience *Astrid's World*, floating over miniature scenes from her books with moving figures, lights, and sound, as familiar figures suddenly pop out of corners.

Heading south on Djurgården, where the island rises in steps to a hilltop, is **Skansen** ⓮ (open May daily 10am–8pm; June–Aug daily 10am–10pm;

Map on pages 230–231

Tunnelbanan, Stockholm's metro system, is described as the "world's longest art gallery". Many stations have paintings, sculptures, mosaics and engravings – and all can be seen for the price of a ticket.

BELOW: winter in the city.

Spinning is one of the many traditional skills still practised at Skansen, the open-air museum.

Sept–Apr daily 10am–4pm; entrance fee; tel: 08 442 80 00), the oldest open-air museum in the world. In 1891, Artur Hazelius decided to preserve the fast-disappearing Swedish way of life by collecting traditional buildings. Today there are some 150, including an 18th-century church, still used for services and weddings. Many of the houses and workshops are grouped together to form the town quarter along a steep cobbled street. They include authentic workshops where tradesmen once practised their craft. During the summer, many of the buildings revive their traditional use.

While on Djurgården it's worth visiting the lovely former home overlooking the sea and collection of the "Painter Prince" **Prins Eugens Waldemarsudde ⑮** (Prins Eugens väg 6; open Tues–Sun 11am–5pm, Thur until 8pm; entrance fee; tel: 08 545 837 00).

If you choose bus instead of boat and enter the island over Djurgårdsbron from Strandvägen, the first museum you come to is the **Nordiska Muséet ⑯** (Nordic Museum; open Tues–Sun 10am–5pm, also Mon late June–Aug; entrance fee; tel: 08 519 560 00), which depicts Nordic life from the 16th century. It has peasant costumes, a collection of bridal gowns and the traditional silver and gold crowns worn by Swedish brides, exhibits on Lapland culture, folk art, and more.

Marine treasure

BELOW: the *Vasa*, a remarkable work of restoration.

To the west of the Nordiska Museet on the waterfront is the huge, oddly shaped **Vasamuséet ⑰** (Vasa Museum, Galärvarvet; open mid-June–mid-Aug daily 9.30am–7pm; mid-Aug–May daily 10am–5pm, Wed until 8pm; entrance fee; tel: 08 519 548 00). Inaugurated in 1990, the museum houses the *Vasa* warship, built in the 1620s for the Thirty Years' War, on the orders of Sweden's warrior

king, Gustav II Adolf. She was a magnificent ship, decorated with 700 sculptures and carvings, but her oak was too solid. In 1628 she sank in Stockholm harbour on her maiden voyage. In 1956 the Swedish marine archaeologist, Anders Franzén, found her and, in 1961, brought her up from the depths. More than 24,000 objects have been salvaged from the sea bed, including skeletons, sails, cannon, clothing, tools, coins, butter, rum and many everyday utensils.

A short walk across the bridge is the spectacular **Guldrummet** (Gold Room), an underground vault featuring more than 3,000 prehistoric gold and silver artefacts at **Historiska Museet** ⓰ (Museum of National Antiquities, Narvavägen; open daily 11am–5pm; entrance fee; tel: 08 519 556 00).

Map on pages 230–231

The King's Garden

It's anyone's guess what the Swedish sculptor John Tobias Sergel (1740–1814) might have thought of the huge illuminated obelisk, fountain and square that bear his name, and of the modern city around it. The heart of this business and commercial area is not large, but it sits somewhat uneasily with the rest. From **Sergels Torg** it is hard to miss the five towering office blocks on Sveavägen, which cast their shadow over the other buildings. In the 1960s, Stockholm City Council, like so many others, succumbed to the temptation to knock things down and build concrete and glass high-rise buildings.

The destruction of many fine old buildings continued until it threatened **Kungsträdgården** ⓱ (King's Garden) with the statue of the warrior king, Karl XII on its southern side. At this point the Stockholmers had had enough. Normally placid and biddable, they mustered at the King's Garden, climbed the trees that were in danger of the axe, and swore that if the trees went so did

BELOW:
Prins Eugens
Waldemarsudde
art gallery and
former home of the
"Painter Prince".

OUTWARD-BOUND IN THE CITY

Ekoparken is the world's first national city park, a huge set of green lungs that stretch out in a 12-km (7-mile) long arch from Ulriksdals Slott (castle) in the north to the Fjäderholmarna archipelago in the south. This green swathe is so large you'll need a full day of serious hiking to explore it, by foot during the warmer months or on skis or long-distance skates in the winter. The inexpensive Brunnsviken Runt (Around Brunnsviken) boat tour is an excellent way of seeing the Ekopark and includes free admission to many attractions.

The Ekopark includes three royal parks, Djurgården, Haga and Ulriksdal, with palaces to tour (Ulriksdals Slott, Gustav III's Paviljong, Rosendals Slott). Visit the tropical Fjärilshuset (Butterfly House) where hundreds of colourful species land lightly upon your shoulder, or the Bergianska (Bergianska Botanical Gardens) and Naturhistoriska Riksmuseet (Museum of Natural History).

For a pleasant retreat on northern Djurgården, you'll find Rosendalsträgård (Rosendals Garden) with orchards, flowers and vegetables, garden shops and a café. For many Stockholmers this has become the ideal retreat after a day on Djurgården. For Ekoparken information, call the Stockholm tourist office (tel: 08 789 24 90).

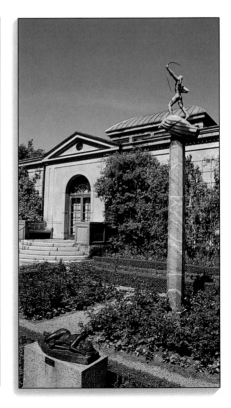

*Prehistoric artefact
in the Gold Room,
Museum of National
Antiquities.*

BELOW: Stockholm's
underground is an
artistic wonder.

the people. The City Fathers retreated and Kungsträdgården survives to soften the edges of the new buildings and harmonise with the older buildings that are left. This is the place to take a leisurely stroll or sit beside the fountains on a summer day and enjoy a coffee at its outdoor café. In summer it is the venue of many outdoor festivals and rock concerts. In winter, part of Kungsträdgården is flooded with water and becomes a popular ice rink, and the restaurant moves indoors.

A short stroll east is the early 20th-century private palace housing one of Stockholm's most unusual museums, **Hallwylska Museet ❷⓿** (Hallwyl Collection, Hamngatan 4; open mid-June–mid-Aug: tours Mon–Fri hourly 11am–4pm, Wed till 6pm; mid-Aug–mid-June: tours Tues–Sun noon–3pm, Wed till 6pm, English tour Sun 1pm; entrance fee; tel: 519 555 99). It's the magpie collection of one person, Countess von Hallwyl, from her ornate piano, to china, beautiful furniture and personal knick-knacks.

On the southern side of Sergels Torg, **Kulturhuset ❷❶** (Culture House; open Mon 11am–6pm, Tues–Sun 10am–7pm) is a popular meeting place and venue for lectures and entertainment with Stockholm's main tourist information centre on the ground floor (open June–Aug Mon–Fri 8am–4pm, Sat & Sun 9am–5pm; rest of year Mon–Fri 9am–6pm, Sat & Sun 10am–3pm; tel: 08 789 24 90). The centre can advise and book tours and other entertainment, sells the Stockholmskortet (Stockholm Card), and has a well-stocked bookshop. One block east on Hamngatan is **Gallerian ❷❷**, a huge covered shopping arcade that stretches to Jakobsgatan. At the south end of Gallerian is the oldest auction house in the world, **Stockholms Auktionsverk** (Stockholm Auction House), Jakobsgatan 10, which has been in business since 1674 (open Mon–Fri

).30am–6pm, Sat 10am–4pm; tel: 08 453 67 00). Everything from china to Chagall and furniture from the 7th century to the 20th is crammed into the storerooms. Many items are small enough to carry, and make unusual Stockholm mementos.

To buy is easy: you just leave a bid in advance for the Tuesday and Wednesday auctions, or you can take part in the auction yourself, no Swedish required. Even if you don't care to bid, browsing among the showrooms sheds light on Swedish homes, the way Swedes live, and what they keep or discard.

Sweden's equivalent of Harrods is **Nordiska Kompaniet (NK) ㉓**, on Hamngatan (just opposite Sweden House), whose rooftop illuminated sign, constantly turning, is visible from far and wide in the city. NK sells everything from shoes to sporting equipment, men's and women's clothing, glass, pottery and silver, jewellery and perfume; its services range from optician to post office and travel agency, and you can get your sightseeing shoes soled and heeled when you come to collect the high-speed prints of your latest roll of film.

Find a bargain

Shopping in Sweden is rarely cheap, but it is always good value. For a bargain, the words to look out for are *rea*, which means sale, and *extrapris*, which does not mean extra, but special low price.

Åhléns City ㉔ is on the corner of Sergels Torg and Drottninggatan. It has a similar range and quality to NK, and a visit to its supermarket food department is a sightseeing tour in itself. The third of this trio of stores is **PUB**, on Drottninggatan at Hötorget, which is a galleria featuring a variety of Swedish and international-brand shops.

Swedish design is world renowned. Wherever you go in the city you'll never be far from shops selling crystal, china and ceramics, and the fashions of designers like Pia, Wallén, Filippa K and Anna Holtblad.

BELOW: enjoying an ice-cream break.

Contemporary Swedish crystal design.

Drottninggatan (Queen's Street), an old street which leads directly through the Riksdagshuset and over the bridge from the Royal Palace, is one of Stockholm's main pedestrian ways. In summer, it is full of casual crowds strolling or sitting at one of the outdoor cafés. Immigrants sell their wares on the pavement. This area is a haven for pickpockets, so be careful.

Not to be missed is **Strindbergsmuséet** ❷ (Strindberg Museum, Drottninggatan 85; open Tues–Sun noon–4pm; entrance fee; tel: 08 411 53 54), housed in the top-floor flat of the **Blåtornet** (Blue Tower) where Sweden's greatest playwright spent his last years and wrote his last epic play, *The Great Highway* in 1908. Even at the end of his life, Strindberg was astonishingly prolific; he produced some 20 books in his four years in the Blue Tower. His study is just as he left it. A Strindberg Festival is held each year in late summer and features plays, concerts, lectures and other events.

Fruit and finery

Walking south along Drottninggatan to Kungsgatan, on your left you'll come to **Hötorget** ❷, with its open-air food stalls and indoor market. This is where Swedes shop for food. Here you can find Swedish delicacies such as elk steak and reindeer and the many varieties of Scandinavian cured herring.

In addition to exploring Gamla Stan's antique shops, take the Tunnelbanan (underground railway) south to Slussen station on **Södermalm** ❷, once the great working-class area of the city; the journey takes just 5–10 minutes. Nowadays, this district is a popular place for artists to live and work. It has become a trendy place to hang out, and new cafés, restaurants and boutiques seem to open daily. The steep slope of **Hornsgatan** ❷ has a cluster of galleries.

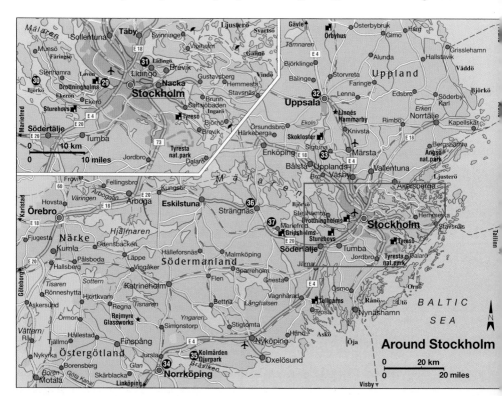

Around Stockholm

0   20 km
0   20 miles

Islands by the thousand

It is a rare city that has 24,000 islands on its doorstep and 100 km (60 miles) of lake at its heart, but this is Stockholm's eternal good fortune. Until the building of the Tunnelbanen, boats were the only means of getting around these vast expanses of water, and today boats are still part of Stockholm life. Boat operators Waxholmsbolaget and Strömma Kanalbolaget transport passengers across Lake Mälaren and around the archipelago *(see page 246)* in a variety of craft from old coal-fired steamers to modern ferries.

The most popular place to visit in the archipelago is the royal palace, **Drottningholms Slot ❷** on Lovön *(see page 245)*, to the west of the city. West of Lovön is **Björkö ❸**, the site of Sweden's oldest city, **Birka**. Between AD 800 and 975, Birka was the trading centre for the 40,000 inhabitants of the rich Mälaren area and the meeting point for traders. This was also where Christianity first came to Sweden, when Ansgar, the Saxon missionary, landed in the 9th century. Almost nothing is left of Birka above ground, but many archaeological digs have revealed the past at sites which include the old town. The **Birka Vikingastaden** (open May–Sept 10am–5pm; entrance fee; tel: 08 560 514 45) features the most recent finds.

Although it is now easy to get there by underground train (T–Ropsten), in summer it is worthwhile taking the boat to the island suburb of **Lidingö ❹**, to visit **Millesgården**, the summer home of the sculptor, Carl Milles and his wife, the Austrian painter Olga Granner (open mid-May–Aug daily 10am–5pm; Sept–mid-May Tues–Fri noon–4pm, Sat & Sun 11am–5pm; entrance fee; tel: 08 446 75 94). Here, Milles patiently reproduced the statues that had made him more famous in his adopted country of the USA than in Sweden. His creations

Maps:
City 230
Area 242

August is the time for a "kräftskiva" (crayfish party). Under the glow of paper lanterns, Swedes enjoy this beloved shellfish, once plentiful in freshwater lakes, but now imported.

BELOW: Stortorget, the square at the heart of Gamla Stan.

Map on page 242

seem to defy gravity: they appear to soar and fly, and step lightly over water, emphasised by their position on terraces carved from the cliffs.

North of Stockholm

Less than an hour's drive north of Stockholm on the E4 lies **Uppsala** ㉜, Sweden's ancient capital, last bastion of heathenism and seat of one of Europe's greatest universities. This is the birthplace of Ingmar Bergman and the setting for his film *Fanny and Alexander*. The town is also an Episcopal See and has the largest Gothic cathedral to be found in Scandinavia, **Domkyrkan** (open daily 8am–6pm). Its vaults, from 1435, house the shrine of Saint Erik, a former king and the patron of Sweden.

Across the town's lush parks rises **Uppsala Slott**, a fortress from the days of the Vasa dynasty (open June–Aug for tours at 1 & 3pm; entrance fee; tel: 018 727 48 00). A few minutes north of the town lies **Gamla Uppsala** (Old Uppsala) the 5th-century bastion of the Yngling dynasty. The three huge grave mounds of kings Aun, Egil and Adils (described in the opening passages of *Beowulf*) dominate the evocative grave fields surrounding **Gamla Uppsalakyrkan** (parish church; open Apr–Sept daily 9am–6pm; Oct–Mar daily 9am–4pm; free; tel: 018 32 70 89).

Near Uppsala, where the sea meets the forest, you'll find **Sigtuna** ㉝, Sweden's oldest town. In the 11th century this was the commercial centre for the Svea and Vandal tribes. Merchant ships from as far away as Asia dropped anchor here; monasteries and abbeys competed with one another in building glorious churches. Today, Sigtuna is a picturesque town with crooked lanes, quaint wooden houses and a miniature town hall. Tant Brun's café on the main pedestrian lane is a lovely place to stop for a cup of strong Swedish coffee and a freshly baked cinnamon bun.

South to Södermanland

To the south of Stockholm is **Norrköping** ㉞, with its tree-lined avenues, outdoor café society, trams and elegant architecture. The town's main attraction is **Kolmården Djurpark** ㉟. This is Scandinavia's wildlife safari, natural habitat and amusement park supreme (open Apr–Sept daily 10am–4pm, later in summer; entrance fee; tel: 011 24 90 00).

Heading north towards Lake Mälaren's bays and inlets you come to **Strängnäs** ㊱, a delightful small town dominated by a magnificent Gothic cathedral. Next to the church at **Boglösa**, 20 km (12 miles) north, are hundreds of Bronze Age rock carvings.

On the lake, about 15 km (9 miles) to the east, lies idyllic **Mariefred** ㊲ and the impressive **Gripsholms Slott** (castle; open mid-May–mid-Sept daily 10am–4pm; mid-Sept–mid-May Sat & Sun noon–3pm; entrance fee; tel: 0159 101 94), which contains the royal portrait collections and a marvellous theatre from the late 1700s. Best of all is the architecture of this fortress, begun in the 1370s and continually updated. Around the edge of the moat is a collection of rune stones carved with serpents, ships and magic inscriptions. Mariefred is a lazy, summer lake town, with cafés and restaurants to suit all tastes and ferry connections to Stockholm. ❑

A Carl Milles sculpture at Millesgården.

BELOW: Uppsala's Gothic cathedral.

A ROYAL TREAT: DROTTNINGHOLM PALACE

Often referred to as Sweden's "mini Versailles", the island palace of Drottningholm with its exquisite gardens and historic theatre is not to be missed

The most popular place to visit in Stockholm's archipelago is Drottningholms Slott (open May–Aug daily 10am–4.30pm; Sept daily noon–3.30pm; Oct–Apr Sat & Sun noon–3.30pm; entrance fee; tel: 08 402 62 80) on Lovön. Now the main home of the Swedish royal family, the 17th-century palace is surrounded by formal Baroque and Rococo gardens of fountains, statues, flowerbeds, box hedges and a variety of trees.

The palace was built for Eleonora, the widow of King Karl X, by the Tessin family of architects headed by Nicodemus the Elder (1615–81). Work began in 1662 and was completed by his son, Nicodemus the Younger.

Although the royal family live at Drottningholm, much of the palace is open to the public. Interior highlights include a magnificent Grand Staircase with *trompe l'oeil* paintings by Johan Sylvius, the baroque Karl X Gallery, Queen Hedwig Eleonora's State Bedroom with its richly painted ceiling, and the library of Queen Louisa Ulrika who married King Adolf Fredrik in 1744.

In the parkland stands the exotic pagoda roofs and ornamental balconies of the Kina Slott (Chinese Pavilion; open May–Aug daily 11am–4.30pm; entrance fee; tel: 08 402 62 70), a birthday present to Queen Louisa Ulrika from her husband. In one of four adjoining pavilions the king had his carpentry workshop. In Kanton, a small village built next to Kina Slott, silkworms that had been introduced perished in the freezing winter, thwarting the court's attempt to produce cheap silk.

The island's greatest treasure is undoubtedly the 18th-century Drottningholms Slottsteater (Court Theatre; May–Sept guided tours only; entrance fee; tel: 08 457 06 00).

The theatre was designed for Queen Louisa Ulrika by Carl Fredrik Adelcrantz and opened in 1766. The queen's son, Gustav III, was an actor and playwright who became known as "The Theatre King". He invited French troupes of actors to perform at Drottningholm and the theatre soon became an influential centre for performing arts. Gustav went on to found Stockholm's Dramatic Theatre and hired Swedish talent to develop a native theatre and opera.

The building fell into disrepair in the 19th century, then in the early 20th century it underwent extensive restoration. Today it is the oldest theatre in the world still using its original backdrops and stage machinery for productions. Attending a performance of opera or ballet here on a summer evening is like experiencing magic from an earlier age. ❑

TOP LEFT: formal gardens at Drottningholm. **ABOVE LEFT:** Chinese Pavilion. **TOP RIGHT:** ballet at the Slottsteater. **RIGHT:** palace entrance.

STEAMING OUT AMONG THE SKERRIES

When summer comes, the Swedes set off by boat to the thousands of idyllic islands that dot the waterways between Stockholm and the Baltic

Every summer thousands of Swedes in boats navigate carefully through waters loaded with 24,000 islands, rocks and islets in the Stockholm archipelago. The brackish waters start in the centre of Stockholm and extend 80 km (50 miles) out into the open Baltic Sea. Close to the mainland, the islands are larger and more lush, the bays and channels wider. Hidden here are idyllic island communities, farmlands and small forests. But as you travel further out, the scenery becomes more rugged, finally ending in sparse windblown islets formed by the last Ice Age.

ISLAND RETREATS

In the middle of the 19th century affluent Stockholm families began to build their second homes along the shores of the various islands in the archipelago. Over the years, "commoners" had more money and leisure time and soon they, too, sought their way to the archipelago. The combination of wilderness, sea, fresh air and closeness to the city satisfied many leisure needs. Today, Swedes either own their cottages or rent them, and enjoy swimming, fishing, boating, nature walks and socialising with friends.

▷ **YOUNG VOYAGER**
Dressed for the ferry ride and a deck-side view of the steam boats and yachts that ply the waters.

△ **ON THE WATERFRONT**
More than 50,000 chalets offering varying degrees of comfort are spread throughout Stockholm's inner archipelago.

▽ **LAZY DAYS**
The archipelago is such an important factor in the Stockholmers' leisure time, that every tenth resident now owns a boat.

▽ HOME FROM HOME
More than 10,000 people live year round on the 150 inhabited islands, working in farming, fishing, boat transport and retailing.

▽ WALK IN THE WILD
Escaping to the islands for summer weekends and holidays, mainly in July, is a perfect antidote to the bustle of city life.

A QUICK GUIDE TO ISLAND HOPPING

The archipelago can be explored on guided tours which can be picked up from Stockholm's city centre. But if you want to travel like the locals, then buy a *Båtluffarkort* (Inter-skerries card), which allows you to see as many islands as you can in 16 days, including:

● Sandön, with its attractive sailing centre village of Sandhamn, sandy beaches and some good restaurants (a 5-hour round trip).

● Fjäderholmarna, featuring a boat museum, aquarium, fish-smoking plant, restaurants and crafts shops (20 minutes by boat from Stockholm).

● Vaxholm, with its famous fortress (1 hour by boat).

● Utö, where a 12th-century iron mine is the principal attraction.

Utö is also a great place for bike-riding (3 hours by boat from the city).

◁ ISLAND HARVEST
Berry and mushroom picking are popular pastimes enjoyed by all ages. Swedes also love nature walks, bird watching and picnicking.

▷ PADDLE POWER
Swedes take time to enjoy the scenery by water. Although sailing is a very popular water sport, canoeing and kayaking come in a close second.

SOUTHERN SWEDEN

Across the Öresund bridge from Denmark, southern Sweden is home to the lively city of Malmö. Castles and Stone Age sites abound, while bathers and birdwatchers head for Öland

Map on page 250

Skåne is Sweden's most southerly province, so close to Denmark across the narrow sound that even the accent is faintly Danish. This isn't surprising because for centuries Swedes and Danes fought over this area, along with the provinces of Halland and Blekinge, until Sweden established its sovereignty in 1658.

Since 2000, however, the two countries have been joined by the Öresund road and rail bridge that links Malmö and Copenhagen. The project has prompted a renaissance for southern Sweden as a centre of the Danish-Swedish Öresund region, with a total of 3 million people and one-fifth of the total combined GNP of Sweden and Denmark.

Skåne is often called Sweden's food store because of its rich farmland, mild climate and good fishing. Along the coast the landscape is undulating and lush and especially spectacular in the southeast corner, Österlen. Inland, there are lakes and three large ridges with lovely walks.

Skåne is renowned for its castles and manor houses. There are said to be 240 in the province, most of which are in private ownership, but it is usually possible to walk round the gardens such as at **Sofiero ❶**, 4 km (2½ miles) north of Helsingborg (open Apr–mid-Sept daily 10am–6pm; entrance fee; tel: 042 14 40 48). Built in 1857, Sofiero was used by King Gustav VI Adolf as his summer palace until his death in 1973. He was a keen botanist and made the gardens a real attraction.

LEFT: markets are a focal point in many Swedish towns.
BELOW: Sweden's Town Hall, Malmö.

Malmö: city of the south

Malmö ❷ is Sweden's third city, a lively place with a population of about 265,000. In the 16th century, Malmö competed with Copenhagen to be Scandinavia's leading capital. In those days it was an important port, not far from rich fishing grounds.

Today, the harbour is still busy and many of the old buildings remain. **Malmöhus**, the dominating castle built by King Christian III when Skåne was still part of Denmark, is Scandinavia's oldest remaining Renaissance castle. It houses the **Malmömuseer** (Malmö Museums; open June–Aug daily 10am–4pm; Sept–May daily noon–4pm; entrance fee; tel: 040 34 44 37), which includes the Art Museum, Museum of Natural History, City Museum, Science & Technology/Maritime Museum, and the **Kommendants Hus** (Commander's House), in Malmöhusvägen.

From the same period is **Rådhuset** (City Hall), which you will find in **Stortorget**, one of the largest squares in Scandinavia. **Stadshuset** (August Palms Plats; open Mon–Fri 8am–4.30pm; tel: 040 34 10 00) was built in 1546 in genuine Dutch Renaissance style. In 1860 it was given a facelift by the architect Helgo Zettervall, with niches, bays, allegorical paintings,

Sweden leads the world in glass-making. Many of the famous glassworks, such as Kosta and Boda, are located in the southeast of the country.

and colonnades. Northeast from Stortorget is **St Petri Kyrka**, Göran Olsgatan 1, built in the Baltic Gothic style and dating from the 13th century, although its towers were built in the 15th century and its copper spires in 1890. This elegant cathedral features a beautiful altar area created by sculptors in 1611.

A particularly idyllic place to sit and relax is **Lilla Torg** (Little Square), with its cobblestones, carefully restored houses and 16th-century charm. Through an arch on the south side of the square is Hemanska Gården. Once a merchant's home and trading yard, it now houses the **Form Design Center** (open Tues–Fri 11am–5pm, Thur until 6pm, Sat–Sun 11am–4pm; free; tel: 040 664 51 50), where Swedish industrial design and handicrafts are displayed.

When you get hungry, head for **Saluhallen** (open 10am–6pm; Sat 10am–2pm), on the northwest corner of Lilla Torg, where you can choose from fish restaurants, cafés, delicatessens and an abudance of fresh food.

Walking east from Lilla Torg, a rewarding visit can be made to **Rooseum**, (Stora Nygatan; open Wed–Fri 2–8pm, Sat–Sun noon–6pm; entrance fee; tel: 040 12 17 16) founded in 1988 by the Swedish art collector and financier Fredrik Roos. Here you'll see the art currently at the centre of international debate, like that of Jean Michel Basquiat, Julian Schnabel and Susan Rothenberg.

Towards Helsingborg

Heading north from Malmö, **Lund** ❸ is a university town with a fine cathedral, **Domkyrkan**, built in the 12th century. Don't miss **Kulturen** (Cultural History Museum, Tegnérs platsen; open May–Sept daily 11am–5pm; Oct–Apr Tues–Sun noon–4pm; entrance fee; tel: 046 35 04 00), an open-air museum with dozens of buildings, silver, textiles, ceramics and art. Along with the University of

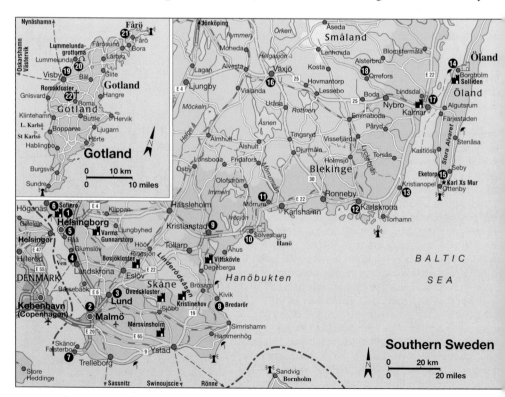

Uppsala, Lund is one of the two ancient Swedish universities. About 30 km (19 miles) north along the coast, **Glumslöv** ❹ offers memorable views. From the hill above the church, on a clear day you can see 30 churches and seven towns, including Copenhagen and Helsingør in Denmark.

Helsingborg ❺, 60 km (37 miles) north of Malmö, is an interesting town of cobbled streets, dominated by the remnants of an old castle, **Kärnan**, and with a bustling harbour. **Höganäs** ❻, 20 km (12 miles) north, is devoted to potters and artists. The large pottery is worth a visit.

Along the south coast

Forty km (25 miles) southwest from Malmö are the summer idylls of **Skanör** and **Falsterbo** ❼. **Skanörs Ljung** is recommended for bird lovers, particularly in September and October, when a large number of migrating birds gather.

Southeast of Kivik is **Bredarör** ❽, site of the Bronze Age **Kiviksgraven** (King's Grave). Scientists wonder about the mysterious markings on the stones. One theory is that Kivik may have been a Phoenician colony in AD 1200.

Kristianstad ❾ is the birthplace of the Swedish film industry, which started around 1910. The original studio is intact and is now a museum where you can watch old films on video (**Filmmuséet**, Östra Storg 53; open Tues–Fri and Sun 1–4pm; tel: 044 13 57 29). Nearby, **Kristianstad Vattenriket** (Water Kingdom) is a rich wetland area on the Helge River, with a diversity of birds, wildlife and plants.

Blekinge is a tiny province with sandy beaches and Sweden's most southerly archipelago. It is excellent for sea fishing. You can enjoy peaceful angling in some of the lakes, or good sport for salmon in the Mörrum River. Canoeing is popular. Driving to Blekinge from Skåne, you first reach **Sölvesborg** ❿, and the ruins of 13th-century **Sölvesborg Slott** (castle).

Mörrum ⓫, 30 km (19 miles) north of Sölvesborg, is noted for its salmon fishing: at **Laxens Hus** you can see salmon and trout at different stages of their development (open Apr–Sept daily 8am–5pm; Oct daily 8am–4pm; entrance fee; tel: 0454 501 23).

The biggest town in Blekinge is **Karlskrona** ⓬, a naval centre built in the 17th century, with wide streets and impressive buildings. In the Björkholmen district you'll find quaint 18th-century cottages built by ships' carpenters. The nearby village of **Kristianopel** ⓭ is renowned for its smoked herring.

Öland: an ornithologist's delight

The island of **Öland**, off the east coast, is one of the most visited areas of Sweden and, with its diverse landscape and superb beaches, it is a paradise for bird-watchers, nature lovers and sun worshippers.

Once you've crossed the Öland bridge from Blekinge, you soon see the ruins of **Borgholm Slott** (castle) rising above the main town of **Borgholm** ⓮, a once splendid residence from the 12th century (open May–Aug daily 10am–6pm; free).

The island has many ancient burial places and there are remains of 16 fortified dwellings from earlier times. The most interesting is **Eketorp** ⓯, in the

TIP

Råå, on the outskirts of Helsingborg, is a picturesque fishing village with an excellent inn.

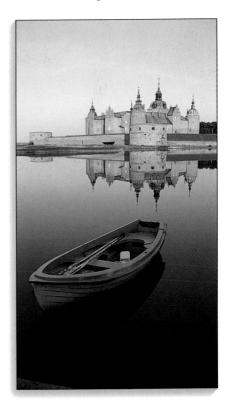

BELOW: Kalmar Castle, Småland.

Map on page 250

Brightly painted timber buildings are a feature of southern Sweden.

south, which has been partly restored. Sweden's prime birdwatching can be enjoyed at the **Ottenby bird station**, on the island's southerly tip, where more than 350 species have been recorded. Nearby, you can see **Karl Xs Mur** (Karl X's Wall), impressive for its sheer size; it was built in 1650 to distinguish Ottenby's domain and keep out the peasants' animals. **Stora Alvaret**, an expanse of bare limestone soil in central southern Öland, is a starkly beautiful landscape offering rare flowers and flocks of cranes in the autumn.

The emigrants

During the late 19th and early 20th centuries, Sweden's population exploded, and many families could no longer eke out a living on the land. So began the years of migration to North America. A popular place to visit is **Utvandrarnas Hus** (House of the Emigrants; open June–Aug Mon–Fri 9am–6pm, Sat & Sun 11am–4pm; Sept–May Mon–Fri 9am–4pm; entrance fee; tel: 0470 201 20) in **Växjö** ⑯, 70 km (43 miles) west of Kalmar, which tells the story of the exodus *(see box page 35)*.

Kalmar ⑰, one of Sweden's oldest cities, was of great importance in the Swedish–Danish wars. Sweden's best-preserved Renaissance castle, **Kalmar Slott** (open June–Aug daily 10am–5pm; Apr, May & Sept daily 10am–4pm; entrance fee), was begun in the 12th century but was completely renovated during the 16th century by the Vasa kings. The castle's coffered ceilings, panelled halls, fresco paintings and magnificent stonework have inspired the Renaissance Festival, held every July, featuring tournament games, market, music and theatre.

Kingdom of glass

BELOW: glass-blowing is a highly valued skill in southern Sweden.

Northwest of Kalmar, about 20 km (12 miles) is **Orrefors** ⑱, part of Sweden's **Glasriket** (Glass Kingdom). The first glass was melted in Sweden in 1556 but it was not established as an industry until 1742, when **Kosta**, the oldest works, was founded to the west of Orrefors. Anders Koskull and Georg Bogislaus Stael von Holstein took the first two syllables of their respective surnames to create "Kosta". The location was ideal because the dense forests provided the timber to keep the furnaces going.

Orrefors started in the glass business by producing windowpanes and bottles. In 1913 the works was taken over by Johan Ekman, an industrialist from Göteborg. Ekman recruited two artists who with their creative flair were to transform Orrefors into one of the world's foremost glassworks: Simon Gate, a portrait and landscape painter, and Edvard Hald, a pupil of Matisse.

Most of the 17 major glassworks are open to visitors for demonstrations and many have shops (open Mon–Fri 9am–6pm, Sat 10am–4pm, Sun noon–4pm; Orrefors Glasbruk, tel: 0481 341 95; Kosta Glasbruk, tel: 0478 345 32; Boda Glasbruk, tel: 0481 240 30).

Look out for *hyttsill* ("glassworks herring") evenings. In bygone times the glassworks were also a social centre where the locals would gather for a chat and bake herrings and potatoes in the furnace, with music provided by an accordionist or fiddler. Some of the works have revived these evenings for the benefit of visitors. ❑

GOTLAND: THE SUNSHINE ISLAND

With its medieval towns, sandy beaches and curious rock formations, tranquil Gotland – the largest island in the Baltic – is a favourite holiday spot

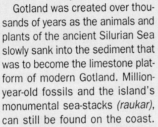

Gotland is an island of gaunt rocks, forests, wild flowers, cliffs and sandy beaches. Blessed with more hours of sunshine than anywhere else in the country, Swedes flock here for their summer holidays.

Gotland was created over thousands of years as the animals and plants of the ancient Silurian Sea slowly sank into the sediment that was to become the limestone platform of modern Gotland. Million-year-old fossils and the island's monumental sea-stacks *(raukar)*, can still be found on the coast.

In the Viking Age the island was a busy trading post. **Visby ⓳**, the principal centre of population, later became a prosperous Hanseatic town. Great stone houses were erected, churches were founded, and a city wall was built. Today, 3 km (2 miles) of the medieval limestone wall remains virtually intact, interspersed with 44 towers and numerous gates. It is now a UNESCO World Heritage site.

Limestone has created one of the island's major attractions – the impressive subterranean tunnels and stalactite caves of **Lummelundagrottorna ⓴** (open May, June & Sept daily 9am–4pm; July–Aug daily 9am–6pm; guided tours only; entrance fee; tel: 0498 27 30 50), 13 km (8 miles) to the north of Visby, which should not be missed. Dress warmly, it's 8°C (46°F) inside.

About 50 km (30 miles) north of Visby lies **Fårö ㉑**, the "island of sheep". Take a ferry to the island from Fårösund, and enjoy sites such as Gamlehamn, a medieval harbour, and the ruins of a chapel to St Olof. You can also see one of Gotland's most bizarrely shaped *raukar*, "The Camel", and visit the beach of Sundersand. After you have been here a while, you will begin to understand why Fårö is the favourite place of Sweden's leading film director, Ingmar Bergman.

Sweden's most primitive horse, the Russ, has lived in the forests of the island from time immemorial. The name Russ comes from the Old Norse *hross*, and it is thought that the horse is a descendant of the wild Tarpan. You can see them, only 123–126 cm (46–52 inches) tall, around the island.

Wherever you travel in Gotland you'll come across at least one of its 92 medieval churches. At **Romakloster ㉒**, in the centre of the island, there is a ruined monastery from the 12th century. There are many other relics of the past including runic stones and burial mounds. If you reach Gotland's southernmost tip, you'll see some of the most impressive *raukar* on the island. ❑

TOP LEFT: Gotland beach. **ABOVE LEFT:** Visby, a Hanseatic town. **TOP RIGHT:** Visby's medieval town wall. **RIGHT:** an unusual sea stack *(raukar)*.

SWEDEN'S WEST COAST

*From the sandy beaches of Halland to the bustling city
of Göteborg and the rocky shores of Bohuslän, the west coast
has long been a summer playground for Swedes*

Map
on page
256

T he west coast of Sweden, generously dotted with beaches and fishing villages, is 400 km (250 miles) of glorious coastline divided in two by the city of Göteborg (Gothenborg). It has been a favourite holiday spot since the early 20th century. The best beaches are in the southern province of Halland. North of Göteborg, in Bohuslän, is a majestic coast of granite rocks and islands.

The E6 connects all the larger cities, but follow the small coastal roads to discover the gems. Starting along the coast in the northwestern corner of the county of Skåne, a number of small towns offer views into the past. **Gamla Viken ❶**, 15 km (9 miles) north of Helsingborg on Highway 22, is a picturesque fishing village. **Torekov**, at the tip of the next peninsula, has a seaside golf course and boats to the island of **Hallands Väderö** where you can spot seals basking offshore.

Sand and salmon

Halmstad ❷, the largest town in Halland, lies on the River Nissan. **Halmstads Slott** (castle), the provincial governor's residence, was built in the 17th century by the Danish king Kristian IV. In front of the castle is moored the old sail-training vessel *Najaden* (open June–Aug Tues & Thur 5–7pm, Sat 11am–3pm), built in 1897. Other sights include **St Nikolai**, a 13th-century church. **Tylösand**, 8 km (5 miles) west of Halmstad, is a popular holiday resort with a predominantly sandy beach and two golf courses. There are good beaches at **Östra Strand, Ringenäs** and **Haverdalsstrand.**

Falkenberg ❸, 40 km (25 miles) north of Halmstad, is on the Ätran, a river famous for its salmon. The old part of the town with its 18th-century wooden houses and cobbled streets is centred on the 14th-century **St Laurenti Church**. There is an old toll bridge *(tullbron)* from 1756 and the oldest pottery in Sweden, **Törngrens Krukmakeri**, which has been run by the Törngren family since 1789 (open Mon–Fri; tel: 0346 103 54). Good beaches are found at **Olofsby** (north of the town) and **Skrea Strand** (south of the town).

Continue 30 km (19 miles) north on the E6 to **Varberg ❹**, a bustling place combining spa, resort, port and commercial centre with a ferry service to Grenå in Denmark. **Varbergs Fästning** (fortress) stands beside the water and houses a youth hostel, restaurant, apartments and a museum. Pride of place goes to the Bocksten Man, the only preserved figure in the world wearing a complete costume from the Middle Ages. Reminders of Varberg's late 19th-century development as a holiday resort include **Societetshuset** (1883), an elaborate wooden pavilion in the park, now a restaurant and a site for outdoor concerts. The bathing station (1903) is a rectangular wooden structure open to the sea in the middle. Around the sides are changing

LEFT: holiday cottage on Klädesholmen.
BELOW: rocky north Bohuslän coast.

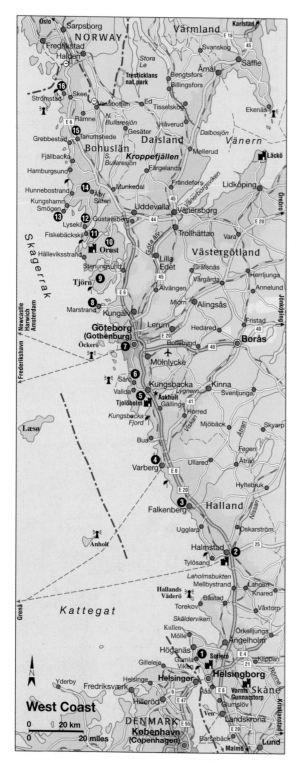

huts and deck chairs where, after a quick plunge in this early version of a sea-water swimming pool, bathers can relax over coffee and waffles.

A taste for Tudor

Heading 30 km (19 miles) north towards **Kungsbacka** you will pass the most out-of-character building along the entire coast. **Tjolöholm Castle ➎** (open mid-June–Aug daily 11am–4pm; April, May, early-June & Sept Sat & Sun only 11am–4pm; Oct Sun 11am–4pm; entrance fee; tel: 0300 54 42 00) was built in the early 20th century in an English Tudor style, with a splendid Art Nouveau interior.

The moment you reach the little seaside resort of **Särö ➏** (immediately north of Kungsbacka), you notice the coastline has changed. Instead of beaches, a dramatic landscape of rocks, inlets and islands takes over. In the early 19th century Särö was a fashionable resort, popular with the Swedish royal family. It remains in a time warp. You can walk along the Strandpromenaden and through **Särö Västerskog**, one of the oldest oak woods on the west coast.

Göteborg

Göteborg ➐ (Gothenburg) is the second-largest city in Sweden (460,000 inhabitants) and home to beautiful parks and a thriving cultural and industrial life. Dutch architects planned the city in the 17th century for King Gustav II Adolf, giving it an architectural character of its own. The shipping industry, particularly trade with the Orient by the Swedish East India Company in the 18th century, shaped the history of the city. Today it is Scandinavia's largest seaport. The harbour area is its soul and a good place to start your sightseeing.

The bold new **Göteborgsoperan ➊** (opera house; tel: 031 13 13 00 for bookings, 031 10 80 00 for info), opened in 1994, stands on the water just west of the commercial centre. Built in ship-like style, it is well worth a visit for its architecture alone. Near the Opera is Göteborg's **Maritima Centrum ➌** (maritime centre; open Mar, Apr, Sept & Oct daily 10am–4pm; May–Aug daily 10am–6pm; Nov Fri & Sun 10am–4pm; entrance fee; tel: 031 10 59 50), on Packhuskajen. Said to be the world's largest floating ship museum, it features 15 ships, including a submarine, destroyer and lightship.

The heart of Göteborg lies along Östra Hamngatan and Kungsportsavenyn. Start at the northern end of Östra Hamngatan; heading south you will pass **Nordstan**, one of northern Europe's largest covered shopping centres. Along the intersecting streets of Norra and Södra Hamngatan are dozens of small and inviting boutiques. Cross Stora Hamnkanalen (Great Harbour Canal) and continue south to **Kungsportsplatsen**, where you can pop into the **Göteborgs Turistbyrå ⊙** (tourist office; open June–Aug daily 9am–6pm; Sept–May Mon–Fri 9am–5pm, Sat & Sun 10am–2pm).

Across the street is **Saluhallen ⊙**, a large indoor marketplace (1886–89) stocked with Swedish specialities such as seafood, cheese and meats. This is a good place to sit and enjoy a cup of coffee, a light snack or a full lunch.

Kungsportsplatsen is also the place to embark on a **Paddan** (Swedish for "toad"), one of the flat-bottomed sightseeing boats that cruise through the old moat, under some 20 bridges, along 17th-century canals, out into the harbour and back again (May–Sept: first departure 10am; tel: 031 60 96 70).

From Kungsportsplatsen, cross the moat into Kungsportsavenyn – known as "**Avenyn**" **⊙** (The Avenue). The Avenyn, 40 metres (130 ft) wide and just under a kilometre long, is a boulevard lined with trees, restaurants, pubs and cafés. Halfway along the Avenyn, you are just a block away from the **Röhsska Museet ⊙** (Vasagatan 37–39; open Wed–Sun noon–5pm, Tues noon–9pm; entrance fee; tel: 031 61 38 50), the Swedish museum for design and handicrafts.

Maps:
Area 256
City 258

A Göteborgskortet (Göteborg Card) gives unlimited travel on city buses and trams, a boat trip and free admission to many museums and to Liseberg.

BELOW: Göteborg's harbourfront and lookout tower.

At the southern end of the Avenyn is Göteborg's cultural centre, **Götaplatsen**, with the Poseidon fountain by the Swedish sculptor Carl Milles. Götaplatsen is flanked by the **Kunstmuseet G** (art museum; open Tues & Thur 11am–6pm, Wed 11am–9pm, Fri–Sun 11am–5pm; entrance fee; tel: 031 61 29 80), with an extensive collection of Scandinavian art, including Anders Zorn's *Bathers*, and work by Munch, Rembrandt and Pissarro. On the west side of the square is the **Konserthuset H** (Concert Hall), home of the Gothenburg Symphony Orchestra.

Lisebergs Nöjespark I (open Apr–Sept; entrance fee; tel: 031 40 01 00), located in the middle of town, is the largest amusement park in northern Europe. Like most amusement parks, it is a great place to take children. For a calmer and non-commercial experience, explore the **Botaniska Trädgården J** (Botanical Gardens) or **Slottsskogen K**, two of the finer among Göteborg's 20 parks.

The rugged coast

The province of **Bohuslän** begins north of Göteborg. To see the coast, head 15 km (9 miles) west from Kungälv on Road 168 past Tjuvkil, where you can catch a ferry to **Marstrand 8**. A town without cars, Marstrand is a popular holiday resort and sailing centre. In summer it is also a good place to buy crafts. **Carlstens Fästning** (fortress) dominates the town and offers the best views of the island. King Oskar II (1872–1907) used to come here every summer to holiday and his statue stands in front of the Societetshuset.

Beyond Marstrand lie the islands of Tjörn and Orust, connected by bridge to the mainland. **Tjörn 9** is beautiful with some barren areas inland and a fascinating coastline. A magnificent curved bridge, which provides good views in either direction, links Tjörn and **Orust 10**. This island, the third-largest in Sweden,

Bohuslän is noted for its fine Bronze Age rock carvings. The "Bridal Pair" at Vitlycke, near Tanumshede, is among the best known of the carvings in the area.

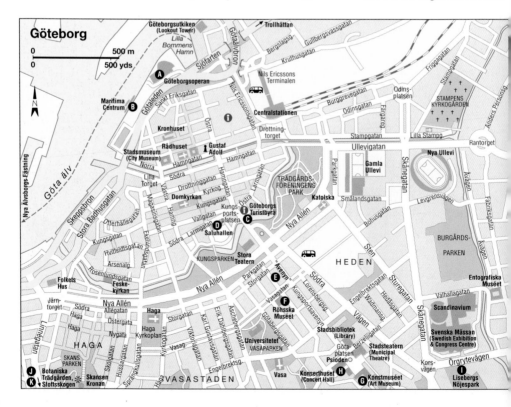

has its quota of fishing villages, including Mollösund, Ellös and Käringön.

Returning to the mainland, take a ferry across the **Gullmarn**, Sweden's only genuine fjord, from **Fiskebäckskil** ⓫ to **Lysekil** ⓬. Lysekil comes to life in the summer with boat excursions to the islands and sea fishing trips. **Havets Hus** (sea aquarium; open July–mid-Aug daily 10am–6pm; mid-Aug–June daily 10am–4pm; entrance fee; tel: 0523 196 70) includes sea life from Gullmarn and the Skagerrak. A tunnel aquarium holds creatures such as rays, sharks, halibut and cod.

North of Lysekil on the Sotenäs peninsula, the small harbour of **Smögen** ⓭ is a favourite stop for boats. The main attraction is the boardwalk, where you can shop, stroll and lounge. The other attraction is fresh shrimp. Watch a fish auction and then go round the corner to buy some of the catch.

At **Åby Säteri** ⓮, 17 km (11 miles) northeast of Smögen, is **Nordens Ark** (open Sept–May daily 10am–4pm; June–Aug daily 10am–7pm; entrance fee; tel: 0523 795 90), a nature park featuring endangered species and old breeds of Nordic farm animals.

Towards Norway

Near **Tanumshede** ⓯, a small town about 50 km (30 miles) north on Route 168, is Europe's largest collection of Bronze Age rock carvings, including depictions of battles, ships, hunting and fishing scenes, and mating couples.

The last town before the Norwegian frontier is **Strömstad** ⓰. A health resort, said to have more hours of sunshine than anywhere else in northern Europe. Strömstad shrimps are considered by the local inhabitants to be in a class of their own, with a distinctive mild flavour. The district has more than a touch of Norwegian about it having been part of Norway until 1717. ❑

Maps:
Area 256
City 258

Thrills for all: Liseberg amusement park in Göteborg.

BELOW: sailing competition on the island of Tjörn.

SWEDEN'S GREAT LAKES

Map on page 262

Two of Europe's largest lakes, Vänern and Vättern, lie at the heart of southern Sweden. In this area of farmland and forests, painted churches, grand castles and literary hideaways abound

Two enormous lakes, Vänern and Vättern, dominate the map of Sweden. The larger of the two is Vänern, a vast stretch of water with an area of 5,585 sq km (2,156 sq miles). It is not only the biggest lake in Sweden but also the largest in Western Europe, and its western shore embraces two provinces, Dalsland and Värmland.

Dalsland is a province of neat farms and prosperous small towns and villages, with empty roads running through its forests. The greatest attraction here is nature and, thus, the most interesting activities are outdoors: namely, camping, hiking and canoeing. West of Mellerud is **Kroppefjällen ❶**, an upland area which is a nature reserve. One of the best ways to explore the region is to hike along the 15-km (9-mile) **Karl XIIs Väg** (trail); maps can be obtained from the tourist office in Mellerud (tel: 0530 183 08).

A local feature is the **Dalslands Kanal**, a network of interconnected lakes and rivers. It was designed by Nils Ericsson and built between 1864 and 1868 to provide better transport for the local ironworks and sawmills. Today, it is popular for sailing and canoeing. The aqueduct at **Håverud ❷**, 14 km (9 miles) north of Mellerud, is a dramatic piece of engineering. Made of iron and 33 metres (108 ft) long, it carries the canal over the rapids of the River Upperud.

LEFT: fishing on the tranquil waters.
BELOW: watery landscape.

Along the Klarälven

An old parish register in Western Värmland states: "Between Sweden and Norway lies Värmland." Even today, a certain rugged independence, plus a slight Norwegian accent, persists. The region has strong traditions and has produced a rich crop of writers of both prose and poetry. Spruce and pine forests cover the county and are often referred to as "Värmland's gold".

The province is crisscrossed with narrow lakes and rivers, and the **Klarälven** can claim to be among its most beautiful rivers. It begins turbulently in Norway, where it is called Trysilelva, but gradually becomes broader, winding and sluggish before emptying into Lake Vänern near the province's largest town, **Karlstad ❸**. Highlights in this 400-year-old town include the cathedral (built in 1730), the longest arched stone bridge in Sweden (168 metres/184 yds) and a popular park, **Mariebergsskogen**.

The Klarälven was the last Swedish river used for floating logs. The practice ended in 1991, but in **Dyvelsten ❹**, 17 km (10 miles) north of Karlstad, the **Flottningsmuséet** (Log Rafting Museum; open mid-June–mid-Aug daily 11am–5pm; entrance fee; tel: 054 87 12 26) shows how it was done.

At **Ransäter ❺**, 40 km (25 miles) north of Karlstad on the Klarälven, the **Hembygdsgården** heritage village (open May–Sept Mon–Fri 9am–5pm; July &

Aug daily 9am–5pm; entrance fee; tel: 0552 303 43) includes museums devoted to mining, forestry, agriculture and rural life, which provide a fascinating picture of the Värmland of yesteryear. Ransäter hosts an annual folk music festival in June and the largest accordion festival in Scandinavia in July.

The Klarälven may no longer be used for floating logs, but many Swedes holiday on the river – drifting along on the gentle current on a raft they assemble themselves. Contact the Karlstad tourist office (tel: 054 14 90 55) for more details.

To the south of Lake Vänern, Lidköping's square is said to be the largest in northern Europe. A big market is held here on Wednesday and Saturday mornings.

Nobel prize-winner

West of Ransäter, on the eastern shore of Mellan-Fryken, is **Mårbacka ❻** (open May–Sept daily 10am–4pm; Oct–Apr guided tours on Sat; entrance fee; tel: 0565 310 27), the manor home of the Swedish writer Selma Lagerlöf, the first woman to receive a Nobel prize for literature, in 1909. Through her books, including *The Wonderful Adventures of Nils* and *The Story of Gösta Berling*, she made the Fryk valley and lakes famous. On the western side of the lake is

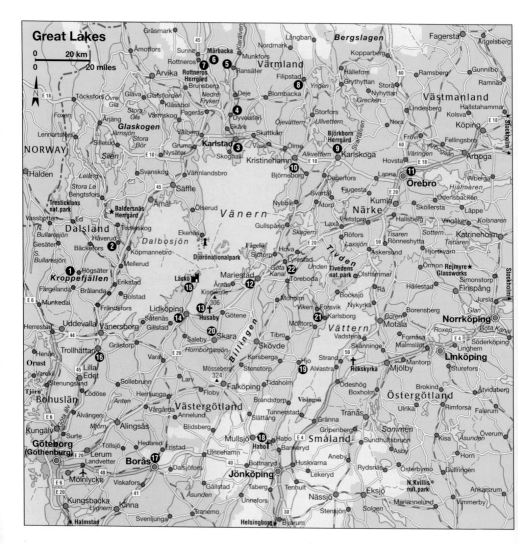

Rottneros Manor ⑦ (open May–Aug daily 10am–5pm; later in July; entrance fee; tel: 0565 602 95), which appears as Ekeby in Lagerlöf's *The Story of Gösta Berling*. One of Sweden's most beautiful parks, it has an arboretum and works by Scandinavian sculptors, including Milles, Eriksson and Vigeland.

Map on page 262

Inventive feats

North of Lake Vänern, the bedrock is rich in minerals and this area has long been associated with Sweden's early industrial development. Many Americans make the pilgrimage to **Filipstad ⑧**, which has the mausoleum of John Ericsson, the gifted inventor and engineer.

Björkborn Herrgård ⑨, near Karlskoga, was the home of the Swedish inventor Alfred Nobel. The manor house is now a museum, **Nobelmuséet** (open June–Aug daily 10.30am–4pm; entrance fee; tel: 0586 834 94). At **Kristinehamn ⑩**, 24 km (15 miles) to the west of Karlskoga, a 15-metre (49-ft) high sculpture by Picasso is the most striking navigational feature on Lake Vänern.

To the east, in the province of Närke, is **Örebro ⑪**, with a dramatic **castle** (open June–Aug, daily tours; entrance fee; tel: 019 21 21 21). Despite its appearance, the building dates from only the late 1800s, but there has been a castle on the site since the 13th century.

Mariestad Slot, on the eastern shore of Lake Vänern.

Between the lakes

The region separating Lake Vänern from Lake Vättern offers rich pickings for the visitor. This is the province of Västergötland. In 1746 the indefatigable Swedish botanist Carolus Linnaeus said: "Truly no one could ever imagine such splendour as in Västergötland who had not seen it for himself."

Heading south along the eastern shore of Vänern, you come to **Mariestad ⑫**, which is dominated by the spire of the 17th-century Renaissance-style cathedral, one of the few churches of this period remaining in Sweden.

Most Swedes learn in school that the king who first united the Svea and Göta tribes, Olof Skötkonung (994–1022), was baptised in 1008 at Husaby Källa (Husaby Spring) at the southern tip of Kinnekulle. Despite disputes, historians would like to establish Husaby as the cradle of the Swedish state. **Husaby Church ⑬** (open May–Sept daily; tel: 0511 34 30 10) has an imposing stone tower with three spires.

Nestled into Kinneviken (Kinne Bay), 51 km (32 miles) south of Mariestad, is **Lidköping ⑭**, a town founded in 1446 and renowned for its porcelain. **Rörstrand** (open Mon–Fri 10am–6pm, Sat 10am–2pm, Sun noon–4pm; tel: 0510 823 46), the second-oldest porcelain factory in Europe and maker of the Nobel china, has its own pottery museum featuring royal pieces, and a large shop. For such a modest-sized town, Lidköping has several fine cafés. The best is Garströms Konditori, established in 1859, on the main square (open daily).

North of Lidköping on the Kållandsö peninsula, stands the restored baroque style 17th-century **Läckö Slott ⑮** (open May–Sept daily 10am–6pm; guided tours only; entrance fee; tel: 0510 103 20), one of the most impressive castles in Sweden. In

BELOW: ready with a smile.

Map on page 262

TIP

On the east of Lake Vättern, historic sites of note include the stone of Rök at Rökeskyrka with its 800 runes (E4 north of Ödeshög) and Alvastra Kloster, Sweden's first Cistercian monastery (Road 50 north of Ödeshög).

BELOW:
cycling along the Göta Kanal.

summer it holds cultural exhibitions and is a venue for outdoor concerts.

Trollhättan 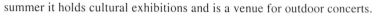, at the southern tip of Lake Vänern, is the home town of Saab Automobile. Long before the invention of the motor car, the town was famous for the magnificent falls of the Göta River. The water level drops by about 32 metres (105 ft), and when the Göta Kanal was built a flight of locks was required to give ships access to Lake Vänern. Today, the river is diverted to generate electricity and the falls are silent. But during the annual Falls Festival in July it is released to follow the old course, providing an impressive spectacle.

The southern part of Västergötland was the heartland of Sweden's textile industry, with the focal point at **Borås** 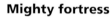, where there is a **Textilmuséet** (Textile Museum; open Tues–Sun times vary; entrance fee; tel: 033 35 89 50).

Around Lake Vättern

Lake Vättern, the second-largest lake in Sweden, covers an area of 1,912 sq km (738 sq miles). Near the southern tip of the lake, on the west side, is the 14th-century timber-built **Habo Kyrka** (church), southwest of Habo village. It features an outstanding painted interior, the work of Johan Christian Peterson and Johan Kinnerus, both of Jönköping, between 1741 and 1743. Their paintings illustrate Luther's catechism and Biblical scenes.

Travelling north along the lake, stop at the small waterside resort of **Hjo** to enjoy freshly smoked whitefish. Then tour the town in a horse-drawn carriage, or cruise on the lake in the 1892 steamer, *Trafik*. In the summer, Hjo hosts Scandinavia's largest handicraft festival. **Skara**, 50 km (31 miles) to the west of Hjo, has Sweden's second-oldest cathedral (after Lund), dating from the 11th century. **Skara Sommarland** (open May–Aug daily 10am–5pm; July–Aug till 6–7pm; entrance fee; tel: 0511 640 00), 8 km (5 miles) east of Skara on Road 49, is a delight for children with numerous attractions from lunar vehicles to a giant water park.

For more relaxed pursuits, head 10 km (6 miles) southeast of Skara on Road 184 to the lake of **Hornborgasjön**, a wildlife area with more than 100 species of birds. The biggest attraction is the annual mating dance of the crane, a graceful long-legged bird, best seen in April.

Mighty fortress

Karlsborg, on the western shore of Lake Vättern, 30 km (19 miles) north of Hjo, is dominated by its huge fortress, **Fästning** (open mid-May–Aug daily 10am–4pm; daily guided tours; entrance fee; tel: 0505 188 30). In 1809, when Sweden lost Finland to the Russians, the Swedes realised that a new defence strategy was required and decided to build two massive fortresses to house the government and the treasury. The first, at Karlsborg, was started in 1819 and required 250,000 tons of limestone. It was quarried by prison labour on the eastern side of the lake and ferried across by boat.

The castle has walls 2 metres (6 ft) thick with 5 km (3 miles) of ramparts, but by the time the building was finally finished, in 1909, fortresses were out of fashion. The second castle was never built. ❑

CROSSING SWEDEN BY CANAL

One of the most leisurely ways of sampling the country's history is to cruise along the Göta Kanal between Stockholm and Göteborg

The challenge of linking the lakes and rivers through the interior of Sweden, from Stockholm on the east coast to Göteborg on the west coast, had exercised the minds of many industrialists and kings before Baltzar von Platen succeeded at the beginning of the 19th century.

At the time, the country needed this new artery from east to west to transport timber, iron and food, and also to build up industry along its banks. For 22 years, 58,000 men laboured to build the **Göta Kanal** ㉒. In 1998, the canal was designated an "International Historic Civil Engineering Landmark", giving it the same status as the Golden Gate Bridge and the Panama Canal. Today, there is no commercial traffic on the canal, but many Swedes travel it in their own boats.

For the visitor, the classic way is to take a cruise between Stockholm and Göteborg on one of the vintage vessels operated by the Göta Kanal Rederiaktiebolaget (Göta Kanal Steamship Company). The oldest of the three vessels is *MS Juno*, built in 1874.

The four-day westbound cruise starts from Stockholm and enters the first lock on the canal at Mem – where the canal was officially inaugurated in 1832. On the second day the boat reaches Berg, with its flight of seven locks, where there is time to visit the historic monastery church at nearby Vreta, once the richest religious establishment in Sweden.

The route crosses two picturesque lakes, Asplången and Roxen, where there are good chances of spotting ospreys and herons during the breeding season. After Lake Roxen

the canal takes you through 15 locks in 3 km (2 miles), lifting you 37 metres (120 ft). The next night is spent at Motala, a town founded by Baltzar von Platen, who started the now thriving engineering industry.

On the third morning the boat crosses Lake Vättern to Karlsborg, site of a huge fortress built at the same time as the canal, and Forsvik, an old metal-working village and the site of the canal's first lock, built in 1813. Here, the boat is often greeted by a local family singing hymns and offering passengers wild flowers. This 100-year-old custom originated as a blessing for passengers as they embarked on what was then regarded as the hazardous crossing of Vättern. In the evening the boat reaches Sjötorp, marking the beginning of Lake Vänern.

At the south side of Lake Vänern, the boat enters the gorge at Trollhättan early the next morning for the last stage of the voyage down the Göta river to Göteborg. ❑

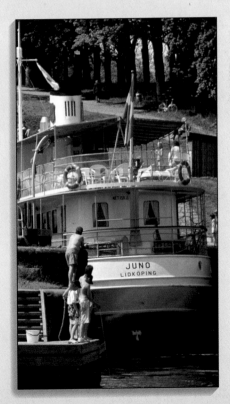

TOP LEFT: safety first. **ABOVE LEFT AND RIGHT:** two of the vintage vessels that cruise the Göta Kanal. **TOP RIGHT:** waiting for a catch.

DALARNA

Map on page 268

Dalarna is Sweden's folklore province, as famous for its scarlet Dala horses as its music and merrymaking at Midsummer. Winter attracts skiers challenged by championship events

Dalarna is often regarded as the heart of Sweden's folklore district, and indeed it represents all that is quintessentially Swedish. With its colourful costumes, centuries-old traditions of music and dance, Midsummer festivals, and evocative rural landscape, its folklore and beauty attract an increasing number of visitors each year.

Dalarna is the third-largest tourist site in Sweden, after Stockholm and Göteborg. The culture that gave us the red-painted Dalahäst (Dala horse) and inspired two of Sweden's most beloved artists, Carl Larsson and Anders Zorn, can best be experienced in the twilight of *fäbodar*, the old pasture cottages nestled in the hills of Dalarna; in the company of some elderly but amazingly energetic fiddlers; or at the magic of Midsummer, when a young woman places nine different flowers under her pillow to dream of the man she will marry.

Music-making

Music is one of the most defining characteristics of Dala culture. Musik vid Siljan (Music on Lake Siljan) and the Falu Folk Music Festival are two annual festivals that attract visitors from all over Sweden and abroad. Distinctly Dala are the *spelmansstämmor*, folk musicians' rallies, particularly the one held each summer in **Bingsjö ❶**, 30 km (19 miles) east of Rättvik, where fiddlers in their eighties turn the classic polka into a musical performance that rivals any blues master.

An exotic setting for listening to music is **Dalhalla** (June–Aug tours Mon–Fri 9am–4.30pm; other times of year, by appointment; tel: 0248 79 79 50), a cavernous outdoor concert arena set in the depths of an abandoned limestone quarry near the town of **Rättvik ❷**. The quarry, abandoned in 1990, was inaugurated as a music arena in 1994, with the first performance, of Wagner's *Der Ring des Nibelungen*, held two years later. The annual summer festivals feature artists of international standing.

Pastoral scenes

For a change of pace, the gentle quiet of the region's *fäbodar* offer a taste of back-to-the-land living. These pasture cottages and surrounding buildings, dating from the 15th and 16th centuries, are found all over Sweden but are most often associated with Dalarna. They constitute a living museum, where cows are milked, butter is churned, *messmör* (a type of goats' cheese) is made, and the classic *tunnbröd* (thin bread) is baked. Many *fäbodar* are open to the public and sell products or serve food.

One worth visiting is **Ljusbodarnas Fäbodar** (open June–Aug) about 20 km (12 miles) south of Leksand on Route 70 towards Mockfjärd, where

LEFT: midsummer celebrations are an annual highlight.
BELOW: folk art telephone box.

children are encouraged to pet the cows, calves, hens, sheep and pigs, and you can enjoy a meal of *sill* (herring) on some nights.

If trying your own hand at 15th-century farming appeals, **Prästbodarna Fäbodar** (open June–Sept daily, book in advance; tel: 0248 141 59), near Bingsjö, has a variety of native Swedish farm animals, and offers one-day courses in butter churning, milking and cheese-making. The farming life seems a natural accompaniment to the breathtaking scenery of the province.

At the northern extremity of Dalarna is the deceptively gentle start of the mountain range which marches north, gaining height all the time until it culminates in the snow-topped peaks of the Kebnekaise range in Lapland. Dalarna is a transition zone between the softer landscapes of southern Sweden and the more dramatic, but harsher landscapes of the north. It is even divided within itself between the more densely populated area south and east of Lake Siljan (dense by Swedish standards) and the relatively uninhabited zones to the north and west of the lake.

Mora on Lake Siljan is best known as the home of the Swedish artist Anders Zorn (1860–1920). His house and studio, Zorngården, and the Zornmuseet are both worth visiting (open daily).

Industrial traditions

Dalarna is by no means exclusively rural. The provincial capital, **Falun ❸**, has been a centre of industry for 1,000 years, and is an attractive town, well worth a stroll to the central square. The **Bergslagen** area to the south developed as an important mining area when minerals including iron, copper and silver were discovered in the 17th century. The manufacture of steel has continued.

Hedemora ❹ claims to be the oldest town in Dalarna, with a charter dated 1459; its privileges as a market town go back even further than that, while parts of the church are 13th century. The locals have devised **Husbyringen**, a 56-km

BELOW:
local musician.

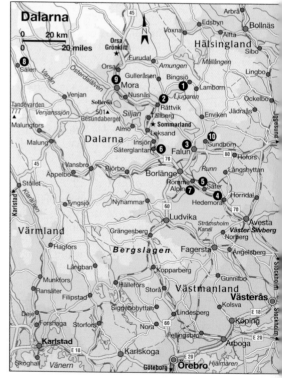

(35-mile) "museum trail" which you can take by car through the area northeast of the town to see a number of industrial archaeology sites.

Also worth visiting is **Säter** ❺, one of the seven best-preserved wooden towns in Sweden. Compared with Hedemora it is quite an upstart, with a town charter dated 1642. The ravines of the Säter Valley were created at the end of the Ice Age and are of interest for their flora.

Map on page 268

Traditional handicrafts

In the province that inspired the distinctive Dala horse, it is not surprising that the region is known for its abundance of carvers, potters, silversmiths, weavers, painters and bakers. This is a mecca for *hemslöjd* (crafts), all of which have their ancient roots in the farming culture. At **Säterglantan** ❻, 3 km (2 miles) south of Insjön Lake, **Hemslöjdens Gård** (tel: 0247 410 45) offers a wide array of handicrafts as well as week-long courses. At **Nittsjö Keramik** (open Mon–Fri 9am–6pm, Sat 9am–2pm; tel: 0248 171 30), 6 km (4 miles) north of Rättvik, clay goods are made following a tradition that goes back 100 years.

The Dalahäst (Dala Horse), a more readily recognised Swedish symbol than the nation's flag.

Cross-country ski challenge

Dalarna's ski resorts are the principal winter tourist attraction, both for cross-country skiing and downhill. **Romme Alpin** ❼ is Sweden's most-visited ski resort outside the proper mountain areas, with some 110,000 visitors annually. Together, **Sälen** ❽ and Idre, in northwest Dalarna, have almost half of Sweden's ski-lift facilities and Sälen is famous for being the starting point for a 53-mile (85-km) cross-country skiing race to **Mora** ❾: the Vasaloppet, the most popular sporting event in Sweden. ❑

BELOW: decorating the Maypole.

LARSSON

Carl Larsson (1853–1919) is Sweden's best-loved artist. The greatest source of inspiration for Larsson was the life he shared with his wife Karin, a textile artist, and their children at their home at **Sundborn** ❿ (open May–Sept daily 10am–5pm; other times by appointment; entrance fee; tel: 023 600 53).

Carl Larsson was born to a poor family in Stockholm and during his youth he suffered all the deprivations of poverty, a period he later described as "hell on earth". He was determined to leave those hard times behind him and thus it was no coincidence that he became the artist who would best portray the happy, harmonious Swedish family, bathed in light, colour, and joyous celebration of home and hearth. In their wooden farmhouse, where Karin and Carl lived with their eight children, they created the simple interiors that were to influence so much of modern design. Stripped floors strewn with rugs, brightly painted furniture and hand-painted friezes were the key elements.

Larsson's paintings were strongly influenced by the local Dalarna folk-art traditions. In his autobiography, Larsson wrote, "My art: it is just like my home; there is no place there for fine furniture... it is simple, but harmonious. Nothing extravagant... just good, strong work."

CENTRAL SWEDEN

*Brilliant blue lakes, rushing rivers, the mysterious outlines of
mountains, and above all the space and silence beckon
hikers and anglers to this untouched landscape*

Map
on page
272

Fiive provinces stretch across central Sweden. In the east are Gästrikland,
Hälsingland and Medelpad, which share the long coastline known as
Jungfrukusten (Virgin Coast). Further inland come Härjedalen and Jämtland, which stretch west to the Norwegian border, the land of lakes and coniferous or birch forests. Härjedalen marks the beginning of the great northern
mountain ranges and the further north you go, the more dramatic the scenery.

The small province of **Gästrikland** has one major town, **Gävle ❶**, in the
southeast corner of the region. Gävle was one of Sweden's great shipping towns,
and the most treasured exhibit at the local museum, **Länsmuséet** (open Tues–Sun
noon–4pm, Wed until 9pm; entrance fee; tel 026 65 56 00), is the Björke boat,
built in AD 100 and among the most notable finds in northern Europe.

Railway enthusiasts should make a point of visiting **Sveriges Järnvägsmuseum** (Railway Museum; open June–Aug daily 10am–4pm; Sept–May closed
Mon; entrance fee; tel 026 144 615) on the outskirts of Gävle. The collection
embraces 29 gleaming locomotives, 30 coaches and wagons and the 1874
coach of King Oscar II.

For children, **Furuviksparken** (open May–early Sept Mon–Fri noon–4pm;
mid-June–mid-Aug till 6pm; entrance fee; tel: 026 17 73 00), 10 km (6 miles)

LEFT: thrill of the
piste, western
Jämtland.
BELOW: lynx,
resident of northern
Scandinavia.

THE INLAND RAILWAY

A trip on the Inlandsbanan (Inland Railway) is an
enjoyable way of seeing some of Sweden's most
dramatic scenery. The route stretches through the Central
Heartlands from Mora in Dalarna to Gällivare in Lapland.

The idea of building such a long railway through a harsh
and inaccessible landscape was first promoted in 1894,
but it was to take another 40 years of hard labour before it
was completed. The 1,100-km (680-mile) line was finally
inaugurated in Jokkmokk in Lapland on 6 August 1937,
and a monument was erected to commemorate the event.

Today the train stops along the way so passengers can
visit local artists and craftspeople or simply admire the
views. Sometimes it has to halt to avoid running into herds
of reindeer resting on the track. With luck, passengers may
also spot elks or bears.

It is possible to make stopovers along the route and stay
for a night or two in local towns and villages to do some
walking in the mountains, or just enjoy the magnificent
landscape. Various packages are available combining rail
travel with hotel accommodation, or trekking. For more
information contact Inlandsbanan AB, Box 561, SE-831 27
Östersund, Sweden. Tel: +46 63 19 44 12; fax: +46 63 19
44 06; www.inlandsbanan.se/

Relive the life of the charcoal burners of old at Albert Vikstens Kojby (Albert Viksten's Cabin Village) at Lassekrog, 40 km (25 miles) northwest of Ljusdal. Visitors can spend a night in a cabin and bake their own "charcoal bread" over the fire (tel: 0651 212 75).

BELOW: folk dancers prepare for the Hälsingehambo festival at Järvsö.

south of Gavle, combines extensive zoological gardens with a variety of other attractions, including a theatre and a circus.

Grilled herring and potatoes with dill butter is a favourite dish all along the Virgin Coast. At **Bönan**, 10 km (6 miles) northeast of Gävle, visit **Engeltofta** to sample the town's famous golden-brown smoked herring, cured over spruce wood – in summer you can catch the boat over from Gävle.

Gästrikland is at the eastern end of the swathe of land which gave Sweden its early mining and smelting industries. Steam trains ply the 4.5 km (2¾ miles) from **Jädraås** ❷, northwest of Gavle, to **Tallås**. The railway is typical of those used to haul minerals or timber, and the coach used by King Oscar II (1872–1907) when he went hunting bears in Dalarna is still in service.

The good-time town

Follow the E4 north to **Söderhamn** ❸, the starting point for boat trips around the archipelago. Söderhamn was founded in 1620 as an armoury for the Swedish army, and the museum is situated in part of what was the gun and rifle factory. Although a commercial centre, the town has an impressive town hall, plus a church to match and a pleasant riverside park.

Around 120 years ago, when the timber industry was at its peak, **Hudiksvall** ❹ had a reputation for high living. A reminder of the era is the town's theatre, opened in 1882. Hudiksvall also has a group of the best-preserved 19th-century wooden buildings in Sweden, the **Fiskarstan**.

The interior of **Hälsingland** has the best scenery, particularly the valley of the river Ljusnandalen , which is laced with lakes along its entire length. West of **Ljusdal** ❺, where the Ljusnan meets the Hennan river, the forests begin.

Dancing in the valley

About 12 km (7 miles) south of Ljusdal is **Järvsö** ❻, a small town in farming and forestry country. Once a year, its peaceful routine is broken by an unforgettable festival: the **Hälsingehambo**, a competitive event involving 3,000 folk dancers. At dawn on a July morning competitors in traditional costumes begin to dance to the tune *Hårgalåten* all the way up the Ljusnan valley, from **Bollnäs** ❼ and Arbrå, to a grand finale 50 km (31 miles) away in Järvsö, in front of Stengård Manor.

Bollnäs has a tradition of sweet-making. In 1919, in a little cottage at **Hållbo**, southeast of the town, Olof Käller invented a special peppermint sweet. Today you can still watch the sweets being boiled, rolled and stretched out in the old way at **Källers Karamellmuseum** (open July daily 2–5pm; tel: 0278 800 23).

Of the mountains around Järvsö, **Gluggberget**, 515 metres (1,689 ft), has a viewing platform at the summit, while **Öjeberget**, 370 metres (1,314 ft), has the advantage that you can drive to the top.

To absorb this region you need to drive first along the minor road 30 km (18 miles) east from Järvsö to **Delsbo** ❽, which attracts large numbers of folk fiddlers for the annual **Delsbostämman**, and then on through Friggesund and Hassela and back to the coast. Surrounded by dark forests, this is **Dellenbygden**, rural Sweden at its best, and includes the Dellen lakes area, with boat and canoe trips, and walking trails.

Anglers' paradise

Together the provinces of **Härjedalen** and **Jämtland** are as big as Denmark, but with a population of only 135,000. To the east and southeast are extensive

Map on page 272

Snow scooters are the most practical form of transport in winter.

BELOW: the dense forests are a good hunting ground.

Map on page 272

The E14 from Östersund to the Norwegian frontier is an age-old route once used by pilgrims on their trek to the grave of St Olav at Trondheim (see page 209).

BELOW: Swedes take to their skis in the winter months. **RIGHT:** "fairy cottage" at Åre.

forests with hills, rivers and lakes. The higher mountains begin in Härjedalen. This heartland has four main rivers, the Ångermanälven, Indalsälven, Ljungan and Ljusnan, all well stocked with fish, especially trout and grayling. Perch, pike and whitefish are the most common in the forested regions, but many tarns have been stocked with trout. You may need a fishing permit, bought cheaply nearby or at the tourist offices. The vast tracts of near-uninhabited territory are also home to wildlife such as bears, wolverine, lynx and the ubiquitous elk.

When tourism was in its infancy, Härjedalen was one of the first Swedish provinces to attract skiers, who still return to pit their skills against its varied terrain, and come back in the summer for mountain walking. The scenery is impressive and, north of **Funäsdalen**, not far from the Norwegian border, the province has Sweden's highest road over the **Flatruet Plateau**, up to 1,000 metres (3,280 ft) high.

At the crossroads of the north–south route, Highway 45, and east–west, Highway 84, is **Sveg**, a small town but Härjedalen's largest at around 4,000 people. **Vemdalen** ❾, 60 km (37 miles) northwest, has an eight-sided wooden church with a separate onion-domed bell tower. Beyond the village the road climbs between two mountains, **Vemdalsfjällen**, before entering Jämtland.

Jämtland is the biggest province in central Sweden, a huge territory of lakes, rivers and mountains. Its heart is the lake of **Storsjön**, the fifth-largest stretch of inland water in the country, which is reputed to have its own monster, a Swedish version of Scotland's "Nessie". Present-day monster-seekers can take a cruise on the lake in the 1875 steamer *Thomée*. On the banks of Storsjön is Jämtland's largest town, **Östersund** ❿, connected by a bridge to the beautiful island of **Frösön**. The island was home to the noted Swedish composer and critic Wilhelm Peterson-Berger (1867–1942). His most popular work, the opera *Arnljot*, is performed every summer on the island.

In Östersund, **Jamtli** (open late June–Aug daily 11am–5pm; Sept–June Tues–Fri 10am–4pm, Sat & Sun 11am–5pm; entrance fee; tel 063 15 01 00), is one of biggest open-air museums in the country, comprising 18th- and 19th-century buildings including a *shieling* (summer farm), baker's cottage, smithy, and an old inn. The food in the café is recommended.

North of Storsjön, on the north bank of Lake Alsensjön at **Glösa** ⓫ are a number of *hällristningar*, primitive rock carvings.

Mountains and canyons

In western Jämtland, the peaks rise up to nearly 1,800 metres (6,000 ft). It is a splendid area for trekking in summer and skiing in winter. Centuries ago, melting ice left many strange and unusual formations such as the deep canyon between the Drommen and Falkfångarfjället mountains. The region is also rich in waterfalls, such as **Ristafallet** near Hålland or **Storfallet**, northwest of Höglekardalen and **Tännforsen**, to the west of Åre ⓬.

Åre is a popular winter sports resort with a funicular railway that goes from the town centre part way up the local mountain, Åreskutan, and a cable car that continues almost to the summit. Lakes and mountains on every side make up a superb view. ❑

NORTHERN SWEDEN

Lapland, land of the Midnight Sun and home to the Sami, offers a richly rewarding experience for the traveller. Fishing villages and holiday islands dot the Bothnian Coast

Map on page 278

In the search for natural landscapes Lapland, which stretches across Northern Sweden and Finland, has become increasingly popular. The uplands, lakes and mountains of the region are among the finest in Europe, and although distances are great there are quality roads and a rail link. Anglers are attracted to the coast of Bottenviken (Gulf of Bothnia), the stretch of water that separates Sweden from Finland. There are excellent opportunities for both river and sea fishing along the coast; holiday-makers and sailors gravitate to its sheltered coves and islands.

The best way to absorb the immensity of Swedish Lapland is to take the inland Highway 45, from south to north. The first town across the border from Ångermanland is **Dorotea ❶**. Its claim to fame is the Dorotea Hotel, which is renowned for its cuisine. **Vilhelmina ❷**, 100 km (60 miles north) on the Ångermanälven river, is of greater interest. It is a well-preserved church village where travellers can find accommodation in its wooden houses.

West of Vilhelmina is the **Kittelfjäll** mountain region and the border with Norway. To the north lies an important road junction at **Storuman ❸** where the 45 is bisected by the E12, known as the Blå Vägen (Blue Highway) because it follows a succession of lakes and the Umeälven river on its route from the east coast. It passes through **Lycksele ❹** where there is a zoo, **Lycksele Djurpark** (open daily from 10am; closing times seasonal; entrance fee; tel: 0950 163 63), that has Nordic species including bear, elk, musk-ox, wolf and reindeer. From Storuman the E12 continues west through Tärnaby to Mo i Rana in Norway.

LEFT: on top of the world in Lapland.
BELOW: Sami in traditional garb.

The Silver Road

From Slagnäs, on Highway 45, a secondary road leads through glorious lakeside scenery to **Arjeplog ❺**, one of Swedish Lapland's most interesting towns. The main attraction is the **Silvermuséet** (Silver Museum; open mid-June–mid-Aug daily 9am–6pm; mid-Aug–mid-June Mon–Fri 10am–4pm, Sat 10am–2pm; entrance fee; tel: 0961 612 90). Housed in an old school, it provides a fascinating insight into the region's history and the Sami people of Lapland. It owes its existence to Einar Wallqvist, "doctor of the Laplanders", who, besides his medical work, collected cultural objects. He established a museum which today has the finest collection of Sami silver in the world. Arjeplog's church is 17th-century and also worth a visit.

Arjeplog is roughly halfway along Highway 95, the Silvervägen (Silver Road) between Skellefteå in the east and Bodø on Norway's west coast. In the 17th century there were silver mines around **Nasafjäll** and the ore was transported, by reindeer and boat, to the east coast. Not until 1974 did it become an asphalted

Northern Sweden

highway opening up an area of outstanding beauty. There are magnificent views from Galtisbuouda, 800 metres (2,620 ft) high, just north of Arjeplog.

West of Arjeplog, at the isolated community of **Laisvall ❻** is **Laisvallsgruvan** (July guided tours Tues and Thur; no children under 15; entrance fee; tel: 0920 202 62), the biggest lead mine in Europe.

Arvidsjaur ❼, once a trading post, now a junction of roads and railways, has the atmosphere of a frontier town. The major attraction is **Lappstaden** (open daily; July guided tours; tel: 0960 175 00), the oldest surviving example of a Sami village, with *kåtor*, tent-shaped wooden huts, and *härbren*, wooden storehouses. In summer, Arvidsjaur is a tourist centre and in winter, when it is intensely cold, both Arjeplog and Arvidsjaur are taken over by the motor industry to test products in sub-zero temperatures.

Map on page 278

Across the Arctic Circle

The **Arctic Circle** is 156 km (97 miles) north of Arvidsjaur and you can buy a certificate to prove you crossed the line at a nearby café. Further north is **Jokkmokk ❽**, the biggest *kommun* (municipal district) in Sweden covering an area of 19,425 sq km (7,500 sq miles) with a population of 7,000.

Jokkmokk is a centre for the Sami culture and in summer you can see nomadic Sami here. An annual outdoor winter market in February attracts thousands of people, although temperatures can drop to –35°C (–31°F). First held in 1605, the market soon became a meeting place for the Sami and merchants from the coastal communities. Today it is as much a social occasion as an opportunity to trade and events such as weddings and baptisms take place. The **Ájtte *Fjäll-och Samemuseum** (Swedish Mountain and Sami Museum; open mid-June–mid-Aug daily 9am–6pm; mid-Aug–mid-June Mon–Fri 10am–4pm, Sat & Sun noon–4pm; Oct–Apr closed Sat; entrance fee; tel: 0971 170 70) portrays the local culture as well as the mountain world, placing mankind in a natural, cultural and ecological perspective.

Highway 45 continues through a sparsely populated area to **Porjus ❾**, a major centre for hydroelectric power. **Stora Sjöfallet**, the largest waterfall in Sweden, is 180 km (112 miles) west of Porjus. To the east of the town is a wild area, **Muddus National Park** (certain areas are closed during the breeding season, mid-Mar–July; tel: 0971 222 50), home of bear, lynx and wolverine. **Dundret Mountain**, 820 metres (2,690 ft) high, northeast of the park, is a bustling holiday centre where you can ride, walk, windsurf, fish, play golf, go white-water rafting, or pan for gold. See the Midnight Sun in June and July from the summit.

Exploring Muddus National Park.

BELOW: the altar at Jukkasjärvi church shows Sami influences.

Gällivare

Gällivare ❿ (pop. 22,000), and its twin town, Malmberget, owe their growth to the discovery of iron ore. Gällivare is the end of the railway line, Inlandsbanan *(see box, page 271)*, that follows Highway 45 north from Östersund. It is a popular tourist route and jumping-off point for treks into the region that include the Padjelanta and Stora Sjöfallet national parks. The town has a mining museum and an 18th-century Sami church. Beyond Gällivare, the 45 joins the E10 and continues

Wolverines thrive in the national parks of Sweden's far north.

north to **Svappavaara**, a former mining centre, and **Karesuando ⑪**, on the Finnish frontier. Many place names in Swedish Lapland owe more to Finnish than to Swedish. In Kiruna, for example, a fifth of the population are Finnish immigrants.

The most northerly church in Sweden can be found in Karesuando which also has the lowest average winter temperatures and Sweden's only tundra. From the top of **Kaarevaara Mountain**, 517 metres (1,696 ft) high, you can see three countries: Sweden, Finland and Norway.

Beyond Svappavaara, the E10 swings northwest to **Kiruna ⑫** (pop. 22,000). Mining began here in 1900 and is still the main industry. The **Kirunavaara Mine** is the world's largest deep mine with 400 km (250 miles) of underground roadways. In summer visitors can tour it by bus. With the decline in mining, Kiruna has turned to tourism and scientific research: there is a rocket testing station on the banks of the Vittangi river at Esrange. For a glimpse of Sami life and history, visit **Samegård** (open mid-June–Sept daily 10am–6pm; Oct–mid-June Mon–Fri 10am–4pm; entrance fee).

Ice Hotel

East of Kiruna, **Jukkasjärvi ⑬** has acquired fame for its Ice Hotel, which is rebuilt every winter. Activities in the region include dog-sledging in the snow-covered wilderness or white-water rafting in summer.

The E10 (Nordkalottvägen), from Kiruna via the Norwegian frontier to Narvik, penetrates one of Europe's last wilderness areas. The mountains southwest of the highway can only be reached on foot or by pony and it is here that **Kebnekaise**, Sweden's highest peak at 2,117 metres (6,945 ft), reigns supreme. **Abisko ⑭**, 150 km (93 miles) from Kiruna, is a popular

BELOW: creating art out of ice.

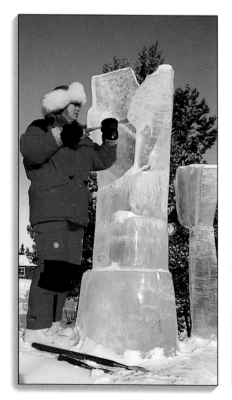

FISHING IN THE FAR NORTH

There is nothing quite like fishing against the impressive backdrop of Sweden's mountains. Creeping silently along a river bank and trying to tempt a shy trout or grayling to the fly is an unforgettable experience. Fishing is well organised in the north. If you are driving along the Northeast Coast there are plenty of opportunities to fish en route, particularly in the unspoilt Piteälven, Kalixälven and Torneälven rivers; just ask at the nearest tourist office.

Further afield, the Tjuonajokk fishing camp on the Kaitumälven river in northwest Lapland is renowned for its grayling fishing. South from there is the Miekak fishing camp, 100 km (60 miles) northwest of Arjeplog (accessible by helicopter from Tjärnberg at Silvervägen, or by snowmobile in winter from Silvervägen), providing arguably the best char fishing in Lapland. At the northernmost extremity of Sweden the fishing centre on Rostojaure lake is renowned for its char and grayling. It is accessible in summer only by helicopter.

Not surprisingly, transport can be expensive, but the cost of fishing permits is relatively low compared with other countries. Permits can be bought at a number of outlets, including tourist offices and some fuel stations. The best month for fishing is usually August.

base from which to set out along the **Kungsleden** (King's Trail) which enables even inexperienced walkers to see the mountains.

The High Coast

*The Bottenviken (Gulf of Bothnia) coastline is low lying and ranges from polished rock to sand and shingle beaches. The major towns along the coast have grown up from trading settlements. Islands form an almost continuous archipelago – a playground for holidaymakers to indulge the Swedish passion for sailing and the sea. Inland, lakes provide tranquil blue oases in the dense forests.

Starting in the south, the main coastal town of Ångermanland is **Härnösand** ⓖ, which is modern except for the town hall, the Domkyrkan (cathedral) and some 18th-century wooden houses. Overlooking the harbour at Murberget there is a large open-air historical museum (open June–Aug daily 11am–5pm; free).

Travelling north, the Höga Kusten (High Coast) Bridge, modelled partly on San Francisco's Golden Gate Bridge, is an impressive structure, 1.8 km (1.1 miles) long. It has a restaurant and visitor centre. Northwest of Härnösand is **Kramfors** ⓰, a leading centre for accordionists. The 13th-century church, near **Ytterlännäs** on Highway 90, is an antiquarian wonder.

The heart of the High Coast is the **Nordingrå Peninsula** ⓱, where the bedrock is an intense red *rapakivi* granite. Scenic treasures include **Omne Bay**, the villages of **Måviken** and **Norrfällsviken**, and the view from the church over Vagsfjärden. **Bönhamn** is a tiny place among the rocks, where **Arnes Sjöbod** is renowned for fresh fish and mashed potatoes and **Café Mannaminne**, near Häggvik, provides home-baked delicacies, handicrafts and musical evenings. The **Höga Kusten walk**, at 25 km (16 miles), starts at Fjordbotten

Map on page 278

TIP

The mosquitoes are rapacious in summer in northern Sweden, so don't forget to pack insect repellent.

BELOW: Bönhamn, on the High Coast.

Map on page 278

with bathing places at Storsand, Norrfällsviken, Hörsång and Noraström.

Between the E4 and the coast lies **Skuleskogen National Park**  (open all year), which is noted for its rare birds and mammals.

Örnsköldsvik ⑲, known as Övik, is an industrial town and one of Sweden's leading winter sports areas*. The islands offshore include *Ulvön with one of the oldest fishermen's chapels in Sweden; **Trysunda**, a favourite with the sailing fraternity; and **Högbonden**, known for its former lighthouse now converted into a cosy clifftop youth hostel accessible by boat from Bönhamn.

Umeå ⑳ is the principal town of Västerbotten. The main attraction here is **Gammlia Friluftsmuseum**, an open-air museum (open mid-June–mid-Aug daily 10am–5pm), which includes the **Västerbotten Museum** (open mid June–mid-Aug daily 10am–5pm; mid-Aug–mid-June Tues–Fri 10am–4pm, Sat noon–4pm, Sun noon–5pm; entrance fee; tel: 090 17 18 00) which explores local history and includes the oldest ski in the world, found nearby, and dated at over 5,000 years old.

Continuing north, **Piteå** ㉑ can come as a culture shock.* Some* wooden houses remain from the 17th century but today it is an industrial centre with timber, paper and pulp industries and a large holiday resort. Norwegians come in flocks from their calm northern fjords to the nearby resort of Pite Havsbad.

From Piteå, the road leads northwest through Älvsbyn to Bredsel and **Storforsen**, Europe's highest natural waterfall with a 81-metre (265-ft) drop.

A traditional Sami hut made from wood and reindeer skins.

BELOW: catch of the day.
RIGHT: winter scene in the frozen north.

World Heritage site

Luleå ㉒, the most northerly major town in Sweden, was moved 10 km (6 miles) by the king in 1649 and stands now at the mouth of the Luleälven river. The old church town, **Gammelstad**, was left on its original site and is a fascinating place to visit with its 400 red-painted cottages and a 15th-century church, still used on important religious occasions. The town is a UNESCO World Heritage site. Beside the original harbour there is an open-air museum, **Friluftsmuséet Hägnan** (open all year; free; tel: 0920 29 38 09), which includes a *hay shed typical of Norrbotten. The **Norrbotten Museum** (open June–Sept Mon–Fri 10am–4pm, Sat & Sun noon–4pm; Oct–Mayclosed Mon; free; tel: 0920 24 35 02) in Hermelin Park provides a picture of the province and has Sami artefacts.

Boden ㉓, 35 km (22 miles) inland from Luleå on the Luleälven river, is the largest garrison town in Sweden. In the 19th century, it was referred to as "one of the strongest fortresses of Europe – that is to say, in the whole world". The **Garnisonsmuséet** (Garrison Museum; open June–Aug: daily 11am–4pm: tel: 0921 683 05) shows 400 years of Sweden's military history.

Sweden's easternmost town, **Haparanda** ㉔, was built opposite Finnish Tornio on the Torneälven river, which forms the border between the two countries.

Road 400 goes north along the river on the Swedish side into the Tornedalen valley to the Kukkolaforsen waterfall. West of the falls, on the Kalixälven river, is **Överkalix** ㉕ with fine views from the top of Brännaberget. At the end of June, this is the place to come and see the spectacular tradition of netting whitefish and salmon. ❏

FINLAND

The urban scene may have undergone a transformation, but the serenity of Finland's lakes and forests remains timeless

From the moment your plane lands at Helsinki airport you are confronted with a scramble for mobile phones. Reserved and reticent Finns? You'd never guess it from the constant telephone prattle. The stereotype of the hesitant, sullen Finn was always questionable, but now Finns are really starting to open up.

In the late 20th century Finland's capital, Helsinki, underwent rapid expansion, draining the enormous, sparsely populated rural areas and maturing into a distinctive and vibrant metropolis with its own identity. Startling new buildings, such as the weird and wonderful Kiasma (Museum of Contemporary Art) and the gleaming National Opera, transformed the city's silhouette; restaurants multiplied; and pavement cafés now open at the first glimpse of spring sunshine, bringing life and colour to the streets.

By the time they celebrated Helsinki's 450th birthday and its status of European City of Culture in 2000, the city's residents had found their place in the European scheme of things. Technological innovations, from the ubiquitous phones to state-of-the-art medical equipment and progressive Internet services, have begun to catch up on, and even overtake, Finland's still substantial pulp and paper industry in terms of economic prestige and significance.

For a country of 5 million people, Finland has produced an astonishing number of architects, artists, sculptors and designers – and it shows. In Helsinki, in particular, almost every corner reveals an intriguing detail: an elegantly carved facade, a statue, a curved window. In cities such as Turku or Porvoo, where the Swedish influence was strongest, some of the oldest buildings remain. Cultural festivals and artistic events are commonplace.

Finland has seemingly endless expanses of untouched landscape, crossed by straight roads running between tall trees. Nobody has managed to count with any degree of certainty how many lakes and islands there are in the country – almost enough, it seems, for every Finnish family to have an island or lake of its own, with plenty of space for visitors, too. No wonder an ideal Finnish summer is based on a waterside wooden cabin and nearby sauna house. With some fishing, swimming, and a small boat, this is Finnish perfection.

As the road heads north, you scarcely realise at first that the rolling farmland of the south has moved into boundless forests and that, gradually, the dark green gives way to the peat and tundra of Lapland. This is the territory of reindeer, bear, wolf, elk and lynx. Along the west coast of the Gulf of Bothnia, the beaches and surprisingly warm waters are ripe for exploration. ❏

PRECEDING PAGES: Sami life as captured by the Sami artist Alariesto; with the onset of winter, artists turn their hand to making ice sculptures; reindeer transport. **LEFT:** lakeside sauna near the town of Jyväskylä.

THE FINNS

Cool, but not humourless, the innovative Finns have fought hard
to preserve their identity and move with the times

People tend mistakenly to describe Finns and their Scandinavian neighbours as cold characters when, in fact, their demeanour can be better described as cool and calm. When one spends some time with Finns in either a social situation or doing business, their dry sense of humour starts to emerge – and it doesn't necessarily need the lubrication of alcohol to loosen things up. Though, of course, the Finns are more at ease away from the work place, in the comfort of their weekend retreat in the country or relaxing in a pub or café.

Finland has come of age since it became a member of the European Union in 1995, taking a more visible, if not more vocal stance. Now successfully a member of the EU, Helsinki is justifiably attracting international recognition as a city to visit rather than just a stopover en route to Russia or other Scandinavian destinations. Helsinki has taken on a more colourful demeanour in recent years, attributable in part to Finland's more relaxed policy towards immigration, which has boosted the foreign population to nearly 5 percent, many of whom are from Vietnam and Senegal.

Well-travelled Finns have long considered themselves cosmopolitan, but they were in the minority. Many younger Finns, shedding their parents' unease, go on to study, work and travel abroad, as well as welcoming all things foreign to Finland.

City versus country

For a traditionally rural country, Finland is becoming more urbanised. Some 80 percent of Finns live on 2 percent of the land. Domestic emigration is accelerating – Finns are moving from small towns to Greater Helsinki, Tampere, Turku and Oulu, although many Helsinki business types are relocating to other countries with warmer climates and lower taxes. The much publicised "*etäyöy*" (distance working via the Internet) has its attractions, but most people still try to escape to the cities.

Nature is sacred

The Finnish state of mind owes a lot to the land itself and the abundance of lakes and forests: more than 400,000 Finns own a plot of forest

LEFT: Thick furs protect the Sami against winter cold.
RIGHT: ice hockey, Finland's national sport.
Champions start training at an early age.

FINLAND: THE ESSENTIALS

Population 5.2 million.
Capital Helsinki (pop. 560,000).
Notable towns Turku, Tampere, Rovaniemi, Oulu.
Climate Northern winters average −13°C (9°F); in the south −5°C (23°F). Summer temperatures average 20°C (68°F).
Top museums Kiasma, Helsinki; Alvar Aalto Museo, Jyväskylä; Suomen Lasimuseo (Finnish Glass), Riihimäki.
Famous homes Hvitträsk (Saarinen); Ainola (Sibelius).
Top events Helsinki Festival; Savonlinna Opera Festival.
Natural wonders Around 190,000 lakes.
Outdoor activities Water sports, hiking, fishing, skiing.
Tourist information www.finland-tourism.com

and everyone has the right of access to the land, which is why Finns take to the woods every summer. Nature is sacred and full of mystery as well as a place of renewal and preparation for the cold, dark months to follow. Which causes one to contemplate whether Finns are manic-depressive by nature, as more suicides are committed after the springtime thaw.

Sisu is a word synonymous with the Finnish character. It mean guts or fortitude, a description which aptly fits the heroic,

> ### SPORTING PROWESS
>
> As a nation, Finns are great lovers of the outdoors and of sport, and some young Finns, following in the footsteps of the great Finnish runner Paavo Nurmi, live for little else but their athletic activities.

Russian regime more than 100 years ago and being long dominated by Sweden. These days Finns are feeling more self-confident. Although they may not forget, they are willing to forgive: across the eastern border, Finnish trucks carry emergency assistance to the struggling Russians who not so long ago were dictating internal issues within Finland.

The Finns are well used to change; it is so deep-rooted in the Finnish soul that the nation accepts almost any new innovation with little resistance, be it

patriotic and noble warriors of Finland's national epic, the *Kalevala*. Yet, in private, these strong men are shy and uncertain, and have great difficulty in waxing poetic when they set out to woo and win the girl. The women, in contrast, are strongheaded, matriarchal, and family-orientated. Perhaps this is why Finland has had so many women in political power in recent years, including their latest president, Tarja Halonen, who was elected for a six-year term in 2000.

No more identity crisis

In the past, Finland struggled to keep its identity, defending its language against the

the Euro, or the latest technological advances in mobile phones.

Change is most visible in nature. With spring in the air everything grows rapidly, the summer months are light and hot, then winter arrives and for a few weeks around the solstice nature stops, frozen, for a pause. Finns prepare for Christmas and their New Year's resolutions. The big wheel keeps turning, another year means new opportunities for change. "The only constant is change," Finns will tell anyone who asks, but despite this, traditions are never completely forgotten.

Indeed, there are so many paradoxes in the Finnish character that it would be hard to convince the sceptical foreigner that there isn't more than a dash of schizophrenia in the national psyche. For every ranting drunk, there's a raving teetotaller. For every patriotic Finn, there's one who leaves as soon as he can afford the fare, never to return. For every shrinking violet, there's an arrogant, cigar-smoking bombast who's never happier than when showing off his possessions and singing his own praises.

Nordic links

The "typical Finn" is the result of a genetic combination that is 75 percent identical to that whose ancestors merged with the gargantuan Vikings. Most Finns are fair-haired (though, overall, Finns are the "darkest" of the Scandi-navians). Some of the most famous Finns are sportsmen and women, taking advantage of their generally strong and healthy physiques.

Finns have entered the 21st century with both style and class. By nature, they are peace-makers. At war, Finns tend to lose, but at peace, Finns certainly seem to be winning. Pinning down their personality is not easy, but if you go to Finland with preconceived stereo-types at the ready, you will no doubt be able to satisfy any or all of them. ❑

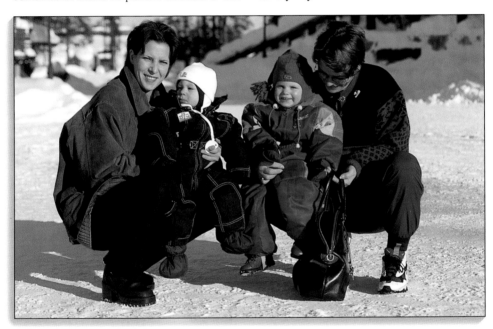

of other Scandinavians, but 25 percent is thought to be derived from tribes that migrated to Finland from east of the Ural Mountains. This more Oriental strain accounts for certain physical traits that set Finns apart from their Nordic neighbours – finely pronounced cheek-bones and quite small slatey-grey or blue eyes.

Laplanders tend to be smaller in stature and sturdily built. Karelians are stockier and have sallower complexions. They are slightly smaller in stature than people from the west coast,

LEFT: with the first sign of summer, cafés spill out onto Helsinki's streets and squares.
ABOVE: enjoying a crisp winter's day in Lapland.

ROMANY GYPSIES

One of the oldest groups in Finland who are not ethnic Finns are the Romany gypsies, whose womenfolk are instantly recognisable by their elaborate embroidered lace blouses and voluminous skirts. Although today most speak only Finnish, few have intermarried, so their dark good looks stand out against fairer Finns.

Most gypsies are no longer nomadic and live instead in houses and flats, subsidised by the government. Some families still tend to wander, especially in autumn, from one harvest festival to another. Little horse-trading is done these days, however, and the gypsies' appearance at these fairs is little more than a vestige of nostagia.

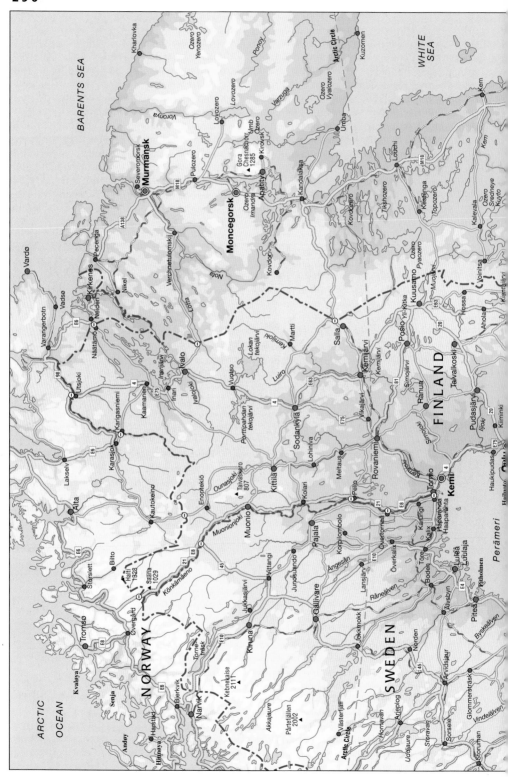

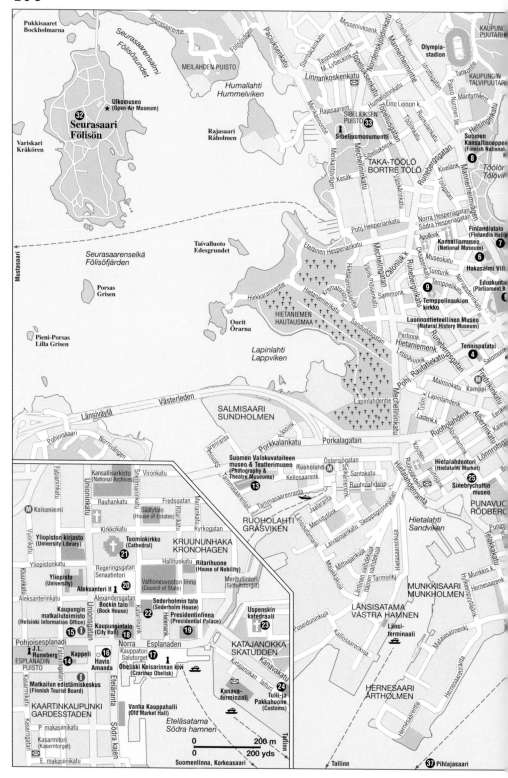

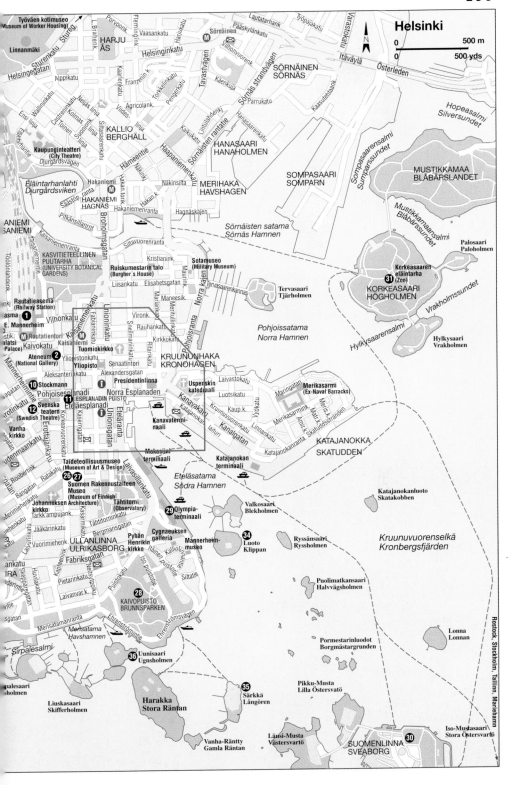

Helsinki

0   500 m

0   500 yds

HELSINKI

*An intriguing mix of Swedish and Russian influences combine
with an ultramodern architectural stamp to make
Finland's capital a gem of the northern Baltic*

Map
on pages
298–299

Flying over Helsinki, one sees nothing but lakes and forests. Arriving in the city centre, there are stately granite buildings and people bustling along, purposefully conversing into mobile phones. Although it appears at first glance to be a city in motion, the Finnish capital is surprisingly quiet, except for the buzz of a skateboard, or a tram making its way across town. In recent years, once the spring light and summer sun appear, pavement cafés have become a pleasant addition to city life.

After a complex 450-year history, Helsinki has grown from a picturesque village with a harbour to a modern, confident capital where the quality of life has been ranked as among the highest in Europe. The "Daughter of the Baltic" has gained her own identity.

Building a capital

Before gaining independence in 1917, Finland lived through 500 years of Swedish rule, and more than 100 years under the Russians. These diverse influences from the west and then from the east have contributed to Helsinki's character. Helsinki was founded in 1550 by the Swedish King Gustav Vasa, but the monumental city centre was built in the early 19th century, thanks largely to

LEFT: monument to Jean Sibelius.
BELOW: young sailor at the harbour.

FACT FILE

Area 338,000 sq km, of which 10 percent is water.
Situation Helsinki is the centre of the Greater Helsinki Area, a region with some 1.2 million inhabitants.
Population 560,000.
Climate July is the warmest month, average temperature: 20°C (68°F); January is the coldest: –5.7°C (22°F).
Finest building Finlandia Hall by Alvar Aalto.
Biggest attraction Annual Helsinki Festival which takes place at the end of August and beginning of September. The festival offers a range of international culture, including classical music, dance, theatre and exhibitions (tel: 6126 5100; www.helsinkifestival.fi).
Newest attraction City Art Museum and Museum of Cultures in Tennispalatsi, the former tennis palace, which also contains a 14-screen cinema complex.
Best excursions City Bus Tour departing from Esplanadi Park, Viking and Olympia terminals (tel: 228 1600); and the 50-minute round trip by Tram 3T.
Best view of the city From the lookout tower and bar of the Hotel Torni, Helsinki's tallest building at 13 storeys.
Meeting place Kappeli café-restaurant, Eteläesplanadi 1.
Tourist information Helsinki City Tourist Office, Pohjoisesplanadi 19 (tel: 169 3757).

Rautatieasema, the railway station designed by Eliel Saarinen in 1905.

the talents of the German-born architect Carl Ludwig Engel. Engel's first commission was a new administrative centre, followed by the cathedral, senate building, university and university library. Engel's neo-classical work can also be seen in St Petersburg and Tallinn. At the same time, Helsinki became the seat of a nationalist movement. Native architects, such as Eliel Saarinen and Alvar Aalto emerged and, after independence in 1917, Finnish Functionalism replaced Art Nouveau as Helsinki's predominant architectural style *(see page 306)*.

Nothing could completely protect the city from the massive Russian air raids of 1944 – nor from fervent, and not always lovely, post-war reconstruction. But Helsinki's position on the sea soon helped it to regain and then increase its stature, not only as a major port, but also as the important site for shipbuilding and international meetings it is today.

Helsinki today

Modern Helsinki is a tranquil but still growing city with some 560,000 occupants. The heart of the city pulses around **Rautatieasema ❶**, the Railway Station, which also contains a metro station and an underground shopping complex. Designed by Eliel Saarinen in 1905 and completed in 1919, it links two of Helsinki's most prevalent styles: National Romanticism and Functionalism.

To the east of the station on the opposite side in another stately building is the **Ateneum ❷** (Museum of Finnish Art, Kaivokatu 2; open Tues, Wed & Fri 9am–6pm; Thur 9am–8pm, Sat & Sun 11am–5pm; entrance fee; tel: 173 36401), built in 1887. The museum's collection of Finnish paintings, sculpture and graphic art covers the years 1750 to 1960 and includes works by such notable Finns as Akseli Gallén-Kallela and Albert Edelfelt.

BELOW: fresh produce on sale in a city market.

Aalto's plan

To get around Helsinki, just remember that all roads lead to **Mannerheimintie**, the city's main thoroughfare and the longest street in Finland. This neighbourhood is evolving based on a plan by Alvar Aalto, which is finally being realised perhaps in ways the great designer would not have anticipated.

From the railway station turn north into Mannerheimintie and on your right you'll see **Kiasma** ❸ (open Tues 9am–5pm, Wed–Sun 10am–8.30pm; entrance fee; tel: 173 36501), a museum of contemporary art, opened in 1998. This remarkable gleaming white structure by the American architect Steven Holl is a symbol of the new Helsinki. Outside, the building's close proximity to the bronze statue of Field Marshal Mannerheim atop his steed, makes a striking reflection at night.

Behind Kiasma is a eye-catching glass building, **Sanomatalo**, which is headquarters for Helsinki's two daily newspapers. Within this striking complex that resembles a space station, is the **Design Forum** (open Mon–Fri 10am–6pm, Sat & Sun 11am–4pm), which hosts a variety of free exhibitions, and an innovative restaurant called **Pulp**.

Joining Kiasma to create a triangle of Functionalist architecture are two other cultural institutions: **Lasipalatsi** (Glass Palace) across Mannerheimintie and the former **Tennispalatsi** ❹ (Tennis Palace) at the other end of the bus station area. Lasipalatsi has been rejuvenated with utmost care to create a media centre which includes an Internet library, television studios, cinema, and fine cafés and restaurants. Tennispalatsi was used during the 1952 Olympic Games and now houses Finland's largest cinema complex (14 screens) and two museums, the **City Art Museum** (open Tues–Sun 11am–8.30pm; entrance fee; tel: 3108

Map on pages 298–299

TIP

See the best of Helsinki with a Helsinki Card, which can be purchased from the Tourist Office, Pohjoisesplanadi 19, hotels and R-kiosks. The card includes free museum admission and free travel on city buses, trams, trains and the metro.

BELOW: Kiasma, the Museum of Contemporary Art.

Traditional Finnish dolls are popular souvenirs.

BELOW: from left, the Parliament Building, Finlandia Hall, and the National Museum.

7001), and the **Museum of Cultures** (open Tues–Fri 11am–8pm; Sat & Sun 11am–6pm; entrance fee; tel 40 501).

Opposite Kiasma is the **Eduskuntatalo** ❺ (Parliament Building), built between 1925 and 1930 and distinguished by an impressive row of steps and a facade of 14 columns of grey granite. Statues of former Finnish presidents scatter the area between the Parliament Building and the **Kansallismuseo** ❻ (National Museum; closed for renovation at the time of writing) two blocks to the north. The museum's decoration, its collection and the stone bear by the entrance are the work of Emil Wikström. The frescoes on the foyer ceiling, depicting scenes from Finland's national epic, the *Kalevala*, are by Gallén-Kallela. The City Museum branch in the fine **Hakasalmi Villa** (open Wed–Sun 11am–5pm; entrance fee; tel: 169 3444) across Mannerheimintie houses a special exhibition on Helsinki's history.

Finlandiatalo ❼ (Finlandia Hall; tel: 40 241), opposite the National Museum, is undoubtedly the most famous building in Helsinki. Alvar Aalto designed it both inside and out, completing the main section in 1971. Home to the Helsinki Philharmonic Orchestra, it is used regularly for concerts and events.

Around the corner is the **Sibelius Academy** (Pohjoinen Rautatiekatu 9; tel: 405 4662), Helsinki's famous musical conservatory, where concerts are given by top students. Continuing north along Mannerheimintie to where Hesperia Park and Töölö Bay come to an end, the **Suomen Kansallisooppera** ❽ (Finnish National Opera House; tel: 4030 2211), which opened in 1993, offers an ambitious season with many international performers.

Nestling, literally, into a small hill west of the Parliament Building behind Mannerheimintie and the winding streets of Töölö, is the ultramodern church, **Temppelinaukion Kirkko** ❾ (open Mon–Fri 10am–8pm, Sat 10am–6pm, Sun

noon–1.45pm & 3.15–5.45pm). It is not only an architectural oddity – built as it is directly into the cliffs, with inner walls of stone – but it is also the site of many good concerts. A service for English speakers is held Sundays at 2pm.

Map on pages 298–299

Shopping and entertainment

Heading south, back to town on Mannerheimintie, you'll find **Stockmann** ⓾, Finland's largest department store, which has an excellent food hall on the lower level. Behind it, on Keskuskatu, is Scandinavia's largest bookshop, **Akateeminen Kirjakauppa**, a great place to browse or to take a break in the stylish café designed by Alvar Aalto. The bookshop faces another Helsinki landmark, **Esplanadin Puisto** ⓫ (Esplanade Park), which was first laid out in 1831 and runs east–west between Mannerheimintie and South Harbour.

The **Svenska Teatern** ⓬ (Swedish Theatre), an elegant semi-circular stone building dating from 1866, commands Esplanade Park's western head on Mannerheimintie. In front of the theatre, Bus 20 will take you just five minutes out of town to the **Ruohalahti** area and the Kaappeli Cable Factory complex, where the **Suomen Valokuvataiteen Museo** and **Teatterimuseo** ⓭ (Photography and Theatre museums, Tallberginkatu 1) are located.

The **Esplanadi**, an old-fashioned promenade, leads from the theatre across the length of the park, past the central statue of J.L. Runeberg, Finland's national poet, to **Kappeli** ⓮ (Eteläesplanadi 1; tel: 681 2440) a café-restaurant. The park is a very popular meeting place and is often the scene of animated fairs, such as the Christmas Fair in December or Night of the Arts in late August. On May Day Eve it is given over to general lunacy as students wearing white caps revel in the streets alongside workers and members of political parties. Two

Helsinki lies at latitude 60°N, and experiences lengthy summer days as a result. At the summer solstice on 22 June, the sun only drops below the horizon for 1 hr 20 mins.

BELOW: two-wheeled transport, a popular way to get around Helsinki.

ON THE TRAIL OF JUGENDSTIL

Helsinki offers a wealth of interest for lovers of architecture, especially among its flamboyant Art Nouveau buildings

For those who love architecture, Helsinki has lots to offer. After becoming Finland's capital in 1812, the Senate Square, designed by Carl Ludwig Engel (1778–1840), was a bold example of the early period of autonomy after Russian rule. Engel's Graeco-Roman-inspired work is found throughout the city in churches, government buildings and the university.

During the second half of the 19th century, the number of architects and designers grew and building styles became more diverse with references to Classicism and Rationalism.

It was after the turn of the 20th century that a younger generation of architects, inspired by

the Arts and Crafts movement, rose in revolt against Classicism and Eclecticism. These included: Lars Sonck (1870–1956), Bertel Jung (1872–1946), and the trio Herman Gesellius (1874–1916), Armas Lindgren (1874–1929) and Eliel Saarinen (1873–1950), who were committed to creating "a more domestic, freer and more authentic world" with their work.

This Art Nouveau, or Jugendstil, as it is called in Finland, is also known as National Romanticism. It is distinguished by its use of stained glass and murals, timber and bronze accents, interesting windows, heavy ornamentation, grey granite, natural colours, and castle-like features. Some of the most famous tourist attractions in Helsinki are Art Nouveau. Their roots go back to the national epic, the *Kalevala*, which inspired the composer Sibelius and the artist Gallén-Kallela. There are many such buildings to be seen in the Katajanokka area near the harbour and in the stylish Eira quarter – look out for Lars Sonck's hospital, Laivurinkatu 27; Lindahl and Thomé's Lord Hotel, Lönnrottinkatu 29, with a granite facade and romantic turrets, and their Otava publishing house at Uudenmaankatu 10. The Pohjola House, Aleksanterinkatu 44, is by Gesellius, Lindgren and Saarinen, as is the National Theatre. Do not miss spending time at the railway station, which is one of Saarinen's masterpieces, especially the murals in the Eliel restaurant.

Private villas were also prominent in this movement and it is worth making an excursion to Hvitträsk *(see page 318)* at Kirkkonummi, just outside Helsinki, which was designed by the architecture trio as a shared living and studio space for themselves and their families. The best-preserved rooms are essentially a museum to Saarinen, who is buried in the wooded, lakeside environs, along with Gesellius. ❑

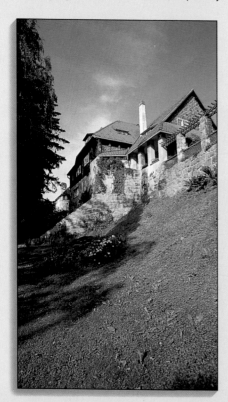

TOP LEFT: Eliel Saarinen's railway station.
LEFT: Hvitträsk studio. **TOP RIGHT:** Art Nouveau detail, Korkeavuorenkatu. **ABOVE:** owl motif.

boulevards stretch east–west along either side of the park. Nowadays, the fine 19th-century stone buildings along **Pohjoisesplanadi** mostly house design shops including Marimekko, Arabia and Aarikka, known respectively for their colourful clothing, distinctive glassware and wooden jewellery. At number 19, the **Helsinki Information Office** and the **City Tourist Board** ⓯ occupy the ground floor. Both offer extensive selections of maps and brochures.

In 1999 the **Hotel Kämp**, Pohjoiseplanadi 29, a popular rendezvous in Helsinki at the end of the 19th century, reopened its doors as a luxury hotel. The **Kämp Galleria** is an exclusive shopping complex on the lower level.

Market days

Across the road from the Kappeli restaurant is the **Havis Amanda Fountain** ⓰, which created quite a stir when it was first erected in 1908. Surrounded by four sea lions spouting water, the bronze statue represents the city of Helsinki rising from the sea, innocent and naked.

Opposite the fountain is the bustling **Kauppatori** ⓱ (Central Market Square; open Mon–Sat 7am–2pm and in summer 3.30pm–8pm). Shoppers wander from stand to stand looking for the perfect new potato, salmon fillet, bunch of dill or flowers. The small tents serve tasty cinnamon or meat pastries and the ubiquitous coffee which seems to fuel the Finns. Other stands proffer interesting goods and handicrafts, many from Lapland.

To the south of the square at the 100-year-old, yellow-and-red brick **Vanha Kauppahalli** (Old Market Hall), one can buy salmon, reindeer cold-cuts, rounds of Oltermanni cheese, or even Vietnamese *loempia* (egg rolls).

Opposite the market stands the long blue **Kaupungintalo** ⓲ (City Hall) designed by Engel in 1833, and **Presidentinlinna** ⓳ (Presidential Palace), designed in 1818 as a private home and turned into a tsarist palace by Engel in 1843. The Finnish president no longer resides here.

Another major landmark, **Senaatintori** ⓴ (Senate Square), stands one block north of here, on the busy **Aleksanterinkatu** shopping street. Over the centuries the square has remained a very impressive spot. Nowadays it functions principally as a byway or as the occasional backdrop for an important event. **Tuomiokirkko** ㉑ (Helsinki Cathedral; open Mon–Sat 9am–6pm, Sun noon–6pm), at the top of a flight of treacherously steep steps on the north side, is a point of pride for Finns, and the exterior – with its five green cupolas, numerous white Corinthian columns and sprinkling of important figurines posing on its roof – is certainly impressive.

The city's oldest stone building, dating from 1757, is the small blue-grey **Sederholmin Talo** ㉒ (open June–Aug daily 11am–5pm; Sept–May Wed–Sun 11am–5pm) on the corner of Aleksanterinkatu and Katariinankatu. Across the street is the **Bockin Talo** (Bock House), also 18th-century, which became the meeting place for Helsinki's City Council in 1818.

Beyond the centre

After exploring Helsinki's centre, venture into one of the surrounding districts, each of which has its own very particular character. **Katajanokka** lies on a small

Map on pages 298–299

Kauppatori market is the place to look for Sami handicrafts, such as this novel hat.

BELOW: Helsinki's fine cathedral, Tuomiokirkko.

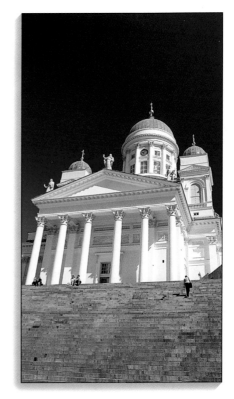

The interior of the Uspensky Cathedral.

BELOW: Kappeli, a popular meeting place on Esplanadi.

promontory sticking out into the sea a few blocks east from Senate Square, connected by two short bridges. The spires and onion-shaped domes of the Russian Orthodox **Uspenskin Katedraali** ㉓ (Uspenski Cathedral), built in 1868, tower above a popular restaurant complex across the street. Helsinki's first Russian restaurant, the **Bellevue**, established in 1917, sits at the base of the cathedral, across from Katajanokka Park.

Jugendstil (Art Nouveau) architecture rules in **Luotsikatu** street, just east of the cathedral. Don't miss the charming griffin doorway at No. 5.

On the southern side of Katajanokka the huge Silja and Viking Line ships from Stockholm tie up, and stylish catamarans ply the route to medieval Tallin, the Estonian capital. In recent years, many of the old warehouses have been converted to restaurants, shops and a hotel. The **Tulli-ja Pakkahuone** ㉔ (Customs and Bonded Warehouse, Katajanokan Laituri 5) from 1900 remains the same, with its inventive Jugendstil architecture.

Finding your way back to Esplanadi, head west on **Bulevardi** and the neighbouring streets like Eerikinkatu, Fredrikinkatu and Uudenmaankatu, which in recent years have become filled with fashionable galleries, boutiques, antique bookshops and restaurants. At the end of Bulevardi, past the old opera house, don't miss the flea market, **Hietalahdentori** ㉕ (open Mon–Fri 8am–2pm, Sat 8am–3pm).To the south of Bulevardi are the exclusive **Eira** and **Ullanlinna** districts. The **Taideteollisuusmuseo** ㉖ (Museum of Art and Design, Korkeavuorenkatu 23; open Tues–Sun 11am–6pm; entrance fee; tel: 622 0540) is an essential stop as it is a showcase for Finland's renowned skills in design, including Alvar Aalto furniture and Lapponia jewellery.

In the same block is the **Suomen Rakennustaiteen Museo** ㉗ (Museum of

Finnish Architecture, Kasarmikatu 24; open Tues– Sun 10am–4pm; entrance fee; tel: 8567 5100), which has an excellent archive of architectural drawings and changing exhibitions focusing on Finnish architectural movements.

The southernmost end of the peninsula is lined by parkland, frequented by joggers, skaters and cyclists. In summer, the city sponsors free concerts in **Kaivopuisto ㉘** (park). In winter, when the sea is frozen, you can actually walk out to some of the closer offshore islands. On the eastern point, embassies fill the chic Ullanlinna district. **Olympiaterminaali ㉙** (Olympia Quay) is a stopping place for Silja and Viking liners and a popular promenade for walkers who find refreshment at **Café Ursula** or **Carousel**.

Map on pages 298–299

Islands abound

Literally hundreds of islands dot the Helsinki coastline. **Suomenlinna ㉚** (Finland's Castle) is undoubtedly the most important. In reality it consists of five islands, over which the ruins of a naval fortress and its fortifications are spread. Suomenlinna has played an integral part in Helsinki's life since its construction started in 1748. It has been listed by UNESCO as a World Heritage site, and functions today as a thriving local artists' community with the restored bastions being used as studios and showrooms. Water buses ferry visitors here from Market Square every half-hour. They dock on **Iso Mustasaari**, from where a hilly path leads up through **Rantakasarmi** (Jetty Barracks), which house art exhibitions and an interesting restaurant and microbrewery known as **Panimo**.

There are several museums on the island (island open daily; entrance to fortress free; museums and restaurants open daily Mar–Oct; entrance fee to museums; tel: 684 1880). The large **Suomenlinna Museum** is the main histor-

Helsinki has a number of public saunas, but the only wood-heated one is Kotiharjun Sauna in Harjutorinkatu (near Sörnäinen metro station; open Tues–Fri 1–8pm, Sat noon–6pm; tel: 735 1535).

BELOW LEFT: taking a break on the harbourside. **BELOW RIGHT:** quiet place for a chat.

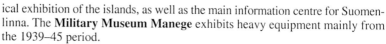

Map on pages 298–299

ical exhibition of the islands, as well as the main information centre for Suomenlinna. The **Military Museum Manege** exhibits heavy equipment mainly from the 1939–45 period.

Cross the bridge to the rambling remains of the **Kruunulinna Ehrensvärd** (Ehrensvärd Crown Castle) and gardens. The castle courtyard is the best-preserved section of the fortress and contains the 1788 sarcophagus of Count Ehrensvärd himself. His former home is now a museum, with old furniture, arms and lithographs. Try to visit the atmospheric summer restaurant **Walhalla**, where on a clear day it is sometimes possible to see Estonia, some 80 km (50 miles) away. There is also the **Rannikotykisto Museo** (Coast Artillery Museum), and the **Vesikko Submarine** to see.

Korkeasaaren Eläitarha ③ (open Mar–Sept daily 10am–6pm; tel: 169 5969) is one of those rare zoos in the world set entirely on an island. In summer you can reach it by boat from Market Square. The zoo, perhaps not surprisingly, specialises in "cold climate animals" although there's an interesting enclosure of South American animals. If you want to learn about indigenous Finnish fauna, you'd do just as well at the **Luonnontieteellinen** (Natural History Museum, Pohjoinen Rautatiekatu 13; open Mon–Fri 9am–5pm, Sat & Sun 11am–4pm; entrance fee; tel: 1912 8800), known for its excellent exhibitions.

The island of **Seurasaari ③** is eminently atmospheric. A pretty, forested place with a national park (open all year), its northeastern side has been made into an **Ulkomuseo** (Open-air Museum; open Mar–Sept daily until 6pm; entrance fee; tel: 4050 9660) containing wooden buildings from provinces all over Finland from the 17th to 19th centuries. The island is connected to the Helsinki shore by a wooden footbridge. Take either bus No. 24 from Erottaja (in front of the Swedish Theatre), or cycle along the Meilahti coastal drive which takes you past **Sibeliuksen Puisto ③** (Sibelius Park) and the silvery tubular **Sibeliusmonumentti** (Monument) to the bridge.

Off the beaten track

Less well known are the smaller islands that form a string around Helsinki's southern peninsula. Across the "Olympic Harbour" are **Luoto ③** and **Valkosaari**, restaurant islands with romantic villas. A long pier outside Kaivopuisto offers a boat service to **Särkkä ③**, another island with a popular restaurant.

Uunisaari ③ is accessible at the southern end of Neitsytpolku street. It's a popular recreational island with a beach, sauna and restaurant.

The **Finnish Sauna Society** situated on the beautiful island of **Lauttasaari** offers wood-heated and smoke saunas and massage (call for times; pre-booking is necessary; tel: 686 0560).

Helsinki's favourite island for swimming is undoubtedly **Pihlajasaari ③**. It actually comprises two islands, with a sandy beach, café and changing cabins on the larger island's western shore. Helsinki's only nudist beach is on the smaller island. Boats to Pihlajasaari depart in summer every 15 to 30 minutes from outside Café Carousel in Eira. The former military island of **Harakka ③**, south of Kaivopuisto, is now a wildlife reserve. ❑

BELOW: military might at the castle of Suomenlinna.
RIGHT: café life, central Helsinki.

THE TRADITIONAL FINNISH SAUNA

An old Finnish proverb says: "First you build the sauna, then you build the house." Even today, there's nothing so uniquely Finnish as a sauna

There are some things along the way which a traveller does not forget – and a real Finnish sauna is one of them. Although its origin is obscure, the sauna came to Finland over 2,000 years ago, and it is a rare Finn who admits to not liking one. Official statistics estimate that there are over 625,000 saunas in Finland, not counting those in private houses or summer cottages that dot the shoreline of the country's lakes. The actual figure could easily be over 1 million in a country of just 5 million people – but then, the sauna is a national institution.

BUSINESS AND PLEASURE

The sauna outgrew its rural roots long ago. Today, be it city or village, you will find public saunas, and it is safe to assume that every new apartment block has a sauna for its tenants. Many companies also have saunas for their employees.

A Finnish sauna is not a meeting place for sex, as it is in some countries; codes of behaviour are strict. Titles and position are, they say, left hanging in the changing room with the clothes. It is not unusual for board meetings and government cabinet meetings to be held in a sauna – perhaps because it's "not done" to swear or raise one's voice. A sauna also leaves you relaxed yet alert.

▽ **FRIENDS AND FOLIAGE**
Tying up birch leaves for the sauna is a social event in summer.

▽ **MORAL CODE**
Despite the nudity, a Finnish sauna is a moral place. Generally, saunas are same-sex only; a mixed sauna is solely a family affair.

▽ **HOT GOSSIP**
There is more to the sauna than just getting clean. It is a happening – a time to meet friends, or to make business deals.

HOW TO TAKE A SAUNA

There is no "right way" to take a sauna – temperature and style vary. The ideal temperature is between 60–80° C (140–175° F) although it can be a cooler 30° C (85° F) on the bottom platform, reserved for children. A common practice is to brush oneself with a wet birch switch, called the *vihta*. This not only gives off a fresh fragrance but increases blood circulation and perspiration.

How long you sit in the sauna is entirely up to you. When you have had enough, you move on to stage two: cooling off. A cold shower is the most common way but, if the sauna is by a lake or the sea, a quick plunge into the cool water is stimulating.

The final stage is to dry off, which should be done naturally, to avoid further perspiration. It is also time for a beer or coffee and a snack to complete the ritual.

△ STEAM HEAT
Water thrown over the hot stones creates a dry steam *(löyly)*, which makes the heat tolerable and stimulates perspiration.

◁ COOLING OFF
In the winter, brave souls jump through holes in the ice or roll around in the snow – not recommended practice for people with high blood pressure.

SAUNA FASHIONS
The sauna has become such an integral part of Finnish life, that there are even "designer" outlets specially geared towards sauna accessories.

ANCIENT USES
In olden days in rural Finland the sauna was not just the place in which to get clean, but also where babies were born and sausages smoked.

SOUTHERN FINLAND

*Follow the route of the Nordic kings from west to east across
Southern Finland through a gentle landscape with painted
villages, ancient castles and an island-studded coast*

Map
on page
316

Helsinki

T o follow the south coast of Finland from west to east is to follow a route
once travelled by Nordic kings and princes to St Petersburg. Known as
The King's Road, the route passes through mainly flat coastal country
covered with farmland and dense forest. The area is heavily settled, and it is also
heavily Swedish-speaking. From Pargas (Parainen), south of **Turku ❶** *(see
page 323)* at the head of the Turunmaa archipelago chain, through Hanko
(Hangö), Ekenäs (Tammisaari), Karis (Karjaa), and further east via Porvoo
(Borgå) through a cluster of small villages on the approach to Kotka, you will
hear a great deal of Swedish being spoken and read it as the first language on
signposts. This is all part of the democracy of bilingualism in Finland.

The eastern portion of the coast, past Helsinki, is riddled with fortifications.
For the Swedes, then the Russians, and finally the independent Finns, the
Russian border has been a crucial dividing line. The Finnish-Soviet borders
still have a no-man's-land running between them, and although travel between
the two countries has become far easier and more popular since the break-up of
the USSR, there is no mistaking the sterner attitude of the Russian customs
guards and immediate deterioration of road conditions as soon as one crosses
over the border to the east.

LEFT: models of
ships traditionally
grace the windows
of Loviisa's
wooden houses.
BELOW:
a summer treat.

Exploring the islands

Richly vegetated but sparsely populated, the archipelago of **Turunmaa ❷** is quieter than the Alands
(see page 321) in terms of tourism, and the islands
are reached more quickly from the mainland. They
are linked by a series of bridges and then ferries. Ferries also service some of the smaller islands that spin
off south from the main chain. Local buses connect
the larger towns. Many Finnish families have their
own islands – the ultimate refuge.

Turunmaa's finest harbour is on the northern spur of
Nagu. An old wooden house overlooking the marina
has been made into a guesthouse-style hotel. Also to
be found in Nagu is the **Borstö Folk Museum** and
the 14th-century **St Olof's Church**.

As you approach **Pargas ❸** (Parainen) from west
or south you come to **Sattmark**, on the island of
Stortervolandet. This tiny log cabin was once a
sailor's quarters. It now serves light meals in its pret-
tily furnished rooms and outside on the dock.

Continuing east towards Piikkiö, it is worth making
a detour to **Kuusiston Linna ❹** on the Kuusisto
peninsula. This medieval bishop's castle stood stoutly
until Gustav Vasa ordered its demolition in 1528, but
enough remains to have encouraged restoration.

Salo ❺, to the east on the mainland in the heart of
the apple-growing Salojoki Valley, has a lively market

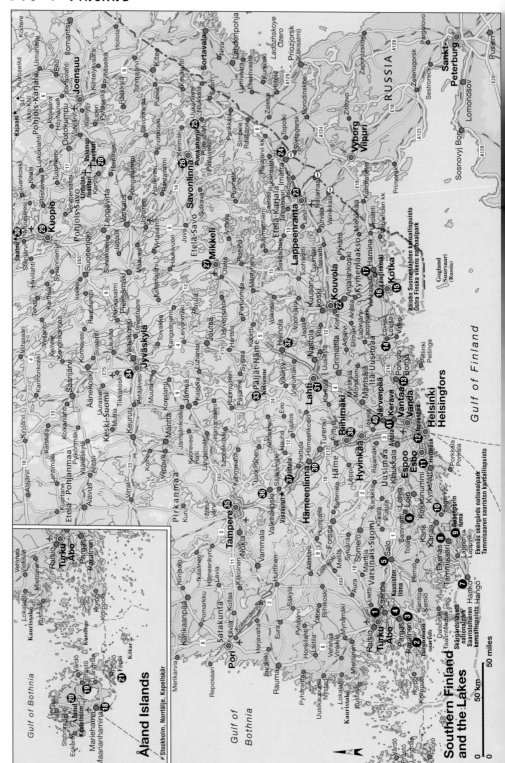

Åland Islands

Stockholm, Norrtälje, Kapellskär

Southern Finland and the Lakes

Gulf of Bothnia

Gulf of Finland

RUSSIA

and is set off by a triad of churches – the Lutheran **Uskela** (1832) by C.L. Engel, the Greek Orthodox **Tsasouna** at its foot, and the stunningly modern **Helisnummen** (Helisnummi Church) about 4 km (2 miles) outside the town. Many of the world-famous Nokia phones are manufactured in Salo. At **Sammatti** ❻, 48 km (30 miles) east of Salo, look out for the sign to **Paikkarin Torppa** (Paikkari Cottage), the home of Elias Lönnrot who collected the legends and tales for the *Kalevala (see page 58)*.

Map on page 316

Marina life

Due south of Salo is **Hanko** ❼ (Hangö), Finland's southernmost town, once a popular spa resort, and now frequented for its annual regatta and its beaches. Hanko is distinguished by an abundance of turreted villas in pastel shades which grace the stretch of beach behind a line of charming white changing huts. These stately homes were built at the turn of the 19th century for the Russian nobility who came for health cures; several offer bed and breakfast accommodation.

Hanko's **Linnoitusmuseo** (Frontline Museum; open May–Aug daily 11.30am–6.30pm), with its wartime bunker is a reminder of the town's strategic history, such as the destruction of the fortifications during the Crimean War. The Municipal Library and Gallery offers a range of exhibitions and there are several art galleries, notably **Loft Gallery E. Pinomaa**, Satamakatu 1, which exhibits contemporary art. **Alan's Cafe**, Raatihuonentori 4, makes divine pastries and shares a charming garden complex with an antiquarian bookshop and crafts gallery. At the harbourfront, housed in some renovated warehouses, are a couple of restaurants featuring locally caught fish. On 26 August, the annual Night of the Bonfires takes place in the main harbour area and launches the Hanko Days Weekend Festival (note that at the end of August hotels and restaurants virtually shut down).

Setting off for a sail from the marina at Hanko.

BELOW: the flat landscape of southern Finland is ideal for cycling.

There are boat excursions to **Bengtskår Lighthouse**, 25 km (15 miles) south of Hanko, which make a memorable day's adventure. Built in 1906, the massive stone structure is Scandinavia's tallest lighthouse at 52 metres (170 ft) high. The walk to the top (252 steps) is worth the extra breaths for the view. There is a café and chapel, and it is possible to lodge here.

Ekenäs ❽ (Tammisaari) is the next main coastal stop along the King's Road. It is a finely laid out old town, with 18th- and 19th-century cobbled streets and charming wooden buildings, and is a great place for a stroll and some delicious Finnish ice cream (*jäätelö*). Just to the south is the **Tammisaaren Saariston Kansallispuisto**, a national park, resplendent with marshes, forests and water birds.

There is an extremely active boating life in and around Ekenäs, and numerous outdoor concerts in summer. The **Knipan** summer restaurant and the steeple of the old granite church (1680) are the town's main landmarks. For an historical background on the town, visit **Porvaristalo** (Ekenäs Museum, Gustav Vasas Gata 13; open June–mid-Aug daily 11am–5pm; mid-Aug–May Tues–Thur evening and Fri–Sun afternoon; tel: 019 263 3161). There are boat tours from the North Harbour in July and early August. A few

Windmills are a feature of the islands and low-lying districts of the south.

kilometres eastwards is **Snappertuna**, a farming village 15 km (10 miles) from the late-14th-century ruined castle at **Raasepori ⑨**. The outdoor theatre in the Raseborg dale stages dramatic and musical evenings and in July you may catch a re-enacted medieval duel. Further east beyond Snappertuna is **Fagervik ⑩**, the site of a tremendous old manor overlooking an inlet. This is the place to picnic, horse ride or enjoy good walking paths.

Approaching Helsinki from the west it would be a shame to miss Eliel Saarinen's home at **Hvitträsk ⑪** (open June–Aug daily 10am–6pm; Sept–May daily 11am–5pm; entrance fee; tel: 4050 9630). The stone and timber buildings seem to blend with the forest, the great cliffs and the White Lake that give the house its name. The main studio, now a museum, saw the planning of 70 projects by the great three architects in recent Finnish history: Saarinen, Herman Gesellius and Armas Lindgren.

Tarvaspää ⑫ was the home of Finland's national artist Akseli Gallén-Kallela (1865–1931). His Jugendstil-inspired studio has been converted into the **Gallén-Kallela Museum** (open June–Aug daily 10am–8pm; Sept–May Tues–Sat 10am–4pm, Sun 10am–5pm; tel: 541 3388) displaying the artist's paintings, stained glass, tools and objects collected on his travels.

Medieval town

BELOW: the former home of Finland's national poet, J.L. Runeberg, Porvoo.

East of Helsinki, **Porvoo ⑬** (Borgå) is one of Finland's most important historical towns. The Swedish king, Magnus Eriksson, gave Porvoo a royal charter in 1346; from this point on it became a busy trading post and, ultimately, it was the place where the Diet of Porvoo (1809) convened to transfer Finland from Swedish to Russian hands. The striking **Porvoo Cathe-**

dral, where this momentous event took place, dates from the 15th century.

While its rich history made the town important, Porvoo's writers and artists gave it its real character. The home of Finland's national poet, **J.L. Runeberg** (open May–Aug Mon–Sat 10am–4pm, Sun 11am–5pm; Sept–Apr Wed–Sat 10am–4pm, Sun 11am–5pm; entrance fee; tel: 019 581 330) has been restored to its original condition. **The Edelfelt-Vallgren Art Museum** (open May–Aug daily 10am–4pm; Sept–Apr Wed–Sun noon–4pm; entrance fee; tel: 019 574 7589) occupies a 1792 merchant's house, formerly the Town Hall, on Rahti-huoneentori (Town Hall Square). It features paintings by Albert Edelfelt – one of Finland's finest 19th-century artists – and works by sculptor Ville Vallgren, as well as a fine Art Nouveau furniture collection. The **Albert Edelfelt Atelier** in Haikko, 6 km (4 miles) south of Porvoo, also exhibits much of Edelfelt's work.

For scenery, the medieval atmosphere of **Old Porvoo** has few rivals: its riverbanks are lined with red-ochre warehouses and the pastel-coloured wooden houses from the 16th century provide a charming backdrop. Today, they house museums, boutiques, cafés and restaurants, as well as private residences. A fine excursion is to take a river cruise to Porvoo from the main harbour in Helsinki.

Towards the border

East of Porvoo, the landscape becomes more rural and less populated. In summer, the grassy hillocks bristle with wildflowers. **Loviisa** ⓮ is a pretty coastal town with an esplanade headed by the New Gothic Church. A town museum tells the local history, including the role of the Rosen and Ungern bastions, built in the 18th century to protect the important trade route between Vyborg and Turku. The Old Town buildings survived the fire of 1855 and tours can be made

Map on page 316

Good stopping points on the journey east from Loviisa to Kotka are the excellent sandy beaches of Pyhtää and the holiday island of Kaunissaari with its interesting fishing village.

BELOW: wooden home typical of southern Finland.

Map
on page
316

Tsar Alexander III,
whose hand-crafted
timber fishing lodge
at Langinkoski
was a gift from the
Finnish state.

BELOW:
strawberries
for sale at a
roadside stall.

of the last spirits factory, which today is an artist's atelier. Just 10 km (6 miles) from the centre of town on an island at the mouth of Loviisa Bay is the **Svartholma** sea fortress, built in 1748.

Kotka ⑮ is the next important destination on the King's Road and is considered one of the most beautifully situated cities in Finland. It is around Kotka that the Kymi River breaks up into five branches before rushing off into the sea, making for perfect salmon and trout fishing. The closest of the spray of islands along the coast can be reached by bridges, the rest by ferry.

Kotka centre is based on an esplanade. One street to the northwest, at Kirkkokatu and Koulukatu, is the main Lutheran church with tremendous brick buttresses; the imposing Orthodox St Nicolai Kirkko complex and park runs along Papinkatu. Kotka has frequent boat services to nearby islands, some of which have old fortifications. The pleasant **Sapokka Harbour** has one of the finest parks in Finland, with a high artificial waterfall. Step aboard a water bus for a tour of this beautiful archipelago.

Apart from the Kotka islands, the **Kymenlaakso** (Kymi river valley) extends further inland, where there are gorgeous forest paths. Details are available from the Kotka Tourist Office at Kirkkokatu 3, tel: 05 234 4424.

Imperial lodge

The impressive Imperial Fishing Lodge of Tsar Alexander III (1845–94) is at **Langinkoski** ⑯ (open May–Aug daily 10am–7pm; Sept–Oct Sat & Sun only; entrance fee; tel: 05 228 1050). The tremendous log building with simple furnishings was crafted by the Finns for the Tsar. Several nature paths begin from Langinkoski. If you walk north for 5 km (3 miles), you'll pass the Kyminlinna fortification, over the Hovinkoski rapids in Huumanhaara, on a branch of the Kymijoki river to Keisarin Kosket. These "tsar's rapids" course around Munkkisaari Island, with its Orthodox chapel (Tsasouna). The spot is also ideal for fishing and rapids-shooting. On the bank is **Keisarin Kosket Lodge**, an Orthodox monastery site from 1650 to 1850, with boats and cabins for hire; fishing licences are also sold (tel: 05 210 7400).

In summer, **Kärkisaari**, just to the west of Kotka, makes for a lovely excursion. The former youth hostel here (originally a villa from the beginning of the 20th century) now provides stylish bed and breakfast accommodation. The long swimming dock leads into the island-filled inlet of the Gulf of Finland. On the adjacent peninsula is **Santalahti**; the crescent-shaped beach has grassy knolls at the edge of a sandy bay.

Kotka is only 70 km (45 miles) from the nearest Russian city, Viipuri (Vyborg) and 270 km (170 miles) from St Petersburg; all varieties of Finland–Russia trips can be arranged with the Kotka Tourist Board, but remember to plan overnight trips well in advance so that your visa will be ready.

Hamina ⑰ is the last of the large Finnish towns before the Russian border. Further east lies **Vaalimaa**, a busy border station with huge supermarkets selling goodies to Russians and Finns alike. ❑

ÅLAND ISLANDS: THE ULTIMATE RETREAT

To the west of Finland, the Ålands are a perfect island-hopping destination. Catch a ferry, hire a bike and discover this little-known paradise

The Åland Islands (Ahvenanmaa in Finnish) are a collection of granite skerries comprising some 6,500 islands off the west coast of Finland.

Ålanders have inhabited their islands for thousands of years, and have a strong ethnic culture and a formidable pride in their identity. The population of 25,000 has had its own flag since 1954 and its own postage stamps since 1984. Today, the islands are an autonomous demilitarised zone represented both in the Finnish parliament and the Nordic Council, with Swedish being the official language. Although part of the EU, Åland remains outside the tax union agreement so tax-free shopping is available to travellers.

June to August is the ideal time to visit. Take a Viking or Silja Line ferry from Turku, Helsinki, or Stockholm to **Mariehamn** ⓲, sailing through the maze of skerries en route. There are also Finnair flights from Helsinki.

Mariehamn is the capital of the main island, Åland, and with 11,000 inhabitants, it is the only town-sized settlement. In the West Harbour, the four-masted museum ship *Pommern*, built in Glasgow in 1904, is worth a visit, as is the nearby Maritime Museum (open May, June & Aug daily 9am–5pm; July daily 9am–7pm; Sept–Apr Tues–Sun 10am–4pm; entrance fee). Other museums feature exhibitions on prehistoric and Ice and Bronze Age life, hunting, fishing and even delivering mail.

The islands are a paradise for hiking, fishing, cycling, golfing, swimming and other water sports, and are best explored by bicy-

cle and ferry. From Åland, there is a daily bike ferry to **Prästö** ⓳. You can hire bicycles from the Mariehamn harbours. Most notable in Åland's northeast are the historic Kastelholm and Bomarsund fortresses. **Kastelholm** ⓴, (open May–Sept) was once the administrative centre for the islands and dates from the 1300s. The Russians began fortifying it in 1829. Adjacent are the Cultural History Museum and Jan Karlsgården Open-Air Museum (open May–Sept daily; Oct–Apr Mon–Fri; entrance fee).

To the southeast of Åland lies **Föglö** ㉑, once an important vodka smuggling destination. In the eastern part of the island there is a natural bird reserve.

Midsummer celebrations are held in almost every village with the traditional raising of the Midsummer pole and dancing.

Hotels, guest houses, cottages and camping facilities are available. For information, contact Ålands Turistinformation, Storagatan 8; tel: 018 240 000; www.mariehamn.aland.fi. ❑

TOP LEFT: figurehead, Åland Maritime Museum. **ABOVE LEFT:** Åland flags. **TOP RIGHT:** riding on the islands. **RIGHT:** sauna on the water's edge.

TURKU

Ancient and modern coexist in Turku, Finland's former historic capital. Colourful restaurant boats line the river; museums, bars and galleries intermingle in the city centre

Map on page 324

Surrounded by islands, river and sea, Turku (Åbo in Swedish) is a summer paradise, yet it is also worth a visit during other seasons. The River Aura divides the modern city in two and you can cross its five main bridges or take the little ferry that still carries pedestrians and bicycles free of charge.

Turku is Finland's oldest city and yet many of the buildings go back only to the Great Fire of 1827 which destroyed a town then largely made of wood. In 1300, when it acquired a new cathedral, Turku became the spiritual centre of Finland. Around the same time, the solid lines of a castle began to rise near the mouth of the River Aura as the heart of royal power in Finland, where the Swedish governor lived and visiting dignitaries paid their respects.

After the Great Fire, the market and town moved away from the cathedral to the west bank of the Aura, much of it designed and built to the plan of Carl Ludwig Engel. Turku had the first university in Finland, founded by the 17th-century Governor General of Finland, Count Per Brahe.

Today, **Turun Linna 🅐** (Turku Castle; Linnankatu 80; open mid-Apr–mid-Sept daily 10am–6pm; mid-Sept–mid-Apr Tues–Sun 10am–3pm; entrance fee; tel: 02 262 0300) looks towards the modern town centre, some 3 km (2 miles) away. Many of its rooms have been preserved as the Turku Historical Museum.

LEFT: Turku's 14th-century cathedral.
BELOW: market day in the main square.

Exploring the town

Begin your walking tour in the colourful market square. Just adjacent is the **Ortodoksinen Kirkko 🅑** (Orthodox Cathedral), built in 1838 on the orders of Tsar Nicholas I. Be sure and visit the 19th-century **Kauppahalli 🅒** (Indoor Markethall), across the street in Eerikinkatu.

Turning down Aurakatu, the Auransilta (bridge), gives the first view of the numerous restaurant boats and the sleek white hull and complicated rigging of the *Suomen Joutsen*, which once plied the ocean between South America and Europe. Nearby at Luostarinmäki is the open-air **Käsityöläismuseo 🅓** (Handicrafts Museum; open mid-Apr–mid-Sept daily 10am–6pm; mid-Sept–mid-Apr Tues–Sun 10am–3pm; entrance fee; tel: 02 262 0350) which features traditional crafts people at work. Coming down the hill, detour via the Observatory on Vartiovuori, now the **Merenkulkumuseo 🅔** (Turku Art Museum; open Sept–May Tues–Thur 11am–6pm, Fri–Sun 10am–4pm; June–Aug Tues–Thur 11am–7pm, Fri–Sun 10am–4pm; entrance fee; tel: 02 274 7570) until 2004, when it will return to its former location on Puolalanmäki. It houses a comprehensive collection of Finnish art.

Tuomiokirkko 🅕 (Turku Cathedral; open daily 9am–7pm) maintains a stately presence. Consecrated in 1300, it is Finland's most important medieval struc-

ture. In the Cathedral Park a statue depicts Governor Per Brahe in a classically proud pose. A complex of cream-hued buildings at Vanha Suurtori 7 houses the **Turku Cultural Centre** with a cosy Book Café and restaurant, Teini (tel: 02 233 0203), offering a reasonably priced luncheon buffet. To the north stands the **Rettig Palace**, today the museum complex, **Aboa Vetus and Ars Nova** (open mid-Apr–mid-Sept daily 11am–7pm; mid-Sept–mid-Apr Thur–Sun 11am–7pm; entrance fee; tel: 02 250 0552). The main house exhibits 20th-century art and the courtyard (with ruins of a medieval town) provides a glimpse of Turku's history.

Along the riverbank

For a riverbank tour, visit **Qwensel House**, named after a judge, J.W. Qwensel, who bought the plot of land in 1695. This is Turku's oldest wooden building, with a popular courtyard café, and now houses the **Apteekkimuseo** (Pharmacy Museum; Läntinen Rantakatu 13; open mid-Apr–mid-Sept daily 10am–6pm; mid-Sept–mid-Apr Tues–Sun 10am–3pm; entrance fee; tel: 02 262 0280). From the front of the museum, the horse-cab *Musta-Hilu* provides leisurely views of the city.

Walk past Myllysilta (Mill Bridge) to the next bridge, Martinsilta, where the *SS Ukkopekka* steamship is moored, and still offers pleasant excursions through the archipelago. Depending on how far you care to walk, you can continue on this side of the river as far as Turku Castle and the modern harbour areas, with merchant tugs and tankers and the terminals of the Viking and Silja lines.

On your way to the harbour at Linnankatu 74 is the **Forum Marinum** (Maritime Centre; open May–Sept daily 11am–7pm; Oct–Apr Tues–Sun 10am–6pm; entrance fee), home of the excellent Maritime Museum and Turku's museum ships, including the barque *Sigyn*.

TIP

A dining experience not to be missed: The Angel Restaurant, Kauppiaskatu 16 (tel: 02 231 9088) serves heavenly meals in a series of dining rooms all featuring seraphic decor.

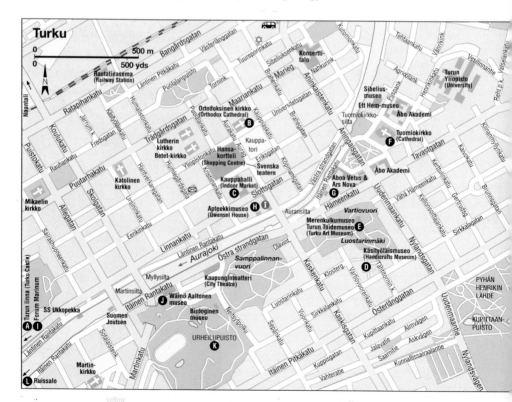

yellow

Heading back towards the centre you come to the **Wäinö Aaltonen Museo ❶** (Itäinen Rantakatu 38; open Tues–Sun 11am–7pm; entrance fee; tel: 02 262 0850). The modern structure contains works by one of Finland's most important sculptors, Wäinö Aaltonen (1894–1966). In **Urheilupuisto ❻**, the surrounding park, the windmill on Samppalinnanmäki is the last of its kind in Turku. Next to it is the running track where the champion long-distance runner and Olympic gold medallist Paavo Nurmi (1897–1973) trained. His statue stands on Auransilta. The polished granite stone on the slopes of Samppalinnanmäki is Finland's independence memorial, unveiled in 1977 on its 60th anniversary.

Ruissalo Island

Boat services depart several times daily for **Ruissalo Island ❼**. An ideal excursion for cyclists, walkers and nature lovers, Ruissalo also has the area's best beaches. The 19th-century **Villa Roma** is typical of the "lace villas" (so-called because of their latticed balconies and windows) built by wealthy merchants. Its owner, the Procultura Foundation, shows summer exhibitions of top-quality Finnish art. In summer, the island is home to Ruisrock, the annual rock festival.

One of the best ways to see the archipelago is with a cruise aboard the *SS Ukkopekka*, which retains something of its steamship past. The bearded skipper, Captain Kangas, is everyone's image of a sea captain. The steamship cruises to different islands and towns, including Captain Kangas's home town of **Naantali**, a charming place north of Turku. Naantali is popular in the summer, when people move into their summer houses and yachts moor in the harbour. Children are attracted by **Moomin World** (open mid-June–mid Aug daily 10am–7pm), based on the characters made famous by the Finnish author Tove Jansson. ❑

Turku has become known for its quartet of bars in the city centre, housed in buildings that have been converted from a pharmacy, bank, schoolhouse, and even a public toilet.

Map on page 324

BELOW: boats moored on the Aura river.

FINLAND'S LAKELAND

A labyrinth of lakes and pine-covered islands extends north from Helsinki. The landscape that was home to Sibelius rewards exploration by lake steamer and canoe

Map on page 316

With some 33,000 islands and peninsulas, the Great Lakes of Saimaa and Päijänne in Central Finland provide a diverse waterscape of lakes, rivers and canals to form Europe's largest inland waterway system. This varied landscape owes its beauty to the Ice Age when glaciers carved out the shape of lakes and ridges. Excellent holiday facilities are offered for most kinds of water sports throughout this region.

The best approach to the lakes is via industrial **Kouvola ㉒**, about 140 km (86 miles) northeast of Helsinki and a junction of road and rail routes into Saimaa. Although not the most interesting town in Finland, Kouvola's Kaunisnurmi quarters house quaint handicraft shops and several museums.

To capture the spirit of Saimaa, ignore the direct routes to Kuopio in the north *and head east on Road 6 to **Lappeenranta ㉓**, South Karelia's main town. The fortress next to the harbour was built by the Russians in 1775. Nearby, the suburb of Linnoitus is the most interesting part of the town, where you will find Finland's oldest **Orthodox Church** (1785) and the **Etelä-Karjalan Museo** (South Karelian Museum; open June–Aug Mon–Fri 10am–6pm, Sat & Sun 11am–5pm; Sept–May Tues–Sun 11am–5pm; entrance fee; tel: 5 616 2255), with a fascinating section on the old city of Vyborg (just a few miles south in Russia). The **Ratsuväkimuseo** (Cavalry Museum; open June–Aug Mon–Fri 10am–6pm, Sat & Sun 11am–5pm; entrance fee; tel: 5 616 2255) details the history and distinctive red uniforms of Finland's proud soldiers. Day cruises to Russia operate from Lappeenranta for which Western visitors do not require visas, although they are obligatory for other visits.

A few miles further east is the industrial city of **Imatra ㉔**, once erroneously described as the "Niagara of Finland", but worth a brief visit to see the impressive **Imatrankoski** (rapids).

High on the ridges

About 50 km (30 miles) north of Imatra, Road 6 passes within a few hundred metres of the Russian border. Switching to Road 14, you soon come to **Punkaharju ㉕**, one of Finland's best-loved beauty spots. Punkaharju is one of countless ridges bequeathed to Finland by the last Ice Age. It's around 7 km (4 miles) long and in places is just wide enough to carry the road; elsewhere it widens to accommodate magnificent pine and birch woods.

Lusto, the superb Forestry Museum (open May & Sept daily 10am–5pm; June–Aug daily 10am–7pm; Oct–Apr Tues–Sun 10am–5pm; entrance fee; tel: 015 345 1030) has a comprehensive exhibition on Finland's forests and associated subjects such as design, wilderness trekking, forestry industry and research.

LEFT: peaceful Lakeland waters.
BELOW: composer Jean Sibelius was born in the town of Hämeenlinna.

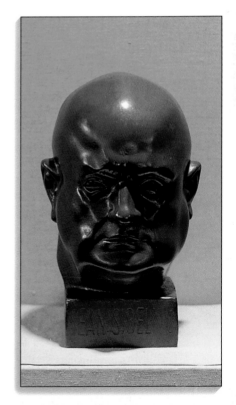

Tucked away among Punkaharju's ridges are well-equipped holiday centres and the **Kesämaa (Summerland) Leisure Centre** for family fun. The **Retretti Arts Centre** (open June–Aug daily 10am–5pm, July until 6pm; entrance fee; tel: 015 775 2200), built into the bedrock on the ridge, is well worth a visit. Its annual exhibition, featuring four usually quite different, internationally acclaimed artists, is a major event in Finland. In summer, a lake steamer sails between Punkaharju and Savonlinna from Retretti. The two-hour trip is a delightful mini-voyage through the islands.

Operatic odyssey

Savonlinna ㉖ ("the castle of Savo") is the most charming of Finland's main lakeland towns and the best base in Saimaa for making trips. It has the medieval castle of **Olavinlinna** (open for tours June–mid-Aug daily 10am–5pm; mid-Aug–May daily 10am–3pm; entrance fee), which is the site of the annual International Opera Festival that takes place throughout July. Tickets for, and accommodation during, the festival should be booked well ahead (tel: 15 47 6750; e-mail: info@operafestival.fi; www.operafestival.fi). With its massive granite walls, ramparts and shooting galleries topped by three great round towers, Olavinlinna has everything you might expect from a medieval castle.

Near the castle, the museum ship *Salama*, a steam schooner built in 1874, shipwrecked in 1898 and raised from the lake in 1971, is one of three converted old ships that form the inland navigation section of the **Savonlinnan Maakunta-museo** (Savonlinna Provincial Museum, Riihisaari; open July–mid-Aug daily 11am–8pm; mid-Aug–June Tues–Sun 11am–5pm; entrance fee; tel: 015 571 4712).

From Savonlinna to Kuopio by lake steamer is a full day's journey. Road travellers have a choice of continuing west from Savonlinna on Roads 14 and 5 to Mikkeli or staying with Saimaa to its northern limits beyond Kuopio.

Mikkeli ㉗, a pleasant provincial capital, is a historic army town. Some 5 km (3 miles) north of Mikkeli, the **Visulahti Family Leisure Centre** is set in a park populated with an automobile exhibition, waxworks and the Dinosauria amusement centre.

Convent culture

The recommended way to Kuopio from Savonlinna is via Varkaus on Road 464, a particularly attractive and watery route. Then take Road 23 heading northeast towards Joensuu in north Karelia, passing by the Orthodox monastery of **Valamon Luostari** ㉘ (open daily 8am–9pm; tel: 017 570 1504: www.valamo.fi) and the convent of **Lintulan Luostari** (tel: 17 563 106). On all three counts of history, culture and scenery, these merit a visit. Monastery cruises run from Kuopio in summer.

The clue to the monastery's history lies in its name. Valamo is the large island on Lake Ladoga, across the Russian border to the east, on which an Orthodox religious foundation was established in the Middle Ages. During the Finn-Russian Winter War, 1939–1940, the handful of elderly monks was forced to leave and eventually settled in the present site of Uusi ("New") Valamo, originally an old manor house. Valamon

BELOW: the lakes attract windsurfers.

Luostari has experienced something of a renaissance in recent years. There is a fine church, completed in 1977, a cafeteria, souvenir shop and a modern hotel. The Lintulan Luostari, a few kilometres away, has a similar but shorter history.

Map on page 316

Music and dance

Kuopio ㉙ has a crowded summer calendar, the highlight of which is the International Dance and Music Festival in June. The town's daily market fills most of the central **Tori** (Market Place) and is one of the most varied outside Helsinki. Sights to see include the **Kuopion Kortellimuseo** (Kirkkokatu 22; open mid-May–mid-Sept daily 10am–5pm, Wed until 7pm; mid-Sept–mid-May Tues & Sun 10am–3pm; entrance fee; tel: 17 182 625), comprising a number of original dwellings complete with authentic furniture, warehouses, and even gardens dating from the 18th century to the 1930s. The **Kuopion Museo** (Kauppakatu 23; open Mon–Sat 9am–4pm, Wed until 8pm, Sun 11am–6pm; Sept–Apr closed Sun; entrance fee; tel: 17 182 603) houses regional collections of a cultural and natural history order in a castle-like building.

Icons – many from the 18th century and some from the 10th century – and sacred objects are on view at the **Ortodoksinen Kirkkomuseo** (Orthodox Church Museum, Karjalankatu 1; open May–Aug Tues–Sun 10am–4pm; Sept–Apr noon–3pm; entrance fee; tel: 17 287 2244). The treasures were brought here from Valamo and Konevitsa monasteries in Karelia and a few from Petsamo in the far north, all territories ceded to the Soviet Union.

At **Iisalmi** ㉚, 80 km (50 miles) north of Kuopio on Road 5, **Evakkokeskus** (Kyllikinkatu 8), a Karelian-Orthodox Cultural Centre, displays valuable relics recovered from territory now in Russia. You can dine on

The 19th century re-created in Lappeenranta.

BELOW: Olavinlinna, a dramatic setting for opera.

Street corner kiosks offer everything from culinary delights to fast food.

the harbour at **Kuappi**, "the smallest restaurant in the world", or at **Olutmestari**, Savonkatu 18, a popular summer restaurant with an attractive terrace.

The western lakes

To the west of the region lies Päijänne, Finland's deepest lake and its longest at 119 km (74 miles). At the southern and northern ends of the lake system are two of Finland's more substantial towns, Lahti and Jyväskylä respectively, which are linked to the west of Päijänne by one of Europe's main highways, E24, and to the east of it by a network of slower more attractive routes.

Lahti ❸ lies 103 km (64 miles) north of Helsinki on Road 4 (E75). The **Lahden Urheilukeskus** sports centre offers some of Finland's best winter sports facilities, and is the venue for the annual Finlandia Ski Race and the Ski Games. Lahti is a modern place, one of its few older buildings being the **Kaupungintalo** (Town Hall) designed by Eliel Saarinen in 1912. Three blocks to the north is the market, and two blocks further north, at Kirkkokatu 4, the highly individualistic **Ristinkirkko** (Church of the Cross; open daily), built in 1978, and the last church in Finland designed by Alvar Aalto.

The **Lahden Historiallinen Museo** (Lahdenkatu 4; open Mon–Fri 10am–5pm, Sat & Sun 11am–5pm; entrance fee; tel: 03 814 4536) in Lahti Manor is an exotic late 19th-century building with very good regional ethnographical and cultural history collections, as well as art and furniture. A few kilometres northwest to Tiirismaa is the tourist centre of **Messilä**, combining an old manor house, downhill skiing in winter and camping.

From Lahti it's only 35 km (21 miles) northeast on Road 4 to the pleasant little town of **Heinola ❷**. Taking the popular summer lake route, it is a lovely

BELOW: dancers perform at Kuopio's annual festival.

four-and-a-half hours by steamer, three and-a-half hours by hydrofoil.

The **Jyrängönkoski** (rapids) provide good sport for local canoeists and for fishermen casting for lake and rainbow trout. Rent a rod at the **Siltasaari Fishing Centre** and have your catch smoked to eat on the spot or take it away.

An attractive route to Jyväskylä is to leave Lahti to the north on Road 24 and after 25 km (15 miles), soon after crossing the Vääksy canal at Asikkala, branch right onto minor Road 314. This will take you along the **Pulkkilanharju** (ridge), which vies with that of Punkaharju for magnificent views. Continue via Sysmä and Luhanka, through various waterscapes that make up Päijänne's contorted eastern shore. To rejoin Road 9 (E63) at Korpilahti for the final leg to Jyväskylä you can use the enormous bridge across Kärkistensalmi, one of Päijänne's many narrow straits. Road 24, of course, provides a more direct main road link all the way from Lahti to Jyväskylä in 174 km (107 miles).

A beauty spot inside the **Päijänteen Kansallispuisto** (Päijänne National Park) is the long, slender island of **Kelvenne** ❸, 60 km (37 miles) north of Lahti, with its lakes, lagoons and curious geological formations. You can reach it from the Ravintola Laivaranta camping area (tel: 03 551 2471) at Padasjoki.

Alvar Aalto's city

Jyväskylä ❸ is situated on the northern shore of Lake Päijänne. Alvar Aalto grew up here and there are no fewer than 30 major buildings by him around the area, including the university, theatre and the Museum of Central Finland. Don't miss the **Alvar Aalto Museo** (7 Alvar Aallonkatu; open Tues–Sun 11am–6pm; Aug until 8pm; entrance fee; tel: 14 624 809) with its collection of architectural plans, photographs, scale models and Aalto's furniture designs. There are a

Map on page 316

BELOW: a boat is an essential part of Lakeland life.

number of winter and summer sports facilities in Jyväskylä, but the town is best known internationally as the venue for the well-attended 1,000 Lakes Rally in August, Finland's premier motor racing event. The Jyväskylä Arts Festival is a major cultural event held every June, always with a different theme.

With over 200 lakes in the area, make sure to take a boat journey from Tampere, either south on the Silverline route, or north on the Poet's Way, or hop on a boat to Viikinsaari to retreat into nature.

Tampere

Tampere ㉟, Finland's industrial capital, lies 150 km (94 miles) southwest of Jyväskylä. It was officially founded in 1779 by King Gustav III of Sweden-Finland and owes its fortunes to the Tammerkoski (rapids), which first brought power and industry to the area. The Tammerskoski have largely lost their working factories, and in their place are hotels, shopping centres and museums.

Significant churches, museums and buildings include the 20th-century **Kirjasto Ⓐ** (City Library) by husband and wife architects, Reima and Raili Pietilä, the design of which is said to be based on the open wings and spread tail feathers of a wood grouse; and **Tampere-talo Ⓑ** (Tampere Hall), a spectacular blue-white structure designed in 1990 by Esa Piiroinen and Sakari Aartelo.

Tuomiokirkko Ⓒ (Tampere Cathedral, Tuomiokirkonkatu 3), designed by Lars Sonck in National Romantic style and completed in 1907, contains some of the best of Finnish art, including Magnus Enckell's altar fresco of the Resurrection and Hugo Simberg's masterpiece, *The Wounded Angel*.

In a park on the eastern side of town is another Pietilä design, the stark-looking **Kalevan Kirkko** (church; Liisanpuisto 1). Built in 1966, its most striking feature is the organ with 3,000 pipes shaped like a sail.

The Tampella foundry, built in 1850, was transformed in 1996 into an impressive museum centre and renamed **Tehdasmuseo Vapriikki Ⓓ** (Veturiaukio 4;

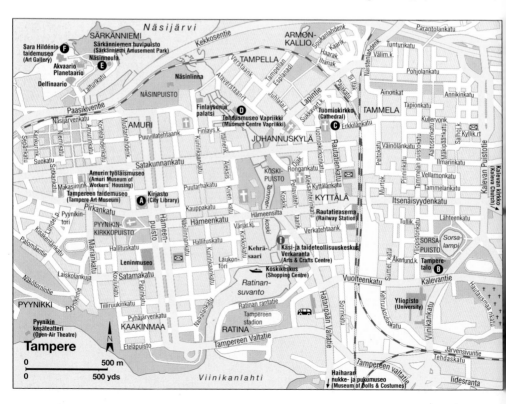

Tampere

0 ⸻ 500 m
0 ⸻ 500 yds

open Tues–Sun 10am–6pm; entrance fee; tel: 03 3146 6966). It features exhibitions on the Tampere region from archaeology to technology. There is a café-restaurant, and museum shop.

Across the northern harbour entrance from Näsinpuisto (park) is the highest viewpoint in Finland, the **Näsinneula Observation Tower** **E** (open daily 10am–midnight; entrance fee). It stands 120 metres (400 ft) high at the centre of Särkänniemi Park. The park is a favourite place for children with its aquarium, dolphinarium, planetarium, children's zoo and amusement park (for opening hours, tel: 03 248 8212; www.sarkanniemi.fi). In the same complex is the **Sara Hildénin Taidemuseo** **F** (Sara Hildén Art Museum; open May–Sept daily 11am–6pm; Oct–Apr closed Mon; entrance fee; tel: 3 214 3134), located in a beautiful building housing Hildén's collection of modern Finnish and foreign art.

South of Tampere

From Tampere, the 175-km (110-mile) route back to Helsinki passes through the industrial centre of **Valkeakoski** **㊱**. In the Middle Ages, Valkeakoski was only a hamlet, later a mining village in the parish of Sääksmäki; but, even then, it had the rapids that meant water power, first to grind corn and then to make paper. In contrast, the 19th-century National Romantic movement brought artists to Sääksmäki and these two ingredients – industry and art – still combine today.

The old **Voipaalan Kartano** (Voipaala Manor; open May–Sept daily; Oct–Apr closed Mon; entrance fee; tel: 3 543 6528) on Rapola Hill has become an art centre. It was once the home of the sculptor Elias Ilkka who owned the manor and farm where the Valkeakoski Summer Theatre performs. Make your way to **Visavuori**, the studio home of one of Finland's best-known sculptors, Emil

Tampere Library houses "Moomin Valley", an exhibition of the characters from Tove Jansson's popular books.

BELOW: Kaleva Church, Tampere.

Map on page 316

Wikström (1864–1942). At the age of 29, he won a competition to design the frieze for Helsinki's House of Estates and in the same year designed this house overlooking the lake, complete with rooftop observatory.

Glass-blowing centre

Of all Finland's glassmakers, **Iittala** ⑤ is probably the most famous. In the **Ittalan Lasimuseo** (museum; open May–Aug daily 9am–8pm; Sept–Apr daily 10am–6pm; entrance fee; tel: 02 0439 3512) beautiful functional glassware and *objets d'art* such as glass birds and fruit shapes are on display, along with designs by Alvar Aalto and Timo Sarpaneva. Visit the Iittala shop where seconds are often indistinguishable to the inexpert eye and less than half the price of perfect work.

It's also worth visiting the **Suomen Lasimuseo** (Finnish Glass Museum; open May–Aug daily 10am–6pm; Sept–Apr Tues–Sun 10am–6pm; entrance fee; tel: 019 741 7494) in **Riihimäki** ⑧, just off Road 3, 35 km (26 miles) south of Hämeenlinna. The museum is housed in an authentic glassworks from 1914. Exhibits trace the history of glassmaking from the early days of windowpane production to the era of glass as a fine art in the 20th century.

Häme Castle, Hämeenlinna, built by the Swedes in the 13th century.

BELOW: keeping up the glassmaking tradition at Iittala.

Sibelius country

Continuing south from Iittala, Road 57 leads to the lake of Hattula and **Hattulan Pyhän Ristin Kirkko** (Hattulan Church of the Holy Cross), one of Finland's best-known and oldest churches, built in 1320. Just off the E12, **Aulangon Puisto** (Aulanko Forest Park) is ideal for a break, overlooking Aulankojärvi (lake). Jean Sibelius, who was born in nearby **Hämeenlinna** ⑨, is said to have commented on Aulanko: "I was thinking of these scenes from my childhood when I composed *Finlandia*."

Hämeenlinna has two claims to fame: first, the early 13th-century Häme Castle (open May–mid-Aug daily 10am–6pm; mid-Aug–Apr daily 10am–4pm; entrance fee; tel: 3 675 6820) and, second, the fact that it was the birthplace of Jean Sibelius. Sibelius was born in December 1865 in the little timberboard house of the town physician, Christian Gustaf Sibelius, now the **Sibeliuksen Syntymäkoti Museo** (Sibelius Home Museum, Hallituskatu 11; open May–Aug daily 10am–4pm; Sept–Apr daily noon–4pm; entrance fee; tel: 03 621 2755). The big dining room is used for recitals, and the house is full of memorabilia.

Heading south through Hyvinkää to **Järvenpää** ⑩, you are only 45 km (30 miles) from Helsinki. The area's **Tuusulanjärvi** (lake) attracted late 19th-century artists and intellectuals away from their city haunts to build studio-villas on the eastern side, just beyond Järvenpää. Among them was the portrait painter Eero Järnefelt, noted for his rural and folk scenes, and Jean Sibelius and his wife Aino. **Museon Nimi Ainola** ⑪ was the Sibelius home for 53 years (open May–Sept Tues–Sun 11am–5pm; entrance fee; tel: 09 287 322). Designed by Lars Sonck, the house is still furnished as it was in Sibelius's time and the drawing room holds the composer's piano. Floral tributes adorn the couple's grave in the garden. ❏

CANOEING THE OPEN WATERS

Paddling a canoe on the lakes and rivers of Finland is one of the most pleasurable ways to explore the country. For the energetic there are annual races

One of the more testing annual events on the European canoeing calendar is the Arctic Circle Race which takes place every summer north of the Arctic Circle from Kilipsjärvi to Tornio along 537 km (334 miles) of the border rivers between Finland and Sweden. Another is the six-day 700-km (430-mile) Finlandia Canoe Relay each June, usually through the complex Saimaa system.

With 187,888 lakes (at the last count) and innumerable rivers, it's surprising that canoeing has only become popular in Finland in recent years. There is a growing range of packages whereby you can canoe well-tried routes of varying lengths with the option of hiring equipment, camping or staying in farmhouse accommodation.

A particularly well-tried series of routes forms an overall 350-km (217-mile) circuit beginning and ending at Heinola. This needs 10–15 days, but can also be divided into shorter sections. Another, along 320 km (200 miles) of the Ounasjoki river in Lapland from Enontekiö to Rovaniemi, features sections of true Arctic wilderness; the rapids are mainly Grade I, but it is possible to portage round the most daunting of these. Yet another follows a 285-km (180-mile) lake-and-river route taken by the old tar boats from Kuhmo to Oulu.

If you're attracted to the idea of pioneering across the lakes the possibilities are legion. Any of the 19 road maps which cover the entire country on a scale of of 1:200 000 will be sufficient for general planning, but absolutely essential for more detail are the special inland water charts, for example, for Saimaa on a scale of 1:40 000/1:50 000. It's not until you are in your canoe, however, that navigation problems become clear. From water level one island of rock and pine trees looks like another with few helpful landmarks. You will appreciate those other vital aids to canoeing the Finnish lakes: a compass and a pair of binoculars.

The greatest inconvenience you are likely to encounter is wind. Squalls blow up quickly and across these great expanses, waters are soon whipp ed up into turbulence. Head for shelter at the first sign.

Seek permission to camp whenever possible, since the right to pitch your tent anywhere has been abused by some foreigners and is no longer permitted. Often, of course, there is no one to ask. It is one of the joys of canoeing in Finland that you may travel for days without sign of humanity, other than a tugboat hauling timber, or a fisherman. ❑

TOP LEFT: canoeists stop for a well-earned rest. **ABOVE:** kayakers in action. **ABOVE RIGHT:** paddle power. **RIGHT:** slalom competitor.

FINLAND'S WEST COAST

*The beautiful Bothnian coastline preserves its rich
maritime heritage and its blend of Finnish-Swedish culture
in the islands and towns along the road to Lapland*

Map
on page
338

T he west coast of Finland is a fascinating mixture of past and present: stately churches and old wooden houses, museums and modern industry. With its close proximity to Sweden, Swedish remains the first language for many communities and some towns have both Swedish and Finnish names.

The first main town north of **Turku** *(see page 323)* on Road 8 is **Uusikaupunki ❶** (Nystad). The **Kulttuuruhistoriallinen Museo** (Museum of Cultural History; open June–Aug Tues–Sun; entrance fee; tel: 02 8451 5399) is in the house of F.W. Wahlberg, a former shipowner and tobacco manufacturer. **Myllymäki Park** is a reminder that many retired sailors became millers and the countryside was once dotted with windmills; four windmills and a tower remain.

Palaces and timber homes

Rauma ❷ is the largest medieval town in Scandinavia, listed as a UNESCO World Heritage Site with 600 or so wooden buildings painted in traditional pastel shades. Many of these are still private homes. Although the dwellings and shops are 18th- and 19th-century buildings, the pattern of narrow streets dates back to the 16th century.

Pori ❸, some 47 km (37 miles) north of Rauma, was founded by Duke Johan of Sweden in 1558. With a population of 76,600, it is one of Finland's chief export harbours and hosts a jazz festival every July. Interesting sights include the **City Hall**, built in the style of a Venetian Palace. More offbeat is the **Jusélius Mausoleum** (open May–Aug daily noon–3pm; Sept–Apr Sun only noon–2pm; free) at Käppärä Cemetery, built by a Pori businessman in memory of his young daughter. Inside is one of the artist Akseli Gallén-Kallela's masterpieces.

Satakunta Museo (open Tues–Sun 11am–5pm; entrance fee; tel: 02 621 1063), dating from 1888, is the largest Finnish cultural history museum and includes a fine collection of 19th- and 20th-century Finnish art. The **Porin Taidemuseo** (Pori Art Museum, Eteläranta; open Tues–Sun 11am–6pm; entrance fee; tel: 2 621 1080) features contemporary art.

The peninsula leading from Pori to **Reposaari** has a long sandy beach and is one of Finland's best resorts. **Kristinestad ❹** (Kristiinankaupunki), 95 km (59 miles) to the north was founded by the Swedish governor, Count Per Brahe, in 1649. A master of diplomacy, he gave the town the name of both his wife and Queen Kristina of Sweden-Finland. **Merimuseo** (open May–Sept Tues–Sun; entrance fee; tel: 06 221 2859), is set in the house of former shipowner S.A. Wendelin and displays his memorablilia.

Vaasa ❺ (Vasa), established in the 14th century, has been devasted by wars and fire. Today it is a handsome

LEFT: sparkling water in the Gulf of Bothnia.
BELOW: Rauma's Franciscan monastery.

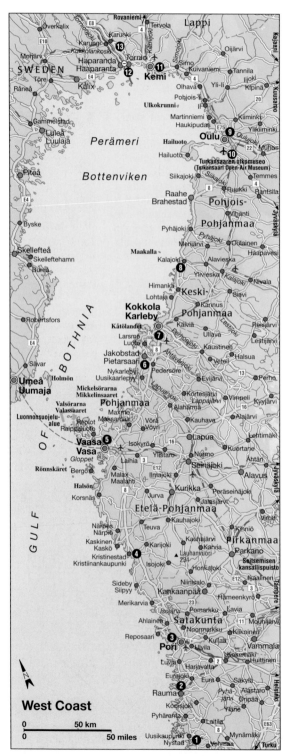

West Coast

0   50 km

0   50 miles

town with wide, attractively laid-out streets and a large market square. Notable buildings include the Orthodox Church, the Court of Appeal (1862), and the Town Hall (1883). For the best view of the town, clamber up the 200 steps in the tower behind the police station headquarters.

Vaasa is well-endowed with museums, the most important being the **Pohjanmaan Museo** (Ostrobothnian Museum; Museokatu 3; open Fri–Tues 10am–5pm, Wed & Thur until 8pm; tel: 06 325 3800), which covers local history and art. **Bragen Ulkomuseo** (Brage Open-Air Museum; open June–Aug Tues–Sun; entrance fee; tel: 6 312 7166) features Ostrobothnian farm life in the 19th century. **Wasalandia** is the town's colourful amusement park (open May–Aug daily noon–6pm; until 8pm in July; entrance fee; tel: 06 211 1200). Offshore islands add to the charms of Vaasa.

Jakobstad ❻ (Pietarsaari) gained repute as the pre-eminent Finnish ship-building centre, producing vessels that opened new trade routes around the world. One of the town's best-known sailing ships *Jakobstads Wapen*, a 1767 galleon, still makes cruises. Some 300 or so restored wooden houses may be seen in the old part of town.

Road of seven bridges

From Jakobstad to **Kokkola** ❼, take the attractive route called the "road of seven bridges", which runs from island to island across the archipelago. Kokkola's Town Hall was designed by Carl Ludwig Engel, who has left his mark on so many Finnish towns, and there is an English park and boathouse commemorating an episode in the Crimean War with the British fleet. On the 230-km (140-mile) road north between Kokkola and Oulu, the town of **Kalajoki** ❽ is a popular spot for fishing, bathing and sailing.

Oulu ❾ is the largest city in northern Finland, with a population of 115,500. **Turkansaaren Ulkomuseo** ❿ (Turkansaari Open-Air Museum; open June–Sept daily 10am–6pm; entrance fee; tel: 08 5586 7191) can be found on a small island in the Oulujoki, 14 km (8 miles) east of Oulu. It has an interesting collection of Ostrobothnian buildings, including a church, farm buildings and windmills. In town, the **Tietomaa Science Centre** (open daily 10am–6pm; entrance fee; tel: 08 5584 1340) offers a wealth of hands-on exhibits. The elegant **Oulun Taidemuseo** (open Tues–Sun 11am–6pm, Wed 11am–8pm; entrance fee; tel: 08 5584 7463) has a permanent exhibition of Finnish contemporary art. Visit **Koskikeskus** (Rapids Centre) on the mouth of the Oulujoki, with 12 fountains.

Map on page 338

Snow and the Midnight Sun

From Oulu to **Kemi** ⓫ one begins the approach to Lapland. Kemi lies at the mouth of the Kemijoki River and is known as the seaport of Lapland. In winter, you can take an excursion on the 1961 icebreaker, *Sampo*. A sight not to miss is **Lumilinna** (Snow Castle; tel: 016 259 502) with its dazzling white walls and illuminated towers. The castle is rebuilt every year and opens in February.

On the border a short distance west is **Tornio** ⓬, near the mouth of the Tornionjoki. The **Aineen Taidemuseo** (Aine Art Museum; open Tues–Thur 11am–6pm, Fri–Sun 11am–3pm; entrance fee; tel: 016 432 438) houses a fine collection of Finnish art from 1814 to the present. For a great view, visit the **Vesitorni** water tower (open daily mid-June–mid-Aug 11am–8pm).

At the **Green Zone Golf Course** (open June–Oct) on the Finnish-Swedish border, you can play nine holes in Sweden and nine in Finland. It is a rare delight to play a night round in summer, thanks to the Midnight Sun.

If you drive 9 miles (15 km) north of Tornio off Road E78, you will come to **Kukkolankoski** ⓭, the longest free-flowing rapids in Finland at 3,500 metres (11,150 ft). Fishermen here still use the traditional long-handled net. ❑

Lumilinna, the annual snow castle at Kemi, makes an impressive sight.

BELOW: tranquil scene on the West coast.

Map
on page
342

Helsinki

BELOW: the
Evakkokesus
Orthodox Centre;
many Karelians
belong to the
Orthodox Church.

KARELIA AND KUUSAMO

*Easterly Karelia with its distinctly Orthodox heritage is the
setting for Finland's epic poem, "Kalevala". Traditions
abound, the air is pure and the landscape untouched*

K arelia is the general name for the area whose westernmost part is still in
Finland and the larger, easternmost part – which was ceded to the Soviet
Union as a result of the Treaty of Paris in 1947 – is in Russia. There are
many holiday options, including renting a cottage or log cabin by the water or
staying in a "working" farmhouse. Depending on the season, one can enjoy a
range of water or winter sports, fishing, hiking, and berry-picking.

Joensuu ❶, the "capital" of North Karelia, is famous for its Festival of Song
every June. The **Pohjois-Karjalan Museo** (North Karelia Museum, Koskikatu
5; open Mon–Fri 10am–5pm, Sat & Sun 11am–4pm; entrance fee; tel: 013 267
5222) features exhibits on the history and the folk culture of this part of Karelia. The museum is housed in the Carelicum tourist centre (tel: 013 267 5223).
Along the same street there is the **Taidemuseo** (Art Museum, Kirkkokatu 23;
open Tues–Sun noon–6pm; entrance fee; tel: 13 267 5388), containing an icon
collection and Finnish paintings from the 19th and 20th centuries.

Before turning north, go east to **Ilomantsi** ❷. Ilomantsi is the oldest inhabited area of North Karelia and a stronghold of the Orthodox Church. Easter is
the most impressive festival here, and other colourful events are held throughout the summer. Ilomantsi was one of the main battle grounds in the wars of

1939–45 and the **Fighter's House** on Hattuvaara Hill has exhibitions about that period. Nearby in the village of **Runokylä** at the Singers Lodge on Parppeinvaara Hill, the ancient folk poems of the *Kalevala* are still sung by women in traditional costume (accompanied by the *kantele*, a zither-like instrument). The **Parppei Pirtti** restaurant (tel: 013 881421) on the hill features Karelian cuisine, including tiny fish *(vendace)*, cold smoked whitefish, hearty meat casseroles and pies, *pirakka* pastries, and baked cheese with cloudberry jam.

Gateway to the wilderness

Heading north from Joensuu, take Route 6 and the eastward fork to Route 73 to **Lieksa ❸**, where the **Ruuankoski** (rapids) must be seen, and possibly experienced, under the supervision of a guide. Lieksa, one of the many forest centres in Finland, is only about 20 years old and has a population of 19,000 in an area larger than London. The **Pielinen Museo** (Pielinen Open-Air Museum, Pappilantie 2; open May–Sept daily; entrance fee; tel: 013 520 2402) has 70 buildings, some dating to the 17th century, which document local settlement.

At **Vuonisjärvi ❹**, 29 km (18 miles) from the centre is **Paateri** (open June–Aug: daily; entrance fee), the studio of Eeva Ryynänen, a wood sculptor noted for her spectacular Wilderness Church.

Lieksa is the gateway to Finland's wilderness. "Never go hiking on your own" is the warning motto of this region, whose dense forests are inhabited by bears, wolves, elk and reindeer. At **Kaksinkantaja**, 40 km (26 miles) from the centre, there is an exhibition of bear skulls and stuffed animals by Väinö Heikkinen, a renowned bear hunter (open June–Aug daily; entrance fee). From Lieksa, Road 73 leads to **Nurmes ❺**. First mentioned in documents in 1556, Nurmes is a beautiful

TIP

Mountain biking is a popular way to explore Karelia. Hire a bike locally, or join a week-long guided trail bike expedition from Lieksa (details from Lieksa Tourist Service, tel: 13 520 2400).

BELOW: traditional way of life on a Karelian farm.

KARELIA: SOUL AND SAUNA

If Finland has a soul, that soul lives on in Karelia. When Finns have gone to war, it has concerned Karelia. A Karelian theme runs through the music of Sibelius and his *Karelian Suite* reaches sublime heights of patriotism.

The Karelians were one of the earliest of the Finnish communities; they are evident in Bronze and Iron Age discoveries. The *Kalevala*, the great epic saga of ancient life in the far north, is really about Karelians. The poem, which in the 18th and 19th centuries became the cornerstone of the struggle for national culture, recounts everyday events and rituals and finally the heroes' joy as they celebrate in song the salvation of the land of Kalevala from its enemies.

True Karelia exists only as a fragment of its former self. The greater part of the region lies east of the Russian border, lost to Finland after the Winter War (1939–40). As a result 400,000 Karelians had to be resettled in the 1940s. Since then, people of Karelian origin can be found in all parts of Finland. They tend to be lively and talkative, in contrast with the more taciturn nature of other Finns.

It is they who are responsible for the sauna. Early Karelians cleared woodland to grow crops and used steam heat to dry their grain. The therapeutic benefits of this heat were later realised and so the sauna was born in Finland.

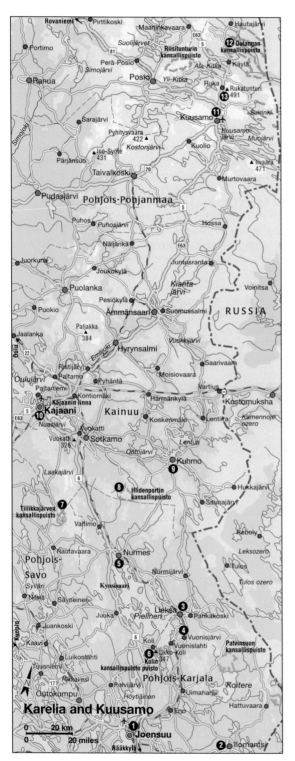

Karelia and Kuusamo

0   20 km
0   20 miles

town. The **Bomba House** (Suojärvenkatu 1; tel: 013 687 200) is a traditional wooden Karelian house at Ritoniemi, about 2 km (1¼ miles) from the town, surrounded by a "Karelian village" which provides visitors not only with comfortable accommodation, but also with delicious meals of local specialities.

Nurmes is the place to leave the car and take a scenic ride on Finland's largest inland waterway ferry down Lake Pielinen to **Kolin Kansallispuisto** ❻ (Koli National Park). Here you will see views that inspired some of Finland's greatest painters as well as the composer, Sibelius.

Before reaching the Oulu area, if your choice is Road 6 north you could detour to the remote national park, **Tiilikkajärven Kansallispuisto** ❼, near Rautavaara. It was established to conserve the uninhabited area of Lake Tiilikka and the surrounding bogs.

Another national park, **Hiidenportin Kansallispuisto** ❽, is southeast of Sotkamo and also best reached from Road 6. This is a rugged area with the narrow Hiidenporti Gorge, a rift valley with rock sides dropping 20 metres (70 ft) to the floor. There are well-marked trails and camp sites in the park.

Both in and outside the parks you may find reindeer. These animals are the main source of income for many people living in the region and it is very important to take special care on roads when reindeer are around, especially at dusk.

The Finnish frontier

Kuhmo ❾ is a frontier town surrounded by dense forests in the wilderness area of Kainuu. It is known for its annual Kuhmo Chamber Music Festival. A fascinating re-created **Kalevala Village** (open mid-June–Aug daily; entrance fee; tel: 08 652 0114) in a wooded park on the outskirts of Kuhmo displays numerous local folk traditions. The aim is to give modern-day visitors an idea of Finnish culture as it was immortalised in Finland's epic poem, *Kalevala*. The **Hotel Kalevala** specialises in regional cuisine (tel: 08 655 4100).

A long straight road through some of Finland's darkest forests leads west out of Kuhmo to Sotkamo and then onwards to **Kajaani** ⑩, the area's main town, on the eastern edge of Oulujärvi (lake). Kajaani still has the ruins of the 1604 castle and its town hall was designed by Carl Ludwig Engel, who was responsible for so much of early Helsinki. The road from Kajaani towards **Oulu** hugs the shores of Oulujärvi, plunging first into thickly wooded hill country. Before entering Oulu, the route goes through **Muhos** which has the second-oldest church in Finland, dating from 1634.

Kuusamo

The only other main centre in this scantily populated area is **Kuusamo** ⑪, almost at the Russian border, some 360 km (225 miles) northeast across the breadth of the country along Road 20. The Kuusamo region is marvellous wilderness country, ideal for canoeing and fishing, and the main sound in these parts is a mixture of rushing water and the wind high in the pines. This is also berry country, with several varieties growing in great profusion on the Arctic tundra. The only snag is the number of mosquitoes: take plenty of protection.

    Karhuntassu Tourist Centre (tel: 08 615 5555) provides information on activities, accommodation and most other aspects of the region. In winter, the area is excellent for skiing and snowmobiling. There are two national parks: the largest, **Oulangan Kansallispuisto** ⑫, to the north, covers a largely untouched region bordering the Oulanka river. **Karhunkierros**, the most famous walking route in Finland, stretches some 100 km (60 miles) through the Oulanka canyon to the **Rukatunturi Fells** ⑬. A smaller national park, **Riisitunturi**, lies to the southwest of Oulanka. Moving further north approaching Lapland, the landscape and culture change from the traditions of Karelia to the ancient ways of the Sami people. ❏

Map on page 342

The Museum of North Karelia at Joensuu traces the region's social history.

BELOW: white-water expedition.

FINNISH LAPLAND

For some travellers, Lapland is the land of the Midnight Sun,
a haven for fell-walkers and anglers. For others, it's the land
of Father Christmas, reindeer racing and dog sledging

Map
on page
346

Helsinki

Whatever the season, Lapland offers a variety of interesting natural phenomena and cultures, from the mysterious Northern Lights and the dark Kaamos skies to the magical contrast of the Midnight Sun. However you choose to arrive – by air, sea, train, or car, be prepared to experience Lapland and the Arctic Circle on foot, whether reindeer spotting, cross-country skiing, snowmobiling, ice-golfing, salmon-fishing, gold-panning, discovering the Sami culture, or simply hiking the rich swampland in search of cloudberries. These activities will only whet your appetite for the delicious Lappish cuisine.

Two main roads bore their way northwards through the province of Lapland (Lappi). Road 4 (E75), sometimes called the Arctic Highway, links Kemi (coming from Oulu) with Rovaniemi before continuing northeastwards into Norway at Utsjoki. The other is Road 21 (E8), which follows the Tornio Valley upstream from Tornio, continuing beside various tributaries that form the border with Sweden, eventually to cross into Norway near Kilpisjärvi.

When exploring this region, the need for proper clothing and equipment cannot be over-stressed: climatic changes are rapid and, for all its magnificence, the Arctic wilderness can be a ruthless place. In summer take plenty of mosquito repellent, preferably purchased from a local *apteekki* (pharmacy), which will be able to recommend the most effective product.

LEFT: a Laplander.
BELOW: tending reindeer.

Rovaniemi, Lapland's capital

From Kemi, Road 4 follows the valley of the Kemijoki. You reach **Rovaniemi ❶** within 115 km (70 miles). This administrative capital of Lapland, on the cusp of the Arctic Circle, is the launching point for most trips into the province.

The town has been completely rebuilt since World War II, almost quadrupling its population to 34,500 in the process. The reconstruction plan for Rovaniemi was made by Alvar Aalto who also designed the fine **Lappia House** complex on Hallituskatu, containing a theatre, library and congress facilities.

Half underground, the eye-catching **Arktikum** (Pohjoisranta 4; open May–Aug daily 10am–6pm; Sept–Apr closed Mon; entrance fee; tel: 016 317 840) houses the Arctic Centre and the Provincial Museum of Lapland. The Arctic Centre has exhibits illustrating Arctic history and culture; the museum gives a good introduction to Lapland's flora and fauna, Sami traditions and Rovaniemi's history. You'll get a better feeling for bygone days in the 19th-century farm buildings at the **Pöykkölä Museum** (open June–Aug Tues–Sun noon–4pm; entrance fee; tel: 016 348 1095), by the Kemi river, 3 km (2 miles) to the south.

Rovaniemen Taidemuseo (Rovaniemi Art Museum, Lapinkävijäntie 4; open Tues–Fri & Sun noon–5pm;

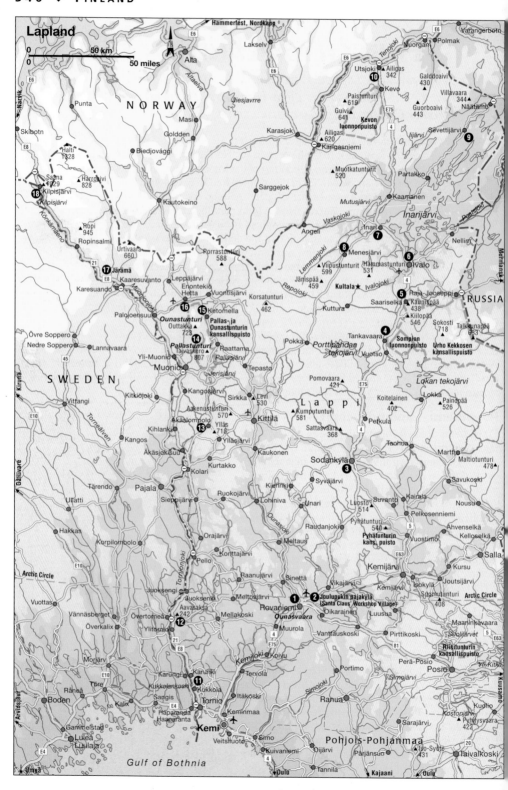

entrance fee; tel: 016 322 2822) has the Wihuri collection of modern Finnish art and various changing exhibitions.

Rising up from the confluence of the Ounasjoki and Kemijoki to the south of Rovaniemi are the wooded slopes of **Ounasvaara**, a well-developed skiing area and the site of annual international winter games. It's also a favourite gathering place on Midsummer Night.

Land of Santa Claus

About 8 km (5 miles) from the town on Road 4, soon after the turn-off for Rovaniemi airport, **Joulupukin Pajakylä ❷** (Santa Claus' Workshop Village; open June–Aug daily 9am–7pm; Sept–May daily 10am–5pm; free; tel: 016 356 2096) straddles the Arctic Circle. Its post office annually handles thousands of letters from children. There are some good shops, a puppet theatre, art exhibitions, a glass factory, a few reindeer and, of course, Santa Claus.

At Syväsenvaara, 5 km (3 miles) from Rovaniemi, is **Santapark** (open mid-June–mid-Aug daily 10am–6pm; Dec–Mar Fri 1–5pm; entrance fee; tel: 016 333 0000), an amusement park which has fun rides and attractions for children.

You will notice that the landscapes – predominantly forested – are becoming progressively emptier as you travel north. However, there are reindeer aplenty and the occasional elk, so do drive slowly; keep your eyes open and your camera handy – they say white reindeer bring good luck. One of the best fell areas east of Road 4 is centred on **Pyhätunturi**, about 135 km (84 miles) northeast of Rovaniemi. Another, just north of it, is **Luostotunturi**, south of Sodankylä.

Sodankylä ❸, 130 km (80 miles) from Rovaniemi, is the first substantial place along this route. It is the home of the Midnight Sun Film Festival held each June. Next to its 19th-century stone church, its wooden predecessor is Lapland's oldest church, dating from 1689.

Gold country

Northwards, there's little to detain you for the next 100 km (60 miles) or so until, a few miles beyond Vuotso, you reach **Tankavaara ❹**. Gold panning has been practised in various parts of Lapland for well over a century, and at **Tankavaara Gold Village**, its **Kultamuseo** (Gold Museum) not only chronicles man's historical endeavours to find gold, but for a modest fee gives tuition and allows you to pan for gold. There are cabins where you may lodge and a simple restaurant (tel: 16 626 171; fax: 16 626 271).

About 40 km (25 miles) further north there is more self-catering accommodation, together with modern hotels and sports facilities, centred on **Laanila** and **Saariselkä ❺**, an immensely popular winter sports centre with good facilities.

Ivalo and Inari

Another 23 km (14 miles) north is the turning for Ivalo airport, Finland's northernmost. **Ivalo ❻** is the largest community in northern Lapland, though in terms of Sami culture it is much less important than Inari. There is, however, an attractive wooden Orthodox church tucked away in the woods, serving the

Map on page 346

Rovaniemi lies just 8 km (5 miles) south of the Arctic Circle.

BELOW: Santa Claus out for a stroll.

Ranua, south of Rovaniemi, is the cloudberry capital of Finland. These unusual berries grow on peat bogs and pine marshes and are ripe for picking in July. Taste them at Ranua's cloudberry markets in early August.

Skolt Sami, a branch of the Sami people who formerly lived in territory ceded to the Soviet Union in 1944. They have different costumes, language and traditions from the Finnish Sami, and some now breed sheep as well as reindeer. Ivalo's Lutheran Church stands near the bridge which carries Road 4 over the Ivalojoki; then it's a further 39 km (27 miles) to **Inari ❼**, much of it a delightful route along parts of the shores of Inarijärvi. Inari village is an excellent base for wilderness exploration; you can lodge at the traditional Hotel Inarin Kultahovi (tel: 016 671 221).

Though smaller than Ivalo, Inari is the administrative centre for a vast if sparsely populated area, and a traditional meeting place for colourfully costumed Sami people, especially during the church festivals of Lady Day and Easter Day.

Inarijärvi is Finland's third-largest lake, covering 1,300 sq km (808 sq miles) and is dotted with 3,000 islands, some of them considered sacred according to Sami tradition. Boat trips and sightseeing flights are available during the summer to the holy **Ukko Island**.

Inari's excellent **Saamelaismuseo** (Siida Sami Museum; open June–Sept daily 9am–8pm; Oct–May Tues–Sun 10am–5pm; entrance fee; tel: 16 665 212; www.samimuseum.fi) comprises a modern museum building and an open-air section *(skansen)* with old buildings and equipment illustrating the traditionally nomadic way of life. There are also some exhibits on early Skolt Sami culture and modern Sami life. The Siida building also houses the **Ylä-Lapin Luontokeskus** (Northern Lapland Visitor Centre), which sells fishing permits and assists in hiking plans for those wishing to explore the wilderness. Be sure to leave time to shop at Inari's many fine handicraft shops that include a silversmith's shop and a knife-making studio.

BELOW: reindeer sledging is a popular activity.

SLEDGING

The easiest way to get across Lapland's vast, icy and largely flat landscape has always been on skis or sledges; the latter less exhausting for longer distances. There are many types of sledging, but the most popular and readily associated with northern Finland is the dog sledge. Four or six husky dogs, hardy beasts naturally acclimatised to snow and ice, are harnessed to the front of the sledge, with passengers standing on the back runners. Unlike horses, the huskies are not readily controllable, so keeping the sledge stationary is done with a hook wedged deep in the snow. Once the hook is withdrawn, the dogs lurch forward.

Reindeer sledging, as epitomised by images of Santa and his sleigh at Christmas, is another method of getting around, with the advantage that these animals can cover longer and more snowy distances, although they travel more slowly than dogs.

Many centres in Lapland now offer the chance of sledging excursions for tourists – contact tourist offices in main towns for more details. It is essential that the right equipment is worn: thermals, waterproofs, hats and goggles are necessary to combat the dampness and bitterness of the snow.

Towards Norway

Road 955 from Inari leads 40 km (25 miles) southwest to **Menesjärvi ❽**, a Sami settlement from which one can continue by road then river boat or on foot up the wild and beautiful **Lemmenjoki Valley** ("river of love") to a remote gold prospectors' camp. From Menesjärvi, Road 955 continues across Lapland to join Road 79 at Kittilä. Around Inari and north of it, the road passes a number of attractive holiday centres, mostly of the self-catering variety. After 26 km (16 miles) you come to Kaamanen from which a minor road branches northeast 100 km (60 miles) to **Sevettijärvi ❾**, the modern main settlement for the Skolt Sami. An interesting time to be there is during the Easter Orthodox festival. While there, visit the Sami graveyard, with its unusual turf-covered graves.

A couple of kilometres north of Kaamanen take the minor road to **Utsjoki ❿**, 94 km (58 miles) away on the border with Norway, passing a series of beautiful lakes close to the eastern fringes of the **Kevon Luonnonpuisto** (Kevo Nature Park). Utsjoki is an important Sami community close to Finland's northernmost point. Its church (built 1860) is one of the few pre-World War II churches still standing in Lapland.

The village and road follow the Utsjoki downstream to join with the Tenojoki, a renowned salmon river. As you approach the Norwegian border at **Kirkenes**, the landscape changes dramatically. You can connect with a variety of routes, eventually returning into western Lapland at Kilpisjärvi or Enontekiö.

Western Lapland

Your route through western Lapland is likely to begin at **Tornio** about 80 km (50 miles) south of the Arctic Circle. The earlier stretches of the **Way of the Four Winds** (E8) present a very different face of Lapland from the Arctic Road, for the lower section of the Tornio valley is much more populated, and served by Finland's northernmost railway branch to Kolari.

In its southern stages the road passes through a string of small communities mainly based, in these marginally milder and more fertile conditions, on agriculture and dairy farming. The Tornionjoki is a good salmon river. Perch, whitefish, grayling, trout and even Arctic char can be found in Lapland's waters. Local travel agencies will organise guided fishing trips complete with gear and permits. At **Kukkola ⓫** look out for the **Kukkolankoski rapids**; people used to ride the rapids while standing on a log.

About 70 km (43 miles) north of Tornio, beyond Ylitornio, is the 242-metre (794-ft) high **Aavasaksa Hill ⓬**, the most southerly point from which the Midnight Sun can be seen, attracting considerable throngs for Midsummer Eve festivities. A few miles nearer Juoksenki, you cross the Arctic Circle. The scenery becomes wilder as you pass between Pello and Kolari.

Fell country

About 10 km (7 miles) north of Kolari, a detour by Road 940 to the right leads to **Akäslompolo ⓭**. This well-equipped tourist resort and skiing centre, on the shores of a small lake, is set among magnificent forested hills and bare-topped fells; the highest is

Map
on page
346

Leather goods and "puukko" knives are among the best buys in Lapland.

BELOW: panning for gold, Tankavaara.

Map
on page
346

In northern Lapland the sun stays above the horizon from late May to late July. Autumn is known as "Ruska", when the leaves turn explosive shades of red, yellow and orange.

BELOW: traditional wooden cabin.
RIGHT: Lemmenjoki National Park.

Ylläs, at 718 metres (2,355 ft), served by chair lifts. A marked trail follows the chain of fells stretching northwards from here, eventually leading in about 150 km (90 miles) to the **Pallastunturi** ❹ fell group. It's a glorious trail with overnight shelter available in untended wilderness huts. Off-road biking is also a possibility with trails for various levels of expertise.

From Akäslompolo you can continue north along minor roads and in 31 km (19 miles) turn left onto Road 79. This is the main road from Rovaniemi, providing an alternative approach to western Lapland. Road 957 to the right is recommended as the best approach to Enontekiö. A further branch left off this route leads from Road 79 to the lonely hotel complex of **Pallastunturi**, magnificently cradled in the lap of five of the 14 fells which make up the Pallastunturi group. From here the choice of fell walks includes the long-distance 60-km (37-mile) trail north from Yllästunturi across the fells to Enontekiö. At **Ketomella** ❺ on Road 957 there's a car ferry across the river.

Enontekiö ❻, also known as Hetta, sprawls along the northern shore of Ounasjärvi (lake), looking across to the great rounded shoulders of the Ounastunturi fells. Most of Enontekiö's buildings are modern, including the pretty wooden church which has an altar mosaic depicting Sami people.

Soaring mountains

From **Palojoensuu**, Road 21 continues northwest along the Muonionjoki and Könkämäeno valleys, the scenery becoming even wilder and more barren. A little north of Kaaresuvanto you cross the coniferous tree line and pass the last of the spindly pines.

At **Järämä** ❼, 10 km (6 miles) further from the tiny settlement of Markkina, German soldiers built fortifications during a standstill in the Lapland War of 1944. Many of these bunkers have been restored and are now open to the public. South and north of **Ropinsalmi**, the mountains reach ever greater heights; the highest, **Halti**, soars up to 1,328 metres (4,357 ft) on the Norwegian border at Finland's northwesternmost point. More accessible and distinctive is Saana, at 1,029 metres (3,376 ft), above the village and the resort of **Kilpisjärvi** ❽.

Kilipisjärvi is an excellent launching pad for wilderness enthusiasts. There is a lake of the same name whose western shore forms the border with Sweden, and a marked trail which takes about a day and leads to the boundary stone marking the triple junction of Finland, Sweden and Norway.

Motorboats take visitors to the **Mallan Luonnenpuisto**, a nature reserve to the north of the lake (entry permit required: details from Kilipsjärven Retkeilykeskus, tel: 016 537 771). Within the reserve, there is a pleasant 15-km (9-mile) trek.

The rest of these immense, empty, rugged acres are as free to all comers as the elements – and as unpredictable. Never set off without proper equipment and provisions and, unless you are experienced in such landscapes, a guide; always inform someone where you are heading and when you expect to return. Simple advice, but it cannot be said often enough. ❑

INSIGHT GUIDES
Travel Tips

CONTENTS

Denmark

The Place 354
Climate 354
Visas and Passports 355
Health 355
Money Matters 355
What to Bring 355
Getting There 356
Tour Operators 356
Public Holidays 357
Telecommunications 357
Business Hours 357
Medical Services 358
Security and Crime 358
Getting Around 359
Hotel Listings 360
Restaurant Listings 363
Nightlife 365
Sport 365
Shopping 366
Language 366
Further Reading 367

Norway

The Place 368
Climate 368
Visas and Passports 369
Health 369
Money Matters 369
What to Bring 370
Tour Operators 370
Getting There 370
Telecommunications 372
Medical Services 372
Security and Crime 373
Public Holidays 373
Business Hours 374
Getting Around 374
Hotel Listings 377
Restaurant Listings 379
Nightlife 381
Sport 382
Shopping 383
Language 383
Further Reading 384

Sweden

The Place 385
Climate 385
Visas and Passports 386
Health 386
What to Bring 386
Getting There 386
Money Matters 386
Tour Operators 387
Telecommunications 388
Public Holidays 389
Medical Services 389
Security and Crime 389
Business Hours 390
Getting Around 390
Hotel Listings 392
Restaurant Listings 397
Nightlife 399
Sport 400
Shopping 401
Language 402
Further Reading 403

Finland

The Place 404
Climate 404
Visas and Passports 405
Health 405
Tour Operators 405
Money Matters 405
What to Bring 405
Getting There 405
Telecommunications 406
Business Hours 407
Public Holidays 407
Medical Services 407
Security and Crime 407
Getting Around 408
Hotel Listings 409
Restaurant Listings 411
Nightlife 414
Sport 414
Shopping 415
Language 415
Further Reading 416

DENMARK

The Place

Area 43,094 sq km (16,659 sq miles).
Capital Copenhagen.
Population 5.4 million, of whom 1.8 million live in the Copenhagen area, 285,000 in Århus and 184,000 in Odense.
Life expectancy 74 years for men and 79 for women.
Language Danish.
Religion 89 percent of Danes are registered as belonging to the Evangelical Lutheran Church, although few attend services.
Time zone Central European Time Zone. One hour ahead of Greenwich Mean Time (GMT), six hours ahead of Eastern Standard Time (EST).
Currency Danish krone (crown); plural kroner; marked kr in shops or DKK internationally; and split into 100 øre.
Weights and measures Metric.
Electricity 220 volts AC, two-pin round plugs.
International dialling code +45.

Geography

The Kingdom of Denmark – the word originally meant "border district of the Danes" – lies between the North Sea on the west and the Baltic Sea on the southeast. Germany borders to the south for 69 km (43 miles), and Sweden is 25 minutes to the east.

Jutland, which makes up about 70 percent of the country, is a peninsula jutting into the North and Baltic Seas. The rest of the land consists of islands, 405 in all. The major islands are Bornholm, Zealand (where Copenhagen is situated), Falster, Fyn and Lolland.

Flat or gently undulating, Denmark has been covered by ice sheets at least four times over the past two million years. The natural vegetation is a mixed forest covering one-eighth of the country. Around seven-tenths of the land is used for farming, with most farms family run. Barley, used for cattle feed, is the main crop. There are few valuable minerals, but limestone and gravel are widely mined. Oil and gas have both been found in the Danish sector of the North Sea.

Greenland and the Faroe Islands are also part of the kingdom of Denmark. Both are self-governing and have their own languages.

Climate

Denmark's temperate marine climate keeps the weather mild, with the North Atlantic Drift, part of the Gulf Stream, providing a warming influence. Average rainfall is 660 mm (26 in) a year.

The swimming season starts (except for true masochists) in the middle of May and ends in September.

Be prepared for a variable climate and remember to dress for cold and wet weather in the winter and spring.

Max. Temperatures

January	2°C (36°F)
February	2°C (36°F)
March	5°C (41°F)
April	10°C (50°F)
May	16°C (61°F)
June	19°C (66°F)
July	22°C (71°F)
August	21°C (69°F)
September	18°C (64°F)
October	12°C (54°F)
November	7°C (45°F)
December	4°C (39°F)

The People

Most Danes are Nordic Scandinavians, although a German minority can be found in south Jutland. Around 85 percent of the population lives in towns or cities.

There is a growing number of foreign residents (in all 7 percent of the population).

Economy

A member of the European Union, Denmark is one of the world's great trading nations. Grain was the major export until the 19th century; dairy products then became dominant. Although they remain the best-known exports, dairy products account for only 30 percent of export turnover, with light industrial goods accounting for the rest.

Denmark has a growing environmental development industry, inventing and producing a wide variety of products that span energy-saving light bulbs to high-tech windmills, which are sold locally and internationally.

As elsewhere in western Europe, service industries provide an increasing proportion of work, and only one-fifth of workers are now engaged in manufacturing.

The average income and benefits provided by the social welfare system are still among the highest in the world – but so are personal income taxes. The average family spends about 30 percent of its net income on rent, 20 percent on food and 15 percent on transport.

Government

A kingdom for over 1,000 years, Denmark is the oldest monarchy in the world. The reigning monarch, Queen Margrethe, has no real political power or influence, yet no laws or governments are recognised without her signature.

Since 1945, most governments have been coalitions, and the dominant political party was the Social Democrats, until the 2001 elections, when they were beaten by the Liberal Party; the anti-immigration Danish People's Party also made significant gains. The parliament has 179 members, including two each from Greenland and the Faroe Islands (Færøerne).

Planning the Trip

Visas and Passports

A valid passport entitles you to a stay of up to three months. Visas are not required for EU citizens, and those from Canada and the US. Other nationalities may need a visa before arriving. If in doubt, ask at a Danish Embassy or Consulate.

If you arrive from a Scandinavian country, your passport probably won't be checked. If you intend to stay longer than three months you have to obtain a resident's permit.

Customs

Danish customs formalities are usually painless. The rules about limits on goods/gifts allowed through customs depend on whether you are coming from an EU country. If in doubt, check with a local Danish consul. Money and cheques may be brought in freely.

DUTY FREE

Visitors from countries outside Scandinavia and the EU are entitled to claim back value added tax (MOMS) when leaving Denmark.

Many shops can mail goods home to you, avoiding MOMS payment. For visitors wishing to take goods away with them, shops displaying Global Refund Denmark emblems offer tourists a personal export service with MOMS refunds on purchases of over 300DKK. You must declare your purchase and get a stamp from customs from the last EU country you leave.

There are Global Refund outlets at almost every international airport in Europe and on some ferry lines.

Information Before You Go

● **UK** The Danish Tourist Board, 55 Sloane Street, London SW1X 9SY. Tel: 020 7259 5959. Fax: 020 7259 5955. www.visitdenmark.com E-mail: dtb.london@dt.dk
● **US** The Danish Tourist Board, 655 Third Avenue, 18th Floor, New York, NY 10017. Tel: 212-885 9723. Fax: 212-885 9726. www.visitdenmark.com E-mail: sbc@dt-nyc.com www.goscandinavia.com
● **Canada**: The Danish Tourist Board, PO Box 115, Station N, Toronto, Ontario M8V 3S4. Tel: 416-823 9620.
● **Australia** The Danish Tourist Board, Level 4, 81 York Street, Sydney NSW 2000. Tel: 02 9262 5832. Fax: 02 9290 1981. www.scandinavia.com.au E-mail: denmark@finnesse.com.au

The following websites provide useful information:
● **Denmark Hotel list** www.dkhotellist.dk
● **Wonderful Copenhagen** Guide to the city: www.visitcopenhagen.dk
● **The Faroe Islands Tourist Board** www.tourist.fo or www.faroeislands.com
● **Greenland Tourism** www.greenland-guide.dk or www.greenland.com

Health

Standards of hygiene in Scandinavia are among the highest in the world. Visitors often comment upon how clean Denmark is. There are no major health hazards and the tap water is safe to drink.

The Danish medical system will assist anyone in an emergency; however you should take out travel insurance before you leave. British nationals should take a form E111, available from any post office in the UK. You will be charged for doctors' consultations and prescriptions. To get a refund, take the receipts together with your E111 and passport to the local health office.

Money Matters

Currency

Notes come in 50, 100, 200, 500 and 1,000 denominations. There are 25 and 50 øre coins (both copper coloured), 1 krone, 2 krone, 5 krone (silver coloured with a hole in the centre), and 10 and 20 krone (solid gold-coloured coins that are similar-looking except the 20 krone piece is a little bigger than the 10 krone).

Changing money

Exchanges are open outside normal business hours at the Copenhagen Central Railway Station, and in the centre of the city.

Den Danske Bank (tel: 32 46 02 80) is open Mon–Sun 6am–8.30pm; and Forex Mon–Sun 8am–9pm.

There are several 24-hour exchange machines near Copenhagen City Hall.

How to pay

Visa and MasterCard are widely accepted in shops. Diner's Club is accepted in many restaurants. American Express cards can sometimes be used in major hotels and shops. All banks and a few shops take travellers' cheques.

What to Bring

The time of year you are most likely to encounter good weather is mid-May to mid-June. Even if you are lucky enough to travel in a year with a fine summer, you should still expect some cold and rainy days. Yet it can also be very hot. Whatever time of year you are visiting, it is wise to bring a sweater and a raincoat.

Danes dress casually both in their free time and at work. When going out for the evening men rarely have to put on a suit and tie.

Getting There

BY AIR

The two main airports in Denmark are Copenhagen Kastrup Airport and Bilund Airport in Jutland. Denmark's national carrier is SAS (Scandinavian Airlines System), which is primarily for international traffic. Maersk Air and Cimber Air serve most of the domestic routes. British Airways flies daily from Heathrow to Kastrup Airport. The low-cost operator easyJet flies daily from London Stansted to Copenhagen.

From the UK
British Airways Tel: 0845 7733377.
www.ba.com
easyJet Tel: 08706 000 000.
www.easyjet.com
Maersk Air Tel: 020 7333 0066.
www.maersk-air.com
SAS Tel: 0845 607 2772.
www.scandinavian.net

From the US
SAS Tel: 1-800-221 2350.
www.scandinavian.net

BY SEA

From Germany and Poland
From Germany, ferries connect Puttgarden and Rødby (Lolland). Ferries also run between Warnemünde and Gedser, and in the summer, Sassnitz and Rønne (Bornholm). Swinoujscie in Poland sends a daily ferry to Copenhagen.

From Sweden
Sweden operates several lines from Helsingborg to Helsingør (North Zealand) and from Varberg to Grenå (East Jutland); other ferries go from Göteborg to Frederikshavn (North Jutland). From Rønne (Bornholm) there is a ferry to Ystad.

From Norway
Boats go from Oslo to Copenhagen or to Hirtshals and Frederikshavn in North Jutland; from Hanstholm there are ferries to Bergen and Egersund. Ferries from Larvik (Norway) go to Frederikshavn.

From the UK
DFDS Seaways *(see below)* ferries run from Harwich to Esbjerg.

BY RAIL

Trains arrive daily from Germany, Britain (via Eurostar to Brussels) and Sweden.
● For trains from Britain:
tel: 08705 848 848.
www.raileurope.co.uk
● For information in Denmark on international trains:
tel: 70 13 14 16.
www.dsb.dk
● For Denmark's inland trains:
tel: 70 13 14 15.
www.dsb.dk

BY COACH

Eurolines is the leading operator of scheduled coach services, including 11 destinations in Denmark with regular departures from London to Copenhagen, Hirtshals, Ålborg, Århus, Padborg and Rødby.
● **Eurolines** Tel: 08705 808080 or 08705 143219.
www.eurolines.co.uk

Tour Operators

● **Scantours**
47 Whitcomb St, London WC2H 7DH.
Tel: 020 7839 2927.
Fax: 020 7839 5891.
www.scantoursuk.com
● **Norwegian Coastal Voyage**
3 Shortlands, London W6 8NE.
Tel: 020 8846 2666.
Fax: 020 8846 2678.
www.norwegiancoastalvoyage.com
● **DFDS Seaways**
Scandinavia House, Parkeston Quay, Harwich, Essex CO12 4QG.
Tel: 08705 333 000 (reservations)
www.dfdsseaways.co.uk

Practical Tips

Media

NEWSPAPERS AND MAGAZINES

English-language newspapers are widely available at all main train stations, as well as kiosks. You can also read them free at the Central Library, Krystalgade 15 or Café Europa, Amagertorv 1, Copenhagen.
 The English-language weekly *The Copenhagen Post* has information, news, entertainment and restaurant guides (from tourist offices).

BOOKS

Many of the public libraries have a good selection of books in English, and Copenhagen has bookshops that specialise in foreign literature *(see Shopping, page 366).*

TELEVISION

There are many satellite/cable channels featuring CNN, BBC and MTV in English. In addition, there are often movies in English without subtitles on the national channels DR1, DR2 and TV2.

RADIO

A high percentage of music on Danish radio is in English. For news

Useful Numbers

● **Police, ambulance, fire** 112
● **Danish directory enquiries** 118
● **International directory enquiries** 113

Public Holidays

- **1 January** New Year's Day (1)
- **March/April** Easter
- **1 May** Workers' Day
- **May/June** Whit Monday
- **May/June** Ascension Day
- **5 June** Constitution Day
- **24–26 December** Christmas

A floating holiday is Prayer Day (Store Bodedag), which falls on a different day each year. All shops and businesses close all day on major holidays, and for half a day on Prayer and Ascension Days.

in English, tune in to Radio Denmark at 1062kHz medium wave Mon–Fri 10.30am, 5.10pm and 10pm.

Postal Services

For opening hours of most post offices, see Business Hours, below. The railway station office in Copenhagen is open Mon–Fri 8am–10pm, Sat 9am–4pm and Sun 10am–5pm.

Telecommunications

Phone calls to foreign countries can be made from Statens Teletjeneste offices, above the post office in the Central Railway Station, and next door to the post office in Købmagergade in Copenhagen.

Tourist Offices

There is a tourist office in almost every city, with knowledgeable and friendly staff. They can assist in planning a trip, make reservations, or provide directions and leaflets.

For access to websites and information about all tourist offices in Denmark, visit the central www.visitdenmark.com. Some of the tourist bureaus are:

Copenhagen

Bernstorffsgade 1, 1577 Copenhagen V (at the main entrance of Tivoli) Tel: 70 22 24 42. Fax: 33 12 97 23 www.visitcopenhagen.dk

North Zealand

Havnepladsen 3, 3000 Helsingør Tel: 49 21 13 33. Fax: 49 21 15 77 www.visithelsingor.dk

Southwest Zealand

Fondens, Bro 3, Postboks 278, 4000 Roskilde Tel: 46 35 27 00. Fax: 46 35 14 74 www.visitroskilde.dk

Bornholm

Munch Petersensvej 4, 3700 Rønne Tel: 56 95 95 00. Fax: 56 95 95 68 www.bornholminfo.dk

Funen

Rådhuset, 5000 Odense C Tel: 66 12 75 20. Fax: 66 12 75 86 www.odense.dk

East Jutland

Rådhuset, 8000 Århus C Tel: 89 40 67 00. Fax: 86 12 95 90 www.visitaarhus.com

North Jutland

Østerå 8, 9000 Ålborg Tel: 98 12 60 22. Fax: 98 16 69 22 www.visitaalborg.com

West Jutland

Nytorv 5, 8800 Viborg Tel: 86 61 16 66. Fax: 86 60 02 38 www.viborg.dk/turisme

South Jutland

Torvet 3–5, 6760 Ribe Tel: 75 42 15 00. Fax: 75 42 40 78 www.ribetourist.dk

Greenland

Greenland Tourism, PO Box 1552, DK-3900 Nuuk, Greenland Tel: 299 32 28 88 Fax: 299 32 28 77 E-mail: tourism@greennet.gl www.greenland-guide.dk

The Faroe Islands

The Faroe Islands Tourist Board, Undir Bryggjubakka 17, PO Box 118 FO-110 Tórshavn, Faroe Islands Tel: 298 31 60 55 Fax: 298 31 08 58 E-mail: tourist@tourist.fo www.tourist.fo

Travelling with Kids

Denmark is a peaceful, safe country with many suitable attractions, such as amusement parks, playgrounds, parks and children's theatres. Many museums have opened children's sections, and music festivals are often arranged so kids can take part. Highlights include:

Copenhagen

Experimentarium (Science Centre) Tuborg Havnevej 7 Tel: 39 27 33 33. A hands-on science museum. Open Mon–Fri 9am–5pm (Tues until 9pm); Sat and Sun 11am–5pm.

Zoologisk Have (Zoo) Roskildevej 32. Tel: 36 30 20 01. Open daily 9am–4pm or 6pm.

Puppet Theatre Over the summer there are free puppet shows in Kongens Have (the Royal Gardens) near Rosenborg Palace. At 2pm and 3pm, Tues–Sun.

Business Hours

Offices: 8/9am–4/5pm.
Shops: Mon–Thurs until 5.30pm; Fri until 7pm (8pm in Copenhagen); Sat 9am–noon or 5pm. All are closed on Sunday except for bakeries and kiosks, some of which are open around the clock.
Pharmacies: As shops except Steno Apotek in Copenhagen

(across the street from the train station) which opens all hours.
Supermarkets: until 7/8pm, at least in Copenhagen. The one at the railway station opens all hours.
Banks: Mon–Fri 10am– 4pm, some till 6pm Thurs.
Post offices: Mon–Fri 9am–5pm, Sat 9am–noon.

Lost Credit Cards

- **MasterCard/Visa**
44 89 25 00 (24 hours)
- **American Express** 70 11 55 00
- **Diners' Club** 36 73 73 73

Tivoli
Vesterbrogade 3. Tel: 33 15 10 01.
The world-famous amusement park,
Tivoli, just across from Central
Station, is a delight, with Italian-style
Commedia dell'Arte twice daily
and a huge variety of rides. Open
Apr–Sept Sun–Thurs 11am–12pm,
Fri and Sat 11am–1am.

Outside Copenhagen

Bakken
A traditional amusement park in the
beautiful Dyrehaven area near
Klampenborg. This is also a perfect
place for a walk in the countryside,
or for a ride in a horse-drawn
carriage. Open daily 25 Mar–30
Aug, noon–midnight.
Benneweis Circus
The largest circus in northern
Europe, in Dronningmølle.
www.cirkus-benneweis.dk
Legoland
An amusement park in Jutland, built
out of 33 million Lego bricks. Open
daily Apr–Oct. Tel: 75 33 13 33.
Lejre Research Centre
Historical-archaeological centre in
Zealand with a reconstructed Iron
Age village. Children can grind their
own flour, cut wood and make
Viking bread. Tel: 46 48 08 78.

Business Travellers

The Danes are not excessively
formal when it comes to business
dress. Punctuality is appreciated
and it's probably best to make
business appointments for morning
or early afternoon. Offices are often
deserted on Friday afternoons. July
and August is holiday-time.

Travellers with Disabilities

The Danish Tourist Board publishes
*Access in Denmark – A Travel Guide
for the Disabled*. Tourist offices
have lists of restaurants and
businesses, and the free *Denmark
Accommodation Guide* lists hotels
with special facilities.

Medical Services

Health care is generally free in
Denmark. Acute illnesses or
accidents will be treated at the
casualty department of the nearest
hospital. You can contact a doctor
on 33 15 46 00; outside normal
business hours, tel: 70 13 00 41.

PHARMACIES

Most operate normal business
hours. But there is also a 24-hour
pharmacy in every region, the
name and address of which is
posted on the door of every
pharmacy (or look in the
Yellow Pages telephone directory
under *Apotek*).

DENTAL SERVICES

Dental care is available by
appointment only. Check the listings
under *Tandlæger* in the *Yellow
Pages*. Outside normal business
hours you can call Tandlægevagten,
tel: 35 38 02 51.

Religious Services

Services are normally on Sunday
at 10am, and they are often
repeated at 2pm. There are several
foreign congregations in
Copenhagen.
English Church
At Esplanaden near Amaliegade.

Copenhagen Card

We recommend that you buy a
Copenhagen Card at your hotel,
the central railway station or the
Copenhagen tourist information
office. The card gives you free
entry to Tivoli and discounts to
other sights, plus free bus/train
rides in the city and an
informative 122-page guide.

Sankt Petri Church
On the corner of Nørregade and Skt
Pedersstræde. In German.
Church of the Reformation
At Gothersgade across the street
from Rosenborg Castle. Shared by a
German and French congregation.
Jewish Synagogue
Krystalgade.
Nusrat Jahan Mosque
Eriksminde Alle 2.
Roman Catholic Church
Skt Ansgars, Bredgade 64.

Security and Crime

Denmark is generally very safe, but
you should not take risks. To
recover lost or stolen property,
contact the nearest police station
for assistance, or try the lost and
found offices at railway stations.
Police stations in Copenhagen
can be found on Central Station,
tel: 33 15 38 01, and at
Polititorvet, tel: 33 14 14 48.

Tipping

Service is included in all bills, but a
sign of appreciation is often
welcomed. In restaurants it is a
friendly gesture to pick up the notes
but leave the coins. Taxi drivers
appreciate it if the fare is rounded
up to the nearest 5 or 10DKK.

Consulates

The following embassies and
consulates are in Copenhagen.
- **Australia**
Dampfaergevej 26
Tel: 70 26 36 76
- **Canada**
Kristen Bernikowsgade 1
Tel: 33 48 32 00
- **Ireland**
Østbanegade 21
Tel: 35 42 32 33
- **UK**
Kastelsvej 40. Tel: 35 44 52 00
- **US**
Daghammarskjölds Allé 24
Tel: 35 55 31 44

Getting Around

On Arrival

Almost all international flights arrive and depart from Copenhagen Airport. Trains run six times an hour directly from Terminal 3, the international terminal at Copenhagen Airport, to Central Station. They take 13 minutes and leave at 06, 11, 26, 31, 46, and 51 minutes past the hour, running from 5.06am to 12.11am.

An intercity express train runs from the airport daily to Frederikshavn, Struer, Herning and Esbjerg.

Trains run between the airport and many major Swedish cities.

The Øresund bridge connects Denmark and Sweden. Starting near Kastrup Airport, you can reach the Swedish city of Malmö in 20–30 minutes, Stockholm in 5 hrs and Gothenburg in 3 hrs 20 minutes.

There is a taxi stand next to Terminal 3.

By Air

If you fly you can be on the other side of Denmark in less than an hour. Maersk Air and Cimber Airways have daily flights from Copenhagen to Bornholm, Odense, Århus (Tirstrup) and several other destinations in Jutland.
Maersk Air
Tel: 73 33 00 66
Fax: 76 50 26 50
www.maersk-air.com
Cimber Air Tel: 74 42 22 23
www.cimber.dk

By Coach (Long-distance Bus)

There is an extensive network of buses throughout Denmark. For details contact HT Customer Service, tel: 36 13 14 15.
www.ht.dk
Open daily 7am–9.30pm.

By Train

There is a very efficient train service linking all major cities and some of the smaller towns.

There is a boat-train link from Copenhagen to Rønne, Bornholm.

Useful numbers
General information
Tel: 33 14 17 01
www.dsb.dk
Trains going out of the country
Tel: 70 13 14 16
Inland trains
Tel: 70 13 14 15

By Car

Rules of the road
Remember to drive on the right, and drive politely. Always give way at pedestrian crossings and look out for bicycles when turning right. Look over your left shoulder every time you open the doors on the driver's side – bicycles are everywhere. Overtake on the left only.

Drivers and passengers must wear seat belts at all times, and dipped headlights are required.

Speed limits
These are standard speed limits, which are enforced:
Built-up areas 50 kph (30 mph)
Main roads 80 kph (50 mph)
Motorways 110 kph (70 mph)
For a car with a trailer, the limits are 50 kph (30 mph), 70 kph (40 mph) and 90 kph (55 mph) respectively.

Roadside assistance
If you break down, use the emergency telephones by roads to call FALCK, the Danish motorists' aid organisation, tel: 70 10 20 30. If FALCK can't repair your car on the spot it will be towed to a garage, for a fee. Open 24 hours a day.

Car rental
It pays to shop around. Ask travel agents about special offers, or try

Yellow Pages. **Avis** (tel: 33 26 80 80) and **Hertz** (tel: 33 17 90 00) have offices all around the country, but it is possible to get a better deal with smaller firm like **Europcar** (tel: 89 33 11 33) and **Lej et Lig** (tel: 39 29 85 05). You need a valid international driving licence and must be at least 20–25 years old.

By Bike

In the centre of Copenhagen you can use bikes free of charge. You pay 20DKK, which is refunded when you deliver the bike back.

Information and advice
Dansk Cyklistforbund
Romersgade 7, 1362
Copenhagen K. Tel: 33 32 31 21
www.dcf.dk

Bike rental in Copenhagen
Cyklebørs
157 Gothersgade. Tel: 33 14 07 17
Københavns Cykler
Central Station. Tel: 33 33 86 13

By Taxi

Taxis are available at airports, central train and bus stations and in the centre of all major cities.
● **Copenhagen Taxi**
Tel: 35 35 35 35
● **Øbrotaxi** Tel: 32 51 51 51
● **HS Taxi** Tel: 38 77 77 77

Tour Operators

Throughout Denmark
Copenhagen Excursions
Tel: 32 54 06 06. Fax: 32 57 49 05
www.cex.dk

Copenhagen
● To hire an authorised guide to the city, contact: **Meet the Danes**, Ravnsborggade 2, DK-2200 Copenhagen N
Tel: 33 46 46 46
E-mail: info@meetthedanes.dk
www.meetthedanes.dk
● *Copenhagen This Week* (www.ctw.dk; available free at most hotels and tourist agencies) has a list of tours.

Where to Stay

Danish hotels are not cheap, but have first-class facilities and are very much business-orientated. They are classified by one to five stars by HORESTA (Danish Hotel, Restaurant and Tourist Employers' Association). Rooms have showers more often than baths, so if you want a bath ask before you book.

Greenland
In Greenland hotels come into the expensive category and there is not a wide selection of alternatives. Make sure of your accommodation before you go. **Greenland Tourism** Tel: 299 32 28 88. www.greenland-guide.dk

Faroe Islands
Hotels here were until recently largely designed for visiting sailors. Apart from a few in Torshavn (of which at least two have good facilities), modern hotels are not plentiful. Private houses and youth hostels provide an alternative. **Faroe Islands Tourist Board** Tel: 298 31 60 55. www.tourist.fo

Information and reservations
The *Denmark Accommodation Guide* is available free from the Danish Tourist Board in London, tel: 020 7259 5958, www.dtb.dt.dk. This lists hundreds of hotels, holiday centres and inns.

You can book a hotel at the tourist information office opposite Central Station in Copenhagen (open daily 9am–4pm; tel: 70 22 24 42). For further information try the Danish Tourist Board in your home country *(see page 355)*.

Hotels are grouped by area, starting with Copenhagen. Within each city or region, they are listed alphabetically in price order, with the most expensive first.

COPENHAGEN

Hotel d'Angleterre
Kongens Nytorv 34, DK-1050
Tel: 33 12 00 95. Fax: 33 12 11 18
E-mail: sales@remmen.dk
www.remmen.dk
Entertains European royalty and the famous. Popular pavement café. 243 beds, suites available. **$$$**

Savoy Hotel
Vesterbrogade 34, DK-1620
Tel: 33 26 75 00. Fax: 33 26 75 01
Carefully restored 1906 building in a garden courtyard. **$$–$$$**

Copenhagen Admiral Hotel
Toldbodgade 24–28
Tel: 33 74 14 14. Fax: 33 74 14 16
E-mail: admiral@admiral-hotel.dk
www.admiral-hotel.dk
Conversion of a 1787 granary with excellent facilities. 815 beds. **$$**

Sophie Amalie Hotel
Sankt Annæ Plads 21, DK-1250
Tel: 33 13 34 00. Fax: 33 11 77 07
E-mail: sales@remmen.dk
www.remmen.dk
Well-renovated building. Some rooms have a harbour view. Quiet. **$$**

Hotel Amager
Amagerbrogade 29, DK-2300
Tel: 32 54 40 08. Fax: 32 54 90 05
www.hotelamager.dk
On the way to the airport but only five minutes' bus ride to the centre. A traditional *pension* hotel. **$**

Hotel Opera
Tordenskjoldsgade 15, DK-1055
Tel: 33 47 83 00. Fax: 33 47 83 01
www.operahotelcopenhagen.dk
Old-fashioned style and charm. Next door to the Opera. **$**

Hotel Fy and Bi
Valby Langgade 62, 2500 Valby
Tel: 36 45 44 00. Fax: 36 45 44 09
www.hotelfyandbi.dk
A charming 100-year-old hotel and restaurant built around a courtyard and painted in traditional Danish yellow. **$**

$$$	955–2,995DKK
$$	725–1,050DKK
$	under 450–835DKK

Price categories are based on the average cost (including tax) of a double room, usually with breakfast.

ZEALAND

Fredensborg
Hotel Store Kro
Slotsgade 6, 3480
Tel: 48 40 01 11. Fax: 48 48 45 61
E-mail: info@storekro.dk
www.storekro.dk
Deluxe and romantic with Fredensborg Castle as its neighbour. **$$**

Frederiksværk
Hotel Frederiksværk
Torvet 6, 3300
Tel: 47 72 22 88. Fax: 47 72 01 13
E-mail: post@frvhotel.dk
www.frvhotel.dk
235 years old and in the centre. **$**

Helsingør
Hotel Hamlet
Bramstræde 5, 3000
Tel: 49 21 05 91. Fax: 49 26 01 30
E-mail: hotelhamlet@internet.dk
www.hotelhamlet.dk
A charming old-fashioned building near Kronborg Castle only two minutes from the train station. **$$**

Køge
Hotel Hvide Hus
Strandvejen 111, DK-4600
Tel: 56 65 36 90. Fax: 56 66 33 14
E-mail: koge@hotelhvidehus.dk
www.hotelhvidehus.dk
Modern hotel with sea views. **$$**

Næstved
Mogenstrup Kro
Præstø Landevej 25, DK-4700
Tel: 55 76 11 30. Fax: 55 76 11 29
www.firsthotels.com
First-class hotel and resort. **$$**

Rødby
Landmands Hotel
Vestergade 6, 4970

Tel: 54 66 07 67. Fax: 55 66 07 67
Quaint roadside inn near ferry. **$**

Roskilde
Hotel Prindsen
Algade 13, DK-4000
Tel: 46 30 91 00. Fax: 46 30 91 50
E-mail: info@hotelprindsen.dk
www.hotelprindsen.dk
Royal-style building 305 years old,
recently renovated and central. **$$**

Slagelse
Hotel Frederik d.11
Idagårdsvej 3, DK-42200
Tel: 58 53 03 22. Fax: 58 53 46 22
E-mail: hotel@fr2.dk
www.fr2.dk
A modern red-brick building near the
Antvorskou ruins. **$$**

Stege
Præstekilde Kro & Hotel
Klintevej 116, Keldby DK-4780
Tel: 55 86 87 88. Fax: 55 81 36 34
Modern hotel in a pretty area 20 km
(12 ½ miles) from Møn cliffs. **$–$$**

Tisvildeleje
Strandhotel "Højbohus"
Hovedgaden 75, 3220
Tel: 48 70 71 19. Fax: 48 70 71 77
On the beach. Popular with both
Danes and tourists in summer. **$$**

Vedbæk
Hotel Marina
Vedbæk Strandvej 391, 2950
Tel: 45 89 17 11. Fax: 45 89 17 22
E-mail: marina@hotelmarina.dk
www.choicehotels.dk
Modern, overlooking the marina. **$$**

FUNEN

Odense
Hotel H.C. Andersen Radisson SAS
Claus Bergs Gade 7, DK-5000
Tel: 66 14 78 00. Fax: 66 14 78 90
www.radisson.com
Good, modern hotel in the old part
of town. Conference facilities. **$$$**
City Hotel Odense
Hans Mulesgade 5, DK-500
Tel: 66 12 12 58. Fax: 66 12 93 64
E-mail: reception@city-hotel-
odense.dk
www.city-hotel-odense.dk

Moderately priced three-star with all
modern comforts. **$$**
Odense Congress Centre
Ørbækvej 350, DK-5220
Tel: 65 56 01 00. Fax: 65 56 01 99
E-mail: konf@occ.dk
www.occ.dk
Both a congress centre and four-
star hotel with 218 beds. **$$**
Motel Brasilia/Blommenslyst Kro
Middelfartvej 420
DK-5491 Blommenslyst
Tel: 65 96 70 12. Fax: 65 96 79 37
Beautiful motel, 8 km (5 miles)
west of Odense, added to an old
kro (inn) with lovely garden.
Excellent traditional food. **$$**
Det Lille Hotel
Dronningensgade 5, DK-5000
Tel: 66 12 28 21
A charming little family hotel on a
quiet street near the centre. **$**
Hotel Ansgar
Østre Stationsvej 32, DK-5100
Tel: 66 11 96 93. Fax: 66 11 96 75
www.hotel-ansgar.dk
One of the old mission hotels with
all facilities. 70 rooms. **$**
Ydes Hotel
Hans Tausensgade 11, DK-5000
Tel: 66 12 11 31. Fax: 66 12 17 82
E-mail: reception@ydes.dk
www.ydes.dk
Small hotel. English breakfast. **$**

Rudkøbing
Rudkøbing Skudehavn
Havnegade 21, DK-5900
Tel: 62 51 46 00. Fax: 62 51 49 40
Modern hotel with many facilities.
Overlooking the harbour. **$**

JUTLAND

Ålborg
Park Hotel
J.F. Kennedys Plads 41, DK-9000
Tel: 98 12 31 33. Fax: 98 13 31 66
E-mail: park.hotel.aalborg@mail.dk
www.park-hotel-aalborg.dk
Built in 1900, central hotel. **$$**

Århus
Radisson SAS Scandinavia
Margrethepladsen 1, DK-8000
Tel: 86 12 86 65. Fax: 86 12 86 75
www.radissonsas.com
A large steel and glass building

and major conference centre. **$$$**
Hotel Royal
Store Torv, Box 43
Tel: 86 12 00 11. Fax: 86 76 04 04
E-mail: royal@hotelroyal.dk
www.hotelroyal.dk
Beautiful building, more than 150
years old, but modernised with a
fine conservatory restaurant. **$$$**
Hotel Marselis
Strandvejen 25, DK-8000
Tel: 86 14 44 11. Fax: 86 14 44 20
www.marselis.dk
Between a beach and forest. With a
café and restaurant. Conference
facilities and live music. **$$–$$$**
Hotel La Tour
Randersvej 139, DK-8200
Tel: 86 16 78 88. Fax: 86 16 79 95
www.latour.dk
200 beds, all private facilities. **$$**
Hotel Ritz
Banegårdsplads 12, Postboks 37
Tel: 86 13 44 44. Fax: 86 13 45 87
www.hotelritz.dk
Very central and close to the station
with interesting decor. **$$**
Scandic Hotel Plaza Århus
Banegårdspladsen 14, DK-8100
Tel: 87 32 01 00. Fax: 87 32 01 99
www.scandic-hotels.com
Central, with a bar, fitness centre,
Jacuzzi and indoor parking. **$$**

Christiansfeld
Brødremenighedens Hotel
Lindegade 25, DK-6070
Tel: 74 56 17 10. Fax: 74 56 17 27
Old guesthouse with a restaurant. **$**

Esbjerg
Palads Hotel
Skolegade 14, DK-6700
Tel: 75 18 16 00. Fax: 75 18 16 24
E-mail: cab-inn@cab-inn.dk
www.cab-inn.dk
Nice, recently renovated. Central. **$**

Fanø
Sønderho Kro
Kropladsen 11, 6720
Tel: 75 16 40 09. Fax: 75 16 43 85
www.sonderhokro.dk
Built in 1722 in idyllic surroundings
perfect for a romantic break. **$$**

Frederikshavn
Hotel Frederikshavn
Tordenskjoldsgade 14, DK-9900

Tel: 98 43 32 33. Fax: 98 43 33 11
E-mail: frederikshavn@scandic-
hotels.com
www.scandic-hotels.com
Modern. Central. Good facilities. **$$**

Hirtshals

Hotel Strandlyst
Tornby Strand, DK-9850
Tel: 98 97 70 76. Fax: 98 97 70 76
Cosy 100-year-old hotel 10 minutes
from the beach. Open summer. **$**

Ribe

Hotel Dagmar
Torvet 1, DK-6760
Tel: 75 42 00 33. Fax: 75 42 36 52
E-mail: dagmar@hoteldagmar.dk
www.hoteldagmar.dk
The oldest hotel in Denmark,
established in 1581. Across the
street from the cathedral. **$$**

Skagen

Danhostel Skagen
Rolighedsvej 2, DK-9990
Tel: 98 44 22 00. Fax: 98 44 22 55
E-mail: danhostel.skagen@adr.dk
www.danhostelnord.dk/skagen
Clean, cosy and near the beach. **$**

Vejle

Munkebjerg Hotel
Munkebjergvej 125, DK-7100
Tel: 76 42 85 00. Fax: 75 72 08 86
E-mail: info@munkebjerg.dk
www.munkebjerg.dk
Modern hotel in the middle of forest
with marvellous views. **$$–$$$**

BORNHOLM

Allinge

Hotel Pepita
Langebjergvej 1 Sandvig, DK-3770
Tel: 56 48 04 51. Fax: 56 48 18 51
E-mail: pepita@post5.tele.dk
Cosy family-run hotel near beach. **$**

Gudhjem

Hotel Casa Blanca
DK-3760
Tel: 56 48 50 20. Fax: 56 48 50 81
E-mail: hotel.casa-blanca.
gudhjem@mail.dk
Modern family hotel with a fantastic
view of the sea. Outdoor pool. **$$**

Price Guide

$$$	955–2,995DKK
$$	725–1,050DKK
$	under 450–835DKK

Price categories are based on
the average cost (including tax)
of a double room, usually with
breakfast.

GREENLAND

Illulisaat

Hotel Arctic
Box 1501, DK-3952
Tel: 299 94 41 53
Fax: 299 94 40 49
www.hotel-arctic.gl
Modern hotel with a superb view
over the bay and Disko Island. The
best way to reach it is by helicopter
from Søndrestrømfjord Airport. **$$$**

Kangerlussuaq

Hotel Kangerlussuaq
Box 1006, DK-3910
Tel: 299 84 11 80
Fax: 299 84 12 84
www.glv.gl
On the tip of one of Greenland's
longest fjords with 269 rooms, and
numerous amenities. **$$**

Narsarsuaq

Hotel Narsarsuaq
The Airport, DK-3921
Tel: 299 66 52 53.
Fax: 299 66 53 70
www.glv.gl
The airport hotel with 192 rooms,
around 16km (10 miles) from the
start of the inland ice. **$$$**

Hotel Perlen
Box 8, DK-3291
Tel: 299 66 17 13/57 20 17
Fax: 299 66 17 13
Family-run hotel with good food and
beautiful views of the sound. **$$**

Nuuk

Hotel Hans Egede
Aqqusinersuaq 1–5,
Box 289, DK-3920
Tel: 299 32 42 22
Fax: 299 32 44 87
www.hhe.gl
Modern conference hotel. Has 250
beds with private facilities. **$$$**

Qaanaaq

Hotel Qaanaaq
Box 88, DK-3971
Tel: 299 97 12 34
A small, simple hotel on the remote
northwest coast of Greenland. **$**
● For further information contact:
Greenland Tourism
Tel: 299 32 28 88
Fax: 299 32 28 77
E-mail: tourism@greennet.gl
www.greenland-guide.dk

THE FAROE ISLANDS

Bordoy, Klaksvík

Hotel Klaksvíkar Sjómansheim
Víkarvegur 59, FO-700 Klaksvík
Tel: 298 45 53 33
Fax: 298 45 72 33
Handy for the ferry. 61 rooms,
some en suite. Restaurant. **$$**

Eystoroy, Eiði

Hotel Eiði
Tel: 298 42 34 56
Fax: 298 42 32 00
Has 31 beds without private
facilities but with mini-bars. **$**
● Eystoroy also has two youth
hostels, as do many other islands.
Details from: **Ferðaráð Føroya**
Tel: 298 31 60 55
Fax: 298 31 08 58
www.farhostel.fo

Mykines

Kristianshús
Tel: 298 31 09 85
Fax: 298 31 09 85
E-mail: mykines@post.olivant.fo
Open May to September. **$**

Tórshavn

Hotel Føroyar
Oggjarvegur, PO Box 3303, FO-110
Tórshavn
Tel: 298 31 75 00
Fax: 298 31 60 19
www.hotelforoyar.com
Modern but built in traditional
style, looking across to the island
of Nolsoy. All private facilities.
$$$
Hotel Hafnia
Áarvegur 4-10, FO-110
Tel: 298 31 32 33
Fax: 298 31 52 50

By the harbour, with 76 beds all with private facilities. Sauna. **$$**
Hotel Vágar
Sørvágur, FO-380
Tel: 298 33 29 55
Fax: 298 33 23 10
E-mail: hotel@ff.fo
www.ff.fo
Restaurant serves local food; conference facilities. **$$**
Hotel Tórshavnar Sjómansheim
Tórsgøta 4,
FO-100 Tórshavn
Tel: 298 35 00 00
Fax: 298 35 00 07
E-mail: hotel@hotel.fo
www.hotel.fo
Comfortable, with 72 rooms, some with private facilities. Restaurant.
$

● For further information contact:
The Faroe Islands Tourist Board
Tel: 298 31 60 55. E-mail:
tourist@tourist.fo
www.tourist.fo

Family Holidays

Camping/caravanning
You can hire stationary caravans or huts on many camp sites (all high standard), or take your own tent. For a list of sites, ask the Danish Tourist Board or contact:
Camping Rådet Tel: 39 27 88 44.
Fax: 39 27 80 44
www.campingraadet.dk
Camping Club Denmark Vonsildvej 19, DK-6000, Kolding.
Tel: 75 52 14 82. Fax: 75 52 45 29
www.ccd.dk

Farm Holidays
For details contact: **Landboferie i Danmark**.www.bondegaardsferie.dk

Youth Hostels

Denmark has around 100 youth hostels. You need to be a member of the Youth Hostel Association in your home country. For details:
Denmarks Vandrerhjem
Vesterbrogade 39, DK-1620, Copenhagen V. Tel: 31 31 36 12
www.danhostel.dk.
Danish tourist offices also have a free list of sites.

Where to Eat

What To Eat

Within the past couple of decades the Danish kitchen has gone through a quiet revolution. Not only have the traditional hearty meals of pork and beef seen new low-calorie, high-fibre varieties, but words like pizza, pasta, quiche and kebab have also gone into the everyday vocabulary.

However, the food that is usually associated with Denmark has not suffered from this clash of cultures: open sandwiches *(smørrebrød)* are still most common for lunch. *Smorgåsbord* is a lunch buffet of cold dishes, where you can pick and choose from a range of Danish specialities. Beer and aquavit are also traditional.

Take advantage of the varieties of fish from the Baltic and North seas. Fowl and game are common, especially in autumn.

Many restaurants offer "a two-course meal of good, Danish food". This is where one finds roast pork, minced beef, meat or fish balls, and other traditional dishes.

Restaurant Listings

Restaurants are grouped by area, starting with Copenhagen. Within each city or region they are listed in price and alphabetical order starting with the most expensive.

COPENHAGEN

Danish
Krogs Fiskerestaurant
Gammel Strand 38, 1202 K
Tel: 33 15 89 15
Fax: 33 15 83 19
Possibly the best (and priciest) fish restaurant in town. **$$$**

Peder Oxe
Grobrødretorv 11
Tel: 31 11 00 77
Good for lunch, with an excellent salad bar and *smørrebrød*. **$$$**
St Gertrude's Kloster
Hauserplads 32d
Tel: 33 14 66 30
Specialises in medieval dishes. **$$$**
Restaurant Olsen
Store Kongensgade 66
Tel: 33 93 91 95
A basement café-bistro serving excellent modern Danish cuisine on candlelit tables. **$$**
Slotskælderen
Fortunstræde 4
Tel: 33 11 15 37
The best open sandwiches in Copenhagen at this small, intimate restaurant popular with politicians from the nearby parliament. **$**

International
Era Ora
Overgaden Neden Vandet 33B
Tel: 32 54 06 93
Gourmet Italian restaurant in the Christianhavn district with top-notch meat and fish dishes. **$$$**
San Giorgio
Rosenborggade 7
Tel: 33 14 89 05
One of the best Italian (Sardinian) restaurants in Copenhagen. **$$$**
El Gusto
Havnegade 47
Tel: 33 11 32 16
Oldest, largest Mexican restaurant in town. **$$**
Indian Taj
Jernbanegade 3–5
Tel: 33 13 10 10
Traditional Indian. Good value. **$$**
Pasta Basta
Valkendorfsgade 22 (between Stråget and Gråbrødretorv), 1151 K
Tel: 33 11 21 31

Price Guide

Price categories are based on an average cost of a two-course meal (excluding drinks but with tax) per head:
$$$ 200DKK or more
$$ 100–200DKK
$ less than 100DKK

Try the first-rate buffet of hot and cold pasta dishes. Reasonable prices. $

ZEALAND

Kongens Lyngby
Restaurant Brede Spisehus
I.C. Modewegsvej,
2800 Kongens Lyngby
Tel: 45 85 54 57
Fax: 45 85 57 67
Danish/French cuisine. $$$

Humlebæk
Sletten Kro
Gl. Humlebækvej, 3050
Tel: 49 19 13 01
Fax: 49 19 13 91
Danish specialities. $$$

Hillerød
Slotskroen
Slotsgade 67, 3400
Tel: 48 26 01 82
Fax: 48 24 08 82
Typical Danish lunch. $/$$

BORNHOLM

Fredensborg
Strandvejen 116, Rønne
Tel: 56 95 44 44.
Fax: 56 95 03 14
High gastronomic standard with a view of the forest and the sea. $$$

Price Guide

Price categories are based on an average cost of a two-course meal (excluding drinks but with tax) per head:
$$$ 200DKK or more
$$ 100–200DKK
$ less than 100DKK

ODENSE

Den Gamle Kro (The Old Inn)
Overgade 23
Tel: 66 12 14 33
Fax: 66 17 88 58
International cuisine in a building dating back to 1683. $$$

Restaurant & Café Vestergade 1
Vestergade 1, 5000 Odense
Tel: 66 12 52 53.
A good choice for brunch and excellent Danish home cooking. $$
Olivia
Vintapperstræde 37
Tel: 66 17 87 44
Cosy café with home-made pies. $

JUTLAND

Aabenraa
Krusmølle
Krusmøllevej 10, Feldstedskov
Tel: 74 68 61 72
Fax: 74 68 62 10
Serves Danish and international cuisine. $$

Ålborg
Restaurant "Mortens Kro"
Algade 37, 9000
Tel/fax: 98 12 48 60
Danish and French cuisine. $–$$

Arden
Rold Gammel Kro
Hobrovej 11, 9510
Tel: 98 56 17 00
Fax: 98 56 25 11
Traditional Danish dishes. $$

Århus
Latin Brasserie & Crêperie
Klostergade 2
Tel: 86 13 78 12
Elegant, romantic French restaurant with chefs of the highest calibre. An arty, bohemian-type setting. $$$
L'Estragon
Klostergade 6
Tel: 86 12 40 66
Top-class classic French food. $$$
Chez Tony
Tordenskjoldsgade 25
Tel: 86 16 88 30
Popular Greek restaurant. $$
Emmery's
Guldsmedegade 24
Tel: 86 13 04 00
Gourmet bakery and tapas. $$
Pind's Café
Skolegade 29
Tel: 86 12 11 02
An Århus institution serving traditional Danish fare. $$

Copenhagen's Cafés

Café Chips
Øster Farimagsgade 53
Tel: 35 38 47 91
Cosy. Music some Sundays. $
Café Dan Turell
Store Regnegade 3, 1110 K
Tel: 33 14 10 47
Artists often frequent this café. $
Café Norden
Østergade 61, 1100 K
Tel: 33 13 59 59
Pretty upstairs, with paintings. $
Krasnapolsky
Vestergade 10, 1456 K
Tel: 33 32 88 00
Popular with the young. $
Park Café
Østerbrogade 79, 2100 Ø
Tel: 35 42 6248
Often has live music. $

Christiansfeld
Den Gamle Gæstgivergård
Lindegade 25, 6070
Tel: 74 56 17 10
Fax: 74 56 36 40
Top-class restaurant specialising in classic Danish cuisine. $$$

Nykøbing Mors
Sallingsund Færgekro
Sallingsundvej 104
7900 Nykøbing Mors
Tel: 97 72 00 88
Fax: 97 72 25 40
French cuisine. $–$$

Randers
Slotskroen
Slotsgade, 8900
Tel: 86 43 56 64
Fax: 86 42 69 41
Danish, French and Italian food. $$$

Skagen
Brøndums Hotel
Anchersvej 3, 9990
Tel: 98 44 15 55
Established in 1840. Good-quality wine and traditional cuisine. $$

Nightlife

Information

The best entertainment is found in Copenhagen, Århus and Odense. Check the local newspapers or call tourist information offices.

BILLETnet is an information network where you can reserve tickets and get details on entertainment events. Tel: 38 48 11 22. www.billetnet.dk

For details about musical events, contact **Danish Music Information Centre**: Tel: 33 11 20 66. Fax: 33 32 20 16. www.mic.dk

Listings

COPENHAGEN

Theatre

Most theatre is in Danish even though the piece may have been written in another language.

The London Toast Theatre, Kochsvej 18. Tel: 33 22 86 86 The only English-language theatre in Copenhagen, showing plays of a high standard.

Det Konglige Teater (The Royal Theatre), Kongens Nytorv. Tel: 33 69 69 69 www.kgl-teater.dk Major operas and symphonies.

Live music

Café Baptof Nodre Fasanvej 46 Tel: 38 86 90 67 Folk, Irish, American.

Copenhagen Jazz House Niels Hemmingsensgade 10 Tel: 33 15 26 00 The place for jazz.

Mojo Løngangsstræde 21C Tel: 33 11 64 53 Live blues every night.

Pumpehuset Studiestræde 52. Tel: 33 93 19 60 Big names in modern music.
Café Svejk Smallegade 31. Tel: 38 86 25 60 Blues, rock and folk.

ODENSE

Badstuen Østre Stationsvej. Tel: 66 13 48 66 Rock, blues, Latin and pop.
Brandts Klædefabrik Bradnst Passage 37–43 Tel: 66 13 78 97 Music, dance and theatre.
Odense Koncerthus Claus Berg Gade 9 Tel: 66 12 44 88 Classical music.
Rytmeposten Østre Stationsvej 35 Tel: 66 13 60 20 Rock blues and pop.

ÅRHUS

Nightlife is centred around Skolegade. Many cafés and bars are near the cathedral and in the streets leading to Guldsmedegade. You should also stroll through Vestergade and Jægersgårdgade.

Fatter Eskild Skolegade 25. Tel: 86 19 44 11 Blues music.
Glazzhuset Åboulevarden 35. Tel: 86 12 13 12 Live jazz.
Jazzbar Bent J Nørre Allé 66. Tel: 86 12 04 92 Famous jazz bar.
Musikcaféen Mejlgade 53. Tel: 86 76 03 44 Rock, blues, folk of all kinds.

Cinema

All foreign films are shown with their original soundtrack. Local newspapers have all the details of what's on where.

Sport

Angling

Anglers must have fishing permits, which can be obtained at any post office or tourist office.

Fishing rights in lakes and streams are usually privately owned but permits can often be hired from the local tourist office.

Golf

There are more than 125 golf courses to choose from in Denmark. Guests are welcomed at Danish golf clubs on presentation of a valid membership card from their home club. Two worth trying are:
Smørem Golf Centre Skebjerg 46. Tel: 44 97 01 11.
Furesø Tel: 42 81 74 44.

Hiking

There are many beautiful places for hiking in Denmark. Local tourist offices have maps of tested walks and will help you to plan routes. Try walking along the lovely chalk-white cliffs of Stevens or through the peaceful forest of Bøgeskov, just an hour south of Copenhagen.

Sailing

Boats and yachts are available for hire on a weekly basis. Visitors should ask to see a certificate from the Shipping Inspection office before hiring a boat. Try:
Nordia Boat Charter Tel: 97 20 99 22. Fax: 97 11 88 70. E-mail: mail@nordiaboatcharter.dk www.nordiaboatcharter.dk

Shopping

What to Buy

Danish design is famous all over the world, especially in kitchenware, furniture and stereo equipment.

Beautiful amber necklaces are to be found in all jewellery stores, along with exquisite replicas of ancient Viking jewellery in silver and gold.

Ceramics and glassware are a tradition in Denmark and, in addition to Royal Copenhagen Porcelain, there are many small ceramic studios scattered throughout the country.

Danish furs are very popular among tourists and countless shops specialise in traditional and modern knitwear.

Lego bricks are known throughout the world, but most Danish children's toys are made of strong, durable wood with designs and functions that are based on educational principles.

Feather bedding is a Danish speciality and many stores sell down duvets, eiderdowns, quilts and pillows and can arrange shipment of bulky items.

Danish pipe makers carve wood and meerschaum pipes with excellent craftsmanship.

Tax-free Shopping

Part of the reason for the high prices is a value-added tax (called MOMS) of 25 percent, added to all sales and services.

Visitors can avoid making this contribution to the Danish state by having their purchases shipped home or, for non-EU residents, by shopping in stores that offer a tax-free service (*see Customs, page 355 for further details*).

Shopping in Copenhagen

The main shopping in Denmark's capital are the pedestrian streets, and first among them Strøget. When there, take a look inside **Illums Bolighus** (at Amagertorv). It sells everything from high-quality furniture to kitchenware. Nearby is **Georg Jensen**'s silver shop at Strøget and Pilestræde.

Visit **Krea** in Vestergade and **BR** across the street from **Magasin** for children's toys. Around the corner in Lars Bjørnstræde are street fashion and secondhand shops.

Pistolstræde is more pricey, and you will notice the influence of Birger Christensen, the owner of **Café Bee Cee**, **Birger Christensen Furs** and several other food and fashion shops in the neighbourhood.

Hennes & Mauritz, originally a Swedish company, is now an enormous success with the younger generation in Denmark.

HANDICRAFTS

There is an information centre for Danish handicrafts at Amagertorv 1,1160 Kbh. K.
Tel: 33 12 61 62.

BOOKS

The following shops are worth trying for foreign-language literature:
Arnold Busck, Købmagergade 49. Tel: 33 73 35 00.
Atheneum Boghandel, Norregade 6. Tel: 33 12 69 70.
Fax: 33 14 69 33.
Boghallen, Radhuspladsen 37.
Tel: 33 11 85 11.
Fax: 33 11 14 10.
English Books and Records, The Book Trader, Skindergade 23.
GAD, At Central Station and Vimmelskaftet 32.
Tel: 33 12 91 48
www.gad.dk
Books in English, German and French.

Language

Pronunciation

The old joke says that Danish is not so much a language as a disease of the throat, and so it sometimes seems. Danish has three extra letters – æ, ø, and å – plus unpronounceable sub-glottal stops, and myriad dialects and accents. Here are a few simple rules of thumb for pronouncing vowels:

a = a, as in bar
å = aw, as in paw
æ = e, as in pear
e = e, as in bed
i = ee, as in sleep
ø = u, as in fur

General

yes/no *ja/nej*
big/little *stor(t)/lille*
good/bad *god(t)/dårlig(t)*
possible/impossible *muligt/umuligt*
hot/cold *varm/kold*
much/little *meget/lidt*
many/few *mange/få*
and/or *og/eller*
please/thank you *vær så venlig/tak*
I *jeg*
you *(formal) du (de)*
he/she *han/hun*
it *den/det*
we *vi*
you *(plural, formal) I (de)*
they *de*
foreigner *udlænding*
foreign *fremmed*

Medical

pharmacy *(et) apotek*
hospital *(et) hospital*
casualty *(en) skadestue*
doctor *(en) læge*

Food and Drink

breakfast *morgenmad*
lunch *(break) frokost (pause)*
dinner *middag*
tea *te*
coffee *kaffe*
beer *(bottle/draught) øl/fadøl*

Getting Around

left *venstre*
right *højre*
street *(en) gade/vej*
bicycle (path) *(en) cykel (sti)*
car *(en) bil*
bus/coach *(en) bus*
train *(et) tog*
ferry *(en) færge*
bridge *(en) bro*
traffic light *(et) trafiklys*
square *(et) torv*
north *nord*
south *syd*
east *øst*
west *vest*

Numbers

1	*en/et*
2	*to*
3	*tre*
4	*fire*
5	*fem*
6	*seks*
7	*syv*
8	*otte*
9	*ni*
10	*ti*
11	*elleve*
12	*tolv*
13	*tretten*
14	*fjorten*
15	*femten*
16	*seksten*
17	*sytten*
18	*atten*
19	*nitten*
20	*tyve*
21	*enogtyve*
30	*tredive*
40	*fyrre*
50	*halvtreds*
60	*tres*
70	*halvfjerds*
80	*firs*
90	*halvfems*
100	*hundrede*

Buying a Ticket

ticket *billet*
adult *voksen*
child *barn*
single *enkelt*
return *retur*

Money

How much is it? *Hvad koster det?*
Can I pay with... *Må jeg betale med...*
travellers' cheques *rejsechecks*
money *penge*
notes/coins *sedler/mønter*
Please may I have...? *Må jeg få...?*
the bill *regningen*
May I have a...? *Må jeg få en...?*
receipt *kvittering*
bank *(en) bank*
exchange *veksle*
open *åben*
closed *lukket*
MOMS *value-added tax (VAT)*

Time

good morning *godmorgen*
good day/evening *goddag*
goodnight *godaften/godnat*
today *i dag*
tomorrow *i morgen*
yesterday *i går*
morning *formiddag*
noon *middag*
afternoon *eftermiddag*
evening *aften*
night *nat*
What time is it? *Hvad er klokken?*
It's five o'clock *Den er fem*

Place Names

Copenhagen *København*
Elsinore *Helsingør*
Zealand *Sjælland*
Funen *Fyn*
Jutland *Jylland*

Days of the Week

Monday *mandag*
Tuesday *tirsdag*
Wednesday *onsdag*
Thursday *torsdag*
Friday *fredag*
Saturday *lørdag*
Sunday *søndag*

Further Reading

General

Complete Hans Christian Andersen Fairly Tales (Gramercy Books). The classic collection of children's tales by Denmark's master storyteller.
The Sixth Floor by Robin Reilly (Cassell). Dramatic account of the Danish resistance in World War II and the tragic consequences of the British RAF raid on the Gestapo's Copenhagen headquarters.
A Conspiracy of Decency by Emmy Werner (Westview Press). The story of how Denmark's Jews were saved from the Nazis, based partly on living eyewitness accounts.
Culture Shock! Denmark by M. Strange (Kuperard). A short guide to Denmark's customs and culture.
The Great Gamble by Dudley Pope (Chatham Publishing). An account of the naval Battle of Copenhagen in 1801, in which Nelson secured victory for Britain.

Scandinavia Connection *(see page 384 for contact details)* offer a selection of books in English about Denmark; categories include art & architecture, nature and culture.

Other Insight Guides

Over 200 titles in the acclaimed Insight Guides series cover every continent. Titles in the northern Europe region include *Denmark, Norway, Sweden,* and *Finland.* Insight Pocket Guides, with an itinerary-based approach, include *Denmark* and *Oslo & Bergen.* Insight Compact Guides to the region include *Denmark, Copenhagen, Norway* and *Finland.*

NORWAY

The Place

Area 386,958 sq km (150,000 sq miles).

Capital Oslo.

Population 4.5 million, of whom 512,000 live in Oslo, 230,000 in Bergen, 110,000 in Stavanger and 151,000 in Trondheim.

Language Norwegian, of which there are two variations: *bokmål* and *nynorsk*. The Sami in north Norway speak Lappish. English is widely understood.

Religion Around 94 percent are Evangelical Lutheran Church of Norway. Other churches, mostly Protestant and Roman Catholic, represent about 4 percent.

Time zone Central European Time, GMT +1 hour, EST +6 hours. The clock is set forward an hour in March, and back an hour in September.

Currency Norwegian krone (NOK), divided into 100 øre.

Weights and measures Metric. Distances are given in kilometres (km) but Norwegians often refer to a *mil* which is 10 km (so 10 mil is 100 km). When talking about land area you will also often hear the word *mål*. This old measure of 984.34m^2 has been rounded up to 1,000m^2 (or 1 decare).

Electricity 220 AC (two-pin plug).

International dialling code +47.

Topography

Norway is a narrow country 2,600 km (1,600 miles) long. At points it narrows down to as little as 6 km (4 miles). Most of the country's 21,465-km (13,330-mile) continental coastline lies along the North Sea. Norway has common borders with Sweden, Finland and Russia. It also has sovereignty over a few islands within the Arctic Circle, the largest being Svalbard (Spitsbergen).

The south is hilly and partially forested. The most fertile food-growing region is the southern quarter. Although indented with fjords all around its coast, the west coast from Stavanger to Bergen and Bergen to Trondheim contains the most-visited fjords.

The Glomma is Norway's longest river, with its source in South Trøndelag and outflow into the Oslofjord. Norway has thousands of glacial lakes, the largest of which is Lake Mjøsa in the southeast.

Climate

Oslo is one of the warmest places in Norway during winter; in January the average 24-hour high is -2°C (28°F) and the low is -7°C (19°F). Up north it's a different story, with sub-zero temperatures reigning for months and a good number of roads shut over winter due to long-term snow. February and March are the best skiing months. March, April and early May are the wet spring months when roads are buckled due to thaws and refreezes; through this period the temperature slowly lifts from about 4°C (39°F) to 16°C (61°F).

Come summertime and the season of the midnight sun, Oslo enjoys average temperatures in the low-to mid-20s°C (70s°F), while the sunlight-bathed north has a perfect hiking temperature, around 20°C (68°F). October is the time for autumn rains as temperatures dip below 10°C (50°F), then continue their slide towards zero. The first snow arrives mid-October.

Government

Norway's national assembly, *Stortinget*, is the mainstay of its political system. There are 165 members who sit in two chambers (*Odelsting* and *Lagting*); elections occur every four years. There are 19 major local government counties (*fylke*), divided into smaller municipalities (*kommune*). The government is headed by a prime minister who leads the majority party or a coalition of parties in the *Stortinget*. The Norwegian monarch is the symbolic head of state.

Across the political spectrum from left to right are the Red Electoral Alliance (RV), the Socialist Left Party (SV), the Labour Party (A), the Centre Party (SP), the Liberal Party (V), the Christian Democratic Party (Kr.F), the Conservative Party (H) and the Progress Party (Fr.P). Norway's constitution dates from 17 May 1814.

Economy

Norway has been a member of NATO and the OECD since 1949, and is a founder member of the UN. The nation spends more money per capita on foreign aid than any other country. It is also a member of the Council of Europe and the EEA (the country turned down European Union membership in referenda in 1972 and 1994).

With Denmark, Sweden, Iceland, Finland, the Faroe Islands and Greenland, Norway is also a member of the Nordic Council (founded in 1952).

Norway's economy has boomed due to North Sea oil. Other long-established industries include timber, pulp and paper, hydro-electric power, gas, shipping and some mining. Fish and agricultural products have long been staples of the economy. The revenue from ocean fisheries has now been surpassed by fish farming, particularly salmon. Commercial whaling is carried out on a modest scale (roughly 600 minke whales a year) against the

Aurora Borealis

The Northern Lights, or Aurora Borealis, are most often seen from November to February during the long Arctic nights. It's best to head north of the Arctic Circle, which cuts Norway just south of Bodø on the Nordland coast.

wishes of the International Whaling Commission (IWC). Newer industry revolves around computers and business services. Tourism is a continually increasing source of capital, too. Some of Norway's most successful ventures include Statoil, Norsk Hydro, Kværner, Aker RGI and Royal Caribbean Cruise Lines.

The People

Norwegians are pleasantly polite. Whenever strangers meet, there is always a handshake and exchange of full names. Whenever you are served you will hear the phrase *Vær så god* ("You are welcome" and "It is a pleasure to serve you" rolled into one). The only equivalent to "please" in Norwegian is *vennligst*, which is formal and not frequently used. Nor do they say *takk* (thank you) as frequently as English-speaking people.

The only thing remotely unruly in Norwegian manners occurs in the busy streets of Oslo. People jostle each other with impunity: don't be offended if there's no apology.

Doing Business

Norwegians have all the state-of-the-art props. Don't be caught out without a good-looking business card, a laptop and mobile phone.

People take work seriously, but also know how to maintain a relaxed business atmosphere. Liquid lunches are unusual, and the work day ends at 3.30 or 4pm. Norwegians take their summer holiday very seriously: from mid-June to the end of July/first week in August, offices and factories empty, and it is almost impossible to do business. May can also be a tricky month.

Norwegians are rarely duplicitous. They may well mention the bad points of something first, to get them out of the way; then it's on to the sell. You won't be drowned in a sea of hype, but the honesty may be hard to get used to.

Planning the Trip

Visas and Passports

A valid passport is all that is necessary for citizens of most countries to enter Norway. Citizens of other countries in the Schengen Agreement do not need passports. Visas are not required. Tourists are generally limited to a three-month visit; it is possible to stay longer, but you must apply for a visa after the initial three months.

Customs

The following can be imported:
● **Money** Notes and coins (Norwegian and foreign) up to NOK 25,000 or equivalent. If you intend to import more, you must fill in a form (available at all entry and exit points) for the Customs Office.
● **Alcohol** 1 litre wine (up to 22 percent proof) and 1 litre of spirits (up to 60 percent proof) or 2 litres wine if no spirits; 2 litres beer. On top of the tax-free quota you may bring in 4 litres wine or liquor against payment of duty.
● **Tobacco** 200 cigarettes or 250 g of other tobacco goods.

Health

The are no major health hazards in Norway. No vaccinations are necessary and the tap water is (generally) good.

Treatment

Norway has reciprocal treatment agreements with the UK and many other European countries; your own National Insurance should cover you to receive free treatment at public hospitals (you will have to pay towards medicine, however). EU members should obtain the relevant documentation to entitle them to this (for British citizens a form E111 from post offices). People from countries without such agreements, and those without an E111, will have to pay a small fee.

Money Matters

The Norwegian krone (NOK) is divided into 100 øre. Notes come in denominations of NOK 50, 100, 200, 500 and 1,000 and coins 50 øre and NOK 1, 5, 10 and 20.

You can change currency at post offices, the Oslo S-train station, international airports, some hotels and commercial banks. Public telephones take phone-cards (from kiosks) or coins.

Info Before You Go

AUSTRALIA
The embassy deals with tourist information.
17 Hunter Street, Yarralumia, Canberra ACT 2600.
Tel: 02 6270 2700
E-mail: noramb@ibm.net
www.scandinavia.com.au

UK
Norwegian Tourist Board
Charles House, 5 Lower Regent Street, London SW1Y 4LR.
(no walk-in service)
Tel: 0906 302 2003 (premium-rate brochure line).
Fax: 020 7839 6014.
E-mail: greatbritain@ntr.no
www.visitnorway.com

USA/CANADA
Norwegian Tourist Board
655 Third Avenue, Suite 1810, New York 10017.
Tel: 212-885 9700.
Fax: 212-885 9710.
E-mail: usa@ntr.no
www.goscandinavia.com

Tour Operators

● **Activity holidays**
Inntravel
Hovingham, York YO62 4ZR.
Tel: 01653 629010.
● **Arctic voyages/whale watching**
Arctic Experience &
Discover the World
29 Nork Way, Banstead,
Surrey SM7 1PB.
Tel: 01737 218800
www.arctic-discover.co.uk.

● **Norway specialists**
Bridge Travel Service
55–59 High Road, Broxbourne,
Herts EN10 7DT.
Tel: 01992 456300
www.bridgetravel.co.uk
Norsc Holidays
The Court, The Street,
Charmouth DT6 6PG.
Tel: 01297 560033
www.norsc.co.uk
Taber Holidays
30A Bingley Road, Saltaire,
Shipley, W Yorkshire BD18 4RS.
Tel: 01274 594642
www.taberhols.co.uk
● **Tailormade holidays**
Specialised Tours
4 Copthorne Bank, Copthorne,
Crawley, West Sussex RH10 3QX.
Tel: 01342 712785
www.specialisedtours.com

● **Tours/Cruises**
Page & Moy
136–140 London Road,
Leicester LE2 1EN.
Tel: 08700 106230
www.page-moy.com or
www.cruisecollection.com

Scantours
47 Whitcomb Street,
London WC2H 7DH.
Tel: 020 7839 2927
www.scantours.co.uk

● **Fjord tours**
Crystal Holidays (see below)
www.crystallakes.co.uk
DFDS Seaways
Scandinavia House, Parkeston
Quay, Harwich, Essex CO12 4QG.
Tel: 08705 333000
www.dfdsseaways.co.uk
Fjord Line
International Ferry Terminal,
Royal Quays, North Shields
NE29 6EG.
Tel: 0191 296 1313
www.fjordline.co.uk
Taber Holidays (see above)
Norwegian Coastal Voyage
3 Shortlands,
London W6 8NE.
Tel: 020 8846 2666
www.norwegiancoastalvoyage.com

● **Skiing/Hiking**
Crystal Holidays
Crystal House, Arlington Road,
Surbiton, Surrey KT6 6BW.
Tel: 0870 8880252
www.crystalski.co.uk
Explore Worldwide
1 Frederick Street,
Aldershot GU11 1LQ.
Tel: 01252 760000
www. exploreworldwide.com
Waymark Holidays
44 Windsor Road,
Slough SL1 2EJ.
Tel: 01753 516477
waymarkholidays.co.uk

Road toll stations are sometimes unmanned and require coins to be inserted (usually NOK 10) to lift the barrier.

How to pay
Use of credit cards is widespread, with Eurocard, Visa, American Express and Diner's Club the most common. Travellers' cheques are accepted. In most banks you can also get cash on a Visa card, up to a certain limit.

What to Bring

Norway is protected by the Gulf Stream so it can get even warmer than its southern neighbours. In the south, temperatures in the upper 20s°C (80s°F) are not unusual. The average temperature for the country as a whole in July is about 16°C (60°F).

Pack the clothes you would normally wear in northern Europe, including jumpers, fleeces and a raincoat and walking shoes. You are not usually required to dress formally for dinner at Norwegian resort hotels.

Spring and autumn are rainy so an umbrella is useful. In winter bring very warm clothing: mittens or gloves and hats (covering the ears) are strongly advised.

A first-aid kit is recommended for those making trips to remote parts. Include potions for preventing and treating mosquito bites.

Getting There

BY AIR

Scandinavia's flagship carrier, SAS, runs a wide range of flights between Oslo Gardermoen Airport and other world capitals, with many direct services to and from Bergen, Oslo, Stavanger, Tromsø and Trondheim.

From the UK
● **SAS** (which now owns Braathens) offers daily non-stop flights from Heathrow to Oslo and Stavanger. In summer there is a twice-weekly non-stop service from Heathrow to Tromsø and daily (except Saturday) flights from Manchester to Oslo and from Aberdeen to Stavanger.
Tel: 0845 60727727.
www.scandinavian.net.
● **Braathens** operates flights from Gatwick to Bergen and from Aberdeen and Newcastle to Stavanger.
Tel: 0845 607 27727.
www.braathens.no
● **British Airways** operate several flights a day from London Heathrow to Oslo and one a day from Manchester to Oslo.
Tel: 0845 773 3377.
www.ba.com
● **Ryanair** offers cut-price flights from Stansted to Torp near Sandefjord, two hours by coach to Oslo, and to Haugesund.
Tel: 0871 246 0000.
www.ryanair.com
● **Norwegian** fly from London Stansted to Oslo five times a week.
Tel: 0191 214 0994.
www.norwegian.no

Charter flights There are also charter flights to various airports in Norway (check with your travel agent for details).

All airports are served by buses and taxis, and Oslo Gardermoen Airport has a high-speed rail link to Sentralstasjon (known as Oslo S, the city's central railway station).

From the US
● **SAS**
Tel: 1-800-221 2350.
www.scandinavian.net

BY SEA

From the UK
Fjord Line operates the only direct year-round service from the UK with sailings from Newcastle to Stavanger, Haugesund and Bergen.
● Fjord Line, Norway House, International Ferry Terminal, Royal Quays, North Shields, Tyne & Wear NE29 6EG. Tel: 0191 296 1313. www.fjordline.co.uk
DFDS Seaways sail from Newcastle to Kristiansand.
● DFDS Seaways, Scandinavia House, Parkeston Quay, Harwich, Essex CO12 4QG.
Tel: 08705 333 000.
www.dfdsseaways.co.uk

BY RAIL

Numerous rail services link Norway with the rest of Scandinavia and Europe. From the Continent, express trains operate to Copenhagen, where inter-Scandinavian trains connect to Oslo. There are train connections in Oslo to other cities in Norway.
Norwegian State Railways (NSB) operates trains from Stockholm and Copenhagen to Oslo usually twice a day. You can also get to northern Norway from Stockholm, with Trondheim and Narvik the principal destinations.

International arrivals and departures are at Oslo S station. Gardermobanen, the high-speed rail

link from/to Oslo Gardermoen Airport, has a terminal at Oslo S.
● For tickets and information, contact NSB Reisesenter, PO Box 673, N-5001 Bergen, Norway. Tel: 81 50 08 88. www.nsb.no
● When in Norway, you can contact NSB directly, tel: 81 50 08 88 and dial 4 to be connected to an English-speaking operator, or contact the nearest railway station. www.nsb.no

BY ROAD

Most major shipping lines to Norway allow passengers to bring cars. Petrol is expensive in Norway. For further information contact:
Norges Automobil Forbund (NAF or Norwegian Automobile Association), Storgt 2, 0105 Oslo.
Tel: 22 34 14 00.
Fax: 22 33 13 72.
www.naf.no
Kongelig Norsk Automobilklub (KNA or Royal Norwegian Automobile Club), Drammensv. 20C PO Box 2425 Solli, 0201 Oslo.
Tel: 22 36 49 10.

Practical Tips

Media

NEWSPAPERS

Most larger kiosks (like the Narvesen chain at railway stations, airports, etc) and some bookshops sell English-language newspapers.
Deichmanske Bibliotek, the main public library, is at Henrik Ibsen's Gate 1 in Oslo, where you'll find a selection of international papers and periodicals, as well as free internet access.

RADIO

English broadcasts on short wave can be picked up if atmospheric conditions are favourable. Best results can usually be heard on short-wave frequency 9410.

During winter BBC Radios 1, 2, 3 and 4 can sometimes be received on AM. Radio 5 can be picked up on 909 and 693 medium wave (best reception in the evening). On Sunday Radio Norway (93 FM) broadcasts news in English.

TELEVISION

Norway has three main television stations: NRK (Norsk Rikskringkasting), TV2 and TVNorge (TVN). Cable TV is widespread.

BOOKS

Oslo has several bookshops with English sections, including:
Erik Qvist, Drammensveien 16.
Tel: 22 54 26 00.
Tanum Karl Johan, Karl Johansgate 37/41. Tel: 22 41 11 00.

Postal Services

The central post office in Oslo, at Dronningensgate 15 (the entrance is on the corner of Prinsensgate), is open Mon–Fri 8am–6pm and Sat 9am–3pm. Other post offices are open weekdays 8am–4pm, Sat 8am–1pm.

Telecommunications

Calls abroad can be made from hotels – with a surcharge – or from phone booths or the main telegraph office at Kongensgate 21 (entrance Prinsensgate), Oslo.

You can also send faxes and telegrams from here.

Norwegian pay-phones take 1, 5 and often 20-kroner pieces; the minimum charge is NOK 2. Phonecards, which can be used in the green phone booths, can be bought in Narvesen kiosks and at post offices. Credit cards (Visa, American Express, Diners, Eurocard and MasterCard) are accepted in some card phones. Cheapest calling time is 5pm–8am.

Local Tourist Offices

General information
The Tourist Information Centre, Fridtjof Nansens Plass 5, Oslo
Tel: 23 11 78 80.
Fax: 22 83 81 50.
www.visitoslo.com
Norwegian Tourist Board
PO Box 722 Sentrum
Stortorvet 10, NO-0150 Oslo
Tel: 24 14 46 00
Fax: 24 14 46 01
www.visitnorway.com/www.nortra.no
Regional information
Regional tourist offices are usually open to callers, and also supply information in writing or by phone.

Oslo/Oslofjord
The Tourist Information Centre
Fridtjof Nansens Plass 5, Oslo
Tel: 23 11 78 80.
Fax: 22 83 81 50.
www.visitoslo.com
Akershus Tourist Board
Schweigaardsgt 4, N-0185 Oslo

Tel: 22 05 58 75
Fax: 22 05 58 99
www.akershus.com
Destinasjon Vestfold AS
Thor Dahls Gate 1-5,
N-3210 Sandefjord
Tel: 33 48 60 00
Fax: 33 46 61 01
www.visitvestfold.com

East Norway
Headmark Tourist Board
Grønnegt 11, N-2300 Hamar
Tel: 62 52 90 06
Fax: 62 52 21 49
www.hedmark.com
Lillehammer Turist
Jernbane Torget 2
2609 Lillehammer
Tel: 61 28 98 00
www.lillehammerturist.no
Fjell og Fjord Ferie
Sentrumsvegen 93, N-3550 Gol
Tel: 32 07 61 35
Fax: 32 07 61 36
www.eventyrveien.com

South Norway
Telemark Travel
PO Box 3233 Handelstortget,
N-3702 Skien
Tel: 35 90 00 20
Fax: 35 90 00 21
www.visittelemark.com
Aust-Agder Tourist Board
Servicebox 606
N-4809 Arendal
Tel: 37 01 73 76
Fax: 37 01 73 65

Fjord Norway
Fjord Norway
PO Box 4108 Dreggen
N-5023 Bergen
Tel: 55 30 26 40
Fax: 55 30 26 50
www.fjordnorway.no
Rogaland Tourist Board
Peder Klows Gate 27,
N-4005 Stavanger
Tel: 51 51 66 00
Fax: 51 51 67 88
www.rogaland-f.kommune.no
Hordaland/Bergen Tourist Board
Vagsallmenningen 1,
N-5014 Bergen
Tel: 55 55 20 00
Fax: 55 55 20 01
www.visitbergen.com

Useful Numbers

- **Fire** 110
- **Police** 112
- **Ambulance** 113
- **Medical problems**
For emergency treatment in Oslo ring 22 11 70 70.
- **Internal directory enquiries** 180
- **International directory enquiries** 181
No coin required in phone boxes

Sogn/Fjordane Tourist Board
PO Box 299,
N-6852 Sogndal
Tel: 57 69 16 17
Fax: 57 69 14 31
www.sognefjord.no
Møre/Romsdal Tourist Board
Fylkeshuset,
N-6401 Molde
Tel: 71 24 50 80
Fax: 71 25 49 18
www.visitmr.com

Central Norway
Central Norway Travel
(Sør/Nord-Trøndelag), PO Box 65,
N-7400 Trondheim
Tel: 73 84 24 40
Fax: 73 84 24 50
ww.visitcentral-norway.com

North Norway
Nordland Reiseliv
PO Box 434, N-8001 Bodø
Tel: 75 54 52 00
Fax: 75 54 52 10
E-mail:
nordland@nordlandreiseliv.no
www.visitnordland.no
Finnmark Tourist Board
Sorenskriverveien 13, N-9511 Alta
Tel: 78 44 00 20
Fax: 78 43 51 84
E-mail: post@visitnorthcape.com
www.visitnorthcape.com

Medical Services

DOCTORS/HOSPITALS

Even in remote areas you should have no problem getting medical help. In emergencies EU members will receive free treatment at state hospitals *(see page 369 for details of reciprocal arrangements)*, but have to pay towards non-hospital costs and for prescriptions.

If you are ill, ask your hotel, tourist office or a pharmacy for the address of an English-speaking GP. Private doctors are in the directory under *Leger* (doctors). Keep receipts if you have insurance.

PHARMACIES

For minor problems, head for a pharmacy, or *Apotek*. Most larger cities have all-night pharmacies. In other cities enquire at your hotel; or try the emergency number in the phone book under *Legevakt* or *Lækjarvakt* (doctor on duty).

DENTISTS

Emergency dental treatment in Oslo is available from: Oslo Kommunale Tannlegevakt, Tøyen Senter, Kolstadgata 18 (near Tøyen T-bane station).Tel: 22 67 30 00. Open Mon–Sat 7am–10pm, Sunday and public holidays 11am–2pm.

Religious Services

Services are held in English at the American Lutheran Church and the Anglican/Episcopalian Church (St Edmund's, Møllergate 30, tel: 22 69 22 14).

Public Holidays

- **1 January** New Year's Day
- **March/April** Palm Sunday, Maundy Thursday, Good Friday, Easter Sunday, Easter Monday
- **1 May** Labour Day
- **17 May** National Independence Day
- **May** Ascension Day (sixth Thursday after Easter)
- **May/June** Whitsun and Whit Monday (seventh Sunday/Monday after Easter)
- **25 December** Christmas Day
- **26 December** Boxing Day

The Jewish synagogue is at Bergstein 13, near St Hanshaugen, tel: 22 69 65 70).

Oslo's Protestant cathedral or *domkirke* (at Storgate, tel: 23 31 46 00) puts on concerts for tourists at 8pm every Wednesday). For up-to-date information, consult the daily press, or latest *Oslo Guide*.

Security and Crime

The streets of Oslo are relatively safe compared with the bigger cities of Europe and North America. Crime against tourists is rare. Park safely and hide valuables.

Norwegian cities late at night are often full of young people who are drunk, but you're more likely to meet verbal harassment than bodily harm. Most bars have good bouncers, and police patrols are supplemented by private-sector security personnel and *Nattravnene* (Night Ravens, a Guardian Angel-type patrol).

Worse than the drunks are drug abusers. Give them and the areas they frequent a wide berth (these are usually the cheaper bars and cafés around railway stations).

Tipping

Hotels include a service charge and tipping is generally not expected. Restaurants usually include a service charge, in which case it's your choice to add anything (5–10 percent is customary). The same applies to taxi drivers. Table service in bars requires tipping.

Travellers with Disabilities

Visitors in need of guidance should contact the Norwegian Association for the Disabled, Oslo Folke Bernadottes vei 2, N-0862 Oslo. Tel: 22 17 02 55. Fax: 22 17 61 77. www.nhf.no

Hotel listings in accommodation guides have symbols denoting disabled access and toilets. In the *Oslo Guide* under Outdoor Activities you'll find some listings that mention accessibility for the disabled.

The Norwegian State Railways (NSB) have carriages specially furnished for the disabled and the Coastal Express ships have lifts and cabins for disabled people. Euro Terra Nova AS, at Rådhusgt 17, N-0158 Oslo, offers brochures on coach tours for wheelchair users, and provides hotel bookings and hire cars. Tel: 22 99 23 99. Fax: 22 99 23 90.

Travelling with Kids

Norway is welcoming and safe for children. Family attractions include:

In and around Oslo
Barnekunstmuseet (International Children's Art Museum; exhibits and workshops), Lille Frøensveien 4. Tel: 22 46 85 73.
Horse riding, mini-golf and Mini-zoo Ekeberg near Ekeberghallen. Tel: 22 68 26 69.
Puppet Theatre Frognerveien 67. Tel: 22 34 86 80 (open May–Sept).
TusenFryd Amusement Park Ås, Østfold. Tel: 64 97 66 99. Open June–Aug (May and Sept weekends only). Transport by bus 541 from Oslo-S or Rådhuset. Attractions include roller-coaster, Spaceshot, flume ride, carousel, magic carpet and climbing wall.
VikingLandet, adjacent to Tusenfryd. Tel: 64 97 66 99. Live like a Viking for a day. Open June–Sept.

Around Norway
The Troll Family Park near Lillehammer. Tel: 61 27 72 22. Attractions include the World's Largest Troll, Fairy Tale Cave, Supervideograph, Photo Adventure, Energy Centre (exhibition centre for oil and gas), Wax Museum and Experience Centre for Ice Cream.
Kongeparken near Stavanger. Tel: 51 61 71 11. More than 40 attractions, including life-sized model of The Giant Gulliver (85 x 7.5 metre, 280 x 25-ft), riding tracks, bob track, farm, car track, Wild West City, birds and fun fair.
Sommarland Bø in Telemark. Tel: 35 95 16 99. Norway's biggest water park, including many

Business Hours

- **Offices** 9am–4pm or 8am–4pm; lunch is taken early, 11.30am–12.30pm, or noon–2pm at a restaurant.
- **Shops** Mon–Fri 9am–5pm, Thurs until 8pm, Sat from 9am until 1, 2 or even 3pm.
- **Shopping centres** Until 8 or 9pm on weekdays, 6pm on Sat.
- **Banks** 9am–3.30pm weekdays, Thurs until 5pm.
- **Pharmacies** Mon–Fri 9am–5pm, Saturday mornings and on a rota basis in larger cities.

waterslides and Stuka, a 26-metre (85-ft) water chute and a floating river. Plus live entertainment, pony rides, Wild West City and playground.
Kristiansand Dyrepark Tel: 38 04 97 00. Norway's largest wildlife park and most-visited tourist attraction. The park has many other attractions: amusement park, water park, show and entertainment park, leisure park and Cardamomaby – a tiny village from a well-known children's book.
Youth Information, at Møllergata 3, Oslo, provides information on all subjects for young people. Open Mon–Fri 11am–2pm. Tel: 22 41 51 32. www.unginfo.oslo.no

Embassies in Oslo

Canada
Wergelandsvn 7
Tel: 22 99 53 00
UK
Thomas Heftyesgate 8
Tel: 23 13 27 00
United States
Drammensveien 18
Tel: 22 44 85 50

Getting Around

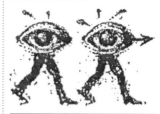

Public Transport

Norway has an excellent network of public transport services. Although covering great distances can be expensive, there are discount tickets for tourists such as the Fjord Pass and Bonus Pass (for all Scandinavia), plus pan-European budget passes such as InterRail and Eurail. Within larger cities, tourist passes cover urban transport and many museums.

From the Airport

Oslo's Gardermoen Airport is roughly 50 km (30 miles) north of the city. The airport bus runs every 15 minutes from the airport to downtown Oslo, taking 47 minutes. A taxi or private vehicle takes 30 minutes. A high-speed rail link runs to Oslo S station in 20 minutes.

If you are coming from London's Stansted you will arrive at Torp Airport (which is at Sandefjord, almost two hours' drive south along the west side of the fjord). From there buses and trains connect with central Oslo.

All other major city airports are served by buses and taxis.

By Air

Considering its size, Norway is well served by airlines, with about 50 airports and airfields. The domestic airlines are SAS, Braathens, Widerøe and Norwegian.

Discount tourist passes

SAS offers a Visit Scandinavia Pass, Braathens a summer Visit Norway Pass (discount-rate flight coupons) and Widerøe the Summer Pass.

SAS Scandinavian Airlines
0080 Oslo
Bookings: 81 52 04 00
Info: 67 59 67 19
Main office: 67 59 60 50
Braathens
Oksenøyveien 3, 1330 Fornebu
Tel: 81 52 00 00
Fax: 67 59 13 09
www.braathens.no
Widerøe's Flyveselskap ASA
Eyvind Lychesvei 10, PO Box 312, N-1301 Sandvika
Tel: 81 00 12 00
Fax reservations: 33 48 26 91
www.wideroe.no
Norwegian
PO Box 115
N-1330 Fornebu
Tel: 67 59 30 00
www.norwegian.no

By Rail

Rail services are far more comprehensive in the south than in the north, and tend to fan out from Oslo, so you will have to supplement your trip with ferries and buses. The Oslo–Bergen line is regarded as one of the world's most spectacular for its scenery.

Oslo S is Norway's busiest railway station, located in central Oslo at the eastern end of Karl Johansgate on Jernbanetorget. Long-distance, express and local suburban trains arrive and depart here. The end of the line in Norway is at Bodø, but the most northerly station is at Narvik, which is reached through Sweden by train or by bus from Fauske.

Most trains are modern and efficient, but the older rolling stock has a touch of nostalgic luxury. New inter-city express (ICE) trains offer one class only. If you plan to take special fast trains, you must book ahead. Ticket sales are from the main hall of the train station.

For information about timetables, ticket prices, bookings and seat reservations, tel: 81 50 01 76 or 177 for operator, or fax: 22 36 64 58. Or contact Trafikanten *(see Tickets and Info box, page 375).*

Discount tourist passes
The Norway Railpass offers three to eight weeks of unlimited rail travel in Norway, or three travel days over one month. The Scanrail Pass offers unlimited travel all over Scandinavia, as well as discounts on certain ferries, buses and hotel chains.

By Coach (Long-distance Bus)
Where the rail network stops, the bus goes further: you can get to practically anywhere you want by bus. Usually it is not necessary to book in advance, just pay the driver when you board.

Discount tourist pass
The NOR-WAY Bussekspress (bus pass) guarantees a seat for all passengers. On sale only outside Norway through the company's agents, the pass is valid all year round and offers two categories for travel on the national network: either unlimited travel within seven consecutive days, or unlimited travel within a 14-day period.
NOR-WAY Bussekspress AS
Karl Johans gt. 2, N-0154 Oslo.
Tel: 82 05 43 01; www.nor-way.no

By Boat

Ferries
Ferries are an invaluable means of transport that allow short cuts across fjords to eliminate many road miles. In Oslo, ferries to the fjord islands leave from the quay near Aker Brygge.

Long-distance boats
Hurtigruten, the Norwegian coastal express service, is a vital means of water transport for Norwegians, and a superb way for visitors to see Norway's dramatic coast. In summer, boats leave daily, travelling between Bergen and Kirkenes in 11 days and putting in at 35 ports.
Travel agents can give details, and sell special Coastal Passes to 16–26-year-olds. The steamers take cars, and should be booked well in advance. Either contact your local travel agent or:

Troms Fylkes Dampskibsselskap AS
Bookings: 77 64 82 00
Fax: 77 64 81 40
E-mail: booking@tfds.no
Ofotens og Vesteraalens Dampskibsselskab ASA
Narvik
Tel: 76 96 76 00
Fax: 76 96 76 01
Bookings: 76 96 76 96
Fax: 76 96 76 11
E-mail: booking@ovds.no
www.hurtigruten.com

City Travel Cards

Oslo
The Oslo Pass (Osloskortet, issued for one, two and three days, with half price for children) is your ticket to unlimited public transport (including city ferries) and free entry to many museums.
If you want a card for travel only, passes include the Minikort (four rides at a discount) and Maxikort (14 rides at a discount).
The Oslo Pass may be purchased at the Oslo S railway station, Trafikanten (see Ticket and Info, below), Narvesen kiosks, hotels, camp sites and tourist offices.

Bergen and elsewhere
Other cities offer similar tourist travel cards: for example, the Bergen Card (24-hour and 48-hour passes from tourist information offices, the railway station, hotels, camp sites and the Hurtigruten terminal) and the Bergen Package (details in the Official Bergen Guide from the Bergen Tourist Board).

Tickets and Info
For tickets, routes, times and all queries about public transport, **Trafikanten** at Oslo S Station offers an information and booking service.
Tel: 81 50 01 76 (lines open Mon–Fri 7am–11pm, Sat–Sun 8am–11pm). Office open Mon–Fri 7am–8pm, Sat–Sun 8am–6pm.
Info line: 177

City Travel

By bus and tram
Oslo has a comprehensive bus and tram system. There are detailed timetables at every stop. There are night buses on some routes and morning buses (starting at 4am).
Bergen and **Trondheim** also have tram systems.

By underground
Oslo's underground is called the T-bane and is very simple to use. There are five lines that converge under the centre of Oslo. You can catch any train to any of the far-flung suburbs from any of the stations between Tøyen and Majorstuen. Station entrances are marked with "T". Trafikanten has route maps. The most scenic route is T-bane 1 up to Frognerseteren.

By Taxi
Taxis are widely available. In Oslo, telephone 023 23 and you will be transferred to the nearest taxi rank. Minibuses can also be booked, tel: 22 38 80 70. Otherwise, you can take a taxi from one of the many ranks around the city. All registered taxis carry a registration number on the roof, which is lit up when the taxi is free.
In Oslo taxis are more expensive at night or if ordered by phone. When everyone leaves the bars and restaurants around 3am, long queues build up at ranks. This has given rise to "pirate" taxis. These either cruise up out of the blue or a "dummy" (usually a foreigner) asks you if you want a taxi without queuing. These taxis, which do not carry a taxi sign on the roof, are not recommended; if you want to take the risk agree a price beforehand.

By Car
Norway's roads are extremely good, particularly in view of the treacherous weather conditions encountered in winter.

Norway in a Nutshell

This is a unique trip that takes you through some of Norway's most beautiful scenery, ascending to altitudes of 866 metres (2,850 ft) with breathtaking views. The usual tour comprises: train from Oslo to Myrdal/Flåm, boat to Gudvangen, bus to Voss and train back to Oslo. But it is also possible to start at Oslo and finish in Bergen or vice versa. Tickets are available from railway stations.

Be prepared for long tunnels. EU driving licences are valid in Norway, but drivers from other countries must carry an International Driving Licence.

You drive on the right, and traffic regulations are strictly enforced (for guidelines, see Rules of the Road box).

Winter driving
With Norway's winters, you should never assume all roads are passable. Small roads in the north are often closed and even the E6 highway from Oslo to Trondheim closes occasionally.

Breakdown and accidents
The British AA and RAC are affiliated to the AIT (Alliance Internationale de Tourisme), so members receive free assistance (with journey planning as well as backup in case of breakdown or accident) from Norway's rescue service, NAF (Norges Automobilforbund). Comprehensive repairs can also be carried out at NAF-contracted garages (for which you will have to pay), and NAF patrol Norway's main roads and mountain passes from 16 June to 14 August.
NAF, Storgt 2, N-0155 Oslo
Tel: 22 34 14 00
Fax: 22 33 13 72
24-hour emergency service
(for members of AIT clubs):
Tel: 22 34 16 00. Fax: 22 42 88 30.
If you are involved in an accident where there are no injuries but you

need help, you can phone either of these 24-hour assistance firms on these freephone numbers:
Falken Redningskorps AS
Tel: 80 03 00 50/22 95 00 00.
Viking Redningstjeneste AS
Tel: 80 03 29 00/22 08 60 20.
It is not necessary to call the police for minor accidents, but drivers must exchange names and addresses; leaving the scene without doing so is a crime. Only call the police (112) or an ambulance (113) in emergencies.

Tolls
Several roads have moderately expensive tolls, and you have to pay to enter larger cities.

CARAVANNING

For information contact:
The Norsk Caravan Club,
PO Box 104, N-1921 Sørumsand
Tel: 63 82 99 90.
Fax: 63 82 99 99.
www.caravanklubben.no.

Rules of the Road

Some of Norway's driving regulations vary significantly from those elsewhere. Here are a few tips, but for further guidance get Velkommen på norske veier (Welcome to Norwegian Roads), which has an English section and is available at tourist offices.
• **Speed limits** The maximum speed limit is usually 80 kph (50 mph), though 90 kph (55 mph) is permitted on dual carriageways. The limit is 50 kph (30 mph), and even 30 kph (20 mph) on certain residential roads. On-the-spot fines are given for speeding.
• **Giving way** Roads marked at intervals by yellow diamond signs indicate that you have priority. On all others you must give way to traffic from the right. Some roads have a series of white triangles across them at junctions: stop and give way.

CAR HIRE

Hiring a car can be expensive. Watch for special weekend and summer prices. Hire firms include:
Avis Bilutleie/Liva Bil AS
PO Box 154, N-1361 Billingstad (near Oslo).
Tel: 66 77 11 11. Fax: 66 77 11 30.
Reservations: 81 53 30 44.
www.avis.no
Europcar/Interrent
Box 7041 Homansbyen, N-0306 Oslo
Tel: 67 16 58 00.
Reservations: 67 16 58 20.
www.europcar.no
Hertz Bilutleie
Box 331, N-1324 Lysaker/Oslo.
Tel: 67 16 80 80.
Reservations: 67 16 80 00.
www.hertz.no

By Bike

A lot of people cycle in Norway. Proceed with caution, however; although there are a few cycle routes, it is not an integrated system. In the countryside cycling

On roundabouts (traffic circles) priority is from the left. Always give way to trams, buses and taxis. Many roads have a lane for buses and taxis only.
• **Documentation/equipment** You must always have the following with you in your car: driving licence, car registration documents, European accident statement form, insurance policy and a reflective warning triangle. A snow shovel and tow rope are useful in winter.
• **Lights** It is obligatory for all vehicles to drive with dipped headlights during the day all year round. Carry spare bulbs.
• **Seat belts** must be worn, both front and back.
• **Tyres** It is obligatory to use winter tyres from October to April. These are either tyres with studs (piggdekk) or specially designed tyres for use in ice and snow.

is easier as you'll find surfaced cycle paths.

Cyclists are not permitted to travel through the larger road tunnels, but bikes are allowed on most trains and buses for a small charge. There are even special cycle trains in summer. Tourist offices have details of tours and can provide suggestions and maps of cycling routes.

Information
The Syklistens Landsforening (Cycling Association), Storg 23C Pb. 8883 Youngstorget, 0028 Oslo. Tel: 22 47 30 30. Fax: 22 47 30 31. E-mail: slf-bike@online.no

Cycle rental
Oslo, Bergen and Trondheim have public cycle-hiring services. You can collect and drop off bikes at various points round the city. Contact tourist offices for details. Bikes can also be hired from hotels, camp sites, tourist offices or sports shops, as well as small cycle-hire shops. In Oslo, contact:
AS Skiservice, Tryvannsveien 2 0394 Oslo. Tel: 22 13 95 00.

Off-road and mountain bikes are for hire in Oslo from:
White Water AS, Cort Adelers g 27. Tel: 22 55 11 07. Fax: 22 55 11 48.

On Foot

Norway is a nation of devout walkers. You can walk wherever you want in forests, mountains, on the seashore and other non-cultivated regions. This should be done with consideration, though – use paths.

The Touring Association (Den Norske Turistforening), Storgate 3, Pb. 7 Sentrum, 0101 Oslo (weekdays only). Tel: 22 82 28 00. Fax: 22 82 28 01. www.turistforeningen.no Provides maps and information. Membership gives you rights to use the association's huts.

Where to Stay

Norwegian hotels are notoriously expensive, but they cut rates in summer and on most weekends. Accommodation ranges from hotels (luxurious to comfortable), to more modest guesthouses, camp sites, cosy self-catering chalets, and youth/family hostels. Facilities and service are international standard.

Choosing a Hotel

There is no central hotel booking service, so you have to go through travel agents and tour operators, or book direct (as practically everyone speaks English this is easy).

In Oslo, the tourist offices at the Information Centre at Fridtjof Nansens, Plass 5 and at Central Station will book accommodation for those arriving in person. It is open every day 8am–11pm.

The *Accommodation in Norway* brochure, available from Norwegian embassies and consulates or the Norwegian Tourist Board (NORTRA) in Oslo, is useful. The Oslo and Bergen guides produced by the cities' tourist boards have good up-to-date listings

The *NRI Guide* is a free book listing around 1,000 establishments, ferry timetables and the coastal express steamer. It is available from tourist offices, or contact Norsk Reiseinformasjon AS, Karl Johansgt. 12A, N-0154 Oslo. Tel: 22 47 73 40. Fax: 22 47 73 69.

Hotel Chains

The major hotel chains are all well represented in the five main congress towns of Oslo, Stavanger, Bergen, Trondheim and Tromsø. Most offer discount cards.
Best Western Hotels Norway, Cort Adelers g 16, N-0254 Oslo. Tel: 22 55 09 10. Fax: 22 55 61 23. Free booking number: 80 01 16 24. www.bestwestern.no
Choice Hotels AS, Sommerogt. 13–15, PO Box 2454, 0201 Oslo. Tel: 22 40 13 00. Fax: 22 40 13 00 www.choice.no
First Hotels Tel: 800 104 10 (in Norway) Tel: +468 442 8400 (international) E-mail: first.res@firsthotels.se www.firsthotels.com
Radisson SAS International Hotels PO Box 185, N-1324 Lysaker. Tel: 67 12 02 20. Fax: 67 12 00 11. Toll-free in Norway: 80 01 60 91. www.radissonsas.com
Rica Hotel og Restaurantkjede AS, Slependveien 108, PO Box 3, 1375 Billingstad. Tel: 66 85 45 60. Fax: 66 85 45 61. www.rica.no
Scandic Hotels AS Sjølyst pl 5, PO Box 173 Skøyen, 0212 Oslo. Tel: 23 15 50 00. Fax: 23 15 50 11. www.scandic-hotels.com

Price Guide

$$$	More than NOK1,700
$$	NOK1,100–1,700
$	Less than NOK1,100

Price categories are based on the average cost (including tax) of a double room with breakfast in high season.

Hotel Listings

Hotels are grouped by area, starting with Oslo. Within each city or region, they are listed alphabetically in price order, with the most expensive first.

OSLO

Bristol Kristian VII's Gate 7, N-0164 Tel: 22 82 60 00. Fax: 22 82 06 01 Patronised by the wealthy, with a superb lobby and antiques. Close to the main shopping street. $$$
Clarion Royal Christiania Hotel Biskop Gunnerus' Gate 3, N-0106

Tel: 23 10 80 00. Fax: 23 10 80 80
Magnificent atrium, spacious rooms,
good service. Near station. **$$$**
Continental
Stortingsgaten 24–26, N-0161
Tel: 22 82 40 40. Fax: 22 82 40 65
Established in 1909, this is where
Norwegian guests of state stay. **$$$**
Grand
Karl Johansgate 31, N-0159
Tel: 23 21 20 00. Fax: 23 21 21 00
Luxurious hotel opposite the
Stortinget. Spacious rooms. **$$$**
Radisson SAS Plaza Hotel
Sonja Henies pl 3, N-0134
Tel: 22 17 10 00. Fax: 22 17 73 00
This is the tall glass structure
between Oslo S and Oslo Spektrum.
Popular among rock stars. **$$$**
Radisson SAS Scandinavia Hotel
Holbergsgate 30, N-0166
Tel: 23 29 30 00. Fax: 23 29 30 01
Luxurious, with fine restaurants and
a rooftop bar. Airport buses. **$$$**
Frogner House Hotel
Skovveien 8, N-0265
Tel: 22 44 79 90. Fax: 22 56 05 00
Beautiful old building just west of
the centre; quiet. **$$**
Holmenkollen Park Hotel Rica
Kongveien 26, N-0390
Tel: 22 92 20 00. Fax: 22 14 61 92
In a leafy district, this grand old
wooden building overlooks a famous
ski jump. Excellent facilities. **$$**
Norrøna Hotell
Grensen 19, N-0159
Tel: 23 31 80 00. Fax: 23 31 80 01
Completely renovated three-star but
century-old atmosphere. Central. **$$**
Golden Tulip Rainbow Hotel Stefan
Rosenkrantz Gate 1, N-0159
Tel: 23 31 55 00. Fax: 23 31 55 55
One of a chain. Couldn't be more
central; buffet lunches are great. **$**

AROUND OSLO

Clarion Oslo Airport Hotel
N-2060 Gardermoen
Tel: 63 94 94 94
Fax: 63 94 94 95
The first of many chain hotels near
Oslo Gardermoen Airport. **$$**
Quality Airport Hotel
N-2050 Jessheim
Tel: 63 92 61 00. Fax: 63 92 61 01
Well situated for the airport. **$$**

Scandic Hotel Høvik/Oslo
Drammensvn 507,
N-1322 Høvik
Tel: 23 15 53 00. Fax: 23 15 53 11
Attractive hotel with good dining
and bar; 6 km (4 miles) from Oslo.
$$
Golden Tulip Hotel Oslofjord
Sandviksvn 184, 1330 Sandvika
Tel: 67 55 66 00. Fax: 67 55 66 88
Set in a handsome fjord town
15 km (9 miles) from Oslo,
with views over the fjord and islands.
$

BERGEN

Radisson SAS Hotel Norge
Ole Bulls Plass
Tel: 55 57 30 00
Fax: 55 57 30 01
In the centre, with 350 quality
rooms/suites, four restaurants,
garden and pool. **$$$**
Radisson SAS Royal Hotel
Bryggen
Tel: 55 54 30 00. Fax: 55 32 48 08
The classic Norwegian building
style makes this an unusually
handsome hotel. With high-grade
facilities. **$$$**
Clarion Admiral
C. Sundtsgate 9–13
Tel: 55 23 64 00
Fax: 55 23 64 64
Part of the Choice chain and
one of Bergen's finest. The
restaurant has superb views and
cuisine. **$$**
Rainbow Hotel Rosenkrantz
Rosenkrantz 7
Tel: 55 30 14 00. Fax: 55 31 50 01
Comfortable and central with
restaurant and nightclub. **$$**
Fagerheim Pension
Kalvedalsveien 49A
Tel: 98 40 40 70
A friendly, central *pension*. **$**
Hotel Park Pension
Harald Hårfagresgt 35
Tel: 55 54 44 00. Fax: 55 54 44 44
Rooms available with or without
facilities. **$**
Strand Hotel
Strandkaien 2B
Tel: 55 59 33 00. Fax: 55 59 33 33
Family-run with restaurant and bar.
$

STAVANGER

Radisson SAS Royal Hotel
Løkkeveien 26
Tel: 51 56 60 00
SAS's usual excellent services. **$$**
Scandic Hotel
Eiganesvn 181, PO Box 570 Madla,
N-4040 Hafrsfjord
Tel: 23 15 50 00. Fax: 23 15 50 01
One of the quality Scandic hotels,
ideal for conferences. Includes
"environmental" rooms made from
97 percent recyclable material. **$$**
Commandør Hotell
Valberggt 9, N-4006
Tel: 51 89 53 00. Fax: 51 89 53 01
Cosy with home comforts. **$**
Havly Hotel
Valberggt 1, N-4006
Tel: 51 89 67 00. Fax: 51 89 50 25
Modest well-appointed rooms. **$**
The Little House
Vaisenhusgt 40, N-4012 Stavanger
Tel: 51 89 40 89
Home-from-home rooms (each with
bath). Central. **$**

Price Guide

$$$	More than NOK1,700
$$	NOK1,100–1,700
$	Less than NOK1,100

Price categories are based on
the average cost (including tax)
of a double room with breakfast
in high season.

Skagen Guesthouse
Skanegt.7
Tel: 51 93 85 00
Great harbour-side location. **$**

TROMSØ

Ishavshotel Tromsø
Fr. Langesgt 2
Tel: 77 66 64 00. Fax: 77 66 64 44
First rate, specialising in
conferences and comfort. **$$$**
Grand Nordic
Storgt 44
Tel: 77 75 37 77. Fax: 77 75 37 78
4 km (2 ½ miles) from airport with
conference facilities. **$$**
Saga Tromsø
Richard Withs Plass 2

Fjord Pass

This pass gives 20 percent discount at 236 hotels, guesthouses, apartments and holiday cottages, plus several hotel chains. It is available from travel agents or tourist offices, as well as hotels and Mix kiosks.

Tel: 77 60 70 00. Fax: 77 60 70 10
Small conference hotel. **$$**
Scandic Tromsø
Heiloveien 23
Tel: 77 75 50 00. Fax: 77 75 50 11
Modest conference hotel close to the airport. Well-appointed rooms. Outside pool. **$$**
With Home Hotel
Sjøgata 35–37, N-9000
Tel: 77 68 70 00. Fax: 77 68 96 16
First-class hotel with beautiful view to the Tromsø Bridge and cathedral. Feels like a maritime museum. **$$**
Tulip Inn Rainbow Tromsø Hotell
Grønneg 45
Tel: 77 75 17 00. Fax: 77 75 17 30
Small, informal and central. **$**

TRONDHEIM

Grand Olav Clarion Hotel
Olavskvartalet
Tel: 73 80 80 80. Fax: 73 80 80 81
Top-class; located right in the heart of town. **$$$**
Prinsen Scandic
Kongensgate 30
Tel: 73 80 7000
A wealth of facilities including a fine restaurant, bistro, bar, grill room, wine tavern and beer garden. **$$**
Radisson SAS Royal Garden Hotel
Kjøpmannsgt 73
Tel: 73 80 30 00
Well-appointed rooms plus pool, gym, sauna and restaurants. **$$**
Elgeseter Bed & Breakfast
Tormodsgate 3
Tel: 73 94 25 40. Fax: 73 82 03 31
Ten minutes' walk from centre. **$**

Chalets

There are abundant holiday *hytter* (cabins or chalets) available for rent. These usually house four to

six people. For details contact:
Den Norske Hytteformidling,
Kierschowsgate 7, PO Box 3404
Bjølsen, N-0406 Oslo.
Tel: 22 35 67 10. Fax: 22 71 94 13.

Fishermen's Cabins

In the Lofoten islands in the north, you can rent a traditional former fisherman's cabin *(rorbu)*. Contact: **Lofoten Tourist Office**, Tel: 76 09 15 99. Fax: 76 09 24 25.

Camping

Norway has more than 1,000 camp sites, classified by one to five stars, depending on the standard and facilities available.

The Norwegian camping card *(Norsk Campingkort)* offers a faster checking-in service and a discount. It is available from participating camp sites. Many camp sites have cabins that may be booked in advance. Some are small and basic, but others are large and well equipped with a sitting room, one or two bedrooms, kitchen, shower and toilet. For more information, write to: **Norwegian Camping Guide**, Essendropsgt. 6, N-0305 Oslo, or visit www.camping.no

B&Bs

Norwegian B&Bs are of a high standard. You can book at local tourist offices or at Oslo's central railway station. Or look out for signs for *Rom* or *Husrom*. A B&B guidebook, *Rom i Norge*, is available from bookshops in Norway or from: **Norsc Holidays** by mail order, tel: 22 27 85 09. The **Norway Bed & Breakfast Book** is on sale at Scandinavia Connection *(see page 384 for contact details)*.

Youth/Family Hostels

There are around 100 youth hostels of a relatively high standard, divided into three categories. You must book in advance in high season.
Hostelling International Norway,
Torggata 1, N-0181 Oslo.
Tel: 23 13 93 00. Fax: 23 13 93 50.
E-mail: hostels@vandrerhjem.no

Where to Eat

What to Eat

Norwegians eat hearty breakfasts, but light lunches; the size of the evening meal depends on the day of the week and the occasion. With the abundant supply of seafood and what can be gleaned from forest and field, the Norwegian diet is in the main healthy and appetising.

The hunting season (early autumn) offers some irresistible temptations: pheasant, grouse, fresh elk and reindeer steaks served with peppercorns and rich wild mushroom sauces. It is also a good time of year for seafood.

Coffee breaks with pastries are popular. *Frokost* (breakfast) is more or less a variation of the lunch *Koldtbord*, a spread including breads (try *grovbrød*) and *flatbrød* (crisp cracker), sausages, cheeses (try the piquant *Gudbrandsalost*, a delicious burnt goats' milk cheese with a dark golden colour), eggs, herrings, cereal, *gravlaks* (marinated salmon), cereals, and coffee and tea. The lunch version has hot dishes, such as sliced roast meats, meatballs or fish. *Øllebrød* (beef marinated in beer and served inside pitta bread with salad) makes a hearty, inexpensive lunch; an open-faced shrimp or ham sandwich is another staple. Dinner in a city restaurant can be anything you wish. In more remote places, menus are limited by availability. *Smørbrød* is a snack (called *aftens* when eaten at night), usually of brown bread with butter, cheese and salami or ham.

Where to Eat

There has been a significant increase in what's on offer if you eat out. Pizza has become very

Sport

If Norwegians can contrive a sport as an excuse to be outdoors, they'll do it. That's why there are such great facilities here. For a full listing of the range of sports and sports facilities in the Oslo region, see the Outdoor Activities pages of the *Oslo Guide*, from tourist offices.

Canoeing

Some of the best canoeing and kayaking lakes and rivers are in the Femund area, Østfold, Aust and Vest Agder, Telemark and suburban Oslo. Contact the local tourist office for details.

Cycling

For details *see Getting Around, page 376–7*.

Fishing

The fishing is excellent in Norway, whether you're at sea or on a fjord, lake or river. You need a local fishing permit to fish sea char, salmon or sea trout and a national fishing licence for inland fishing in Norway. You can buy a fishing permit at or near to your holiday spot. See the tourist board's *Angling in Norway* for full details.

Golf

Norwegian golf courses are by and large difficult and challenging. Most require either a Green Card or a handicap under 20. Green fees are in line with most European golf courses. Some nine-hole courses offer day fees.

In the Oslo region professional competitions are held at Bogstad, Larvik, Borre and Vestfold golf

clubs, but by far the most beautifully situated is the Tyrifjord golf links. For information, contact: **Norges Golfforbund**, PO Box 163, Lilleaker N-0216 Oslo. Tel: 22 73 66 20. Fax: 22 73 66 21. E-mail: nfg@golf.no. www.ngf@golf.no

Hiking

The country's extensive mountain ranges and high plains make ideal walking terrain. The most popular areas include the Jotunheim, Rondane and Dovrefjell mountains; the Hardangervidda plateau in the Trollheimen district; and the Finnmarksvidda plain. Mountain cabins are open from the end of June until mid-September, plus over the Easter holiday.

The Norwegian Mountain Touring Association (DNT) runs about 300 guided hikes in summer, and glacier walks in winter. Membership includes hut access. For details: **Den Norske Turistforening** Storgate 3, PO Box 7 Sentrum, 0101 Oslo. Tel: 22 82 28 00. Fax: 22 82 28 01.

Horse Riding

There are riding centres and hotels all over Norway where you can hire a horse for organised trekking or take lessons. For further details contact tourist offices, or: **Norges Rytterforbund** Serviceboks 1 Ullevål Stadion. Tel: 21 02 96 50. Fax: 21 02 96 51.

Skiing

Along with hiking, this is the primary participant sport in Norway. Even in summer Norwegians take to the slopes (as a rule from June to September), and the sight of people swooping down the slopes in bikinis and trunks is something to behold.

The main ski resorts are at Lillehammer, Trysil, Geilo, Hemsedal, Norefjell (the nearest to Oslo) and Voss, but there are many more; all tourist offices can advise on local ski facilities for cross country and slalom. Also check the Norwegian ski guide on www.skiinfo.no

Glacier Hiking

Glacier hiking is an exhilarating and exciting experience – which should be attempted only with an experienced local guide. Several Norwegian tour companies offer guided glacier walks *(breer)*, particularly in the following areas:

Fjord Norway: Hardangerjøkulen, Folgefonna, Buarbre, Bondhusbre, Smørstabbre, Fannaråkbre and Nigardsbre. **Oppland:** Styggebre. **Norland Reiseliv:** Svartisen and Engenbreen.

For details, contact **Glacier Information Centres** in western Norway at Oppstryn (tel: 57 87 72 00), Fjærland (tel: 57 69 32 88) and Josterdalen (tel: 57 68 32 50).

Sailing

Foreign visitors are always welcome in boating circles, and there are sailing and boating clubs and associations throughout Norway. Without your own boat, sailing of any sort can be expensive, and the closest you may get is a small catamaran or even a windsurfer. In Oslo you can hire equipment from: **Seasport Oslo AS** Dronning Mauds g 1/3. Tel: 22 83 79 28. Fax: 22 83 92 95. **Norges Seilforbund** Serviceboks 1, Ullevål Stadion. Tel: 21 02 90 00. Fax: 21 02 90 17.

Swimming

Temperatures along the coast and inland reach 20°C (68°F) in summer, and even in the north it can be warm enough to swim. Nude beaches are to be found in Oslo, Moss, Halden, Tønsberg, Larvik, Molde, Ålesund, Bergen, Trondheim and Salten. Most larger hotels have pools and there are numerous leisure centres throughout Norway.

There are several possibilities for waterskiing and windsurfing along the coast, as well as on Norway's numerous lakes.

White-water rafting is available on the following rivers: Sjoaelva in Oppland, Trysilelva in Hedmark and Driva in Sør-Trøndelag.

The Norwegian coast offers very good conditions for diving. There are several diving centres along the west coast, particularly in the counties of Møre and Romsdal.

Norwegian Diving Federation Sognsveien 75L, Serviceboks 1 Ullevål Stadion, N-0480 Oslo.

Norwegian Wildlife & Rafting AS Randsverk, 2680 Vågå. Tel: 61 23 87 27. Fax: 61 23 87 60.

Winter Sports

Skiing is just one of Norway's winter attractions. There are snowmobile trips to the North Cape, reindeer safaris and dog-sled races over the plane of Finnmarksvidda. You can go on horse-drawn sleigh rides, or try your hand at ice fishing, snow boarding or ice skating. Several companies offer winter train journeys along the spectacular coast. *For details, see Tour Operators on page 370* or contact the Norwegian tourist board.

Spectator Sports

Skiing is the primary spectator sport with annual competitions, such as the Holmenkolen Ski Festival. In summer large crowds come to see athletics during the Bislet Games. There are several horse trotting and race tracks in Norway. Other popular spectator sports include marathon running, football, ice hockey and boat races. Check Oslo or local area guides or tourist offices for details.

Shopping

What to Buy

Popular souvenirs from Norway include knitted jumpers, cardigans, gloves and mittens, pewter, silver jewellery and cutlery, hand-painted wooden objects (like bowls with rose designs), trolls and fjord horses carved out of wood, goat and reindeer skin, enamel jewellery, woven wall-designs, furs, handicrafts, glassware and pottery – to name just a few *(see Tax-free Shopping for how to reclaim value-added tax).*

The major department stores are Christiania Glasmagasin and Steen & Strøm, both of which have a good selection of most of these items.

Anyone interested in buying Norwegian art will have ample prospects – from south to north, Norway abounds in galleries.

Tax-free Shopping

The Norwegian Tax-free Shopping scheme covers around 3,000 stores. For purchases over NOK 308, the store issues you with a tax-free slip for the amount of value-added tax paid. When you leave Norway, a refund of 11–18 percent (depending on sale price) will be refunded (in your local currency) on presentation of the goods, the tax-free slip and your passport, on condition that the item has not been used while in Norway. Norway Tax-free Shopping has its own representatives at airports, on all international ferries and at the main border crossings. Check opening times, however, as they are not open 24 hours. Leaflets are at participating stores.

Enquiries to Global Refund Norge PO Box 48. N-1332 Østerås. Tel: 67 15 60 10. Fax: 67 15 60 29.

Language

There are two variations of the Norwegian language: *bokmål* and *nynorsk.* Both belong to the western group of the Scandinavian branch of the Germanic languages, one of the subfamilies of the Indo-European languages.

The Sami population (Lapps) in north Norway speak Lappish. English is widely understood in the towns.

The following is a list of useful words and phrases.

General

yes *ja*
no *nei*
good morning *god morgen*
good afternoon *god ettermiddag*
good evening *god kveld*
today *I dag*
tomorrow *I morgen*
yesterday *I går*
hello *hei*
How do you do? *God dag/Morn*
goodbye *adjø/ha det (bra)*
thank you *takk*
How much is this? *Hvor mye koster det?*
It costs... *Det koster...*
What time is it? *Hvor mye er klokken?*
It is (The time is...) *Den er... (Klokken er...)*
Could I have your name please? *Hva er navnet?*
My name is... *Mitt navn er...*
Do you speak English? *Snakker du engelsk?*
I only speak English *Jeg snakker bare engelsk*
May I help you? *Kan jeg hjelpe deg?*
I do not understand *Jeg forstår ikke*
I do not know *Jeg vet ikke*
It has *Den har*
to rent *leie*

free *ledig*
room to rent *rom til leie*
chalet *hytte*
Could I have the key please? *Kan jeg få nøkkelen?*

Directions

How do I get to...? *Hvordan kommer jeg til...?*
Where is...? *Hvor er...?*
right *høyre*
to the right *til høyre*
left *venstre*
to the left *til venstre*
straight on *rett frem*

Emergencies

hospital *sykehus*
doctor *lege*
police station *politistasjon*

Signs

Parking *Parkering*
Toilet *Toalett/WC*
Gentlemen *Herrer*
Ladies *Damer*
Vacant *Ledig*
Engaged *Opptatt*
Entrance *Inngang*
Exit *Utgang*
No entry *Ingen adgang*
Open *Åpent*
Closed *Stengt*
Push *Skyv*
Pull *Trekk*
No smoking *Røyking forbudt*

Eating Out

breakfast *frokost*
lunch *lunsj*
dinner *middag*
eat *spise*
drink *drikke*
Cheers! *Skål!*
Can I order please? *Kan jeg få bestille?*
Could I have the bill please? *Kan jeg få regningen?*

Getting Around

aeroplane *fly*
bus/coach *buss*
car *bil*
train *tog*

Numbers

1	en
2	to
3	tre
4	fire
5	fem
6	seks
7	syv or sju
8	åtte
9	ni
10	ti
11	elleve
12	tolv
13	tretten
14	fjorten
15	femten
16	seksten
17	sytten
18	atten
19	nitten
20	tjue
21	tjue-en
22	tjue-to
30	tretti
40	førti
50	femti
60	seksti
70	sytti
80	åtti
90	nitti
100	hundre
200	to hundre
1,000	tusen

Shopping

money *penger*
department store *hus/atormagasin*
chemist *apotek*
grocery store *(in countryside) landhandel*
shop *butikk*
food *mat/kost*
to buy *kjøpe*
sauna *badstue*
off-licence/liquor store *vinmonopol*

Buying a Ticket

adult *voksen*
child *barn*
single *énveisbillett*
return *tur-retur-billett*

Further Reading

Tourist Publications

Some useful publications from the Norwegian Tourist Board include: *Accommodation in Norway, Norwegian Camping Guide and Tourist Timetables in Norway.* These booklets are issued free by the Tourist Board or the nearest Norwegian embassy or consulate.

Guides

Adventure Roads in Norway: Where is the Best Scenery? A selection of fascinating routes chosen by some of Norway's foremost travel experts. The routes and places of interest are marked on maps and the book is illustrated with beautiful colour photographs.
Norway's Coastal Voyage. A description of the popular coastal voyage from Bergen to Kirkenes in Arctic Norway and back.
Angling in Norway. A 160-page illustrated guide covering salmon, sea trout and freshwater fishing, as well as information on fishing regulations and conservation.
A Journey Through Norway: Unique Places to Dine and Stay. Full-colour photos and recommendations on unusual accommodation.
Highlights of Norway. A colourful cultural/historical guide to what Norway has to offer apart from fjords and midnight sun.

The above books can be ordered from: **Scandinavia Connection**, 26 Woodford Square, London W14 8DP. Tel: 020 7602 0657; www.scandinavia-connection.co.uk; or **Nortrabooks**, PO Box 2893 Solli, N-0230 Oslo, Norway. E-mail: nortra@online.no

Rutebok for Norge is a complete list of ferry, train, bus and plane timetables for Norway, together with details of hotels, guesthouses and other accommodation.

Order from: **Norsk Reiseinformasjon AS**, Tollbugt 32, 0157 Osloy. Tel: 22 47 73 40. Fax: 22 47 73 69.

Living in Norway by Michael Brady (Palamedes Press). The A to Z source book for anyone living and working in the country.

History

Norway: A History from the Vikings to our own Times by Rolf Danielsen (Scandinavian University Press, Oslo). An account of social and economic development in Norway.

Fiction

Dakota: Four Inspirational Love Stories in the Northern Plain by Lauraine Snelling (Barbour Publishing). Four contrasting tales about Norwegian women living in the US.

Norwegian Folk Tales by Peter Christen Asbjørnsen and Jørgen Moe (Grøndahl og Dreyers Forlag; Oslo). The ultimate collection of Norwegian folk tales, superbly illustrated.

The Werewolf by Aksel Sandemose, translated by Gustaf Lannestock (University of Wisconsin Press). Powerful novel set against the backdrop of Norwegian society from World War I to the 1950s.

Other Insight Guides

Over 200 titles in the acclaimed **Insight Guides** series cover every continent. Titles in the region include *Norway, Denmark, Sweden,* and *Finland.* **Insight Pocket Guides**, with an itinerary-based approach, include *Oslo & Bergen.* **Insight Compact Guides** to the region include *Norway, Denmark, Copenhagen* and *Finland.* **Insight Fleximaps** combine clear, detailed cartography with essential travel information. The laminated finish makes the maps durable, weatherproof and easy to fold. Scandinavian titles include *Norway, Copenhagen* and *Stockholm.*

SWEDEN

The Place

Area 449,790 sq km (173,620 sq miles).

Capital Stockholm.

Population 8.9 million, of whom 750,000 live in Stockholm, 466,000 in Göteborg *(Gothenburg)* and 265,000 in Malmö.

Languages Swedish, Finnish and Sami.

Religion 94 percent of Swedes are Evangelical Lutheran.

Time zone Central European Time Zone. One hour ahead of Greenwich Mean Time (GMT), six hours ahead of Eastern Standard Time. Clocks go forward one hour from the end of March to the end of October.

Currency Swedish krona (plural kronor, marked "kr" or "Skr" in shops, or SEK internationally, and split into 100 öre.

Weights and measures Metric.

Electricity 220 volts AC, two-pin round plugs.

International dialling code: +46, then 8 for Stockholm, 31 for Göteborg or 40 for Malmö.

Climate

In summer Sweden's weather is similar to that in Britain – and just as unpredictable – although in a good year some remarkably high temperatures can be recorded in the Arctic regions. The area round Piteå on the Gulf of Bothnia is known as the Northern Riviera because of its warmth. But in the north, autumn and winter arrive early and spring comes in late May.

Winter can be cold; even in Stockholm, maximum temperatures in the day are likely to remain below freezing in January and February.

Government

Sweden is a constitutional monarchy, with a parliamentary government and a one-chamber legislature. The prime minister is appointed by a majority of the Swedish Parliament and heads a cabinet with about 12 ministries.

The country is divided into 24 provinces, headed by a governor appointed by the cabinet. Regionally elected provincial councils are responsible for medical care and local planning, and the lowest tier of local government is exercised by the 284 municipalities, whose remit includes planning, welfare and local education.

Sweden joined the European Union in January 1995.

Economy

Sweden's rich natural resources of ore deposits, forests and hydro-electric power have made it a highly industrialised country. Companies like Volvo, Saab and Electrolux are household names worldwide.

The old mining region of Bergslagen is still the home of the iron and steel industry, and electronics is thriving in Stockholm and Västerås.

Farming is still important, above all in southern Skåne, but only some 5 percent of Sweden's workforce is involved in agriculture and less than 10 percent of the country is farmland.

Forestry and the pulp and paper industries are important, particularly along the Gulf of Bothnia and Lake Vänern. Telecommunications and Internet related business is booming.

Planning the Trip

Visas and Passports

A valid passport entitles you to stay up to three months, and visas are not normally required. If you arrive from another Scandinavian country, passports aren't usually checked. If you intend to stay longer than three months you will need to obtain a resident's permit, which you can do once you are in Sweden.

Customs

Swedish Customs formalities are usually painless.

Duty free
Visitors from EU countries aged 18 or over can import duty free 400 cigarettes/200 cigarillos/100 cigars or 550g tobacco. Visitors aged over 20 can import 5 litres of spirits or 6 litres of dessert wine, 52 litres of wine plus 64 litres of beer.

Visitors from non-EU countries aged 18 or over can import duty free 200 cigarettes/100 cigarillos/50 cigars or 250g tobacco. Visitors aged over 20 can import 1 litre of spirits or 2 litres of dessert wine, 2 litres of wine plus 15 litres of beer.

Gifts
For visitors from non-EU countries presents up to a value of 1,700 Skr may be taken into the country, but the value of any food you are bringing is included in this limit.

Health

Standards of hygiene in Sweden are among the highest in the world. No inoculations are needed, and tap water is safe to drink.

However, in the far north of Sweden in high summer, strong precautions need to be taken against mosquitoes. Consult your pharmacist at home, and on arrival at your destination it is also advisable to ask the local pharmacist to recommend the most effective product.

MEDICAL TREATMENT

Sweden has reciprocal agreements with the UK and other countries, under which visitors are entitled to the same medical treatment as Swedes. But it is very important for EU nationals to bring a form E111 (available in the UK at post offices) which allows visitors to pay the same fees as Swedes.

Visitors from outside the EU pay higher consultation fees, although these are modest compared with those charged in North America.

For hospital visits you have to pay the actual cost. Therefore, it is important to take out medical insurance before travelling (and to keep receipts for any treatment you have so you can reclaim the money on your return home).

Money Matters

There is no limit on the import of Swedish and foreign currency.

Travellers' cheques can be exchanged without difficulty at banks all over Sweden. A foreign exchange service is also provided by about 500 post offices with the "PK Exchange" sign.

Forex and Wexex, *bureaux de change* with branches in most major towns, usually have better exchange rates than the banks and post offices and don't charge any commission.

All the leading credit cards are accepted by most hotels, restaurants and shops throughout the country, and you can also take out cash on these cards at foreign exchange offices and banks.

What to Bring

Sweden's weather is unpredictable, so plan for any eventuality. In summer, even in the Arctic north, you could have hot, sunny days that call for shorts and T-shirts, or sweaters and rainwear may be needed.

Winters can be very cold, but this is dry cold. Still, you should take a heavy coat and warm headgear as well as sturdy footwear for the slushy streets.

Tourist Info at Home

● **UK**
Swedish Travel & Tourism Council, 11 Montagu Place, London W1H 2AL.
Tel: 020 7870 5600.
Fax: 020 7724 5872
www.visit-sweden.com

● **USA**
Scandinavian Tourist Board, PO Box 4649, Grand Central Station, New York, NY 10163-4649.
Tel: 212-885 9700.
Fax: 212-885 9710.
www.visit-sweden.com

● There are no Swedish tourist offices in Canada, Australia and New Zealand, but the Swedish Consulate/Embassy supplies information and literature.

Getting There

BY AIR

Scandinavian Airlines (SAS) and British Airways operate frequent direct flights from London Heathrow to Stockholm and Göteborg. Ryanair also operates daily direct services from London Stansted to Stockholm Skavsta (100km, 62 miles southwest of Stockholm), Västerås, Malmö and Göteborg City, as well as a service from Glasgow Prestwick to Stockholm Skavsta. From Manchester, Finnair and Skyways fly to Stockholm and City

Airline operates to Göteborg. Birmingham is connected to Stockholm and Göteborg by Maersk.

Since Copenhagen airport is now linked directly by train to Malmö (journey time 20 mins) it can also be useful if visiting southern Sweden to fly to the Danish capital. There are daily flights to Copenhagen from London Heathrow (SAS, BA and Varig), London Gatwick (Maersk), London Stansted (easyJet), Birmingham (BA), Manchester (SAS) as well as both Edinburgh and Glasgow (bmi). KLM also fly from 13 regional UK airports via Amsterdam to Copenhagen, Göteborg and Stockholm.

From the UK

Braathens
Tel: 0191 214 0991
www.braathens.no
British Airways
Tel: 0845 773 3377
www.ba.com
Finnair
Tel: 020 7408 1222
www.finnair.co.uk
KLM
Tel: 0870 507 4074
www.klmuk.co.uk
Ryanair
Dublin, tel: 01 249 7851
UK, tel: 0870 246 0000
www.ryanair.com
SAS
Tel: 0845 607 2772
www.scandinavian.net

From the US

Finnair
Tel: 1-800-950 5000
www.finnair.com
Icelandair
Tel: 1-800-223 5500
www.icelandair.com
SAS
Tel: 1-800-221 2350
www.scandinavian.net

BY SEA

DFDS Seaways (tel: 08705 333000 in the UK) has a year-round service twice a week to Göteborg from

Tour Operators

Arctic Experience
29 Nork Way, Banstead, Surrey SM7 1PB.
Tel: 01737 214214.
www.artic-experience.co.uk
Bridge Travel Service
55–59 High Road, Broxbourne, Herts EN10 7DT.
Tel: 0870 191 7277.
www.bridgetravel.co.uk
Crystal Holidays
Crystal House, Arlington Road, Surbiton, Surrey KT6 6BW.
Tel: 0870 888 0252.
www.crystalholidays.co.uk
DFDS Seaways
Scandinavia House, Parkeston Quay, Harwich, Essex CO12 4QG
Tel: 08705 333000.
www.dfdsseaways.co.uk
Explore Worldwide
1 Frederick Street, Aldershot GU11 1LQ.
Tel: 01252 760000.
www. exploreworldwide.com
Norvista
31–35 Kirby Street,
London EC1N 8TE
Tel: 0870 744 7315.
Fax: 020 7409 7733.
www.norvista.co.uk
Norwegian Coastal Voyage
3 Shortlands, London W6 8NE.
Tel: 020 8846 2666
www.norwegiancoastalvoyage.com
Scantours
47 Whitcomb Street, London WC2H 7DH
Tel: 020 7839 2927
Fax: 020 7839 5891
www.scantoursuk.com

Newcastle (about 25 hours). This is ideal for motoring holidays in Sweden as it cuts out the long drive across Europe. You can also take the ferry from Harwich to Esbjerg in Denmark (three or four times a week) and then drive up to Grenå or Frederikshavn and catch another ferry from there to Sweden. Or you can drive through Denmark and cross the Öresund Bridge that connects Copenhagen and Malmö.

BY TRAIN

The fastest rail route from the UK to Sweden is via the Eurostar service through the Channel Tunnel from London Waterloo International or Ashford International in Kent to Brussels, with onward trains to Copenhagen and connecting services to Sweden.

For further information call:
Rail Europe, tel: 08705 848848, www.raileurope.co.uk

BY COACH (LONG-DISTANCE BUS)

Eurolines is the leading operator of scheduled coach services to 16 destinations in Sweden. Coaches depart up to three times a week from London Victoria Coach Station. Eurolines offers competitive fares with reductions for children, young people and senior citizens.

For information call:
Eurolines, tel: 08705 143219, www.eurolines.com, or gobycoach.com

BY CAR

With the 16-km (10-mile) Öresund road and rail bridge connecting Copenhagen with Malmö, you can drive all the way to Sweden from Denmark. The drive from Copenhagen Airport to Malmö takes about 45 minutes.

Practical Tips

NEWSPAPERS AND MAGAZINES

English-language newspapers are widely available at kiosks in larger cities, usually on the day of publication. **Kulturhuset** (the cultural centre) at Sergels Torg, Stockholm, has a good selection of English publications that can be read for free, as does the **City Library** in Göteborg on the main square, Götaplatsen.

TELEVISION

Sweden's state-run SVT1, SVT2 and Kanal 4 show foreign films (with subtitles) most evenings. The commercial TV3 and Kanal 5 run American chat shows, sport, movies and soap operas. Plus there are many satellite/cable channels, featuring CNN, BBC and MTV, broadcast in English with subtitles.

RADIO

Radio Sweden has programmes in English with news and information about Sweden on medium wave 1179KHz (254m), and also in the Stockholm area on FM 89.6MHz. A variety of BBC and NPR programmes is also available on FM 89.6.

Postal services are now found at supermarkets and petrol stations rather than at dedicated post offices although the post office at Stockholm's Central Station (open Mon–Fri 7am–10pm and weekends 10am–7pm) still exists.

Stamps *(frimärken)* are also on sale at Pressbyrån newsstands, bookstalls and stationers' shops. You will find two different postboxes, blue for local letters and yellow for all other destinations.

There are plenty of payphones, credit card phones (signposted CCC) and special telegraph offices (marked Telia or Telebutik) throughout Sweden. Most of the payphones operate only with a telephone card *(Telia telefonkort)* available in Pressbyrån, kiosks, bookstalls and stationers' shops.

You can send faxes from hotels, motels and youth hostels, or (in larger towns), from Telia shops.

A good starting point for national tourist information is:
The Swedish Tourist Federation (Svenska Turistföreningen).
Box 25, 101 20 Stockholm
Tel: 08 46 32 10 0.
Fax: 08 67 81 95 8.
E-mail: info@stfturist.se
www.meravsverige.nu

LOCAL TOURIST OFFICES

Sweden has a countrywide network of *Turistbyrå* (tourist information offices) that can be identified by the international "i" sign. They usually have a hotel booking service, *rumsförmedling* or *hotellcentral*, and supply information about local sightseeing and sporting activities. Some are open during the summer only. A complete list can be obtained from The Swedish Travel & Tourism Council www.visit-sweden.com.

Stockholm
Kulturhuset, Sergels Torg
Tel: 789 2490
Fax: 789 2491
E-mail: info@stoinfo.se
www.stockholmtown.com
This is the country's busiest tourist office. Run by the Stockholm Information Service (SIS), it has its own Excursion Shop for booking sightseeing tours.

SIS also publishes the monthly *What's On* brochure, which lists current cultural attractions as well as useful travel tips and telephone numbers.

Dalarna
Trotzgatan 10–12, SE-791 83 Falun
Tel: 023-830 50
Fax: 023-833 14
www.siljan.se
Göteborg
Kungsportsplatsen 2, SE-411 10
Tel: 031 61 25 00
Fax: 031 61 25 01
www.goteborg.com
Gotland
Hamngatan 4, Box 1403,
SE-621 25 Visby
Tel: 0498 20 17 00
Fax: 0498 20 17 17
www.gotland.com
Lapland
Lars Janssonsgatan 17, Box 113,
SE-981 22 Kiruna
Tel: 0980-188 80
Fax: 0980-182 86
www.lappland.se
Skåne
Kyrkogatan 11, SE-222 21 Lund
Tel: 046 35 50 40
Fax: 046 12 59 63
www.skaneturist.nu
Småland
Resecentrum, Järnvägsstationen,
55189 Jönköping
Tel: 036 10 50 50
Fax: 036 10 77 68
E-mail: info@visit-smaland.com
www.visit-smaland.com

The Swedes are good at devising excellent attractions for the whole family, like amusement parks such as **Liseberg** (www.liseberg.se) in Göteborg and **Gröna Lund Tivoli** (www.gronalund.com) in Stockholm.

Astrid Lindgren fantasies

The famous Swedish author Astrid Lindgren is a master at creating fantasy characters that appeal to children. Pippi Longstocking, Emil and Karlsson on the Roof are just some of the attractions at Junibacken.

Junibacken, Galärvarvsvägen
Tel: 08 58 72 30 00
Fax: 08 58 72 30 99
www.junibacken.se

In Vimmerby in the province of Småland you can also visit Astrid Lindgren's World, another fairy-tale land with living characters from her books. Open May–Aug.

Astrid Lindgren's World
Tel: 0492 79 80 0
Fax: 0492 15 88 5
E-mail: info@alv.se
www.alv.se

Sommarland Centres

There are several Sommarland developments in Sweden, the largest of which is at Skara (www.sommarland.se), northeast of Göteborg. It has 50 attractions, including a waterslide, a grand prix race track, a mini-zoo, a railway and three boating lakes.
Tel: 0511 770 300.
Fax: 0511 641 15.

Zoos

The best-known zoo/safari park is at Kolmården (www.kolmarden.com) near Norrköping. It has lions, giraffes and so on, as well as Sweden's only dolphinarium.
Tel: 011 24 90 00.

Santaworld

Not far from Mora is Santaworld, where children can explore Santa's house, workshop and animals and the Snow Queen's Palace, and place orders for Christmas.
Tel: 025 02 12 00.

Business Travellers

The Swedes tend to be rather formal about business. There is little small talk and few lengthy business lunches. Formal business dress, punctuality and preparation are essential. If invited to a client's home for dinner, a gift like a bottle of malt whisky – very expensive in Sweden – is welcomed, and flowers or chocolates for your hostess.

Useful Numbers

- **Police, fire, ambulance**
  112 (calls are free)
- **Swedish directory enquiries**
  118 118
- **International directory enquiries** 118 119

Travellers with Disabilities

In line with its enlightened social attitudes, Sweden has long been a pioneer in accommodating travellers with disabilities. Many hotel rooms and facilities are adapted for the needs both of people with mobility problems and those suffering from allergies. Toilets with the handicap symbol can be found almost everywhere. In Stockholm, most buses are designed for easy access for people with wheelchairs and pushchairs (one parent can travel for free on buses if the baby is in a pushchair). Mainline and underground trains have lifts or ramps.

The annual guide *Hotels in Sweden* lists facilities and chalet cabins with wheelchair access.

Gay Travellers

Sweden is renowned for its liberal attitudes to sex, and its age of consent is 15 for heterosexuals and gays. But there is nevertheless little open affection between gay couples and the gay scene is less apparent in Stockholm than in other capitals, with few places for gays only.

Medical Services

HOSPITALS

Sweden does not have a GP system, so the place to go for any type of treatment is the nearest hospital. Casualty *(Akutmottagning)* deals with serious problems, but Vårdcentral or Husläkarmottagning out-patients clinics are a better option since you will normally be seen within an hour. Take your passport with you.

PHARMACIES

Chemists *(apotek)* should be your first port of call for minor ailments. Generally, they open Mon–Fri 9am–6pm, although some also open on Saturdays, usually 9.30am–1pm. If you need medicine outside office hours, go to the nearest hospital. There is also one all-night pharmacy in Stockholm (C.W. Scheele, Klarabergsgatan 64; tel: 08 45 48 13 0).

DENTISTS

Dental surgeries are indicated by the sign *Tandläkare*. In Stockholm there is an emergency dental service at St Eriks Sjukhus, Fleminggatan 22; tel: 08 54 55 12 20 (open daily 8.45am–8.30pm).

Security and Crime

Sweden is generally a law-abiding country. Crime figures are low, and the streets are by and large safe. Since Sweden is one of the most progressive countries in the world, with the highest percentage of women in the workforce and half its

Public Holidays

- **1 January** New Year's Day
- **6 January** Epiphany
- **March/April** Good Friday and Easter Monday
- **1 May** Labour Day
- **May** Ascension (usually second part of the month); Pentecost (10 days after Ascension)
- **June** Midsummer's Day (around the 24th)
- **November** All Saints' Day (usually at start of the month)
- **25 and 26 December** Christmas

Note: If the holiday is one day away from the weekend, offices tend to be closed the day between (known as klämdag or "squeeze day").

It is virtually impossible to transact business during July.

ministers women, lone female travellers rarely encounter problems.

A far less permissive attitude is, however, taken to drinking. Sweden's drink/driving laws are strict and it is an offence to drink alcohol or be found drunk in any public place. Drug trafficking is also a very serious offence, which carries heavy prison sentences.

For emergency assistance anywhere within Sweden (police, fire service or ambulance) dial 112. Calls are free from pay phones.

Religious Services

The Swedish State Church is in the Lutheran tradition and has churches throughout the country.

Stockholm has the widest range of places of worship, including a Greek Orthodox church, several synagogues and three Islamic mosques.

Protestant services in English are usually held once a week in major cities. Inquire at your hotel for more information.

Tipping

Restaurants A service charge is included in the bill and a further tip is not expected, although it's usual

Embassies/Consulates

Australia
Sergels Torg 12, Stockholm
Tel: 08 613 29 00
Fax: 08 24 74 14
www.sweden.embassy.gov.au
Canada
Tegelbacken 4, Stockholm
Tel: 08 453 30 00
Fax: 08 453 30 16
www.canadaemb.se
UK
Skarpögatan 6–8, Stockholm
Tel: 08 671 30 00
Fax: 08 662 99 89
www.britishembassy.com
US
Dag Hammarskjölds Väg 31
Tel: 08 783 53 00
Fax: 08 661 19 64
www.usemb.se

Business Hours

● **Shops** mainly 9.30am–6pm weekdays and until between 1 and 4pm Sat. In the larger cities many shops open on Sun, usually noon–4pm. Shops generally close early the day before a public holiday.
● **Department stores** may remain open until 8pm or 9pm and possibly also on Sundays.
● **Banks** Mon–Fri 9.30am–3pm (6pm in some cities). The bank at Stockholm Arlanda Airport's arrival and departure halls are open daily 6am–10.30pm.

to round up the bill to the nearest 10–20 Skr.
Taxis Drivers usually get an extra 10 Skr but this is optional.
Cloakrooms at restaurants and clubs charge about 15-20 Skr.
Hotels Tipping for special services by staff is fine but not expected.

Getting Around

On Arrival

All three of Sweden's major international airports – Stockholm (Arlanda), Göteborg (Landvetter) and Malmö (Sturup) – have excellent links to the city centre. From Arlanda, passengers can use the Arlanda Express high-speed train which operates four times an hour to Stockholm Central Station and takes only 20 minutes. There are also frequent bus services, from Västerås *Flygbussarna*, from Arlanda's international and domestic terminals as well as from Skavsta Airport to the city terminal at Klarabergsgatan above Central Station. In Göteborg and Malmö, coaches (long-distance buses) operate from the airport to the cities' central stations.

Taxis are always available but make sure that you get a price before getting into the taxi. At Arlanda Airport, Taxi Stockholm, Taxi Kurir and other companies have fixed fares for rides into the city centre.

By Air

All major cities and towns are linked by an efficient network of services operated mainly by SAS and Skyways.

Cheap flights are available on selected domestic services all year, as well as standby flights for under 25s and special fares for senior citizens. But many of the best deals are during the summer peak season in July when few business executives are travelling.

The Scandinavia/Nordic Air Pass, for eight one-way flights over three months, is available to foreigners.

Details from travel agents, or contact
Skyways Tel: 020 95 95 00.

By Train

Swedish State Railways, or SJ (tel: 0771 75 75 75; www.sj.se), operate an efficient network, mostly electrified, covering the entire country. Trains are frequent, particularly on the main trunk route linking Stockholm with Göteborg, on which there is an hourly service. The high-speed train X2000 travels at up to 200 kph (125 mph) and is a good choice if you want to travel long distances; the journey from Göteborg to Stockholm takes only three hours.

Rail passes
Swedish State Railways offer a wide range of fares for both business and leisure travellers. Conditions and prices may depend on whether you buy your ticket in Sweden or abroad. A number of discount fares are available, including:
● **Sweden Rail Pass** offers travellers from North America unlimited rail travel within Sweden, either first or second class for 3, 4 or 5 days in one month. You can buy your Sweden Rail Pass from: DER Travel Services, www.der.com, or Rail Europe, www.raileurope.com.
● **ScanRail Pass** gives you unlimited rail travel within the Nordic countries. It is available for first- and second-class for five or 10 travel days over a two-month period,

Scenic Train Route

The *Inlandsbanan* (Inland Railway) runs for more than 1,300 km (800 miles) down the spine of Sweden from Gällivare, north of the Arctic Circle, to Mora in the south. The ticket is valid for 10 days and you may stop and continue wherever you please in the direction in which you are heading. For more details contact: **Inlandsbanan AB**, Köpmangatan 22B, S-831 27 Östersund. Tel: 0771 53 53 53.

or 21 consecutive days of travel. This pass is available from DER and in the UK from Rail Europe *(see above)*.
● **Tågplus** If you want to combine rail, bus and boat in one ticket, the best way is probably to buy a Tågplus ticket that enables you to reach over 3,000 destinations within Sweden. For more details and to book, call: 0771 75 75 75.
   To get a *förköpsbiljett* (reduced-rate ticket) in Sweden, you must book seven days in advance. For more information, prices and bookings call: 0771 75 75 75.
   For rail travel in Lapland, call Connex, tel: 0771 26 00 00.

By Coach (Long-distance Bus)

Travelling by bus is usually cheap, and an efficient network of express services links all major towns and cities, operated mainly by:
Svenska Buss Tel: 0771 67 67 67.
Swebus Express Tel: 0200 21 82 18.

In Stockholm
The bus network in Stockholm is claimed to be the world's largest and is run by the Stockholm Transit Authority, which also operates the *Tunnelbanan* (underground) and local mainline rail services.
   Instead of paying cash on the bus, it is cheaper to buy a *Förköpshäfte* (from Pressbyrån and on the underground), which is a voucher for 10 rides within the centre. The driver stamps your ticket when you board and you can travel freely within one zone on the bus, train and underground for an hour on the same ticket. There is no self- service system for buying tickets on the *Tunnelbanan*; use the *Förköpshäfte* or pay cash when you pass the ticket office which is always staffed. You can also buy the SL Tourist Card, which gives free public transport in the Greater Stockholm area for 24 or 72 hours.

In Göteborg
Göteborg has a superior tram system, as well as a good network of bus routes. The *Göteborgskortet*

By Underground

Stockholm is justifiably proud of its underground, known as T-banan (identified by the "T" sign). It is spotless, with almost 100 stations covering more than 95 km (60 miles). Commuter trains *(pendeltåg)* take you quickly to the suburbs of Stockholm and to Nynäshamn, where you can board the ferry to the island of Gotland.

pass gives free public transport, admission to Liseberg Tivoli, some museums, free boat trips and free parking. Valid for 24 hours.

In Malmö
Malmökortet, available for one, two or three days, gives free public transport, discounts or free admission to museums, free parking, discounts on sightseeing tours and on trains to Copenhagen.

By Boat or Ferry

There are innumerable commuter services in the Stockholm archipelago operated by the famous white boats of the Waxholm Steamship Company. During the summer, visitors can buy a 16-day season ticket *(Båtluffarkortet)*, which gives unlimited travel on the Waxholm boats. For information call: 08 67 95 83 0, www.waxholmsbolaget.se. Strömma Kanalbolaget's website also has information on sightseeing and excursions in Stockholm: www.stromma.se. The Baltic island of Gotland has services from Nynäshamn and Oskarshamn. For details check with a tourist office or call Destination Gotland, tel: 04 98 20 18 00 www.destinationgotland.se.

By Taxi

Swedish taxis are usually efficient, but rely more on telephone bookings than being flagged down. Fares are steep. There is a minimum charge, and the meter starts as soon as the taxi arrives at your address. The bigger firms accept credit cards.

In Stockholm, some companies have a maximum fare for rides within the centre. This is good value if you want to travel, for example, from the north to the south of town or if there is a traffic jam.

To book a taxi, call:
Taxi Stockholm Tel: 08-15 00 00
Taxi Kurir Tel: 08-30 00 00
Taxi Tel: 020-93 93 93

By Bicycle

Many of Sweden's towns are ideal for exploring by bike, with good cycle lanes. Cycling holidays are also popular. Bikes can be hired in most places; just enquire at the local tourist office.
Cykelfrämjandet, Tulegatan 43, SE-113 53 Stockholm, tel: 08-54 59 10 30, www.cykelframjandet.a.se, publishes cycling guides in English.

On Foot

Stockholm, Malmö and Göteborg are compact enough to explore on foot. An age-old Swedish law, *Allemansrätten* (Everyman's Right) states that you can venture into the countryside anywhere you like and pick berries and flowers, fish, camp, swim in the lakes and roam at will – as long as you don't harm crops or animals. Hitchhiking is discouraged.

By Car

Main routes
Sweden's roads are uncrowded, with toll-free motorways covering more than 1,100 km (700 miles), and trunk roads some 80,500 km (50,000 miles). There are thousands of kilometres of often picturesque byroads.

Rules of the road
● Traffic gives way to approaching traffic from the right, unless signs indicate otherwise, and gives way to traffic already on a roundabout (traffic circle).
● Everyone must wear seat belts.

● Headlights are obligatory both day and night.
● Drivers are not required to call the police after accidents but must exchange names and addresses. If you do not stop at all you may be liable to a fine or imprisonment.
● In the event of a breakdown, contact the police or Larmtjänst, a 24-hour set-up run by insurance companies (telephone numbers are listed in directories). The emergency number 112 should be used only for accidents or injury.
● Sweden's drink-drive laws are strictly enforced, with spot checks and heavy fines.
● A new law requires drivers to stop at pedestrian crossings when a person is crossing or even indicates an intention to cross.

Speed Limits

Motorways 110 kph (70 mph)
Dual carriageways 90 kph (55 mph)
Unsigned roads 70 kph (43 mph)
Built-up areas 50 kph (31 mph), 30 kph (19 mph) in school areas

CAR HIRE

Stockholm
Avis, Vasagatan 10B.
Tel: 020-78 82 00.
Europcar, Hotel Sheraton, Tegelbacken 6.
Tel: 08-611 45 60.
Hertz, Vasagatan 26.
Tel: 020-21 12 11/08-454 62 50.
Sixt, Klarabergsviadukten 92.
Tel: 08-411 15 22.
All of the above car-hire companies have offices at Arlanda airport.

Where to Stay

Choosing a Hotel

Swedish hotels are of a uniformly high standard, although expensive. However, hotel rates do come down in high summer when the expense-account business travellers are on holiday. Scandic and Sweden Hotels are the country's leading multiples. Away from the big cities, there are plenty of privately owned hotels with the individuality lacking in chains.

Visit www.hotelsinsweden.net for details on hotels in most towns and cities.

DISCOUNTS

All the hotel groups run discount schemes during summer. Stockholm, Göteborg and Malmö also offer special discount packages at weekends year-round and daily in summer. These often include free public transport and free admission to visitor attractions.

Nationwide Chains

The big international hotel chains like Hilton or Sheraton have made little impact. Accommodation is dominated by Scandinavian chains such as Scandic or Sweden Hotels.
Best Western Hotels
Skyheholmsvägen 2, Box 28, SE-171 11 Solna.
Tel: 020 792 752
Fax: 08 566 293 50
www.bestwestern.se
Choice Hotels
Vasagatan 46, SE-111 20 Stockholm. Tel: 08-440 44 40/ 020-66 60 00
First Hotels
Linnégatan 87D
SE-104 51 Stockholm

Tel: 08-442 84 00/020-41 11 11
E-mail: info@firsthotels.se
www.firsthotels.com
Ibis
Tel: 020 44 48 88
www.ibishotel.com
Scandic Hotels
Hälsingegatan 40, Box 6197,
SE-102 33 Stockholm
Tel: 08 51 75 17 00.
www.scandic-hotels.com
Sweden Hotels
Sveavägen 39, SE-111 34
Stockholm. Tel: 08 701 79 00 or
0771 77 70 00
www.swedenhotels.com

Hotel Listings

Hotels are grouped by area, starting
with Stockholm. Within each city or
region, they are listed alphabetically
in price order, with the most
expensive first.

STOCKHOLM

Hotell Diplomat
Strandvägen 7C, SE 104 40
Tel: 08 459 68 00
Fax: 08 459 68 20
E-mail: info@diplomathotel.com
www.diplomathotel.com
Beautiful waterside location on the
city's most exclusive street. **$$$**
Lydmar Hotel
Sturegatan 10, SE-114 36
Tel: 08 566 113 00
Fax: 08 566 113 01
E-mail: info@lydmar.se
www.lydmar.se
One of the best soul and jazz
stages in Stockholm. Central with
an excellent restaurant. **$$–$$$**
Villa Källhagen
Djurgårdsbrunnsvägen 10,
SE-115 27

Price Guide

$$$ 1,800–2,600Skr
$$ 1,000–1,800Skr
$ up to 1,000Skr
Price categories are based on
the average cost (including tax)
of a double room for two, usually
with breakfast.

Tel: 08 665 03 00
Fax: 08 665 03 99
E-mail: villa@kallhagen.se
www.kallhagen.se
Modern, charming hotel with good
restaurant. Close to parks. **$$**
First Hotel Crystal Plaza
Birger Jarlsgatan 35, SE-111 45
Tel: 08 406 88 00
Fax: 08 24 15 11
E-mail:
bokning@crystalplazahotel.se
www.crystalplazahotel.se
Centrally located. Different room
rates on offer. **$–$$**
Gustav Vasa Hotel
Västmannagatan 61, SE-113 25
Tel: 08 34 38 01
Fax: 08 30 73 72
E-mail: gustav.vasa@wineasy.se
www.hotel.wineasy.se/
gustav.vasa
In popular residential area near
restaurants and shops. Three
underground stops from centre. **$**
Hotell Tre Små Rum
Högbergsgatan 81, SE-118 54
Tel: 08 641 23 71
Fax: 08 642 88 08
E-mail: info@tresmarum.se
www.tresmarum.se
Simple but very good-value B&B
in the trendy suburb of Södermalm.
$

AROUND STOCKHOLM

Grythyttan
Grythyttans Gästgivaregård
Prästgatan 2, SE-712 81
Tel: 0591 147 00
Fax: 0591 141 24
E-mail: info@grythyttan.com
www.grythyttan.com
Sweden's best-known inn in a lovely
setting. Expensive but exquisite
restaurant and wine list. **$$**

Mariefred
Gripsholms Värdshus & Hotel
Kyrkogatan 1, SE-647 23
Tel: 0159 347 50
Fax: 0159 347 77
E-mail: info@gripsholms-
vardshus.se
www.gripsholms-vardshus.se
Carefully renovated. Beautiful indiv-
idually furnished rooms. **$$–$$$**

Skokloster
Skokloster Wärdshus & Hotel
SE-746 96 Skokloster
Tel: 018 38 61 00
Fax: 018 38 60 55
E-mail: info@skokloster.se
www.skokloster.se
Beautiful surroundings close to
the castle. **$**

Uppsala
First Hotel Linné
Skolgatan 45, SE-750 02
Tel: 018 10 20 00
Fax: 018 13 75 97
E-mail: linne@firsthotels.se
www.firsthotels.com
Modern hotel with a view over
Linnaeus Garden. Situated in a
quiet area. **$$**

GÖTEBORG

Elite Plaza Hotel
Västra Hamngatan 3, SE-404 22
Tel: 031 720 40 00
Fax: 031 720 40 10
E-mail: info@gbgplaza.elite.se
www.elite.se
New luxury hotel in the centre. **$$$**
Hotel Eggers
Drottningtorget, Box 323, SE-401 25
Tel: 031 80 60 70
Fax: 031 15 42 43
E-mail: hotel.eggers@telia.com
www.hoteleggers.se
Classic 19th-century railway hotel
with individually furnished rooms.
By the station and near the city
centre. **$$**
Mornington Hotel
Kungsportsavenyn 6, SE-411 36
Tel: 031 17 65 40
Fax: 031 711 34 39
E-mail: goteborg@mornington.se
www.mornington.se
First-class with generous breakfast,
right in the centre on Avenyn. **$$**
Novotel Göteborg
Klippan 1, SE-414 51
Tel: 031 14 90 00
Fax: 031 42 22 32
E-mail: info@novotel.se
www.novotel.se
Overlooking the harbour, near good
public transport. **$$**
Hotel Excelsior
Karl Gustavsgatan 7, SE-411 25

Tel: 031 17 54 35
Fax: 031 17 54 39
E-mail: info@hotelexelsior.nu
www.hotelexelsior.nu
Charming old-style hotel with individually furnished rooms, within easy walking distance of Avenyn. **$–$$**

Price Guide

$$$	1,800–2,600Skr
$$	1,000–1,800Skr
$	up to 1,000Skr

Price categories are based on the average cost (including tax) of a double room for two, usually with breakfast.

St Jörgens Hotell & Pensionat
Gamla Lillhagsvägen 127B,
SE-422 04
Tel: 031 55 39 81
Fax: 031 55 39 82
E-mail: hotellet@st-jorgen.nu
www.st-jorgen.nu
Charming and small in rural setting within easy reach of the centre. **$**

MALMÖ

Hilton Malmö City
Triangeln 2, SE-200 10
Tel: 040 693 47 00
Fax: 040 693 47 11
www.hilton.com
Modern high-rise glass building. Most rooms have a nice view. **$$$**

Hotel Noble House
Gustav Adolfstorg 47, SE-211 39
Tel: 040 664 30 00
Fax: 040 664 30 50
E-mail: info@hkchotels.se
www.hkchotels.se
Right in the centre. **$$**

Scandic Hotel St Jörgen
Stora Nygatan 35, SE 20312
Tel: 040 693 46 00
Fax: 040 693 46 11
www.scandic-hotels.com
A comfortable and well-appointed central hotel with its own restaurant and bar. **$$**

Hotell Royal
Norra Vallgatan 94, SE-211 22
Tel: 040 664 25 00
Fax: 040 12 77 12

E-mail: info.royal@swedenhotels.se
www.swedenhotels.com
Small hotel in an old building close to shops, station and ferries. **$**

SOUTHERN SWEDEN: SMÅLAND & ÖLAND

Åhus
Åhusstrand
Kolonivägen, SE-296 01
Tel: 044 28 93 00
Fax: 044 24 94 80
E-mail: info@ahusstrand.com
www.ahusstrand.com
Right on the beach, with a 200-metre (650-ft) landing outside. **$–$$**

Helsingborg
Hotel Mollberg
Stortorget 18, SE-251 10
Tel: 042 37 37 00
Fax: 042 37 37 37
E-mail: info.mollberg@elite.se
www.elite.se
Classic, well-known and beautiful hotel right in the centre of town. **$$**

Kalmar
Scandic Stadshotell
Stortorget 14, SE-392 32
Tel: 0480 49 69 00
Fax: 0480 49 69 10
www.scandic-hotels.com
Beautiful building with individually furnished rooms in the centre. **$$**

Lund
Grand Hotel
Bantorget 1, SE-221 04
Tel: 046 280 61 00
Fax: 046 280 61 50
E-mail: hotel@grandilund.se
www.grandilund.se
Recently renovated old building, right in the centre. **$$–$$$**

Öland
Guntorps Herrgård
Guntorpsgatan, SE-387 36
Borgholm
Tel: 0485 130 00
Fax: 0485 133 19
E-mail: guntorp.herrgard@swipnet.se
www.guntorp.oland.com
Beautiful manor house just outside Borgholm, with lovely restaurant, pool and charming rooms. **$**

Västervik
Best Western Västervik
Stadshotell, Storgatan 3,
SE-593 30
Tel: 0490 820 00
Fax: 0490 820 01
E-mail: stadshotellet@stadshotellet.nu
www.bestwestern.se
Modern hotel right in the centre of town, close to the waterfront. **$–$$**

Vimmerby
Vimmerby Stadshotell
Sevedegatan 39, SE-598 37
Tel: 0492 121 00 (136 30)
Fax: 0492 146 43
E-mail: info@vimmerbystadshotell.se
www.vimmerbystadshotell.se
Pleasant and on town square. **$$**

Ystad
Ystads Saltsjöbad
Saltsjöbadsvägen 6, SE-271 39
Tel: 0411 13 63 00
Fax: 0411 55 58 35
E-mail: info@ystadssaltsjobad.se
www.ystadssaltsjobad.se
Newly renovated with panoramic Baltic view. Relaxing. **$$**

GOTLAND

Visby
Wisby Hotell
Strandgatan 6, SE-621 24
Tel: 0498 25 75 00
Fax: 0498 25 75 50
E-mail: info@wisbyhotell.se
www.wisbyhotell.se
Old hotel with modern rooms in the centre of town. **$$**

THE WEST COAST

Halmstad
Hotel Tylösand
Tylöhusvägen, SE-301 16
Tel: 035 305 00
Fax: 035 324 39
E-mail: info@tylosand.se
www.tylosand.se
First-class hotel overlooking the beach with top-class golf courses nearby. **$$**

Lysekil
Hotel Lysekil
Rosvikstorg 1, SE-453 30
Tel: 0523 66 55 30
Fax: 0523 155 20
www.hotellysekil.se
Modern hotel with all facilities.
Situated near the water and a wide
range of water activities. **$**

Marstrand
Grand Hotel Marstrand
Rådhusgatan 2, SE-440 30
Tel: 0303 603 22
Fax: 0303 600 53
E-mail: info@grandmarstrand.se
www.grandmarstrand.se
Attractive late-19th-century hotel.
Located by the water. **$$**

Varberg
Varbergs Stadshotell & Asia Spa
Kungsgatan 24–26, SE-432 41
Tel: 0340-69 01 00
Fax: 0340-69 01 01
E-mail: info@varbergsstads
hotell.com
www.varbergsstadshotell.com
Carefully renovated hotel from the
turn of the 20th century. Centrally
located. **$$**

THE GREAT LAKES

Borås
First Hotel Grand
Hallbergsgatan 14, SE-503 05
Tel: 033 10 82 00
Fax: 033 41 07 69
E-mail: info@firsthotelgrand.se
www.firsthotelgrand.se
First-class and modern. **$$**

Karlstad
Rasisson SAS Plaza
Västra Torggatan 2, SE-652 25

Tel: 054 10 02 00
Fax: 054 10 02 24
E-mail:
info.karlstad@radissonsas.com
www.plaza-karlstad.nu
First-class hotel in the centre. **$$**

Lidköping
Stadt Lidköping
Gamla Stadens Torg 1, SE-531 02
Tel: 0510 220 85
Fax: 0510 215 32
www.stadtlidkoping.se
www.ekoxen.se
Old waterfront hotel. **$$**

Nora
Nora Stadshotell
Rådstugugatan 21, SE-713 31
Tel: 0587 31 14 35
Fax: 0587 31 13 00
E-mail: norastadshotel@home.se
Family-owned hotel with
good restaurant in the town
square. **$**

GÖTA KANAL

Karlsborg
Kanalhotellet
Storgatan 94, SE-546 32
Tel: 0505 121 30
Fax: 0505 127 61
www.kanalhotellet.se
Late 19th-century hotel. **$**

Söderköping
**Romantik Hotel Söderköpings
Brunn**
Skönbergsgatan 35, SE-614 21
Tel: 0121 109 00
Fax: 0121 139 41
E-mail: info@soderkopingsbrunn.se
www.soderkopingsbrunn.se
Charming hotel in a park. **$–$$**

DALARNA

Falun
First Hotel Grand
Trotzgatan 9–11, SE-791 71
Tel: 023 79 48 80
Fax: 023 14 14 33
E-mail: grand.falun@firsthotels.se
www.firsthotels.se
Dalarna's biggest hotel; central. **$$**

Mora
First Hotel Mora
Strandgatan 12, SE-792 30
Tel: 0250 59 26 50
Fax: 0250 189 81
E-mail: mora@firsthotels.se
www.firsthotelmora.com
Modern hotel in the centre close to
Zorn museum and finishing line of
Vasaloppet ski race. **$$**

Tällberg
Hotell Klockargården
Siljansvägen 6, SE-793 70
Tel: 0247 502 60
Fax: 0247 502 16
www.klockargarden.com
Charming traditional timber houses
with an exhibition of art and
craftwork nearby and great views of
Lake Siljan. **$–$$**

THE CENTRAL HEARTLANDS

Åre
Åregården
SE-830 13
Tel: 0647 178 00
Fax: 0647 179 60
E-mail: reservations.are@diplomat-
hotel.se
www.diplomathotel.com
First-class family-owned hotel with

Camping

There are about 750 officially approved sites, many in pretty locations. Most open from early June to the end of August. Rates are claimed to be among the cheapest in Europe.

You can also rent camping chalets and cottages, caravans and motor homes. For fast check-in and check-out plus insurance while at the site, you should get the Swedish Camping Card. This is free, and you can apply for it before you leave for Sweden, but you have to pay a small validation fee at your first site. The card is available (allow one month for delivery) from: **Sveriges Camping – och Stugföretagares Riksorganisation**, Box 255, S-451 17 Uddevalia. Fax: 0522 64 24 30. E-mail: ck@camping.se. Or visit the very useful www.camping.se

---

skiing facilities, shops and nightclubs nearby. **$–$$$**

Sundsvall

First Hotel Strand
Strandgatan 10, SE-851 06
Tel: 060 64 19 50
Fax: 060 61 92 02
E-mail: strand.sundsvall@
firsthotels.se
www.firsthotels.se
Marine-style hotel with a popular bar and restaurant. **$$**

LAPLAND

Arvidsjaur

Laponia Hotel
Storgatan 45, SE-933 33
Tel: 0960 555 00
Fax: 0960 555 99
E-mail: laponia@laponia-gielas.se
www.laponia-gielas.se
Modern. Offers a range of winter sports. **$$**

Kiruna

Hotell Vinterpalatset
Järnvägsgatan 18, SE-981 21

Tel: 0980 677 70
Fax: 0980 130 50
E-mail: vinterp@kiruna.se
www.kiruna.se/~vinterp
Small privately owned hotel built in 1904 but fully renovated. **$–$$**

Riksgränsen

Riksgränsen
SE-981 94
Tel: 0980 400 80
Fax: 0980 431 25
E-mail: reservation@riksgransen.nu
www.riksgransen.nu
Rooms and self-catering, by the side of a lake with skiing facilities and opportunities for hiking nearby. **$$**

THE NORTHEAST COAST

Haparanda

Haparanda Stadshotell
Torget 7, SE-953 31
Tel: 0922 614 90
Fax: 0922 102 23
E-mail:
info@haparandastadshotell.se
www.haparandastadshotell.se
Early 20th-century hotel in the town centre. The restaurant's specialities include reindeer, elk and grouse. **$$**

Piteå

Piteå Stadshotell
Olof Palmes Gata 1, SE-941 21
Tel: 0911 23 40 00
Fax: 0911 23 40 20
E-mail: info@piteastadshotell.com
www.piteastadshotell.com
Restored late 19th-century hotel in the centre of town. **$$**

Umeå

First Hotel Grand
Storgatan 46, SE-903 26
Tel: 090 77 88 70
Fax: 090 13 30 55
E-mail: umea.grand@firsthotels.se
www.firsthotels.se
Renovated hotel with a nightclub on Friday and Saturday. Central. **$$**

Where to Eat

Choosing a Restaurant

Sweden, once known as the land of *husmanskost* (homely fare), is enjoying a culinary renaissance, thanks to a new generation of chefs who know how to give a sophisticated twist to classic Swedish dishes such as reindeer, elk, lingonberries, salmon or herring.

Eating out has become increasingly popular, but can seem expensive if you drink a lot of wine or beer. Stockholm has more than 700 restaurants covering at least 30 national cuisines. Göteborg is particularly good for seafood, and Malmö claims to have more restaurants per head than any other Swedish city.

For travellers on a tight budget there is no shortage of inexpensive places to eat. Look for the *dagens rätt* (dish of the day), a lunch that usually includes bread, a simple salad and soft drink for around 65–75Skr. Traditional Swedish food like meatballs, *pytt i panna* (fried potatoes, onions, meat and sausage served with beetroot), and pea soup is widely available. The famous *sill* (pickled herring) is served mostly around midsummer with new potatoes. You can find all kinds of pickled herring; with onions, mustard, barbecue sauce, garlic or herbs, or *matjessill* (with sour cream and chives).

Salmon has less of a luxury connotation than in other countries. *Gravad lax* (marinated salmon) and *rökt lax* (smoked salmon) can be found on the *smörgåsbord* and on most Swedish menus.

Fast food outlets are everywhere. The ubiquitous *korvkiosk* sells grilled chicken, sausages, hamburgers and *tunnbrödsrulle* (a parcel of mashed potato, sausage and ketchup or mustard wrapped in soft bread). Some serve *strömming* (fried herring) and mashed potato. The Swedes generally eat fairly early. Restaurants start serving lunch at about 11am and some small hotels, particularly in country areas, serve evening meals around 6pm. In country areas they often stop serving early, but at motels and in the cities you can eat later.

Restaurant Listings

Restaurants are grouped by area with Stockholm first. They are listed alphabetically in price order, with the most expensive first.

STOCKHOLM

Gondolen
Stadsgården 6
Tel: 08 641 70 90
Highly recommended. Offers traditional Swedish cuisine with a great view over the city. **$$$**

Bon Lloc
Regeringsgatan 111
Tel: 08-660 60 60
Catalan-inspired food, featuring the best of fresh Swedish produce. Run by famous chef Mathias Dahlgren, who recently received a *Guide Rouge* star. **$$$**

Operakällaren
Operan (Royal Opera House)
Tel: 08 676 58 00
Arguably Stockholm's best-known restaurant. Its Christmas *smörgåsbord* was nominated by Jan Morris in London's *Times* as "the best meal in the world". **$$$**

PA & Co
Riddargatan 8
Tel: 08 611 08 45

Price Guide

Price categories are based on an average cost per head of a three-course meal (excluding drinks but with tax):

$$$ more than 400Skr
$$ 200–400Skr
$ up to 200Skr

Well-known restaurant, so reserve your table in advance. **$$**

Sturehof
Stureplan 2
Tel: 08 440 57 30
Stylish Swedish food. Has a popular bar and live music. **$$**

Farbror Frej
Frejgatan 79
Tel: 08 32 05 25
Intimate restaurant run by a cycling legend. Great food and a warm welcome. **$-$$**

Indian Curry House
Scheelegatan 6
Tel: 08 650 20 24
Small, basic restaurant with good Indian food at reasonable prices. **$**

AROUND STOCKHOLM

Grythyttan
Grythyttans Gästgivaregård
Prästgatan 2
Tel: 0591 147 00
Well-known romantic inn. Excellent modern Swedish food. **$$-$$$**

Södertälje
Oaxen Skärgårdskrog
Oaxen (30km/19 miles from Södertälje)
Tel: 08 551 531 05
Excellent Swedish cooking. **$-$$**

SOUTHERN SWEDEN & SMÅLAND

Malmö
Restaurang Johan P
Lilla Torg, Landbygatan 3
Tel: 040 97 18 18
Excellent and beautifully presented fish dishes. **$$**

Restaurang Möllan
Bergsgatan 37C
Tel: 040 12 10 15
A good choice for filling, good-value Swedish home cooking. **$$**

Skeppsbron 2
Börshuset
Tel: 040 36 62 02
Modern and inventive cuisine in a building overlooking the sea. **$$**

Brogatan
Brogatan 12
Tel: 040 30 77 17

Popular among the famous. Organic Swedish food and live music. **$-$$**

There is an area worth visiting in Malmö called Lilla Torg, where the market hall is located and new restaurants are opening all the time offering various cuisines.

Helsingborg
Elinor
Kullagatan 53
Tel: 042 12 23 30
Charming restaurant specialising in fish and seafood. **$$**

Kalmar
Calmar Hamnkrog
Skeppsbrogatan 30
Tel: 0480 41 10 20
Gourmet restaurant with a sea view. Classic and international food. **$$**

Simrishamn
Karlaby Kro
In the village of Tommarp, 7km/4 miles from Simrishamm
Tel: 0414 41 13 60
Cosy restaurant serving fresh local produce. **$$-$$$**

GOTLAND

Visby
Donners Brunn
Donners Plats
Tel: 0498 27 10 90
Friendly gourmet restaurant with "Best Lamb Chef" in Sweden. **$$**

Bakfickan
Stora Torget 1
Tel: 0498 27 18 07
Cosy restaurant; excellent fish. **$-$$**

THE WEST COAST

Göteborg
Fiskekrogen
Lilla Torget 1
Tel: 031 10 10 05
Best fish restaurant in town; exciting wines at good prices. **$$$**

Trädgår'n
Nya Allén
Tel: 031 10 20 80
Exotic award-winning international restaurant. Has live music. **$$$**

Price Guide

Price categories are based on an average cost per head of a three-course meal (excluding drinks but with tax):

$$$ more than 400Skr
$$ 200–400Skr
$ up to 200Skr

Hemma Hos
Haga Nygata 12
Tel: 031 13 40 90
Cosy local restaurant serving great fish dishes and desserts. $$
Bliss Resto
Magasinsgatan 3
Tel: 031 13 85 55
Swedish and Oriental dishes. $$
Noon
Viktoriagatan 2B
Tel: 031 13 88 00
Asian bar/restaurant. Friendly and professional. Good desserts. $$

Halmstad
Pio & Company
Storgatan 37
Tel: 035 21 06 69
Traditional Swedish food. $$

Hamburgsund
Skäret
Strandvägen 10
Tel: 0525 345 80
Charcoal-grilled fish. $$

Tanumshede
Tanums Gestgifveri
Apoteksv 7, 30km (19 miles) from Strömstad
Tel: 0525 290 10
Swedish food. $$

THE GREAT LAKES

Jönköping
Svarta Börsen
Kyrkog 4
Tel: 036 71 22 22
Traditional with excellent fish. Good-value business lunches. $$–$$$

Karlstad
Tiffany
Västra Torggatan 19
Tel: 054 15 33 83

Stylish restaurant specialising in local fish and game. $$–$$$

GÖTA KANAL

Dalarna
Borlänge
Värdshuset Dala Floda
Badvägen 6, Dala Floda (40km/25 miles from Borlänge)
Tel: 0241 220 50
Excellent well-known inn/restaurant. International menu. $–$$

Falun
Dössbergets Värdshus
Bjursås (20km/12 miles from Falun)
Tel: 023 507 37
Beautifully located with traditional Swedish and gourmet food. $$

Leksand
Åkerblads Hotell & Gästgiveri
Sjögattu 2, Tällberg (13km/8 miles from Leksand
Tel: 0247 508 00
Traditional Swedish. Buffet lunch and *smörgåsbord* at weekend. $$

Söderköping
Romantik Hotel Söderköpings Brunn
Skönbergsgatan 35
Tel: 0121 109 00
Fine Swedish and international cooking; some veggie dishes. $$

What to Drink

Alcohol is a luxury in Sweden due to the high taxes. Alternatives include low- or medium-strength beer, Ramlösa mineral water, or one of the excellent indigenous schnapps.

There is no difficulty in ordering a drink with your meal, although the stronger Class III beer *(starköl)* may not be available in restaurants and bars until noon.

The Swedish authorities have a puritanical attitude towards drinking: you can buy alcohol only through branches of the State-controlled monopoly

Vadstena
Starby Kungsgård
Ödeshögsvägen
Tel: 0143 751 00
Excellent. Traditional Swedish and gourmet international cuisine. $$

THE CENTRAL HEARTLANDS

Åre
Villa Tottebo
Parkvägen 1
Tel: 0647 505 99
Pleasant restaurant serving mostly local products. $$

Östersund
Mikado
Grytan, Brunflo (10km/6 miles from Östersund)
Tel: 063 209 08
Prettily served Japanese cuisine. $$–$$$

Sundsvall
Fem Rum och Kök
Östra Långgatan 23
Tel: 060 17 62 62
Cosy restaurant with Swedish food and a variety of single malts. $$

LAPLAND

Jukkasjärvi
Jukkasjärvi Wärdshus
Marknadsvägen 63
Tel: 0980 668 80

Systembolaget, open Mon–Fri 9am–6pm and Sat 10am–2pm but closes early the day before a public holiday.

The minimum age for buying alcohol is 20; you may be asked for proof of your age if you are in your early 20s.

It's worth looking out for bars and cafés advertising a reduced-price happy hour. This may be at any time of the day, but is worth finding as it can bring the cost of half a litre of lager down to half the price charged in nightclubs.

Excellent restaurant specialising in local products such as reindeer, grouse, char and cloudberries.
$$

Tärnaby
Sånninggården Restaurang & Pensionat
Klippen, Hemavan (25km/15 miles from Tärnaby),
Tel: 0954 330 00
Beautifully located; specialising in local game and poultry.
$–$$

THE NORTHEAST COAST

Luleå
Margaretas Värdshus
Lulevägen 2, Gammelstad (10km/6 miles from Luleå)
Tel: 0920 25 42 90
Picturesque inn with a restaurant, serving local specialities. **$–$$**

Umeå
K-A Svensson Kök och Matsalar
Blå Huset, Vasaplan
Tel: 090 77 98 00
Serves Swedish dishes with an interesting twist. **$–$$**

Cafés

STOCKHOLM

Vete-Katten
Kungsgatan 55
Tel: 08 21 84 54
Traditional café in shopping area.
Rosendals Trädgård
Rosendalsterrassen 12, Djurgården
Tel: 08 545 812 70
Delicious foods within the garden by Rosendal Palace on Djurgården.

GÖTEBORG

Ahlströms Konditori
Korsgatan 2
Tel: 031 13 48 93
Founded in 1905.
Junggrens Café
Kungsportsavenyn 37
Tel: 031 16 17 51
A classic café for young people.

Nightlife

There is an active nightlife in the larger cities but nothing particularly hectic in the smaller communities. Many of the hotels listed have bars, nightclubs and sometimes even live dance music. The university cities like Uppsala, Lund, Linköping and Umeå have quite a busy nightlife, at least for the students.

Skiing resorts like Åre and Sälen are also good for nightlife (mostly for younger people) during the season, from December to April. Apres-ski is often very lively with bands playing covers of well-known tunes to packed crowds.

Out in the countryside and in smaller towns *dansband* (Swedish country-style music) is very popular.

Given the high cost of drinking in Sweden, a night out on the town can be expensive.

Nightclubs & Discos

Nightclubs and discos usually close around 3am, but in Stockholm some places extend this to 5am.

Stockholm
Café Opera
Operahuset. Tel: 08 676 58 07
Expensive but ever-popular.
Spy Bar
Birger Jarlsgatan 20
Tel: 08 611 65 00
Trendy with recent dance music.
Biblos
Biblioteksgatan 9
Tel: 08 54 51 85 00
Popular restaurant with large bar and small dance floor downstairs.

Göteborg
Park Lane
Kungsportsavenyn 36–38
Tel: 031 20 60 58
Fancy nightclub with international

atmosphere. Three bars, casino restaurant and live performances.
Trädgår'n
Nya Allén
Tel: 031 10 20 80
Restaurant with live performances.
Valand
Vasagatan 41
Tel: 031 18 30 93
Three bars and a restaurant with live performances most nights.

Malmö
Slagthuset
Jörgen Kocksgatan 7A
Tel: 040 10 99 31
Three dance floors. House, classic old hits and Top 40 (disco).
Kulturbolaget
Bergsgatan 18.
Tel: 040 30 20 11
A popular haunt among hard rock lovers, but also features pop.
Privé
Malmborgsgatan 7
Tel: 040 97 46 66
Disco popular among the older generation; people dress up.

Bars and Live Music

Stockholm
Fasching
Kungsgatan 63. Tel: 08 21 62 67
Stockholm's largest and probably most popular jazz club.
Lydmar
Sturegatan 10. Tel: 08 566 113 00
Popular bar and jazz club.
Pelikan
Blekingegatan 40
Tel: 08 556 090 90
Unpretentious bar and beer hall.
Nalen
Reyeringsgatan 74
Tel: 08 453 34 00
Jazz, swing and big band can all be found here.

Göteborg
Brasseri Lipp
Kungsportsavenyn 8
Tel: 031 10 58 30
French bistro/bar. Older crowd.
Palace
Södra Hamngatan 2
Tel: 031 80 75 50
Classic bar, popular among business people on Friday.

Trädgår'n
Nya Allén. Tel: 031 10 20 80
Restaurant with live performances.

Malmö
Hipp
Kalendegatan 12
Tel: 040 97 40 30
Beautiful restaurant/bar with club
arrangements. Salsa evenings.
Kulturbolaget
Bergsgatan 18. Tel: 040 30 20 11
Popular with tough rock lovers.

Music

The musical scene is busiest in
autumn, winter and spring, but
there is still a lot on in summer. In
Dalarna several communities
organise music festivals.

Stockholm
The main concert hall is the
Konserthuset (tel: 08 10 21 10),
home of the Stockholm Philharmonic
Orchestra, whose season runs from
September to May or June.
 Berwaldhallen (the Berwald
Concert Hall, tel: 08 784 18 00) is
the base for Swedish National
Radio's musical activities, with
regular performances by the Radio
Symphony Orchestra.
 Stockholm's famous **Kungliga
Operan** (Royal Opera House,
tel: 08 24 82 40) has top
international performances
mid-August to June.

Göteborg
Konserthuset (the Concert Hall,
tel: 031 726 53 10) hosts the
Göteborg Symphony Orchestra,
which is known worldwide and
performs every week, often with
guest artists, from August to June.
 The modern **Göteborgsoperan**
(Göteborg's Opera House, tel: 031
13 13 00) offers a varied
programme (including opera, ballet
and musicals) from August to
June.

Malmö
The 1,300-seat **Konserthuset**
(Concert Hall, tel: 040 34 35 00) is
permanent home for the Symphony
Orchestra.

Theatre

Sweden has a lively theatrical life in
the major cities, but many theatres
tend to be closed during the peak
summer months. Performances are
usually in Swedish.

Stockholm
The most prestigious theatre is
Dramaten (Royal Dramatic Theatre,
tel: 08 667 06 80) on Nybroplan,
with four auditoriums. The most
unusual one is **Drottningholms
Slottsteater** (Drottningholm Court
Theatre at Drottningholm Palace,
tel: 08 665 14 00) founded by King
Gustav III in 1766. Many sets from
the 18th century are still in use
today. In summer there are ballet
and opera performances.
 Current performances are listed
in the *Stockholm This Week*
booklet. There is a booth on
Norrmalmstorg Square where you
can buy last-minute theatre seats at
prices at least 25 percent below
normal box-office rates.

Göteborg
The two main theatres are
Stadsteatern (tel: 031 61 51 00)
and **Folkteatern** (tel: 031 60 75
75), both open from late August to
early June.

Malmö
The **Musikteatern** (tel: 040 20 85
00) stages plays in Swedish, but
you can often catch an opera or
musical performance.

Cinema

Virtually all foreign films are shown
with their original sound tracks and
Swedish subtitles. Local
newspapers have full details of
programmes and times. In
Stockholm, cinemas showing first-
run international films include
Filmstaden Sergel, Filmstaden
Söder, Rigoletto, Biopalatset and
Astoria. The two dominating film
companies, SF and Sandrews, have
websites where you can book your
ticket for any cinema:
SF: www.sf.se
Sandrews: www.sandrews.se

Sport

Spectator Sports

Göteborg is probably the most sport-
conscious town in Sweden, and its
Scandinavium (tel: 031 81 10 20) is
the venue for many major events,
including tennis, ice hockey and
table tennis. The city's other main
arena is Ullevi Stadium (tel: 031 81
10 20), where international
tournaments in football, athletics
and speedway are staged regularly.
 Tennis is Sweden's top spectator
sport. The main tournaments are
the Swedish Open at Båstad on the
southwest coast in mid-July and the
Stockholm Open which is held in
early November.
 Athletics meetings are usually in
early July. Stockholm also stages a
large marathon in early June.
 The famous Globen arena
(tel: 08 600 34 00) in Stockholm
holds sporting events and concerts.
 Horse racing and trotting are
popular, with courses at Stockholm
(Täby), Göteborg (Åby) and Malmö
(Jägersro). The Swedish Derby is in
July at Jägersro, which is also the
venue for a major horse show in
August. Another important annual
international horse show is held at
the Göteborg Scandinavium in April.

Canoeing

Svenska Kanotförbundet
Idrottens Hus, Storforsplan 44, SE-
123 87 Farsta. Tel: 08 605 60 00.
Fax: 08 605 65 65.

Cycling

Svenska Cykelförbundet
Drakslingan 1, SE-193 40 Sigtuna
Tel: 08-592 525 50
Fax: 08-592 529 36
www.svenska-cykelforbundet.se

Fishing

Swedish Angling Federation
Box 2, SE-163 21 Spånga.
Tel: 08 795 33 50.
Fax: 08 795 96 73.
E-mail: hk@sportfiskarna.se

Golf

Svenska Golfförbundet
Kevingestrand 20, SE-182 11
Danderyd. Tel: 08 622 15 00.
Fax: 08 753 05 22.
E-mail: sgf@golf.se; www.golf.se

Hiking

**Swedish Walking and Hiking
Association**, Idrottens Hus,
Storforsplan 44, SE-123 87 Farsta.
Tel: 08 605 64 49.
Fax: 08 605 64 46.
National Parks
www.environ.se and www.fjallen.nu

Horse Riding

Svenska Ridsportförbundet
Herroskogsvägen 2
SE-730 40 Kolbäck
Tel: 0220 456 00
Fax: 0220 456 70
www.ridsport.se

Sailing

Svenska Seglarförbundet
Af Pontinsvägen 6, SE-115 21
Stockholm. Tel: 08 459 09 90.
Fax: 08 459 09 99.
E-mail: ssf@ssf.se

Skiing

Svenska Skidförbundet
Riks Skidstadion, SE-791 19 Falun
Tel: 023-874 40
www.skidor.com

Tennis

Svenska Tennisförbundet
Lidingövägen 75, SE-115 94
Stockholm. Tel: 08 667 97 70.
E-mail: info@tennis.se
www.tennis.se

Shopping

What to Buy

Sweden is famous the world over
for its elegant design, and you will
find plenty of good buys in
glassware, stainless steel, silver,
pottery, ceramics, textiles and
leather goods. Department stores
such as NK and Åhléns have
branches all over the country and
are noted for their high-quality,
inexpensive kitchenware.
Glass The best bargains are to be
found in "Glass Country" – Småland,
in the southeast – where there are
more than 15 glassworks. Major
glassworks like Orrefors, Kosta-
Boda, Älghult and Skruf have shops
adjoining their factories where you
can pick up seconds. For flawless
glass products you need to shop at
the major department stores like
NK, Crystal Art Centre or Nordiska
Kristall in Stockholm.
Porcelain Sweden is also renowned
for its high-quality porcelain, and
bargains can be found at the
Gustavsberg factory outside
Stockholm and at the Rörstrand
factory in Lidköping.
Fashion Clothing at inexpensive
prices can be found at Hennes &
Mauritz (H&M), Lindex, JC and
KappAhl. But the best place to pick
up good buys in textiles is probably
Borås, 60 km (37 miles) from
Göteborg. Knallebygden is a large
shopping centre in Borås.
Books English-language books are
widely available. In Stockholm,
excellent bookshops include:
Sweden Bookshop, Slottsbacken
10, Box 74 34, SE- 10391. Tel: 08
453 78 00. Fax: 08 20 72 48,
www.swedenbookshop.com
Hedengrens Bokhandel, Stureplan
4. www.hedengrens.se
Akademibokhandeln, Mäster

Samuelsgaten 32, on the corner
of Regeringsgatan.
www.akademibokhandeln.com
English Book Centre,
Surbrunnsgatan 51.
www.engbookcen.se

Markets

Stockholm has markets at
Östermalmstorg and Hötorget, while
Göteborg has its Fish Church fish
market. Stockholm has what is
claimed to be northern Europe's
largest flea market at Skärholmen,
20 minutes on the underground
from the city (open daily, but
Saturday and Sunday are best).

Local Crafts

In the countryside, it's worth
looking out for Hemslöjd handicraft
centres, where you can buy
attractive locally produced items.
Women's and children's clothes are
especially good buys, as well as
furs and needlework.
Below is just a small selection of
outlets in Stockholm and Göteborg:
Svensk Hemslöjd
Sveavägen 44, Stockholm.
Tel: 08 23 21 15.
Svenskt Vistra
Kungsgatan 55, Stockholm.
Tel: 08 21 47 26.
Bohusslöjd
Kungsportsavenyn 25, Göteborg.
Tel: 031 16 00 72.
There's also a website for *Gula
Sidorna (Yellow Pages)* listing shops
throughout Sweden: www.gulas
idorna.se (search for *hantverk*).

Design

Several shops in Stockholm are
worth visiting:
DesignTorget
Kulturhuset, Sergels Torg 3.
Tel: 08 508 315 20 and
Götgatan 31.
Tel: 08 462 35 20.
Norrgavel
Birger Jarlsgatan.
Tel: 08 545 220 50.
Svenskt Tenn
Strandvägen 5.
Tel: 08 670 16 00.

Language

The Alphabet

The Swedish alphabet has 29 letters. The additional three are å, ä and ö and come after the letter Z. To find Mr Åkerblad in the telephone book, therefore, look at the end of the listings.

Getting By

yes *ja*
no *nej*
hello *hej*
goodbye *hejdå*
please *tack/var så god*
good morning *god morgon*
good afternoon *god eftermiddag*
good evening *god kväll*
how do you do *goddag*
excuse me *ursäkta*
thank you *tack*
Do you speak English? *talar du engelska?*
I only speak English *jag talar bara engelska*
I do not understand *jag förstår inte*

Getting Around

aeroplane *flygplan*
bus/coach *buss*
car *bil*
train *tåg*
How do I get to...? *hur kommer jag till...?*
Where is ...? *var finns ...?*
right *höger*
to the right *till höger*
left *vänster*
to the left *till vänster*
straight on *rakt fram*

Eating and Drinking

breakfast *frukost*
lunch *lunch*
dinner *middag*
eat *äta*
drink *dricka*
Cheers! *skål!*
off-licence *systembolaget*
Can I order, please? *får jag beställa?*
I would like *jag skulle vilja*
Could I have the bill please? *kan jag få notan?*
hot *varm*
cold *kall*

Shopping

Can I help you? *kan jag hjälpa till?*
to buy *att köpa*
money *pengar*
How much is this? *vad kostar det?*
It costs *det kostar*
shop *affär*
department store *varuhus*
supermarket *snabbköp*
grocery store *(in countryside) lanthandel*

Numbers

1	*en/ett*
2	*två*
3	*tre*
4	*fyra*
5	*fem*
6	*sex*
7	*sju*
8	*åtta*
9	*nio*
10	*tio*
11	*elva*
12	*tolv*
13	*tretton*
14	*fjorton*
15	*femton*
16	*sexton*
17	*sjutton*
18	*aderton*
19	*nitton*
20	*tjugo*
21	*tjugoen*
22	*tjugotvå*
30	*trettio*
40	*fyrtio*
50	*femtio*
60	*sextio*
70	*sjuttio*
80	*åttio*
90	*nittio*
100	*hundra*

bakery *bageri*
chemist *apotek*
bookshop *bokhandel*
food *mat*
big *stor*
small *liten*

Accommodation

do you have any vacancies? *har ni några lediga rum?*
twin room *dubbelrum med två sängar*
single room *enkel rum*
chalet *stuga*
to rent *att hyra*
room to rent *rum att hyra*
Could I have the key please? *kan jag få nyckeln?*

Clothes/Laundry

clothes *kläder*
coat/overcoat *kappa/överrock*
jacket *jacka*
suit *kostym*
shoes *skor*
skirt *kjol*
blouse *blus*
jumper *tröja*
wash *tvätta*
launderette *tvättomat*
dry cleaning *kemtvätt*
dirty/clean *smutsigt/rent*

Signs

Toilet *Toalett*
Gentlemen *Herrar*
Ladies *Damer*
Vacant *Ledig*
Engaged *Upptagen*
No smoking *Rökning förbjuden*
Entrance *Ingång*
Exit *Utgång*
No entry *Ingen ingång*
Open *öppen/öppet*
Closed *Stängt*
Push *Tryck*
Pull *Drag*

Time

today *idag*
tomorrow *i morgon*
yesterday *i går*
morning *morgon*
afternoon *eftermiddag*
evening *kväll*

In an Emergency

accident and emergency
akutmottagning
clinic *vårdcentral*
hospital *sjukhus*
doctor *doktor*
police station *polisstation*

What time is it? *hur mycket är klockan?*
it is... *den är...*
the time is... *klockan är...*
Sunday *söndag*
Monday *måndag*
Tuesday *tisdag*
Wednesday *onsdag*
Thursday *torsdag*
Friday *fredag*
Saturday *lördag*

Further Reading

Good books on Sweden are few and far between, but the best source of information on publications in English is the Swedish Institute, which itself publishes a good range of guides. Its website has a good list and has an ordering service.
Svenska Institutet
Slottsbacken 10
Box 7434, SE-103 91 Stockholm.
Tel: 08 453 78 00.
Fax: 08 20 72 48.
www.si.se (also search under Sweden bookshop.)

History

Sweden: A Traveller's History by Eric Elstob (Boydell Press). Swedish history from its beginnings.
Swedish History in Outline by Jörgen Welbull (Swedish Institute).
The Vikings, Lord of the Seas by Yves Cohat (Thames & Hudson). History of the Vikings, with excellent colour photography.

Architecture

A Home by Lena Rydin (Cari Larsson Gården/Dalaförlaget). Artist Carl Larsson's farm in Sundborn in the Dalarna region in photographs and paintings.
Great Royal Palaces of Sweden by Göran Alm (M.T. Train/Scala Books). A dozen castles, palaces and pavilions belonging to Swedish royalty over the past 500 years.

Art and Design

Carl and Karin Larsson: Creators of the Swedish Style by Michael Snodin and Elisabet Stavenow-Hidemark (eds.). A profile of two of Sweden's most influential designers.
A History of Swedish Art by Mereth Lindgren, Louise Lyberg, Birgitta Sandström and Anna Greta

Wahlberg (Bokförlaget Signum). A bird's-eye view of Swedish painting, sculpture and architecture.
The Swedish Room by Lars Sjöberg and Ursula Sjöberg (Frances Lincoln Limited). Some of Sweden's most classic interiors.

Food

The Swedish Kitchen: A Culinary Journey by Lennart Hagerfors (Norstedts). A cookbook by one of the best-known chefs in Sweden, with 198 modern Swedish recipes.
Smörgasbord: A Swedish Classic by Kerstin Torngre (Swedish Institute). A short guide to Sweden's traditional buffet spread.

Fiction

The Wonderful Adventures of Nils and *The Further Adventures of Nils* by Selma Lagerlöv. Captivating stories about a boy who flies around Sweden on a goose, have made Lagerlöv one of the nation's most popular children's authors. As travelogues, they're enjoyable for adults too.

Guides

Live and Work in Scandinavia by Andre de Vries et al (Vacation Work Publications). Jobs and how to obtain them.
National Parks in Sweden: Europe's Last Wilderness edited by Ingvar Bingman (The National Environment Protection Board, available through the Swedish Institute). Details of Sweden's vast forest land.

Other Insight Guides

Over 200 titles in the acclaimed **Insight Guides** series cover every continent. Titles in the region include *Sweden, Norway, Denmark,* and *Finland.* **Insight Compact Guides** to the region include *Norway, Denmark, Copenhagen* and *Finland.* **Insight Fleximaps** are durable, weatherproof and easy to fold. Scandinavian titles include *Stockholm, Copenhagen* and *Norway.*

FINLAND

The Place

Area 338,000 sq km
(130,600 sq miles).
Capital Helsinki.
Population 5.2 million, of whom
about 40 percent live in rural
areas and around 1.2 million in
Greater Helsinki.
Language Finnish and Swedish;
Sami is spoken by the indigenous
people of Lapland.
Religion About 87 percent are
Evangelical Lutheran, with 1 percent
Finnish Orthodox and
12 percent unaffiliated.
Time zone GMT + 2 hours; EST + 7
hours.
Currency the euro (€).
Weights and measures Metric.
Electricity 220 AC (two-pin plug).
International dialling code: +358.

Geography

Finland is set on the Baltic Sea. Its
neighbouring countries are Sweden,
Norway, Russia and on the opposite
shore of the Baltic, Estonia. Finland
is 65 percent covered by forest, 10
percent by lakes, and 8 percent by
cultivated land.

Climate

Finland has cold winters and fairly
warm summers. In July, the south
has similar temperatures to
southern England, with less rain
and more sunshine. The hottest
months are Jul–Aug, when
temperatures average 18°C
(65°F); the coldest are Jan–Feb,
averaging -4°C (25°F). In south
and central Finland snow settles
at the start of Dec and melts
mid–late Apr (or May in the
forests). In the north snow comes
about five weeks earlier and ends
about three weeks later.

Economy

Until the end of World War II
Finland received a modest income
from agriculture and the textile
trade. Since then the lords of
Finnish industry have been pulp
and paper products/machinery,
forestry, a few electronics and
engineering giants (such as Nokia
mobile telephones) and Neste oil
refining. Today only 10 percent of
the population is involved in
farming.

Government

Finland is a parliamentary
democracy with a president, a
prime minister and a 200-member,
single-chamber parliament. The
president is elected, while the
prime minister is chosen by a
conference of parties participating
in the current government.
Coalition governments led by
Social Democrats have dominated
Finland's short history as an
independent republic. In 2000,
Tarja Halonen, a Social Democrat,
was elected president for a six-
year term and is Finland's first
woman to hold this office. With
several other women in positions
of power, this was not considered
unusual.

Tourist Info at Home

● **UK**
Finnish Tourist Board
PO Box 33213, London W6 8JX
Tel: 020 7365 2512 (UK)
Tel: 01 407 3362 (Ireland)
Fax: 020 8600 5681
Email: finlandinfo.lon@mek.fi
No personal callers.
● **US/Canada**
Finnish Tourist Board
PO Box 4649
Grand Central Station
New York NY 10163-4649
Tel: 212 885 9700 or 800-FIN-
INFO (North America)
Email: mek.usa@mek.fi
● **Australia**
The Embassy supplies tourist
information.
12 Darwin Avenue
Yarralumla, ACT 2600
Tel: 02 6273 3800
Fax: 02 6273 3603
Email:
finland@austarmetro.com.au
www.finland.org.au/
● **Websites**
Finland: www.finland-tourism.com
Helsinki: www.hel.fi/english

The People

Finland is the sixth-largest land area
in Europe, but the population is
sparse with only 16 inhabitants per
sq km (6 per sq mile).
In general Finns are courteous,
particularly to foreign guests, about
whom they are quite curious. If you
are going to a Finn's house for
dinner, take a plant or flowers; and
a bottle of wine or other spirits is
always appreciated considering the
high cost of alcohol.

Planning the Trip

Visas and Passports

Citizens of most Western countries do not need visas to travel to Finland; a valid passport will suffice. EU citizens may enter with a valid ID card.

Customs

The following items may be brought into Finland.

Cigarettes/tobacco

Non-EU citizens over 17 years of age may bring in 200 cigarettes, 50 cigars or 250 g (1–2 lb) tobacco products duty free. Europeans aged 17 or over can bring in 300 cigarettes, 75 cigars or 400 g of tobacco products.

Alcohol

Any visitor aged 20 or over can bring in 15 litres of beer, 2 litres of other mild alcohol (drinks containing not more than 22 percent by volume of alcohol) and 1 litre of strong alcohol (spirits). For visitors of 18 years of age, the quantity limit is the same, but must not include strong alcohol.

Health

You'll have little to worry about healthwise in Finland. However, you may have an uncomfortable time with the mosquitoes in northern and central parts in July and August. Ask your GP about mosquito treatment before you go and enquire at chemists in Finland about the most effective repellent.

Finland's medical facilities have an excellent reputation worldwide. The country has reciprocal health arrangements with other EU members, so visitors are entitled to the same treatment as Finns (UK citizens must provide an E111 form, available from post offices).

Money Matters

Finland's unit of currency is the euro (€). Notes are available in 500, 200, 100, 50, 20, 10 and 5 euros and coins in 2 and 1 euros, 50, 20, 10, 5, 2, and 1 cents.

How to pay

Credit cards MasterCard, Visa, Diner's Club and American Express are accepted in most establishments in main cities.
Travellers' cheques and common currencies can easily be exchanged in banks.
ATMs Automatic Teller Machines marked OTTO give local currency if you have a card with an international PIN number (Visa, Cirrus, PLUS, MasterCard and so on).

What to Bring

The best advice on packing for Finland is to bring layers of clothes, no matter what the season. In winter, gloves, long underwear, hats, woollen tights and socks, and several layers of cotton topped by wool and something waterproof are recommended. Bring heavy-duty footgear not only to keep out damp but to avoid good shoes being ruined by salt and gravel put down to melt the ice on pavements. Spring and autumn are rainy, and summers are usually pleasantly dry and sunny, but occasionally wet.

Getting There

BY AIR

Finnair, the national carrier of Finland, operates internationally and has national routes to more than 20 cities. Both Finnair and British Airways connect London and Helsinki with daily flights; Finnair fly from Manchester to Helsinki. Finnair (and many other airlines) fly direct between Helsinki and most European capitals, and Finnair also links with several North American cities, including New York.
British Airways Tel: 0845 773 3377.
www.ba.com
Finnair Tel: 020 7408 1222 (UK).
Tel: 212 499 9026 (US)
Tel: 08 8306 8411 (Australia)
www.finnair.com
SAS Tel: 0845 607 2772.
www.scandinavian.net

BY SEA

The Silja Line and Viking Line operate daily ferries between Stockholm and Helsinki that are reasonably priced, luxurious and well equipped with restaurants,

Tour Operators

● **Bridge Travel Service**
Bridge House, 55–59 High Street, Broxbourne, Herts EN10 7DT.
Tel: 0870 191 7277.
bridgetravel.co.uk
● **Crystal Holidays**
Crystal House, Arlington Road, Surbiton, Surrey KT6 6BW.
Tel: 0870 160 6040.
www.crystalholidays.co.uk
● **Norvista**
31–35 Kirby Street, London EC1N 8TE.
Tel: 0870 744 7315.
www.norvista.co.uk

● **Page & Moy**
136–140 London Road, Leicester LE2 1EN.
Tel: 0870 010 6212
www.page-moy.com.
● **Scantours**
47 Whitcomb Street, London WC2H 7DH.
Tel: 020 7839 2927.
www.scantoursuk.com
● **Norwegian Coastal Voyage**
3 Shortlands, London W6 8NE.
Tel: 020 8846 2666
www.norwegiancoastalvoyage.com

saunas, swimming pools, tax-free shops and children's playrooms. Journey time is around 16½ hours.
Silja Line Tel: 09 18041.
www.silja.com
Viking Line Tel: 09 123 577
www.vikingline.fi

BY RAIL

It's a long haul to Finland from just about anywhere by rail, because you inevitably finish the trip north with a 15-hour journey by boat and train from Stockholm to Helsinki. From Britain, the handiest route is by ferry from Harwich to the Hook of Holland, overland to Copenhagen, then connecting train to Stockholm and boat or boat and train to Helsinki. Total travel time is about 45 hours. To get to north Finland you have to end the journey by bus as Finnish rail lines run only as far as Rovaniemi and Kemijärvi (or Kolari in winter).

Practical Tips

Media

NEWSPAPERS AND BOOKS

With the exception of the *International Herald Tribune*, which arrives on the afternoon of its publication date, you'll have to wait a day and a half for English-language newspapers to get to Helsinki. Foreign papers are sold at **Helsinki railway station** and **Akateeminen Kirjakauppa** (Academic Bookstore) at Pohjoisesplanadi 39, where you can also get books in English, and at the **larger hotels** in other cities, as well as at **main airports**.

TOURIST PUBLICATIONS

Helsinki This Week, free from the tourist office at Vantaa Airport and most hotels, is an English-language guide to cultural and tourist events in the capital.
City, a weekly newspaper with a calendar of cultural events and restaurant listings in Helsinki, publishes a quarterly edition in English available at most hotels.
Helsinki This Week is published by the Finnish Tourist office and available at most hotels.

RADIO AND TELEVISION

For news in English, you can tune in to 103.7 FM in Helsinki or to Channel 1 at around 9am on weekdays. Transmission time changes with the season, so ask the tourist board for an updated schedule; they will also supply information on broadcasts in other

parts of Finland. Many hotels subscribe to British or US cable news networks.

Postal Services

Post offices are open 9am–5pm. Services include stamps, registered mail and *poste restante*. The *poste restante* address is Elielinaukio, 00100 Helsinki. It's on the railway square side of the main post office (Mannerheiminaukio 1) and is open Mon–Fri 7am–9pm, Sat 9am–6pm and Sun 11am–9pm.

Telecommunications

Finland is a world leader in telecommunications, with a highly sophisticated, deregulated phone system. Public call boxes take either coins or phonecards (on sale at most kiosks and tourist offices). The best way to call overseas cheaply is at post and telegraph offices in main cities. Look for the *Lennätin* (telecommunications) section. To make a call, use any booth with a green light and pay the cashier afterwards. You must dial 990 to get an overseas line. Hotels usually add a surcharge for calls made from your room.

MOBILE PHONES

Finland is the home of Nokia and has the world's highest ownership of mobile phones – around 60 percent of Finns own one. There are several operators; two major ones are Radiolinja and Sonera.

Business Travellers

Doing business in Finland does not differ greatly from elsewhere in Europe, with a few exceptions.
Business hours: Lunch can be as early as 11am. Offices operate from 8am to 4pm, and in summer until 3pm.
Business style: Finns tend to present things as they are, warts and all. They do not go in for exaggeration, so their way of selling things might seem a bit subdued.

Business entertaining: You are as likely to be invited on a ski outing or sailing trip as on a night out on the town. These days, Finns tend not to drink at lunch, but after-hours drinking is still *de rigueur*.
Etiquette: Finns are punctual and courteous, though formal. Hand-shakes are good for all occasions
Holidays: Try to avoid business in July and early August. Other blackout periods for business are the spring skiing break in late February (southern Finland) or early March (northern Finland), plus two weeks over Christmas and a week at Easter.

Medical Services

HOSPITALS

If you need medical treatment, almost any *Terveysasema* (health clinic) or *Sairaala* (hospital) will treat you for a nominal fee or will bill your insurance firm. All doctors speak English. Casualty is generally called *Ensiapu*. Visitors needing hospital care in Helsinki should contact the following:
For surgery and medicine:
Meilahti Hospital, Haartmaninkatu 4, Helsinki. Tel: 09 4711, or the 24-medical advice hotline *(see Emergency Numbers, page 408)*.
For serious accidents:
Helsinki University Hospitals' Töölö Hospital, Topeliuksenkatu 5, Helsinki. Tel: 09 4711.

Business Hours

Shops In larger cities generally 9am–5pm, with late-night opening on Thursday. In Helsinki, many open until 9pm on weekdays and 6pm on Saturday. Larger food stores usually open 9am–8pm weekdays and 9am–4pm on Saturday. The only really late shops are in the tunnel under the Helsinki railway station: open weekdays 10am–10pm and weekends noon–10pm.
Banks Mon–Friday 9.15am–4.15pm, *bureaux de change* open a bit later. The one at the airport opens daily 6am–11pm.

For 24-hour private medical care:
Mehiläinen, Runeberginkatu 47a, Helsinki. Tel: 09 431 4444.

PHARMACIES

A pharmacy is called *apteekki*. There is usually at least one open late at night in larger towns. In Helsinki, the Yliopiston Apteekki at Mannerheimintie 96 is open 24 hours a day.

DENTISTS

In emergencies: Dentarium, 6th Floor, 7A Mikonkatu.
Tel: 09 622 1533

Tourist Information

Finland has over 50 main tourist information offices, marked with an "i", as well as many summer tourist offices. The following are the main tourist offices, but a full list can be obtained at most offices:
Finnish Tourist Board
Eteläesplanadi 4, 00130 Helsinki. Tel: 09 4176 9300. Fax: 4176 9301. Postal address: PO Box 249, 00131 Helsinki.
Helsinki City Tourist Office
Pohjoisesplanadi 19, 00100. Helsinki. Tel: 09 169 3757. Fax: 09 169 3839.
Rovaniemi Tourist Information
Koskikatu 7, 96200 Rovaniemi. Tel: 016 346 270. Fax: 016 347 351.
Tampere City Tourist Office
Verkatehtaankatu 2, FIN-33101 Tampere. Tel: 03 3146 6800. Fax: 03 3146 6463.
Turku City Tourist Office
Aurakatu 4, 20100 Turku. Tel: 02 262 7444. Fax: 02 262 7674.

Security and Crime

Until recently, vandalism was the only noticeable sign of crime. But now lone pedestrians may encounter groups of inebriated young men looking for a challenge

Public Holidays

- **1 January** New Year's Day
- **6 January** Epiphany
- **March/April** Good Friday, Easter Sunday
- **1 May** May Day
- **May/June** Ascension Day
- **May/June** Whitsun
- **end of June** Midsummer's Eve and Day
- **early November** All Saints' Day
- **6 December** Independence Day
- **24–26 December** Christmas Eve and Day, Boxing Day

late at night. Try to walk on busy streets and keep out of their way.
There is also occasional pickpocketing on the Helsinki metro and at main railway stations. Be on your guard and avoid using these forms of transport after 11pm.

Religious Services

In Helsinki, services in English are held at the Temppeliaukio Church, and the Church in the Rock on Lutherinkatu. There is one mosque and one synagogue in Helsinki.

Disabled Travellers

Travelling should not pose big problems. The Finnish Tourist Board has a list of travel agencies that specialise in tours for the disabled traveller. Most newer buildings have access for disabled people, and the Tourist Board's *Finland Hotel Guide* indicates which hotels have access and facilities for disabled people. When ordering a taxi, specify your needs (wheelchair is *pyörätuoli*). Some city buses "kneel", making it easier to board.

Travelling with Kids

In Helsinki, the Tourist Board can provide a list of babysitters.

ATTRACTIONS

Heureka, the Finnish Science Centre (in Tikkurila 15 minutes by train from downtown Helsinki), has permanent and temporary "hands-on" exhibitions, a planetarium and an IMAX theatre. Tel: 09 85799.

There are several good spots in the Lakeland region:

The Messilä Vacation Centre, in Hollola near Lahti, features many supervised activities, including pony riding and (in winter) skiing.

The Musta and Valkea Ratsu Dollshouse and Puppet Theatre is north from Hollola, towards Hartola, on Road 52 (signposted), 19230 Onkiniemi. Tel: 03 718 6959.

The Land of the Mountain Troll, in Outokumpu, north of Savonlinna, is an amusement park and mineral and mining exhibition.

Santa Claus's Village, Rovaniemi, near the Arctic Circle. Rumour has it Santa stops off here when travelling from his secret hideaway. Open daily year round.

Åland Islands Check out the amusement park by the west harbour, Pommern ship museum at the west harbour, and Lilla Holmen bird park on the east harbour.

Emergency Numbers

Ambulance, rescue services, fire department and police 112
24-hour medical advice hotline (Helsinki only) 10023

Embassies/Consulates

UK
Itäinen Puistotie 17
Tel: 09 228 65100
US
Itäinen Puistotie 14, Helsinki
Tel: 09 171 931
CANADA
Pohjoisesplanadi 25B, Helsinki
Tel: 09 288 530
SOUTH AFRICA
Rahapajankatu 1 A 5, Helsinki
Tel: 09 686 03130

Getting Around

On Arrival

Finland's main international airport, Helsinki-Vantaa, is connected by Finnair bus to the main railway station in Helsinki. Yellow taxis are slightly cheaper than other types because they take a minimum of four passengers and take longer to reach destinations.

By Air

Finnair and Air Botnia both operate domestic flights. Fares are relatively inexpensive all year round, but particularly cheap in July. For more information, contact:
Finnair *(see page 405 for details)*
Air Botnia In Finland, tel: 020 386 000. www.airbotnia.fi

By Rail

The Finnish train network offers good services to major places such as Turku and Helsinki.

Passes
Finnrail passes are available for three, five or 10 days within a one-month period. Alternatively, you can buy a EuroDomino pass outside Finland, valid for travel within Finland for 3–8 days in one month. For information, contact:
Finnish State Railways
PB 488, 00101 Helsinki.
Tel: 0307 20 902
www.vr.fi

By Water

The Silverline and Poet's Way begins in Tampere and covers much of the western Lakelands, with tours in the Päijänne region and

over the country's largest lake, Saimaa, in eastern Finland. Many other operators run trips on the lakes. For details, contact local tourist offices, or the following:
Silverline and Poet's Way
Tel: 03 212 4804
www.silverline.com
Lake Päijänne Cruises
Tel: 014 263 447
www.paijanne-risteilythilden.fi
Roll Cruises of Kuopio
Tel: 017 182 584
www.kuopioinfo.fi
Helsinki's only real commuter island is Suomenlinna, with ferries travelling roughly every half hour.

By Bus

There are bus services on 90 percent of public roads (with 40,000 long-distance departures a day) that cover the areas that trains don't, particularly in the north.
For details about buses, contact:
Matkahuolto, tel: 0200 4000.
www.matkahuolto.fi

By Car

Finland's roads are not too plagued by traffic, although they do get very busy between the capital and the countryside on Friday and Sunday during summer.
Foreign cars entering Finland should carry a nationality sticker. In most cases, your own insurance with a green card will suffice to drive in Finland, but check ahead to be sure. If you are driving a foreign car and are involved in an accident, contact the Finnish Motor Insurers' Bureau. Tel: 09 680 401.
Pay attention to road signs showing elk and reindeer zones, as collisions with these animals are usually serious. Be especially careful at dusk when the animals are most active.

Rules of the road
● Drive on the right and overtake on the left. Exceptions are on roads marked by a triangle sign; if this is facing you, you must give right of way; if you are on a major road it is likely that the feed-in streets will

have triangles, giving you the right of way. The first vehicle to reach the roundabout (traffic circle) has right of way.
● Headlights are obligatory outside built-up areas, at dusk, at night or in bad weather (UK cars must have stickers over their lights to divert the beam).
● Seat belts are compulsory for both drivers and passengers.
● Speed limits are signposted, and range from 30 kmph (18 mph) in school zones to 100 kmph (62 mph) on motorways.
● Studded tyres are compulsory from 1 December to 28 February or when weather conditions require.
● Do not drink drive. Fines are steep and imprisonment possible.

By Taxi

Taxis run throughout the country. City centres, as well as most major airports, bus and railway stations, have stands. Otherwise, local telephone books list the number of the nearest firms (under *Taksi* in the *White Pages*). It is worth finding the closest one as taxis charge from their point of departure (and add an order fee). In a few places you can also hail a cab in the street.

By Bicycle

Finland is a good cycling country. Some hotels, holiday villages, camp sites, tourist information offices and most youth hostels hire out bicycles. The Finnish Youth Hostel Association offers planned routes – including accommodation *(see Choosing a Hotel, opposite)*.

Where to Stay

Choosing a Hotel

Hotels throughout Finland are clean and well equipped, though expensive. A good breakfast buffet is usually included and one can find bargains at the chain hotels (generally up to 60per cent of standard prices) at weekends, and in summer when they lose their business and conference trade.

Budget accommodation includes youth and family hostels, farmhouses, guesthouses, family villages, camping and various forms of self-catering. During the summer holidays, some student residences become Summer Hotels, opening on 1 June. Details of youth hostels are available from:
The Finnish Youth Hostel Association, Yrönkatu 38B, 00100 Helsinki. Tel: 09 565 7150. Fax: 09 565 71510. E-mail: info@srm.inet.fi www.srmnet.org

Local tourist offices and booking centres will provide up-to-date prices, including details of weekend and summer discounts. General information on accommodation is available from the Finnish Tourist Board in your home country, or from the head office in Helsinki *(see Tourist Information, page 407)*. Or Helsinki has its own booking centre at the railway station:
Hotel Booking Centre, Central Railway Station
Tel: 09 2288 1400.
Fax: 09 2288 1499
www.helsinkiexpert.fi

Hotel Chains

Finland has many large hotel chains of its own, as well as foreign ones. Scandic, Sokos and Cumulus offer

fairly comfortable standard services in most big towns; Radisson SAS and others have even more comfortable facilities. Most are reliable, with clean rooms and restaurants with identical menus. Some of the best known are:
Best Western Finland
Köydenpunojankatu 7, 00180 Helsinki
Tel: 08001 2010
www.bestwestern.fi
Cumulus
Restel Hotel Group
Tel: 08001 2868
www.cumulus.fi
Scandic
Tel: 08000 6969
www.scandic-hotels.com
Sokos Hotels
Tel: 020 1234 600
www.sokoshotels.fi

Discounts

A systematic way to get discounts is to enrol in the Finncheque scheme, in which some 250 hotels participate. By spending around €34 on a Finncheque, you get a night's free accommodation in these hotels.

Further details can be obtained from the Finnish Tourist Office in Helsinki *(see page 407)*.

HELSINKI

Scandic Hotel Continental
Mannerheimintie 46, 00260
Tel: 09 40551
Fax: 09 4737 2211
www.scandic-hotels.com
One of Helsinki's oldest upmarket hotels. Well-furnished rooms with all amenities, many with park views. Sauna, massage and pool.
$$$

Scandic Hotel Simonkenttä
Simonkatu 9
Tel: 09 68380
Fax: 09 683 8111
www.scandic-hotels.com
Recently opened hotel in the city
centre. Comfortably furnished;
some rooms have their own sauna
and terrace with magnificent
views. **$$$**

Sokos Hotel Klaus Kurki
Bulevardi 2–4, 00120
Tel: 09 43340
Fax: 09 4334 7100
www.sokoshotels.fi
On a pretty street with a popular
bar, restaurant and deli. Attracts a
modern urban crowd. **$$$**

Hotel Anna
Annankatu 1, 00120
Tel: 09 616 621
Fax: 09 602 664
www.hotelanna.com
Quiet, comfortable and centrally
located with 64 rooms with all
amenities. Excellent breakfast
buffet. **$$**

Radisson SAS Plaza
Mikonkatu 23, 00100
Tel: 09 77590
Fax: 09 7759 7100
www.radisson.com
All modern amenities. **$$**

Sokos Hotel Torni
Yrjönkatu 26, 00100
Tel: 09 433 60
Fax: 09 4336 7100
www.sokoshotels.fi
Gracious 13-storey hotel with an
older Art Deco-style section. **$$**

Academica
Hietaniemenkatu 14, 00100
Tel: 09 1311 4334
Fax: 09 441 201
www.hostelacademica.fi
Basic summer hotel providing
small, modern rooms with their
own kitchen. Family rooms
available. **$**

Eurohostel
Linnankatu 9, 00160
Tel: 09 622 0470
Fax: 09 655 044
www.eurohostel.fi
Located on Katajanokka Island by
the ferry terminals, this no-frills
hostel has shared facilities
including kitchen, laundry, sauna
and café. **$**

THE SOUTH

Hanko

Pensionat Garbo
Raatimiehenkatu 8, 10900
Tel/Fax: 019 248 7897
Like a Hollywood museum – each
themed room features a star from
the silver screen. **$$**

Villa Maija
Appelgrenintie 7, 10900 Hanko
Tel: 019 248 2900
Fax: 019 248 3900
This fine 19th-century villa is one of
many on this attractive street. **$$**

Kotka

Sokos Hotel Seurahuone
Keskuskatu 21, 48100
Tel: 05 35 035
Fax: 05 350 0450
www.sokoshotels.fi
This very central hotel has superb
rooms and a fine restaurant. **$$$**

Naantali

Naantali Spa & Congress Hotel
21100 Naantali
Tel: 02 445 5100
Fax: 02 445 5101
www.naantalispa.fi
In a charming seaside town near
Turku, this unique hostelry offers
luxury in a yacht next to the spa. **$$**

Turku

Scandic Hotel Marina Palace
Linnankatu 32, 20100
Tel: 02 336 300
Fax: 02 336 32211
www.scandic-hotels.com
Picturesque riverside spot, with all
amenities and attractive rooms. Bar,
restaurants, meeting rooms. **$$$**

Quality Hotel Ateljee
Humalistonkatu 7, 20100
Tel: 02 233 6111
Fax: 02 233 6699
www.choicehotels.fi
Designed by Alvar Aalto. Two of the
230 well-equipped rooms contain
furniture by the master. Many
artists display their works here. **$$**

Scandic Hotel Plaza Turku
Yliopistonkatu 29
Tel: 02 33200
Fax: 02 332 0111
www.scandic-hotels.com
Designed in 1929 by Erik

Bryggman, a friend of Alvar Aalto,
this hotel has 107 comfortable and
simply styled rooms. Good
restaurant and popular bar. **$$$**

Park Hotel
Rauhankatu 1, 20100
Tel: 02 273 2555
Fax: 02 251 9696
www.parkhotelturku.fi
This elegant Jugenstil building
(1902) was once a private mansion.
Each of the well-furnished rooms is
different, some with a park view. **$$**

Turku City Hostel
Linnankatu 39
Tel: 02 262 7680
Fax: 02 262 7675
E-mail: hoteltk@saunalahti.fi
A reasonably priced alternative
within walking distance of sights. **$**

Best Western Hotel Seaport
Matkustajasatama (Passenger
Harbour), 20100
Tel: 02 283 3000
Fax: 02 283 3100
E-mail: hotel.seaport@kolumbus.fi
By the castle, a 19th-century
warehouse with red-brick facade in
original neo-Gothic style with
beautiful wooden beams inside. **$**

Price Guide

Price categories are based on
the average cost (including tax)
of a double room with breakfast.

$$$	215–285 euros
$$	145–215 euros
$	70–145 euros

LAKELAND

Imatra

Scandic Hotel Imatran Valtionhotelli
Torkkelinkatu 2, 55100
Tel: 05 68881
Fax: 05 688 8888
E-mail: imatra@scandic-hotels.com
Art Nouveau castle, next to the
Imatra rapids. **$$$**

Jyväskylä

Hotelli Yöpuu
Yliopistonkatu 23, 40100
Tel: 014 333 900
Fax: 014 620 588
www.hotelliyopuu.fi
Best of this chain. **$$$**

Kuopio
Scandic Hotel Kuopio
Satamakatu 1
Tel: 017 195 111
Fax: 017 195 2211
www.scandic-hotels.com
This large hotel on the waterfront is
one of the finest in town. **$$$**
Sokos Hotel Puijonsarvi
Minna Canthinkatu 16, 70100
Tel: 017 170 111
Fax: 017 170 117
E-mail: sales.puijonsarvi.sok.fi
www.sokoshotels.fi
Modern, pleasant ambience. **$$$**
Spa Hotel Rauhalahti
Katiskaniementie 8, 70700
Tel: 017 473 473
Fax: 017 473 470
E-mail: myynti@rauhalahti.com
This fine spa hotel includes a wing
with budget apartments. **$–$$**

Lappeenranta
Scandic Hotel Patria
Kauppakatu 21, 53100
Tel: 05 677 511
Fax: 05 451 2441
www.scandic-hotels.com
Modern hotel close to the harbour
and fortress area; 130 rooms,
restaurants and saunas. **$$$**

Punkaharju
Punkaharjun Valtionhotelli
58450 Punkaharju 2
Tel: 015 739 611
Fax: 015 441 784
E-mail: punkaharjun.myynti@
lomaliitto.fi
Wooden Russian-style villa with
lots of atmosphere and 24 rooms.
$$

Savonlinna
Spa Hotel Casino
Kasinosaari, 57130
Tel: 015 739 5430
Fax: 015 272 524
E-mail: casino.myynti@
svlkylpylaitos.fi.
Large complex, on an island. Cheap
hostel beds in summer. **$$$**
Perhehotelli Hospitz
Linnankatu 20, 57130
Tel: 015 515 661
Fax: 015 515 120
Cosy, family-run hotel. Often fully
booked in summer. **$$**

Tampere
Cumulus Koskikatu
Koskikatu 5, 33100
Tel: 03 242 4111
Fax: 03 242 4399
E-mail: www.cumulus.fi
Modern with good bar and food.
$$
Sokos Hotel Tammer
Satakunnankatu 13, 33100
Tel: 03 262 6265
Fax: 03 262 6266
www.sokoshotels.fi
Dramatic hotel, part Art Deco. Set
in a green, hilly district. **$$**
Hotel Victoria
Itsenäisyydenkatu 1, 33100
Tel: 03 242 5111
Fax: 03 242 5100
www.hotelvictoria.fi
Simple hostel with a lively bar and
restaurant. **$** (group discounts)

WEST COAST

Oulu
Holiday Club Oulun Eden
Nallikari, 90500
Tel: 08 884 2000
Fax: 08 554 4103
www.holidayclub.fi
Spa facilities in a beach area. **$$$**

KARELIA

Joensuu
Sokos Hotel Kimmel
Itäranta 1, 80100
Tel: 013 277 111
Fax: 013 277 2112
www.sokoshotels.fi
The town's liveliest evening spot.
Request a quiet room. **$$$**

LAPLAND

Rovaniemi
Rantasipi Pohjanhovi
Pohjanpuistikko 2, 96200
Tel: 016 33 711
Fax: 016 313 997
www.restel.fi
E-mail: pohjanhovi.rantasipi@restel.fi
Legendary luxury riverside hotel
with swimming pool, nightclub and
casino. **$$$**

Where to Eat

What to Eat

Finnish cuisine has broadened and
improved enormously in recent
years. The wild game dishes are a
real treat and are usually served
with exquisite mushroom and berry
sauces. In summer, you are strongly
recommended to try *ravut* (crayfish).
Crayfish feasts are often held in
hotel restaurants and include lots
of *schnapps* and songs.

Finns tend to eat a large hot
lunch, then a smaller cold meal in
the evening. Dining out has become
more popular, with Italian, Chinese
and French restaurants in almost all
major towns. The best Russian
cuisine outside of Russia is found
in Helsinki.

Where to Eat

In the past, it was difficult to get a
really cheap meal in Finland, but
you can find places where you will
definitely get value for money. Fixed-
price lunches are often very good
deals and are usually advertised on
boards outside restaurants. The
Sokos and Stockmann department
stores have excellent food halls;
otherwise, for snacks there are
more and more cafés sprouting up
that supply sandwiches, quiche,
soups and salads at reasonable
prices.

Many hotels (particularly Sokos
and Scandic) in Helsinki, Turku,
Tampere and elsewhere have good
places to eat, ranging from gourmet
restaurants to wine bars and cafés.

Restaurant Listings

Restaurants are listed in
alphabetical order by region, with
the most expensive first.

HELSINKI

Bellevue
Rahapajankatu 3. Tel: 09 179 560
Superb cuisine in Helsinki's oldest
and most refined Russian
restaurant. **$$$**
George
Kalevankatu 17. Tel: 09 647 662
Excellent, with Finnish ingredients
served elegantly and originally. **$$$**
Pääkonttori (Radisson SAS)
Mikonkatu 23. Tel: 09 775 96001
Seasonal Finnish ingredients
prepared in a refined manner. The
Bistro offers more casual fare. **$$$**
Walhalla
Suomenlinna. Tel: 09 668 552
Open in summer, this restaurant is
set in the old fortress. Seafood and
game are specialities. **$$$**
Babushka Ira
Uudenmaankatu 28
Tel: 09 680 1405
Charming restaurant with adjoining
café serving an extensive buffet of
Russian delicacies. **$$**
Kynsilaukka Garlic Restaurant
Fredrikinkatu 22. Tel: 09 651 939
Specialises in garlicky food. **$$**
Lappi
Annankatu 22. Tel: 09 645 550
Authentic Lapland food. **$$**
Maxill
Korkeavuorenkatu 4
Tel: 09 638 873
Has a loyal clientele who come for
the consistently good menu. **$$**
Namaskaar
Bulevardi 6A. Tel: 09 6220 1155
Top-quality Indian dishes on
Helsinki's main street. **$$**
Bar Tapasta
Uudenmaankatu 13. Tel: 09 640 724
Where the young and hip come for
snacks, pasta and good wine. **$**
KarlJohan
Yrjönkatu 21. Tel: 09 612 1121
Traditional Finnish dishes at fair
prices. Homely atmosphere. **$**

THE SOUTH

Turku
Summer in Turku is not complete
without a session in one of the
dozen boat restaurants on the River
Aurajoki.

Enkeliravintola
Kauppiaskatu 16. Tel: 02 231 9088
Fine restaurant serving delicious
food. Desserts are excellent.
$$$
Pinella
Porthaninpuisto. Tel: 02 251 0001
Popular place serving delicious
crêpes and seafood. Just below is
Ribs, serving steaks and grilled ribs
in a cave-like area. **$$**
Samppalinna
Itäinen Rantakatu. Tel: 02 311 165
Continental cuisine. **$$**
Panimoravintola Herman
Läntinen Rantakatu 37
Tel: 02 230 3333
This brewery-restaurant serves
a popular inexpensive lunch
buffet on its ground level, while
upstairs more gourmet food is
offered. **$–$$**
Pizzeria Dennis
Linnankatu 17
Tel: 02 469 1191
Tasty and authentic pizzas. **$**

Price Guide

Price categories are based on an
average cost per head of a three-
course meal (excluding drinks but
with tax):
$$$ more than 35 euros
$$ 15–35 euros
$ under 15 euros

LAKELAND

Kuopio
The small *muikku* (whitefish) is a
speciality in Kuopio, although more
famous is the *kalakukko* (loaf of rye
bread crust filled with fish and pork)
that can be found at the market.
Musta Lammas
Satamakatu 4. Tel: 017 5810 458
A pleasant restaurant, considered
Kuopio's best. **$$$**
Vapaasatama Sampo
Kauppakatu 13.
Tel: 017 261 4677
Informal; serving excellent fish. **$$**
Wanha Satama
Tel: 017 197 304
Rustic and lively; located by the
passenger harbour. Serves tasty
muikku. **$$**

SAVONLINNA

The market is busy and popular.
Prices are steep during the opera
festival, but the market is also at
its liveliest then.
Majakka
Satamakatu 11. Tel: 015 531 456
A popular place near the market
serving good fish and meat. **$$**
Sillansuu
Verkkosaarenkatu 1
Tel: 015 531 451
Popular pub near Market Bridge. **$$**

Tampere
Astor
Aleksis Kivenkatu 26
Tel: 03 260 5700
Live piano music every night. **$$$**
Hella & Huone
Salhojankatu 48
Tel: 03 253 2440.
Genuine French gourmet restaurant.
$$$
Näsinneula
Särkänniemi
Tel: 03 248 8234
Revolving restaurant high in the
Näsinneula Observation Tower
serving fine Finnish cuisine. **$$$**
Eetvartti
Sumeliuksenkatu 16
Tel: 03 3155 5300
Run by the Pirkanmaa Hotel and
Restaurant School. High-quality food
cooked by the students. **$**
Plevna
Itäinenkatu 8. Tel: 03 260 1200
Lively pub/café specialising in
steaks, sausages and beers. **$**
Salud
Tuomiokirkonkatu 19
Tel: 03 366 4460
Popular tapas restaurant with a fine
wine selection. **$**

WEST COAST

Vaasa
Gustav Wasa
Raastuvankatu 24. Tel: 06 326 9200
Cellar restaurant serving excellent
meat portions and some fish. **$$$**
Kanttarellis
Kauppapuistikko 15
Tel: 06 361 0000
Worth visiting for the decor. **$$**

LAPLAND

Rovaniemi

Restaurant Puolukka
Valtakatu 20. Tel: 016 310 222
Popular and central, specialising in
fish with some international fare. **$$**

Drinking Notes

Alcohol is expensive in Finland due
to high taxes.
Beer The Finnish *tuoppi* is about 30
percent larger than the British pint;
and a *pieni tuoppi* is about two-
thirds of that quantity. If you don't
specify, you will be served a
relatively, strong (number 4, which
is 4.5 percent alcohol) beer. You
must say if you want the 3.5
percent beer, known as *keski-olut*
(medium). Number 1 beer *(ykkss-
olut)* is the weakest, just over 1
percent proof.
Wine in Finland is imported and
very costly in restaurants, but there
is more choice in Alko outlets (the
state alcohol monopoly).

Where to buy

Spirits and wine can be bought only
from Alko shops (Stockmann
department store in Helsinki has a
unit on the ground floor). Medium-
and lower-alcohol beer can be
bought in supermarkets.

Licensing laws

A restaurant marked *B-oikeudet*
is licensed only to serve beer
and wine. Most bars are open
until at least midnight in Helsinki,
and some stay open until
3am or 4am.

Culture

Museums

Finland is a country of small
museums, the grandest of which is
the Ateneum in Helsinki. The Helsinki
Card includes free entrance to many
museums as well as free public
transport. Turku recently introduced a
similar card. Opening hours are
reduced in winter, and most
museums close on Monday.

Classical Music/Opera

Most larger cities have a steady
round of concerts throughout the
year, but music festivals abound in
summer. The most famous, in July,
are: **Savonlinna Opera Festival** at
Olavinlinna Castle, in eastern
Finland; **Kuhmo Chamber Music
Festival**, also in eastern Finland;
and **Kaustinen Folk Festival**, in
western Finland. The festivals have
Finnish and international stars.
    Opera has a great following, and
much of it features Finnish
composers and performers.

HELSINKI

In late summer Helsinki has its
Juhlaviikot (Festival Weeks)
featuring broad-ranging programmes
with artists from Finland and
abroad. Information from: Helsinki
Festival Office, Casipalatsi,
Mannerheimintie 22–24, 00100
Helsinki, Tel: 09 6126 5100;
www.helsinginjuhlaviikot.fi
    Also, try the weekday evening
concerts at the **Temppeliaukio**
(Church in the Rock) in Töölö,
Helsinki.
    During the rest of the year, the
Finlandia Concert Hall features
major performances. The national

opera (and ballet) company perform
at the Opera House.

TAMPERE

Since 1975 the city has held an
international choir festival each
year and the **Tampere Biennale** is a
festival of new Finnish music. The
Tampere Hall is a prestigious
venue. For information contact:
Tel: 03 243 4500.

TURKU

Turku is a lively musical city, and
the **Turku Musical Festival** in
August is one of the oldest in
Finland, attracting visiting
composers and international
musicians. Further information from
the Foundation for the Turku Music
Festivals, Uudenmaankatu 1,
20500 Turku.
Tel: 02 2511 162.

Theatre

Tampere rivals Helsinki and Turku
for year-round theatrical events but
most performances are in Finnish.
One exception is the **Pyynikki
Outdoor Summer Theatre** where
you can see plays from mid-June to
mid-August, with synopses in
English. Booking is necessary.
Tel: 03 216 0300.
    The **Tampere Theatre Festival** in
August includes many international
companies. Tel: 03 214 0992.

Cinema

Finns do not dub foreign films, and
you can enjoy as good a selection
of movies here as in any other
European city of moderate size.
    In Helsinki, there are large
complexes like the **Tennispalatsi**
and **Forum** as well as intimate art
houses like the **Orion Film Archive**,
Eerikinkatu 15 (tel: 09 615 40201)
and the **Andorra**, Eerikinkatu 11
(tel: 09 612 3117).
    In Turku and Tampere, there are
several **multiscreen cinemas** in the
city centres.

Nightlife

Pubs, Bars and Clubs

Pub crawling remains popular and there are several clubs that attract the best pop bands. Occasionally a good jazz or rock act will make it to Helsinki's **Hartwall Arena**, but the city is certainly not on the itinerary of most major performers.

The minimum age for drinking alcohol is 18 but some clubs have an age limit of 21. Entrance fees vary. It is normal to pay the doorman/bouncer a fee (around €1-1.50) to hang up your coat.

Nightclubs and discos have become more popular in recent years. The popular **Copacabana** salsa club, the **Helsinki Club** and **Tenth Floor** dance bar at the Hotel Vaakuna in Helsinki are good examples. For good nightlife try:

HELSINKI

Highlight Café
Frederikinkatu 42. A sports-theme pub with American-style food.
Corona Bar
Eerikinkatu 11. Tel: 09 642 002
Attracts a young hip crowd who come to talk, drink beer, eat toasted sandwiches and play pool.
Kuu
Töölönkatu 27. Tel: 09 2709 0973
An intimate, older, small bar serving excellent Finnish cuisine. The adjacent Kuu Kuu bar is a hangout of Finnish writers and artists.
O'Malleys
Yrjönkatu 28. Tel: 09 13 11 31
Irish, mellow, small and usually crowded tavern. Some live music.
Storyville
Museokatu 8. Tel: 09 408 007
A cosy jazz club to have a late drink. There is a cover charge.

Tavastia
Urho Kekkosenkatu 4.
Tel: 09 69 48 51 1.
This university-owned club attracts some of Helsinki's best live music.
Torni
Yrjönkatu 26. Tel: 09 13 11 31
Try the Ateljee Bar on the 13th floor of this hotel for light meals and drinks (outdoor seating in summer) offering the best view in Helsinki.
Vanha Kellari
Vanha Yliopisto, Mannerheimintie 3.
Tel: 09 68 44 90 0
The students' union-owned Vanha is set in a Neo-Classical building and flows with the traffic of devoted beer-drinkers year-round. Occasional live music.
Zetor
Kaivopiha. Tel: 09 666 966
This "tractor-style" rock 'n' roll disco has to be seen to be believed. Experience the surrealism of the Finnish countryside.

TAMPERE

Nightlife is very evident on the main street, **Hämeenkatu**. Bar hopping is easy, although more "traditional" pubs are elsewhere, such as **Salhojankadun Pub** on Salhojankatu, and **Ohranjyvä** at Näsilinnankatu 15. Locally brewed beer is available at **Plevna** (Itäinenkatu 8) and **Wanha Posti** (Hämeenkatu 13A).

TURKU

Panimoravintola Koulu
Eerikinkatu 18. Tel: 02 274 5757
This former school has a brewery and the classrooms are now pubs or restaurants.
Old Bank
Aurakatu 3. Tel: 02 274 5700
Once a very fine bank, this pub serves more varieties of beer than any other in town.
Uusi Apteekki
Kaskenkatu 1. Tel: 02 250 2595
Literally "new pharmacy", this pub is set in an old chemist.

Sport

Participant Sports

Orienteering, golf, hunting, fishing, tennis, badminton and squash are a few of the popular sports. For details on any sport, contact:
Suomen Valtakunnan Urheiluliitto (The National Sports Association), Radiokatu 20, 00240 Helsinki. Tel: 09 348 121. Fax: 09 348 12602.

Cycling
The countryside is ideal for cyclists: flat on the west coast leading to gently rolling hill areas. For suggested cycle routes, contact:
The Finnish Youth Hostel Association (see page 409).

Sailing
Most harbours have guest marinas where you can dock for reasonable overnight fees. Canoeing is also popular in the Lakelands region.

Spectator Sports

Popular spectator sports include ski jumping, sailing and hockey.

In early July the Hanko sailing regatta takes place off Finland's south coast. Kotka also sponsors a yearly Tall Ships event. The biggest inland sailing regatta is on Lake Päijänne, in July. Details from the **Finnish Yachting Association** Vattuniemenkatu 13, 00210 Helsinki. Tel: 020 733 8881. Fax: 020 733 8888.

In mid-June the Finlandia Canoeing Relay is held in the Lakelands (the venue changes annually).

In mid-February, the 75-km (47-mile) Finlandia Ski Race is one of the top events. For details contact:
Finlandia Ski Race Office Urheilukeskus, 15110 Lahti. Tel: 03 816 813. Fax: 03 751 2079.

Shopping

FINNISH DESIGN

Choose from jewellery, woodwork, clothing, glass or kitchenware. **Lapponia Aarikka** and **Kaleva Koru** jewellery are particularly Finnish, the first being a mainly contemporary collection and the second a collection based on designs from the Finnish epic poem *Kalevala*, rendered in silver, gold, and brass. Aarikka also supplies some fine woodwork products, including chopping boards, Christmas decorations, toys and wooden jewellery.

The most impressive ceramic work is commissioned by **Arabia**, one of the older Finnish firms. Its factory (about 20 minutes' tram ride from Helsinki centre) has a small museum upstairs, and pristine goods as well as seconds on sale downstairs. **Pentik** is known for its ceramics as well as beautifully crafted leather clothing.

Iittala makes beautiful glassware at its factory. **Marimekko** is the quintessential Finnish clothing designer, with its typical brightly coloured fabrics for men, women and children, as well as more elegant clothing for women and textiles for home use. These companies can be found both in their own stores and department stores in most Finnish towns of any size, including three shops on the Pohjoisesplanadi in Helsinki.

HELSINKI

Apart from mainstream department stores, shopping centres (**Aleksi 13**, **Forum** and **Kämp Galleria**) and boutique shopping in Helsinki, there are several market squares that sell both fresh food and a range of other consumer goods of greatly varying quality, from second-hand clothes and records to designer jewellery, Sami mittens and fur hats.

Kauppatori is the main market, followed by **Hietalahdentori** and **Hakaniementori**, all near the centre. Note that markets have extended hours in summer and are open until about 8pm, but close briefly from about 2pm. Otherwise, **the Esplanade** is the hub of shopping delights in Helsinki.

TURKU

Turku has its own **Stockmann** store at Yliopistonkatu 22. Also on Yliopistonkatu are **Pentik** (No. 25), famous for ceramics, and **Aarikka** (No. 27), for handmade wooden crafts and decorations.

For crafts, look into **Sylvi Salonen**, specialising in linens and decorative crafts at Yliopistonkatu 29. The markets are generally open daily except Sunday. Turku's **open-air market** features flowers, fish, fruit, vegetables and some crafts. The **indoor market hall** offers all that and more, including bread, cheese, coffee, tea, spices, snacks and many handicrafts.

TAMPERE

Tampere has most of the medium-sized department stores found in Helsinki and Turku, as well as a host of smaller boutiques. A good collection is at **Kehräsaari Boutique Centre**, Laukontori 1, Keräsaari, in a converted textile mill.

Visit the **Verkaranta Arts and Crafts Centre** at Verkatehtaankatu 2 for a good selection of handicrafts and toys. The main **Tampere Market Hall**, at Hämeenkatu 19, is open Mon–Fri 8am–6pm, Sat 8am–4pm.

Language

good morning *hyvää huomenta*
good day *hyvää päivää*
good evening *hyvää iltaa*
today *tänään*
tomorrow *huomenna*
yesterday *eilen*
hello *päivää* or *terve*
How do you do? *kuinka voit*
goodbye *näkemiin* or *hei hei*
yes *kyllä* or *joo*
no *ei*
thank you *kiitos*
What time is it? *paljonko kello on?*
It is... (the time is...) *kello on...*
Could I have your name? *saisinko nimesi?*
My name is... *nimeni on...*
Do you speak English? *puhutko englantia?*
I only speak English *puhun vain englantia*
Can I help you? *voinko auttaa sinua?*

chemist *apteekki*
hospital *sairaala*
doctor *lääkäri*
police station *poliisilaitos*
parking *paikoitus*
phrase book *turistien sanakirja*
dictionary *sanakirja*
car *auto*
bus *bussi*
coach *linja-auto*
train *juna*
aeroplane *lentokone*
Cheers! *kippis!*
to rent *vuokrata*
for sale *myytävänä*
free, no charge *ilmainen*
room to rent *vuokrattavana huone*

I do not understand *en ymmärrä*
I do not know *en tiedä*
Could I have the key? *saisko avaimen?*

Directions

How do I get to..? *miten pääsen..?*
Where is...? *missä on...?*
right *oikealla*
to the right *oikealle*
left *vasemmalla*
to the left *vasemmalle*
straight on *suoraan*

Eating Out

breakfast *aamiainen*
lunch *lounas*
dinner *illallinen*
to eat *syödä*
to drink *juoda*
I would like to order... *haluaisin tilata...*
Could I have the bill? *saisko laskun?*

Signs

Toilet *vessa*
Gentlemen *miehet*
Ladies *naiset*
Vacant *vapaa*
Engaged *varattu*
Entrance *sisäänkäynti*
Exit *uloskääynti*
No entry *pääsy kielletty*
Open *avoinna, auki*
Closed *suljettu, kiinni*
Push *työnnä*
Pull *vedä*

Days of the Week

Monday *maanantai*
Tuesday *tiistai*
Wednesday *keskiviikko*
Thursday *torstai*
Friday *perjantai*
Saturday *launantai*
Sunday *sunnuntai*

Shopping

money *raha*
How much does this cost?
paljonko tämä maksaa?
It costs... *se maksaa...*

handicraft *käsityö*
grocers *ruoka kauppa*
shop *kauppa*
food *ruoka*
to buy *ostaa*
off-licence *alko*

Clothes/Laundry

clothes *vaatteet*
overcoat *päällystakki*
jacket *takki*
suit *puku*
shoes *kengät*
skirt *hame*
blouse *pusero*
jersey *puuvilla or villapusero*
launderette *pesula*
dry cleaning *kemiallinen pesu*
dirty *likainen*
clean *puhdas*
stain *tahra*
A Guide to Finnish Architecture by

Numbers

1	*yksi*
2	*kaksi*
3	*kolme*
4	*neljä*
5	*viisi*
6	*kuusi*
7	*seitsemän*
8	*kahdeksan*
9	*yhdeksän*
10	*kymmenen*
11	*yksitoista*
12	*kaksitoista*
13	*kolmetoista*
14	*neljätoista*
15	*viisitoista*
16	*kuusitoista*
17	*seitsemäntoista*
18	*kahdeksantoista*
19	*yhdeksäntoista*
20	*kaksikymmentä*
30	*kolmekymmentä*
40	*neljäkymmentä*
50	*viisikymmentä*
60	*kuusikymmentä*
70	*seitsemänkymmentä*
80	*kahdeksankymmentä*
90	*kahdeksankymmentä*
100	*sata*
200	*kaksisataa*
1,000	*tuhat*

Further Reading

General Interest

Kaipia & Putkonen (Otava).
A fascinating town-by-town guide to buildings, with plenty of photographs and illustrations.
Facts about Finland (Otava). The most comprehensive coverage of Finland's history and culture, by a range of Finnish authors.
Food from Finland by Anna-Maija and Juha Tanttu (Otava). An excellent guide to Finnish food, including recipes and colourful features on raw ingredients, such as berries and fungi.
A Brief History of Finland by Matti Klinge (Otava, 1999). This revised edition offers a concise account of the nation's history.
The Maiden Who Rose from the Sea by Helena Henderson (Hisarlik Press). An entertaining collection of Finnish folk tales.

Scandinavia Connection *(see page 384 for contact details)* offer a selection of books in English about Finland; categories include art & architecture, nature and culture.

Scandinavia

Scandinavia by Tony Griffiths. Two hundred years' worth of Scandinavian history, culture and art in this highly readable volume.
In Forkbeard's Wake: Coasting Around Scandinavia by Ben Nimmo. A very lively and up-to-date account of sailing around the region. With an array of colourful and amusing characters.
The Cambridge History of Scandinavia Vol. 1 by Knut Helle et al. An academic look at the early years of Scandinavian history to 1520 with further volumes to come.
Kitchen of Light by Andreas Viestad. A Wonderful collection of

Scandinavian recipes that will reassure you that it's not all herring and anchovies.

Scandinavian Design by Charlotte Fiel. A survey *circa* 1900 to the present day that illustrates virtually all areas of design: furniture, glass, ceramics, textiles, jewellery, lighting, industrial and product design.

The Oxford Illustrated History of the Vikings by Peter Sawyer (ed). This colourful book, by leading international scholars, takes a considered look at the latest research and presents a compelling picture of the Vikings and their age.

Other Insight Guides

More than 500 Insight Guides, Insight Pocket Guides, Insight Pocket Guides and Insight Maps cover every continent.

Insight Guide titles in the region covered by this book include *Finland, Norway, Denmark* and *Sweden*. **Insight Pocket Guides**, with an itinerary-based approach, include *Oslo & Bergen*. **Insight Compact Guides** to the region include *Finland, Norway, Denmark* and *Copenhagen*. **Insight Flexi Maps** are specially laminated, making them durable, weatherproof and easy to fold. Scandinavian titles include *Norway, Copenhagen* and *Stockholm*.

Feedback

We do our best to ensure the information in our books is as accurate and up-to-date as possible. The books are updated on a regular basis, using local contacts, who painstakingly add, amend and correct as required. However, some mistakes and omissions are inevitable and we are ultimately reliant on our readers to put us in the picture.

We would welcome your feedback on any details related to your experiences using the book "on the road". Maybe we recommended a hotel that you liked (or another that you didn't), as well as interesting new attractions, or facts and figures you have found out about the country itself. The more details you can give us (particularly with regard to addresses, e-mails and telephone numbers), the better.

We will acknowledge all contributions, and we'll offer an Insight Guide to the best letters received.

Please write to us at:
Insight Guides
PO Box 7910
London SE1 1WE
United Kingdom
Or send e-mail to:
insight@apaguide.co.uk

ART & PHOTO CREDITS

Denmark

*Numbers in italics refer to
photographs*

a

Absalon of Roskilde, Bishop 31, 98
Æbelø 126
Ærø 126
Ærøskøbing 126
agriculture 44
Åkirkeby 120
  Åkirke (church) 120
Ålborg 134
  Jomfru Ane Gade 134
  Stenhus (Stone House) 134
Almindingen forest 119
Als Island 131
amber 133
Ancher, Anna and Michael 52–3,
134
  The Girl in the Kitchen (Anna
   Ancher) *50*
Andersen, Hans Christian 36, 51,
100, 104, 116, 117, 123, *127*
  Hans Christian Andersen
   Museum (Odense) *122*, 124
  *Shadow Picture of a Journey to
   the Harz Mountains and
   Saxony* 127
  The Emperor's New Clothes 51
  The Improvisatore 127
  The Little Match Girl 117
  The Little Mermaid 51
  The Nightingale 127
  The Princess and the Pea 51,
   127
  The Tinder Box 117, 127
  The Ugly Duckling 51, 116
Århus 129
  Århus Kunstmuseum (Museum of
   Art) 129
  Den Gamle By (Old Town) 129
  Domkirken (Cathedral of St
   Clement) 129
  Rådhus (City Hall) 129
art and crafts 51–3
  in Bornholm 119
  CoBrA movement 53, 131, 132
  Danish Design 54, 99, *110–11*
  Danish Design Centre
   (Copenhagen) 99, 110
  in Funen 123
  Royal Academy of Fine Arts
   (Copenhagen) 102
  Scandinavian design 54
  Skagen painters 52–3, 107, 134
arts and entertainment

Danish Film Institute
  (Copenhagen) 102
Det Kongelige Teater (Royal
  Theatre) (Copenhagen) 51,
  102, 103
Faroese Cultural Evening 143
Nordisk Film Kompagni 52
Royal Danish Ballet 51
Royal Danish Opera 51
Royal Danish Orchestra 51
Royal Theatre Orchestra 127
Sjællands Symphony Orchestra
  99
Aurora Borealis *see* **Northern
  Lights**
Avernakø 126

b

Bagenkop 126
Bagger, Erik 111
Balka 121
Bang, Jens 134
beaches 65–6
  Bagenkop (Langeland) 126
  Balka 121
  Dueodde 121
  Hennes Strand *135*
  Hvide Sande 133
  Køge 116
  Liseleje 115
  Marielyst (Falster) 117
  Risting (Langeland) 126
  Tisvilde 115
  in Western Jutland 133
Billund 131
  Legoland 131
Blåvands Huk (lighthouse) 133
Blixen, Karen *51*, *115*, 126
  Out of Africa 51, 115
Bogense 126
  Gyldensteen castle 126
Bohr, Niels 99
Borðoy Island 143
Bornholm 118–21
  see also individual place names
Bournonville, August 51–2
Brahe, Tycho 102

c

Caroline Matilde 35
castles and fortresses
  Aalholm Slot (Nysted) 117
  Absalon's Old Fortress
   (Copenhagen) 97, 107
  Egeskov Slot (Funen) 125, *126*
  Gamleborg (Almindingen Skov,
   Bornholm) 118–9

Gamleborg (Paradisbakkerne,
  Bornholm) 118–9
Gavnø Slot 116
Gissfeld Slot 116
Gyldensteen (Bogense) 126
Hammershus (Bornholm) 119
Kalø Slot (Jutland) 129
Kronborg Castle (Helsingør) 35,
  115, 116
Liselund Slot 117
Nyborg Slot (Nyborg) 123
Rosenborg Slot (Copenhagen)
  97, 107
Ruins of Absalon's Old Fortress
  (Christiansborg, Copenhagen)
  107
Shackenborg Slot (Møgeltønder)
  132
Sønderborg Slot (Sønderborg)
  131
Valdemars Slot (Tåsinge) 126
Vikingeborgen Trelleborg (Viking
  fortress) 116
Christian IV 161
churches and cathedrals
  Åkirke (Åkirkeby) 120
  Alexander Nevski Russian
   Orthodox Church
   (Copenhagen) 103
  Chapel (Frederiksborg, Hillerød)
   113
  Den Tilsandede Kirke (Sand-
   Covered Church) *134*
  Domkirke (Cathedral) (Roskilde)
   115
  Domkirken (Cathedral of St
   Clement) (Århus) 129
  Frederikskirken (Marble Church)
   (Copenhagen) 103–4, *104*
  Københavns Domkirke
   (Cathedral) (Copenhagen) 101
  Østerlars Kirke (St Laurentius)
   (Gudhjem) 120
  Palace Chapel (Christiansborg,
   Copenhagen) 107
  Ribe Domkirke (Cathedral) (Ribe)
   132
  "round churches" of Bornholm
   120–21
  round church (Olsker) *118*, 120
  Sankt Petri Kirke (St Peter's)
   (Copenhagen) 100
  Skt Knuds Domkirke (Odense)
   124
  Skt Mariæ Kirke (Helsingør) 115
  Skt Nikolai Kirke (Køge) 116
  Skt Nikolai Kirke (Rønne) 120
  Vor Frelsers Kirke (Church of Our
   Saviour) (Copenhagen) 97, 108

Christiansen, Ole Kirk 131
Christiansfeld 131
climate 89, 97, 354
  of the Faroe Islands 141
  of Greenland 139
Copenhagen 77, 97–108, 113
  Absalon's Old Fortress, ruins 97, 107
  Alexander Nevski Russian Orthodox Church 103
  Amagertorv 86, 100
  Amaliehaven 104
  Amalienborg Slot (Palace) 104, 104
  Børsen (Stock Exchange) 98, 108
  Botanisk Have (Botanical Gardens) 107, 108
  canal boat trips 97, 107
  Carlsberg Brewery and stables 102, 108
  Charlottenborg 102
  Christiania 106, 108
  Christiansborg 98, 107–8
    Folketinget (House of Parliament) 107
    Kongelige Stalde & Kareter (Museum of the Royal Stables and Coaches) 108
    Palace Chapel 107
    Ridebanen 107
    Royal Reception Chambers 107
    Teatermuseet 108
    Thorvaldsens Museum 107
  Christianshavn 108
  Christianskirke 108
  Churchillparken 105
  Danish Design Centre 99, 110
  Danish Film Institute 102
  Dansk Arkitektur Center (Danish Architecture Centre) 108
  Den Hirschsprungske Samling (Hirschsprung Collection) 105, 107
  Den Lille Havfrue (Little Mermaid) 104, 105
  Det Kongelige Bibliotek (Royal Library) 105, 108
  Det Kongelige Teater (Royal Theatre) 51, 102, 103
  Fiolstræde 101
  Frederikskirken (Marble Church) 103–4, 104
  Frederiksstaden 103
  Frihavnen (Free Harbour) 105
  Frihedsmuseet (Danish Resistance Museum) 40, 105
  Gammeltorv (Old Square) 100
  Gefionspringvandet fountain 104

Georg Jensen 101
Gråbrødretorv (Greyfriars Square) 101
"Guided Walking Tour of Copenhagen" 103
Hotel d'Angleterre 102, 103
Hotel Kong Frederik 98
Hovedbanegården (Central Railway Station) 99
Illums Bolighus 101, 110
Istedgade 100
Kastellet (The Citadel) 105
Københavns Domkirke (Cathedral) 101
Købmagergade 100
Kompagnistræde 100
Konditori La Glace 100
Kongens Have 107
Kongens Nytorv (King's New Square) 102
Kunstindustrimuseet (Danish Museum of Decorative Art) 103, 110
Krystalgade 101
Latin Quarter 101
Little Mermaid see Den Lille Havfrue
Museet Louis Tussaud's 98–9
Museum Erotica 102
Nationalmuseet (National Museum) 22, 97, 100
Nyboder 105
Ny Carlsberg Glyptotek 97, 99, 100
Nyhavn 102, 103
Palace Hotel 98
Paustians Hus 105
Rådhuset 97, 98
  Jens Olsen's World Clock 98
Rådhuspladsen (City Hall Square) 98, 99
Royal Academy of Fine Arts 102
Rundetårn (Round Tower) 97, 101–2, 103
Rosenborg Slot (Castle) 97, 107
Royal Copenhagen Porcelain 101, 103
Sankt Petri Kirke (St Peter's Church) 100
shopping 97, 100–101
Slagteren ved Kultorvet (Coal Square) 101
Slotsholmen (Castle Island) 107
Sømod's Bolcher 101
Statens Museum for Kunst (National Museum for Fine Arts) 97, 105
Strandgade 108

Strøget 100
Tivoli Gardens 96, 97, 98
Tobaksmuseet (Tobacco Museum) 101
tourist information 97, 100
transport 97
University of Copenhagen 101
Use It 100
Vesterbro 99–100
Vestergade 100
Vor Frelsers Kirke (Church of Our Saviour) 97, 108
culture and traditions
  of the Faroe Islands 143
  Greenland traditional costume 138

d

"Daisy Routes" 126
Dinesen, Isak see Blixen, Karen
Dreyer, Carl Th. 52
Dueodde 121
Dybbøl 131–2
  Dybbøl Mill and museum 132

e

Ebeltoft 129
Eckersberg, C.W. 52
economy 43–4
Egeskov Slot 125
  maze 125
  Veteranmuseum (Veteran Motor Museum) 125
Eiríksson, Leifur 26
Eiríksson, Thorvaldur 26
Elmelund 117
Enniberg 142
Eriksen, Edvard 104
Ertholmene Islands 120
  Christiansø 120
  Frederiksø 120
Esbjerg 133
Esturoy 143

f

Fåborg 125
  Fåborg Museum for Fynsk Kunst 125
  Klokketårnet 125
Falster 117
  see also individual place names
Fanefjord 117
Fanø 133
Faroe Islands 77, 140, 141–3
  see also individual place names
Fensmark 116

Holmegård Danish Glassvæk (glassworks) and museum 116
festivals and events
Århus festival week 129
Bornholm Classical Music Festival 120
Folk Music Festival (Tórshavn, Faroe Islands) 143
Horsens Middle Ages Festival 131
Midsummer's Eve celebrations 117
Summartonar Music Festival (Faroe Islands) 143
Tórshavnar Jazz, Folk and Blues Festival (Faroe Islands) 143
Viking life re-enactments 132
food and drink 62–3, 363
alcohol restrictions in Faroe Islands 143
aquavit/schnapps 62, 134, 143
Bornholm specialities 121
Greenland specialities 139
smørrebrød 61–2
Sønderborg sausages 131
Fredensborg (palace) 115
Freydis 26
Funen 28, 123–7
see also individual place names
cycling tours 123
Fyrkat 28, *29*, 132

g

Gammel Skagen (Old Skagen) 134
Gilleleje 115
Hos Karen og Marie restaurant 115
Greenland 40, 77, 137–9
see also individual place names
climate 137
tourism 137
Grenen 134
Gudhjem 120
Bornholms Model Jernbane (model train) Museum 120
Østerlars Kirke (St Laurentius) 120

h

Hærvejen cycle and walking trail 69
Harald Bluetooth 26, 132
Haslev 116
Hastings 25–6
Helsingør 115
Carmelite Kloster (Convent) 115
Kronborg Castle 35, 115, 116
Skt Mariæ Kirke 115
Henne 133

Henne Kirkeby Kro 133
Henningsen, Poul 110
Hillerød 115
Frederiksborg 115
Chapel *113*
Natural History Museum 115
Himmelbjerget (Sky Mountain) 131
Hobro 132
Hobro Museum 132
Holberg, Ludvig 51
Høm, Poul 121
Horsens 131
Høst, Oluf 120
Hov 131
Hoyvik 143
Fornminnisavn (National Museum) 143
Humlebæk 115
Louisiana Museum for Moderne Kunst (Louisiana Museum of Modern Art) 52, 115
Hvide Sande 133

i

industry
film 52
fishing 61, 141
oil 44
Ishoj 116
Arken Museet for Moderne Kunst *116*
Ittoqqortoormiit 137
Ivar the Boneless 26

j

Jacobsen, Arne 54, 110, 111, 129
Jelling 28, 132
Jellingstenene (Jelling Stones) *132*
Johansen, Viggo 134
Jorn, Asger 53, 131
Jutland 28, 53, 129–34
see also individual place names

k

Kangerlussuaq 137
Keldby 117
Kerteminde 123, 124
Johannes Larsen Museum 124
Kierkegaard, Søren 36, 51, 100
Kirkjubøur 142, 143
Smoke Room 143
Klaksvík 143
Nordoya Fornminnisavn (North Islands Museum) 143
Klampenborg 113

Klampenborg Dyrhavn (deer park) 113
Bakken fun fair 113
Ordrupgaard 113
Peter Lieps' restaurant 113
Køge 116
Hugo's Vinkælder inn 116
Skt Nikolai Kirke 116
Knud of Denmark and England 207, 209
Knud II 124
Knuthenborg safari park 117
Kolding 131
Koldinghus Slot 131
Kunstmuseet Traphold (Trapholt Museum of Art) 131
Kristian II *31*, 33, 34, 234
Kristian IV 34, 98
Kristian VII 34
Krøyer, P.S. 52–3, 134

l

Ladby 123
Viking Burial Ship Museum 28, 123
Langeland 126
language 21–2, 91, 143, 366
Lassen, Anders 40
Lego *131*
Lind, Jenny 127
Lindholm Høje 28, *29*, 132
Liseleje 115
literature 51
see also individual writers' names
Anglo-Saxon Chronicle 23, 26
Beowulf 22
Hamlet 115, 116
Lolland 117
see also individual place names
Lønstrup 134
Lunkebugten Bay (Tåsinge) 126
Lyø 126

m

Margrethe II *42*
Marielyst 117
Marstal 126
Melsted 120
Landbrugsmuseet Melstedgård (agricultural museum) 120
Middlefart 126
Midnight Sun 138
Moesgård 129
Forhistorisk Museum (Museum of Prehistory) 129
Møgeltønder 132
Shackenborg Slot 132

Mols Bjerge 129
Møn 116–7
    see also individual place names
    Grønjægers Høj barrow grave 117
monarchy 42
Møns Klint 112
Munch-Petersen, Ursula 110
museums and galleries
    Århus Kunstmuseum (Museum of
        Art) (Århus) 129
    Arken Museet for Moderne Kunst
        (Ishoj) 116
    Bornholms Model Jernbane
        (model train) Museum
        (Gudhjem) 120
    Bornholms Museum (Rønne) 120
    Carl Nielsen Museet (Odense)
        124–5
    Danmarks Grafiske Museum
        (Danish Museum for Printing)
        (Odense) 125
    Dansk Arkitektur Center (Danish
        Architecture Centre)
        (Copenhagen) 108
    Den Fynske Landsby (Funen
        Village) (Odense) 125
    Den Gamle By (Old Town) open-
        air museum (Århus) 129
    Den Hirschsprungske Samling
        (Hirschsprung Collection)
        (Copenhagen) 105, 107
    Dybbøl Mill and museum (Dybbøl)
        132
    Fåborg Museum for Fynsk Kunst
        (Fåborg) 125
    Forhistorisk Museum (Museum
        of Prehistory) (Moesgård) 129
    Fornminnissavn (National
        Museum) (Hoyvik) 143
    Forsvarsmuseet (military
        museum) (Rønne) 120
    Frihedsmuseet (Danish
        Resistance Museum)
        (Copenhagen) 40, 105
    Glass Museum (Fensmark) 116
    Hans Christian Andersen
        Museum (Odense) 122, 124
    Hobro Museum (Hobro) 132
    Johannes Larsen Museum
        (Kerteminde) 124
    Kongelige Stalde & Kareter
        (Museum of the Royal Stables
        and Coaches) (Christiansborg,
        Copenhagen)107–8
    Kunsthallen (art gallery)
        (Odense) 125
    Kunstindustrimuseet (Danish
        Museum of Decorative Art)
        (Copenhagen) 103, 110

    Kunstmuseet Traphold (Trapholt
        Museum of Art) (Kolding) 131
    Landbrugsmuseet Melstedgård
        (agricultural museum)
        (Melsted) 120
    Lindholm Høje museum 28, 29,
        132
    Louisiana Museum for Moderne
        Kunst (Louisiana Museum of
        Modern Art) (Humlebæk) 52,
        115
    Museet for Fotokunst (Museum
        of Photographic Art) (Odense)
        125
    Museet Louis Tussaud's
        (Copenhagen) 98–9
    Museum Erotica (Copenhagen)
        102
    Nationalmuseet (National
        Museum) (Copenhagen) 22,
        97, 100
    Natural History Museum
        (Frederiksborg, Hillerød) 115
    Norðoya Fornminnissavn (North
        Islands Museum) (Klaksvík)
        143
    Silkeborg Kunstmuseum
        (Museum of Art) (Silkeborg)
        131
    Skagens Museum (Skagen) 134
    Statens Museum for Kunst
        (National Museum for Fine
        Arts) (Copenhagen) 97,
        105
    Teatermuseet (Christiansborg,
        Copenhagen) 108
    Thorvaldsens Museum
        (Christiansborg, Copenhagen)
        107
    Tidens Samling (Time Collection)
        (Odense) 125
    Tobaksmuseet (Tobacco
        Museum) (Copenhagen) 101
    Tønder Museum (Tønder) 132
    Veteranmuseum (Veteran Motor
        Museum) (Egeskov Slot) 125
    Viking Burial Ship Museum
        (Ladby) 28, 123
    Vikingeskibshallen (Viking Ship
        Museum) (Roskilde) 115–6
Mykines Island 142

Næstved 116
Narsarsuaq 139
national parks and nature reserves
    Rebild Bakker 68
    Svanninge Bakker 68, 125

nature and outdoor life 65–69,
    71–2
Nielsen, Anne Marie 125
Nielsen, Carl 124–5, 127
    Carl Nielsen Museet (Odense)
        124–5
    My Childhood 127
Nordby 131
    Samsø Labyrinten (maze) 131
Northern Lights 138
Nuuk (Godthåb) 137
Nyborg 123
    Nyborg Slot 123
Nyker 120
Nykøbing 117
    Czarens Hus (Tsar's House) 117
Nylars 120
Nysted 117
    Aalholm Slot 117

Odense 123–5
    Brandt's Klædefabrik 125
    Carl Nielsen Museet 124–5
    Danmarks Grafiske Museum
        (Danish Museum for Printing)
        125
    Den Fynske Landsby (Funen
        Village) 125
    Hans Christian Andersen
        Museum 122, 124
    Kunsthallen (art gallery) 125
    Munkemøllestræde 124
    Museet for Fotokunst (Museum
        of Photographic Art) 125
    Nørre Lyndelse 125
    Skt Knuds Domkirke 124
    Tidens Samling (Time Collection)
        125
Oehlenschläger, Adam 51
Olsker 120
    round church 118, 120
Oresund bridge 44, 45, 77, 249
Ørsted, H.C. 126

Paradisbakkerne (Hills of Paradise)
    118, 119
people
    Danes 89–91
    Faroe Islanders 141
    Inuit of Greenland 137
Petersen, Carl-Henning 132
plant life 119
population
    of Copenhagen 97
    of Denmark 89

Poskjær Stenhus barrow 132
Qeqertarsuaq (Disko Island) 137

r

Råbjerg Mile 134
religion 26
Ribe 132
  Ribe Domkirke (Cathedral) 132
Ringkøbing Fjord 133
Risting 126
Rolf ("Rolo") the Ganger 26
Rønne 119–20
  Bornholms Museum 120
  Kastellet (Citadel) 120
  Forsvarsmuseet (military
    museum) 120
  Skt Nikolai Kirke 120
Roskilde 115–6
  Domkirke (Cathedral) 115
  Vikingeskibshallen (Viking Ship
    Museum) 115–6
Rudkøbing 126
Rungsted
  Rungstedlund 113, 115

s

Samsø 129, 131
Silkeborg 131
  Silkeborg Kunstmuseum
    (Museum of Art) 131
Sisimiut 137
Skagen 134
  see also Gammel Skagen
  Anchers Hus (Ancher's House)
    134
  Skagens Museum 134
Sønderborg 131
  Café Druen 131
  Sønderborg Slot 131
Sønderho 133
Spodsbjerg 117
sport 365
  angling and ice fishing 70, 138,
    142
  boating and sailing 14, 65–6,
    97, 138
  football 71
  hiking and walking 66–7, 69,
    138, 141
  ice skating 99
  pony trekking 138
Stege 117
Stevns Klint 116
Struensee, Johann Friederich
  34–5
Svaneke 120
Svendborg 125

Syv Haver, De (The Seven Gardens)
  125, 125

t

Tårs 117
Tasiilaq 137
Tåsinge island 126
Thorvaldsen, Bertel 107
Thyborøn 133–4
  shell-covered house 133, 134
Tisvilde 115
Tønder 132
  Tønder Museum 132
Tórshavn 141
tourist information 89
transport
  bicycles 68–9, 98, 120, 121
  boat trips and cruises 131,
    137–8, 141
  dog-sled trips in Greenland 137,
    138
  helicopter tours in Greenland 138
  IC3 Train 111
Trelleborg 28
Troense 126
  Troense Inn 126
Tybrind Vig 126

u–v

Uppsala 26
Valdemar I 31
Valdemar II 31
Valdemar IV 32
Vestmanna 142
Vestmannabjørgini 142

w–z

Wegner, Hans J. 54, 110
wildlife 138, 141
  Arctoc Fox 138
  Puffin 142
windmills 68
Zealand 113–7
  see also individual place names

Finland

Numbers in italics refer to
photographs

a

Aalto, Alvar 57, 331
Aaltosen, Wäinö 324–5
Aavasaksa Hill 349
  Midsummer Eve festivities
    (Aavasaksa Hill) 349
accommodation
  camping 68, 335, 409
  wilderness huts 68
Akäslompolo 349
  Ylläs fell 349
Åland Islands 321
  see also individual place names
Alexander III 320
architecture 57, 291, 302, 306
  Jugendstil (Art Nouveau) 306,
    308
  Suomen Rakennustaiteen Museo
    (Museum of Finnish
    Architecture) (Helsinki) 308–9
  traditional wooden buildings 337,
    338
Arctic Circle 345, 347, 349
art and craft 57–8
  Finnish Design 57
  Scandinavian design 54
  tradtional Finnish dolls 304
arts and entertainment
  Finlandiatalo (Finlandia Hall)
    (Helsinki) 57, 301, 304
  Helsinki Philharmonic Orchestra
    (Helsinki) 304
  Suomen Kansallisooppera
    (Finnish National Opera
    House) (Helsinki) 291, 304
  Sibelius Academy (Helsinki) 58,
    304
  Svenska Teatern (Swedish
    Theatre) (Helsinki) 305
  Teatterimuseo (Theatre Museum)
    (Helsinki) 305
  Valkeakoski Summer Theatre
    (Valkeakoski) 333
Aulangon Puisto (Aulanko Forest
  Park) 334
Aurora Borealis see Northern
  Lights

b

beaches 65, 291
  Hanko (Hangö) 317
  nudist beach 310

Pihlajasaari 310
Pyhtää 319
Reposaari 337
of Ruissalo Island 325
Santalahti 320
Bobrikov, Nikolai Ivanovich 39

c

churches and cathedrals
Hattulan Pyhän Ristin Kirkko
(Hattulan Church of the Holy
Cross) 334
Helisnummen (Salo) 317
Kaleva Kirkko (Tampere) 332
Orthodox (Lappeenranta) 327
Ortodoksinen Kirkko (Orthodox
Cathedral) (Turku) 323
Porvoo Cathedral 319
Ristinkirkko (Church of the
Cross) (Lahti) 330
St Olof's (Nagu) 315
Temppelinaukion Kirkko
(Helsinki) 304–5
Tsasouna (Salo) 317
Tuomiokirkko (Cathedral)
(Helsinki) 307
Tuomiokirkko (Cathedral)
(Tampere) 332
Tuomiokirkko (Cathedral) (Turku)
323
Uskela (Salo) 317
Uspenskin Katedraali (Cathedral)
(Helsinki) 308
climate 293, 301, 404
culture and traditions 57

e

economy 43
Edelfelt, Albert 57, 319
Ekenäs (Tammisaari) 317–8
boat tours 317–8
Porvaristalo (Ekenäs Museum)
317
Engel, Carl Ludwig 57, 302, 306,
323, 338
Enontekiö 350

f

Fagervik 318
festivals and events
Christmas Fair (Helsinki) 305
Easter Orthodox festival
(Sevettijärvi) 349
Festival of Song (Joensuu) 340
Hanko Days Weekend Festival
(Hanko) 317

Helsinki Festival 301
International Dance and Music
Festival (Kuopio) 329
International Opera Festival
(Savonlinna) 58, 328
jazz festival (Pori) 58, 337
Jyväskylä Arts Festival (Jyväskylä)
332
Kuhmo Chamber Music Festival
(Kuhmo) 342
May Day Eve (Helsinki) 305
Midnight Sun Film Festival
(Sodankylä) 347
midsummer celebrations in the
Åland Islands 321
Night of the Bonfires (Hanko)
317
Ruisrock (Ruissalo Island) 325
Föglö 321
bird reserve 321
food and drink 62–3, 411
aquavit 62
cloudberry 348
Panimo microbrewery
(Suomenlinna) 309
smörgåsbord 62

g–h

Gallén-Kallel, Akseli 57–8, 318,
337
Gesellius, Herman 57, 306, 318
Gulf of Bothnia 291
Halti mountain 350
Hämeenlinna 334
Häme Castle *334*
Sibeliuksen Syntymäkoti Museo
(Sibelius Home Museum) 334
Hamina 320
Hanko (Hangö) 317
Alan's Café 317
boat trips to Bengtskår
Lighthouse *317*
Hanko Days Weekend Festival 317
Linnoitusmuseo (Frontline
Museum) 317
Loft Gallery E. Pinomaa 317
Night of the Arts (Helsinki) 305
Night of the Bonfires 317
regatta 317
Harakka wildlife reserve 310
health 405
mosquitoes 343, 345
Heinola 330
Helsinki 77, 291, 301–10
see also **Harakka, Lauttasaari,
Luoto, Pihlajasaari, Särkkä,
Seurasaari, Suomenlinna,
Uunisaari, Valkosaari**

Akateeminen Kirjakauppa
bookshop 305
Aleksanterinkatu 307
Ateneum (Museum of Finnish Art)
302
Bellevue Russian restaurant 308
Bockin Talo (Bock House) 307
Bulevardi 308
Café Ursula 309
Carousel café 309
Christmas Fair 305
City Art Museum 301, 303–4
Design Forum 303
Eduskuntatalo (Parliament
Building) *304*
Eira 308
Esplanadi 305
Esplanadin Puisto (Esplanade
Park) 305
Finlandiatalo (Finlandia Hall) 57,
301, *304*
Hakasalmi Villa 304
Havis Amanda Fountain 307
Helsinki Festival 301
Hietalahdentori (flea market) 308
Hotel Kamp 307
Kamp Galleria 307
Hotel Torni 301
Kaivopuisto park 309
Kansallismuseo (National
Museum) *304*
Kappeli café-restaurant 301,
305, *308*
Katajanokka 307–8
Kauppatori (Central Market
Square) 307
Kaupungintalo (City Hall) 307
Kiasma (Museum of
Contemporary Art) 291, *303*
Lasipalatsi (Glass Palace) 303
Luotsikatu 308
Mannerheimintie 303
May Day Eve 305
Museum of Cultures 301, 304
Night of the Arts 305
Olympiaterminaali (Olympia Quay)
309
Pohjoisesplanadi 307
Presidentinlinna (Presidential
Palace) 307
Pulp restaurant 303
Rautatieasema (Railway Station)
302, 306
Ruohalahti 305
Sanomatalo 303
Sederholmin Talo 307
Senaatintori (Senate Square)
307
shopping 305, 307

Sibelius Academy 58, 304
Sibelius Monument 310
Sibeliuksen Puisto (Sibelius Park) 310
Stockmann 305
Suomen Kansallisooppera (Finnish National Opera House) 291, 304
Suomen Rakennustaiteen Museo (Museum of Finnish Architecture) 308–9
Suomen Valokuvataiteen Museo (Photography Museum) 305
Svenska Teatern (Swedish Theatre) 305
Taideteollisuusmuseo (Museum of Art and Design) 308
Teatterimuseo (Theatre Museum) 305
Temppelinaukion Kirkko 304–5
Tennispalatsi (Tennis Palace) 303
tourist information 301, 307
Tulli-ja Pakkahuone (Customs and Bonded Warehouse) 308
Tuomiokirkko (Helsinki Cathedral) 307
Ullanlinna 308
Uspenskin Katedraali (Uspenski Cathedral) 308
Vanha Kauppahalli (Old Market Hall) 307
Hildén, Sara 333
Hvitträsk 318

i

Iisalmi 329
Evakkokeskus Cultural Centre 329
Kuappi restaurant 329
Olutmestari beer hall 329
Iittala 334
glass museum 334
Ilkka, Elias 333
Ilomantsi 340–41
Fighter's House 341
Imatra 327
Imatrankoski (rapids) 327
Inari 348
Saamelaismuseo (Siida Sami Museum) 348
Ylä-Lapin Luontokeskus (Northern Lapland Visitor Centre) 348
Inarijärvi Lake 348
boat trips 348
Ukko Island 348

industry
fishing 61
pulp and paper 291
Ivalo 347–8

j

Jakobstad (Pietarsaari) 338
historic sailing ship trips 338
Jansson, Tove 58, 325, 333
Järämä 350
World War II bunkers 350
Järnefelt, Eero 334
Järvenpää 334
Ainola 334
Tuusulanjärvi (lake) 334
Joensuu 340
Festival of Song 340
Pohjois-Karjalan Museo (North Karelia Museum) 340
Taidemuseo (Art Museum) 340
Joulupukin Pajakylä (Santa Claus Workshop Village) 347
Jung, Bertel 306
Jyrängönkoski 330–31
Siltasaari Fishing Centre 330–31
Jyväskylä 331–2
1,000 Lakes Rally 332
Alvar Aalto Museo 57, 331
Jyväskylä Arts Festival 332

k

Kajaani 343
Kaksinkantaja 341
Kalajoki 338
Karelia 77, 340–43
see also individual place names
Karelian Circle Trek 68
Karhunkierros walking route 343
Karhuntassu Tourist Centre 343
Kärkisaari 320
Kastelholm fortress 321
Cultural History Museum 321
Karlsgården Open-Air Museum 321
Kaunissaari Island 319
Keisarin Kosket Lodge 320
Kelvenne Island 331
Kemi 339
icebreaker excursions 339
Lumilinna (Snow Castle) 339
Ketomella 350
Kilipsjärvi 335, 350
Kirkenes 349
Kivi, Aleksis 58
Leah 58
Seven Brothers 58
Kokkola 338

Kotka 320
boat trips 320
Sapokka Harbour 320
Kouvola 327
Kristinestad (Kristiinankaupunki) 337
Merimuseo 337
Kuhmo 342
Hotel Kalevala 342
Kalevala Village 342
Kuhmo Chamber Music Festival 342
Kukkola 349
Kukkolankoski rapids 339, 349
Kuopio 329
International Dance and Music Festival 329
Kuopion Kortellimuseo 329
Kuopion Museo 329
Ortodoksinen Kirkkomuseo (Orthodox Church Museum) 329
Tori (Market Place) 329
Kuusamo 343
see also individual place names
Kuusistan Linna 315
Kymenlaakso (Kymi river valley) 320

l

Laanila 347
Lahti 330
Kaupungintalo (Town Hall) 330
Lahden Historiallinen Museo 330
Lahden Urheilukeskus sports centre 330
Ristinkirkko (Church of the Cross) 330
lakes 66, 327–35, 343
Langinkoski 320
Tsar Alexander III's fishing lodge 320
language 21–2, 36, 294, 315, 321, 337, 415
Lapland 70, 77, 291, 339, 345–50
see also individual place names
Lappeenranta 327, 329
day cruises to Russia 327
Etelä-Karjalan Museo (South Karelian Museum) 327
Orthodox Church 327
Ratsuväkimuseo (Cavalry Museum) 327
Lauttasaari 310
Finnish Sauna Society 310
Lemmenjoki Valley 348
Lieksa 341
Pielisen Museo (Pielinen Open-Air Museum) 341

Ruuankoski (rapids) 341
Lindfors, Stefan 54
Lindgren, Armas 57, 306, 318
Lindroos, Peter 58
Lintulan Luostari 328–9
literature
  see also individual writers'
  names
  Anglo-Saxon Chronicle 23, 26
  Beowulf 22, 244
Lönnrot, Elias 34, 58
  Kalevala 34, 58, 294, 317, 340,
  341, 342
Loviisa 319–20
Luostotunturi 347
Luoto 310

m

Mäkinen, Tommi 71
Mannerheim, Marshal 41
Mariehamn 321
  Maritime Museum 321
  Pommern museum ship 321
Marti Ahtissari *19*
Mattila, Karita 58
media 303
Menesjärvi 348
Messilä 330
Midnight Sun 77, 339, 345, 349,
  350
Mikkeli 328
  Visulahti Family Leisure Centre
  328
Mikkola, Hannu 71
Muhos 343
museums and galleries
  Aboa Vetus and Ars Nova (Turku)
  324
  Aineen Taidemuseo (Aine Art
  Museum) (Tornio) 339
  Alvar Aalto Museo (Jyväskylä) *57*,
  331
  Apteekkimuseo (Pharmacy
  Museum) (Turku) 324
  Arctic Centre (Rovaniemi) 345
  Ateneum (Museum of Finnish Art)
  (Helsinki) 302
  Borstö Folk Museum (Nagu)
  315
  Bragen Ulkomuseo (Brage Open-
  Air Museum) (Vaasa) 338
  City Art Museum (Helsinki)
  303–4
  Cultural History Museum
  (Kastelholm fortress) 321
  Design Forum (Helsinki) 303
  Edelfelt-Vallgren Art Museum
  (Porvoo) 319

Etelä-Karjalan Museo (South
  Karelian Museum)
  (Lappeenranta) 327
Evakkokeskus Cultural Centre
  (Iisalmi) 329
Forum Marinum (Maritime
  Centre) (Turku) 324
Gallén-Kallela Museum
  (Tarvaspää) 318
glass museum (Iittala) 334
Helsinki Art Museum (Helsinki)
  301
Kalevala Village (Kuhmo) 342
Kansallismuseo (National
  Museum) (Helsinki) *304*
Karlsgården Open-Air Museum
  (Kastelholm fortress) 321
Käsityöläismuseo (Handicrafts
  Museum) (Turku) 323
Kiasma (Museum of
  Contemporary Art) (Helsinki)
  291, *303*
Kultamuseo (Gold Museum)
  (Tankavaara) 347
Kulttuuruhistoriallinen Museo
  (Museum of Cultural History)
  (Uusikaupunki) 337
Kuopion Kortellimuseo (Kuopio)
  329
Kuopion Museo (Kuopio) 329
Lahden Historiallinen Museo
  (Lahti) 330
Linnoitusmuseo (Frontline
  Museum) (Hanko) 317
Luonnontieteellinen (Natural
  History Museum)
  (Suomenlinna) 310
Lusto (Forestry Museum)
  (Punkaharju) 327
Maritime Museum (Mariehamn)
  321
Merenkulku-Museo (Turku Art
  Museum) (Turku) 323
Merimuseo (Kristinestad)
  337
Military Museum Manege
  (Suomenlinna) 310
Museum of Cultures (Helsinki)
  301, 304
Ortodoksinen Kirkkomuseo
  (Orthodox Church Museum)
  (Kuopio) 329
Oulun Taidemuseo (Art Museum)
  (Oulu) 339
Pielisen Museo (Pielinen Open-Air
  Museum) (Lieksa) 341
Pohjanmaan Museo
  (Ostrobothnian Museum)
  (Vaasa) 338

Pohjois-Karjalan Museo (North
  Karelia Museum) (Joensuu)
  340
Pommern museum ship
  (Mariehamn) 321
Porin Taidemuseo (Art Museum)
  (Pori) 337
Porvaristalo (Ekenäs) 317
Pöykkölä Museum (Rovaniemi)
  345
Provincial Museum of Lapland
  (Rovaniemi) 345
Rannikotykisto Museo (Coast
  Artillery Museum)
  (Suomenlinna) 310
Ratsuväkimuseo (Cavalry
  Museum) (Lappeenranta)
  327
Retretti Arts Centre (Punkaharju)
  328
Rettig Palace (Turku) *see* Aboa
  Vetus and Ars Nova
Saamelaismuseo (Siida Sami
  Museum) (Inari) 348
Sara Hildénin Taidmuseo (Sara
  Hildén Art Museum) (Tampere)
  333
Satakunta Museo (Pori) 337
Savonlinna Maakuntamuseo
  (Provincial Museum)
  (Savonlinna) 328
Sibeliuksen Syntymäkoti Museo
  (Sibelius Home Museum)
  (Hämeenlinna) 334
Suomen Lasimuseo (Finnish
  Glass Museum) (Riihimäki)
  334
Suomenlinna Museum
  (Suomenlinna) 309–10
Suomen Rakennustaiteen Museo
  (Museum of Finnish
  Architecture) (Helsinki) 308–9
Suomen Valokuvataiteen Museo
  (Photography Museum)
  (Helsinki) 305
Taidemuseo (Art Museum)
  (Joensuu) 340
Taideteollisuusmuseo (Museum
  of Art and Design) (Helsinki)
  308
Teatterimuseo (Theatre Museum)
  (Helsinki) 305
Tehdasmuseo Vapriikki museum
  (Tampere) 332–3
Tietomaa Science Centre (Oulu)
  339
Turkansaaren Ulkomuseo
  (Turkansaari Open-air
  Museum) (Oulu) 338–9

Ulkomuseo (Open-air Museum) (Seurasaari) 310
Voipaalan Kartano (Voipaala Manor) (Valkeakoski) 333
Wäinö Aaltosen Museo (Turku) 324–5
Ylä-Lapin Luontokeskus (Northern Lapland Visitor Centre) (Inari) 348
Rovaniemi Art Museum 345, 347

n

Naantali 325
Moomin World 325
Nagu 315
Borstö Folk Museum 315
St Olof's Church 315
national parks and nature reserves 68
Hiidenporttin Kansallispuisto 68, 342
Kevon Luonnonpuisto 349
Koli Kansallispuisto 342
Mallan Luonnenpuisto nature reserve 350
Oulangan Kansallispuisto 343
Päijänteen Kansallispuisto 331
Ramsholmen Nature Reserve 68
Riisitunturi 343
Seurasaari 310
Tammisaaren Saariston Kansallispuisto 317
Tiilikkajärven Kansallispuisto 342
nature and outdoor life 65–69, 71–2
Noras, Arto 58
Northern Lights 345
Nuovo, Frank 54
Nurmes 341–2
Bomba House 342
scenic boat trips 342
Nurmi, Paavo *43*, 71, 294, 325

o

Oulu 338–9, 343
Koskikeskus (Rapids Centre) 339
Oulun Taidemuseo (Art Museum) 339
Tietomaa Science Centre 339
Turkansaaren Ulkomuseo (Turkansaari Open-air Museum) 338–9
Oulujärvi lake 343

p

Pallastunturi fells 349–50
Pallastunturi Hotel complex 349
Palojoensuu 350
Pargas (Parainen) 315
people 293–5
Karelians 341
Romany Gypsies 295
Sami 21, *37*, 55, 70, *292*, 343, 347–8, 349
Pihlajasaari 310
Pori 337
City Hall 337
jazz festival 58, 337
Jusélius Mausoleum 337
Porin Taidemuseo (Art Museum) 337
Satakunta Museo 337
Porvoo (Borgå) 318–9
Albert Edelfelt Atelier 319
Edelfelt-Vallgren Art Museum 319
J.L. Runeberg home 319
Old Porvoo 319
Porvoo Cathedral 319
river cruises 319
Prästö 321
Pulkkilanharju (ridge) 331
Punkaharju 327–8
lake steamer trip to Savonlinna 328
Lusto (Forestry Museum) 327
Kesämaa (Summerland) Leisure Centre 328
Retretti Arts Centre 328
Pyhätunturi 347
Pyhtää 319

r

Raasepori 318
castle ruins 318
Rauma 337
Rautio, Erkki 58
Reposaari 337
Riihimäki 334
Suomen Lasimuseo (Finnish Glass Museum) 334
rivers
Aura 323
Kemijoki 339
Kymi 320
Kymijoki 320
Oulujoki 339
Tornionjoki 349
"road of seven bridges" 338
Ropinsalmi 350
Rovaniemi 345

Arktikum 345
Arctic Centre 345
Provincial Museum of Lapland 345
Lappia House 345
Pöykkölä Museum 345
Rovaniemi Art Museum 345, 347
Ruissalo Island 325
Ruisrock festival 325
steamship cruises 325
Villa Roma 325
Rukatunturi Fells 343
Runokylä 341
Parppei Pirtti restaurant 341
Singers Lodge 341
Ryynänen, Eeva 341

s

Saana mountain 350
Saarinen, Eliel 57, 306, 318
Saariselkä 347
Salo 315, 317
Helisnummen (Helisnummi Church) 317
Tsasouna Church 317
Uskela Church 317
Salonen, Esa-Pekka 58
Sammatti 317
Paikkarin Torppa (Paikkari Cottage) 317
Santa Claus 347
Santa Claus Workshop Village *see* Joulupukin Pajakylä
Santapark 347
Santalahti 320
Särkkä 310
Sattmark café 315
saunas *290*, 309, *312–3*, 341
Finnish Sauna Society (Lauttasaari) 310
Savonlinna 328
International Opera Festival 58, 328
lake steamer trips 328
Olavinlinna castle 328
Savonlinna Maakuntamuseo (Provincial Museum) 328
Schauman, Eugen 39
Seurasaari 310
Seurasaari National Park 310
Ulkomuseo (Open-air Museum) 310
Sevettijärvi 349
Easter Orthodox festival 349
shopping
tax-free shopping 321, 415
Sibelius, Jean *58*, 334, 341
Finlandia 58, 334

Karelian Suite 341
Kullervo 58
monument *300*
Sillanpää, F.E. 58
Snappertuna 318
Sodankylä 347
Midnight Sun Film Festival 347
Sonck, Lars 306
sports and pastimes 294, 414
1,000 Lakes Rally (Jyväskylä)
332
Arctic Circle Race 335
canoeing 335
dog-sledging and reindeer
sledging 70, 348
Finlandia Canoe Relay 335
Finlandia Ski Race and Ski
Games 330
fishing and ice fishing 70, 320,
321, 330–31
football 71
gold-panning 345, 347
golf 321
golf under the Midnight Sun 70,
71, 339
hiking 66, 68, 321, 341, 343,
345, 349–50
Ice Hockey 72, *293*
Kesämaa (Summerland) Leisure
Centre (Punkaharju) 328
Koskikeskus (Rapids Centre)
(Oulu) 339
Lahden Urheilukeskus sports
centre (Lahti) 330
motor racing 71, 332
mountain biking 341
regatta (Hanko) 317
skiing and other winter sports
72, 330, 345, 347, 349
snowshoe trekking 70
Visulahti Family Leisure Centre
(Mikkeli) 328
water sports 321
Stahlberg, Kaarlo Juho 40
Suomenlinna (Finland's Castle)
309, *310*
Iso Mustasaari 309
Korkeasaaren Eläitarha zoo 310
Kruunulinna Ehrensvärd
(Ehrensvärd Crown Castle)
310
Luonnontieteellinen (Natural
History Museum) 310
Military Museum Manege 310
Panimo microbrewery 309
Rannikotykisto Museo (Coast
Artillery Museum) 310
Rantakasarmi (Jetty Barracks)
309

Suomenlinna Museum 309–10
Vesikko Submarine 310
Walhalla restaurant 310
Svartholma sea fortress 320

Tampere 332–3
boat trips 332
Kaleva Kirkko (church) 332
Kirjasto (City Library) 332
Näsinneula Observation Tower
333
Sara Hildénin Taidmuseo (Sara
Hildén Art Museum) 333
Särkänniemi Park 333
Tammerkoski (rapids) 332
Tampere-talo (Tampere Hall) 332
Tehdasmuseo Vapriikki museum
332–3
Tuomiokirkko (Tampere
Cathedral) 332
Tankavaara 347
Kultamuseo (Gold Museum) 347
Tankavaara Gold Village 347
Tarvaspää 318
Gallén-Kallela Museum 318
Tornio 335, 339, 349
Aineen Taidemuseo (Aine Art
Museum) 339
Vesitorni water tower 339
transport
cycling in the Åland Islands 321
Turku 315, 323–5, 337
Aboa Vetus and Ars Nova
museums 324
Angel Restaurant 324
Apteekkimuseo (Pharmacy
Museum) 324
Forum Marinum (Maritime
Centre) 324
horse cabs 324
Käsityöläismuseo (Handicrafts
Museum) 323
Kauppahalli (Indoor Market Hall)
323
Merenkulku-Museo (Turku Art
Museum) 323
Ortodoksinen Kirkko (Orthodox
Cathedral) 323
Rettig Palace *see* Aboa Vetus
and Ars Nova
steamship excursions 324
Tuomiokirkko (Turku Cathedral)
323
Turku Cultural Centre 324
Turun Linna (Turku Castle) 323
Urheilupuisto park 325
Wäinö Aaltosen Museo 324–5

Turunmaa archipelago 315
see also individual place names

Utsjoki 349
Uunisaari 310
Uusikaupunki (Nystad) 337
Kulttuuruhistoriallinen Museo
(Museum of Cultural History)
337
Myllymäki Park 337

V

Vaalimaa 320
Vaasa (Vasa) 337–8
Bragen Ulkomuseo (Brage Open-
Air Museum) 338
Pohjanmaan Museo
(Ostrobothnian Museum) 338
Wasalandia 338
Valamon Luostari (monastery)
328–9
Valkeakoski 333–4
Valkeakoski Summer Theatre
333
Visavuori 333–4
Voipaalan Kartano (Voipaala
Manor) 333
Valkosaari 310
Vatanan, Ari 71
Vuonisjärvi 341
Paateri 341

W

Way of the Four Winds 349
wildlife 341
reindeer 70, 341, 342, 347
Wikström, Emil 333–4
windmills *318*

Norway

Numbers in italics refer to photographs

a

accommodation
  hytta 65, 196, 377
Ålesund 190, 199
Alta 213
  Alta Museum 213
Amundsen, Roald 166, 170
Archer, Colin 170
architecture
  Art Nouveau at Ålesund 199
  stave churches 56, 153, 170,
    176–7, 189, 197
Arctic Circle 208
  Polarsirkelsenteret (Arctic Circle
    Centre) 208
Arendal 173, 176
  Arendal Bymuseum (Town
    Museum) 173, 176
  Rådhus (Town Hall) 176
art and crafts 55–6
  prehistoric pictographs 168, 213
  rose painting 56, 193
  Scandinavian design 54
  wood carving 193
arts and entertainment
  Grieghallen (concert hall)
    (Bergen) 186
  Hardanger fiddle 181, 182
  Harmonien orchestra 186
  Nationaltheatret (National
    Theatre) (Oslo) 164
  traditional music and dance 182,
    193
Åsgårdstrand 170
  Munch's Lille Hus (Munch's Little
    House) 169–70
Askøy 182
Atlanterhavsveien (Atlantic Road)
  200
***Aurora Borealis* see Northern
  Lights**
Aursunden lake 193
Averøya 200

b

balestrand 197
Barents, Willem 214
Bergen 77, 178, 182, 185–9
  Bergen Akvariet (Aquarium)
    187–8
  Bergen Billedgalleri (Municipal
    Art Gallery) 188–9

Bergen International Music
    Festival 56, 186
Bryggen 184, 187
Bryggens Museum 187
Domkirke (Cathedral) 187
Fisketorget (Fish Market) 185,
    187
Fløibanen (funicular) 188
Fløyen mountain 188
Gamle Bergen 153
Grieghallen (concert hall) 186
Håkonshallen 188
Hanseatiske Museum 187
Korskirken 187
Mariakirken (St Mary's Church)
    187
Raftohuset –
  Menneskerettighetenes Hus
  (Rafto Human Rights House)
    189
Rasmus Meyers Samlinger
  (Rasmus Meyer Collection) 189
shopping 187
Stenersens Samling 189
Torgalmenningen 187
Bodø 207, 208
Borre Nasjonalpark 169
Brønnøysund 208
Brundtland, Gro Harlem 153
Bud 200
Buekorps 186
Bull, Ole 56, 181, 189
  statue in Bergen 187

c

churches and cathedrals
  Domkirke (Cathedral) (Bergen)
    187
  Domkirken (Cathedral)
    (Stavanger) 181
  Drøbak Kirke (Drøbak) 168
  Fantoft Stave Church (Paradis)
    189
  Ishavskatedralen (Arctic Ocean
    Cathedral) (Tromsø) 203, 212
  Korskirken (Bergen) 187
  Mariakirken (St Mary's) (Bergen)
    187
  Nidarosdom (Nidaros Cathedral)
    (Trondheim) 153, 205, 206,
    209
  stave church (Borgund) 56, 153
  stave church (Heddal) 56, 153,
    176–7, 182
  Urnes Stavkirke (stave church)
    (Luster) 56, 197
  Utstein Kloster (Mosterøy Island)
    178

climate 153, 161, 368
  arctic 212, 214
culture and traditions 55–6
  trolls 191

d–e

Dombås 193–4
Drøbak 168, 169
  Drøbak Kirke (church) 168
  Follo Museum (Heritage
    Museum) 168
  Oscarsborg Festning (Fort)
    168
Du Chaillu, Paul Belloni 194
  Land of the Midnight Sun 194
Duun, Olav 154
economy 43–4
Eid 198
Eidsvoll 167
  Eidsvollbyningen (Memorial
    Building) 167–8
Elverum 193
Erik of Pomerania 33, 115

f

Fåberg 192
  Norsk Vegmuseum (Road
    Transport Museum) 192
Fedje 182
festivals and events
  Battle of Stiklestad re-enactment
    (Stiklestad) 209
  Bergen International Music
    Festival (Bergen) 56, 186
  blues festival (Hell) 153, 207
  Emigration Festival (Stavanger)
    179
  Haugesund International Film
    Festival 155
  Hollmenkollen Ski Festival (Oslo)
    161, 165
  Ibsen Festival (Oslo) 164
  International Trad Jazz Festival
    (Haugesund) 179
  Jazz Festival (Oslo) 161
  Lofotfiske (Kabelvåg) 211
  Molde International Jazz Festival
    (Molde) 200
  National Day 189
  Norwegian Film Festival
    (Haugesund) 179
  Olsok (St Olav's day) 169
  Olsokspelet (St Olav's Play)
    (Stiklestad) 207–8
  St Olav Festival (Trondheim)
    208
Finse 67, 195

Fjærland 197
  Norsk Bremuseum (Norwegian
    Glacier Museum) 197
fjords 66, 76, 153, 177, 181–2,
  187, 191, 196–200
  cruises 187, 202–3
Flåm 197
  scenic railway 197
Flekkefjord 173
Florø 198
  Sogn og Fjordane Kystmuseet
    (Coastal Museum) 198
food and drink 62–3, 379
  alcohol restriction 41
  aquavit 62
  Arctic Ale 212
  distilleries 191–2
  geitost (goat's cheese) 193
  Løten Brænderi distillery (Løten)
    191–2
  Mack brewery (Tromsø) 212
Førde 197
Førdefjord 198
  Sunnfjord Museum 198
Fosse, Jon 154
Foyn, Svend 170
Frederikstad 168
  Oldtidsveien (Highway of the
    Ancients) 168
Frederiksten 34

g

Gaup, Nils 213
  Pathfinder 213
Geirangerfjorden 198–9
Gjende lake 195
glaciers 67
  Briksdalsbreen 198
  Jostedalsbreen 67, 196, 197,
    198, 201
  Norsk Bremuseum (Norwegian
    Glacier Museum) (Fjærland)
    197
Grieg, Edvard 36,56, 181, 182,
  185–6, 195
  Peer Gynt 195
Grimstad 173
  Grimstad Bymuseum (Town
    Museum) 173
Gudbrandsdalen 191, 193–4

h

Haav, Anne 193
Hafjell 192
Håkon Håkonson 170, 206
Håkon VII 39, 43
Halden 168

Frederiksten Festning (Fort)
  museums 168–9
Haldenkanal (canal) 169
  see also Ørje
Hamar 191
  Hedemarksmuseet og
    Domkirkeodden (Hedemark
    Museum and Cathedral Point)
    191
  Jernbanemuseet (National
    Museum of Railway Transport)
    191
Hamsun, Knut 167
  Sult (Hunger) 167
Harald Fairhair 25
Harald I Hårfagre 181
Harald V 42
Harald Hardrade 26, 161
Hardangerfjorden 181
Haugesund 179
  International Trad Jazz Festival
    179
  Norwegian Film Festival 179
Heddal 176–7
  Heddal Bygdetun (Rural Museum)
    177
  stave church 56, 153, 176–7,
    182
Helberg, Claus 180
Hell 153, 207
  blues festival 153, 207
Hella 197
Heyerdahl, Thor 166, 170
Hidra Island 173
Hjemmeluft 213
Honningsvåg 214
  Nordkappmuséet (North Cape
    Museum) 214
Hordaland 173, 181–2, 183
  see also individual place names
Horten 169
  Marinemuseet (Naval Museum)
    169
Hovig, Jan Inge 212
Husaby, Hallvard see St Hallvard

i–j

Ibsen, Henrik 36, 56, 164, 173,
  176
immigration issue 154–5, 162
industry
  fishing and fish farming 61, 182,
    199, 211
  metal foundries 208
  oil 44, 151, 153, 179, 181,
    182
Jan Mayen 40
Jonsson, Tor 154

k

Kabelvåg 211
  Lofotfiske 211
Karasjok 213
Karmøy Island 177
Kautokeino 213
Kierulf, Halfdan 56
Kinsarvik 181–2
Kragerø 171, 176, 178
Kristiansand 173
  Christiansholm Festning
    (fortress) 173
  Kristiansand Dyrepark 173
Kristiansund 200
Kvaløya 212
Kvinesdal 173
Kvinnfoss (Lady's Waterfall) 197

l

Laksestudioet 178
  Kolbeinstveit Museum (Rural
    Museum) 178
language 21–2, 36, 154, 213,
  383
Lapland 70, 77
Larvik 170
  Farriskilde (Farris Spring) 170
Lillehammer 192
  Maihaugen open-air museum
    192
  Winter Olympic facilities 192
Lillesand 173
Lindesnes Fyr (lighthouse) 173
literature
  see also individual writers'
    names
  Anglo-Saxon Chronicle 23, 26
  Beowulf 22, 244
Lofoten Islands 153, 203, 211
  see also individual place names
Longyearbyen 214
Longyear, John 214
Løten 192
  Løiten Lys candle factory 192
  Løten Brænderi distillery 191–2
Luster 197
  Urnes Stavkirke (stave church)
    56, 197
Lysøen (Island of Light) 189

m

Maelstrom 211
Magnus 31
Mandal 176
Margarethe 32–3
Mellemverftet 200

Memurubu 196
Midnight Sun 203, 212
Mjøsa lake 191
Mo i Rana 208
Molde 200
Molde International Jazz Festival 200
Morgedal 176
Mosjøen 208
Moskenesøya 211
Moskenstraumen 211
Mosterøy Island 178
Utstein Kloster (church) 178
mountains
Besseggen ridge 195
Dovrefjell (Dovre Mountains) 193–5
Galdhøpiggen 67
Glitterind 67
Gråkallen (Old Man) 205
Gvepseborg 177
Hardangervidda 181, 195
Jotunheimen Mountains 67, 195, 196
Rondane range 196
Snøhetta 194
Munch, Edvard 36, 56, 163
Shrik (Scream) 56, 163
museums and galleries
Alta Museum (Alta) 213
Arendal Bymuseum (Arendal) 173, 176
Bergen Billedgalleri (Municipal Art Gallery) (Bergen) 188–9
Borgarsyssel Museum (Sarpsborg) 169
Bryggen Museum (Bergen) 187
Det Internasjonale Barnekunstmuseet (International Museum of Children's Art) (Oslo) 161, 163, 164
Emanuel Vigeland Museum (Oslo) 164
Follo Museum (Heritage Museum) (Drøbak) 168
Frammuseet (Fram Museum) (Oslo) 166
Frederiksten Festning museums (Halden) 168–9
Grimstad Bymuseum (Town Museum) (Grimstad) 173
Hardanger Folkemuseum (Utne) 181
Hanseatiske Museum (Bergen) 187
Heddal Bygdetun (Rural Museum) (Heddal) 177

Hedemarksmuseet og Domkirkeodden (Hedemark Museum and Cathedral Point) (Hamar) 191
Hermetikkmuséet (Canning Museum) (Stavanger) 181
Ibsen-museet (Ibsen Museum) (Oslo) 164
Jernbanemuseet (National Museum of Railway Transport) (Hamar) 191
Kanalmuseum (Ørje) 169
Kolbeinstveit Museum (Rural Museum) (Laksestudioet) 178
Kon-Tiki Museum (Oslo) 166
Maihaugen open-air museum (Lillehammer) 192
Marinemuseet (Naval Museum) (Horten) 169
Munch-museet (Munch Museum) (Oslo) 163
Nasjonalgalleriet (National Gallery) (Oslo) 56, 153, 163
Nordkappmuséet (North Cape Museum) (Honningsvag) 214
Nordnorsk Kunstmuseum (North Norway Art Museum) (Tromsø) 212
Norges Hjemmefrontmuseum (Norway's Resistance Museum) (Oslo) 40, 164–5
Norsk Bremuseum (Norwegian Glacier Museum) (Fjærland) 197
Norsk Folkemuseum (Oslo) 161
Norsk Industriarbeidermuseum (Norwegian Industrial Workers Museum) (Rjukan) 177
Norsk Oljemuseum (Norwegian Petroleum Museum) (Stavanger) 181
Norsk Sjøfartsmuseum (Norwegian Maritime Museum) (Oslo) 166
Norsk Vegmuseum (Road Transport Museum) (Fåberg) 192
Norwegian Crown Jewels (Trondheim) 206
Polarsirkelsenteret (Arctic Circle Centre) 208
Rasmus Meyers Samlinger (Rasmus Meyer Collection) (Bergen) 189
Skimuseet (Ski Museum) (Oslo) 161, 165
Sogn og Fjordane Kystmuseet (Coastal Museum) (Florø) 198

Sunnfjord Museum (Førdefjord) 198
Telemark Museum (Skien) 176
Tromsø Museum (Tromsø) 212
Vikingskipshuset (Viking Ship Museum) (Oslo) 28, 153, 161, 166
Myrdal 197
scenic railway 197

n

Nansen, Fridtjof 166
National Parks 68
Jostedalsbreen 196
nature and outdoor life 65–69, 71–2
Nordfjorden 198
Nordhordland 182
Nordkapp (North Cape) 153, 213–4
Children of the World Monument 214
Nordkapphallen (North Cape Hall) 214
Norheim, Sondre 72, 176
Northern Lights 203, 212, 214
Notodden 176
Nøtterøy 170
Ny Ålesund 214
Svalbard Rocket Range 214

o

Olav Haraldsson (St Olav) 154, 205, 206, 207, 209
Olav V 177, 206
Olav Tryggvason 26, 209
statue (Trondheim) 206
Oluf 32–3
Opsvik, Peter 54
Oseberghaugen Viking site 170
Oslo 77, 161–70
Aker Brygge (Aker Quay) 161, 167
Akershus Slott og Festning (Castle) 161, 164–5
Norges Hjemmefrontmuseum (Norway's Resistance Museum) 40, 164–5
Bygdøy peninsula 166
Det Internasjonale Barnekunstmuseet (International Museum of Children's Art) 161, 163, 164
Det Kongelige Slott (Royal Palace) 162–3
Det Norske Utvandrersenteret (Emigration Centre) (Stavanger) 179

Emanuel Vigeland Museum 164
Frammuseet (Fram Museum) 166
Frogner Park 161, 163, *168*
Holmenkollbakken
(Hollmenkollen Ski Jump) *165*
Hollmenkollen Ski Festival 161,
165
Ibsen Festival 164
Ibsen-museet (Ibsen Museum)
164
Jazz Festival 161
Kon-Tiki Museum 166
Munch-museet (Munch Museum)
163
Nasjonalgalleriet (National
Gallery) 56, 153, 163
Nationaltheatret (National
Theatre) 164
Norsk Folkemuseum 161
Norsk Sjøfartsmuseum
(Norwegian Maritime Museum)
166
Oslomarka (Oslo's fields)
165–6
Oslo Sentralstasjon (Oslo Central
Station) 163
Rådhuset (City Hall) 163
Skimuseet (Ski Museum) 161,
165
Stortinget (Parliament) 162
tourist information 161
transport 161, 166–7
Tryvannstårnet (Tryvann Tower)
161
Vigelandsparken (Vigeland Park)
160, 162, 163
Vikingskipshuset (Viking Ship
Museum) *28,* 153, 161,
166
Oslomarka 161
Østerdalen 191, 193
Osterøy 182

p-q

Paradis 189
Fantoft Stave Church 189
Peer Gyntveien (Peer Gynt Way)
196
people 151, 153–5, 170, 179, 181
Sami 21, *37,* 55, *70,* 213, *214*
plant life 214
Polarsirkel see **Arctic Circle**
polar winter 214
politics 153, 167–8
population 153
Preikestolen (Pulpit Rock) 153,
172, 177
Quisling, Vidkun 43

r

Rafto Prize for Human Rights 189
Rafto, Thoralf 189
Reine 211
rivers
Glomma 193
Jølstra 1978
Lågen 193
Nidelva 205–6, 209
Suldalslågen 178
Rjukan 40, 177, 180
Norsk Industriarbeidermuseum
(Norwegian Industrial Workers
Museum) 177
Rogaland 173, 177–8
see also individual place names
Røros 153, *192,* 193
Runde 199–200

s

St Hallvard 166
Sandefjord 170
Badeparken 170
Gokstadhaugen Viking burial site
170
Preståsen 170
Sandvig, Anders 192
Sarpsborg 169
Borgarsyssel Museum 169
Skien 176
Telemark Museum 176
Skipper, Essau and John 196
Three in Norway by Two of Them
196
Skykkjedalsfossen waterfall 182
Sogndal 197
Sognefjorden 196–7
Sogn og Fjordane 196, *197*
see also individual place names
Sørlandet 173
see also individual place names
Sotra 182
Sparre, Victor 212
Spitsbergen see **Svalbard**
sports and pastimes 71, 381
Birkebeiner race 192
cycling and mountain-biking 170
dog-sledging and reindeer sleigh
rides 70
fishing and ice fishing 69, 70,
71, 178, 182
football 71
golf under the Midnight Sun 70,
71
hang gliding and paragliding 182
hiking and walking 67, 165–6,
170, 182, 194, 195–6, 205

Holmenkollbakken
(Hollmenkollen Ski Jump)
(Oslo) *165*
Hollmenkollen Ski Festival (Oslo)
161, 165
sailing and boating *14,* 165,
170, 177, 178
skiing and other winter sports
72, 165, 166, 178, 182, 192,
195–6, 199, 205
Skimuseet (Ski Museum) (Oslo)
161, 165
snowshoe trekking 70
Styrkeprøven (Trial of Strength)
bicycle race (Trondheim) 207
Telemark skiing 72, 176
watersports 165, 182
Winter Olympics facilities
(Lillehammer) 192
Stavanger *179,* 181
Alexander Kielland Minnesmerke
(monument) 181
Breiavatnet 181
Det Norske Utvandrersenteret
(Emigration Centre) 179
Domkirken (Cathedral) 181
Emigration Festival 179
Gamle Stavanger (Old Stavanger)
181
Hermetikkmuséet (Canning
Museum) 181
Kvernevik 181
Norsk Oljemuseum (Norwegian
Petroleum Museum) 181
Sverd i fjell monument 181
Steinkjer 208
Stiklestad 207, 209
Battle of Stiklestad re-enactment
209
Olsokspelet (St Olav's Play)
207–8
Stryn 199
Svalbard (Spitsbergen) archipelago
40, 214
Svalbard Satellite Station 214
Svendsen, Johan 56
Svolvær 211

t

Telemark 176–7
see also individual place names
"Telemark, Heroes of" 40, 177, *180*
Telemarkskanal 1 76
Tjøme 170
Todalfjorden 200
Svinvik Arboret (Arboretum) 200
Tønsberg 170
island tours 170

Nordbyen 170
Slottsfjellet fortress 170
Storgata 170
transport
boat services and sightseeing
trips 169, 178–9, 191,
194–5, 200, 202–3, 208
mountain railway *197*
Troldhaugen 186
Trollfjorden *203*
Trollheimen 200
Tromsø 203, 211–2
Fjellheisen cable car *212*
Ishavskatedralen (Arctic Ocean
Cathedral) *203*, 212
Mack brewery 212
nightlife 211
Nordnorsk Kunstmuseum (North
Norway Art Museum) 212
Tromsø Museum 212
Tromsø Satellite Station 212
Trondheim *204*, 205–7
cycling in the city 206–7
Erkebispegården (Archbishop's
Manor) 206
Nidarosdomen (Nidaros
Cathedral) 153, *205*, 206,
209
Norwegian Crown Jewels 206
St Olav Festival 208
Styrkeprøven (Trial of Strength)
bicycle race 207
Trampe bicycle lift 207
TusenFryd amusement park 168

u

Ulefoss 176
Ullensvang 182
Ulsteinvik 200
Uppdal, Kristofer 154
Utne 181
Hardanger Folkemuseum 181
Utne Hotel 181

v–w

Vardø 213
Verdens Ende (World's End) 170
Vesaas, Halldis Moren 154
Vesterøy peninsula 170
Vigeland, Emanuel 164
Vigeland, Gustav 163
Voss 182
wildlife
bird-watching 178, 199, 203
polar bears *214*
reindeer 70, 195, *214*
Salmon leaping 178

Sweden

*Numbers in italics refer
to photographs*

a

Abisko 280–81
Kungsleden (King's Trail) 67,
281
Åby Säteri 259
Nordens Ark nature park 259
accommodation 392
Ice Hotel (Jukkasjärvi) 70, 223,
280
Miekak fishing camp 280
mountain stations 67
Tjuonajokk fishing camp 280
Albrecht 32–3
**Alvastra Kloster (Cistercian
monastery)** 264
architecture
fäbodar 267
of Southern Sweden 252
Arctic Circle 279
Åre winter sports resort 72,
274
Arjeplog 277
Silvermuséet (Silver Museum)
277
art and crafts 53–5
Dalahäst (Dala horse) 267,
269
Dalarna folk art 269
Nittsjö Keramik (pottery) (Rättvik)
269
Scandinavian design 54
Swedish design 223, 233, 241
Törngrens Krukmakeri pottery
(Falkenberg) 255
traditional crafts 238, 269
arts and entertainment
Dalhalla outdoor concert arena
(Rättvik) 267
Drottningholms Slottsteater
(Stockholm) 53, *245*
folk music 267, 281
Götaplatsen cultural centre
(Göteborg) 258
Göteborgsoperan (Opera House)
(Göteborg) 256
Göteborg Symphony Orchestra
(Göteborg) 223, 258
Konserthuset (Concert Hall)
(Göteborg) 258
Kulturhuset (Culture House)
(Stockholm) 240
Arvidsjaur 279
Lappstaden Sami village 279

b

beaches 65
Blekinge 251
of Gotland 253
Haverdalsstrand 255
Öland Island 251
Olofsby 255
Östra Strand 255
Ringenäs 255
Skrea Strand 255
West Coast 255
Bellman, Carl 53
Berg 265
Bergman, Ingmar 55, *244*, 253
Fanny and Alexander 244
Bergman, Ingrid 55, *59*
Bernadotte, Count Folke 43
Bernadotte, Jean-Baptiste 35–6,
42
Bingsjö 267
spelmansstämmor (folk
musicians' rallies) 267
Birka 28, 29
Björg, Björn 71
Björkborn Herrgård 263
Nobelmuséet 263
Björkliden 72
Blå Vägen (Blue Highway) 277
Blekinge 251
Boden 282
Garnisonsmuséet (Garrison
Museum) 282
Boglösa 244
Bohuslän archipelago 65, 258
Bollnäs 273
Bönan 272
Engeltofta 272
Bönhamn *281*
Arne's Sjöbod restaurant 281
Borås 264
Textilmuséet (Textile Museum)
264
Borgholm 251
Borgholm Slott (Castle) 251
Bredarör 251
King's Grave (Kiviksgraven)
251

c

Carl Gustaf 42
Carl XVI Gustaf 72
castles
Borgholm Slott 251
Carlstens Fästning (Fortress)
(Marstrand) 258
Drottningholms Slott (Stockholm)
34, 233, 243, *245*

Gripsholms Slott (Mariefred) 244
Halmstad Slott 255
Kalmar Slott *251, 252*
Karlsborg 264, 265
Kärnan (Helsingborg) 251
Läckö Slott 263–4
Malmöhus (Malmö) 249
Mariestad Slott 263
Örebro 263
Sölvesborg Slott 251
Tjolöholm 256
Uppsala 244
Varbergs 255
Visborg 33
churches
Domkyrkan (Cathedral) (Lund) 250
Domkyrkan (Cathedral) (Uppsala) *244*
Habo Kyrka (Habo) 264
Husaby Church (Husaby) 263
monastery church (Vreta) 265
St Laurenti (Falkenberg) 255
St Nikolai (Halmstad) 255
St Petri Kyrka (Cathedral) (Malmö) 250
Sami church (Gällivare) 279
Storkyrkan (Cathedral) (Stockholm) 234
climate 225, 234, 385
customs and folklore 223, 267
see also **etiquette, festivals and events**
Lake Storsjön monster 274

d

Dalarna 77, 267–9
see also individual place names
Dalsland province 261
see also individual place names
Dalslands Kanal 261
Dellenbygden 273
Delsbo 273
Delsbostämman folk fiddlers' festival 273
Dorotea 277
Dyvelsten 261
Flottningsmuséet (Log Rafting Museum) 261

e

economy 43–4, 227
Eketorp ancient burial site 251
Ericsson, John 263
Erik I 31, 32, 244
etiquette 226

f

Falkenberg 255
St Laurenti Church 255
Törngrens Krukmakeri pottery 255
Falkoping 33
Falsterbo 251
Falun 268
Bergslagen 268
Fårö 253
festivals and events
Delsbostämman folk fiddlers' festival (Delsbo) 273
Equestrian Week (Malmö) *249*
Falls Festival (Trollhättan) 264
Falu Folk Music Festival 267
folk music festival (Ransäter) 262
Hälsingehambo folk dance festival (Järvsö) *272, 273*
handicraft festival (Hjo) 264
hyttsill ("glassworks herring") evenings (Orrefors) 252
Midsummer celebrations 233, *266*
Music on Lake Siljan 267
Renaissance Festival (Kalmar) 252
St Lucia celebrations (Stockholm) 233
spelmansstämmor (folk musicians' rallies) (Bingsjö) 267
summer festivals (Rättvik) 267
Walpurgis Night (Stockholm) 233
Filipstad 263
Fiskebäckskil 259
Flatruet Plateau 274
food and drink 62–3, 226, 396
alcohol restrictions 41, 226
aquavit 62
confectionary 273
crayfish 243
schnapps 227
smörgåsbord 62
Strömstad shrimps 259
Swedish specialities 272
Forsvik 265
Fröson 274
Funäsdalen 274
Furuviksparken 271–2

g

Gällivare 279
mining museum 279
Sami church 279
Gamla Viken 255

Gammelstad 282
Friluftsmuséet Hägnan open-air museum 282
Garbo, Greta 55
Gästrikland 271–2
see also individual place names
Gävle 271
Länsmuséet 271
Sveriges Järnvägsmuseum (Railway Museum) 271
Glasriket (Glass Kingdom) *252*
Glösa 274
prehistoric rock carvings 274
Glumslöv 251
Göta Kanal 77, 223, *264, 265*
cruises 265
cycle trails 69
Göteborg (Gothenburg) 223, 256–8, 265
"Aveyn" (The Avenue) 257
Botaniska Trädgården (Botanical Gardens) 258
Götaplatsen cultural centre 258
Göteborgsoperan (Opera House) 256
Göteborgs Turistbyrå (Tourist Office) 257
harbourfront *257*
Konserthuset (Concert Hall) 258
Kungsportsplatsen 257
Kunstmuséet (Art Museum) 258
Lisebergs Nöjespark amusement park 258, *259*
Maritima Centrum (Maritime Centre) 257
Nordstan shopping centre 257
Padden sightseeing boats 257
Röhsska Muséet 257–8
Saluhallen market 257
Slottskogen park 258
transport *257*
Gotland 33, *253*
see also individual place names
Granner, Olga 243
Gullmarn fjord 259
Gustavus II Adolphus 34
Gustav III *52,* 53
Gustav VI Adolf 249
Gustav Vasa *18, 30,* 234, 301

h

Habo 264
Habo Kyrka (church) 264
Hallands Väderö 255
Hållbo 273
Källers Karamellmuseum 273
Hälsingland 272–3
see also individual place names

Halmstad 255
  Halmstad Slott (Castle) 255
  St Nikolai Church 255
Haparanda 282
Härjedalen province 273–4
  see also individual place names
Härnösand 281
  open-air museum 281
Håverud 261
health
  mosquitoes 281
Hedemora 268–9
  Husbyringen museum trail 268–9
Helsingborg 249, 251
  Kärnan (Castle) 251
  Sofiero Palace gardens 249
  Hemavan 67
Hjo 264
  handicraft festival 264
  lake cruises 264
Höga Kusten Bridge 281
Höga Kusten walk 282
Höganäs 251
Hudiksvall 272
  Fiskarstan 272
Husaby 263
  Husaby Church 263
Hydman-Vallien, Ulrika 54

immigration issues 227
industry
  engineering 265
  fishing 61
  glass 252
  mining 277, 279, 280
  motor 44, 264
  shipping 256
  iron and steel 268, 272
  Swedish film industry 251
  textiles 264
  timber, paper and pulp 282

Jädraås 272
  steam trains to Tallås 272
Jämtland province 273, 274
  see also individual place names
Järvsö 273
  Hälsingehambo folk dance
    festival *272*, 273
Johnson, Eyvind 55
Jokkmokk 279
  Ájtte Svenskt Fjäll-och
    Samemuseum (Swedish
    Mountain and Sami Museum)
    279

Jukkasjärvi 280
  Ice Hotel 280
Jungfrukusten (Virgin Coast) 271

Kalmar 33, 252
  Kalmar Slott (Castle) *251*, 252
  Renaissance Festival 252
Karesuando 280
Karl XII 34
Karl XIIs Väg (Trail) 261
Karlfeldt, Erik Axel 55
Karlsborg 264, 265
  Fästning (Fortress) 264, 265
Karlskrona 251
Karlstad 261
  Mariebergsskogen park 261
Kiruna 280
  Kirunavaara Mine 280
  Samegård 280
Klädesholmen *254*
Konghelle 31
Kramfors 281
Kristianopel 251
Kristianstad 251
  Filmmuséet (film museum) 251
Kristinehamm 263
Kungsbacka 256

Lagerkvist, Pär 55
Lagerlöf, Selma 53, 55, 262
  Gösta Berlings Saga 53, 262,
    263
  The Wonderful Adventures of Nils
    55, 262
Laisvall 279
  Laisvallsgruvan lead mine 279
lakes
  Asplången 265
  Hornborgasjön 264
  Mälaren 69, 243, 244
  Rostojaure 280
  Roxen 265
  Siljan 268
  Storsjön 274
  Vänern 77, 261–4, 265
  Vättern 77, 261, 264, 265
language 21–2, 402
Lapland 70, 77, *276*, 277–82
Larsson, Carl and Karin 54, 55,
  223, 267, 269
Lassekrog 272
  Albert Vikstens Kijby (Cabin
    Village) 272
Lidköping 262, 263
  market 262

Rörstrand porcelain factory 263
Lindgren, Astrid 55, 237
  Emil in Lönneberga 55
  Pippi Longstocking 55
Linnaeus, Carl 36
literature
  see also individual writers'
    names
  Anglo-Saxon Chronicle 23, 26
  Beowulf 22, 244
Ljusbodarnas Fäbodar 267–8
Ljusdal 272
Luleå 282
Lummelundagrottorna caves 253
Lund 250–51
  Domkyrkan (Cathedral) 250
  Kulturhistoriska Muséet (Cultural
    History Museum) 250
Lycksele 277
  Lycksele Djurpark (zoo) 277
Lysekil 259
  boat trips 259
  Havets Hus (Sea Aquarium) 259

Malmö 249–50
  Equestrian Week *249*
  Form Design Centre 250
  Lilla Torg (Little Square) 250
  Malmöhus (castle) 249
  Kommendants Hus
    (Commander's House) 249
  Malmömuseer 249
  Rådhuset (City Hall) 249
  Rooseum 250
  St Petri Kyrka (Cathedral) 250
  Saluhallen 250
  Stadshuset 249–50
  Stortorget 249
Mårbacka 262
Mariefred 244
  Gripsholms Slott (Castle) 244
Mariestad 263
  Mariestad Slott (Castle) 263
Marstrand 258
  Carlstens Fästning (Fortress)
    258
Martinson, Harry 55
Måviken 281
Mem 265
Midnight Sun 279, *282*
Milles, Carl 243–4
Moberg, Vilhelm 55
  Kristina from Duvemåla 55
  The Emigrants 55
monarchy 42
Mora 268, 269
  Zorngården 268

Zornmuséet 268
Mörrum 251
Laxens Hus 251
Motala 265
mountains 274
Dundret 279
Galtisbuouda 279
Gluggberget 273
Kaarevaara 280
Kebnekaise 280
Kittelfjäll 277
Öjeberget 273
Vemdalsfjällen 274
museums and galleries
Ajtte Svenskt Fjäll-och
Samemuseum (Swedish
Mountain and Sami Museum)
(Jokkmokk) 279
Birka Vikingastaden (Stockholm)
243
Bruksmuséet (ironworks
museum) (Iggesund) 272
Carl and Karin Larsson museum
(Sundborn) 54
Filmmuséet (film museum)
(Kristianstad) 251
Flottningsmuséet (Log Rafting
Museum) (Dyvelsten) 261
Friluftsmuséet Hägnan open-air
museum (Gammelstad) 282
Gammlia Friluftsmuseum open-air
museum (Umeå) 282
Garnisonsmuséet (Garrison
Museum) (Boden) 282
Guldrummet (Gold Room)
(Stockholm) 239
Hallsylska Muséet (Hallwyl
Collection) (Stockholm) 240
Hembygdsgården heritage village
(Ransäter) 261–2
Historiska Muséet (Museum of
National Antiquities)
(Stockholm) 233, 239
Husbyringen museum trail
(Hedemora) 268–9
Jamtli open-air museum
(Östersund) 274
Källers Karamellmuseum (Hållbo)
273
Konstmuséet (Art Museum)
(Göteborg) 258
Kulturen (Cultural History
Museum) (Lund) 250
Länsmuséet (Gävle) 271
Malmömuseer (Malmö) 249
Maritima Centrum (Maritime
Centre) (Göteborg) 257
Medeltidsmuseum (Medieval
Museum) (Stockholm) 236

mining museum (Gällivare)
279
Moderna Muséet (Stockholm)
55, 233, 236–7
Nationalmuseum (National
Museum of Fine Arts)
(Stockholm) 237
Naturhistoriska Riksmuséet
(Museum of Natural History)
(Stockholm) 239
Nobelmuséet (Björkborn
Herrgård) 263
Nordiska Muséet (Nordic
Museum) (Stockholm) 238
open-air museum (Härnösand)
281
Röhsska Muséet (Göteborg)
257–8
Silvermuséet (Silver Museum)
(Arjeplog) 277
Skansen open-air museum
(Stockholm) 233, 237, 238
Stadsmuséet (City Museum)
(Stockholm) 236
Strindbergsmuséet (Strindberg
Museum) (Stockholm) 242
Sveriges Järnvägsmuseum
(Railway Museum) (Gävle)
271
Textilmuséet (Textile Museum)
(Borås) 264
Utvandrarnas Hus (House of the
Emigrants) (Växjö) 252
Vasamuséet (Vasa Museum)
(Stockholm) 233, 238,
239
Zornmuséet (Mora) 268

n

Nasafjäll 277
national parks and nature reserves
68
Dalby Söderskog 68
Kristianstad Vattenriket (Water
Kingdom) 251
Kroppefjällen nature reserve 261
Muddus 279
Nordens Ark nature park (Åby
Säteri) 259
Padjelanta 70, 279
Skuleskogen 282
Stora Sjöfallet 279
Store Moss 68
nature and outdoor life 65–69, 71–2
Nobel, Alfred 36, 263
Nobel Prizes
literature 55, 58, 167, 262
peace 154

Nordingrå Peninsula 281
Norra Ulvön 282
Norrfällsviken 281
Norrköping 244
Kolmården Djurpark 244

o

Öland Island 251
see also individual place names
Olof Skötkonung 263
Omne bay 281
Örebro 263
castle 263
Oresund bridge 44, 45, 77, 249
Örnsköldsvik 282
Orrefors 252
glass factory visits 252
hyttsill ("glassworks herring")
evenings 252
Orust 259
Östberg, Ragnar 234
Östersund 274
Jamtli open-air museum 274
Ottenby bird station 252
Karl Xs Mur (Karl X's Wall) 252
Överkalix 282
Övik see Örnsköldsvik
Palme, Olof 44
people 225–7
Sami 21, 37, 55, 70, 223, 277,
279, 282
Peterson-Berger, Wilhelm 274
Arnljot 274
Piteå 282
Porjus 279
Prästbodarna Fäbodar 268

r

Ransäter 261
folk music festival 262
Hembygdsgården heritage village
261–2
Rättvik 267
Dalhalla outdoor concert arena
267
Nittsjö Keramik (pottery) 269
summer festivals 267
rivers
Ångermanälven 274
Ätran 255
Göta 264, 265
Indalsälven 274
Kaitumälven 280
Kalixälven 280, 282
Klarälven 261–2
Ljungan 274
Ljusnan 274

Ljusnandalen 272
Mörrum 69, 251
Nissan 255
Piteälven 280
Torneälven 280, 282
Upperud 261
Rökeskyrka 264
stone of Rök 264
Romakloster 253
Romme Alpin ski resort 269
Rottneros Manor 263

S

St Erik 244
Sälen winter sports resort 72, 269
Särö 256
Särö Västerskog 256
Säter 269
Säterglantan 269
Hemslöjdens Gård 269
Sergel, John Tobias 239
Sidén, Ann-Sofi 55
Sigtuna 244
Silvervägen (Silver Road) 277
Sjötorp 265
Skåne 249–52
see also individual place names
Skanör 251
Skanörs Ljung 251
Skara 264
Skara Sommarland 264
Smögen 259
Söderhamn 272
boat trips 272
Södra Ulvön 282
Sölvesborg 251
Sölvesborg Slott (Castle) 251
Sörmlandsleden (Sörmland Route) 67
sports and pastimes 438
dog-sledging and reindeer sleigh rides 70, 280
fishing and ice fishing 69, 70, 251, 274, 277, 279, 280
football 71
gold-panning 279
golf 255, 279
golf under the Midnight Sun 70, 71
hiking and walking 66, 67, 261, 273, 274, 279
sailing and boating 14, 251, 261, 273
skiing and other winter sports 71–2, 269, 274, 282
snowshoe trekking 70
Vasaloppet cross-country ski race 72, 269

white-water rafting 279, 280
Stenmark, Ingemar 71
Stockholm 77, 233–44
Åhléns City 241–2
Aquaria 233
Björkö 243
Birkamuséet 243
Blasieholmen 237
Blåtornet (Blue Tower) 242
boat trips 243, 265
Djurgården see Ekoparken
Drottninggatan (Queen's Street) 242
Drottningholms Slott 34, 233, 243, 245
Drottningholms Slottsteater (theatre) 53, 245
Ekoparken 233, 236, 239
Bergianska Botanical Gardens 239
Fjärilshuset (Butterfly House) 239
Naturhistoriska Riksmuséet (Museum of Natural History) 239
Rosendalsträgård (Rosendals Garden) 239
Gallerian shopping arcade 240–41
Gamla Stan (Old Town) 232, 233–4
Grand Hotel 237
Gröna Lund amusement park 233, 237
Guldrummet (Gold Room) 239
Haga park 239
Hallsylska Muséet (Hallwyl Collection) 240
Historiska Muséet (Museum of National Antiquities) 233, 239
Hornsgatan 243
Hötorget 242
Junibacken 233, 237
Kaknästornet (Kaknäs Television Tower) 233
Katarinahissen 236
Kulturhuset (Culture House) 240
Kungliga Slottet (Royal Palace) 222, 233, 235
Kungsträdgården (King's Garden) 239–40
Lidingö 243–4
Millesgården 243–4
Medeltidsmuseum (Medieval Museum) 236
Midsummer celebrations 233
Moderna Muséet 55, 233, 236–7
Nationalmuseum (National Museum of Fine Arts) 237
nightlife 233

Nordiska Kompaniet (NK) 241
Nordiska Muséet (Nordic Museum) 238
Prins Eugens Waldemarsudde 238, 239
PUB 242
Riddarholmen island 235
Riddarhuset (House of Nobility) 235
Riksdaghuset (Parliament building) 235–6
St Lucia celebrations 233
Sergels Torg 239
shopping 234–5, 240–42
Skansen open-air museum 233, 237, 238
Skeppsholmen 236
Södermalm 242–3
Stadshuset (City Hall) 233, 234, 236
Stadsmuséet (City Museum) 236
Stockholm card 233, 234
Stockholms Auktionsverket (Stockholm Auction House) 241
Storkyrkan (Cathedral) 234
Stortorget 233, 234, 243
Strindbergsmuséet (Strindberg Museum) 242
Strömmen channel 69
Sverigeleden (Sweden Bicycle Route) 69
tourist information 233
transport 233, 237, 240
Ulriksdal see Ekoparken
Vasamuséet (Vasa Museum) 233, 238, 239
Våsterlånggatan 234–5
Walpurgis Night 233
Stockholm archipelago 65
Stora Alvaret 252
Storuman 277
Strängnäs 244
Strindberg, (Johan) August 53, 55, 242
The Great Highway 242
The Red Room 53
Strömstad 259
Sundborn 54, 55, 269
Carl and Karin Larsson museum 54
Svappavaara 279–80
Sveg 274

t

Tallås 272
Tanumshede 258, 259
Bronze Age rock carvings 258, 259

Taube, Evert 235
Tjörn 258–9
Torekov 255
transport
  cycle routes 69
  Inlandsbanan (Inland Railway)
    271, 279
  snow scooters *273*
Trollhättan 264, 265
  Falls Festival 264
Trysunda 282
Tylösand 255

u–v

Umeå 282
  Gammlia Friluftsmuseum open-air
    museum 282
Uppsala 26, 244
  Domkyrkan (Cathedral) *244*
  Gamla Uppsala 244
  Gamla Uppsalakyrkan (parish
    church) 244

Linnaeus house and botanical
  garden 36
Uppsala Slott 244
Varberg 255–6
  Societetshuset 255
  Varbergs Fästning (Fortress)
    255
Värmland 261
Vasa, Gustav 33–4
Västerbotten Museum 282
Västergötland 263–4
  see also individual place names
Växjö 252
  Utvandrarnas Hus (House of the
    Emigrants) 252
Vemdalen 274
Vilhelmina 277
Visby 32, *253*
von Hausswolff, Carl Michael 55
von Heidenstan, Verner 55
von Linné, Carl *see* Linnaeus
Vreta 265
  monastery church 265

w–z

Wallenberg, Raoul 43
Wallqvist, Einar 277
waterfalls
  Kukkolaforsen 282
  Ristafallet 274
  Stora Sjöfallet 279
  Storfallet 274
  Storforsen 282
  Tännforsen 274
Wiberg, Pernilla 71–2
Wikström, Elin 55
wildlife 68, 274
  bird watching 251, 252,
    264
  lynx *271*
  reindeer 70, 271
  Russ horses of Gotland 253
  of the wetlands 251
  wolverine *280*
Ytterlännäs 271
Zorn, Anders 267, 268

A B C E F G H I J a b c d e f g h i j k l

Insight Guides Website
www.insightguides.com

*Don't travel the
planet alone.
Keep in step with
Insight Guides'
walking eye,
just a click away*

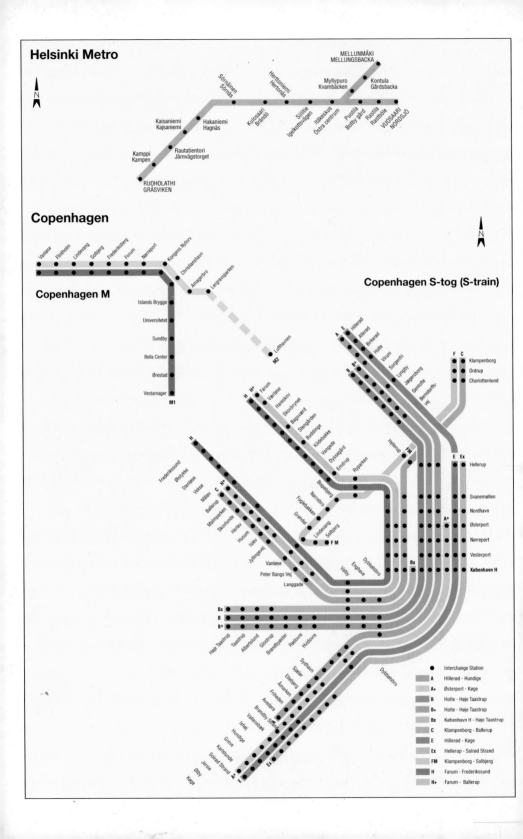